Major Problems in American
Foreign Relations

MAJOR PROBLEMS IN AMERICAN HISTORY SERIES

GENERAL EDITOR

THOMAS G. PATERSON

Major Problems in American Foreign Relations
Volume II: Since 1914

DOCUMENTS AND ESSAYS

SIXTH EDITION

EDITED BY
DENNIS MERRILL
UNIVERSITY OF MISSOURI–KANSAS CITY

THOMAS G. PATERSON
UNIVERSITY OF CONNECTICUT

HOUGHTON MIFFLIN COMPANY
Boston   New York

For
Theresa Hannon
Aaron M. Paterson

Publisher: Charles Hartford
Senior Consulting Editor: Jean L. Woy
Senior Development Editor: Frances Gay
Project Editor: Reba Libby
Editorial Assistant: Rachel Zanders
Manufacturing Coordinator: Carrie Wagner
Senior Marketing Manager: Sandra McGuire

Cover image: Mural reproduced by courtesy of Erni Vales Designs/photograph by
Alan Schein Photography/Corbis.

Printed in the U.S.A.

Library of Congress Catalog Card Number: 2003109912

ISBN: 0-618-37039-0

123456789-MP-08 07 06 05 04

Contents

C H A P T E R   5
Defeating the Axis, Planning the Peace:
The Second World War
Page 153

C H A P T E R   6
The Origins of the Cold War
Page 186

CHAPTER 7
The Korean War and Containment in Asia
Page 245

CHAPTER 10
Cuba and the Missile Crisis
Page 367

CHAPTER 11
The Vietnam War
Page 414

C H A P T E R   1 4
September 11, 2001, and Anti-Americanism in the Muslim World
Page 536

Maps

Preface

The terrorist attacks that struck United States soil on September 11, 2001, forcefully illustrated that we live in a global age. No barrier is unbreachable, it seems, for we are inextricably linked to the rest of the world. Newspaper headlines and television reports from around the globe bombard Americans every day, reminding us, sometimes to our discomfort, that the United States participates in an international community. In a world made interconnected and interdependent by instant communications, rapid transportation, information revolution, economic partnerships, travel and tourism, and a shared natural environment, we have discovered that everything—from gas at the pump to the clothes we buy to the air we breathe—carries the "global" tag. We know that a sizable portion of our tax dollars pays for foreign economic, military, and humanitarian aid; for overseas military and intelligence installations; and for interventions, wars, and covert operations intended to change the behavior of other people and governments. News of massacres, famines, and violent uprisings constantly arouses Americans' moral sensibilities. Terrorist cells operate through global networks and obtain international reach. Families worry about the hundreds of thousands of U.S. military personnel stationed abroad, many of them in harm's way. Holidays commemorate international events. The American people have long participated in international affairs—and so has their government; this book seeks to explain why, how, and where.

This book explores America's many intersections with the world from World War I to the present. It shows how Americans from various walks of life participate in the world community. It examines why and how American leaders devised policies to protect, manage, and extend U.S. interests abroad. The documents and essays in *Major Problems in American Foreign Relations* reveal that searching debate—among Americans and foreign peoples, and among scholars who study the past—has surrounded most issues. Indeed, Americans have spiritedly debated one another about their place in the world, their wars, their territorial expansion, their overseas commitments, their trade policies, and the status of their principles and power; and with comparable vigor, they have debated the people of other nations about the spread of U.S. interests, culture, and ideologies. This book captures the reasoning and the passion that informed these debates by probing the factors that influenced decision-makers, the processes by which decisions are made, and the impact of those decisions on the United States and other nations.

We use the phrase *American Foreign Relations* in the title because the subject matter encompasses the myriad of ways in which peoples, cultures, economies, national governments, nongovernmental organizations, regional associations, and international institutions interact. The term *foreign policy* seems inadequate to account for this wide array of activities and actors because it focuses largely on governmental decisionmaking and on policy itself. *Diplomacy* falls short because it refers primarily to negotiations or communications among states and organizations. *International history* seems so broad a term that it loses meaning, while at the same time it underplays an appropriate emphasis on *American* foreign relations. The phrase *foreign relations* comes closest to the new emphases because it explains the totality of interactions—economic, cultural, political, military, environmental, and more—among peoples, organizations, states, and systems.

For this sixth edition we have integrated into our chapters some of the very best recent scholarship. In this volume, more than half the essays are new or revised, including selections by Gerald C. Horne, Melvyn P. Leffler, Garry Clifford, Tony Smith, Benjamin D. Rhodes, Leila J. Rupp, Gerhard Weinberg, Bruce M. Russett, Jonathan G. Utley, Arnold A. Offner, Mary Ann Heiss, Elizabeth Cobbs Hoffman, Dennis Merrill, Robert Dallek, Robert Buzzanco, Fredrik Logevall, Robert K. Brigham, John Lewis Gaddis, Joseph S. Nye Jr., Bernard Lewis, Ussama Makdissi, and Robert Wright. This edition includes recently released Cold War documents from former Communist archives and increased coverage of the post-Cold War era, including an expanded and updated analysis of America's place in the international system at the beginning of the twenty-first century. We have added a new chapter on the terrorist attacks of September 11, 2001, the George W. Bush administration's war against terrorism, and the roots of anti-Americanism in the Muslim World (Chapter 14). Selected essays and documents continue to reflect the growing scholarship on international cultural relations, and the impact of attitudes about gender, race, and national identity on world affairs—including a new chapter on Cold War culture and the Third World (Chapter 9). As always, we have included foreign voices and statements by people of color, so as to illuminate the wide array of participants in foreign relations and to suggest ways in which America influences other peoples and nations. We have also accented the importance of groups who share transnational commonalities—such as women's rights activists, relief and development workers, and international peace organizations—to illustrate how cultural, economic, and political internationalism have transformed foreign relations and spurred globalization.

Like other volumes in this series, *Major Problems in American Foreign Relations* approaches its subject in two ways: first, through primary sources; and second, through the interpretations of scholars. We invite readers to contend with a diversity of viewpoints and approaches on critical issues. Documents introduce each chapter's problem, identify key questions, reveal the flavor of the times, and convey the intensity of the debate. Through encounters with documents, students can immerse themselves in the historical moment, shape their own perspectives, and test the explanations of others. The essays demonstrate that different scholars read documents differently, come to quite different conclusions, or choose to focus on different aspects of an issue. Students' interaction with the documents and essays builds an appreciation for the complexity of historical problems, a fascination about historical inquiry, and a recognition that events and personalities once buried in the past carry contemporary meaning for students as both scholars and citizens. Introductions and headnotes in each chapter start this empowering and rewarding process. And suggestions for further reading at the end of each chapter provide resources for students who would like to do additional research.

Instructors and students who want to continue their study of foreign relations history are invited to join the Society for Historians of American Foreign Relations

(SHAFR). This organization publishes a superb journal, *Diplomatic History*, as well as an informative newsletter, offers book, article, and lecture prizes and dissertation research grants, and holds an annual conference where scholars present their views and research results. Dues are reasonable. The organization has recently published an updated bibliographical work entitled *American Foreign Relations Since 1600: A Guide to the Literature* (2003), edited by Robert L. Beisner and Kurt W. Hanson, which is available for purchase. This indispensable guide includes citations of journal articles, books, memoirs, document collections, and other sources, organized by topic and period. For information on SHAFR, contact the SHAFR Business Office, Ohio State University, Department of History, 106 Dulles Hall, 230 West 17th Avenue, Columbus, OH 43210; email shafr@osu.edu or visit the official website at www. shafr.com. For on-line discussion of topics in the history of U.S. foreign relations, consult the electronic journal *H-DIPLO* web page at http://h-net2.msu.edu/~diplo.

We are very pleased to acknowledge the many generous people who have helped us with both documents and essays, advised us about content, and pointed out errors. Detailed and constructive written reviews for this edition were provided by Stanley J. Adamiak, University of Central Oklahoma; David L. Anderson, University of Indianapolis; Diane Shaver Clemens, University of California, Berkeley; John W. Coogan, Michigan State University; Gordon E. Harvey, University of Louisiana at Monroe; Robert B. Kane, Troy State University, Montgomery; Sharon Murphy, Nazareth College of Rochester; Kenneth E. Shewmaker, Dartmouth College; and Amy L. S. Staples, Middle Tennessee State University. The talented Houghton Mifflin staff deserves special thanks. Imaginative, thorough, and understanding, Houghton Mifflin's editors shaped this book for the better. We thank Senior Consulting Editor for History and Political Science Jean L. Woy; Senior Development Editor Frances Gay; Project Editor Reba Libby; Editorial Assistant Rachel Zanders; and Permissions Editor Tracy Metivier.

We are also grateful to friends, colleagues, and students who contributed in various ways to the first five editions: Lloyd E. Ambrosius, Harold Barto, Miriam Biurci, Richard Dean Burns, J. Garry Clifford, Richard H. Collin, Bruce Cumings, Joe Decker, Bruce dePyssler, John Dobson, Gregory E. Dowd, Michael Ebner, Jim Falls, Miriam Formanek-Brunell, Mark Gilderhus, Mary A. Giunta, James Goode, Gerald Gordon, Laura Grant, Kenneth J. Hagan, Peter L. Hahn, Paul W. Harris, James Hindman, Elizabeth Cobbs Hoffman, Michael Hunt, Jane Hunter, Holly Izard, Donald Johnson, Lawrence Kaplan, Ellen Kerley, Warren Kimball, Carla Klausner, Karen Kupperman, Melvyn Leffler, Douglas Little, Jean Manter, Frederick Marks, James Matray, John Merrill, Jean-Donald Miller, Nancy Mitchell, Carl Murdoch, Brian Murphy, Charles Neu, Patrick Peebles, Stephen Pelz, Alan Perry, Carol Petillo, Joel Rhodes, Eileen Rice, Andrew Rotter, Reneé Schloss, Thomas Schwartz, Kenneth E. Shewmaker, Katherine S.W. Siegal, Martha Lund Smalley, Mark Stoler, Harry Stout, William Steuck, John Sylvester, Nancy Bernkopf Tucker, Paul Varg, Mary Wolfskill, Marvin Zahniser, and Thomas Zoumaras.

We welcome comments, suggestions, and criticisms from students and instructors so that we can continue to improve this book.

D. M.
T. G. P.

Approaching the Study of

American Foreign Relations

The study of American foreign relations raises several central questions. What are the key characteristics of U.S. foreign relations, and what shaped them? What is the relationship between the nation's domestic setting—its ideology, culture, politics, geography, social structure, and economy—and its foreign relations? To what extent do American foreign relations owe their character not to domestic conditions and attitudes but to interaction with the wider world? Does the United States behave like other powers in international relations, or does it have defining, exceptional qualities? What weight should we assign to the several ways—political, strategic, economic, military, cultural—in which peoples, societies, and nations relate to one another? How is power distributed in the international system?

Most scholars agree that the United States built on a tradition of expansion to emerge as a predominant, even hegemonic global power in the twentieth century. But how, and why? Was the expansionist course calculated and coherent, or accidental and haphazard? Did economic interests fuel the drive toward hegemony—a quest for foreign markets and investment opportunities, or what the historian William Appleman Williams called "Open Door" expansionism? Or did America's engagement with the world reflect a defensive mindset, or foreign policy "realism," that sanctioned the use of power to protect U.S. security interests against external threats—a posture that necessitated the acquisition of overseas bases, strategic raw materials, and military allies? Some analysts argue that the urge to spread American power and the American way of life arose from an ideological canon: an aspiration to promote democracy and the international rule of law throughout the world—what the consummate realist George Kennan derisively labeled "moralism-legalism." Others focus on the cultural roots of American expansionism. Culture differs from ideology in that it is less self-conscious and less rigid. By "culture" we mean a constellation of values, beliefs, myths, language, symbols, and assumptions about what it means to be American, what it means to be foreign, and how U.S. leaders and citizens should conduct themselves on the world stage. These perceptions grow out of cultural constructions of class, race, gender, sexuality, age, and national identity that are always being reconsidered and negotiated by different groups within society and refashioned in light of international experiences. Finally, contemporary scholars also have to grapple with the phenomenon of globalization, the increasing political, economic, cultural, technological, and environmental interconnectedness of the world. How has globalization reshaped American foreign relations? To what extent has the globalizing process blurred boundaries and identities, and undermined the nation-state structure?

Related to the many questions about U.S. expansionism and the larger world are others that highlight how policy is made and how the process of decisionmaking shapes both the policy and the outcome. How have U.S. leaders gone about deciding to use the nation's power abroad, and has that exercise of power produced the results intended? Scholars also explore domestic politics and elections, presidential-congressional relations, the Constitution, bureaucracies, interest groups and elites, the media and public opinion, and individuals whose personalities mold perceptions and influence decisions. What role have nongovernmental organizations (NGOs) and transnational advocates for human rights, international peace, environmental protection, and other global reforms played in U.S. foreign policy?

One way to think about the different approaches presented very briefly in this opening chapter is to ask how each would explain specific events or relations, such as the United States entry into the First World War, the Japanese-American clashes that led to World War II in the Pacific, the origins and escalation of the Cold War, the launching of the Peace Corps, U.S. engagement in the Middle East, or the daunting specter of global terrorism. Does one approach or a combination of approaches carry more explanatory power?

The diversity of viewpoints in this introductory chapter affords us an opportunity to discover and understand the complexity of major problems in American foreign relations whose legacies persist today.

E S S A Y S

In the first essay, Thomas J. McCormick of the University of Wisconsin, Madison, introduces the "world systems theory" of international relations and emphasizes U.S. economic hegemony or dominance in a capitalist world system comprising core, periphery, and semi-periphery countries. In the twentieth century, the United States has possessed preponderant economic and military power and exercised political-ideological leadership, rising to the status of preeminent core country. But McCormick notes that hegemony is "impermanent"; great powers become rentier and warfare states, and decline inevitably sets in. In the second essay, Emily Rosenberg of Macalaster College explores a subject that is in many ways connected to global economics: international cultural relations. She emphasizes that the export of American ideas, news headlines, music, film, and other popular culture—promoted both by government agencies and private initiative— have contributed to American hegemony abroad and generated backlashes of cultural nationalism. Yet U.S. domination, and world-wide cultural homogeneity, have been mitigated by various classes and interest groups within recipient societies who have often reshaped American cultural exports to suit their own tastes and needs. Globalization and the information revolution of the late twentieth century, she concludes, have further blurred national boundaries and complicated cultural interaction.

In the third essay, Andrew Rotter of Colgate University explores a specific aspect of culture: gender. Using U.S. relations with India as an example, he explains that cultural constructions of femininity and masculinity influence the ways in which diplomats perceive and relate to other peoples. For example, the gendered language of international relations undergirded a negative view of nonaligned India during the Cold War era and helped justify a vigorous policy of anti-Communist containment on the Indian subcontinent. Rotter further notes that constructions of gender have been linked historically to Western imperialism, and have played an important role in U.S. relations with Asia, Latin America, and the Middle East. Gerald C. Horne of the University of North Carolina, Chapel Hill, emphasizes that America's rise to world power in the twentieth century cannot be understood without an examination of race. U.S. policymakers embraced doctrines of white supremacy to justify overseas imperialism at the start of the twentieth century, and articulated the language of anti-communism to "contain" the aspirations of recently decolonized people of color during the Cold War era. Paradoxically, the domestic African-American civil rights movement, Japan's Great Power status, and revolutionary social movements abroad have also spurred U.S. leaders to shun racism and endorse human rights. Pointing to the escalating clash between Western and non-Western cultures at the dawn of the twenty-first century, Horne predicts that international relations will continue to be shaped by race.

Melvyn P. Leffler of the University of Virginia, in the fifth essay, argues that the pursuit of national security—the defense of domestic core values and interests against external threats—best explains U.S. behavior abroad. According to Leffler, the national security approach demands that analysts distinguish between real and perceived threats and probe the inner meaning of the term "core values"—a label that refers to America's bedrock cultural, economic, ideological, and political identity and institutions. He maintains that one of the principal strengths of the national security paradigm is its ability to merge traditional examinations of material interests, territory, and power with new studies of culture and ideology. In the sixth selection, J. Garry Clifford of the University of Connecticut explains how bureaucratic politics—the give-and-take bargaining within the U.S. government—shapes the pacing, implementation, and therefore the outcome of foreign policy. Because of all the tugging and hauling in the policy process, U.S. foreign relations do not always conform to its leader's intentions.

The World-System, Hegemony, and Decline

THOMAS J. McCORMICK

Since modern history began in the late fifteenth century, the earth's inhabitants have lived in three distinct types of environments: the capitalist world-system (or world economy), the external world (empires), or the minisystems of subsistence communities. For the past five hundred years, the dynamic growth and expansion of the world-system has been at the expense of the other two. The Ottoman Empire of the Turks disappeared, the Russian Empire of the Romanovs and the empire of the Manchus in China collapsed in revolutionary disarray, all victims of their archaic political systems and the inability of their quasi-feudal economies to compete with or alternatively to insulate themselves from the more dynamic and efficient economies of the capitalist world-system. Likewise, the minisystems of Eastern Europe, Ireland, the Americas, Africa, and Asia were, over time and despite great resistance, wrenched away from their subsistence, village agriculture and integrated into a cash nexus and the world market. By the late twentieth century, the remnants of the external world of empires, the Soviet Union and the Peoples' Republic of China, had

Thomas J. McCormick, *America's Half-Century: United States Foreign Policy in the Cold War and After,* pp. 1–7. Copyright © 1995 by Johns Hopkins University Press. Reprinted with permission of The Johns Hopkins University Press.

emerged from the containment and self-isolation of the Cold War and begun to experiment with market economies in place of command (planned) economies. Also by that time, the remaining isolated pockets of subsistence systems had virtually disappeared from the face of the earth. The revolutionary expansion of European capitalism and Mediterranean civilization, begun a half-millennium earlier, seemed about to reach its final, all-encompassing frontier. The world-system and the world itself seemed almost one—one world rather than three. . . .

During the last decade, a number of academic observers have concluded that capitalism's tendency toward international fluidity eventually produced a configuration that could properly be described as a system, a combination of parts forming a complex, unitary whole. Fernand Braudel and Immanuel Wallerstein, in their epic studies of early European capitalism, concluded that such a system was in place by 1650. Others feel that it was not until the nineteenth century that an integrated global division of labor allowed capitalism to merit characterization as a system.

Studies advancing a world-system analysis (including this study) argue that there are three constants about that world system, even though the particular forms it takes are always changing. First, there are always implicit geographical boundaries within that system, and they are essentially defined by the spatial limits of the world market economy at any given time. In our contemporary period, the term *free world* is essentially a synonym for the capitalist world-system. Cold War rhetoric may impart a more ideological twist to the phrase, but Nelson Rockefeller's chief aide got at its root in late 1941 when he declared that America was "committed to the fight for freedom of economic life and for freedom of the seas, in a word, the fight for a free world." Second, there is always a center or pole to the system, a dominant city that acts as the coordinating point and clearing house of international capital. Its location has shifted historically from the Mediterranean to Northern Europe to North America (and perhaps yet to Northeast Asia), but there is always a central metropolis, be it London in 1845 or New York in 1945.

Finally, the system consists of three successive zones, each performing a specialized function in a complex, international division of labor. *Core* countries (the First World) own most of the high-tech, high-profit enterprises. The *periphery* (the Third World) specializes in primary production of agricultural commodities and raw materials—they are the "hewers of wood and carriers of water." Between them, the *semiperiphery* (the Second World) performs intermediate functions of transport, local capital mobilization, and less complex, less profitable forms of manufacturing. Historically, there has been some limited mobility of individual nations between zones, including America's own transformation from a semiperipheral country in 1790 to a core country by 1890. Likewise, changing technology continually redefines what constitutes high-, intermediate-, or low-value enterprises. Textiles, steel, and shipbuilding might have been high-value activities in an earlier era but have become low- or intermediate-value in the contemporary age of electrical equipment. What remains constant are the zones themselves and the specialized (and unequally rewarded) division of labor among them. Hence, in 1988 there is a world-system in which North America, Japan, and Europe constitute the core and specialize in electronics, capital goods, diversified agriculture, and finance; the less developed countries (LDCs) of Africa, Southeast Asia, and the Caribbean basin, as the periphery, specialize in non-petroleum raw materials and single-crop agriculture; and the newly industrializing countries (NICs), Mexico, Brazil, South Africa, Israel, Iran, India, China, and those of Eastern Europe and the Pacific rim, as the semiperiphery, specialize in shipping, petroleum, credit transactions, and consumer goods manufacturing.

The emergence of a capitalist world economy coincided with the emergence of the modern nation-state as the prevailing political unit of governance, and the nation-state has both fostered and inhibited the capitalist world economy. On one hand, nation-states have often provided crucial stimulation of economic growth and development: their banking, taxation, credit, and internal improvement policies have frequently aided domestic entrepreneurs in accumulating capital and minimizing risks. On the other hand, those same nation-states have often interfered with and impeded the fluidity and mobility of capital, goods, and labor across national boundaries. This nationalist bias is caused in part by nation-states being, by definition, wedded to specific territories and committed to the defense and sustenance of their citizens. In part, too, it reflects the uneven pace of capitalist development among countries, and the unequal division of labor and rewards that results from it. The frequent consequence has been an attempt by "have-not" countries to overtake "have" countries through nationalistic economic measures, often referred to as mercantilistic policies in earlier periods and, in our own time, as import-substitution policies (i.e., substitution of indigenous products for those previously imported). Whatever the cause of this nationalist bias, the resulting farm subsidies, military spending, protective tariffs, navigation laws, capital controls, and restricted currency convertibility have constituted serious obstacles to a free world of economic internationalism and interdependence in which capitalism, as a purely economic system, can realize its maximum efficiency and profitability. So, too, have the policies of territorial expansion that often accompany economic nationalism interfered, by seeking to monopolize whole regions of the earth for the benefit of a single national economy. Examples are the British mercantile empire of the eighteenth century and the Japanese Greater East Asian Co-Prosperity Sphere of the twentieth. In sum, nation-states have tended to pursue policies of economic autarky—capitalism in one country or one self-contained trading bloc—and such approaches limit the options of capital in pursuit of maximum rewards.

Hegemony historically has operated to soften the contradiction between the internationalist imperatives of capitalism and the nationalist biases of political nation-states. In the context of the world-system, hegemony means that one nation possesses such unrivaled supremacy, such predominant influence in economic power, military might, and political-ideological leadership, that no other power, or combination of powers, can prevail against it. Economic supremacy is the indispensable base of hegemony, for all other forms of power are possible with it and no others possible, for very long, without it. Any hegemonic power must, simultaneously, contain the dominant financial center, possess a clear comparative advantage in a wide range of high-tech, high-profit industries, and function commercially as both the world's major exporter and its major importer. Beyond mere economic power, it must possess clear military superiority and ideological hegemony as well. By fear or respect, it must be able to exert its political will over the rest of the system and command deference to its principles and policies.

Hegemony and the balance of power have been on opposing sides of the contradiction between economic internationalism and national autarky or self-sufficiency.

The balance of power attempts to use the alignment of forces and, if necessary, war, to prevent any one power from achieving such preponderance that it could impose economic internationalism on autarkic-minded nations. A single hegemonic power, however, has a built-in incentive to force other nations to abandon their national capitalism and economic controls and to accept a world of free trade, free capital flows, and free currency convertibility. As the world's dominant economic power, a hegemonic power has the most to gain from such a free world and the most to lose from nationalistic efforts to limit the free movement of capital, goods, and currencies. So the preponderant world power is unequivocally self-interested in using its economic power, as workshop and banker of the free world, to create institutions and ground rules that foster the internationalization of capital. It finds it inherently advantageous to use its political power as ideologue of the world-system to preach the universal virtues of freedom of the seas, free trade, open door policies, comparative advantage, and a specialized division of labor. It finds it necessary to use its military power as global policeman to protect the international system against external antagonists, internal rebellions, and internecine differences: to be judge, jury, and executioner, insuring that the ground rules of internationalism are not impeded by either friend or foe.

Only twice in the history of the capitalist world economy has hegemony triumphed over balance of power as the prevailing structure of the international system. Great Britain functioned as hegemonic center between roughly 1815 and 1870, and the United States did so between roughly 1945 and 1970. (Others argue that the Dutch republic did so as well, in the late seventeenth century, but the argument seems rather forced.) In each instance, world war was crucial to the formation of hegemony. It radically redistributed power and wealth in ironic fashion, denying hegemony to a European continental power while bestowing postwar supremacy on its balance of power adversary.

In the first instance, France attempted through its Napoleonic Wars (constituting the first truly world war) to impose its dominance on the Eurasian heartland, the very center of European capitalism. Great Britain attempted to thwart that ambition through its traditional balance of power politics, and it ultimately prevailed. But the wars and attendant revolutions were so long, so destructive, so destabilizing that they temporarily obliterated the old balance of power system and left Great Britain the tacit sovereign of the post-Napoleonic world. In the second instance (as we shall see in detail later), Germany, under both the Kaiser and Hitler, attempted to impose its dominance on the same Eurasian heartland, while Anglo-American balance of power diplomacy sought to prevent it. But the ironic consequence of World Wars I and II was, by denying hegemony to the Germans, to make it possible for the Americans to become the acknowledged leaders of the free world. In each case, hegemony made it nearly impossible for other core powers to use war as an instrument of diplomacy against each other—a Pax Britannica for the mid-nineteenth century and a Pax Americana for the mid-twentieth. In each case, hegemony blunted the forces of economic nationalism and facilitated greater global interdependence, enabling a freer and easier *exchange* of goods in the nineteenth century and the multinational *production* of goods in the twentieth.

Hegemony is always impermanent, as Great Britain discovered and the United States is discovering. Indeed, hegemony undermines the very economic supremacy upon which it necessarily must rest. Two related tendencies lead the preponderant power to neglect investment in its civilian research and production and to transform itself into a *rentier* nation and *warfare* state. There is a tendency to overinvest and lend overseas and to live off dividends and interests (renting out one's money, hence *rentier*). It happens because it is easy to do, since the hegemonic power is in a position to secure favorable treatment for its capital throughout the free world. It happens also because it is necessary, since higher wage bills make it more profitable to invest overseas than at home. The higher wage bills themselves are part of the burden of power: the necessity to demonstrate to managers and workers that there are ample economic rewards for supporting an internationalist foreign policy with their votes, tax dollars, and conscription.

The tendency to overinvest abroad is compounded by the tendency to overinvest in military production. Essential to the hegemonic power's capacity to act as global policeman, military research and production receive favored treatment from the government in the form of state-subsidized high profits. The government becomes a more predictable and more profitable customer than private individuals and corporate consumers. The end result is to divert capital from civilian to military production, to the neglect of modernization needs of the domestic industrial plant. This disinvestment, as some term it, erodes over time the economic underpinnings of hegemony and makes it more difficult to compete with other core powers who have avoided the pitfalls of similar disinvestment. Moreover, like a snowball rolling downhill, the problems compound as the hegemon grows aware of its decline. Confronted with declining profitability in the civilian sector, it is likely to stress military spending even more as the easiest way to assure its capitalists of adequate returns—often spending far in excess of any plausible military purposes. Relatedly, it is likely to exploit its continuing function as world policeman to extort special privileges from its competitors: favored treatment for its currency, its trade, and its investments in exchange for continued police protection. In short, it is likely to become even more of a rentier or warfare economy and speed up the very decline it is trying to retard.

Cultural Interactions

EMILY S. ROSENBERG

During the early conquest of the New World, a scientist in Europe prophesied that "The New World, which you have conquered, will now conquer you." The United States in the twentieth century, having become the most powerful of the states created in the New World, did indeed launch what many Europeans considered a reverse conquest. What Englishman W. T. Stead in 1901 called the "Americanization of the World," however, came less through armaments, armadas, and mass movements of population than through the exportation of cultural products. In recent years, scholars of American foreign relations, taking cues from social and cultural history, have given increased attention to this history of cultural expansion. . . .

"Cultural Interactions," by Emily Rosenberg from Stanley Kutler, ed., *Encyclopedia of the United States in the Twentieth Century,* Volume II. (New York: Charles Scribner & Sons, 1996), pp. 695, 698–708, 710–715. Reprinted with the permission of Macmillan Library Reference USA, a division of Ahsuog, Inc. Copyright © 1996 by Charles Scribner & Sons.

This essay . . . neither portrays America's growing cultural dominance as inexorably uplifting nor implies that cultural implantation has destroyed the world's rich cultural diversity and turned everyone into passive recipients of American capitalism. Influenced by poststructuralist theory, this essay assumes that cultural exchanges are contextually negotiated, vary considerably according to time and place, and are marked by both acceptance and resistance. It also suggests that U.S. cultural products have been important purveyors of trends that now ironically seem "international." In the late twentieth century it may be that Americanization and internationalization have actually become blended phenomena, both characterized by the simultaneous globalization and cultural fragmentation associated with postmodernity. . . .

Exportation of mass cultural products predated the Great War [World War I], but the national emergency enlarged governmental promotion of America's entertainment and informational industries. The war, and governmental assistance, formed the basis for rapid international expansion of American mass culture in the 1920s.

President Woodrow Wilson appointed George Creel, a journalist and progressive reformer, as head of the Committee on Public Information (CPI), charged with selling the war at home and abroad. Creel did not see these promotional activities as propaganda or manipulation. Rather, he insisted that he was purveying truth, information, and education. Firmly believing in what he termed the Gospel of Americanism, Creel shared Wilson's conviction that the United States had a special mission in the world to promote international harmony and peace, even if the means involved war. Creel did not try to sell the war so much as he tried to sell America as a symbol of progress and of social and industrial fairness. . . .

Creel appreciated the persuasive power of the printed word, but his true genius lay in marshaling moving images to serve the national cause. America's motion pictures were already fairly popular exports. Developed in the United States by an immigrant-influenced film industry for a largely immigrant audience, Hollywood's films of the silent era easily crossed boundaries of language and culture. . . .

During the war, . . . [t]he film industries of Britain, France, and Germany collapsed under the pressures of financially strapped governments, shortages of material such as film, and disruption of export trade. Creel, meanwhile, made sure that Hollywood producers received allotments of carefully controlled nitrate, a scarce component vital to both the film and munitions industries. Moreover, the technical and stylistic innovations of American filmmakers attracted audiences. Unlike their European counterparts, American films owed more to the streetwise influences of vaudeville and the lavish extravaganzas of nineteenth-century popular pageants (including Wild West shows) than to elite art and culture. With or without governmental assistance, Hollywood had laid the basis for a global entertainment empire. . . .

American film exports boomed throughout the 1920s and came to dominate world markets: American films constituted 95 percent of those shown in Britain and Canada, 70 percent of those in France, 80 percent of those in South America. Even the advent of talkies, which many people had predicted would bring the death of film exports, had little effect. After a short period of experimentation, subtitles and dubbing began to work satisfactorily, adding little additional production cost. . . .

Like the motion picture industry, America's radio industry also received a jumpstart from government during World War I and then expanded during the 1920s.

Before World War I, Britain dominated international cable lines, the chief form of international communications, and could easily invade the confidentiality of both commercial and strategic cables originating in the United States. For the U.S. government, promoting a new network of point-to-point wireless communications became a priority. During the war, the government nationalized the radio industry, rapidly enlarged its capacities, and worked with business leaders to forge a global communications network. When broadcasting (as distinguished from point-to-point transmissions) of radio messages emerged as a major medium of entertainment and information after the war, American technology was in the forefront. . . .

Exports of information, film, and radio were part of a much broader outflow of products associated with American mass culture. American specialty products in the post–World War I era—electrical goods, automobiles, oil—were strong carriers of cultural values. America's giant electrical companies, for example, sold the hardware for the growth of radio broadcasting, made illumination more widespread, and pushed home consumer items such as refrigerators. The American automobile, oil, and rubber industries all reinforced each other in promoting internationally a car culture that was also developing at home. And modern advertising, given a boost by the example of Creel's wartime success in salesmanship and by new studies on the psychology of selling, introduced these lifestyle-transforming products to international markets in more compelling ways than ever before. . . .

American tourists and intellectuals of the 1920s (even those who often denounced America for its materialism) also spread consumer values. The age of mass tourism was just dawning. By the late 1920s, many middle-class Americans could afford foreign travel. Numbers of tourists to Europe—the favored destination—rose from 15,000 in 1912 to more than a quarter of a million in 1929. American intellectuals also had a growing impact, especially in Europe. The American writers and artists who migrated to Paris in the interwar period contributed to what Jean-Paul Sartre described as France's greatest literary experience. American Studies developed respectability, as the Sorbonne, inspired by the World War I alliance between France and the United States, became the first European university to establish a permanent teaching position in American Civilization (in 1917). Universities in England, Germany, Austria, the Soviet Union, and elsewhere also instituted American Studies. . . .

The American cultural invasion of the interwar years brought a backlash of cultural nationalism. Influential, sensational books in many countries around the world assailed the rising cultural power of the United States. . . . Critiques such as these leveled an array of charges, from German disgruntlement at a country that would enforce a constitutional ban against beer drinking to broader jabs against America's alleged crass materialism, soulless individualism, and worship of technology. A board of concerned British citizens, including the novelist Thomas Hardy, warned that the tasteless melodramatics of American films imperiled the Empire by portraying whites as fools who worshiped money and fashion and had no stable home life. . . .

The discourses of anti-Americanism that accumulated as American cultural influence grew, however, need to be treated cautiously. In the countries of Europe, and also of Asia and Latin America, the "meaning" of America came to be encoded within cultural and political debates that often had little to do with the United

States itself. The European avant-garde, for example, greeted American jazz and some consumer goods as democratic impulses that could help sweep away class pretensions in a new Europe. (Many of the most fervent admirers of America, however, had never visited the country; and many others did not like it when they did.) Similarly, anti-Americanism created a foil against which presumed national virtues or characteristics could be reinforced and applauded. Anti-American critics stressed U.S. crime and violence (frequently mentioning Al Capone), materialism, and licentiousness to argue for cultural preservation at home. . . .

If economic hard times and cultural nationalism during the 1930s challenged American expansiveness, World War II brought new and unparalleled opportunities for extending U.S. influence. New wartime propaganda agencies [such as the Office of War Information], the presence of U.S. army troops around the globe, the Americanization associated with postwar occupations, postwar aid and informational programs, and the anticommunist cultural offensive launched in the early 1950s all helped the United States attain preeminent cultural, as well as military, power in the post–World War II era. . . .

The global anticommunist cultural offensive of the 1950s arose together with the economic, political, and military mobilization recommended in the important 1950 National Security Council document NSC-68. Immediately after World War II, the OWI had been disbanded and the State Department, settling into peacetime, emphasized "cultural" rather than "informational" (i.e., propaganda) initiatives. Congress provided direct funding for educational exchanges under the Smith-Mundt Act of 1948, which created the Fulbright program. As Soviet-American antagonism grew, however, those advocating more aggressive promotion of Americanism attacked expenditures for slow, elite-based cultural exchanges. In 1950 President Truman, responding to the recommendations of NSC-68 and to the Korean War, initiated a "Campaign of Truth.". . . The new initiative expanded Fulbright exchanges but also laid the foundations for more targeted propaganda by placing information offices, libraries, and mass media products in countries around the world. Nearly 300 centers were established by the late 1950s, offering English and stressing the value of American-style democracy, labor unions, and technological accomplishments. . . .

The new activism in informational diplomacy gathered even greater momentum during the Korean War. President Dwight Eisenhower, taking an aggressive stand, decided to institutionalize the Campaign of Truth in a new agency, the United States Information Agency (USIA), formed in 1953. . . .

Creation of a permanent peacetime propaganda apparatus to spread American culture marked a significant departure for U.S. policy, but America's cultural influence abroad did not come solely from governmental design. America's mass culture seemed to have almost boundless appeal, especially to youth. Although USIA officials sometimes complained about movies that portrayed Americans as gangsters, racists, foolish millionaires, and corrupt materialists, Hollywood's America packed box offices and fed the fascination with American life. Like movies, privately sponsored radio programs, such as *Hit Parade* and *The Jack Benny Show,* attracted audiences and won friends. U.S. television networks, fearing saturation in domestic markets, aggressively invested in foreign stations and arranged syndication. . . .

As in the 1920s, U.S. consumer products continued to be successful missionaries for the American Way. American-style self-service grocery stores, chain-store retailing, and installment buying developed in Europe as well as in parts of Latin America and Asia in the 1950s. America's mass-marketed magazines, especially Henry Luce's *Life,* fed the identification between America and consumer abundance, between "freedom" and purchasing power. *Life's* 1946 feature entitled "Dreams of 1946," for example, pictured a dishwasher, radio, power lawnmower, and other household technologies. Magazines featured women with leisure time provided by electric kitchens and new prepackaged foods. Glamorous housewives with the time to dote on their husbands became another icon for "freedom" during the Cold War. . . .

Some people eagerly embraced American models. Around the world, commentators remarked about the special appeal of American culture to youth. If older generations had seen Britain or France as preeminent cultural centers, the generation born during World War II increasingly looked to the United States. The lingua franca of this global youth culture emanated from the United States in words such as "bar," "DJ," "rock 'n' roll," "sex appeal," "teenager," "be-bop," "glamour girls," "minibar." . . .

[Yet] the fear that U.S. "cultural imperialism" would facilitate its political and economic domination became even more widespread during and after the generally unpopular Vietnam War. In the 1970s, the global dominance of the American media and the formation of a "nonaligned movement" in Cold War politics prompted some international politicians to try to redefine "free flow" as having to do with the balance of information sources rather than simply with private ownership. Urho Kekkonen, the president of Finland, for example, noted in a 1973 speech that the global flow of information is "one-way, unbalanced traffic and in no way possesses the depth and range which the principles of freedom of speech require." . . .

The backlash against American "cultural imperialism" seemed to peak in the 1970s and early 1980s. Resistance to American power, however, often had a twist. Just as young protestors in the United States used rock 'n' roll songs as their protest anthems, so did youth abroad. Crowds who might one day throw stones at U.S. embassies might, the next day, gather to listen to American rock music. The worldwide student unrest of 1968 seemed interwoven in a kind of global youth culture, often with origins in the United States itself. Ironically, even when America's international policies failed to bring goodwill, its popular culture often gained converts for the future. . . .

The domino-like fall of communist governments in Eastern Europe during 1989 and 1990 opened even more opportunities for U.S. cultural expansion. As Pepsi developed ads that associated their cola with images of the crumbling Berlin Wall, McDonald's gloated over the taste that Eastern Europeans were developing for American cuisine. Billboards in Prague carried the message "I am a billboard, I sell your products." *Playboy,* in a full-page ad in the *New York Times* (15 December 1989) proclaimed itself to be in the forefront of "EXPORTING THE AMERICAN DREAM.". . .

In the late twentieth century, international flows of finance, information, and entertainment—managed by computers, digitalized information networks, and satellites—are rendering national boundaries less important. Whereas major media industries in the past were clearly anchored within the nation-state system, the information revolution that will extend into the twenty-first century transcends state boundaries. . . .

The very consumer-oriented specialty commodities upon which America built both economic and cultural power in the 1920s now comprise the sectors that best exemplify the new transnational, globalized economy and culture: automobiles, electrical appliances, food processing. During the 1980s, most giant American manufacturing firms substantially cut jobs in the United States and added to their labor forces abroad. Ford now builds a "world car" from parts manufactured and assembled on four continents. Even America's signature specialty product, the Hollywood film, is now a globalized phenomenon. . . .

Throughout much of the twentieth century, Americans exported, often with significant assistance from government, a distinctive mass culture that identified America with the future and served the country's geopolitical interests. As technologies of information and entertainment have spread in the late twentieth century, however, cultural interactions are less and less amenable to an analytical frame focused on the nation state. In this postmodern era, marked by simultaneous globalization and fragmentation, Americanization and internationalization increasingly overlap, and sites of cultural interaction multiply with less and less relationship to national boundaries. One might paraphrase the older prophecy that opened this essay and direct it to the United States itself: "The world, which you have conquered, will now conquer you."

The Gendering of Peoples and Nations

ANDREW ROTTER

An analysis of gender illuminates important aspects of relations between nations; here the concern is with the United States, in relation to India and, tangentially, to Pakistan. [The scholar] Mrinalini Sinha has written, "Empires and nations are gendered ideological constructs," to which one might add that nations—reacting to the real differences between them—also construct each other. For the purposes of this article, gender, or gendering, is not a static idea, but a transnational process: it is the assignment of certain characteristics based on prevailing ideas of masculinity and femininity to a people and nation by another people and nation. Masculinity and femininity are not, in this view, biologically determined categories, but culturally and socially conditioned constructs. Nations and the people who constitute them become gendered, and this affects the policies that other nations pursue toward them.

The history of United States foreign relations is not generally held to be susceptible to gender analysis. The makers of American foreign policy, mostly men, do not talk explicitly about gender issues or intentionally use a gendered vocabulary when they discuss their policies toward other countries. They talk about strategy and geopolitics, economics and access to raw materials, and systems, ours versus theirs. Because of this, as [the historian] Joan W. Scott has written, most historians believe that gender "refers only to those areas . . . involving relations between the sexes. Because, on the face of it, war, diplomacy, and high politics have not been explicitly about those relationships, gender seems not to apply and so continues to be irrelevant to the thinking of historians concerned with issues of politics and power."

Scott herself argues that "high politics itself is a gendered concept," and at least one diplomatic historian has pursued this insight. In her two important essays, Emily S. Rosenberg has suggested that historians of United States foreign relations

Reprinted by permission from Andrew Rotter, "Gender Relations, Foreign Relations: The United States and South Asia, 1947–1964," *Journal of American History* (81) September 1994.

undertake "a quest to understand the ever-changing ideologies related to gender, and their social and political implications." . . .

Examination of the gender issue requires the use of sources not often studied by diplomatic historians, among them anthropology and psychology texts, photographs, popular literature, travelers' accounts, films . . . and plays. The study also demands an unconventional reading of conventional sources on policy making. One must look at the usual published documents, in the State Department *Foreign Relations* volumes and elsewhere, and also make the rounds of American presidential libraries and national archives in the United States, Great Britain, and India. But the researcher with gender in mind must look for odd things in the documents: stray remarks about personal style or gesture, comments about a people's alleged "emotionalism" or "effeminacy," and even references to the kinds of parties American hosts put on for their Indian or Pakistani guests. What would seem a collection of marginalia to most diplomatic historians becomes a treasure trove of information demanding thick description to someone interested in culture.

Begin with the Western idea, which persists over time, that India is a female country. One of the most influential books about India written by a Westerner was Katherine Mayo's *Mother India,* published in 1927, a scathing attack on Hindu customs and practices. Mayo's choice of title was no accident; it built on a long tradition of representing India as female. The early twentieth-century American traveler Sydney Greenbie noted, apparently without irony, that on a map India "looked like the ponderous milk-bags of a cow holding the very living essence of Asia." Writers contrasted the West and India in ways that evoked gender. The West was grasping, materialistic, scientific, and calculating; India was spiritual, impulsive, and even irrational. "The masculine science of the West," wrote Greenbie, "has found out and wooed and loved or scourged this sleepy maiden of mysticism." In the discourse of India's relations with the West, concludes Richard Cronin, "one metaphor emerges as dominant. The West is a man, the East is a woman."

The Western representation of India as female conferred effeminacy on most Indian men. Caught in the enervating web of Hinduism, which Westerners regarded as less a religion than a pathology, the majority of Indian men had been deprived of their manliness and their virility. In the context of gender, it is possible to discern three features that Westerners historically assigned to most Indian men. The first of these was passivity and its more exaggerated forms; the second was emotionalism; the third was a lack of heterosexual energy. All of these features were associated with femininity, which Westerners regarded as effeminacy if exhibited by a man, and all imposed on India the Western constructions of the feminine and the masculine.

The first of these features amalgamated passivity, servility, and cowardice. Nothing, argued Westerners, could stir Hindu men out of their passive torpor. Indian men could endure anything, evidently without suffering from a sense of shame because of their inaction. They did not resist oppressors but rather regarded them with stupefying indifference. In *Mother India* Mayo wrote: "India was . . . the flaccid subject of a foreign rule. . . . Again and again conquering forces came sweeping through the mountain passes down out of Central Asia, and the ancient Hindu stock, softly absorbing each recurrent blow, quivered—and lay still." There was a "Hindu craze" in the United States during the 1920s and 1930s, and thousands of Americans became familiar with the "three levels of conduct" of Vedanta, the type of Hinduism most often brought to the country by Indian spiritual leaders, or swamis. Level one was "obedient activity"; level two "desireless activity"; the third and highest level was "pure passivity." It is not hard to imagine that such exhortations to obedience, renunciation, and quiescence could have been borrowed from prescriptive literature written for early twentieth-century American women. . . .

The idea that Indian men were passive, servile, and cowardly persisted into the Cold War period. British and American policy makers condemned Indian foreign policy makers for their unwillingness to take a stand in the conflict between the United States and the Soviet Union. A British official characterized Indian policy toward Indochina in 1950 as "non-interference i.e. doing nothing." Sir Archibald Nye, the perceptive British high commissioner in India during the late 1940s and early 1950s, blamed "Gandhian ethics" for what he called India's "quietist policy of non-resistance to aggression" and noted that Indian leaders were inclined to make "pronouncements which, when trouble appears on the horizon, are not acted upon." Americans agreed with this view. Officials in the Eisenhower administration reported that the Indians were "fearful" of United States arms sales to [its more openly anti-Soviet neighbor] Pakistan because "physically they are weak and fear aggression," a fear policy makers thought irrational and alarmist. . . .

A second trait that according to Americans and other Westerners revealed the effeminacy of Hindu men was emotionalism, usually associated with hypersensitivity. Rather than deal with issues logically and coolly, Hindu men flew off the handle—just as American women were allegedly apt to do. Americans constantly found verification for the cliché that the West was rational and tough, the East emotional and sensitive. In a 1948 profile, the Central Intelligence Agency (CIA) described Jawaharlal Nehru, the Indian prime minister: "Nehru is a man of broad vision and of integrity, but his character is weakened by a tendency toward emotionalism which at times destroys his sense of values. He is gracious as well as brilliant, but volatile and quick-tempered." A sense of pride came naturally with independence, but the Indians were an especially sensitive people—or so claimed ambassadors to India Loy Henderson (1948–1951) and Chester Bowles (1951–1953). In 1954, the former law partner of Secretary of State John Foster Dulles wrote that Indians had "an almost feminine hypersensitiveness with respect to the prestige of their country." President Dwight D. Eisenhower agreed. Reading of Indian objections to the administration's plan to provide arms for Pakistan, Eisenhower wrote Dulles: "This is one area of the world where, even more than most cases, emotion rather than reason seems to dictate policy." . . .

Where did these American representations of India come from? Who constructed gendered India, and why? One answer, perhaps the simplest, is that the representations came from the British and were deployed to serve the purposes of empire. Americans often saw India through British eyes, and the British made a clear distinction between hard-fighting, masculine, Indian men from the north and west—usually Muslims—and weak, effeminate Hindus from the south and Bengal. These images were popularized by Rudyard Kipling, whose stories made archetypes of the loyally militant Muslim and the craven, underhanded Bengali. Kipling's verse "East is East, and West is West, and never the twain shall meet" is well known, but few remember the next two lines: "But there is neither East nor West, Border, nor Breed, nor birth / When two strong men stand face to face, though they come from the ends of earth!" Kipling was referring to the camaraderie between British soldiers and the Muslim Pathans of the northwest frontier. The British who lived in India regarded the Bengali, on the other hand, as "litigious" and "effeminate," a "trouble-maker" who "doesn't appeal to many British people in the same way as the very much more manly, direct type from upper India." . . .

[T]he British characterized Bengali men as effeminate as part of the project of imperialism. Gendered British thinking about India emerged simultaneously with the rise of British imperialism. Gender inspired imperialism, allowed it to grow, and justified its frequently tortuous evolution. [The scholar] Ashis Nandy has argued that pre-modern Europe, with its agrarian economy and "peasant cosmology," valued the attributes of "femininity, childhood, and . . . 'primitivism.' " The emergence of capitalism and its concomitants "achievement and productivity" resulted in the re-jection of feminine, agrarian values and caused their projection onto the so-called "low cultures of Europe" and cultures in America, Africa, and Asia. By this process, Nandy writes, west Europeans came to see "uncivilized" others paradoxically, as innocent children but also as "devious, effeminate, and passive-aggressive." In com-bination particularly with economic factors—it was the East India Company, not the British government, that established its rule over much of India in the late eighteenth and early nineteenth centuries—gender explained to Britons why India needed their help. The innocent children of India required the protection of the strong men of the West. Other nations, especially Russia, threatened India. Within the country, the British saw their presence as essential to protect the weakest elements of Indian society. They argued that despite their effeminate cowardliness—or perhaps because of it—Hindu men frequently brutalized the lower castes and women especially. . . . As a matter of fact, they presided over a system that promoted child marriage, abused brides who married with insufficient dowries, and encouraged *sati,* the self-immolation of widows. British imperialists argued that interposing their power be-tween the upper castes and the helpless masses was their only humane course. . . .

Americans learned much of what they knew about empire from the British. The United States became an imperialist nation in its own right, but like the British raj, the American empire was undergirded by perceptions based on gender. Gendered imagery, linked to discourses on race, figured prominently in the white subjugation of Native Americans. The image of the noble savage, childlike and innocent and in com-munion with Mother Earth, largely gave way to the image of the bloodthirsty savage who threatened white womanhood and therefore had to be controlled. When Ameri-can policy makers looked abroad in the late nineteenth century, they beheld nations whose populations seemed to cry out for the protection, guidance, and discipline that only white men could provide. As [the historian] Emily Rosenberg notes, "Women, nonwhite races, and tropical countries often received the same kinds of symbolic characterizations from white male policy makers: emotional, irrational, irresponsible, unbusinesslike, unstable, and childlike." Concerned, perhaps, that their own mascu-linity was at risk—a concern of American men at least as far back as the Revolution, when Tom Paine had charged men to awaken from "fatal and unmanly slumbers"—policy makers developed patriarchal designs on the weaker members of the family of nations. There were figurative children out there who needed help, and there were figurative women who were too soft or emotional to take care of themselves. . . .

Like the señoritas who so often represented them in cartoons, the Latin Ameri-can nations could be wooed by an appropriate suitor—Uncle Sam—and also required male protection from the lecherous Spanish. American gender perceptions of East

Asian nations swung on weights and counterweights. For officials at the United States legation in Peking (Beijing) in the late nineteenth century, China was inert, weak, and therefore vulnerable to European imperialism. Chinese mandarins were soft and indolent, surrounded by eunuchs and more concerned with palace intrigue than with putting some necessary steel into the military. That vision changed with the Boxer Rebellion in 1899 and 1900; a cartoon drawn in the latter year shows Uncle Sam and President William McKinley moving against the Boxers with sword and bayonet, though too late for an American woman and child who lie dead before them. Americans viewed the Japanese with ambivalence during the first decades of the twentieth century, but American unease turned to loathing following the "Rape of Nanjing" in 1937.

In Vietnam, the United States fought for and against allegedly unmanly men. Vietnamese men were slight of build and smooth skinned. They held hands, which according to Gen. William Westmoreland, struck the American solders as "odd and effeminate." Who could feel manly fighting for men like these? Why die (in Loren Baritz's ironic phrase) "in defense of perverts"? Vietnamese women also fought the Americans, increasing the humiliation of defeat. President Lyndon B. Johnson, whose efforts to assert his manhood through his foreign policy were at least as pronounced as those of Kennedy, first castrated his chief adversary: "I have Ho Chi Minh's pecker in my pocket"; then effeminized him: "I'm going up old Ho Chi Minh's leg an inch at a time." The inability of the United States to win in Vietnam caused great frustration, and American cultural discourse after 1973 attempted to reconstruct the shattered masculinity of American men. It may be that American manhood was restored with the United States–led coalition victory over Iraq in the 1991 Gulf War. Saddam Hussein was punished, said George Bush, for having "raped, pillaged, and plundered" Kuwait. As a result, the United States had finally "kicked the Vietnam syndrome." During the brief ground war a *New York Times* reporter saw an American soldier brandish a pair of women's underpants and exult: "*This* is what we are fighting for!" Women were thus symbolically returned to their rightful place in American society, and Kuwait joined the ranks of nations gathered under the protective arm of United States paternalism.

Race and the American Century

GERALD C. HORNE

[O]ne cannot begin to understand U.S. foreign policy during this century without contemplating race and racism, just as one cannot begin to understand the ebb and flow of race and racism in this nation without contemplating the global context. Indeed, just as some have suggested that "class struggle" is the motive force of history, this insight should be complemented with the idea that relations—or "struggles"—between and among nations is the locomotive of history and, most definitely, is the leading factor determining the advance and retreat of "white supremacy." . . .

Gerald C. Horne, "Race from Power: U.S. Foreign Policy and the General Crisis of White Supremacy," *Diplomatic History* 23 (Summer 1999), 438–440, 442–443, 448–451, 453–457, 459–461. Copyright © 1999 by Blackwell Publishing. Reprinted with permission.

W. E. B. Du Bois announced almost one hundred years ago that "the problem of the twentieth century is the problem of the color line." Yet, this founder of the NAACP pointedly did not limit this formulation to "black-white" relations; in fact, he went on to state forcefully what he did mean in words that too often have been forgotten: this "problem" included "the relation of the darker to the lighter races of men [*sic*] in Asia and Africa, in America and the islands of the sea." In some ways today's era has seen a retreat from the more expansive racial discourse of a century ago, which not only refused to view race as bipolar but also insisted on its global nature. This more expansive approach inherently is more appropriate when considering U.S. foreign policy and the question of "white supremacy." . . .

Theodore Roosevelt, the man who led this nation into the American Century, was an admirer of some of the most notorious white supremacists of his era. He was among those who were obsessed with notions of race and, particularly, what was called "race suicide," that is, the idea that those of European descent were a global minority whose birth rates portended even steeper declines. Men and women—who were "white"—should be "eager lovers," he thought, in order to arrest this development; these conceptions of race, which implicated gender, were also intended to undergird class privilege. An indication of Roosevelt's beliefs was his friendship with Madison Grant, one of the leading racial theorists of that era.

Another leading racial theorist was Lothrop Stoddard, who in turn was quite friendly with Madison Grant. Unlike many today who speak of race solely in the domestic context, Stoddard saw race as a global phenomenon. "The first real challenge to white world supremacy," he thought "was the Russo-Japanese War of 1904." As a result of an Asian nation's victory over a European power, this holder of a Harvard doctorate argued that "throughout Asia and even in Africa, races hitherto resigned or sullenly submissive began to dream of throwing off white control." The United States as one of Europe's "white outposts" was viewed as central to reversing this "rising tide of color." Instead, Moscow's defeat at the hands of Tokyo marked a crucial turning point in the general crisis of "white supremacy," just as it accelerated the crisis of Czarist Russia. . . .

From the point of view of "white supremacy," there was justifiable concern about Russia's defeat. Japan's victory "electrified the atmosphere in India. It shattered the illusion of European invincibility." India as well as other colonized nations learned another lesson that did not augur well for the hegemony of European colonialism; for Tokyo's victory revealed that the "state played an indispensable and large part in the development of a nation . . . and therefore that good government by a foreign nation was no substitute for self-government." . . .

This paradoxical situation came clear in the aftermath of World War I when Japan clamored at Versailles for the establishment of principles of international discourse favoring racial equality. Needless to say, this development was viewed with more than mild concern by the Southerner—Woodrow Wilson—who occupied the White House, not to mention his Dixiecrat comrades. There was a fierce debate on this Japanese resolution on the "equality of nations"; the U.S. delegation feared what this might mean concerning immigration, particularly to California. The United States viewed itself not just as an Atlantic nation but as a Pacific one as well; a key difference between the two, of course, was that racial tensions were more prominent in the latter region. Reputedly, "the President said that he did not trust the Japanese."

They very existence of Japan—a modern capitalist nation in Asia—called into question the essential premises of "white supremacy" and, as a partial consequence, was viewed as a dire threat to the United States. Japan's existence also hindered the execution of U.S. foreign policy during this era, as Tokyo established friendly relations with the leaders of a sector of the U.S. body politic that was not necessarily favorable to "white supremacy"—African Americans. After World War I, A. Philip Randolph—the legendary black labor leader—"concluded that Japan, plus the power of other free nations 'combined with an international league of workingmen' could effectively pressure the Western powers." Randolph backed up his rhetoric by joining in 1919 with Marcus Garvey and others at the home of one of the nation's few black women millionaires—C. J. Walker—to form the International League of Darker Peoples. The league was short lived but one thing it did do was to arrange a meeting with a visiting Japanese publisher and editor at the Waldorf-Astoria in New York City in order to seek Tokyo's assistance in raising the question of racial equality at Versailles. Tellingly, the league not only encompassed those of African descent but those of Asian—particularly Japanese—descent as well.

Increasingly, a growing sector of those in the African diaspora felt that they could play upon the contradictions between Washington and London on the one hand and Tokyo on the other to their own advantage. Both British and U.S. military intelligence took careful note of an editorial in Garvey's newspaper, *Negro World,* which said as much: "With the rising militarism of Asia and the standing militarism of Europe one can foresee nothing else but an armed clash between the white and yellow races. When this clash of millions comes, an opportunity will have presented itself to the Negro people of the world to free themselves. . . . The next war will be between the Negroes and the whites, unless our demands for justice are recognized. With Japan to fight with us we can win such a war." Eliminating the more egregious aspects of "white supremacy" was increasingly seen in Washington as a question of national security, though this forced march away from the power of race was often cloaked in the disguise of morality. . . .

Similarly, World War I led directly to another development that can be said to have contributed to the general crisis of "white supremacy": the Bolshevik Revolution. And, like Tokyo, this new "threat" was linked with the staunchest domestic opponent of "white supremacy": African Americans. Reportedly, Woodrow Wilson felt that the "American Negro" troops "returning from abroad would be our greatest medium in conveying bolshevism to America." In addition to the question of "reds," the president was also deathly concerned with the question of "whites." Thus, he added, the "French people have placed the Negro soldier in France on [a level of] equality with the white man, and 'it has gone to their heads.'"

"White supremacy" was producing ever more complex complications for U.S. foreign policy. Early in 1919 one harried U.S. intelligence agent argued that increasingly African-American radicalism was aiming at a "combination of the other colored races of the world. As a colored movement it looks to Japan for leadership; as a radical movement it follows Bolshevism and has intimate relations with various socialistic groups throughout the United States." The "combination" of this "Colored Scare" and "Red Scare" was taken quite seriously by Washington.

As ever, U.S. elites had to worry that "white supremacy" at home had a noticeable downside: those not sharing in its bounty might feel obligated to align with the real and imagined enemies of Washington, thereby jeopardizing national security. Even France, of all nations, whose exploitation of Africans was noticeably egregious, often took a different tack toward African Americans, which provided it with leverage in Washington.

Still—Japan and France notwithstanding—it was the advent of the Soviet Union that stirred the most concern, not only because this nation quickly attracted a number of leading African-American intellectuals but, in addition, it also made inroads in Africa itself by pledging to assist those nations struggling to throw off the yoke of colonialism. Yet even here Japanese played a pivotal role. Sen Katayama helped to organize Communist parties in Japan, Mexico, Canada, and the United States. Eventually he was elected to the leading body of the Communist International, based in Moscow, where in 1928 he helped to formulate the official position of the Reds on the "Negro Question," which included the "right of Negroes to self-determination in the Southern States." The "Comintern" pledged to assist African-Americans in their effort to discard the yoke of Jim Crow and third-class citizenship—a promise that could not be easily disregarded. Katayama was also a close friend of the Jamaican-American poet Claude McKay during this writer's sojourn with the organized left. McKay was just one of a host of leading black intellectuals—a list that was to include W. E. B. Du Bois, [the author and playwrite] Shirley Graham Du Bois, [the singer] Paul Robeson, [the writer] Langston Hughes, and [the feminist and journalist] Claudia Jones, among others—who were to align with the forces of socialism: the pestilence of "white supremacy" was no small factor in helping to explicate this crucial decision.

As Tokyo, then Moscow in jujitsu fashion began to turn "white supremacy" back against those in the United States that benefited from it, it was beginning to dawn that racialist thinking could carry the seeds of its own destruction. Just as capitalism itself inexorably spawned its own gravediggers, the same could be said for "white supremacy." This realization helped to guarantee that ultimately Washington could gain an advantage over its erstwhile allies in Paris and Brussels and Lisbon by taking positions on colonialism in Africa that were not in total accord with those of Western Europe; this realization also helped to ensure that Jim Crow itself would not survive the American Century. . . .

World War II, inter alia, represented a true crisis of "white supremacy." It was becoming evident that Washington and London particularly were finding it ever more difficult to explain why lives must be sacrificed so that they would not be dominated by Tokyo and Berlin, while the United States and United Kingdom continued to maintain racialized systems of oppression at home and abroad. Ineluctably, World War II compelled these great powers to endure a "race" away from the "power" that the more outlandish versions of "white supremacy" represented. Even though powerful forces in the United States had significant influence on Nazi ideology, there was a sobering realization in Washington that doctrines of racial and ethnic supremacy—if left unchecked—could lead to a holocaust of unimaginable proportions. Still, like the cowboys of old, the United States began to exit the saloon of "white supremacy" with their guns blazing, dropping atomic bombs in a final flourish on Japan as a concluding reminder of what would befall those so bold as to challenge the existing racial order. Then they turned their attention to Moscow, which too had been seeking to take advantage of "white supremacy"—the once

proud system of racial privilege that now was being seen as a major liability threatening the continued existence of the American Century.

Though the praxis of "white supremacy" was castigated officially and eroded
substantially during the Cold War, it was not extinguished altogether. Instead, it was
buttressed by an aggressive anticommunism that had the advantage of being—at
least formally—nonracial. The anticolonial upsurge, however, was designed to overturn the racialized system of oppression—and underdevelopment—that colonialism
represented. In turn, the unjust—and racialized—enrichment that colonialism represented could be better defended in this new era by terming anticolonial opponents as
"Communist." The tagging of anticolonialists as "red" slowed down the movement
against colonialism and—perhaps not coincidentally—gave "white supremacy" a
new lease on life.

In the United States this battle against "white supremacy" had a certain unique-
ness. [The historian] Mary Dudziak is largely correct in asserting that "desegregation" was a "Cold War imperative." Without slighting at all the heroic contribution
of those who participated in the "civil rights movement," it is long past time to recognize that—just like the anti-apartheid movement—the international community
played a substantial role in compelling the United States to move away from the
more outrageous aspects of "white supremacy." How could Washington credibly
charge Moscow with human rights violations when minorities in this nation were
treated so horribly? The pressure from the international community was felt most
directly—and powerfully—during the 1957 school desegregation crisis in Little
Rock. It is clear in retrospect that President Dwight Eisenhower's decision to commit troops to this racial tinderbox in Arkansas was motivated substantially by his
sensitivity to the damage this crisis was having on the global image of the United
States, particularly at a time when the Soviet launching of Sputnik was causing
severe doubts about Washington's overall position. Simultaneously, these domestic
maneuvers affected U.S. foreign policy as Washington found it more difficult to
align with erstwhile allies in South Africa and Rhodesia as recently enfranchised
African Americans and a newly energized anticolonial movement began to object.

The importance of the international community in the battle against segregation
can be detected by examining the travails of those in the vanguard of this struggle
on this side of the Atlantic. The attack on Paul Robeson accelerated when he was
reported to have cast doubt on the desire of African Americans to participate in a
war against the Soviet Union, thus reminding U.S. rulers of the unease they had
felt about waging war against Japan a few years earlier. Martin Luther King's difficulties accelerated after he began to denounce the war in Vietnam more forcefully.
African Americans—and their opponents—implicitly recognized that a formidable
weapon in the conflict with domestic racism was international leverage.

Still, Robeson, King, and others persevered and helped to keep global issues on
the front burner at a time when the domestic struggle against Jim Crow was preoccu-
pying most. Africa generally and Southern Africa particularly became the epicenter
of the struggle against "white supremacy" during the Cold War. Moscow—the much
reviled "evil empire" of U.S. propaganda—actually provided diplomatic and material assistance to the Africans, much to the consternation of Washington: the United
States had to be concerned that African Americans particularly would be moved
by this development, which could present a ticklish domestic and international

problem for Washington. Thus, during the decisive stages of the Algerian Revolution, Moscow—according to Soviet leader Boris Ponomarev—"supplied free to the People's Liberation Army . . . 25 thousand rifles, 21 thousand machine guns and sub-machines guns, 1300 howitzers, cannons and mortars, many tens of thousands of pistols and other weapons. Over 5 million rubles' worth of clothes, provisions and medical supplies were supplied to Algeria by Soviet social organizations alone. Hundreds of wounded from the Algerian Liberation Army were saved and treated in the Soviet Union. Soviet wheat, sugar, butter, conserves, condensed milk, etc., streamed into Algeria." Moscow provided similar assistance to those fighting colonialism and other forms of exploitation in IndoChina, Southern Africa, and Cuba, which too had a substantial population of African descent. Indeed, this assistance to those fighting racialized systems of oppression was no small factor in sparking an economic and political crisis that led to the collapse of the USSR.

Many in the United States felt such aid violated the basic norms of "peaceful co-existence" and "detente," though without this Soviet aid, Asians and Africans—and Cubans—would have faced more difficulty in confronting their opponents. These opponents—particularly those in Washington—continually asserted that their opposition to this Third World-Moscow alliance was based not on some outdated devotion to "white supremacy" but the Cold War creed of anticommunism.

Southern Rhodesia, the colony that [the famous American Indian fighter] Frederick Russell Burnham had helped to found decades earlier, provides an illustrative case study of the fate of "white supremacy" during a Cold War era when this doctrine was officially denounced. The fact is that despite these official bromides, racialist thinking continued to exert a powerful influence on U.S. foreign policy, even when it was not disguised in the finery of the newer philosophy of anticommunism.

Dean Acheson, by his own admission, was "present at the creation" of the Cold War confrontation. His anti-Communist credentials were impeccable and he was a member in good standing of the U.S. ruling class. Yet, in his private communications—and at times those in public as well—he conceded that "white supremacy" was no negligible factor in explaining his support for the minority regimes in Southern Africa. Often that support was expressed directly to Sir Roy Welensky, a prominent member of the Rhodesian elite.

In 1965 this colony had refused to accede to the winds of change blowing through the continent and declared a "unilateral declaration of independence" in defiance of the movement toward decolonization. Though denounced by many in the international community, Acheson—and many other influential U.S. leaders—adamantly backed the rebel regime in Rhodesia. Why? Sir Roy hinted at one reason in 1971 when Richard Nixon was cozying up to China, a maneuver that was decisive in creating a bloc that ultimately brought down the Soviet Union. One would have thought that the usually far-sighted Rhodesian leader would have sensed the obvious geopolitical implications of this strategem but he had other important issues on his mind—namely the impact the Nixon maneuver had on "white supremacy"—as he informed Acheson: "We Whites seldom appreciate the extent to which the Black and the Brown man order their thinking on how strong or weak they think one is, and it is, therefore always unwise to start off on a basis they think one is afraid of them. This may sound childish to you Dean, but I've lived all my life where the Whites have been outnumbered many times. I don't know the Yellow man, but I'm told that he is even more concerned about his dignity and face-saving than the Black man and will always interpret our casual ways as being weak." Acheson fed and reflected this racialist thinking, telling his interlocutor, "I still cling to Bret Harte's aphorism, 'That for ways that are dark And for tricks that are vain The Heathen Chinese is peculiar.' But no more so than the heathen Japanese."

Welensky, Acheson, and many other leaders from the Pan-European world were not simply driven by anticommunism during the Cold War—they were driven by "white supremacy" as well. It did appear that as the Pan-African ideal took hold in the midst of the Cold War, a revived "Pan-Europeanism" arose to counter it. This was particularly the case in the United States. . . .

For a good deal of the American Century, "race" was seen as a global concern with Japan rarely far from calculations about this concept. Tokyo had proved to be a nettlesome foreign policy concern for Washington, as the Pacific war amply demonstrated. With the Cold War, however, Japan became a U.S. ally and its ability to attract disgruntled African Americans searching for leverage against their own government virtually disappeared. Correspondingly, "race" was reduced to a domestic concern—or at most, a concern that implicated Africans generally.

Yet, Washington's Cold War policy of anticommunism undercut the antiracists of the left in Tokyo as it provided leverage to those Japanese who were the ideological descendants of the purveyors of prewar racialist thinking, particularly "anti-white" thinking. When the Soviet Union collapsed, the adhesive that had bound many of the Japanese right—as well as many Chinese elites—to the United States eroded and what emerged was a troubling eruption of racialist thinking.

Mahatir Mohamad, prime minister of Malaysia, was a direct beneficiary of the protracted Cold War campaign—spearheaded by London and assisted by Washington—that routed the left in his country. Shintaro Isihara, a leading Japanese conservative, was the kind of anticommunist that the United States smiled on during the Cold War. Recently they produced a volume that raises intriguing questions about the future of "race"—and "white supremacy"—in the twenty-first century. They approvingly cite "Lenin who said that European prosperity was based on exploiting the cheap labor and abundant resources of the colonies. When that rapacious plunder became impossible, the sun began to set on Europe. . . . Europe 'surpassed' Asia through plunder and exploitation." "Western civilization" itself, they state, "was built on war." This broad assertion includes the United States. "Europeans and Americans are still dreaming of past glory," they suggest; they go on to warn that "Asians"—not just Japanese and Malaysians—"are fed up with the blustering and threats of American trade negotiators." "Asia," they warn, "presents a more serious threat to the West than even militaristic Japan did earlier this century." With bluntness, they charge that the Gulf War was no more than another expression of white supremacy: "If the United States can get away with this—peddling arms throughout the Middle East, intervening militarily to protect its supply of oil, and arm-twisting Japan to foot the bill—then the white race still rules the world"; "it is impossible to communicate with Americans as well as we do with Asians," they conclude. Why? "Color is one reason . . . the perception that white people are better than colored people." They pointedly observe that it may "take a cataclysmic event" to "shake the great majority of Americans out of their hubris and self-righteousness" and suggest that "we may have to form an Asian united front against Americanization." . . .

The brusque reassertion of racial thinking in Asia has emerged just as the United States finds that relations with both China and Japan are not the best; it is strategically impractical to maintain prickly relations with both of these Asian giants simultaneously, though the bluntness of "white supremacy" makes it difficult to forge subtle distinctions between and among "non-whites." Simultaneously, influential thinkers in this nation are warning of a "clash of civilizations"—warnings that bear an eery resemblance to the racial maunderings of Lothrop Stoddard and Madison Grant in the early part of this American Century. As ever, the contours of race in this nation will be shaped by developments in the global arena and, it appears, U.S. foreign policy will continue to be shaped by racial considerations.

National Security, Core Values, and Power

MELVYN P. LEFFLER

National security policy encompasses the decisions and actions deemed imperative to protect domestic core values from external threats. This definition is important because it underscores the relation of the international environment to the internal situation in the United States and accentuates the importance of people's ideas and perceptions in constructing the nature of external dangers as well as the meaning of national identity and vital interests.

By encouraging students of American foreign policy to examine both the foreign and the domestic factors shaping policy, by obligating them to look at the structure of the international system as well as the domestic ideas and interests shaping policy, the national security approach seeks to overcome some of the great divides in the study of American diplomatic history. . . . Generally, realist historians believe that diplomatic behavior responds (or should respond) to the distribution of power in the international system; most revisionist and corporatist scholars and most historians who dwell on ideas and ideology assume that domestic economic requirements, social and cultural forces, and political constituencies are of overwhelming importance. By relating foreign threats to internal core values, the national security model encourages efforts to bridge the gaps between these divergent interpretative approaches, or, more precisely, to see that these variables must be studied in relation to one another and nuanced judgments made about how they bear on one another.

Although the national security approach acknowledges that power plays a role in the functioning of the international system and that interests shape the behavior of nations, it does not reify the salience of power or the centrality of interest in the construction of foreign policy. Indeed, in one of the most sophisticated approaches to the study of national security, Barry Buzan points out that realists who dwell on power and idealists who focus on peace often have obscured the meaning of national security, defined as the protection of core values from external threats. More recently, the most sophisticated approach to national security reconceptualizes the concept and takes explicit cognizance of the impact of culture and identity. National interests, argues Peter Katzenstein, "are constructed through a process of social interaction"; "security interests are defined by actors who respond to cultural factors." States are social actors operating in social environments. National identity is constructed as a result of human agency, and external threats are measured in relation to their perceived impact on core values. . . .

External dangers come in many varieties. The historian of U.S. foreign policy must appraise the intentions and capabilities of the nation's prospective foes. But that step is only the beginning. Views of a potential adversary, after all, are heavily influenced by perceptions of other variables such as the impact of technological change, the appeal of one's own organizing ideology, the lessons of the past, and the structural patterns of the international system itself. . . .

In studying the systemic sources of foreign policy behaviors, the national security approach demands that analysts distinguish between realities and perceptions. This task, as simple as it sounds, is fraught with difficulty because it is often harder for historians to agree on what constitutes an actual danger than on what is a perceived threat. Nancy Mitchell shows, for example, that German imperial actions in the early 1990s engendered enormous feelings of insecurity and hostility among Americans, but that, in fact, German actions and policies were fare less threatening than widely perceived. She analyzes how rhetoric, military images, and trade competition conjured up fears and shaped perceptions that were inconsistent with the realities of German behavior. Likewise, the very different interpretations of American diplomacy in the 1920s and 1930s between "realists" on the one hand and "revisionists" or "corporatists" on the other hand rests in part on assessments of the degree of threat to vital U.S. security interests in the interwar years. If there were no real threats before the middle or late 1930s, then contemporary proponents of arms limitation treaties, arbitration agreements, and non-aggression pacts can be viewed as functional pragmatists seeking to create a viable liberal capitalist international order rather than as naïve idealists disregarding the realities of an inherently unstable and ominous balance of power.

Perceptions of events abroad, however, are themselves greatly influenced by the ideas, ideals, and core values of the perceiver. The national security approach demands that as much attention be focused on how the American government determines its core values as on how it preceives external dangers. The term *core values* is used here rather than *vital interests* because the latter implies something more material and tangible than is appropriate for a national security imperative. The United States has rarely defined its core values in narrowly economic or territorial terms. Core values usually *fuse* material self-interest with more fundamental goals like the defense of the state's organizing ideology, such as liberal capitalism, the protection of its political institutions, and the safeguarding of its physical base or territorial integrity. . . .

The protection and pursuit of core values requires the exercise of power. Power is the capacity to achieve intended results. Power may be an end in itself as well as a means toward an end. In the twentieth century, power (including military power) derives primarily from economic capabilities. Power stems from the scale, vigor, and productivity of one's internal economy and its access to or control over other countries' industrial infrastructure, skilled manpower, and raw materials. Power is relative.

The chief characteristic of twentieth-century American foreign policy has been the willingness and capacity of the United States to develop and exert its power beyond its nineteenth-century range to influence the economic, political, and military affairs of Europe and Asia. This trend has manifested itself in the evolution of the Open Door policy, in the aid to the Allies in both world wars, in the wielding of American financial leverage, in the assumption of strategic obligations, in the deployment of troops overseas, in the provision of economic and military assistance, in the undertaking of covert operations, in the huge expenditures on armaments, in the growth of the American multinational corporation, and in the assumption of a hegemonic role over the world capitalist system. The national security approach helps to make sense out of these developments. Alterations in the distribution of power, changes in the international system, and developments in technology influence the perception of threat and the definition of core values and impel American officials to exercise power in varying ways. . . .

Although occasionally criticized for its disregard of ideological and cultural concepts, the national security approach to the study of American foreign relations should be conceived as perfectly congruent with these new directions of scholarship. Central to the national security approach is the concept of core values. National security is about the protection of core values, that is, the identification of threats and the adoption of policies to protect core values. The new studies on culture and ideology mesh seamlessly with the synthetic qualities of a national security paradigm because they help to illuminate the construction and meaning of core values. In his insightful book on social scientists and nation building in the Kennedy era, Michael Latham writes that "A larger, more deliberate analysis of ideology and identity . . . can open new areas of inquiry by introducing a less reductive analysis of the 'interests' that critics have typically discerned behind official discourse." And he concludes that "in the midst of a collapsing European colonial order, social scientists and Kennedy administration policymakers conceived of [modernization] as a means to promote a liberal world in which the development of 'emerging' nations would protect the security of the United States."

The fervor with which the United States waged the Cold War can only be grasped by understanding the role of ideology in the construction of American national identity. In his succinct, valuable volume on Manifest Destiny in American history, Anders Stephanson reminds us of the puritannical, millenarial, and religious impulses that infuse America's approach to the world. Other factors might have influenced the Cold War, he writes, "but the operative framework in which they all fit is the story of American exceptionalism, with its missionary implications." And this emphasis on American nationalist ideology, sometimes conflated with notions of an American century or a Wilsonian century, pulsates through the new foreign policy literature. "American nationalist ideology," writes John Fousek, "provided the principal underpinning for the broad public consensus that supported Cold War foreign policy."

But when translated into policy, the ideological fervor was always calibrated. . . .

Preponderance [overwhelming global power] and hegemony, as Paul Kennedy and Robert Gilpin have written, confer advantages and impose costs. If threats are exaggerated and commitments overextended, if one's credibility is vested in the achievement of too many goals, one's relative power will erode and one's core values may become imperiled. There is an ominous dynamic influencing the behavior patterns of great powers. Whether or not the United States will succumb to it will depend on whether groups, bureaucracies, and individual policymakers can find a means of restoring a viable equilibrium among threats, core values, and the exercise of power.

Bureaucratic Politics and Policy Outcomes

J. GARRY CLIFFORD

In the mid-1960s, when members of the Harvard Faculty Study Group on Bureaucracy, Politics, and Policy began to write their scholarly tomes, their sometime colleague in the mathematics department, the irreverent folk singer Tom Lehrer, inadvertently gave song to what came to be called the "bureaucratic politics" approach to the study of U.S. foreign policy. In his ballad about a certain German emigre rocket scientist, Lehrer wrote: "Once the rockets are up / Who cares where they come down? / That's not my department! / Said Wernher von Braun." Lehrer's ditty, by suggesting that government is a complex, compartmentalized machine and that those running the machine do not always intend what will result, anticipated the language of bureaucratic politics. The dark humor also hinted that the perspective might sometimes excuse as much as it explains about the foreign policy of the United States.

The formal academic version of bureaucratic politics came a few years later with the publication in 1971 of Graham T. Allison's *Essence of Decision.* Building on works by Warner R. Schilling, Roger Hilsman, Richard E. Neustadt, and other political scientists who emphasized informal bargaining within the foreign policy process, and adding insights from organization theorists such as James G. March and Herbert A. Simon, Allison examined the 1962 Cuban Missile Crisis to counter the traditional assumption that foreign policy is produced by the purposeful acts of unified national governments. Allison argued that instead of behaving like a "rational actor," the Kennedy administration's actions during the crisis were best explained as "outcomes" of standard operating procedures followed by separate organizations (the navy's blockade, the Central Intelligence Agency's U-2 overflights, and the air force's scenarios for a surgical air strike) and as a result of compromise and competition among hawks and doves seeking to advance individual and organizational versions of the national interest. Allison soon collaborated with Morton H. Halperin to formalize the bureaucratic politics paradigm. Other scholars followed with bureaucratic analyses of topics including American decision making in the Vietnam War, the nonrecognition of China, the Marshall Plan, U.S.-Turkish relations, the Antiballistic Missile (ABM) decision, nuclear weapons accidents, and U.S. international economic policy, as well as refinements and critiques of the Allison-Halperin model. The John F. Kennedy School of Government at Harvard made bureaucratic politics the centerpiece of its new public policy program, and Allison became its dean. In 1999, his framework long since hailed as "one of the most widely disseminated concepts in all of social sciences," Allison and Philip Zelikow prepared an extensive, revised edition of *Essence of Decision* to refute political science theorists who "explain state behavior by system-level or external factors alone."

The Allisonian message holds that U.S. foreign policy has become increasingly political and cumbersome with the growth of bureaucracy. Diversity and conflict permeate the policy process. There is no single "maker" of foreign policy. Policy flows instead from an amalgam of organizations and political actors who differ substantially on any particular issue and who compete to advance their own personal and organizational interests as they try to influence decisions. Even in the aftermath of such national disasters as Pearl Harbor or the terrorist attacks of September 2001, turf wars proliferate because agencies reflexively resist reorganization and scapegoat others to avoid blame. The president, while powerful, is not omnipotent; he is one chief among many. For example, President Ronald Reagan may have envisaged his Strategic Defense Initiative (or "Star Wars") as a workable program to shield entire populations from the threat of nuclear war, but hardliners in the Pentagon saw it primarily as an antiballistic missile defense that would gain a technological advantage over the Soviet Union and stifle public agitation for more substantial arms control proposals.

Even after a direct presidential decision the "game" does not end because decisions are often ignored or reversed. Just as Jimmy Carter thought he had killed the B-1 bomber, only to see it revived during the Reagan years, so too did Franklin D. Roosevelt veto a "Pacific First" strategy in 1942, whereupon the Joint Chiefs of Staff, in historian Mark Stoler's words, "formally submitted to his [FDR's] orders but did so in such a way as to enable them to pursue a modified version of their alternative strategy" for the rest of World War II. Because organizations rely on routines and plans derived from experience with familiar problems, those standard routines usually form the basis for options furnished the president. Ask an organization to do what it has not done previously, and it will usually do what the U.S. military did in Vietnam: It will follow existing doctrines and procedures, modifying them only slightly in deference to different conditions.

Final decisions are also "political resultants," the product of compromise and bargaining among the various participants. As Allison puts it, policies are "resultants in the sense that what happens is not chosen . . . but rather results from compromise, conflict, and confusion of officials with diverse interests and unequal influence; political in the sense [of] . . . bargaining along regularized channels among individual members of government." Similarly, once a decision is made, considerable slippage can occur in implementing it. What follows becomes hostage to standard operating procedures and the parochial interests of the actors and agencies doing the implementing. Even when a president personally monitors performance, as John F. Kennedy tried to do during the missile crisis, organizational routines and hierarchies are so rigid and complex that the president cannot micromanage all that happens. Not only did Kennedy not know that antisubmarine warfare units were routinely forcing Soviet submarines to the surface, thus precipitating the very confrontations he wanted to avoid, but the president was also unaware that NATO's nuclear-armed fighter-bombers had been put on a nuclear Quick Reaction Alert (QRA), thus escaping the tight personal controls he had placed on Jupiter missiles in Turkey and Italy.

The bureaucratic politics perspective also suggests that intramural struggles over policy can consume so much time and attention that dealing with external realities can become secondary. Virtually every study of nuclear arms negotiations from the Baruch Plan to START confirms the truism that arriving at a consensus among the various players and agencies within the U.S. government was more complicated, if not more difficult, than negotiating with the Soviets. Ironically, officials who are finely attuned to the conflict and compartmentalization within the American government often see unitary, purposeful behavior on the part of other governments. Recall the rush to judgment about the Soviet shooting down of a Korean airliner in autumn 1983 as compared to the embarrassed and defiant explanations emanating from Washington when a U.S. navy spy plane collided with a Chinese jet and crash-landed on Hainan Island in 2001. When NATO forces carried out long-planned war games (Operation Able Archer) in the aftermath of the KAL 007 shoot-down, Washington experts scoffed at intelligence reports that Soviet leaders genuinely feared a nuclear first strike, calling it a disinformation ploy. Only President Reagan, as one scholar has noted, worried that "[Andrei] Gromyko and [Yuri] Andropov are just two players sitting on top of a large military machine" and that panic and miscalculation might lead to Armageddon, so he told his startled senior advisers. Reagan's very next speech called for "nuclear weapons" to be "banished from the face of the earth."

Several important criticisms have been leveled at the bureaucratic politics approach. Some critics contend that ideological core values shared by those whom Richard J. Barnet has called "national security managers" weigh more in determining policy than do any differences attributable to bureaucratic position. The axiom "where you stand depends on where you sit" has had less influence, they argue, than the generational mindset of such individuals as McGeorge Bundy, Paul Nitze, John J. McCloy, and Clark Clifford, whose participation in the foreign policy establishment spanned decades and cut across bureaucratic and partisan boundaries. Because, as Robert S. McNamara later observed of the missile crisis, "you can't manage" crises amidst all the "misinformation, miscalculation, misjudgment, and human fallibility," other critics suggest that the framework lets decisionmakers off the hook by failing to pinpoint responsibility. Indeed, the president can dominate the bureaucracy by selecting key players and setting the rules of the game. Even though President Reagan once joked that "sometimes our right hand doesn't know what our far right-hand is doing," his defenders erred in absolving Reagan by blaming the Iran-contra affair on insiders "with their own agenda" who allegedly deceived the detached president by feeding him false information. Yet, as Theodore Draper has clearly demonstrated, at all top-level meetings on Iran-contra, President Reagan spoke more than any of his advisers, forcefully steered discussions, and made basic decisions, whether or not he subsequently approved every operational detail. The historian must be careful in each case to judge how much of the buck that stops with the president has already been spent by the bureaucracy. . . .

Yet such defeats in the bureaucratic politics approach may not hamper historians, who do not need models that predict perfectly. Unlike political scientists, they do not seek to build better theories or to propose more effective management techniques. Because the bureaucratic politics approach emphasizes state-level analysis, it cannot answer such system-level questions as why the United States has opposed revolutions or why East-West issues have predominated over North-South issues. It is better at explaining the timing and mechanics of particular episodes, illuminating proximate as opposed to deeper causes, and showing why outcomes were not what was intended. The bureaucratic details of debacles such as Pearl Harbor and the Bay of Pigs invasion are thus better understood than the long-term dynamics of war and peace. . . .

When can the framework be most helpful? Because organizations function most predictably in a familiar environment, major transformations in the international system (wars and their aftermaths, economic crises, the Sino-Soviet split) require the analyst to study how these changes produce, however belatedly, institutional adjustments in U.S. policies. Equally propitious, even for the pre-Cold War era, are military occupations wherein the often clashing missions of diplomats and military proconsuls ("striped pants" versus "gold braid," in Eric Roorda's formulation) complicate the management of empire from Managua to Manila. So too are political transitions that bring in new players pledged to reverse the priorities of their predecessors, and particularly those administrations in which the president, deliberately or not, encourages competition and initiative from strong-willed subordinates. Fiascos such as the U.S. failure to anticipate the attack on Pearl Harbor and the Iran-contra affair not only force agencies to reassess procedures and programs but, even better, often spawn official investigations that provide scholars with abundant evidence for bureaucratic analysis. Budget battles, weapons procurement, coordination of intelligence, war termination, alliance politics—in short, any foreign policy that engages the separate attentions of multiple agencies and agents—should alert the historian to the bureaucratic politics perspective.

Consider, for example, the complex dynamics of American entry into World War II. Looking at the period through the lens of bureaucratic politics reveals that FDR had more than Congress in mind when making his famous remark: "It's a terrible thing to look over your shoulder when you are trying to lead—and to find no one there." The institutional aversion to giving commissioned naval vessels to a foreign power delayed the destroyers-for-bases deal for several weeks in the summer of 1940, and only by getting eight British bases in direct exchange for the destroyers could Roosevelt persuade the chief of naval operations, Admiral Harold Stark, to certify, as required by statute, that these destroyers were no longer essential to national defense. According to navy scuttlebutt, the president threatened to fire Stark if he did not support what virtually every naval officer opposed and the admiral agonized before acquiescing. The army's initial opposition to peacetime conscription, FDR's dramatic appointment of Henry L. Stimson and Frank Knox to head the War and Navy departments in June 1940, his firing of Admiral James O. Richardson for his opposition to basing the Pacific fleet at Pearl Harbor, the refusal of the army and navy to mount expeditions to the Azores and Dakar in the spring of 1941, the unvarying strategic advice not to risk war until the armed forces were better prepared—all suggest an environment in which the president had to push hard to get the bureaucracy to accept his policy of supporting the Allies by steps short of war. Even the navy's eagerness to begin Atlantic convoys in spring 1941 and the subsequent Army Air Corps strategy of reinforcing the Philippines with B-17s were aimed in part at deploying ships and planes that FDR might otherwise have given to the British and the Russians. . . .

In sum, this essay should be read as a modest plea for greater attention to bureaucratic politics. The perspective can enrich and complement other approaches. By focusing on internal political processes we become aware of the tradeoffs within government that reflect the cooperative core values posited by the corporatists or neo-realists. In its emphasis on individual values and tugging and hauling by key players, bureaucratic politics makes personality and cognitive processes crucial to understanding who wins and why. Bureaucratic hawks, as Frank Costigliola has noted, often use emotion-laden, gendered language to prevail over their dovish colleagues. Although bureaucratic struggles may be over tactics more than strategy, over pace rather than direction, those distinctions may matter greatly when the outcome is a divided Berlin and Korea, a second atomic bomb, impromptu hostage rescue missions that fail, or a military "exit strategy" that precludes occupation of the enemy's capital. Too easily dismissed as a primer for managing crisis that should be avoided, the bureaucratic politics perspective also warns that when "governments collide," the machines cannot do what they are not programmed to do. Rather than press "delete" and conceptualize policy only as rational action, it is incumbent on historians to know how the machines work, their repertories, the institutional rules of the game, the rosters, and how the box score is kept. The peculiarities of the U.S. checks-and-balances system of governance make such analysis imperative. The British ambassador Edward Lord Halifax once likened the foreign policy processes in Washington to "a disorderly line of beaters out shooting; they do put the rabbits out of the bracken, but they don't come out where you would expect." Historians of American foreign relations need to identify the beaters and follow them into the bureaucratic forest because the quarry is much bigger than rabbit.

 F U R T H E R   R E A D I N G

(In addition to the following, see works mentioned in the essays above.)

Shigeru Akita and Takeshi Matsuda, eds., *Look Backward at the Twentieth Century* (2000) (on world systems theory)
Graham Allison and Philip Zelikow, *Essence of Decision: Explaining the Cuban Missile Crisis,* (1999)
Benedict Anderson, *Imagined Communities,* revised edition (1991) (on culture and nationalism)
Bonnie S. Anderson, *Joyous Greetings* (2000) (on international women's movement)
Carol Anderson, *Eyes Off the Prize* (2003) (on African Americans and the UN)
Giovanni Arrighi, *The Long Twentieth Century* (1994) (on world capitalism)
William H. Becker and Samuel F. Wells, eds., *Economics and World Power* (1984)
Gail Bederman, *Manliness and Civilization* (1995)
Thomas Bender, *Rethinking American History in a Global Age* (2002)
Thomas Borstelmann, *The Cold War and the Color Line* (2000)
Paul H. Buhle, *William Appleman Williams: The Tragedy of Empire* (1995)
David Campbell, *Writing Security* (1992) (on postmodern theory)
John M. Carrol and George C. Herring, eds., *Modern American Diplomacy* (1995)
J. Garry Clifford and Samuel R. Spencer Jr., *The First Peacetime Draft* (1986)
Carol Cohn, "War, Wimps, and Women: Talking Gender and Thinking War," in Miriam Cooke and Angela Woolacott, eds., *Gendering War Talk* (1993), 227–246
Robert Dallek, *The American Style of Foreign Policy* (1983)
Alexander DeConde, *Presidential Machismo* (2000)
Mary L. Dudziak, *Cold War and Civil Rights* (2000)

Cynthia Enloe, *Bananas, Beaches, and Bases* (1989) (on gender)
James Fallows, *More like Us* (1989)
Heidi Fehrenbach and Uta G. Poiger, eds., *Transactions, Transgressions, Transformations: American Culture in Western Europe and Japan* (2000)
Eric Foner, *Who Owns History?* (2002)
Frank Füred, *The Silent War* (1998) (on race)
John Lewis Gaddis, *The Landscape of History* (2002)
Marc Gallichio, *The African American Encounter with Japan and China* (2000)
Lloyd C. Gardner, ed., *Redefining the Past* (1986)
Jessica C. E. Gienow-Hecht et al., eds., *Culture and International Relations* (2003)
Craig Gorden, *Force and Statecraft* (1995)
Andre Gunder Frank and Barry Gills, *The World System* (1996)
Gerald K. Haines and J. Samuel Walker, eds., *American Foreign Relations* (1981)
Morton Halperin, *Bureaucratic Politics and Foreign Policy* (1974)
Michael J. Hogan, ed., *The Ambiguous Legacy* (1999)
———, *Paths to Power* (2000)
——— and Thomas G. Paterson, eds., *Explaining the History of American Foreign Relations* (2004)
Kristin Hoganson, "Cosmopolitan Domesticity: Importing the American Dream, 1865–1920," *American Historical Review,* 107 (February 2002), 55–83
———, *Fighting for American Manhood* (1999)
Ole Holsti, *Public Opinion and American Foreign Policy* (1996)
Gerald C. Horne, *From the Barrel of a Gun: The U.S. and the War Against Zimbabwe, 1965–1980* (2001)
Michael H. Hunt, *Ideology and U.S. Foreign Policy* (1987)
G. John Ikenberry, ed., *American Foreign Policy: Theoretical Essays* (1999)
Peter J. Katzanstein, ed., *The Cult of National Security* (1996)
George F. Kennan, *American Diplomacy, 1900–1950* (1951)
Charles Kindleberger, *The World Economy and National Finance in Historical Perspective* (1995)
Christina Klein, *Cold War Orientalism* (2003) (on U.S. and Asia)
Gabriel Kolko, *Century of War* (1994)
———, *The Roots of American Foreign Policy* (1969)
Michael Krenn, *Black Diplomacy* (1999)
Rob Kroes, *If You've Seen One, You've Seen the Mall: Europeans and American Mass Culture* (1996)
Michael E. Latham, *Modernization as Ideology* (2000)
James N. Leiker, *Racial Borders* (2002)
Charles S. Maier, "Consigning the Twentieth Century to History: Alternative Narratives for the Modern Era," *American Historical Review,* 105 (June 2000), 807–831
———, "Marking Time: The Historiography of International Relations," in Michael Kammen, ed., *The Past Before Us* (1980)
Gordon Martel, ed., *American Foreign Relations Reconsidered* (1994)
Thomas J. McCormick, *America's Half Century: United States Foreign Policy in the Cold War* (1999)
James McDougall, *Promised Land, Crusader State* (1995)
Margaret H. McFadden, *Golden Cables of Sympathy* (1999) (on transatlantic feminism)
James K. Merriwether, *Proudly We Be Africans* (2002)
Charles E. Neu, "The Rise of the National Security Bureaucracy," in Louis Galambos, ed., *The New American State* (1987)
Richard E. Neustadt, *Presidential Power* (1990)
——— and Ernest R. May, *Thinking in Time* (1986)
Frank A. Ninkovich, *The Wilsonian Century* (1999)
Thomas J. Noer, *Cold War and Black Liberation* (1985)
Peter Novick, *That Noble Dream: The "Objectivity Question" and the American Historical Profession* (1988)

Ruth Roadh Pierson and Nupur Chaudhuri, *Nation, Empire, Colony* (1998) (on gender and race)

Brenda Gayle Plummer, *Rising Wind: Black Diplomats and U.S. Foreign Policy, 1935–1960* (1996)

———, ed., *Window on Freedom* (2003)

Mary A. Renda, *Taking Haiti* (2001) (on cultural paternalism)

Walter Rodney, *How Europe Underdeveloped Africa* (1972)

Emily S. Rosenberg, *Financial Missionaries to the World* (2000)

———, *Spreading the American Dream* (1982)

Andrew J. Rotter, "Saidism Without Said: *Orientalism* in U.S. Diplomatic History," *American Historical Review,* 105 (October 2000), 1205–1217

"Roundtable: Cultural Transfer or Cultural Imperialism," *Diplomatic History,* 24 (Summer 2000), 465–528

David Ryan, *U.S. Foreign Policy in World History* (2000)

Edward Said, *Culture and Imperialism* (1993)

———, *Orientalism* (1978)

Joan W. Scott, *Gender and the Politics of History* (1999)

Robert Shaffer, "Race, Class, Gender and Diplomatic History," *Radical History Review,* 70 (1998), 156–168

Mrinalini Sinha, "Reading *Mother India:* Empire, Nation, and the Female Voice," *Journal of Women's History,* 6 (1994), 6–44

Richard Slotkin, *Gunfighter Nation: The Myth of the Frontier in Twentieth Century America* (1992)

Tony Smith, *Foreign Attachments* (2000) (on ethnic groups and foreign relations)

Anders Stephanson, *Manifest Destiny* (1995)

Ann Laura Stoler, *Carnal Knowledge and Imperial Power* (2002)

"Symposium: African Americans and U.S. Foreign Relations," *Diplomatic History,* 20 (1996), 531–650

"Symposium: Gender and U.S. Foreign Relations," *Diplomatic History,* 18 (1994), 47–124

Penny Von Eschen, *Race Against Empire* (1997)

Immanuel Wallerstein, *The Capitalist World Economy* (1979)

Kathryn Ward, ed., *Women Workers and Global Restructuring* (1990)

James Westheider, *Fighting on Two Fronts: African Americans and the Vietnam War* (1997)

Donald W. White, *The American Century* (1996)

William Appleman Williams, *Empire as a Way of Life* (1980)

———, *The Tragedy of America Diplomacy* (1959)

CHAPTER
2

Woodrow Wilson,
the First World War,
and the League Fight

In August 1914 Europe descended into war. Then an imperial power and an active trader on the high seas, the United States became ensnared in the deadly conflict. Until April 1917, however, President Woodrow Wilson struggled to define policies that would protect U.S. interests and principles, end the carnage, and permit him to shape the terms of the peace settlement. The president protested violations of U.S. neutral rights (dramatized by the sinking of the Lusitania *by a German submarine in May 1915), lectured the belligerents to respect international law, and offered to mediate a "peace without victory." When his peace advocacy faltered and Germany launched unrestricted submarine warfare, Wilson asked a divided but ultimately supportive Congress for a declaration of war.*

Once the United States became a belligerent, Wilson strove not only to win the war but to shape the postwar peace. He called for a nonvindictive peace treaty and urged the creation of an association of nations to deter war. The president's Fourteen Points outlined his plans for shelving balance-of-power politics in favor of disarmament, open diplomacy, Open Door trade, and self-determination. Having tipped the balance in favor of the Allies, the United States helped to force Germany to surrender on November 11, 1918. In January of the following year, Wilson journeyed to the Versailles Palace near Paris to negotiate a peace treaty and a covenant for the League of Nations that he believed would sustain a stable world order. European leaders sneered that Wilson was a dreamer, but millions of people on the Continent cheered his arrival and his high-minded appeals for a democratic and peaceful future.

At home, however, many Americans began to question Wilson's handling of foreign policy, especially after they learned that he had compromised many of his principles to win approval for his League. Some critics listened to his lofty rhetoric and wondered if the president had deluded himself into thinking he was the world's savior. Republican leaders, who had defeated Democrats in the 1918 congressional elections, calculated that Wilson was politically vulnerable. Supreme nationalists feared that an international organization would undermine American sovereignty and violate George Washington's venerable advice to avoid permanent alliances. Wilson battled back in an intense national debate, denouncing the naysayers as narrow, backward-looking people who did not understand humanity's demand for a new world order. He refused to abandon the collective security provision of Article 10 of the League covenant, insisting that the covenant would ensure American prosperity and help the United States takes its place as world leader. Unwilling to bargain with senators who demanded "reservations" (amendments), opposed by "irreconcilables" who would accept no league whatsoever, and laid low by a debilitating stroke suffered in the summer of 1919, Wilson lost the fight. The Senate rejected the peace treaty and U.S. membership in the League of Nations.

In spite of the rejected treaty, America's participation in the First World War elevated the nation to great power status and transformed U.S. foreign relations. Moreover, the ideals that Woodrow Wilson espoused became a cornerstone of modern American foreign policy. Thus, it is not surprising that scholars have disagreed strongly in assessing "Wilsonianism." Why did Wilson's diplomacy fail? Some have labeled Wilson a messianic idealist, whose arrogant moralism led him to adopt an inconsistent neutrality during the early stages of World War I and to underestimate the great power nationalism of the Allies—and Senate Republicans—at war's end. Others have praised Wilson for his breadth of vision, his willingness to make America assume a vital role in the postwar peace, and his noble—and arguably far-sighted—crusade against power politics. Still others have analyzed the impact of the adversarial two-party system, the confrontational interplay between the executive and legislative branches of the U.S. government, and the toll taken by Wilson's deteriorating health.

Wilson's diplomacy sparked a debate over fundamental issues in American foreign policy. How engaged in the world should the nation be, and how should foreign policy be conducted? Because his policies weighed so heavily on the future, historians continue to debate Wilson's legacy. Should he be credited with designing a multilateral international system that, once adopted after World War II, preserved the peace for over a half-century? Or was Wilson's principal legacy the flawed Versailles treaty, which unwisely punished Germany, left the United States absent from the League of Nations, and set the stage for the Second World War? To grapple with Wilsonianism and its legacy is to reach for an understanding of America's place in twentieth-century world affairs.

🌐 D O C U M E N T S

When a German U-boat sank the British liner *Lusitania* on May 7, 1915, killing 1,198, including 128 Americans, President Woodrow Wilson sent a strong note to Berlin. The May 13 warning, Document 1, demands that Germany disavow submarine warfare and respect the right of Americans to sail on the high seas. In January 1917, Germany declared unrestricted submarine warfare, and Wilson broke diplomatic relations with Berlin. On April 2, after the sinking of several American vessels, the president asked Congress for a declaration of war. His war message, Document 2, outlines U.S. grievances against Germany. One of the few dissenters in the Senate—the war measure passed, 82 to 6—was Robert M. La Follette of Wisconsin. In his speech of April 4, Document 3, the great reform politician reveals his fear of an American "war machine."

President Wilson issued his Fourteen Points in a speech on January 8, 1918, reprinted here as Document 4. Articles 10 through 16 of the Covenant of the League of

Nations hammered out at the Paris Peace Conference in 1919 are included as Document 5. Wilson explained during his busy western U.S. speaking tour in September 1919 that these provisions would prevent wars. Excerpts from his speeches are featured in Document 6. Led by Senator Henry Cabot Lodge of Massachusetts, critics worked to add "reservations" to the covenant through a Lodge resolution dated November 19, 1919, Document 7. But neither an amended peace treaty (which contained the covenant) nor an unamended treaty passed the Senate.

1. The First *Lusitania* Note Requests Germany to Halt Submarine Warfare, 1915

The Government of the United States has been apprised that the Imperial German Government considered themselves to be obliged by the extraordinary circumstances of the present war and the measures adopted by their adversaries in seeking to cut Germany off from all commerce, to adopt methods of retaliation which go much beyond the ordinary methods of warfare at sea, in the proclamation of a war zone from which they have warned neutral ships to keep away. This Government has already taken occasion to inform the Imperial German Government that it cannot admit the adoption of such measures or such a warning of danger to operate as in any degree an abbreviation of the rights of American shipmasters or of American citizens bound on lawful errands as passengers on merchant ships of belligerent nationality; and that it must hold the Imperial German Government to a strict accountability for any infringement of those rights, intentional or incidental. It does not understand the Imperial German Government to question those rights. It assumes, on the contrary, that the Imperial Government accept, as of course, the rule that the lives of noncombatants, whether they be of neutral citizenship or citizens of one of the nations at war, can not lawfully or rightfully be put in jeopardy by the capture or destruction of an unarmed merchantman, and recognize also, as all other nations do, the obligation to take the usual precaution of visit and search to ascertain whether a suspected merchantman is in fact of belligerent nationality or is in fact carrying contraband of war under a neutral flag.

The Government of the United States, therefore, desires to call the attention of the Imperial German Government with the utmost earnestness to the fact that the objection to their present method of attack against the trade of their enemies lies in the practical impossibility of employing submarines in the destruction of commerce without disregarding those rules of fairness, reason, justice, and humanity, which all modern opinion regards as imperative. It is practically impossible for the officers of a submarine to visit a merchantman at sea and examine her papers and cargo. It is practically impossible for them to make a prize of her; and, if they can not put a prize crew on board of her, they can not sink her without leaving her crew and all on board of her to the mercy of the sea in her small boats. These facts it is understood the Imperial German Government frankly admit. We are informed that, in the instances of which we have spoken, time enough for even that poor measure of safety was not given, and in at least two of the cases cited, not so much as a

This document can be found in U.S. Department of State, *Papers Relating to the Foreign Relations of the United States, 1915, Supplement* (Washington, D.C.: Government Printing Office, 1928), pp. 393–396.

warning was received. Manifestly submarines can not be used against merchant-men, as the last few weeks have shown, without an inevitable violation of many sacred principles of justice and humanity.　　　*

American citizens act within their indisputable rights in taking their ships and in traveling wherever their legitimate business calls them upon the high seas, and exercise those rights in what should be the well-justified confidence that their lives will not be endangered by acts done in clear violation of universally acknowledged international obligations, and certainly in the confidence that their own Government will sustain them in the exercise of their rights.

2. President Woodrow Wilson Asks Congress to Declare War Against Germany, 1917

On the third of February last I officially laid before you the extraordinary announce-ment of the Imperial German Government that on and after the first day of February it was its purpose to put aside all restraints of law of humanity and use its submarines to sink every vessel that sought to approach either the ports of Great Britain and Ireland or the western coasts of Europe or any of the ports controlled by the enemies of Germany within the Mediterranean. That had seemed to be the object of the Ger-man submarine warfare earlier in the war, but since April of last year the Imperial Government had somewhat restrained the commanders of its undersea craft in con-formity with its promise then given to us that passenger boats should not be sunk and that due warning would be given to all other vessels which its submarines might seek to destroy, when no resistance was offered or escape attempted, and care taken that their crews were given at least a fair chance to save their lives in their open boats. The precautions taken were meagre and haphazard enough, as was proved in dis-tressing instance after instance in the progress of the cruel and unmanly business, but a certain degree of restraint was observed. The new policy has swept every restriction aside. Vessels of every kind, whatever their flag, their character, their cargo, their destination, their errand, have been ruthlessly sent to the bottom without warning and without thought of help or mercy for those on board, the vessels of friendly neutrals along with those of belligerents. Even hospital ships and ships carrying relief to the sorely bereaved and stricken people of Belgium, though the latter were provided with safe conduct through the proscribed areas by the German Government itself and were distinguished by unmistakable marks of identity, have been sunk with the same reckless lack of compassion or of principle.

I was for a little while unable to believe that such things would in fact be done by any government that had hitherto subscribed to the humane practices of civilized na-tions. International law had its origin in the attempt to set up some law which would be respected and observed upon the seas, where no nation had right of dominion where lay the free highways of the world. By painful stage after stage has that law been built up, with meagre enough results, indeed, after all was accomplished that could be accomplished, but always with a clear view, at least of what the heart and conscience of mankind demanded. This minimum of right the German Government

This document can be found in *Congressional Record,* LV (April 2, 1917), Part 1, 102–104.

has swept aside under the plea of retaliation and necessity and because it had no weapons which it could use at sea except these which it is impossible to employ as it is employing them without throwing to the winds all scruples of humanity or of respect for the understandings that were supposed to underlie the intercourse of the world. I am not now thinking of the loss of property involved, immense and serious as that is, but only of the wanton and wholesale destruction of the lives of noncombatants, men, women, and children, engaged in pursuits which have always, even in the darkest periods of modern history, been deemed innocent and legitimate. Property can be paid for; the lives of peaceful and innocent people cannot be. The present German submarine warfare against commerce is a warfare against mankind.

It is a war against all nations. American ships have been sunk, American lives taken, in ways which it has stirred us very deeply to learn of, but the ships and people of other neutral and friendly nations have been sunk and overwhelmed in the waters in the same way. There has been no discrimination. The challenge is to all mankind. Each nation must decide for itself how it will meet it. The choice we make for ourselves must be made with a moderation of counsel and a temperateness of judgment befitting our character and our motives as a nation. We must put excited feeling away. Our motive will not be revenge or the victorious assertion of the physical might of the nation, but only the vindication of right, of human right, of which we are only a single champion. . . .

With a profound sense of the solemn and even tragical character of the step I am taking and of the grave responsibilities which it involves, but in unhesitating obedience to what I deem my constitutional duty, I advise that the Congress declare the recent course of the Imperial German Government to be in fact nothing less than war against the government and people of the United States; that it formally accept the status of belligerent which has thus been thrust upon it; and that it take immediate steps not only to put the country in a more thorough state of defense but also to exert all its power and employ all its resources to bring the Government of the German Empire to terms and end the war. . . .

Does not every American feel that assurance has been added to our hope for the future peace of the world by the wonderful and heartening things that have been happening within the last few weeks in Russia? Russia was known by those who knew it best to have been always in fact democratic at heart, in all the vital habits of her thought, in all the intimate relationships of her people that spoke their natural instinct, their habitual attitude towards life. The autocracy that crowned the summit of her political structure, long as it had stood and terrible as was the reality of its power, was not in fact Russian in origin, character, or purpose; and now it has been shaken off and the great, generous Russian people have been added in all their naive majesty and might to the forces that are fighting for freedom in the world, for justice, and for peace. Here is a fit partner for a League of Honour.

One of the things that has served to convince us that the Prussian autocracy was not and could never be our friends is that from the very outset of the present war it has filled our unsuspecting communities and even our offices of government with spies and set criminal intrigues everywhere afoot against our national unity of counsel, our peace within and without, our industries and our commerce. . . . That it means to stir up enemies against us at our very doors the intercepted note to the German Minister at Mexico City is eloquent evidence.

We are accepting this challenge of hostile purpose because we know that in such a government, following such methods, we can never have a friend; and that in the presence of its organized power, always lying in wait to accomplish we know not what purpose, there can be no assured security for the democratic governments of the world. We are now about to accept gauge of battle with its natural foe to liberty and shall, if necessary, spend the whole force of the nation to check and nullify its pretensions and its power. We are glad, now that we see the facts with no veil of false pretense about them, to fight thus for the ultimate peace of the world and for the liberation of its peoples, the German peoples included: for the rights of nations great and small and the privilege of men everywhere to choose their way of life and of obedience. The world must be made safe for democracy. . . .

It is a distressing and oppressive duty, Gentlemen of the Congress, which I have performed in thus addressing you. There are, it may be, many months of fiery trial and sacrifice ahead of us. It is a fearful thing to lead this great peaceful people into war, into the most terrible and disastrous of all wars, civilization itself seeming to be in the balance. But the right is more precious than peace, and we shall fight for the things which we have always carried nearest our hearts—for democracy, for the right of those who submit to authority to have a voice in their own governments, for the rights and liberties of small nations, for a universal dominion of right by such a concert of free peoples as shall bring peace and safety to all nations and make the world itself at last free. To such a task we can dedicate our lives and our fortunes, everything that we are and everything that we have, with the pride of those who know that the day has come when America is privileged to spend her blood and her might for the principles that gave her birth and happiness and the peace which she has treasured. God helping her, she can do no other.

3. Senator Robert M. La Follette
Voices His Dissent, 1917

The poor, sir, who are the ones called upon to rot in the trenches, have no organized power, have no press to voice their will upon this question of peace or war; but, oh, Mr. President, at some time they will be heard. I hope and I believe they will be heard in an orderly and a peaceful way. I think they may be heard from before long. I think, sir, if we take this step, when the people to-day who are staggering under the burden of supporting families at the present prices of the necessaries of the life find those prices multiplied, when they are raised a hundred percent, or 200 percent, as they will be quickly, aye, sir, when beyond that those who pay taxes come to have their taxes doubled and again doubled to pay the interest on the nontaxable bonds held by Morgan and his combinations, which have been issued to meet this war, there will come an awakening; they will have their day and they will be heard. It will be as certain and as inevitable as the return of the tides, and as resistless, too. . . .

Just a word of comment more upon one of the points in the President's address. He says that this is a war "for the things which we have always carried nearest to our hearts—for democracy, for the right of those who submit to authority to

This document can be found in *Congressional Record*, LV (April 4, 1917), Part 1, 226, 228.

have a voice in their own government." In many places throughout the address is this exalted sentiment given expression. . . .

But the President proposes alliance with Great Britain, which, however liberty-loving its people, is a hereditary monarchy, with a hereditary ruler, with a hereditary House of Lords, with a hereditary landed system, with a limited and restricted suffrage for one class and a multiplied suffrage power for another, and with grinding industrial conditions for all the wageworkers. The President has not suggested that we make our support of Great Britain conditional to her granting home rule to Ireland, or Egypt, or India. We rejoice in the establishment of a democracy in Russia, but it will hardly be contended that if Russia was still an autocratic Government, we would not be asked to enter this alliance with her just the same. Italy and the lesser powers of Europe, Japan in the Orient; in fact all of the countries with whom we are to enter into alliance, except France and newly revolutionized Russia, are still of the old order—and it will be generally conceded that no one of them has done as much for its people in the solution of municipal problems and in securing social and industrial reforms as Germany. . . .

Who has registered the knowledge or approval of the American people of the course this Congress is called upon in declaring war upon Germany? Submit the question to the people, you who support it. You who support it dare not do it, for you know that by a vote of more than ten to one the American people as a body would register their declaration against it.

In the sense that this war is being forced upon our people without their knowing why and without their approval, and that wars are usually forced upon all peoples in the same way, there is some truth in the statement; but I venture to say that the response which the German people have made to the demands of this war shows that it has a degree of popular support which the war upon which we are entering has not and never will have among our people. The espionage bills, the conscription bills, and other forcible military measures which we understand are being ground out of the war machine in this country is the complete proof that those responsible for this war fear that it has no popular support and that armies sufficient to satisfy the demand of the entente allies can not be recruited by voluntary enlistments.

4. Wilson Proclaims U.S. War Aims: The Fourteen Points, 1918

I. Open covenants of peace, openly arrived at, after which there shall be no private international understandings of any kind but diplomacy shall proceed always frankly and in the public view.

II. Absolute freedom of navigation upon the seas, outside territorial waters, alike in peace and in war, except as the seas may be closed in whole or in part by international action for the enforcement of international covenants.

III. The removal, so far as possible, of all economic barriers and the establishment of an equality of trade conditions among all the nations consenting to the peace and associating themselves for its maintenance.

This document can be found in *Congressional Record,* LVI (January 8, 1918), Part 1, 680–682.

IV. Adequate guarantees given and taken that national armaments will be reduced to the lowest point consistent with domestic safety.

V. A free, open-minded, and absolutely impartial adjustment of all colonial claims, based upon a strict observance of the principle that in determining all such questions of sovereignty the interests of the populations concerned must have equal weight with the equitable claims of the government whose title is to be determined.

VI. The evacuation of all Russian territory and such a settlement of all questions affecting Russia as will secure the best and freest cooperation of the other nations of the world in obtaining for her an unhampered and unembarrassed opportunity for the independent determination of her own political development and national policy and assure her of a sincere welcome into the society of free nations under institutions of her own choosing; and, more than a welcome, assistance also of every kind that she may need and may herself desire. The treatment accorded Russia by her sister nations in the months to come will be the acid test of their good will, of their comprehension of her needs as distinguished from their own interests, and of their intelligent and unselfish sympathy.

VII. Belgium, the whole world will agree, must be evacuated and restored, without any attempt to limit the sovereignty which she enjoys in common with all other free nations. No other single act will serve as this will serve to restore confidence among the nations in the laws which they have themselves set and determined for the government of their relations with one another. Without this healing act the whole structure and validity of international law is forever impaired.

VIII. All French territory should be freed and the invaded portions restored, and the wrong done to France by Prussia in 1871 in the matter of Alsace-Lorraine, which has unsettled the peace of the world for nearly fifty years, should be righted, in order that peace may once more be made secure in the interest of all.

IX. A readjustment of the frontiers of Italy should be effected along clearly recognizable lines of nationality.

X. The peoples of Austria-Hungary, whose place among the nations we wish to see safeguarded and assured, should be accorded the freest opportunity of autonomous development.

XI. Rumania, Serbia, and Montenegro should be evacuated; occupied territories restored; Serbia accorded free and secure access to the sea; and the relations of the several Balkan states to one another determined by friendly consul along historically established lines of allegiance and nationality; and international guarantees of the political and economic independence and territorial integrity of the several Balkan states should be entered into.

XII. The Turkish portions of the present Ottoman Empire should be assured a secure sovereignty, but the other nationalities which are now under Turkish rule should be assured an undoubted security of life and an absolutely unmolested opportunity of autonomous development, and the Dardanelles should be permanently opened as a free passage to the ships and commerce of all nations under international guarantees.

XIII. An independent Polish state should be erected which should include the territories inhabited by indisputably Polish populations, which should be assured a free and secure access to the sea, and whose political and economic independence and territorial integrity should be guaranteed by international covenant.

XIV. A general association of nations must be formed under specific covenants for the purpose of affording mutual guarantees of political independence and territorial integrity to great and small states alike.

5. Articles 10 Through 16 of the League of Nations Covenant, 1919

Article 10.   The Members of the League undertake to respect and preserve as against external aggression the territorial integrity and existing political independence of all Members of the League. In case of any such aggression or in case of any threat or danger of such aggression the Council shall advise upon the means by which this obligation shall be fulfilled.

Article 11.   Any war or threat of war, whether immediately affecting any of the Members of the League or not, is hereby declared a matter of concern to the whole League, and the League shall take any action that may be deemed wise and effectual to safeguard the peace of nations. . . .

It is also declared to be the friendly right of each Member of the League to bring to the attention of the Assembly or of the Council any circumstance whatever affecting international relations which threatens to disturb international peace or the good understanding between nations upon which peace depends.

Article 12.   The Members of the League agree that if there should arise between them any dispute likely to lead to a rupture, they will submit the matter either to arbitration or to inquiry by the Council, and they agree in no case to resort to war until three months after the award by the arbitrators or the report by the Council.

In any case under this Article the award of the arbitrators shall be made within a reasonable time, and the report of the Council shall be made within six months after the submission of the dispute.

Article 13.   The Members of the League agree that whenever any dispute shall arise between them which they recognise to be suitable for submission to arbitration and which cannot be satisfactorily settled by diplomacy, they will submit the whole subject-matter to arbitration. . . .

Article 14.   The Council shall formulate and submit to the Members of the League for adoption plans for the establishment of a Permanent Court of International Justice. The Court shall be competent to hear and determine any dispute of an international character which the parties thereto submit to it. The Court may also give an advisory opinion upon any dispute or question referred to it by the Council or by the Assembly.

This document can be found in U.S. Department of State, *Papers Relating to the Foreign Relations of the United States, 1919* (Washington, D.C.: Government Printing Office, 1942–1947), XIII, 83–89.

Article 15.   If there should arise between Members of the League any dispute likely to lead to a rupture, which is not submitted to arbitration in accordance with Article 13, the Members of the League agree that they will submit the matter to the Council. . . .

Article 16.   Should any Member of the League resort to war in disregard of its covenants under Articles 12, 13 or 15, it shall *ipso facto* be deemed to have committed an act of war against all other Members of the League, which hereby undertake immediately to subject it to the severance of all trade or financial relations, the prohibition of all intercourse between their nationals and the nationals of the covenant-breaking State, and the prevention of all financial, commercial or personal intercourse between the nationals of the covenant-breaking State and the nationals of any other State, whether a Member of the League or not.

It shall be the duty of the Council in such case to recommend to the several Governments concerned what effective military, naval or air force the Members of the League shall severally contribute to the armed forces to be used to protect the covenants of the League.

6. Wilson Defends the Peace Treaty and League, 1919

Indianapolis, Indiana, September 4

You have heard a great deal about article 10 of the covenant of the league of nations. Article 10 speaks the conscience of the world. Article 10 is the article which goes to the heart of this whole bad business, for that article says that the members of this league, that is intended to be all the great nations of the world, engage to respect and to preserve against all external aggression the territorial integrity and political independence of the nations concerned. That promise is necessary in order to prevent this sort of war from recurring, and we are absolutely discredited if we fought this war and then neglect the essential safeguard against it. You have heard it said, my fellow citizens, that we are robbed of some degree of our sovereign independent choice by articles of that sort. Every man who makes a choice to respect the rights of his neighbors deprives himself of absolute sovereignty, but he does it by promising never to do wrong, and I can not for one see anything that robs me of any inherent right that I ought to retain when I promise that I will do right, when I promise that I will respect the thing which, being disregarded and violated, brought on a war in which millions of men lost their lives, in which the civilization of mankind was in the balance, in which there was the most outrageous exhibition ever witnessed in the history of mankind of the rapacity and disregard for right of a great armed people. We engage in the first sentence of article 10 to respect and preserve from external aggression the territorial integrity and the existing political independence not only of the other member States, but of all States, and if any member of the league of nations disregards that promise, then what happens? The council of the league advises what should be done to enforce the respect for that covenant on the part of the nation

This document can be found in *Congressional Record,* LVIII (September 1919): Part 5, 5001–5002, 5005; Part 6, 5593, 6244–6245, 6249, 6254; Part 7, 6417, 6422.

attempting to violate it, and there is no compulsion upon us to take that advice except the compulsion of our good conscience and judgment. So that it is perfectly evident that if in the judgment of the people of the United States the council adjudged wrong and that this was not a case of the use of force, there would be no necessity on the part of the Congress of the United States to vote the use of force. But there could be no advice of the council on any such subject without a unanimous vote, and the unanimous vote includes our own, and if we accepted the advice we would be accepting our own advice, for I need not tell you that the representatives of the Government of the United States would not vote without instructions from their Government at home, and that what we united in advising we could be certain that the American people would desire to do. There is in that covenant not only not a sur- render of the independent judgment of the Government of the United States, but an expression of it, because that independent judgment would have to join with the judgment of the rest.

But when is that judgment going to be expressed, my fellow citizens? Only after it is evident that every other resource has failed, and I want to call your attention to the central machinery of the league of nations. If any member of that league or any nation not a member refuses to submit the question at issue either to arbitration or to discussion by the council, there ensues automatically, by the engagements of this covenant, an absolute economic boycott. There will be no trade with that nation by any member of the league. There will be no interchange of communication by post or telegraph. There will be no travel to or from that nation. Its borders will be closed. No citizen of any other State will be allowed to enter it and no one of its citizens will be allowed to leave it. It will be hermetically sealed by the united action of the most powerful nations in the world. And if this economic boycott bears with unequal weight, the members of the league agree to support one another and to relieve one another in any exceptional disadvantages that may arise out of it. . . .

I want to call your attention, if you will turn it up when you go home, to article 11, following article 10 of the covenant of the league of nations. That article, let me say, is the favorite article in the treaty, so far as I am concerned. It says that every matter which is likely to affect the peace of the world is everybody's business; that it shall be the friendly right of any nation to call attention in the league to anything that is likely to affect the peace of the world or the good understanding between na- tions, upon which the peace of the world depends, whether that matter immediately concerns the nation drawing attention to it or not.

St. Louis, Missouri, September 5

There can hereafter be no secret treaties. There were nations represented around that board—I mean the board at which the commission on the league of nations sat, where 14 nations were represented—there were nations represented around that board who had entered into many a secret treaty and understanding, and they made not the least objection to promising that hereafter no secret treaty should have any validity whatever. The provision of the covenant is that every treaty or international understanding shall be registered, I believe the word is, with the gen- eral secretary of the league, that the general secretary shall publish it in full just so soon as it is possible for him to publish it, and that no treaty shall be valid which is not thus registered. It is like our arrangements with regard to mortgages on real estate, that until they are registered nobody else need pay any attention to them. And so with the treaties; until they are registered in this office of the league nobody, not even the parties themselves, can insist upon their execution. You have cleared the deck thereby of the most dangerous thing and the most embarrassing thing that has hitherto existed in international politics.

Sioux Falls, South Dakota, September 8

I can not understand the psychology of men who are resisting it [the treaty]. I can not understand what they are afraid of, unless it is that they know physical force and do not understand moral force. Moral force is a great deal more powerful than physical. Govern the sentiments of mankind and you govern mankind. Govern their fears, govern their hopes, determine their fortunes, get them together in concerted masses, and the whole thing sways like a team. Once get them suspecting one another, once get them antagonizing one another, and society itself goes to pieces. We are trying to make a society instead of a set of barbarians out of the governments of the world. I sometimes think, when I wake in the night, of all the wakeful nights that anxious fathers and mothers and friends have spent during those weary years of this awful war, and I seem to hear the cry, the inarticulate cry of mothers all over the world, millions of them on the other side of the sea and thousands of them on this side of the sea, "In God's name, give us the sensible and hopeful and peaceful processes of right and of justice."

America can stay out, but I want to call you to witness that the peace of the world can not be established without America. America is necessary to the peace of the world. And reverse the proposition: The peace and good will of the world are necessary to America. Disappoint the world, center its suspicion upon you, make it feel that you are hot and jealous rivals of the other nations, and do you think you are going to do as much business with them as you would otherwise do? I do not like to put the thing on that plane, my fellow countrymen, but if you want to talk business, I can talk business. If you want to put it on the low plane of how much money you can make, you can make more money out of friendly traders than out of hostile traders. You can make more money out of men who trust you than out of men who fear you.

San Francisco, California, September 17

The Monroe doctrine means that if any outside power, any power outside this hemisphere, tries to impose its will upon any portion of the Western Hemisphere the United States is at liberty to act independently and alone in repelling the aggression; that it does not have to wait for the action of the league of nations; that it does not have to wait for anything but the action of its own administration and its own Congress. This is the first time in the history of international diplomacy that any great government has acknowledged the validity of the Monroe doctrine. Now for the first time all the great fighting powers of the world except Germany, which for the time being has ceased to be a great fighting power, acknowledge the validity of the Monroe doctrine and acknowledge it as part of the international practice of the world.

They [critics] are nervous about domestic questions. They say, "It is intolerable to think that the league of nations should interfere with domestic questions," and whenever they begin to specify they speak of the question of immigration, of the question of naturalization, of the question of the tariff. My fellow citizens, no competent or authoritative student of international law would dream of maintaining that these were anything but exclusively domestic questions, and the covenant of the league expressly provides that the league can take no action whatever about matters which are in the practice of international law regarded as domestic questions.

San Francisco, California, September 18

In order that we may not forget, I brought with me the figures as to what this war [First World War] meant to the world. This is a body of business men and you will understand these figures. They are too big for the imagination of men who do not handle big things. Here is the cost of the war in money, exclusive of what we loaned one another: Great Britain and her dominions, $38,000,000,000; France, $26,000,000,000; the United States, $22,000,000,000 (this is the direct cost of our operations); Russia, $18,000,000,000; Italy $13,000,000,000; and the total, including Belgium, Japan, and other countries, $123,000,000,000. This is what it cost the Central Powers: Germany, $39,000,000,000, the biggest single item; Austria-Hungary, $21,000,000,000; Turkey and Bulgaria, $3,000,000,000; a total of $63,000,000,000, and a grand total of direct war costs of $186,000,000,000—almost the capital of the world. The expenditures of the United States were at the rate of $1,000,000 an hour for two years, including nighttime with daytime. The battle deaths during the war were as follows: Russia lost in dead 1,700,000 men, poor Russia that got nothing but terror and despair out of it all; Germany, 1,600,000; France, 1,385,000; Great Britain, 900,000; Austria, 800,000; Italy, 364,000; the United States, 50,300 dead. The total for all the belligerents, 7,450,200 men—just about seven and a half million killed because we could not have arbitration and discussion, because the world had never had the courage to propose the conciliatory methods which some of us are now doubting whether we ought to accept or not.

San Diego, California, September 19

It is feared that our delegates will be outvoted, because I am constantly hearing it said that the British Empire has six votes and we have one. I am perfectly content to have only one when the one counts six, and that is exactly the arrangement under the league. Let us examine that matter a little more particularly. Besides the vote of Great Britain herself, the other five votes are the votes of Canada, of South Africa, of Australia, of New Zealand, and of India. We ourselves were champions and advocates of giving a vote to Panama, of giving a vote to Cuba—both of them under the direction and protectorate of the United States—and if a vote was given to Panama and to Cuba, could it reasonably be denied to the great Dominion of Canada? Could it be denied to that stout Republic in South Africa, that is now living under a nation which did, indeed, overcome it at one time, but which did not dare retain its government in its hands, but turned it over to the very men whom it had fought? Could we deny it to Australia, that independent little republic in the Pacific, which has led the world in so many liberal reforms? Could it be denied New Zealand? Could we deny it to the hundreds of millions who live in India? But, having given these six votes, what are the facts? For you have been misled with regard to them. The league can take no active steps without the unanimous vote of all the nations represented on the council, added to a vote of the majority in the assembly itself. These six votes are in the assembly, not in the council. The assembly is not a voting body, except upon a limited number of questions, and whenever those questions are questions of action, the affirmative vote of every nation represented on the council is indispensable, and the United States is represented on the council.

Salt Lake City, Utah, September 23

I am not going to stop, my fellow citizens, to discuss the Shantung provision [which shifted control of the area from Germany to Japan] in all its aspects, but what I want to call your attention to is that just so soon as this covenant is ratified every nation in the world will have the right to speak out for China. And I want to say very frankly, and I ought to add that the representatives of those great nations themselves admit, that Great Britain and France and the other powers which have insisted upon similar concessions in China will be put in a position where they will have to reconsider them. This is the only way to serve and redeem China, unless, indeed, you want to start a war for the purpose. At the beginning of the war and during the war Great Britain and France engaged by solemn treaty with Japan that if she would come into the war and continue in the war, she could have, provided she in the meantime took it by force of arms, what Germany had in China. Those are treaties already in force. They are not waiting for ratification. France and England can not withdraw from those obligations, and it will serve China not one iota if we should dissent from the Shantung arrangement; but by being parties to that arrangement we can insist upon the promise of Japan—the promise which the other Governments have not matched—that she will return to China immediately all sovereign rights within the Province of Shantung. We have got that for her now, and under the operations of article 11 and of article 10 it will be impossible for any nation to make any further inroads either upon the territorial integrity or upon the political independence of China.

Denver, Colorado, September 25

The adoption of the treaty means disarmament. Think of the economic burden and the restraint of liberty in the development of professional and mechanical life that resulted from the maintenance of great armies, not only in Germany but in France and in Italy and, to some extent, in Great Britain. If the United States should stand off from this thing we would have to have the biggest army in the world. There would be nobody else that cared for our fortunes. We would have to look out for ourselves, and when I hear gentlemen say, "Yes; that is what we want to do; we want to be independent and look out for ourselves" I say, "Well, then, consult your fellow citizens. There will have to be universal conscription. There will have to be taxes such as even yet we have not seen. There will have to be concentration of authority in the Government capable of using this terrible instrument. You can not conduct a war or command an army by a debating society. You can not determine in community centers what the command of the Commander in Chief is going to be; you will have to have a staff like the German staff, and you will have to center in the Commander in Chief of the Army and Navy the right to take instant action for the protection of the Nation." America will never consent to any such thing.

7. Senator Henry Cabot Lodge Proposes Reservations to the League Covenant, 1919

1. . . . In case of notice of withdrawal from the league of nations, as provided in said article [Article 1], the United States shall be the sole judge as to whether all its international obligations . . . have been fulfilled, and notice of withdrawal . . . may be given by a concurrent resolution of the Congress of the United States.

2. The United States assumes no obligation to preserve the territorial integrity or political independence of any other country . . . under the provisions of article 10, or to employ the military or naval forces of the United States under any article of the treaty for any purpose, unless in any particular case the Congress, which . . . has the sole power to declare war . . . shall . . . so provide.

3. No mandate shall be accepted by the United States under article 22 . . . except by action of the Congress of the United States.

4. The United States reserves to itself exclusively the right to decide what questions are within its domestic jurisdiction. . . .

5. The United States will not submit to arbitration or to inquiry by the assembly or by the council of the league of nations . . . any questions which in the judgment of the United States depend upon or relate to . . . the Monroe doctrine; said doctrine is to be interpreted by the United States alone and is . . . wholly outside the jurisdiction of said league of nations. . . .

6. The United States withholds its assent to articles 156, 157, and 158 [Shantung clauses]. . . .

7. The Congress of the United States will provide by law for the appointment of the representatives of the United States in the assembly and the council of the league of nations, and may in its discretion provide for the participation of the United States in any commission. . . . No person shall represent the United States under either said league of nations or the treaty of peace . . . except with the approval of the Senate of the United States. . . .

9. The United States shall not be obligated to contribute to any expenses of the league of nations . . . unless and until an appropriation of funds . . . shall have been made by the Congress of the United States.

10. If the United States shall at any time adopt any plan for the limitation of armaments proposed by the council of the league . . . it reserves the right to increase such armaments without the consent of the council whenever the United States is threatened with invasion or engaged in war. . . .

14. The United States assumes no obligation to be bound by any election, decision, report, or finding of the council or assembly in which any member of the league and its self-governing dominions, colonies, or parts of empire, in the aggregate have cast more than one vote.

This document can be found in *Congressional Record,* LVIII (November 19, 1919), Part 9, 877–878.

 *E S S A Y S*

In the first essay, Thomas J. Knock of Southern Methodist University delivers a sympathetic but not uncritical assessment of Wilson. Knock argues that Wilson drew upon both progressive and conservative internationalists in pursuing neutrality toward Europe's war but rallied a left-of-center coalition to win reelection in 1916, advance his liberal domestic agenda, and mediate a "peace without victory." Once America entered the war, however, the president failed to win support for his controversial peace treaty, including the League of Nations, primarily because the backing of the progressives he needed for victory eroded in the face of wartime reaction both at home and abroad. In the second essay, the Dutch scholar Jan Wilhelm Schulte-Nordholt presents a more biting critique of Wilson and Wilsonianism. While admiring the president's commitment to peace, Schulte-Nordholt depicts a strong-willed dreamer who lost touch with reality. Driven by his culturally arrogant belief that the United States could provide an appropriate model for world peace, Wilson underestimated the complexities of international politics. At Paris, the Versailles negotiators manipulated the president, who conceded too much in order to save the League. The flawed peace, Schulte-Nordholt concludes, helped sow the seeds of the Second World War. Tony Smith of Tufts University takes on Wilson's critics in the last essay. Focusing on the Treaty of Versailles and the League, Smith praises Wilson's blueprint for a new world order based on the principles of liberal internationalism. Wilsonianism, he observes, wedded the urge for national self-determination to democracy and called for collective security and a liberal economic regime to contain German power and guarantee the peace. Answering foreign-policy "realists" who have accused Wilson of failing to comprehend power politics, Smith asks if there was a better way at the time for America to defend its interests and stabilize Europe. Smith downplays Wilson's impact on the international crises of the 1920s and 1930s and points to the Wilsonian resurgence after World War II as proof of Wilson's far-sightedness.

From Peace to War: Progressive Internationalists Confront the Forces of Reaction

THOMAS J. KNOCK

As the historian Frederick Jackson Turner once remarked, the age of reform in the United States was "also the age of socialistic inquiry." Indeed, by 1912, the Socialist Party of America and its quadrennial standard-bearer, Eugene Debs, had attained respectability and legitimacy. The party's membership exceeded 115,000, and some 1,200 socialists held public office in 340 municipalities and twenty-four states. As many as three million Americans read socialist newspapers on a regular basis. Julius Wayland's *Appeal to Reason,* with 760,000 weekly subscribers, ranked among the most widely read publications in the world.

The general cast of the four-way presidential campaign of 1912 also lent credence to Turner's observation. Notwithstanding the conservatism of the incumbent, William Howard Taft, the impact of progressivism on the two main parties, in tandem with the success of the Socialist party, caused a certain blurring of traditional political lines. To millions of citizens, a vote for either Woodrow Wilson, the progressive

This is an original essay written for this volume based on *To End All Wars: Woodrow Wilson and the Quest for a New World Order* (New York: Oxford University Press, 1992).

Democrat, Theodore Roosevelt, the insurgent "Bull Moose" who bolted the Republicans to form the Progressive party, or Debs, the Socialist, amounted to a protest against the status quo of industrial America. And that protest, from top to bottom, sanctioned an unfolding communion between liberals and socialists practically unique in American history.

In this new age of progressive reform and socialistic inquiry, it would be Woodrow Wilson's opportunity and challenge to reconcile and shape domestic and foreign concerns in ways that no previous chief executive had ever contemplated. . . .

Feminists, liberals, pacifists, socialists, and reformers of varying kinds filled the ranks of the progressive internationalists. Their leaders included many of the era's authentic heroes and heroines: Jane Addams of Hull House, the poet-journalist John Reed, Max Eastman of the *Masses,* the civil-rights crusader Oswald Garrison Villard, and Lillian Wald of New York's Henry Street Settlement, to name a few. For them the search for a peaceful world order provided a logical common ground. Peace was indispensable to change itself—to the survival of the labor movement, to their campaigns on behalf of women's rights and the abolition of child labor, and to social justice legislation in general. If the war in Europe were permitted to rage on indefinitely, progressive internationalists believed, then the United States could not help but get sucked into it; not only their great causes, but also the very moral fiber of the nation would be destroyed should its resources be diverted from reform to warfare. Thus, their first goal (and one in keeping with Wilson's policy of neutrality) was to bring about a negotiated settlement of the war.

The Woman's Peace party, founded in January 1915, in Washington, D.C., and led by Jane Addams, played a pivotal role in the progressive internationalist movement. Guided by the principle of "the sacredness of human life," the platform of the Woman's Peace party constituted the earliest manifesto on internationalism advanced by any American organization throughout the war. The party's "program for constructive peace" called for an immediate armistice, international agreements to limit armaments and nationalize their manufacture, a reduction of trade barriers, self-determination, machinery for arbitration, and a "Concert of Nations" to supersede the balance-of-power system. The platform also pressed for American mediation of the war. Its authors made sure that the president received all of their recommendations. . . .

Many progressive internationalists regarded the reactionary opponents of domestic reform and the advocates of militarism and imperialism as twins born of the same womb; they watched with alarm as the champions of "preparedness" mounted what they viewed as an insidious offensive to thwart social and economic progress at home, as well as disarmament and the repudiation of war as an instrument of foreign policy. In response to the preparedness movement, liberal reformers and leading socialists joined forces to establish the American Union Against Militarism (AUAM). Within months, the AUAM had branches in every major city in the country. When, in the wake of the *Lusitania* disaster, Wilson introduced legislation to increase substantially the size of the army and navy, it appeared that he had surrendered to the enemy. Then, too, a competing, conservative vision of internationalism was vying for national attention.

The program of the conservative internationalists was different in both subtle and conclusive ways. It was developed by the organizers of the League to Enforce Peace (LEP), founded in June 1915, and led by former president William Howard

Taft and other Republicans prominent in the field of international law. Within two years, they had established four thousand branches in forty-seven states. The LEP's platform, "Warrant from History," called for American participation in a world parliament, which would assemble periodically to make appropriate changes to international law and employ arbitration and conciliation procedures to settle certain kinds of disputes. While more or less endorsing the general principle of collective security, most conservative internationalists also believed that the United States should build up its military complex and reserve the right to undertake independent coercive action whenever the "national interest" was threatened. Unlike progressive internationalists, the LEP did not concern itself with self-determination or advocate disarmament or even a military standoff in Europe. These internationalists were openly pro-Allied; in fact, the slogan, "The LEP does *not* seek to end the present war," appeared on their letterhead in the autumn of 1916.

Throughout that year, Wilson met and corresponded with representatives of both wings of the new internationalist movement. In May 1916, for example, he delivered an important address before a gathering of the LEP, the occasion for his first public affirmation on behalf of American membership in some kind of postwar peacekeeping organization. Yet Wilson's sympathies lay decidedly with the progressive internationalists. Two weeks earlier, for the first time, he had articulated to persons other than his absolute confidants his ideas for a "family of nations," during a lengthy White House colloquy with leaders of the AUAM.

The AUAM stood neither for "peace at any price" nor against "sane and reasonable" military preparedness, Lillian Wald explained to the president; but they were anxious about those agents of militarism who were "frankly hostile to our institutions of democracy." Wilson contended that his preparedness program conformed to his interlocutors' criteria—that it would provide adequate security "without changing the spirit of the country" and that one of his motives for it was to achieve a league of nations. "[I]f the world undertakes, as we all hope it will undertake, a joint effort to keep the peace, it will expect us to play our proportional part," he said. "Surely that is not a militaristic ideal. That is a very practical, possible ideal." . . .

Wilson could not have made a truly plausible case for a new diplomacy and a league—nor would he have been continued in office—if, at the same time, he had not been willing and able to move plainly to the left of center in American politics. Indeed, the array of social justice legislation he pushed through Congress on the eve of his reelection campaign gave legitimacy to his aspirations in foreign affairs like nothing else could have. Wilson could boast of a number of accomplishments for his first two years in office: the Underwood Tariff, the Clayton Antitrust Act, the Federal Reserve System, and the Federal Trade Commission. Then, as his polestar moved comparatively leftward with the approach of the 1916 campaign, he put two "radicals" (Louis D. Brandeis and John Hessin Clarke) on the Supreme Court. Over the protests of conservatives in and out of Congress, he secured passage of the Adamson Act, which established the eight-hour day for railroad workers, and the Keating-Owen bill, which imposed restrictions on child labor. Finally, he had defused the conservatives' appeal to jingoism with his "moderate" preparedness program, which, in conjunction with the Revenue Act of 1916, yielded the first real tax on wealth in American history. . . .

But this was only the half of it. As the complement to his advanced progressivism, Wilson also made American membership in a league of nations one of the cardinal themes of his campaign, a theme that complemented the Democratic chant, "He Kept Us Out Of War!" His utterances on the league exerted a significant impact on the outcome. [The leftist journalist] Max Eastman predicted that Wilson would win reelection because "he has attacked the problem of eliminating war, and he has not succumbed to the epidemic of militarism." Indeed, his speeches on the league constituted "the most important step that any President of the United States has taken towards civilizing the world since Lincoln." Herbert Croly, the influential editor of the *New Republic,* threw his support to Wilson not only on the grounds of the president's domestic record but also because he had "committed himself and his party to a revolutionary doctrine": American participation in a postwar league of nations. . . .

In any event, the election returns suggested that Wilson and the progressive internationalists had not merely checked the reactionaries; they had presided over the creation of a left-of-center coalition that seemed to hold the balance of political power in the United States. Precisely what all of this portended for future domestic struggles could hardly be predicted. As for foreign policy, the deeper meaning of their victory was unmistakable. "[T]he President we reelected has raised a flag that no other president has thought or perhaps dared to raise," [the left-liberal journalist] Amos Pinchot submitted. "It is the flag of internationalism."

American neutrality was a fragile thing. Wilson had always shared the conviction of fellow peace seekers that the best way to keep the country out of the war was to try to bring about a negotiated settlement. Twice, to that end, in 1915 and 1916, he had sent his personal emissary, Colonel Edward M. House, to Europe for direct parlays with the heads of all the belligerent governments. These appeals had proved futile. Now, fortified by reconfirmation at the polls, he decided on a bold stroke. In a climactic attempt to end the war, he went before the Senate on January 22, 1917, and called for "peace without victory." In this address, Wilson drew together the strands of progressive internationalist thought and launched a penetrating critique of European imperialism, militarism, and balance-of-power politics—the root causes of the war, he said. In their stead, he held out the promise of a "community of nations"—a new world order sustained by procedures for the arbitration of disputes between nations, a dramatic reduction of armaments, self-determination, and collective security. The chief instrumentality of this sweeping program was to be a league of nations. Thus, Wilson began his ascent to a position of central importance in the history of international relations in the twentieth century.

Responses to the address varied. The governments of both warring coalitions, still praying for decisive victory in the field, either ignored it or received it with contempt. Many pro-Allied Republicans, such as Senator Henry Cabot Lodge of Massachusetts, heaped scorn upon the very notion of "peace without victory" and wondered exactly what membership in a league might entail. Nonetheless, Wilson's manifesto met with an unprecedented outpouring of praise from progressive groups at home and abroad. . . .

One week later, Germany announced the resumption of unrestricted submarine warfare against all flags. After three American ships were sunk without warning, public opinion shifted markedly. On March 20, the cabinet unanimously recommended full-fledged belligerency. Wilson, too, had concluded that after some thirty months of neutrality, war had "thus been thrust upon" the United States. "But," the secretary of interior recorded in his diary, "he goes unwillingly."

In his address to Congress on April 2, 1917, the president explained why neutrality no longer seemed tenable and outlined the measures necessary for getting the country on a war footing. He then turned to more transcendent matters. His goals were the same as when he had addressed the Senate in January; he said, "The world must be made safe for democracy. Its peace must be planted upon the tested foundations of political liberty. We have no selfish ends to serve. We desire no conquest, no dominion. We seek no indemnities for ourselves, no material compensation for the sacrifices we shall freely make." He implied that Americans would be fighting to establish some degree of "peace without victory," or, as he put it, "for a universal dominion of right by such a concert of free nations as shall bring peace and safety to all nations and the world itself at last free"—a program now attainable apparently only through the crucible of war. . . .

Then, just as the United States entered the war, Russia, staggering under the relentless blows of the German army, was seized by revolutionary upheaval. By the end of 1917, the Bolshevik leaders, V. I. Lenin and Leon Trotsky, pulled their ravaged nation out of the war. They thereupon issued proclamations on behalf of a democratic peace based on self-determination and summoned the peoples of Europe to demand that their governments—the Allies and the Central Powers alike—repudiate plans for conquest.

In the circumstances, Wilson really had no choice but to respond to the Bolshevik challenge. In his Fourteen Points Address, of January 8, 1918, the most celebrated speech of his presidency, he reiterated much of the anti-imperialist "peace without victory" formula and once again made the League of Nations the capstone. In answer to Lenin's entreaty to stop the war, he argued that German autocracy and militarism must be crushed so that humanity could set about the task of creating a new and better world. Wilson's endeavor to remove the suspicions hanging over the Allied cause and rally doubters to see the war through to the bitter end succeeded magnificently. The popular approbation that greeted the Fourteen Points in both Europe and America approached phenomenal proportions. (Even Lenin hailed the address as "a great step ahead towards the peace of the world.") But as before, the Allied governments declined to endorse or comment on Wilson's progressive war aims.

At home, Wilson's own immediate priorities inexorably shifted toward the exigencies of war mobilization. And, in part owing to stinging Republican criticism of "peace without victory" and, later, the Fourteen Points as the basis for the postwar settlement, he refused to discuss his plans for the League in any concrete detail throughout the period of American belligerency. He also neglected to lay essential political groundwork for it at home. By the autumn of 1918, important segments among both conservative and progressive internationalists had grown disenchanted with Wilson, albeit for entirely different reasons.

This development would prove to be as unfortunate as the partisan opposition led by the president's arch-nemeses, Theodore Roosevelt and Henry Cabot Lodge. For example, Wilson grievously offended Taft by frustrating the wartime efforts of the LEP and other conservative internationalists, who wanted to make formal plans for the League of Nations in cooperation with the British government. (There were, of course, serious ideological differences between his and Taft's conception of the League, but Wilson might have found a way to use the Republican-dominated LEP to defuse some of the incipient senatorial criticism.)

Perhaps just as consequential, Wilson failed to nurture the left-of-center coalition of 1916, a dynamic political force that, had it remained intact, might have made it possible for him to secure and validate American leadership in a peace-keeping organization intended to serve progressive purposes. But he began to lose his grip on his former base of support as a tidal wave of anti-German hysteria and superpatriotism swept over the country in 1917–1918. Like a giant wrecking machine, "One Hundred Percent Americanism," as it was known, had the potential to batter the progressive wing of the American internationalist movement to ruins. In every part of the United States, acts of political repression and violence (sanctioned by federal legislation) were committed against German-Americans as well as pacifists and radicals. Only at risk of life or limb did antiwar dissenters express their views in public. For example, for speaking out against American participation in the war, Eugene Debs was sentenced to ten years in prison. The postmaster general denied second-class mailing privileges to such publications as the *Milwaukee Leader,* the *Appeal to Reason,* and the *Masses,* virtually shutting them down. The majority of progressive internationalists steadfastly supported the war effort, but they could not abide these kinds of violations of basic First Amendment rights, for which, ultimately, they held Wilson responsible. And so, because he acquiesced in the suppression of civil liberties, Wilson himself contributed to a gradual unraveling of his coalition.

The circumstances in which the war ended compounded the larger problem. By September 1918, the combined might of the Allied and American armies had pushed the enemy back toward Belgium. On October 6, German Chancellor Max von Baden appealed to Wilson to take steps for the restoration of peace based on the Fourteen Points. The armistice was signed on November 11. Meanwhile, a midterm congressional election more important than most presidential elections in American history had taken place. Against the Wilsonian peace plan, the Republicans launched a fiercely partisan, ultraconservative campaign. This time around, endorsements on behalf of the administration by leading progressives outside the Democratic party hardly matched those of the 1916 contest. Even so, the centralization of the wartime economy and the core of Wilson's foreign policy placed him far enough to the left to make all Democrats vulnerable to Republican charges that they were "un-American." Most historians maintain that Wilson committed the worst blunder of his presidency in countering the attacks: He asked the public for a vote of confidence—an ostensibly partisan appeal to sustain the Democrats' control of Congress. When the Republicans won majorities of forty-five in the House and two in the Senate, they could claim that the president, who planned to attend the Paris Peace Conference personally, had been repudiated. The Republicans also thereby gained control over congressional committees, including the Senate Foreign Relations Committee, which would be chaired by Lodge.

Yet despite these political setbacks, the Fourteen Points had acquired the status of sacred text among the war-weary peoples of Europe, and "Wilson" was becoming something more than the name of a president. Italian soldiers placed his picture in their barracks. An old woman said she heard that in America "there was a great saint who is going to make peace for us." Romain Rolland, the French Nobel laureate, pronounced him the greatest "moral authority" in the world. The whole world seemed to come to a halt to honor Wilson when he arrived in Europe. Into the streets and piazzas of Paris, London, Rome, and Milan, millions of people turned out to hail "the Moses from Across the Atlantic." . . .

Whereas he could not have prevailed without the massive outpouring of public support, Wilson still had to pay a heavy price for the League. If he was adored by the "common people," the statesmen of Europe—David Lloyd George, Georges Clemenceau, and Vittorio Orlando—held grave reservations about a Wilsonian peace. They were also keen students of American politics. Fully aware of the arithmetic of the Senate, they used their acceptance of the covenant as a lever to gain concessions on other vital and contentious issues.

For instance, Wilson was compelled to swallow a less-than-satisfactory compromise on the disposition of captured enemy colonies, which the Allies (in particular, Australia and South Africa) coveted for themselves. Clemenceau, on threat of withdrawal of his certification of the League, demanded for France military occupation of the Rhineland; Orlando claimed for Italy the Yugoslav port city of Fiume; and the Japanese insisted on retaining exploitative economic privileges in China's Shantung province. On several occasions, Wilson was able to moderate the more extreme Allied demands and uphold at least the spirit of the Fourteen Points. But, then, on verge of physical collapse, he permitted the Allies to impose upon Germany a huge reparations burden and, on top of everything else, a "war-guilt" clause—saddling it with the moral responsibility for allegedly having started the war. Wilson tried to take comfort in the hope that, once the "war psychosis" had receded, the League would be in position to arbitrate and rectify the injustices contained in the peace treaty itself. After six long months of often acrimonious deliberations, however, the signing of that document in the Hall of Mirrors at Versailles, on June 28, 1919, was at best a fleeting triumph for the exhausted president.

By the time Wilson returned to the United States in the summer of 1919, thirty-two state legislatures and thirty-three governors had endorsed the covenant. According to a *Literary Digest* poll, the vast majority of nearly 1,400 newspaper editors, including a majority of Republican editors, advocated American membership in some kind of league. Had a national referendum been held at just that moment, the country almost certainly would have joined. The reasons for its failure to do so are still debated by historians. To begin, Wilson had already lost the active support of most left-wing progressives, not to mention that of the socialists. Many liberals, too, shook their heads in dismay upon reading the Versailles settlement. They believed that, regardless of his motives, he had forsaken the Fourteen Points; that he had conceded too much to the Allies in the territorial compromises; and that vindictiveness, not righteousness, had ruled at the Paris conclave. In short, they feared that the League of Nations would be bound to uphold an unjust peace.

The great debate also coincided with the opening phase of the Red Scare, an even more hysterical and pervasive manifestation of "One Hundred Percent Americanism" whose focus had shifted from the German menace to the threat of bolshevism. Deterioration of civil liberties continued to discourage many progressive internationalists from giving Wilson's crusade their full devotion. . . .

In the Senate on the one hand sheer partisanship motivated much of the opposition. Until the autumn of 1918, Wilson had been the most uniformly successful (if controversial) president since Lincoln. What would become of the Republican party, a friend asked Senator Lodge, if Wilson got his League and the Democrats could boast of "the greatest constructive reform in history"? On the other hand, many of the senatorial objections were grounded in ideological principles. Most Republicans acknowledged that the United States should cooperate with the Allies and play its part in upholding the peace settlement; but they also believed that Wilson had consigned too many vital national interests to the will of an international authority. (At one point, Wilson had frankly admitted, "Some of our sovereignty would be surrendered.") The Republicans found Article X of the covenant particularly troubling. It obliged contracting nations to "preserve as against external aggression the territorial integrity and political independence of all Members of the League." Thus, at least on paper, the United States might be required to take part in some far-flung military intervention in which it had no compelling interest; at the same time, the United States apparently would be prevented from using its military power unilaterally whenever it wanted to. Although during the peace conference he had responded to early criticisms and amended the covenant—to provide for withdrawal from the League and nominally to exempt the Monroe Doctrine and domestic matters (such as immigration) from its jurisdiction—Wilson had not done enough to assuage the anxieties of the majority of Republicans.

Then, too, a small but sturdy knot of senators known as the "irreconcilables" flat-out opposed the League in any form. Not all of the fifteen or so irreconcilables were partisans or reactionaries (though most, like Albert Fall, were); several of them, including Robert La Follette and George Norris, were bona-fide progressives who based their opposition on convictions similar to those of many liberals and socialists. Irreconcilable or no, only a few of Wilson's opponents were strict isolationists. No one had cut through to the crux of the debate with more discernment than Gilbert M. Hitchcock of Nebraska, the Democratic leader in the Senate, when he observed, "Internationalism has come, and we must choose what form the internationalism is to take." The *Appeal to Reason,* though disillusioned with the president and highly dubious of his labors, was harsher: Republicans feared Wilson's League because it placed restrictions on "America's armed forces . . . [and] the commercial and territorial greed of American capitalists." The Lodge crowd hardly advocated isolationism, but rather "the internationalism of unrestrained plunder and competition."

By summer's end, the Senate Foreign Relations Committee, dominated by Republicans and irreconcilables and with Lodge at the helm, had formulated forty-six amendments as the conditions for ratification; by autumn, these had evolved into formal reservations—curiously, fourteen in number. The most controversial one pertained to Article X of the covenant: "The United States assumes no obligation to preserve the territorial integrity or political independence of any country . . . unless in any particular case the Congress . . . by act or joint resolution [shall] so provide." . . .

Meanwhile, Wilson held a series of White House meetings with groups of Republicans known as "mild reservationists" and tried to persuade them to ratify the treaty as it was written. In fact, there was very little difference between their views and those of the senators called "strong reservationists." Hence, none of these conferences changed anyone's mind. Then, against the advice of his personal physician and the pleading of the First Lady, Wilson determined that he must take his case directly to the American people and let them know what was at stake. For three weeks in September 1919, he traveled ten thousand miles by train throughout the Middle and Far West, making some forty speeches to hundreds of thousands of people.

Wilson appealed to his audiences on both the intellectual and the emotional level. Despite the importance of Article X, he told them, military sanctions probably would not have to come into play very often—in part because of the deterrent manifest within the threat of collective force, in part because of the cooling-off provisions in the arbitration features of the League, and in part because disarmament, which he heavily emphasized, would help to eliminate most potential problems from the start. He also addressed the question of sovereignty, as it related to the Senate's concern over arbitration and the hindrance to unilateral action that League membership implied: "The only way in which you can have impartial determinations in this world is by consenting to something you do not want to do." And the obvious corollary was to agree to refrain from doing something that you *want* to do, for there might be times "when we lose in court [and] we will take our medicine."

But there could be no truly effective League without America's participation. Should Americans turn their backs, he said, they would have to live forever with a gun in their hands. And they could not go in grudgingly or on a conditional basis. The "Lodge Reservations" would utterly "change the entire meaning of the Treaty." If the League were thus crippled, he would feel obliged to stand "in mortification and shame" before the boys who went across the seas to fight and say to them, "'You are betrayed. You fought for something that you did not get.'" . . .

As the crowds grew larger and the cheers louder, Wilson looked more haggard and worn out at the end of each day. His facial muscles twitched. Headaches so excruciating that he could hardly see recurred. To keep from coughing all night, he slept propped up in a chair. At last, his doctor called a halt to the tour and rushed him back to Washington. Two days later, on October 2, he suffered a stroke that nearly killed him and permanently paralyzed the left side of his body. From that point onward, Wilson was but a fragile husk of his former self, a tragic recluse in the White House, shielded by his wife and doctor.

The Senate roll was called three times, in November 1919 and March 1920. But whether on a motion to ratify the treaty unconditionally or with the fourteen Lodge reservations attached to it, the vote always fell short of a two-thirds majority. In November 1920, Warren G. Harding, the Republican presidential candidate, won a landslide victory over the Democrat, James M. Cox. The Republicans were only too happy to interpret the returns as the "great and solemn referendum" that Wilson had earlier said he had wanted for his covenant. "So far as the United States is concerned," Lodge now declared, "that League is dead."

In surveying the ruins, many historians have cited the president's stroke as the primary factor behind the outcome. A healthy Wilson, they argue, surely would have grasped the situation and strived to find a middle ground on the question of reservations. Other historians have maintained that his refusal to compromise was consistent with his personality throughout his life, that he would never have yielded to the Republicans (especially to Lodge), regardless of the state of his health. Although there is merit in both of these interpretations—the stroke and Wilson's personality are of obvious relevance—neither provides a complete explanation. They do not take adequate account of the evolution of the League idea, the ideological gulf that had always separated progressive and conservative internationalism, or the domestic political conditions that had taken shape long before the treaty was in the Senate.

In a very real sense, Wilsonian, or progressive, internationalism had begun at home, as part of the reform impulse in the "age of socialistic inquiry." By the touchstone of Wilson's advanced reform legislation and his synthesis of the tenets of the New Diplomacy, progressive internationalists had been able to define the terms of the debate and claim title to the League until 1917–1918—that is, until "One Hundred Percent Americanism" released uncontrollable forces that overwhelmed them. Wilson contributed to this turn of events by losing sight of the relationship between politics and foreign policy—by refusing to acknowledge his administration's culpability in the wartime reaction and by declining to take any action to combat it. . . .

Whatever the central cause of his historic failure, Wilson's conservative and partisan adversaries earnestly believed that his was a dangerously radical vision, a new world order alien to their own understanding of how the world worked. His severest critics among progressive internationalists believed he had not done enough to rally the people to his side and resist the forces of reaction—either in America or at the Paris Peace Conference. Wilson's response to them was a cry of anguish. "What more could I have done?" he asked historian William E. Dodd shortly before leaving the presidency. "I had to negotiate with my back to the wall. Men thought I had all power. Would to God I had had such power." His voice choking with emotion, he added, "The 'great' people at home wrote and wired every day that they were against me."

On all counts, and no doubt for all concerned, it had been, as Dodd himself concluded, "one long wilderness of despair and betrayal, even by good men."

The Peace Advocate Out of Touch with Reality

JAN WILHELM SCHULTE-NORDHOLT

We are in many respects Woodrow Wilson's heirs. That is why it is of great importance to us to make out what kind of man he was, how he came to his exalted and advanced ideas, and why in the end he failed. That is my purpose. . . . I want to examine more closely the life of a man who sought a solution to problems that are still ours, and who was therefore the first great advocate of world peace. He was, as it were, a whole peace movement all by himself.

I almost wrote "apostle of peace," but this phrase is too strong. It makes it seem that I had at least to some extent a work of hagiography in mind. Far from it! History is about people, their dreams and their failures. It would be all too easy to paint Woodrow Wilson as the great prophet who was always wiser than his fellow men. The purpose of a biography ought not to be to turn a human being into a figure of puppetry; to change the metaphor, to press him into flat uniformity. Was Wilson a prophet, an idealist, a dissembler, a practical man, a revolutionary reformer? He was to some small extent all of these. Like most great men, indeed like

From *Woodrow Wilson: A Life for Peace* (1991) by Jan W. Schulte-Nordholt, trans./ed. by Rowen, Herbert. Reprinted by permission of the University of California Press.

most people, Wilson was a bundle of contradictions. That is what makes him so fascinating. He was many things: a scholar driven by deep feelings; a poet who found his vocation in politics; a Christian consumed by his need for recognition; a lonely man who thought he understood mankind; a practical man who became fossilized in all too lofty dreams; a reasonable man full of turbulent passions. It is this paradoxical personality that I have tried to respect, . . . the irritating, moving grandeur of a self-willed man who played an immense role in history and whose importance has become extraordinarily great in our own times, even though he failed so wretchedly. That is why his life story is a dramatic tale, almost a Greek tragedy, with a catharsis at the end that still drains and raises our emotions. . . .

The outbreak of the war [in 1914] affected the president deeply. It shocked his sensitive nature. We read for example in a letter to [his assistant Edward] House in August: "I feel the burden of the thing almost intolerably from day to day." Two months later he wrote in the same vein but at greater length to Walter Page, the ambassador in London:

> The whole thing is vivid in my mind, painfully vivid, and has been almost ever since the struggle began. I think my thought and imagination contain the picture and perceive its significance from every point of view. I have to force myself not to dwell upon it to avoid the sort of numbness that comes from deep apprehension and dwelling upon elements too vast to be yet comprehended or in any way controlled by counsel.

Here we see once again in Wilson the tension between feeling and detachment.

This only emphasizes the importance of the question of how neutral he really was or wanted to be. His first personal reactions were emotionally favorable to the Allies. He was, after all, imbued with English values and ideals. The French ambassador to Washington, Jules Jusserand, wondered what "the great doctrinaire" in the White House was thinking, but the president soon gave his answer, as it were, to the English ambassador, Sir Cecil Spring-Rice. Spring-Rice informed Sir Edward Grey, the English foreign secretary, that Wilson had admitted to him that everything he held dear was now at stake. The president, he added, spoke with deep emotion. The ambassador, who knew the man he was dealing with, quoted a few lines from Wordsworth's sonnets about English freedom written during the Napoleonic wars. He knew them by heart, Wilson said with tears in his eyes. (Spring-Rice, as it happened, was also playing up to Grey, who, like Wilson, was passionately fond of Wordsworth.)

In his personal feelings Wilson was not in the slightest neutral. House heard him inveigh against everything German—government and people and what he called abstract German philosophy, which lacked spirituality! But he was quite able to separate his personal opinions and his official duties. In the first place, he understood that neutrality was necessary, that the American people were totally set against intervention. But he was also moved by the great goal that he had glimpsed since the beginning of the war, a possibility that fitted his character like a glove. It makes its appearance in his call for neutrality, for he did not merely issue a scrupulously formal official declaration, as any other president would have done. He did more, accompanying this declaration with a personal call to the people to remain truly neutral in thought and words. America, he reminded them, was composed of many peoples and too great sympathy for one or the other side could bring division among them.

Unity was even more necessary for another reason as well. This was the grand ideal that he now made public officially for the first time and which henceforth would inspire him and more and more involve him in international complications. America, he announced, was chosen to mediate, as only America could, just because it was neutral. He spoke in an exalted, religious tone, as he liked to do on so many other occasions. It was as if the war at last made possible things that all his life he had dreamed of—his country as the model and the very leader of the whole world, and himself called and chosen as the leader of his country and the maker of the future. . . .

One thing led to another. The arms shipments [to the Allies] led to loans. [William Jennings] Bryan, the pacifist-minded secretary of state, doubted that this flow of funds, which went almost entirely to the Entente, was really neutral. In good biblical fashion, he saw money as the root of all evil. Was it not written in Scripture that where one's treasure was, one's heart was too? He was able to convince Wilson that steps had to be taken against these loans, and American bankers were therefore warned on August 15, 1914, that such credits were "inconsistent with the true spirit of neutrality." But such a splendid position could not be maintained in the long run. Arms deliveries continued to grow, and the American economy could not do without them. In the spring of 1915 Bryan's idealistic approach was abandoned and one loan after another was floated in the United States. When America entered the war in 1917, the loans to the Allies had risen to more than two billion dollars, while those to the Central Powers amounted to no more than $27,000,000. . . .

War brings all international agreements into question, for war is unpredictable and full of surprises, always different from what anyone could have imagined. This was never so painfully evident as in the question of submarine warfare, since submarines were a weapon without equal, but operated effectively only by surprise. A multitude of notes discussed and debated the question of their surprise attacks. What was the status of the fine agreements about merchant ships in wartime? The answer was clear: a warship might halt, search, seize, and even sink a merchantman, but only after prior warning and giving civilian travelers the opportunity to leave safely. But a submarine that adhered to such rules would of course become defenseless and useless.

When the war broke out, German ships were swept off the seas, Germany was blockaded, and the Germans desperately turned to the submarine as a means of breaking the Allied stranglehold. The initial successes of the U-boats in the autumn of 1914 brought a sudden resurgence of hope, and the German military command slowly realized what a powerful weapon it had in its hands. On February 4, 1915, the German government published an official declaration putting a blockade around the British islands: in a zone around Great Britain, all enemy ships, including merchant vessels, would be attacked without warning. Neutral ships were advised to avoid these regions, since the Allied ships could always be disguised with neutral flags. . . .

The submarine weapon made it much more difficult for the United States, like all nonbelligerents, to remain neutral. Neutrality became a dilemma as never before. Was it neutral to waive fundamental rights of free navigation? Wasn't this itself a serious breach of international law, a grave derogation of morality in a world where morality seemed more and more on the wane?

Wilson, a man of principle, protested, but in so doing he reduced his chances for mediation. A sharp note was sent to Berlin, declaring that the policy set forth in the German note was "so unprecedented in naval warfare that this Government is reluctant to believe that the Imperial Government of Germany in this case contemplates it as possible." The American government would hold the German government fully responsible for the consequences. This seemed like plain talk, but what would happen if American rights were really challenged could not be foreseen. It was nonetheless probable that once such a stand on principle was taken, a conflict would result. . . .

Wherever the inspiration for the phrase ["peace without victory"] came from, the address that the president made to the Senate on January 22 [1917] was genuine Wilson from beginning to end. It was a plea, splendid, grandiose, and vague, for America's involvement in a future world order. That order—an organization of the peoples with its own force—had to come, he said. The question was, what kind of force? This was and remained the point of difficulty. For Wilson, the moralist who knew that without human inspiration and dedication the finest promises are empty, had in mind a "force" that was greater than the force of any country or alliance, which was "the organized major force of mankind." The nations must come to an agreement and then the old system of the "balance of power" would give way to a "community of power." And that could happen only if there was true reconciliation, upon the basis of a "peace without victory," a peace among equals.

That did not bring pleasure to everyone's ears, he realized. But he had to say it, for his intention was "only to face realities and to face them without soft concealments." Dreamers want so much to be taken for realists! . . .

He spoke in the name of the United States of America, the unique and superior country, as he himself liked to call it, forward-looking and in the lead in the service of mankind. All liberal-thinking people everywhere, in Europe and in America, rejoiced at his words. But conservatives (must we call them the realists?) on both sides of the ocean shook their heads over such empty phrases. Among the first of these, as we know, were persons in Wilson's own backyard, his closest advisers. [Secretary of State Robert] Lansing had warned against the term "peace without victory." What did it really mean? And, most of all, how would these words be taken in the Allied countries? But, Lansing tells us, Wilson did not want to listen. "I did not argue the matter, especially as I knew his fondness for phrasemaking and was sure that it would be useless to attempt to dissuade him." . . .

As was to be expected, [Republican Senator Henry Cabot] Lodge surpassed all the others in his hostility to Wilson. In an angry speech to the Senate he wielded the full resources of his logic to tear apart the arguments of his enemy. What did it mean to say that America had no interest in the peace terms but only in the peace? How can men be required to wage war not to win, so that all their sacrifices were in vain, "a criminal and hideous futility"? . . . How could the "organized major force of mankind" be applied? Voluntarily, or automatically, or compulsorily? When the idea of a league was broached two years earlier, he had been greatly attracted to it, but the more he thought about it, the more problems he saw. It could not be made effective by "high-sounding phrases, which fall so agreeably upon the ear, when there is no thought behind it." Does it mean that the small nations can, by majority vote, involve the large nations in war? "Are we prepared to commit ourselves to a purely general proposition without knowing where we are going or what is to be demanded of us, except that we shall be compelled to furnish our quota of military and naval forces to the service of a league in which we shall have but one voice?" A league for peace meant readiness to wage war against any country that did not obey its decisions. What if it decided that Japan and China should have the right of migration anywhere, and Canada, Australia, and New Zealand declined to accept the decision? Or California, for that matter?

The points made by Lodge were fundamental, which is why I present them at such length. Already at this time, in January 1917, the lines of division were drawn which would define the great debate and the great tragedy of 1919. On one side stood the idealist, on the other the realist, and on both sides more than personal animosity was involved. Furthermore, a political alliance was beginning to take shape that slackened during the war years but operated with full force in 1919; it brought together the Republican isolationists from the West, who were also idealists, for the most part from the Progressive camp, and the Republican internationalist realists, [Senator William] Borah on the one side and Lodge on the other. It was an alliance that would bring disaster to Wilson, but in 1917 he could not foresee that. . . .

Wilson shrank from taking the final step [after the German decision in late January 1917 to launch unrestricted submarine warfare], not out of fear, not out of unsullied pacifism, but because his whole conception of mediating between the belligerents (and thereby saving white civilization) would be shattered. This was the principal reason for his hesitation. And so he talked during these weeks in almost pacifist terms about war and imperialism, spoke out in anger against the support for war from right-wing circles, which he described as "Junkerthum trying to creep in under the cover of the patriotic feeling of the moment." . . .

[The journalist] Walter Lippmann, who looked at him with cool rationality and was among those bitterly disappointed with him after 1919, draws for us nonetheless a portrait of Wilson in his book *Men of Destiny,* showing the orator of light learning about darkness. He gazed in March 1917, says Lippmann, "in the bottomless pit." He was "an anguished prophet," full of compassion and doubt, a man who experienced the tragedy of his time and therefore was able, with overwrought absoluteness, to see the league of nations as the only justification of his action.

With this as his justification he went into the war, not out of economic interest, not because of the violation of the neutral rights of the United States, although these played a part, but in order to bring about genuine peace. Only if America took part could it have a voice in the peace. Mediation through participation would be more effective than neutrality, he now believed. To a delegation of pacifists led by Jane Addams, he said on February 28 that "as head of a nation participating in the war, the President of the United States would have a seat at the Peace Table, but that if he remained the representative of a neutral country he could at best only 'call through a crack in the door.'" Personal ambition and general interest concurred in what we may call a mission. The man and his times seemed to fit each other like the two halves of a piece of fruit. . . .

Of all the impressive sermons that Wilson preached to his people and to the world, none became so famous as his "Fourteen Points" speech of January 8, 1918. It attained a breadth and depth, in space and in time, greater than that of all the others. Not that it is his finest address; there are others, such as the "peace without victory" speech of a year earlier and the declaration of war of April 1917, which are more splendid in rhetoric and wider in vision. But this time Wilson was more practical, adding as it were deed to words; he developed a practical program that was of importance for the whole world. . . .

All in all, the Fourteen Points seemed practical and responsible. How lightly they skipped over historical problems would only become evident in Paris. But there was also a fourteenth point, a panacea for all the shortcomings now and later, a League of Nations: "A special association of nations must be formed under specific covenants for the purpose of affording mutual guarantees of political independence and territorial integrity to great and small states alike." This short sentence carried a heavy burden, too heavy as it turned out. In these few words the future world peace was settled, totally and permanently. For Wilson everything revolved around it; he did not see the difficulties and he did not want to see them, and this would in the end bring his downfall. . . .

In general Wilson's principles more and more broke loose from reality and lived their own lives. Self-determination was one such principle. During the war it became one of the major foundations of Wilson's new world order. We shall never subject another people, he had said back in 1915, "because we believe, we passionately believe, in the right of every people to choose their own allegiance and be free of masters altogether."

Only very slowly, as the reality of Europe began to come closer, did he discover the dangerous consequences of the principle. In the discussion with Spring-Rice on January 3 . . . , he wondered whether it was in fact possible to apply it consistently. The example of the threatening dismemberment of Austria-Hungary was probably in his thoughts when he said: "Pushed to its extreme, the principle would mean the disruption of existing governments to an undefinable extent. Logic was a good and powerful thing but apart from the consideration of existing circumstances might well lead to very dangerous results." The Englishman must have heard this with satisfaction, for the British Empire was not about to grant self-determination to all its peoples.

Later, in Paris, many began to realize the difficulties and dangers in this splendid principle. Lansing hit the nail on the head in a confidential memorandum, in which he wondered what self-determination would mean for the Irish, Indians, Egyptians, and South African Boers. What would happen with the Muslims in Syria and Palestine, and how did that fit in with the idea of Zionism, to which Wilson was very sympathetic. "The phrase is simply loaded with dynamite. It will raise hopes which can never be realized." It was the dream of an idealist, he said, and it is clear whom Lansing really had in mind.

As Wilson himself came to see, he had to be very cautious in Paris when trying to put his great principles into practice. He acknowledged that when he had first spoken of self-determination he had not realized that there were so many peoples who would claim it as their right. . . .

Wilson did not underestimate the devastation in Europe, but he retained his nineteenth-century American optimism. His whole existence was tied up with it; he could not live without hope. He clung to the idea of a grand radical cure, to a mystical faith in the mankind of the future, who were purified by events and repented. He had to represent that mankind; he had to make a new peace.

That is why he had to go to Paris [after the German surrender in late 1918]. . . . He was overwhelmed by his mission. His Czech colleague Thomas Masaryk, who understood him well ("now, we were both professors") warned him about the European statesmen: "But he wouldn't listen, for he was too filled with his plan for a League of Nations to take obstacles into account." . . .

Wilson's triumphal tour of Europe took him from Paris to London and then to Rome. Everywhere he was greeted as a savior, as the "Redeemer of Humanity" (*Redentore dell' Humanità*) and "God of Peace" (*Dio di Pace*), in the words of the Italian banners. He spent weeks indulging in this pomp and circumstance, immersed in a sea of flags and songs, carried along by beautiful words that promised so much for the future. Justice! Peace! When we hear Wilson speak in these first weeks, everything is radiant. Sometimes a harsh sound breaks through, as when he replies to [Raymond] Poincaré, the president of France, who wants no reconciliation with the foe, that there exist "eternal principles of right and justice" which bring with them "the certainty of just punishment." But for the most part his outlook is peaceful. He speaks of the peoples who form "the organized moral force of men throughout the world," of the tide of good will: "There is a great tide running in the hearts of men. The hearts of men have never beaten so singularly in unison before. Men have never been so conscious of this brotherhood." . . .

Alas, there was in fact no moral tide that carried all with it. There was rather a divided Europe in which the peoples were driven at least as much by muddled feelings of rage and revenge as by lofty thoughts of right and reason. Wilson himself had experienced the impact of such vindictiveness during the off-year elections in the United States, and it was at least as prevalent in Europe. [French premier Georges] Clemenceau told the Chamber of Deputies at the end of December that he disagreed with Wilson, although he had, he said, the greatest admiration for the American president's "noble candor" (which was changed in the parliamentary journal to "noble grandeur"); he thereupon won a vote of confidence by a majority of 380 to 134. [British prime minister] Lloyd George triumphed equally convincingly in elections for the House of Commons just before Christmas. His coalition of Liberals and Tories, in which the latter were dominant, ran on an electoral program of hate and revenge against Germany with slogans like "Hang the Kaiser" and "Make Germany Pay," received no less than 526 of the 707 seats. It was not Lloyd George himself but the navy minister Sir Eric Geddes who uttered the notorious words, "We shall squeeze the German lemons until the pips squeak."

Wilson's moral majority therefore existed only in his poetic imagination. He was totally out of touch with reality. The Europeans did not know what to make of his fine words. They asked themselves whether he actually meant what he said. "I am one of the few people who think him honest," said Lloyd George to his friends. But he too was exasperated when the president blew his own horn loudly and gave no sign that he understood the sacrifices England had made: "Not a word of generous appreciation issued from his lips." Wilson, the American, could not establish an accepted character and place in Europe. The Europeans thought he was American, with his smooth, streamlined face, showing no emotion behind his shining glasses. . . .

In a word, the European leaders did not like Woodrow Wilson. From the start there was tension between them. Clemenceau, an old hand in politics, was not the man to come under the influence of Wilson's lofty words. He knew the United States; he had lived there just after the Civil War, spoke English well, and had married an American woman. He had no high opinion of American idealism, as was evident in the witticisms he made at Wilson's expense. God had needed only ten commandments, but Wilson fourteen, he jibed. . . . And, in reaction to the "peace without victory" speech, he wrote: "Never before has any political assembly heard so fine a sermon on what human beings might be capable of accomplishing if only they weren't human." In brief, this was classic realism confronting classic idealism. . . .

Wilson believed in his League of Nations as a remedy for all troubles, a miraculous cure that would work precisely because it was so entwined with the peace treaty itself. The treaty might not be perfect, he said in April, but with the League of Nations as an integral part of the treaty, there was a mechanism to improve its operation.

But actually it worked the other way round, a fact that Wilson completely missed. The delegates of the Allied countries exploited his League of Nations proposal to extract concessions from him; the peace turned out very badly because he repeatedly made compromises in order to save his beloved plan, carrying it through the bustling debates to safe harbor. . . . "The fact is," wrote the deeply disappointed [diplomat Henry] White in May, "that the League of Nations, in which he had been more deeply interested than anything else from the beginning, believing it to be the best if not the only means of avoiding war in the future, has been played to the limit by France and Japan in extracting concessions from him; to a certain extent by the British too, and the Treaty as it stands is the result." . . .

The history of the Versailles peace has called forth a welter of difficult questions. Was it too harsh, a *Diktatfrieden* that automatically elicited a reaction of revanche? Or was it, on the contrary, too mild a settlement, enabling the old forces in Germany to continue? In any case, is there a direct causal link between 1919 and 1933? Does the guilt for the disastrous consequences lie with the men who, in Paris, laid down the rules for the future? These are all questions that in their nature cannot be given a conclusive or logically satisfactory answer. But they are also questions that cannot be evaded. If this peace were not accepted, Wilson said many times on his swing through the West in the fall, there would be another war in twenty years. . . .

How horribly right he proved to be! What he predicted came about just as he said. But was he himself guiltless? Hadn't he written the whole scenario for that future? The defeat [of Germany] was a humiliation, not intended as such by him in his noble naïveté, but nonetheless felt as such by the vanquished. Humiliation led to dreams of revenge; the seeds of a new war were put into the soil. Of course, they would only grow when the climate was favorable, when events, primarily the Great Depression that began in 1929, permitted. But beyond question the seeds were planted by the peace of Versailles. . . .

Historians, in their quest for consistency, have to fit Wilson into some pattern, if need be, one that takes time into account. This provides a way out: in the long run, in the future (but with what a frightful intermezzo!), Wilson would be right. This is the way Arthur Link, Wilson's outstanding biographer, approaches the question. For him, Wilson's vision might seem foolish at first sight, because it clashed with reality, but there is in fact a "higher realism." This adds a wider dimension to the problem of Wilson; his deeds then must be judged within the perspective of the future. In it his deeds accord with his words; if they were failures in the short run, all is reconciled in the perspective of a better future. It is a quite Wilsonian idea, paralleling the way Wilson himself saw the League of Nations as the panacea for all temporary compromises.

But is it possible to separate today and tomorrow from each other in this way? Is this how the relationship between realism and idealism actually works? What is the value of a prophet in politics? These are the questions we constantly encounter.

There is a deep tragedy within them. Let me repeat: Wilson himself saw and warned that if there was not a just peace, there would be war again in twenty years. Does it follow from this that he personally shared in the responsibility for the horrors that would break out two decades later? Link's reply is that he did not. At Versailles there was the familiar tension between the ideal and reality, but it is inherent in all human striving. One can only ask why Wilson failed. There are more than enough reasons. After the armistice he had no means to compel France and England; he had been weakened in his own country by the elections; he had formidable opponents in Clemenceau, Lloyd George, [Italian prime minister] Orlando, and [Italian foreign minister Sidney] Sonnino; his ideal of "open covenants" was frustrated. And yet, Link maintains, he gained a reasonable peace that worked and created a new international order. He snaps at the critics:

> It is time to stop perpetuating the myth that the Paris settlement made inevitable the rise to power of Mussolini, the Japanese militarists, and Hitler, and hence the Second World War. That war was primarily the result of the Great Depression.

All the same, questions persist. If the war that came in twenty years was not the consequence of a bad peace, or if it wasn't such a bad peace after all, was Wilson's forecast just a stab in the dark? But then why reproach the others who opposed him?

Wilsonianism: A Workable Blueprint for a Broken World

TONY SMITH

The essential genius of Wilson's proposals for a new world order after World War I was that it had a vision of the proper ordering of domestic as well as international politics that was well suited to the development of political and economic forces worldwide in the twentieth century. Here was a period in Germany, Russia, and Eastern Europe where social forces were struggling over the modernization of the state, where rival conceptions of national unity were trying to make government responsive through party government to nationalistic appeals for popular sovereignty. In domestic terms, Wilson respected the power of nationalism and favored national self-determination. States were presumed to be legitimate when they were democratically constituted, and it was expected that in most instances ethnic boundaries would make for the frontiers of countries. In the context of the world of 1918, such a proposal was radical; it accepted the dismemberment of empires (those of Austria-Hungary, Russia, and Turkey immediately; those of the Western European powers by implication thereafter), and it worked for the replacement of autocracies with democracies in Germany and the new nation-states to the East.

For international relations, Wilson called for a liberal economic regime and a system of collective security designed to preserve the peace. Again, his initiative was radical for it challenged the competitive mercantilistic practices that dictated much of world commerce with a more open trading system, just as it proposed to replace competitive balance of power thinking politically with what he called "a convenant of cooperative peace."

In short, the foundation of Wilson's order was the democratic nation-state; its superstructure was an international order of economic, military, and moral interdependence. Nationalism wed to democracy; democracies wed in peace, prosperity, and mutual respect embodied in international law and institutions: such was Wilson's essential vision, a form of liberalism he felt to be both necessary and appropriate for his era and essential to guarantee American national security. . . .

Wilson failed in his efforts both to root democratic forces in countries where they were struggling to take power and to establish a stable new configuration of power among the states of the continent. German democracy was not robust; Franco-German rapprochement did not occur; outside Czechoslovakia, democratic forces were weak in Eastern Europe; the Russian Revolution remained militant; communist parties in Western Europe sapped democratic forces; fascism came into power in Italy in 1922, encouraging like-minded movements to duplicate its success; no way was found to counter economic nationalism and the destructive impact of the Depression that began in 1929; collective security proved unable to halt Italian aggression in Ethiopia or Japanese attacks on China; and the American people and Congress refused to identify the national security with an active hand in the protection of liberal democracy in Europe.

Was there a better guide than Wilsonianism as to how America should defend its legitimate concerns in the founding of a stable European order friendly to this country's interests? Between 1940 and the early 1950s, the most influential thinkers in this country on the proper conduct of American foreign policy . . . took special pains to use Wilson as a negative example, a textbook study of how foreign policy should not be formulated. For these analysts, Wilsonianism stands for the American penchant to conduct its foreign conduct by moralizing about it, by assuming that somehow democracy is a panacea for the world's problems. In their eyes, liberal democratic internationalism betrays a vein of naive and utopian idealism ill-fitted to effective participation in global politics. The affliction did not start with Wilson nor end with him, but his presidency marks its high-water point. Realism, the dominant school of international relations theory in the United States, was founded at this time by these men and built its concepts by consciously pitting itself against the basic tenets of Wilsonianism.

Thus, referring to the settlement of 1919, [the diplomat and scholar] George Kennan wrote:

> This was the sort of peace you got when you allowed war hysteria and impractical idealism to lie down together in your mind, like the lion and the lamb; when you indulged yourself in the colossal conceit of thinking that you could suddenly make international life over into what you believed to be your own image; when you dismissed the past with contempt, rejected the relevance of the past to the future, and refused to occupy yourself with the real problems that a study of the past would suggest. . . .

[The journalist] Walter Lippmann's charges were even harsher, for they allege that Wilson's mistakes set the stage for the rise of fascism and the inability of the democracies to rally effectively to the challenge. . . .

How, then, should American foreign policy have been formulated? These writers consider themselves realists. They insist that the national interest should be determined rather strictly by calculations of the relative amount of power among states, with a view of preventing threats to the existence or independence of the United States. Seen from this perspective, the only obvious antagonist of the United States in world affairs at that time was Germany, which Washington should forthrightly have mobilized to contain. They have no patience with the "idealism" of a "utopian," "moralistic" crusade to change the character of international relations by making states democratic, such as Wilson advanced, for this talk only put a smokescreen over the essential matter of dealing with German power. . . .

In a word, the realists maintained that Wilson did not adequately appreciate the character of "power politics" or the "balance of power" in his deliberations, by which they meant the need to contain German power so that it would not dominate the continent, a turn of events that would have been seriously threatening to American national security. In Lippmann's view, for example, Wilson failed to explain to the American people why the country went to war: "The reasons he did give were legalistic and moralistic and idealistic reasons, rather than the substantial and vital reasons that the security of the United States demanded that no aggressively expanding imperial power, like Germany, should be allowed to gain the mastery of the Atlantic Ocean."

These charges ask for an indictment that the evidence does not warrant. Thus, Wilson was not a pacifist, and his proposals for disarmament are best understood as confidence-building measures among states, not as a reluctance to back commitments with force, as Lippmann suggested. Again, the League of Nations was not to have either financial or military resources independent of the states that participated in it, and its Council had to act by unanimous agreement; the League was not to be a world government. More, the call for self-determination was not intended as a blank check for secessionist movements. Wilson respected economic, strategic, and historical considerations that had to be weighed against nationalist feelings; it was only toward the end of the war that he finally resigned himself to the dismemberment of the Austro-Hungarian empire rather than to seeing it reconstituted as a democratic federalist structure.

But most importantly, Wilson intended the League to be the vehicle to bind the United States permanently to a management role in world affairs. Whatever the shortcomings of the details in his plan, American membership in the League might well have provided the check on Germany that Wilson's critics allege his naivete and moralizing prevented him from establishing.

For Wilson, the vital issue at the Peace Conference was the League; for his critics, it was Germany. Yet the League's very existence implicitly addressed the essential issue for Europe from 1871 until 1945 (and perhaps once again today): the German question. Given Germany's population, economic strength, militaristic history, political structure, and geography, could it live peacefully with its neighbors? Were the only alternatives to destroy it or be conquered by it? American leadership of the League portended that Germany might be contained by American power. Once contained, domestic reforms might be consolidated so that Germany could live with its neighbors by progressively shedding its militaristic elements in favor of developing itself as a democracy capable of interacting peacefully with the other states of Europe. But even without German reforms, membership in the League would automatically tie America into the European balance of power and so safeguard American national security.

Wilsonianism, did, therefore, meaningfully address the critical issue of what to do about Germany. If the League's fundamental purpose was to check aggression against weaker states created by the dismemberment of the Russian, Ottoman, and Austro-Hungarian empires after 1918, if its collateral ambition was to foster democratic government and liberal international economic exchange, then what better safeguard could be put on German power? As a way of addressing the growing presence of the Soviet Union in world affairs, it offered a useful forum as well.

In addition to the League, Wilson had two other ways of influencing Germany. His preferred approach was to control German power by absorbing it into a liberal economic, political, and military arrangement that would effectively integrate Germany with its neighbors (especially France) and the United States. Here was the germ of the American idea after 1945 to push for European integration based on Franco-German rapprochement. Wilson also agreed to join the British in guaranteeing France against German attack in a treaty independent of the League. The Senate defeated this latter project along with barring American membership in the League. . . .

Fail though it did at the time, the virtues of Wilson's policy for the postwar world were threefold. First, it acknowledged the fundamental political importance of nationalism, seeking to direct rather than to repress its energy. Second, it sought to channel the demands for popular sovereignty contained in nationalism in the direction of democratic government, and away from authoritarian or totalitarian regimes (though the latter—a particular curse of the twentieth century—was not yet clearly visible when Wilson was in office). Third, it attempted to provide a structure of international institutions and agreements to handle military and economic affairs among democratically constituted, capitalist states. In all of these respects, American national security thinking followed Wilson's lead after 1945. Again today, in the aftermath of the cold war, we can see the prescience of his proposals as we deliberate the problems of nationalism in Eastern Europe, the course of Western European integration based on Franco-German understanding, and the need for organizational mechanisms to provide for the peaceful formulation of a gamut of issues from the economic to the military.

It is commonly observed that politics as an art requires pursuing the desirable in terms of the possible. The dilemma of leadership is to decide when it is weakness to fail to exploit the inevitable ambiguities, and therefore possibilities, of the historical moment, and when it is foolhardy to attempt to overcome immovable constraints set by a combination of forces past and present. Since options are always open to some extent, greatness requires creating opportunities and taking risks within the limits set by history.

While the constraints of history nullified Wilson's hopes, his efforts did not totally contradict the forces of his time. Democratic nationalist forces did exist in Germany and parts of Eastern Europe. If it was unlikely that the Bolshevik Revolution would ever have turned in a democratic direction, it was not until 1921 (with the Tenth Party Congress, which established iron discipline within the Communist party, and with the crushing of the Kronstadt mutiny, a sailors' uprising against Lenin's rule) that its totalitarian cast was definitely set. If it was unlikely that democracy would consolidate itself in Germany given the rancors of the right, the splitting of the left, and the rigors of the Depression, it certainly was not until after 1930 that this became manifestly evident. Again, although the Senate had repudiated the League in 1919–20, it could reconsider its position, as at times the American government seemed interested in doing. In short, Wilson's gamble on the forces of democracy and collective security (which in practice would have been the balance of power under another name) was not totally unrealistic. And what were his other options? Indeed his greatness as a visionary comes from how close to success his program came. Suppose America had joined the League in good faith, an organization basically of his devising? By that single act, the course of history might have been changed, for it would have committed the United States to the maintenance of a European equilibrium containing Germany.

The best evidence of the power of Wilsonianism, however, comes from its resurgence in American foreign policy in the aftermath of World War II. Bretton Woods, the initial plans for the United Nations, the hopes for Western European integration that lay behind the occupation of Germany and the Marshall Plan—all this was essentially Wilsonian in inspiration (even when operationalized by people like [British economist John Maynard] Keynes and Kennan who saw themselves as opponents of Wilson's position in Paris in 1919). In the late 1940s, Wilsonianism was thus to have a success that it was denied in the early 1920s. But it was in the late 1980s that Wilson's time truly arrived. Of all the extraordinary developments connected with the end of the cold war in 1989, surely one of the most noteworthy was the way Soviet leader Mikhail Gorbachev's "new thinking" for Europe—with its insistence on the importance of national self-determination, democratic government, and collective security—echoed Wilson's appeals of seventy years earlier. . . .

Unlike most statesmen, then, Wilson deserves to be measured not on the basis of achieving the ends of his policy in their time, but by the magnitude of his efforts and the influence they continued to have in later years. Seen from the perspective of the mid-1990s, three-quarters of a century since he left office, Wilson's concern that nationalism abroad be turned in the direction of democratic government for the sake of the American national interest seems soundly conceived. Writing in 1889 on "Leaders of Men," Wilson had declared:

> Great reformers do not, indeed, observe time and circumstance. Theirs is not a service of opportunity. They have no thought for occasion, no capacity for compromise. They are early vehicles of the Spirit of the Age. They are born of the very times that oppose them. . . . Theirs to hear the inarticulate voices that stir in the night-watches, apprising the lonely sentinel of what the day will bring forth.

🌐 *F U R T H E R   R E A D I N G*

Lloyd Ambrosius, *Wilsonian Statecraft* (1991)
———, *Woodrow Wilson and the American Diplomatic Tradition: The League Fight in Perspective* (1987)
———, *Woodrow Wilson and His Legacy in American Foreign Relations* (2002)
John M. Blum, *The Progressive Presidents* (1980)
H. W. Brands, *Woodrow Wilson* (2003)
Frederick S. Calhoun, *Power and Principle: Armed Intervention in Wilsonian Foreign Policy* (1986)

John W. Chambers III, *The Tyranny of Change: America in the Progressive Era, 1890–1920* (1992)

Kendrick A. Clements, *The Presidency of Woodrow Wilson* (1992)

———, *Woodrow Wilson: World Statesman* (1987)

G. R. Conyne, *Woodrow Wilson: British Perspectives* (1992)

John W. Coogan, "Wilsonian Diplomacy in War and Peace," in Gordon Martel, ed., *American Foreign Relations Reconsidered, 1890–1993* (1994)

———, *The End of Neutrality: The United States, Britain, and Maritime Rights, 1899–1915* (1981)

John Milton Cooper Jr., *Breaking the Heart of the World* (2001)

———, *The Warrior and the Priest: Woodrow Wilson and Theodore Roosevelt* (1983)

David E. Davis and Eugene P. Trani, *The First Cold War* (2000)

Richard R. Doerries, *Imperial Challenge: Ambassador Count von Bernstorff and German-American Relations, 1908–1917* (1989)

David M. Esposito, *The Legacy of Woodrow Wilson* (1996)

Byron Farrell, *Over There* (1999)

Robert H. Ferrell, *Woodrow Wilson and World War I* (1985)

David S. Foglesong, *America's Secret War Against Bolshevism* (1995)

Lloyd C. Gardner, *Safe for Democracy* (1984)

Hans W. Gatske, *Germany and the United States* (1980)

Ross Gregory, *The Origins of American Intervention in the First World War* (1971)

Ross A. Kennedy, "Woodrow Wilson, World War I, and American National Security," *Diplomatic History,* 25 (Winter 2001), 1–31

William R. Keylor, *The Legacy of the Great War* (1998)

Henry Kissinger, *Diplomacy* (1994)

Antony Lentin, *Lloyd George, Woodrow Wilson, and the Guilt of Germany* (1985)

N. Gordon Levin, *Woodrow Wilson and World Politics* (1968)

Arthur S. Link, *Wilson,* 5 vols. (1947–1965)

———, *Woodrow Wilson: Revolution, War, and Peace* (1979)

David W. McFadden, *Alternative Paths: Soviets and Americans, 1917–1920* (1993)

Margaret MacMillan, *Paris, 1919* (2003)

Herbert F. Margulies, *The Mild Reservationists and the League of Nations Controversy in the Senate* (1989)

John H. Mauer, *The Outbreak of the First World War* (1995)

Ernest R. May, *The World War and American Isolation, 1914–1917* (1959)

Arno Mayer, *Politics and Diplomacy of Peacemaking* (1967)

Bert E. Park, *Ailing, Aging, Addicted: Studies of Compromised Leadership* (1993)

Ann R. Pierce, *Woodrow Wilson and Harry Truman* (2003)

Diane Preston, *"Lusitania": An Epic Tragedy* (2001)

Gregory Ross, "To Do Good in the World: Woodrow Wilson," in Frank J. Merli and Theodore A. Wilson, eds., *Makers of American Diplomacy* (1974)

Norman E. Saul, *War and Revolution* (2001)

Klaus Schwabe, *Woodrow Wilson, Revolutionary Germany, and Peacemaking, 1918–1919* (1985)

David Steigerwald, "The Reclamation of Woodrow Wilson," *Diplomatic History,* 23 (Winter 1999), 79–99

Ralph A. Stone, *The Irreconcilables* (1970)

John A. Thompson, *Woodrow Wilson* (2001)

Marc Trachtenburg, *Reparations in World Politics* (1980)

Barbara Tuchman, *The Zimmermann Telegram* (1958)

Robert W. Tucker, "The Triumph of Wilsonianism?" *World Policy Journal,* 10 (1993–1994), 83–99

Edwin A. Weinstein, *Woodrow Wilson: A Medical and Psychological Biography* (1981)

William C. Widenor, *Henry Cabot Lodge and the Search for an American Foreign Policy* (1980)

Robert H. Zeiger, *America's Great War* (2001)

The International
History of the 1920s

The embittering experience of the First World War and the Versailles peacemaking bred a distaste for Europe's old problems, and world politics in general, in the United States. Yet by the 1920s the world had become more interconnected and interdependent than ever before, and growing numbers of Americans enjoyed the benefits of international engagement. American participation in the world market-place, through both trade and investment, accelerated; mass communications and entertainment internationalized culture; and national leaders, often at the behest of private citizens, worked together to promote economic growth, stabilize a troubled world, and try to prevent another Armageddon. Throughout the 1920s, the Republican administrations of Warren G. Harding, Calvin Coolidge, and Herbert Hoover—often with the help of America's leading financiers—attempted to use nonmilitary methods, including economic arrangements and disarmament agreements, to construct a new world order. They devised plans to promote trade and currency exchange and to facilitate repayment of loans and war reparations, curb political extremism, reduce armaments, tame national rivalries, protect imperial interests, and prevent war. The United States worked diligently with European states to restore postwar Germany's economy, reassure France about its security, and contain the Soviet Union's communism. Internationalism also found expression at the grassroots level in the United States and around the world. Educators internationalized curriculums, universities established programs in international studies, private foundations supported transnational collaborations and exchange programs, and tourists traversed the globe. Women's organizations, with memberships that spanned the globe, worked to place disarmament, human rights, world hunger, and sexual equality on the international relations agenda.

As the 1930s opened, however, devastating events demonstrated that the quest for peace, prosperity, and understanding had failed. The Great Depression began to cripple the world marketplace, debts and reparations went unpaid, and trade wars broke out. Militarists in Germany and Japan preached racial chauvinism and vowed destruction of the Versailles settlement and nonaggression pacts, and the League of Nations struggled to define its role in world affairs. As fervent nationalism drove countries away from the once high hopes of Wilsonian internationalism, a second world war seemed possible.

What went wrong? In the immediate aftermath of World War II, historians usually condemned America's interwar behavior. For the generation that had suffered economic want and global war, the 1920s fixation with peace seemed naive and irresponsible. The decade's disarmament treaties, antiwar pacts, and modest military budgets became objects of ridicule—denounced for their disregard of power realities. Washington's maintenance of high tariff rates, critics charged, had undermined global trade in the name of business greed and short-term advantage. Reliance on private bankers and investors, instead of public funds, to provide overseas loans prevented Republican officials from ensuring that American capital served the national interest. And when the global depression that followed produced dictatorships and war, America's refusal to participate in the League of Nations and World Court prevented effective collective security against aggression. Some writers blamed America's failures on a narrow-minded nationalism and postwar "isolationism," a term that implied nearly total disengagement from international affairs. Others noted that twentieth-century global interdependence made isolation virtually impossible by the 1920s but that nonetheless Washington preferred to go it alone, or exercise its unilateral power, to stem threats to U.S. interests. The result was the continued pursuit of hegemony in Latin America, the negotiation of disarmament pacts, and the flexing of U.S. economic muscle—all outside the parameters of international alliances and the League of Nations. Scholars have called such thinking "independent internationalism" and contrast it with the commitment to multilateralism that accompanied the creation of the United Nations following World War II.

Much of the familiar critique remains prominent and persuasive in contemporary scholarship. However, the accelerating pace of globalization today—in the marketplace, politics, and culture—has also spurred historians to revisit the international history of the twenties. Some have highlighted how the Republican administrations of the decade understood the linkages between economic stability and international security, particularly in responding to trade imbalances and international debt. Others have come to view the disarmament treaties of the decade as an indication of international engagement and activism, rather than isolationism and retreat. Still other scholars have examined the rising international consciousness of Americans, both elites and commoners, that arose out of growing overseas commercial and cultural contacts. At times the export of popular culture during the twenties met foreign resistance, and at other times "Americanization" was warmly embraced. Either way, U.S. influence spread. The collapse of international structures and the coming of world war in the 1930s might be attributed to economic forces that no nation could withstand or to troubles endemic to the international system—national rivalries and legacies of Versailles, for example—that were impervious to outside solution. Perhaps more effective international economic policies awaited the ideological shift of the New Deal, which condoned greater government intervention in the capitalist system. Or perhaps the Republican leaders of the twenties were hamstrung by a minority of "irreconcilable" isolationists within their own party, rather than by a pervasive national mentality of isolationism.

How international were Americans during the twenties? In what ways did U.S. diplomacy during that decade contribute to the disastrous 1930s and the coming of World War II? What can the 1920s teach us about the global age in which we now live?

🌎 D O C U M E N T S

In Document 1, dated November 12, 1921, Secretary of State Charles Evans Hughes addresses the Washington Conference on naval disarmament. In making the case that arms reductions would permit public funds to be more wisely applied to economic re-habilitation and growth, Hughes boldly asks the major powers to scrap great numbers of warships. The Five Power Treaty of 1922 did just that. Document 2, a *Chicago Tribune* editorial of November 13, 1921, expresses what many Americans believed after the First World War: that Europe was hopelessly entrapped in rivalries and the United States ought to stay clear until the Continent set its house in order. Not all peace advo-cates, however, imbibed the *Tribune*'s isolationist sentiment. Recently enfranchised to vote, women activists from the United States joined women from other nations to champion international cooperation on behalf of peace and human rights. Document 3 is an excerpt from the Progressive reformer Jane Addams's book *Peace and Bread in Time of War* (1922), a history of the Women's International League for Peace and Freedom (WILPF). Addams, who served as the WILPF's president and attended the League of Nations Assembly in Geneva, Switzerland, in 1920–1921, reflects on the League's shortcomings and its potential as a mechanism for global humanitarianism and reform. In Document 4, a speech before the American Historical Association on December 29, 1922, Secretary Hughes identifies German reconstruction and the repa-rations issue as keys to European stability and recommends the mobilization of private experts to devise solutions. Hughes's proposals came to fruition in the Dawes Plan of 1924, which set a schedule for German reparations payments and provided for private American loans to alleviate Germany's economic plight.

Document 5 is a selection by the prolific Argentine anti-imperialist writer Manuel Ugarte, who identifies the United States as a "New Rome" that annexes wealth rather than territory, manipulates native politics, and creates a detrimental dependency among Latin Americans. Document 6, Edward G. Lowry's article "Trade Follows the Film" (*Saturday Evening Post,* November 7, 1925), reveals the link between economic and cul-tural expansion in the 1920s as American-made movies penetrated world markets. Secre-tary of Commerce Herbert Hoover, an ardent economic expansionist, establishes the value of foreign trade to the U.S. economy and dismisses critics of America's protective tariffs in Document 7, a speech of March 16, 1926. Document 8 is the antiwar Kellogg-Briand Pact, signed by the United States and most of the world's nations in August 1928.

1. Secretary of State Charles Evans Hughes Advocates Naval Disarmament, 1921

We not only have the lessons of the past to guide us, not only do we have the reaction from the disillusioning experiences of war, but we must meet the challenge of im-perative economic demands. What was convenient or highly desirable before is now a matter of vital necessity. If there is to be economic rehabilitation, if the longings for reasonable progress are not to be denied, if we are to be spared the uprisings of peoples made desperate in the desire to shake off burdens no longer endurable, com-petition in armament must stop. The present opportunity not only derives its advan-tage from a general appreciation of this fact, but the power to deal with the exigency

---

This document can be found in the U.S. Congress, *Senate Documents,* 67th Congress, 1st Session (Washington, D.C.: Government Printing Office, 1921), Doc. No. 77, pp. 13–17.

now rests with a small group of nations, represented here, who have every reason to desire peace and to promote amity. . . . Is it not plain that the time has passed for mere resolutions that the responsible Powers should examine the question of limitation of armament? We can no longer content ourselves with investigations, with statistics, with reports, with the circumlocution of inquiry. The essential facts are sufficiently known. The time has come, and this Conference has been called, not for general resolutions or mutual advice, but for action. . . .

It is apparent that this can not be accomplished without serious sacrifices. Enormous sums have been expended upon ships under construction and building programs which are now under way can not be given up without heavy loss. Yet if the present construction of capital ships goes forward other ships will inevitably be built to rival them and this will lead to still others. Thus the race will continue so long as ability to continue lasts. The effort to escape sacrifices is futile. We must face them or yield our purpose. . . .

In making the present proposal the United States is most solicitous to deal with the question upon an entirely reasonable and practicable basis, to the end that the just interests of all shall be adequately guarded and that national security and defense shall be maintained. Four general principles have been applied:

1. That all capital-ship building programs, either actual or projected, should be abandoned;
2. That further reduction should be made through the scrapping of certain of the older ships;
3. That in general regard should be had to the existing naval strength of the Powers concerned;
4. That the capital ship tonnage should be used as the measurement of strength for navies and a proportionate allowance of auxiliary combatant craft prescribed.

The principal features of the proposed agreement are as follows:

Capital Ships

United States.   The United States is now completing its program of 1916 calling for 10 new battleships and 6 battle cruisers. One battleship has been completed. The others are in various stages of construction; in some cases from 60 to over 80 per cent of the construction has been done. On these 15 capital ships now being built over $330,000,000 have been spent. Still, the United States is willing in the interest of an immediate limitation of naval armament to scrap all these ships.

The United States proposes, if this plan is accepted—

1. To scrap all capital ships now under construction. This includes 6 battle cruisers and 7 battleships on the ways and in course of building, and 2 battleships launched.

The total number of new capital ships thus to be scrapped is 15. The total tonnage of the new capital ships when completed would be 618,000 tons.

2. To scrap all of the older battleships up to, but not including, the *Delaware* and *North Dakota*. The number of these old battleships to be scrapped is 15. Their total tonnage is 227,740 tons.

Thus the number of capital ships to be scrapped by the United States, if this plan is accepted, is 30, with an aggregate tonnage (including that of ships in construction, if completed) of 845,740 tons.

Great Britain.   The plan contemplates that Great Britain and Japan shall take action which is fairly commensurate with this action on the part of the United States.
It is proposed that Great Britain—

1. Shall stop further construction of the 4 new Hoods, the new capital ships not laid down but upon which money has been spent. These 4 ships, if completed, would have tonnage displacement of 172,000 tons.
2. Shall, in addition, scrap her pre-dreadnaughts, second line battleships, and first line battleships up to, but not including, the *King George V* class.

These, with certain pre-dreadnaughts which it is understood have already been scrapped, would amount to 19 capital ships and a tonnage reduction of 411,375 tons.

The total tonnage of ships thus to be scrapped by Great Britain (including the tonnage of the 4 Hoods, if completed) would be 583,375 tons.

Japan.   It is proposed that Japan

1. Shall abandon her program of ships not yet laid down, viz., the *Kii, Owari, No. 7* and *No. 8* battleships, and *Nos. 5, 6, 7,* and *8,* battle cruisers.

It should be observed that this does not involve the stopping of construction, as the construction of none of these ships has been begun.

2. Shall scrap 3 capital ships (the *Mutsu* launched, the *Tosa,* and *Kago* in course of building) and 4 battle cruisers (the *Amagi* and *Akagi* in course of building, and the *Atoga* and *Takao* not yet laid down, but for which certain material has been assembled).

The total number of new capital ships to be scrapped under this paragraph is seven. The total tonnage of these new capital ships when completed would be 289,100 tons.

3. Shall scrap all pre-dreadnaughts and battleships of the second line. This would include the scrapping of all ships up to, but not including, the *Settsu*; that is, the scrapping of 10 older ships, with a total tonnage of 159,828 tons.

The total reduction of tonnage on vessels existing, laid down, or for which material has been assembled (taking the tonnage of the new ships when completed), would be 448,928 tons.

Thus, under this plan there would be immediately destroyed, of the navies of the three Powers, 66 capital fighting ships, built and building, with a total tonnage of 1,878,043.

It is proposed that it should be agreed by the United States, Great Britain, and Japan that their navies, with respect to capital ships, within three months after the making of the agreement shall consist of certain ships designated in the proposal and numbering for the United States 18, for Great Britain 22, for Japan 10. . . .

With the acceptance of this plan the burden of meeting the demands of competition in naval armament will be lifted. Enormous sums will be released to aid the progress of civilization. At the same time the proper demands of national defense will be adequately met and the nations will have ample opportunity during the naval holiday of 10 years to consider their future course. Preparation for offensive naval war will stop now.

2. The Isolationist *Chicago Tribune* Denounces Europe's Folly, 1921

It is natural that pacifists and excited humanitarians should stress the evil consequences of the world war at this time. It is equally natural that foreign statesmen and public agencies should join them in keeping this phase of the European situation [of famine and insurrections] before us. It gives a tremendous momentum to the pacifist propaganda, and it relieves the governments and peoples of Europe of a large part of their responsibility for the present condition of their affairs.

But the American mind should clear itself on this point. No one will deny that the war is responsible directly for a vast wastage of life and property. But what needs recognition and emphasis at this moment . . . is that had common sense and self-control governed the policies of the governments and the sentiments of the peoples of Europe their affairs would not be tottering now on the rim of chaos.

On the contrary, were there wisdom and courage in the statesmanship of Europe, were there the same selfless devotion in chancelleries and parliaments as was exhibited on the battlefield, Europe would have been today well on the way to recovery.

The expenditures of the war and the intensification of long existing animosities and jealousies undoubtedly have complicated the problems of statecraft and of government. Undoubtedly the temporary depletion of man power and the temporary exhaustion of body and spirit among the war worn peoples were a burden which recovery has had to assume. Undoubtedly the wastage of wealth and diversion of productive agencies were a handicap to expeditious restoration.

But that these are chiefly responsible for the present state of Europe we do not admit and the future judgment of history, we are confident, will deny.

It is chiefly the folly which has been persistently demonstrated by governments and people since the war that is responsible for Europe's condition today. It is because the moment hostilities ceased and the enemy was disarmed, victors and vanquished turned their backs on the healing and constructive principles they had solemnly asserted from time to time when matters were going against them at the battle front, that the European nations almost without exception have been going down hill. There never in history has been a more perfect illustration of the ancient sarcasm: "When the devil is sick, the devil a monk would be; when the devil is well, the devil a monk is he."

If we wish to know why Europe is in the present state, we cannot do better than to draw a parallel between the assertions of purpose and principle of the allies and "associated" powers in 1916, '17, and '18, and what has actually happened since Nov. 11, 1918.

This document appeared in *Chicago Tribune*, November 13, 1921.

The war was a gigantic folly and waste. No one will deny that. But it was not so foolish nor so wasteful as the peace which has followed it. The European governments, those who come at our invitation and those who remain away, would have us believe they are mere victims of the war. They say nothing of what the war did for them. We might remind them that they profited as well as lost by the war. Many of them were freed from age long tyranny. They got rid of kaisers and saber clattering aristocracies. They were given freedom, and their present state shows how little they have known how to profit by it. They have been given new territories and new resources, and they have shown how little they deserve their good fortune. The last three years in Europe have been given not to sane efforts to heal wounds, remove hostilities, develop cooperation for the common economic restoration which is essential to the life of each. On the contrary, they have been marked by new wars and destruction, by new animosities and rivalries, by a refusal to face facts, make necessary sacrifices and compromises for financial and economic recovery, by greedy grabbing of territory and new adventures in the very imperialism which brought about the war.

It is well for Americans and their representatives to keep this in mind. The appeal to America's disinterestedness is unfairly fortified by the assumption that Europe is the innocent victim of one egotist's or one nation's ruthless ambition. We can take due account of the disastrous effects of the Prussian effort at dominance, but that should not overshadow the stubborn errors which began over again on the very threshold of peace, and which have made the peace more destructive than the war. When the European governments and peoples are ready to make a real peace, which cannot arrive until they give over the policies and attitudes that produced the world war, America will then not fail to give generous aid. But America would be foolish to contribute to the support of present methods or give any encouragement to the spirit which now prevails in the old world.

3. Reformer Jane Addams Assesses the League of Nations, 1922

While the first year of the League held much that was discouraging for its advocates, the first meeting of the Assembly convened in Geneva in November, 1920, resolved certain doubts and removed certain inhibitions from the minds of many of us. The Assembly demonstrated that after all it was possible for representatives from the nations of the earth to get together in order to discuss openly, freely, kindly for the most part, and even unselfishly, the genuine needs of the world. In spite of the special position of the Great Powers, this meeting of the Assembly had so increased the moral prestige of the League of Nations that it was reasonable to believe that an articulate world-opinion would eventually remove the treaty entanglements which threatened to frustrate the very objects of the League. The small nations, . . . not by insistence on the doctrine of the sovereignty and equality of states, but through sheer devotion to world interests, were making the League effective

From Jane Addams, *Peace and Bread in Time of War* (New York: Macmillan, 1922), pp. 215–222.

and certainly more democratic. Perhaps these representatives were acting, not only from their own preferences or even convictions, but also from the social impact upon them, from the momentum of life itself.

In many ways the first meeting of the Assembly had been like the beginning of a new era, and it seemed possible that the public discussion, the good-will, and the international concern, must eventually affect the European situation.

During the following year the League of Nations itself inaugurated and carried out many measures which might be designated as purely humanitarian. In the "Report to the Second Assembly of the League on the Work of the Council and on the measures taken to execute the decisions of the First Assembly" in Geneva on September 7th, 1921, under the heading of General International Activities of the League was the following list:

    C. 1. The repatriation of prisoners.
    C. 2. The relief of Russian refugees.
    C. 3. General relief work in Europe.
    C. 4. The protection of children.

Under "the measures taken in execution of the resolutions and recommendation of the Assembly," in addition to the reports of the Heath Organizations, were others such as the campaign against typhus in Eastern Europe, and the relief of children in countries affected by the war. From one aspect these activities were all in the nature of repairing the ravages of the Great War, but it was obvious that further undertakings of the League must be greatly influenced and directed by these early human efforts.

The International Labor Organization, from the first such a hopeful part of the League of Nations, had just concluded as we reached Geneva in August 1921, a conference upon immigration and possible protective measures which the present situation demanded. For many years I had been a Vice President of the American Branch of the International Association for Labour Legislation and had learned only too well how difficult it was to secure equality of conditions for the labor of immigrants. . . .

There was something very reassuring in this plain dealing with homely problems with which I had been so long familiar. I had always been ready to admit that "the solemn declaration of principles which serve to express the unanimity of the aspirations of humanity have immense value," but this was something more concrete, as were other efforts on the part of the Office to defend labor throughout the world and to push forward adequate legislation on their behalf.

In the reaction, which had gained such headway during the two years of peace, against the generous hopes for a better world order the International Labour Organization as well as the League of Nations was encountering all the hazards of a great social experiment. We could but hope that the former might gain some backing from the international congress, to be held in October, 1921, of working women, bringing their enthusiasms and achievements from all parts of the world.

The food challenge was put up fairly and squarely to the Second meeting of the Assembly of the League of Nations by the Russian famine due to the prolonged drought of 1921. A meeting to consider the emergency had been called in Geneva in August, under the joint auspices of the International Red Cross and the League of Red Cross Societies. We were able to send a representative to it from our Woman's International League almost directly from our Third International Congress in Vienna. There was every possibility for using the dire situation in Russia for political ends, both by the Soviet Government and by those offering relief. On the other hand, there was a chance that these millions of starving people, simply because their need was so colossal that any other agency would be pitifully inadequate, would receive help directly from many governments, united in a mission of good-will. It was a situation which might turn men's minds from war and a disastrous peace to great and simple human issues; in such an enterprise the governments would "realize the failure of national coercive power for indispensable ends like food for the people," [and] they would come to a cooperation born of the failure of force.

Dr. Fridjof Nansen, appointed high commissioner at the Red Cross meeting in August, after a survey of the Russian Famine regions returned to Geneva for the opening of the Assembly on September 5th, in which he represented Norway, with a preliminary report of Russian conditions. He made a noble plea, which I was privileged to hear, that the delegates in the Assembly should urge upon their governments national loans which should be adequate to furnish the gigantic sums necessary to relieve twenty-five million starving people.

As I listened to this touching appeal on behalf of the helpless I was stirred to a new hope for the League. I believed that, although it may take years to popularize the principles of international cooperation, it is fair to remember that citizens of all the nations have already received much instruction in world-religions. To feed the hungry on an international scale might result not only in saving the League but in that world-wide religious revival which, in spite of many predictions during and since the war, had as yet failed to come. It was evident in the meeting of the Assembly that Dr. Nansen had the powerful backing of the British delegates as well as others, and it was therefore a matter for unexpected as well as for bitter disappointment when his plea was finally denied. This denial was made at the very moment when the Russian peasants, in the center of the famine district, although starving, piously abstained from eating the seed grain and said to each other as they scattered it over the ground for their crop of winter wheat; "We must sow the grain although we shall not live to see it sprout."

Did the delegates in the Assembly still retain the national grievances and animosities so paramount when the League of Nations was organized in Paris or were they dominated by a fear and hatred of Bolshevism and a panic lest the feeding of Russian peasants should in some wise aid the purposes of Lenine's government? Again I reflected that these men of the Assembly, as other men, were still held apart by suspicion and fear, which could only be quenched by motives lying deeper than those responsible for their sense of estrangement.

4. Debts and German Reparations: Hughes Calls on Private Experts for Help, 1922

The economic conditions in Europe give us the greatest concern. They have long received the earnest consideration of the administration. It is idle to say that we are not interested in these problems, for we are deeply interested from an economic standpoint, as our credits and markets are involved, and from a humanitarian standpoint, as the heart of the American people goes out to those who are in distress. We cannot

---

This document can be found in *Annual Report of the American Historical Association for the Year 1922* (Washington, D.C.: Government Printing Office, 1926), I, 265–268.

dispose of these problems by calling them European, for they are world problems and we cannot escape the injurious consequences of a failure to settle them.

They are, however, European problems in the sense that they cannot be solved without the consent of European Governments. We cannot consent for them. The key to the settlement is in their hands, not in ours.

The crux of the European situation lies in the settlement of reparations. There will be no adjustments of other needs, however pressing, until a definite and accepted basis for the discharge of reparation claims has been fixed. It is futile to attempt to erect any economic structure in Europe until the foundation is laid.

How can the United States help in this matter? We are not seeking reparations. We are, indeed, asking for the reimbursement of the costs of our army of occupation; and with good reason, for we have maintained our army in Europe at the request of the Allies and of Germany, and under an agreement that its cost with like army costs should be a first charge upon the amounts paid by Germany. Others have been paid and we have not been paid.

But we are not seeking general reparations. We are bearing our own burden and through our loans a large part of Europe's burden in addition. No demands of ours stand in the way of a proper settlement of the reparations question.

Of course we hold the obligations of European Governments and there has been much discussion abroad and here with respect to them. There has been a persistent attempt ever since the Armistice to link up the debts owing to our Government with reparations or with projects of cancellation. This attempt was resisted in a determined manner under the former administration and under the present administration. The matter is plain enough from our standpoint. The capacity of Germany to pay is not at all affected by any indebtedness of any of the Allies to us. That indebtedness does not diminish Germany's capacity, and its removal would not increase her capacity. For example, if France had been able to finance her part in the war without borrowing at all from us, that is, by taxation and internal loans, the problem of what Germany could pay would be exactly the same. Moreover, so far as the debtors to the United States are concerned, they have unsettled credit balances, and their condition and capacity to pay cannot be properly determined until the amount that can be realized on these credits for reparations has been determined. . . .

We have no desire to see Germany relieved of her responsibility for the war or of her just obligations to make reparation for the injuries due to her aggression. There is not the slightest desire that France shall lose any part of her just claim. On the other hand, we do not wish to see a prostrate Germany. There can be no economic recuperation in Europe unless Germany recuperates. There will be no permanent peace unless economic satisfactions are enjoyed. There must be hope, and industry must have promise of reward if there is to be prosperity. We should view with disfavor measures which instead of producing reparations would threaten disaster.

Some of our own people have suggested that the United States should assume the role of arbiter. There is one sufficient answer to this suggestion, and that is that we have not been asked to assume the role of arbiter. There could be no such arbitrament unless it were invited, and it would be an extraordinary and unprecedented thing for us to ask for such an invitation.

I do not think that we should endeavor to take such a burden of responsibility. We have quite enough to bear without drawing to ourselves all the ill-feeling which would result from disappointed hopes and a settlement which would be viewed as forced upon nations by this country which at the same time is demanding the payment of the debts owing to it. . . .

Why should they [statesmen] not invite men of the highest authority in finance in their respective countries—men of such prestige, experience and honor that their agreement upon the amount to be paid, and upon a financial plan for working out the payments, would be accepted throughout the world as the most authoritative expression obtainable? Governments need not bind themselves in advance to accept the recommendations, but they can at least make possible such an inquiry with their approval, and free the men who may represent their country in such a commission from any responsibility to Foreign Offices and from any duty to obey political instructions. In other words, they may invite an answer to this difficult and pressing question from men of such standing and in such circumstances of freedom as will ensure a reply prompted only by knowledge and conscience. I have no doubt that distinguished Americans would be willing to serve in such a commission.

5. Argentine Writer Manuel Ugarte Identifies the United States as the "New Rome," 1923

The flexibility of North American imperialism in its external activities, and the diverse forms which it adopts according to circumstances, the racial composition and the social conditions of the peoples upon which its action is exercised, is one of the most significant phenomena of this century from the point of view of political science. Never in all history has such an irresistible or marvellously concerted force been developed as that which the United States are bringing to bear upon the peoples which are geographically or politically within its reach in the south of the Continent or on the shores of the sea. . . . At times imperious, at other times suave, in certain cases apparently disinterested, in others implacable in its greed, pondering like a chess-player who foresees every possible move, with a breadth of vision embracing many centuries, better-informed and more resolute than any, without fits of passion, without forgetfulness, without fine sensibilities, without fear, carrying out a world activity in which everything is foreseen—North American imperialism is the most perfect instrument of domination which has been known throughout the ages.

By adding to what we may call the scientific legacy of past imperialisms the initiative born of its own inspiration and surroundings, this great nation has subverted every principle in the sphere of politics just as it had already transformed them in the sphere of material progress. Even the European powers, when confronted with North American diplomacy, are like a rapier pitted against a revolver. In the order of ideas with which we are dealing, Washington has modified the whole perspective. The first conquerors, with their elementary type of mind, annexed the inhabitants in the guise of slaves. Those who came afterwards annexed territories without inhabitants. The United States . . . inaugurated the system of annexing wealth, apart from inhabitants or territories, disdaining outward shows in order to arrive at the essentials of domination without a dead-weight of areas to administrate and multitudes to govern. . . .

From Manuel Ugarte, *The Destiny of a Continent,* Catherine A. Phillips (tr.), with an introduction by J. Fred Rippy (ed.) (New York: Knopf, 1925), pp. 139–148.

Thus there has arisen within their spheres of influence an infinite variety of forms and shades. The new imperialism, far from applying a formula or a panacea, has founded a system of special diagnosis for every case, taking into account the area of the region, its geographical situation, the density of its population, its origin, predominating racial composition, level of civilisation, customs, neighbours, whatever may favour or hinder resistance, whatever may induce assimilation or alienation by reason of affinities or differences of race, whatever has to be brought about with a view to future contingencies. The higher motives of force or healthy activity which give direction to expansionist energy, watch particularly over the racial purity of the group and reject every addition which is not identical with it. To annex peoples is to modify the composition of one's own blood, and the invader who does not desire to be diluted, but to perpetuate himself, avoids as far as possible any impairing or enfeebling of the superiority which he claims. . . .

That species of action which makes itself felt in the form of financial pressure, international tutelage, and political censorship admits of every advantage with no risk. In the development of these tactics imperialist policy has given evidence of that incomparable dexterity which is admired even by its victims. In the financial sphere its tendency is to control the markets to the exclusion of all competition, to take upon itself the regulation of any production to which it attaches any value, and to lead the small nations on to contract debts which afterwards provoke conflicts, give rise to claims, and prepare the way for interference favourable to the extension of its virtual sovereignty. In the sphere of external policy it appoints itself the defender of these peoples, obliging the world to accept its intervention in treating with them, and drawing them as satellites into its orbit. In the internal order it encourages the diffusion of whatever increases its prestige, forwards the ambitions of those men who favour its influence, and opposes the spread of all influences of a different nature, blocking the way peremptorily to those who, from a superior sagacity or patriotism, try to maintain their nationality unimpaired. . . .

Here it foments tyrannies, there it supports attempts at revolution, always constituting itself the conciliator or the arbiter, and indefatigably pressing events in the direction of the two ends which it sets before it: first in the moral order, to increase anarchy, so as to bring discredit upon the country; and second, in the political order, to get rid of national representatives who are refractory to the dominant influence, till they meet with a weak or not very enlightened man who, out of inexperience or impatience, will make himself the accomplice of its domination. . . .

The greatest triumph of this system has consisted in the fact that it has come to be a cause of success within our own life. As the source of expedients in our civil struggles, as the dispenser of favours in official life, it has driven not only those who are impatient, but even the most incorruptible and upright to the utmost limit of what can be granted without abdication. In this manner it has proceeded to create subconsciously, in the countries it has "manipulated," a peculiar state of mind, which admits the collaboration in its civil struggles of forces not arising from their own surroundings, and allows an element of foreign life and interest to enter into every national act or project. . . .

When we consider the work of imperialism in America as a whole, it is impossible to refrain from a certain admiration for the magnitude of its effort and the clearness of its conceptions. Never in all history has such subtlety been seen, combined with such a capacity for sustained action. It is evident, I repeat, that from the Spanish-American point of view we have to do with a policy which we ought all to work together to check. A good number of us have been writing and speaking in this sense without intermission for long years. But if we are to stem the advance, our most urgent task is to arrive at a full knowledge of the truth, and to give up vain speech-making. Every strong people extends its ambitions as far as its arms can reach, and every weak people lasts just so long as its energy for defending itself endures. In sacrificing doctrines in order to favour its present and future greatness, the new Rome believes itself to be accomplishing a duty, since it is thus preparing that world dominion for which it considers itself to be set apart. By developing to its full volume and protecting itself against these risks, Latin America would preserve its personality.

6. "Trade Follows the Film," 1925

The sun, it now appears, never sets on the British Empire and the American motion picture. It is a droll companionship, and one which is beginning to evoke comment and provoke inquiry in exalted quarters in foreign parts. The world at large has become so accustomed to seeing the British Empire take this daily promenade in the sun alone that it now lifts its eyebrows and regards the scene with what the fictionists of another day used to call mixed emotions.

In the British the spectacle calls forth a touch of asperity. The French are puzzled and ask, "Is it an amour?" The Germans have begun to dig in and erect barriers. All of them are in varying degrees alarmed by the portent. They are just a teeny bit afraid of this gay, laughing, amusing hussy who parades the whole wide world with such assurance and to such applause from the diverse races and breeds of men. . . .

Our pictures are doing for us what the Prince of Wales so frankly and so capably is doing for the British. International trade is, of course, based on good will. The Prince for some years now has been going about all over the world promoting good will for his countrymen and subjects. Incidentally he has helped trade. Everybody remembers when he was last in New York he set a vogue for blue shirts with soft collars, for a style of hat that blossomed in the shop windows even before he departed, and for gray flannels. Every day what he wore was chronicled in the newspapers, and the youth who set store by styles were quick to copy him. The same thing, it is fair to suppose, happened in the colonies and in South America. The heir apparent did something to introduce and popularize English clothes, shoes, hats, pipes and what not.

Happily, or unhappily—just as you choose—we have no royal family to do that sort of thing for us. But now the word comes from abroad, from many quarters and in increasing volume, that the movie stars and their associates, and the happy and handsome environment in which they are displayed in the films are creating and stimulating a demand for American wares. We now hear that the old saying that trade follows the flag is archaic and out of joint.

"Trade follows the film" is the cry from overseas. It is the discovery of this new factor in international relationships that has caused the flutter. When the movies were simply an amusement and a relaxation and a form of entertainment

Edward G. Lowry, "Trade Follows the Film," *Saturday Evening Post,* 198 (November 7, 1925), 12–13, 151, 158.

for the millions, they could be laughed at by the sophisticates as examples of crude American taste, and no harm was done. But once it became clear that the films directly influenced the currents of trade—that from Spain, the Near East, Chile, the Argentine and Brazil were coming demands for American office furniture, shoes, hardware, clothing and types of California bungalows "like those we see in the movies," then the pictures became a menace and a peril to the foreign trader. His pocketbook touched, he became aroused and began to appeal to his government.

The Prince of Wales himself, as a promoter of trade and good will for his people, was among the earliest to declare and disclose the potency of our pictures as a competitor in securing foreign trade. As long ago as 1923 the Prince was saying in a speech before the British National Film League that the importance of the film industry deserved attention. There was the imperial aspect, he urged. Trade followed the film, he said, and films were a real aid both to the development of imperial trade and the work of individual firms. The film helped to bring together nations speaking different languages. It had no one language of its own, but could convey its ideas in all languages. And so on to the extent of nearly a column in the *London Morning Post,* in which the speech was reported. The same newspaper, commenting on the Prince's outgiving, said: "If the United States abolished its diplomatic and consular services, kept its ships in harbor and its tourists at home, and retired from the world's markets, its citizens, its problems, its towns and countryside, its roads, motor cars, counting houses and saloons would still be familiar in the uttermost corners of the world. . . . The film is to America what the flag was once to Britain. By its means Uncle Sam may hope some day, if he be not checked in time, to Americanize the world." . . .

For whatever may be said about our movies, the stubborn fact stands up that millions of all sorts of people all over the world like them and are willing to pay habitually and constantly to see them. Neither in Germany, England, France, Italy nor Scandinavia can they make pictures with such a universal appeal. I will not be put in the light of a defender or champion of the quality of the American movie; I am not a fan. But their world dominance is an incontestable fact. They are popular, they are affecting trade, they are coloring the minds and changing the desires of foreign peoples, they are the most vivid and potent projection—however distorted—of life in the United States that foreigners receive. The stay-at-homes abroad get their conception of us from our pictures. Whether that condition is or is not deplorable, it is a proved fact.

Now what is the secret of this great popularity and success? It is built on a firm economic basis. For that, the motion-picture industry can take no credit. Lady Luck dealt our producers a hand all aces. The great domestic market afforded in the United States makes it possible to have $1,000,000 superfeatures. Here we have 40 per cent of all the motion-picture theaters in the world. The average weekly attendance at these theaters in the United States is something more than 50,000,000. This great throng pays admissions of about $500,000,000 annually. That is the solid-rock basis on which the American producer has built his world-wide dominion.

With this great supporting, pleasure-loving, money-spending public at home he can afford to experiment, to develop, to lavish expenditures on his productions. If he only just breaks even on a $1,000,000 picture at home, he is still in a comfortable position, for he can count on his export for a profit. It is this domestic market, which no foreign producer has, that gives our industry its solid base. The figures prove it. In 1913, 32,000,000 linear feet of film were exported. In 1928, 200,000,000 feet were sent abroad. On the other hand, only 425 foreign pictures were sent here in 1922, and of these only six were sold and exhibited. The number of imported films has increased in the past three years, but the proportion of imports to exports remains about the same. The foreign and the domestic fan are as one in preferring the American picture to all others.

Now what quality is inherent in the American picture that causes every sort of foreigner—English, German, French, Italian, South American, Central European and Asiatic—to prefer it to his own? What is it in the American picture that has made it a trade and political factor? There is no definite answer, but the industry offers suggestions and possible explanations. One of these, made to me, is this:

> There is no laughter in the European films. They lack gayety, light-heartedness, sprightliness. They do not portray happiness. There is not in them anywhere any sense of irresponsible children at play. These lacking qualities are supplied in almost every American film. Our pictures show people having fun. They reflect freedom, prosperity, happiness, a higher standard of living in clothing, houses, interiors, motor cars—all the material appurtenances of good living.
>
> The European intelligentzia criticize the happy endings of our stories as bad art. But to peoples recovering from the shock of war, and whose financial, economic and social problems are not yet solved, these happy pictures are beacon lights of hope. They seem to show the way to peace, prosperity and happiness. They make the spectators forget their cares and worries and anxieties. They bring relaxation and give entertainment. They are an escape from the daily routine of work. They open a fresh new world of play where there are no class restrictions or the inertia that comes of despair. That is why American pictures are popular abroad. I think, too, we know more of what can be done with the camera.

It may be that that is the true reason. We are at that particular period of our history and growth that gives us happiness in youth and strength and wealth. We are an extraordinarily fortunate and blessed people. Not all of us realize it. But the rest of the world does and is constantly reminded of it by our movies. It has awakened desires in them for some of the things we possess. That is what has made the movie a factor in trade and in our international relationships. That is why trade begins to follow the film.

And it all began as a five-cent peep show. An astonishing evolution, isn't it?

7. Secretary of Commerce Herbert Hoover Extols U.S. Foreign Trade, 1926

Foreign trade has become a vital part of the whole modern economic system. The war brought into high relief the utter dependence of the life of nations upon it. The major strategy of war is to crush the enemy by depriving him of it. In peace time our exports and imports are the margins upon which our well-being

---

This document can be found in U.S. Department of Commerce, *The Future of Our Foreign Trade* (Speech by Herbert Hoover, March 16, 1926, to the Export Manager's Club of New York), Washington, D.C.: Government Printing Office, 1926.

depends. The export of our surplus enables us to use in full our resources and energy. The creation of a wider range of customers to each production unit gives to that unit greater stability in production and greater security to the workers.

And we may quite well view our exports from the other side of the trade balance sheet. They enable us to purchase and import those goods and raw materials which we can not produce ourselves. We could probably get along as a nation if we had to suppress the 7 to 10 per cent of our production which goes to export, but our standard of living and much of the joy of living is absolutely dependent upon certain import commodities. We could not carry on our material civilization without some of the fibers, rubber, and some metals. Without diamonds we would not be able to get satisfactorily engaged to marry. The prosperity of our people in many ways can be measured by the volume of imports. . . .

The Government can chart the channels of foreign trade and keep them open. It can assist American firms in advancing their goods. In the improvement of all the foreign services the Department of Commerce has made great progress in the past five years, and it has been developed into organizing in internal cooperation and consultation with our industries and our merchants. . . .

I believe the effect of the efforts of the department [of Commerce] in establishment of standards, elimination of waste, and the provision of wider information has been to expand the possibilities of foreign trade to many concerns not hitherto able to extend into this field. One of the interesting and encouraging facts is the rapid increase in the number of small concerns participating in export business. The surprisingly large number of inquiries now being received by the department from such firms amply proves that the virtues of high quality, specialized production, good service, precise export technique, and farsighted policy are by no means monopolized by big corporations. Literally thousands of small dealers and manufacturers, whose commodities have a strong specialty appeal and meet a definite need, are now successfully cultivating overseas markets. Foreign trade is thus becoming a national asset in the fullest sense of the word. . . .

Without entering upon any partisan discussion of the protective tariff, which I, of course, support, there is one phase of the tariff which I believe experience shows has less effect upon the volume of international movement of commodities than had at one time been assumed.

As a result of the hardships suffered by many people of both combatant and neutral nations during the war, there came to all nations a deep resolution, in so far as the resources of their countries permitted, to produce as far as possible their essential commodities. The struggle to overcome post-war unemployment has added to this impulse. The result is that 52 of the 70 nations of the world, including almost every important trading nation, increased their tariffs after the war. It might seem that these widespread protective policies would tend to localize industry and thus decrease the total volume of international trade. But it certainly appears that internal economic and social currents which make for prosperity or depression in a nation have a much larger effect upon the total volume of imports than the tariffs and thus more largely affect world trade as a whole. In our case, far from our present tariff diminishing our total imports, they have increased about 35 per cent since the higher tariff came into effect. This has also been the case with other nations which have progressed in internal economy. In any event our experience surely indicates that in considering the broad future of our trade we can dismiss the fear that our increased tariff would so diminish our total imports as to destroy the ability of other nations to buy from us.

The most commonly remarked revolution in our foreign economic relations is our shift from a debtor to a creditor nation upon a gigantic scale. It is the father of much speculative discussion as to its future effect upon our merchandise trade. Alarm has been repeatedly raised that repayment of the war debts must necessitate the increase of imports of competitive goods in order to provide for these payments—to the damage of our industry and workmen. These ideas are out of perspective. Our war debt when settled upon our own views of the capacity to pay will yield about $300,000,000 per annum, although as yet the actual payments are much less than this. The private foreign loans and investments to-day require repayments in principal and interest of about $600,000,000 annually, or nearly twice the war debt. I have heard of no suggestion that interest and repayment of these private debts will bring the disaster attributed to the war debt. The question is of importance, however, as to how this $800,000,000 or $900,000,000 of annual payments may affect our merchandise movement. There is a compensating factor in American trade relations unique to our country which has a large bearing upon this question—that is, the vast dimension of our invisible exports in the form of tourist expenditure, emigrants' remittances, and other forms of American expenditure abroad. These items in 1925 amounted to about $900,000,000, or about $100,000,000 more than our incoming payments on debts of all kinds. In other words, at this stage of calculation the balance of trade should be in our favor by about $100,000,000. But beyond this we are making, and shall long continue to make, loans abroad. For the last four years these loans have averaged nearly $700,000,000 a year, and in fact the merchandise balance in our favor has been running just about this amount.

Now the summation and purpose of all these words is the conclusion that there is no disastrous shift in our imports and exports of merchandise in prospect from debt causes. . . .

By contributing to peace and economic stability, by the loan of our surplus savings abroad for productive purposes, by the spread of inventions over the world, we can contribute to the elevation of standards of living in foreign countries and the demand for all goods.

8. The Kellogg-Briand Pact Outlaws War, 1928

Article 1.　The High Contracting Parties solemnly declare in the names of their respective peoples that they condemn recourse to war for the solution of international controversies, and renounce it as an instrument of national policy in their relations with one another.

Article 2.　The High Contracting Parties agree that the settlement or solution of all disputes or conflicts of whatever nature or of whatever origin they may be, which may arise among them, shall never be sought except by pacific means.

This document can be found in U.S. Department of State, *Papers Relating to the Foreign Relations of the United States, 1928* (Washington, D.C.: Government Printing Office, 1942), I, 155.

ESSAYS

In the first essay, Benjamin D. Rhodes, who teaches at the University of Wisconsin, Whitewater, critiques the Republican foreign policy of the twenties. Rhodes acknowledges that U.S. foreign relations during the 1920s cannot be categorized as isolationist, but he nonetheless concludes that the Harding and Coolidge administrations remained politically detached from other nations and failed to build a viable and lasting world order. Secretary of State Charles Evans Hughes in particular placed too much faith in principles and signed documents in pursuit of peace, rather than working with allies and the League of Nations to create a system of collective military security. The Washington treaties on naval disarmament, the American failure to join the League of Nations and the World Court, the refusal to forgive foreign debts, and the continuing nonrecognition of the Soviet Union destabilized the international system and paved the way for crisis in the 1930s. In the second essay, Frank Costigliola of the University of Connecticut presents a more favorable view of U.S. policies. According to Costigliola, the twenties were a time of relative peace and prosperity when American leaders worked for orderly growth of the world capitalist system to manage the systemic economic, political, and cultural upheaval that arose out of World War I. Once the world descended into chaos in the 1930s, there was little American officials could do because neither Europeans nor Americans would have tolerated massive U.S. intervention. One of Costigliola's contributions to our understanding of the 1920s is the spotlighting of American cultural expansion through Hollywood films and other cultural exports—a phenomenon that calls into question the "isolationist" label and accents the era's internationalizing trends. In the third essay, Leila J. Rupp of the University of California, Santa Barbara, examines another source of internationalism in the interwar period: women's activism. According to Rupp, the horror of World War I, combined with a string of victories in the campaign for suffrage, led feminists in the United States and Europe toward international engagement. The newly established League of Nations provided an imperfect but nonetheless effective forum for internationally minded women to address issues such as equal suffrage, occupational discrimination, and traffic in women and children—as well as disarmament and the mediation of armed conflicts. In addition to influencing League policy, women internationalists forged a collective, transnational female identity, joining a growing number of transnational occupational, professional, and philanthropic organizations in the world system.

The Republican Retreat from International Responsibilities

BENJAMIN D. RHODES

"Republican" foreign policy began with the inauguration of Warren G. Harding on March 4, 1921. Except for the partisan disagreement about the League of Nations, there were many points of similarity between the foreign policies of the two parties. From the Democrats the Republicans inherited and continued to possess an attitude of skepticism toward Britain, France, and Japan. The new administration continued

Benjamin D. Rhodes, *United States Foreign Policy in the Interwar Period: The Golden Age of American Diplomatic and Military Complacency* (New York: Praeger, 2001), pp. 39–43, 45–47, 59–62, 64–65, 69–71. Copyright © 2001 by Praeger Publishers. Reproduced with permission of Greenwood Publishing Group, Inc., Westport, CT.

Wilson's policies on war debts and reparations, refused to recognize Russia, and sought, without spending any money, to improve relations with Latin America. Even on the topic of the League of Nations, the Republicans demonstrated some flexibility, establishing a policy of informal cooperation, but refraining from active membership. And, to the dismay of the irreconcilables [Republicans who had opposed U.S. membership in the League of Nations on any terms], the new administration advocated joining the World Court, an institution established under the auspices of the League of Nations. . . .

Harding did not intend to be his own secretary of state. He made that clear when he named the fastidiously bearded New York lawyer Charles Evans Hughes to the post. "From the beginning," announced Harding, "the Secretary of State will speak for the State Department." . . . In selecting Hughes, Harding followed Wilson's example of 1913 when Bryan was chosen as secretary of state. Both Hughes and Bryan were former presidential candidates who were named secretary of state to unify their respective parties. For all his expertise as a technical lawyer, Hughes was almost as naive and moralistic in his approach to foreign policy as had been Bryan. A practitioner of the legal-moralistic approach, Hughes hoped to establish international rules and agreements promoting such worthy goals as conciliation, arbitration, and disarmament. The good faith of the signatories would ensure the sanctity of the resulting agreements.

Hughes's reputation as a great secretary of state is largely based on a dramatic speech he delivered at the opening of the Washington Conference of 1921. That Hughes, through oratory and force of personality, took the conference by storm is indisputable. Less certain is whether the naval limitations Hughes negotiated were in the long-term national interest of the United States. Actually it was neither Harding nor Hughes, but the unpredictable Senator William E. Borah of Idaho who took the first steps to head off a world naval race. Even before Harding's inauguration Borah introduced a Senate resolution (December 14, 1920) proposing a naval limitation conference. The United States, Great Britain, and Japan would be invited, with the goal being a fifty percent reduction in naval construction over a five-year period. In a second resolution (January 25, 1921) Borah proposed a six-month moratorium on American naval construction while the nation pondered whether to concentrate on reducing battleships, submarines, or aircraft carriers. When Hughes (on July 11) invited four major powers (Great Britain, Japan, France, and Italy) and four lesser powers (China, Portugal, Holland, and Belgium), he included not just disarmament as a topic for discussion, but the stability of the Chinese mainland and the Pacific as well. . . .

In his opening address to the conference Hughes rose magnificently to the occasion by dramatically spelling out the sacrifices he expected from each participant. Hughes took the delegates by surprise; they were expecting a typically harmless welcome to the national capital. And to be sure, Hughes's opening was mundane enough, but before he was through he had proposed the abandonment of 1.8 million tons of existing and planned capital ships; the American contribution was to be 845,740 tons. A common cliché held that Hughes in thirty minutes had destroyed more ships than had gone down in all the naval battles in world history. Fearing a possible leak, Hughes boldly decided to announce his proposals at the very beginning of the conference. The ratio he proposed for limiting battleships (5:5:3:1.75:1.75

for the United States, Great Britain, Japan, France, and Italy respectively) roughly maintained the status quo. Hughes's idea was to extend the battleship ratio to other classes of ships, combined with a ten-year moratorium on further construction.

Three months of bargaining elapsed before Hughes's efforts met success. Three principal treaties were signed by the time the conference adjourned in February 1922. First of all, the Five Power Treaty limited battleships according to the "Rolls Royce: Rolls Royce: Ford" ratio proposed by Hughes. In the process Hughes made several compromises, such as permitting Great Britain to construct two new battleships and agreeing that Japan might retain the battleship *Mutsu,* the sister ship of the infamous *Nagato,* which served as Admiral Isoroku Yamamoto's flagship during the Pearl Harbor attack and which was sunk by an underwater atomic blast at Bikini Atoll in 1946. The agreement provided for a ten-year "holiday" on the new construction of capital ships. Furthermore, aircraft carriers were limited to 135,000 tons for the United States and Great Britain, 81,000 tons for Japan, and 60,000 tons for France and Italy. An effort to limit submarines failed, due to the opposition of France.

The key to the success of the conference was the willingness of the western powers to accept the Four Power Treaty, which replaced the Anglo-Japanese Alliance by, in effect, expanding it into a four-power arrangement between the United States, Great Britain, Japan, and France. Specifically the treaty guaranteed the status quo in the Pacific "with regard to fortifications and naval bases." In practical terms this meant that the United States and Great Britain were forbidden from fortifying such bases as Hong Kong, the Philippines, or Guam. The final major treaty, the Nine Power Treaty, was signed by all the Washington participants. Principally drafted by Elihu Root, the document guaranteed the independence and territorial integrity of China and proclaimed the principle of equal commercial opportunity for all in China. And, in separate agreements negotiated outside the conference, Japan agreed to return Shantung to China and to withdraw all its remaining soldiers from Siberia.

At the time, Hughes was hailed as the greatest secretary of state in the history of the United States. Hughes was praised for his open diplomacy and credited with singlehandedly ending the naval race. . . . Yet, when tension with Japan intensified after 1931, the quest for naval disarmament seemed less and less farsighted because the United States found itself lacking in adequate bases, ships, carrier planes, and workable torpedoes to back up an increasingly tough policy toward Japan. Belatedly it dawned on Americans that a high price had been paid for the Washington treaties. Japan had acquired de facto naval superiority in the Pacific and had prevented the United States and Great Britain from fortifying their bases in the region. In view of the enormous human and financial expenditures of World War II, Hughes did not seem so clever after all. However, in defense of Hughes it can be argued that depression economy measures also explained American naval weakness, leaving the Unites States Navy more than 100 ships short of treaty strength by 1934. Hughes, in defending himself from criticism after Pearl Harbor, contended that his diplomacy had averted a naval race between the United States and Great Britain. He further held that the United States had ample time under the New Deal to modernize the fleet and to fortify Guam, but that Washington complacently failed to take action. Human reputations are fragile, and by the end of the interwar era Hughes's reputation as a miracle worker had faded badly, even though it was hardly fair to have blamed America's glaring military weakness solely on one man. . . .

Harding and Hughes were not isolationists in the sense that they wanted to bury their heads in the sand and abolish the Department of State. Unlike the irreconcilables, Harding and Hughes were not sullen and selfish in purpose. They were representatives of a party that had rejected Wilson's internationalism at great political profit. Considering the entrenched isolationism within their own party, the new leaders showed imaginative practicality in promoting peace through disarmament as an alternative to Wilson's program of peace through world government. They looked upon themselves as inheritors of traditional American concepts of non-entanglement in European politics, not as isolationists. Culturally and intellectually the vast majority of Americans and their leaders during the 1920s were anything but isolationist as they vigorously exported American films, music, and art, as well as concepts of business efficiency and peace through international cooperation. Economically, Americans were extroverted; they invested over $80 billion in Europe, Latin America, and Asia. When Germany experienced difficulty in making reparations payments, it was American, not European, bankers who arranged the Dawes Plan in 1924 and the Young Plan in 1928. Prodded by the Department of Commerce, American exporters made American goods ubiquitous abroad: American foreign trade doubled between 1913 and 1929 despite the maintenance of an illogically high tariff policy. To the extent that there was an American plan to establish world order, it was understated and unstructured. Politically Americans still took as little responsibility as possible for international stability. The country was essentially hoping for the best by neglecting to maintain close ties with the League of Nations and the British Empire, by taking a hard line against its World War I debtors, and by seeking to isolate Soviet Russia while waiting for communism to collapse. If America was internationally engaged culturally and economically during the interwar period, the nation was politically disengaged.

America's platonic political relationship with Europe during the interwar period can be illustrated by the hesitant connection established by the Harding administration with the League of Nations. Harding's overwhelming election victory in 1920 had decisively settled in the negative the question of American membership in the League of Nations. Although thirty-one prominent Republicans, including Hughes and Hoover, had signed a manifesto advocating membership in a revised league, Harding had no intention of wrecking his administration at the beginning by starting a bitter fight with the irreconcilables. The new president, therefore, ignored "The Thirty-One" and told Congress the League "can have no sanction by us." Hughes likewise had no stomach for a fight that he believed was unwinnable. Nevertheless, without American participation, the League of Nations was organized at the neutral site of Geneva, Switzerland. By the spring of 1921 forty-three nations had already joined. At first, as revealed by a series of embarrassing articles in the *New York Times,* the State Department refused even to acknowledge communications from the League; a minor State Department official had relegated all League mail to the dead-letter file. Even though the error was rectified, Hughes's correspondence with the League was as technical, legalistic, and impersonal as possible. By the second year of the Harding administration, Hughes permitted Joseph Grew, the American minister to Switzerland, to establish direct contacts with League officials and to convey informally the American point of view without committing the United States in any way. Under Harding the United States began to participate in League humanitarian activities such as the control of anthrax in cattle and suppression of traffic in opium, prostitutes, and obscene publications. The United States quietly participated in League activities that were in America's interest while holding the League at arm's length. The idea of membership or the assumption of financial responsibility for League activities was anathema.

Less stealthy was the new administration's attitude toward the World Court, which was established in 1922 under the auspices of the League of Nations. Both Harding and Hughes, and later [Calvin] Coolidge, were unambiguously in favor of American participation. Hughes had long supported the principle of international adjudication of disputes. As the leading advocate of American membership in the World Court, Hughes showed flashes of the brilliance he had displayed at Washington. But this time there was to be no miracle at Washington. The irreconcilables were waiting in ambush to employ the same tactics against the World Court that had previously defeated Wilson's League of Nations. Led by Borah and Hiram Johnson, the opponents of the World Court saw American membership as a traitorous first step toward joining the League itself. The struggle began in February 1923, when Hughes recommended to Harding that the United States join the World Court and proposed four reservations designed to disarm the irreconcilables. Hughes's reservations were: first, that membership in the World Court carried with it no legal obligation to the League; second, that America could participate equally with the members of the League in the selection of judges; third, that Congress would determine America's fair share of World Court expenses; and fourth, that the regulations establishing the World Court could not be altered without American approval. Harding risked much of his political capital in challenging his former Senate colleagues and forwarding Hughes's proposal to the Senate. Henry Cabot Lodge, still chairman of the Senate Foreign Relations Committee, responded with determined tactics of delay. Taking his cue from Borah, Lodge tried to trap Hughes by demanding that he explain whether the United States would be required to submit to the judgment of the court all disputes that could not be settled through diplomacy. Lodge added that, as Congress was about to complete its session, a reply was not expected prior to adjournment. Hughes then scored heavily by immediately responding. First, he rejected Lodge's thesis that it was necessary for the United States to submit every dispute to the World Court; that would be futile and a waste of time, he contended. Hughes then pointedly denied that international arbitration of disputes would constitute an entanglement in European politics. Instead, he argued, membership in the World Court was in the national interest of the United States and was consistent with America's past support of arbitration (a point that Hughes exaggerated, since the United States had usually arbitrated only if dealing with minor matters or with stronger powers). Despite Hughes's heroics, the irreconcilables held together and were able to delay a vote during the tenure of Harding and Hughes. The opponents of the World Court retained a potent weapon of their own which they were prepared to unleash in due course—namely, crippling irreconcilable reservations after the model of those employed by Lodge in 1919–1920. . . .

As long as Hughes headed the State Department, he dominated the formulation of foreign policy. That was made plain when, in his carefully prepared 1923 State of the Union message, Coolidge, at the urging of Raymond Robins [of the Red Cross], included a conciliatory overture to the Soviets. The United States, said the president, ought to be "the first to go to the economic and moral rescue" of Russia, provided the Soviets ended revolutionary propaganda, paid for confiscated property, and recognized repudiated debts. "We have every desire to help and no desire to injure," Coolidge concluded. Grigori Chicherin, the Soviet Commissar for Foreign Affairs, expressed a "complete willingness" to discuss outstanding problems. However, instead of unconditionally accepting Coolidge's conditions, Chicherin called for basing discussions upon reciprocity and the principle of non-intervention in the internal affairs of others. The legalistic Hughes then decisively intervened and ruled out any thought of negotiation until Moscow first restored confiscated property, recognized its debt, and promised not to spread propaganda. Hughes's nonrecognition stance prevailed despite the decision of the British to recognize the Soviets in the spring of 1924. On July 1 Hughes reaffirmed his hard-line nonrecognition position, contending that the Soviets had refused to pay valid debts, engaged in subversive efforts to undermine the United States government, and had imposed the will of a small minority upon the Russian people. . . .

Much of Hughes's final year as secretary of state was devoted to seeking a solution to the German financial crisis, caused by runaway inflation and a default of German reparations payments to the Allies. Hughes had to move cautiously to avoid the scrutiny of the irreconcilables. Theoretically reparations were not a concern of the United States since, from the time of the Peace Conference, the official American position had been that the payment of German reparations to the Allies was unrelated to the Allies' payment of war debts to the United States. To everyone else the connection seemed clear enough. Hughes first suggested, in a speech to the American Historical Association on December 29, 1922, that the United States should assist in an adjustment of reparations. Specifically he suggested that "distinguished Americans" should prepare a payment plan. Behind the scenes Hughes engineered the appointment of Chicago banker Charles G. Dawes as chairman of a commission of experts to study currency stabilization. The plan proposed by Dawes provided for a sliding scale of German payments beginning with one million marks the first year, increasing to two and a half million marks annually after five years. An essential feature of the Dawes Plan was a $200 million loan to Germany to be extended by American and European bankers. Both Hughes and [his successor Frank B.] Kellogg played crucial roles in convincing the Allies and Germany to accept the arrangement. At London in mid-July, Kellogg used a Dawes Plan conference to pressure France and Germany to accept. Simultaneously Hughes made an unofficial European visit, masquerading in his role as president of the American Bar Association, to promote a reparations settlement. The American squeeze play paid off handsomely when French Premier Edouard Herriot capitulated and the Dawes Plan temporarily relieved the German financial crisis. Typically the American role had been indirect, unofficial, and involved no governmental commitment. . . .

Hughes was easily the most dominating secretary of state of the interwar era. He left office having won the respect of his associates for his hard work and keen legal mind. . . . To contemporaries, Hughes seemed the greatest of American secretaries of state, with the possible exception of John Quincy Adams. But Hughes's reputation, like those of such other American interwar leaders as Harding, Coolidge, Mellon, and Hoover, faded badly with the collapse of prosperity and the perception that Hughes's legal and moralistic vision, as represented by the Washington Conference treaties, was irrelevant and impotent in meeting the fascist challenge of the 1930s. If

Hughes was not quite the miracle worker described in legend, his was unquestionably a tough act to follow.

Former Minnesota Senator Frank B. Kellogg, sixty-eight years old, was Hughes's hand-picked successor. In terms of direct contact with foreign affairs, Kellogg was better prepared than his predecessor. A wealthy Minnesotan corporation lawyer, he was the successful Republican candidate for the Senate in 1916. He served on the Foreign Relations Committee, and during the debate over the Versailles Treaty he was a mild reservationist. . . .

To contend that the Department of State was in mothballs during Kellogg's tenure would be going too far. But Kellogg had little direct influence on two major foreign policies of the period that made the United States appear narrow-minded as well as sullen and selfish in purpose. In fairness to Kellogg, both the question of joining the World Court and the conflict over repayment of European war debts were issues so enmeshed in partisan politics that probably no secretary of state could have made a difference. Both Coolidge and Kellogg advocated United States membership in the World Court. In his first State of the Union message, Coolidge urged the Senate to approve participation in the World Court with the four reservations suggested by Hughes. Likewise Kellogg, speaking to the American Society of International Law, endorsed American participation. All appearances were that the World Court proposal would pass, especially after the House of Representatives overwhelmingly approved membership by a vote of 302 to 28.

Senator Borah, taking his cue from the deceased Henry Cabot Lodge, denounced what he called the "League Court." He contended, rather transparently, that he favored the concept of a world court, but opposed one related to the League of Nations. Borah, and other World Court opponents, found a solution by adding a fifth reservation stating that the World Court could not, without American approval, hand down an advisory opinion on any matter involving the United States. (According to the League constitution, the League Council could request advice from the World Court on current matters that were before it.) In reality, rendering advisory opinions was a minor function of the World Court, but the strategy worked for the irreconcilables. With five reservations the proposal passed the Senate on January 27, 1926, by a vote of 76 to 17. But it proved impossible to secure acceptance of the reservations by all forty-seven World Court members. With good reason, Coolidge abandoned hope, and the World Court issue faded into oblivion until debated for a final time in 1935. Given the determination and skill of the World Court opponents, it is hard to see what more Coolidge and Kellogg could have done to join the World Court; it is equally difficult to see whether American membership would have affected world events to any great extent.

It was during Coolidge's presidency that America's image abroad sank disastrously. The immediate cause was clear enough: European resentment against the United States' closing of the New York loan market and simultaneously imposing war debt settlements under duress. Instead of the war-time image of generous "Uncle Sam," the United States was widely stereotyped abroad as the sinister creditor "Uncle Shylock." The role played by the State Department in settling the war debts was only a peripheral one inasmuch as the basic collection policy had been established by Congress and was implemented through the World War Foreign Debt Commission headed by Treasury Secretary [Andrew] Mellon. Nevertheless, the unpopular debt settlements imposed by the Debt Commission complicated Kellogg's conduct of foreign policy and reinforced the American impression that Europeans were ungrateful. . . .

To later generations Kellogg's reputation as a muddleheaded statesman was established because he lent his name to what was one of the most bizarre treaties ever conceived: the Kellogg-Briand Pact for the renunciation of war as an instrument of national policy. Originally conceived as a Franco-American pact, it was endorsed by sixty-four nations when it went into effect. Even Kellogg in his retirement became disillusioned and suspected that the treaty, for which he had received the 1930 Nobel Peace Prize, had become (to use a phrase coined by Senator James A. Reed) an "international kiss."

In retrospect it seems incredible that two such experienced statesmen as French Foreign Minister Aristide Briand and Kellogg could have associated themselves with such a strange document. In truth they brought much of the problem upon themselves through opportunistic political maneuvering on the part of Briand and misplaced idealism on the part of Kellogg. Skillful and energetic pressure generated by dedicated pacifists completed the picture. Just who originated the concept of outlawing war is still a subject of some dispute. Among American pacifists, Columbia University President Nicholas Murray Butler, Columbia University historian James T. Shotwell, and Chicago attorney Salmon O. Levinson played the major organizational and public relations roles. Levinson and Raymond Robins combined to enlist the critical support of Senator Borah behind the cause of renouncing war. Briand, at the suggestion of Shotwell, took the first step by proposing a Franco-American treaty outlawing war. His motive was primarily political: to elevate French prestige and to send a message to Germany that the United States' backing of France was unwavering. Briand followed up his proposal by submitting a draft treaty.

Kellogg, who was at first skeptical of the outlawry concept, became by 1928 an enthusiastic convert. A barrage of pacifist pleading and the realization that a renunciatory pact could be his historical legacy as well as the likely route to the Nobel Peace Prize accounted for his change of heart. The fifteen signatories, "deeply sensible of their solemn duty to promote the welfare of mankind," pledged "that they condemn recourse to war for the solution of international controversies, and renounce it as an instrument of national policy in their relations with one another." Only a few Latin American nations failed to attach their approval when the document went into effect in 1929; even today it remains harmlessly in force. Senators James A. Reed of Missouri and George Moses of New Hampshire led a movement to attach reservations so as to protect the Monroe Doctrine and America's right of self-defense. Foreign Relations Committee Chairman Borah, demonstrating his formidable ability as a debater and parliamentary tactician, outmaneuvered the opposition. In the closing weeks of the Coolidge administration the opponents were routed as the Senate approved the pact by a vote of 85 to 1. No American reservations were attached, although Borah read into the record a report of the Senate Foreign Relations Committee explaining that the committee understood that the pact in no way abridged the United States' right of self-defense. Kellogg treated the report as merely an expression of opinion that required no legal action or exchange of notes.

The Coolidge administration departed office indulging in expressions of self-congratulation and praising itself for having brought peace and prosperity to mankind. Condescendingly Coolidge, in his final State of the Union message, announced: "We must extend to other countries the largest measure of generosity, moderation, and patience. In addition to dealing justly, we can well afford to walk humbly." A few skeptics such as Senator Carter Glass of Virginia regarded the Pact of Paris as a "worthless, but perfectly harmless peace treaty." Privately many senators agreed with Glass but hesitated in a presidential election year to go on record against the sacred cause of peace. Hailed by pacifists as the triumph of conciliation, arbitration, and the rule of law, the outlawry movement expressed the near isolationist hope of the 1920s that war would just go away without the inconvenience and cost of binding obligations. The jubilation was short-lived once new conflicts broke out in the Far East—not only dooming the reputations of the authors, but making it clear that the world had bought not peace, but a mess of pottage.

U.S. Cultural Expansion in an Era of Systemic Upheaval

FRANK COSTIGLIOLA

In the quarter-century following the Great Crash, many historians wrote the 1920s off as a decade of amusing antics, precarious prosperity, and isolationist diplomacy. One example of such an approach is Frederick Lewis Allen's *Only Yesterday,* published in the midst of the Depression, which poked fun at a silly decade of flat-chested flappers, narrow-minded businessmen, and tight-fisted diplomats. All this, Allen suggested, especially when mixed with bathtub gin, had to end in a crash. Though his focus was broad, Allen denigrated the achievements of the 1920s.

However historians evaluate the years 1919–33, they must come to grips with the period's central force: political, economic, and cultural upheaval. That systemic instability has often blinded historians to the real accomplishments of the era. Much of the recent historical literature performs a valuable corrective by considering the decade on its own terms, as a period of relative peace and prosperity. These works remind us that most Americans and Europeans of the 1920s believed they could avoid the catastrophes of war and depression. To disparage the 1920s as a period of "false" prosperity and peace because those happy conditions did not endure is to distort history. Certainly the economic and political collapse in the Great Depression evidenced a terrible failure. Yet it is impossible to show how the disaster could have been avoided. By 1929 it was probably beyond the power of the United States to save the international order short of massive intervention—something neither Americans nor Europeans would have tolerated. Moreover, the dissolution of post–World War II prosperity should make us more humble and sympathetic in our criticism of those who were unable to preserve post–World War I prosperity. . . .

In the political realm, instability emerged from the Versailles, St. Germain, and Trianon treaties which made up the 1919 peace settlement. The key point was that these treaties *were* an international issue, an object of debate and struggle that ended only with the outbreak of war in 1939. The treaties imposed a settlement that the defeated nations—Germany, Austria, and Hungary—did not accept and that three of the four main victors—the United States, Great Britain, and Italy—soon saw as at least partially unwise and unsatisfactory. In opposition to the defeated nations, which wanted to overthrow the treaties, France and its eastern allies—Poland, Czechoslovakia, and Rumania—sought to preserve the 1919 settlement.

American pressures and sympathies, both official and unofficial, lay toward moderate treaty revision. Most Americans opposed a total overthrow of Versailles. They did not want to see Germany free of all fetters, nor did they appreciate any change, political, economic or social, that was drastic and destabilizing. Yet the peace treaties were too harsh, many Americans believed, and hampered integration of the defeated powers, particularly Germany, into a stable, prosperous, and peaceful Europe. Although the United States refused to form political alliances with Europeans after 1919, it consistently favored slow, moderate peace treaty revision that would ease the burdens on Germany. In the reparations conferences of 1924 and 1929, the unofficial American representatives who dominated the proceedings substantially transformed reparations from a club with which to beat Germany to a contractual debt owed by Germany. In 1924, at American and British insistence, France reluctantly relinquished its right under Versailles to march into Germany in case of reparations default. Americans encouraged Europeans to accept Germany into the Locarno Pacts and the League of Nations. In 1931, President Herbert Hoover and Secretary of State Henry L. Stimson went so far as to urge the French to pressure their Polish ally to revise the Polish corridor in Germany's favor. . . .

This American solution of peaceful change, of moderate Versailles revision, fit with the Progressive reform tradition such policymakers as Herbert Hoover and Charles E. Hughes carried with them into the postwar years. Like the Progressives of the previous decade, makers of American foreign policy in the 1920s sought stability and order through slow reform that would give repressed groups (workers in the 1910s, Germans in the 1920s) a stake in the improved, fairer system.

American leaders opposed sudden overthrow of the peace treaties just as they opposed socialist revolution at home or anywhere else. Taken in its widest context, the policy of peaceful change was part of America's effort throughout the twentieth century to combat revolutionary upheaval with moderate reform. Pacifying and rebuilding Germany was integral to containing the Bolshevik revolution. Bolshevik Russia presented both a symbolic and a substantive threat to the peaceful change alternative. Most American leaders viewed the Soviet Union as revolution incarnate, despite Moscow's caution and conservatism. If Germany's political and economic structure collapsed, its people, Americans feared, might in desperation forge a Russian alliance to overthrow both Versailles and capitalism. Their very opposition to revolution led Hoover, Hughes, and other American leaders to combat the French policy of rigidly enforcing Versailles, which would only build up pressures for change until they exploded in revolutionary upheaval. . . .

Americans preferred the middle road of democratic capitalism. Yet when faced with the options of revolutionary socialism or fascist order, Americans consistently picked the latter. The United States maintained cordial relations with Benito Mussolini, funding Italy's war debt on favorable terms, allowing private bankers to make large loans, and cooperating closely in 1931 on disarmament and political issues. . . .

Confronted with disorder in the European and world economies, the United States responded with a solution parallel to the political answer of peaceful change.

Orderly growth in the international capitalist economy, Americans believed, would reduce political tensions and the threat of revolution while expanding markets and investment opportunities for United States business. Although the United States carefully measured its political entanglements in Europe, its economic involvement was broad and deep. In the 1920s, moreover, economics and business enjoyed enormous popular prestige in both America and Europe. For reasons of conviction and of expedience, the United States government approached basically political questions such as reparations from an economic or business perspective. This economic emphasis was particularly suited to American policy's decentralized implementation and to its goal of a prosperous Europe. By 1923–24, government officials, central bankers, and top private businessmen forged a loose alliance. Although tactical differences often separated these leaders, they usually cooperated enough to present Europeans with a united front on war debt, loan, and other issues.

Before the crash, Americans pressed the Europeans to adopt the international gold standard, reduce government expenditures, and fund war debts and reparations. This financial program, the Yankees believed, would lay the foundation for Europe's recovery and reestablish an orderly flow of goods and capital. Responding to American and internal pressures, most European governments adopted the gold standard in the 1920s. This move boosted both international business and the power of America's huge gold reserve, but also burdened the world economy with a rigid monetary system that probably depressed prices. Similar consequences followed from American efforts to impose order upon the chaos of war debts and reparations. Under U.S. prodding, by 1929 the Allies and Germany settled these political debts on a fixed, reduced basis. This helped stabilize the world credit system, but the rigid debt settlements, like the rigid gold standard, proved brittle in the Depression. . . .

These political and economic relations can only be understood in their cultural context. The term *culture* is here comprehensively defined to include high culture such as literature, painting, and formal music; popular entertainment forms such as jazz, dancing, film, and sports; mundane matters such as household appliances, foods, and gadgets; more abstract concerns such as religion, philosophy, and language; attitudes toward work, play, money, and war; and finally technological innovations that had sociological implications, such as increased emphasis on machines, statistics, and mass assembly-line production.

Europeans interpreted virtually every manifestation of American culture, whether it was music, films, or automobiles, as the product of a society dominated by technology and the machine. America's technological superiority, moreover, made other aspects of its culture more attractive to Europeans. And it was this technological influence that persisted in Europe after the fad for Americans faded in the Great Depression. In virtually every cultural aspect, there was significant interchange between America and Europe during the 1919–33 period, with most, but not all, of the influence flowing eastward.

To war-weary Europe, struggling to cope with the problems of modern mass society, the United States, emerging from the war rich and buoyant, seemed to have the answers. Since the machine civilization was most advanced and apparently most successful in the United States, many European artists, businessmen, and politicians alike looked westward for models. To help Europe deal with the turbulence of modernization, America offered its own institutions and values, or what contemporaries termed *Americanism*.

Americanism meant a pragmatic, optimistic outlook on life; a peaceful, rational compromise of political differences; an efficient, modern way of organizing work that emphasized machines and mass assembly production; rising standards of living with declining class antagonisms; scientific use of statistics and other information; and the predominance of mass society (this meant democratic politics, widespread consumption, and popular entertainment). Many Europeans welcomed Americanism; others railed against it or were ambivalent, but nearly all believed it was in Europe's future.

In 1630, Governor John Winthrop predicted that America would become a model for the world—"a Citty Upon a Hill" with "the eies of all people" upon it. Three hundred years later Paul Claudel, ambassador from France and himself a man of letters, told Americans: "Your movies and talkies have soaked the French mind in American life, methods, and manners. American gasoline and American ideas have circulated throughout France, bringing a new vision of power and a new tempo of life. The place in French life and culture formerly held by Spain and Italy, in the nineteenth century by England, now belongs to America. More and more we are following America." Hans Joachim, a German writer, recalled the powerful influence in the 1920s of the United States as a land and as a symbol: "America was a good idea; it was the land of the future. It was at home in its age . . . we loved it. Long enough had . . . technology appeared only in the forms of tank, mine, shell-gas. . . . In America, it [technology] was at the service of human life. Our interest in elevators, radio towers, and jazz was . . . expressive of the wish to beat the sword into a plowshare. It was against cavalry but for horsepower. . . . It was an attitude that wanted to convert the flame thrower into a vacuum cleaner. . . . Our belief in America demonstrated where we stood." Europeans in the 1920s were entranced by the image of that city upon the hill.

America's cultural influence was both a product of and a contributor to the United States' economic, political, and (in 1917–19) military power in Europe. In 1917–18 the American economy's size and technological superiority made a psychological as well as military impact on Europe. Exhausted Europeans watched as the Americans quickly raised, equipped, and transported across the Atlantic a two-million-man army. Allies and Germans alike marveled at the Yankees' modern, efficient modes of transportation and organization.

The U.S. Committee on Public Information directed propaganda campaigns at war-weary Europeans eager for new, better answers. Other agencies, such as Herbert Hoover's American Relief Administration, made promotion of America and its way of life an integral part of their operation. Hoover made sure that relief recipients understood their food was coming from a beneficent America. When labor-management strife threatened to stop coal production in central Europe, Hoover's men introduced more liberal labor practices coupled with emphasis on increased labor productivity. President Woodrow Wilson was an enormously effective propagandist, even though—like his chief rival, Vladimir Lenin—he excited European expectations which he could not fulfill.

Indeed, the propaganda war between the United States' liberal capitalism and Russia's revolutionary socialism contained not only antagonistic but complementary aspects that prepared the ground for Europe's Americanization in the 1920s. Wilson and Lenin had both told the European masses that the old imperialist regimes with their balance-of-power politics had produced the war and had to be replaced. Both proclaimed a new era of popular sovereignty, mass society, economic growth, and technological improvement. By the early 1920s, most Europeans were disillusioned with both Wilson's and Lenin's millennial visions. Yet America's enormous economic power and apparent success as a society ensured that many Europeans looking for social solutions, including some of those who had been inspired by Lenin, would turn to the United States for models. Even the Russian Bolsheviks, despite continued hostility toward capitalism, tried to adopt many of America's technological wonders. The United States government ceased propaganda efforts in 1919, but in the ensuing decade private Americans advertised their ideas, institutions, and products in Europe.

Yankee merchandise, films, aviators, artists, entertainers, and above all dollars flooded the Old World, bringing Europeans direct evidence of the United States' position as the leader of Western civilization. Economic and cultural factors intertwined in various ways. . . .

Two elements lay at the source of these cultural interactions: the United States' economic power, which captured European markets and imaginations while financing a flood of tourists and expatriate artists and giving Americans the money to buy what they wanted; and the process of Americanization. Contemporaries used *Americanization* to refer to both the United States' cultural penetration of Europe and the overlapping process of Europe's indigenous modernization. That America became a metaphor and a symbol for modernization testified to the nation's leading position in Western civilization.

In subtle yet important ways, this cultural influence and prestige enhanced the ability of the United States to conduct its political and economic policies in Europe with minimal cost and entanglement. This was especially important after 1919, when the United States government, under both Democratic and Republican administrations, shifted away from direct, official involvement in European politics. The new diplomacy was unofficial rather than official, economic rather than political, limited rather than open-ended, cautious rather than crusading. The respect that many Europeans held for American ideas and methods made such diplomacy easier to implement. At the 1924 Dawes reparations conference, for example, the unofficial American representatives conducted a successful publicity campaign in Europe that presented their plan as a pragmatic and businesslike—that is, an American—solution. Recognizing the importance of prestige (or what they termed moral power), American leaders tried to limit their intervention to instances where it would be successful, thereby enhancing their reputation for effectiveness. . . .

Just as America's prestige flowered with its impressive performance in World War I and in the 1920s, so did its cultural influence, economic power, and political leverage wilt with the Depression and the dissolution of its economy. European artists became disillusioned with their Americanist dream of permanent prosperity and progress and, with the flow of checks and tourists drying up, most American artists went home. The Depression also revealed flaws in the American reconstruction of the world economy. The United States had stabilized trade and financial relations in ways that both protected American interests and enabled Europe to recover, and Americans confidently believed that the beneficent change of economic growth would make the system work. The gold standard, the political debt settlements, the private loans, and the high U.S. tariff were burdens Europe probably could have borne had prosperity continued. But in hard times the economic structure proved too rigid and too tilted toward American interests. It collapsed. . . .

The rise of Nazi Germany and Soviet Russia during this turbulent period of a revolutionary century made mock of American attempts to implement policies of peaceful, moderate political reform and orderly, capitalist economic growth. By 1933, only the cultural leg of the triad was left standing at all, and here too both the Nazis and Soviets demonstrated that technological modernization was easily separated from the rest of the Americanization process. America could not control the chaos unloosed in 1914 after all. . . .

After 1917 American culture penetrated Europe in various ways. The American Expeditionary Force prepared the way for post-war cultural exchange by introducing Europeans to jazz and doughboys to the charm of the Old World. The doughboys' machines, their efficiency, energy, and innovativeness, impressed Europeans. Exhausted by the war, disillusioned with their own societies, many Europeans wondered whether they should not adopt the methods of these highly successful Americans. After the war, many former soldiers returned to the Old World as artists, tourists, or businessmen, each in his own way spreading U.S. culture. Along with Herbert Hoover's American Relief Administration, smaller private aid teams initiated Progressive reforms. Hollywood films stimulated demand for America's products while exposing Europeans to its speech, its manners (and mannerisms), and its values. Fads swept Europe as boxers and dance troupes pioneered this cultural and economic frontier.

Yankee popular culture excited many European artists, particularly avant-garde Germans of the *neue Sachlichkeit,* or new objective school, who sought modern cultural models to replace discredited imperial ones. Although many of these artists, like other Europeans, feared domination by the machine, they welcomed Americanism as a way to increase the Old World's economic productivity while resolving its social and ideological conflicts.

America's mass culture seemed democratic and progressive, the wave of the future. Many German leftist artists saw little contradiction in paying simultaneous allegiance to Bolshevism and Americanism. Both creeds preached popular sovereignty, mass culture, and technological development. In the heyday of U.S. influence, such German artists as Bertolt Brecht decided that Americanism, not bolshevism, offered the surer and more comfortable road to progress.

The United States was not only Europe's competitor, creditor, and occasional political mediator, but also the leader of Western civilization; and what happened in America was of intense, often personal interest to many Europeans. They watched closely, and reacted with near-hysterical joy, to [the aviator] Charles Lindbergh's solo flight across the Atlantic and, only a few months later passionately repudiated the Massachusetts trial and execution of Nicola Sacco and Bartolomeo Vanzetti.

America's influence in Europe had great impact also on its own artistic development. American painters, writers, composers, and other artists made pilgrimages to Europe, looking for freedom and esthetic inspiration. There they found many artists fascinated with the technologically dominated culture they had scorned. Moreover, significant numbers of expatriate artists ended up financing their adventures by working for compatriot businessmen and tourists. In the Old World, then, many Yankee artists found both esthetic validation and financial support for developing an indigenous American art.

Just as America's power led Europeans to heed American culture, so too did such prestige or moral power enhance the effectiveness of the United States' unofficial economic diplomacy. Washington officials realized that America's reputation for success and efficiency, coupled with its lack of interest in most European political rivalries, gave the nation a subtle but important moral authority in the Old World.

The State Department valued this asset because it yielded influence abroad with minimal cost or responsibility. Department officials tried to maximize America's moral power by making sure their foreign policy initiatives would succeed. In 1927, the department countered European resentment of U.S. power by using Charles Lindbergh as a goodwill ambassador. Like the AEF [American Expeditionary Force] a decade earlier, Lindbergh riveted Europeans' attention on Yankee boldness and technology, and thus quickened the pace of Americanization. . . .

Tourists constituted the largest and economically most important American group in Europe. The number of United States visitors jumped from roughly 15,000 in 1912 to 251,000 in 1929. In the latter year, American citizens in Europe spent close to $323 million and immigrants visiting home expended an additional $87 million. By the end of the 1920s, foreign travel became possible for middle-class Americans.

Visits to Paris nightclubs and the Louvre seemed a painless answer to America's balance-of-payments dilemma. Tourists' dollars helped Europe pay its debts and the United States maintain its tariff. Herbert Hoover's Commerce Department noted happily that worldwide American tourist expenditures of $770 million in 1927 more than matched $714 million in war and private debt receipts. In addition to the financial dividend, tourism had a beneficial "political effect," American officials told the Germans, "leading to a normal resumption of relations" between the two nations.

The flood of travelers generated resentment as well as dollars. Always the tourists' favorite, France in 1926 attracted foreigners who picked up bargains as the franc fell. Americans commonly asked waiters and shopkeepers "How much is that in real money?" A few even papered their train compartments or luggage with franc notes. Such insensitivity aggravated tensions over the war debt, and in July Paris erupted in several antiforeign, and especially anti-American demonstrations. Both French and American officials tried to calm emotions. Calvin Coolidge balanced a rebuke of "bumptious" tourists with a warning that badly treated Americans would stay home. But probably the majority of visitors had pleasant tours that never made newspaper headlines—in any case, France remained the number one American tourist attraction in Europe.

In 1929, the combined expenditure of American tourists and residents in France totaled over $137 million, creating an American economy in Paris. In the French capital one could be born in the American hospital, attend one of several American schools and churches, belong to the American Legion, the YMCA, the Cornell, Harvard, or American Women's Club; read one of three Parisian-American newspapers, in a favorite café or at the American Library; sip whiskey in the many American bars, drink milk delivered by American milkmen, eat sweet corn and ice cream produced by local Americans; go to hockey games, boxing matches, and other imported sport events; receive care from American dentists and doctors and be buried by an American undertaker. With fewer United States tourists or permanent residents, Berlin still supported an American church, student association, newspaper and, intermittently, chapters of the American Medical Association, Daughters of the American Revolution, and the Harvard Club. . . .

During the Great War, Hollywood invaded European and other world markets. YMCA representatives entertained Allied troops with American films, and the "movie habit" caught on among civilians and soldiers. In the 1920s, American films were an international box-office hit. Assured of the domestic market, which netted 60 percent of total world film revenue, Hollywood produced extravaganzas with which Europeans could not compete. By 1925, United States films made up 95 percent of the total shown in Britain, 60 percent of the total in Germany, 70 percent in France, 65 percent in Italy, and 95 percent in Australia and New Zealand. In Germany, the number of cinemas increased by 35 percent from 1920 to 1929, while the production dropped from 646 films to 175 films. Americans owned three-fourths of the most fashionable movie threatres in France. Hollywood's profits depended on foreign screenings, since domestic revenues covered only production costs, and frequently not even that.

"Trade follows the film," Americans and Europeans agreed. Greek appliance wholesalers and Brazilian furniture dealers found that their customers demanded goods like those pictured in the American movies. Although direct correlation between films and trade was hard to prove, Congress, parsimonious in most matters, established a Motion Picture Section in the Bureau of Foreign and Domestic Commerce in 1926. Bureau chief Julius Klein and his officials attested that United States films "stimulat[ed] the desire to own and use such garments, furnishing, utensils, and scientific innovations as are depicted on the screen." Will H. Hays, Hollywood czar, boasted of the power of these "silent salesmen of American goods."

American films not only sold United States goods, but, many Europeans feared, threatened independent national identity. "America has colonized us through the cinema," one Frenchman complained. Another French critic testified to the secularization of John Winthrop's city upon the hill: "Formerly US preachers . . . deluged the world with pious brochures; their more cheerful offspring, who pursue the same ends, inundate it with blonde movie stars; whether as missionaries loaded with bibles or producers well supplied with films, the Americans are equally devoted to spreading the American way of life." Charles Pomaret, a member of the Chamber of Deputies, remarked that Europeans had become "galley-slaves" to American finance and culture—appropriately, an image taken from the Hollywood hit *Ben-Hur.* British groups worried that the many Hollywood films shown throughout the empire led to "American domination in the development of national character or characteristics." After a concerned speech by the Prince of Wales, the London *Morning Post* warned: "The film is to America what the flag was once to Britain. By its means Uncle Sam may hope some day, if he be not checked in time, to Americanize the world."

After 1925, Britain, Germany, and France tried to check the trend. Governments enacted measures to limit the number of imported Hollywood films and encourage domestic production. This policy diminished but did not eliminate Hollywood's dominance in Europe. Required by law to produce domestic films if they wanted to import the popular American ones, German and other European producers responded with "quota quickies," often subgrade efforts produced only to meet the letter of the law. American filmmakers circumvented the restrictions by investing in Europe, especially Germany. They imported European directors and performers and remained preeminent in world film exports. The State and Commerce departments vigorously supported Hollywood's diplomacy. In the late twenties film exporters faced a new danger, with talkies. How could they screen English-language movies in polyglot Europe? Hollywood responded with multilanguage production. In collaboration with a Berlin company, Paramount filmed *The Blue Angel* in English and German versions. In France, Paramount worked on an assembly-line basis: sixty-six features in twelve languages for the first year. Dubbed sound tracks helped, and by 1931 United States films had regained all but 10 percent of their 1927 market in England and Germany.

Hollywood films were a hit in Europe because they projected modern culture in a vivid and attractive light. Film embodied the era's emphasis on mechanical, simultaneous, and concentrated production. The message was mass entertainment. As Adolf Behne, a German avant-gardist, recognized, "Film is . . . democratic. . . . This ha[s] been recognized by the German masses, which flock to see Charlie Chaplin films." As the industry's global leaders, Hollywood producers had budgets large enough to pay for the casts of thousands and other spectacular effects calculated to please those masses. Finally, the films portrayed an image of life in fabulous America, the giant of the contemporary world and the pioneer of Europe's own future.

From Switzerland to the Soviet Union, Europeans acknowledged America's cultural leadership. "Mrs. Lenin," Anna Louise Strong reported from Moscow, "wants . . . American ideas on education through doing; manuals about . . . various things." Jean-Paul Sartre reflected, "Skyscrapers . . . were the architecture of the future, just as the cinema was the art and jazz the music of the future." André Siegfried, a French sociologist, concluded that America had replaced Europe as "the driving force of the world." . . .

What happened in America affected the whole world. The United States had become John Winthrop's city upon the hill, though not for the religious reasons that he had expected, and Europeans could not avert their gaze. Whether they welcomed the prospect or dreaded it, most Europeans believed that American civilization portrayed the future course of their own societies. The United States was the metropolis, the hub of the modern cultural system, and Europe now figured as a satellite.

Women's Internationalism

LEILA J. RUPP

We have traced the development of the International Council of Women [(ICW)], the International Alliance of Women [(the Alliance)], and the Women's International League for Peace and Freedom [(WILPF)] from their origins, and we have witnessed their interactions with the proliferating transnational women's organizations in the period after the First World War. Activity on the international stage was picking up. It was a time when national women's movements in the Euro-American arena—fresh from suffrage victories in some cases, frustrated by continued failure in others, and besieged by attacks on women's rights at a time of Depression-era unemployment

From Leila J. Rupp, *Worlds of Women: The Making of an International Women's Movement* (Princeton: Princeton University Press, 1997), pp. 207–215, 217, 225–229. Copyright © 1997 by Princeton University Press. Reprinted by permission of Princeton University Press.

and the rise of fascism—slumped. At the same time, the decline of European dominance of the world system sparked the formation of women's movements, generally
in connection with nationalist movements of liberation, in the areas just shaking off
colonial control. Because feminist internationalists had developed an ideology that
so explicitly denied any responsibility for warmongering, the First World War energized rather than debilitated them. The wave of enfranchisements freed women's energies for international work and shifted attention to goals more international than
suffrage, especially peace. And the establishment of the League of Nations, which
stimulated international organizing among a wide range of constituencies, proved
particularly enticing to women, for the doors to the diplomatic corps within countries
had traditionally slammed in their faces. . . .

The increasing movement of women into the public world in industrialized societies at the turn of the century and the inclusion of members and national sections
from dependent and formerly colonial countries in the 1920s and 1930s complicated the process of constructing a collective identity. Unity on the basis of political
powerlessness declined after 1920 as women's fundamental difference from men
came more and more into question and women's suffrage increasingly divided
women into "haves" and "have-nots." Yet the international women's movement
held together. Given the common assumption of women's disadvantage relative to
men, gender cohesion remained firm. We can even hear the muted beginnings of
the present-day call for solidarity around naming and preventing gender-specific
violence against women. The bold proclamations against global violence that issued from the 1995 United Nations Fourth World Conference on Women in Beijing
have roots . . . that go back to the First World War. . . .

It was through the League of Nations that feminist internationalists succeeded in
putting their issues on the international agenda. By exploring women's participation
in the establishment of the League, organizational attitudes toward the international
body, and the campaign to win women a role in League policymaking, we can see
that the history of international governance would not have been the same without
the participation of the transnational women's groups. . . .

Internationally minded women eagerly anticipated the silencing of the guns at
the end of the great global conflagration and determined to have a hand in forging a
lasting and equitable peace. But when the victorious men announced plans for the
Versailles conference, women found that they had no place at the peace table. In
response, the Union Française pour le Suffrage des Femmes (the French auxiliary
of the International Woman Suffrage Alliance) invited delegates from other auxiliaries in the Allied countries to come to Paris in February 1919 to "bring feminist
pressure," in the words of the IWSA, to bear on the men at Versailles. That women
from only the winning side were included caused some consternation in the IWSA,
but the French suffrage group held firm in their conviction that such a gathering
had to precede a more general one.

The Allied suffragists decided to ask the Peace Congress to appoint a special
commission of women to report on women's issues. The proposal they presented to
[U.S. President Woodrow] Wilson called for international women's organizations to
submit names to individual governments for inclusion on the commission. Wilson
received the delegation "with the greatest sympathy" but reminded the women that
only questions with "an *international* bearing" could be considered, thus ruling out

suffrage. He suggested that they lobby the delegates to the Peace Conference to appoint a commission to investigate the situation of women and that they themselves form a commission of women to advise and instruct "the men's commission." This plan the women accepted.

The Inter-Allied Conference—what British suffragist Margery Fry called "the ladies' conference ([observing] you *can't* call them women, they are *so* well dressed!)"—went on to pass resolutions calling for equal suffrage in all countries, equal nationality and other legal rights for women, all occupations to be opened up to women, wages and salaries based on work rather than the sex of the worker, and acceptance of an equal moral standard for men and women. Then the women set about lobbying the delegates to the Peace Congress. Margery Corbett Ashby, working alongside Lady [Isabel] Aberdeen [(a Scottish aristocrat, wife of the British governor general of Canada and head of the ICW)], confided to Millicent Garrett Fawcett in March 1919 that "things are not going very well just at the moment." But women did win an official hearing before the commission of the League of Nations, where, foreshadowing the later agendas of the coalitions, they called for the admission of women into all permanent bodies of the League, the granting of woman suffrage "as soon as the civilization and democratic development of each country might permit," the suppression of the traffic in women and children, and the establishment of bureaus of education and hygiene. When Article 7 of the Covenant of the League of Nations proclaimed that all positions would be open to women, feminist internationalists rejoiced and rightfully claimed credit. This was a victory facilitated by the connections of elite women such as Aberdeen; as political outsiders, women had to rely on personal influence over male insiders.

The formation of the League of Nations, as we have seen, focused the attention of the international women's organizations on Geneva. They opened offices in the international city and formed coalitions to pursue a variety of goals. But attitudes toward the League differed from group to group. The ICW expressed the greatest enthusiasm. At the 1920 congress, the Council endorsed the principle of the League of Nations and proposed the inclusion of all self-governing states as soon as possible, but also, in accordance with its traditional concern for national autonomy, called for full consideration of "national peculiarities . . . so as to prevent valuable national individuality in ethics, manners, and customs from being interfered with." The ICW *Bulletin* regularly carried upbeat reports from Geneva, including praise for the entry of Germany into the League as "nothing less than a victory for civilization." At the 1925 congress, Princess Gabrielle Radziwill, the League official responsible for relations with voluntary organizations, insisted that the "League needs the work of women, and we women need the League of Nations' help, because the work that we are doing can only bear fruit if it is really sanctioned by our Governments and we women must help this sanction to be given." As late as 1936, in an article titled "The World Needs 'Mothering,'" an ICW member noted that they clung to the League of Nations, despite disappointments, because it represented the first milestone on the road to a system of international law. Not surprisingly, League officials tended to smile upon the ICW, Radziwill describing it as "the most influential women's organization."

The Alliance also evinced great enthusiasm for the work of the League of Nations at the outset, but the relationship grew more troubled, largely because of the

League's dismal record on the inclusion of women. The first postwar congress proceedings reported proudly that the "Alliance has not been slow to recognise that just as hitherto its political work has had to be directed towards the education of individual national parliaments, so in future its work must also include the organising of international co-operation in order to influence the League of Nations." [President of the Alliance] Margery Corbett Ashby insisted in 1928 that "the organisation of the League has rendered the work of the international organisations more fruitful," and she detailed the Alliance's successes with the League in a 1940 report in *Jus Suffragii.* But underneath official zeal, the leadership harbored doubts. [Brazilian] Bertha Lutz confided to [U.S. suffragist] Carrie Chapman Catt that "I have no faith in any international edifice of arbitration that is built on the assumption of separate sovereign ties. The trouble with the League is not the League, it is the Nations." And, true to the Alliance's central commitment to feminism, Corbett Ashby became, according to Gabrielle Radziwill, "one of the prime movers" behind the accusations that the League was not living up to the provisions of Article 7.

As we have seen, skepticism about the League on almost every count thrived within the most radical of the organizations, the Women's International League. The terms of peace, which became public on the first day of WILPF's Zurich congress, prompted a vigorous denunciation by the assembly. From the beginning WILPF members divided on the question of whether or not the League as constituted could be salvaged. While one faction insisted that it represented a step toward peace, the other argued that it violated certain basic principles, especially by excluding some nations. For the critics, the League could, at best, accomplish nothing and, at worst, would simply enforce the victors' unjust peace. WILPF never could resolve these differences. [The U.S. reformer] Jane Addams admitted that the "League is a man-made affair" but nevertheless wanted "to bring to it our woman's understanding, our warmth, our human point of view, our 'generous impulses.'" Others wanted to sever all connections. . . .

At the same time, all three organizations interacted with the League of Nations in a variety of ways. In the wake of international congresses, to which the League Secretariat invariably sent representatives, officers forwarded resolutions concerning the League to the secretary-general. The three bodies as well as the coalitions sponsored luncheons, receptions, and dinners for League officials and for women delegates to the League. Lobbying took the form of both official visits and informal conversations. Until the League moved to a new building in 1937 and required passes for entry, women could buttonhole delegates in the hallways. . . .

What impact such visits had is hard to determine. [WILPF member] Gertrud Baer complained about the attitude of Secretary-General Joseph Avenol, manifested during a meeting with members of the Liaison Committee: "I get completely paralyzed when men start to talk to women in that reassuring and calming way as a husband talks to his wife when she first starts to worry about his business affairs," she wrote. Lady Aberdeen, not surprisingly, saw the interaction between the ICW and the League in a more positive light. She cited Secretary-General Sir Eric Drummond's praise for the ICW's "impressive record of activity" with regard to the International Labor Organization and League of Nations. And Aberdeen claimed that the ICW had earned the title of "the Mother of the League of Nations," having as early as 1888 adopted the objects, methods, and policies that the League later developed.

Yet a member of the British Foreign Office described the pressure from women's organizations as "embarrassing," and Radziwill's successor, Mary Craig McGeachy, noted that too often "delegates in Geneva are urged to take some action in the name of women when they have had no indication whatever that the women of their own country would be interested in such action."

One way that the international organizations made a difference was to be sure that women, however few in number, had a presence at the League of Nations. Just being there mattered. Despite the official opening of all positions to women, very few governments appointed female delegates to the Assembly, and no women served on the League Council. Where women did find a place was in the League Secretariat, the civil service section, in which they held the majority of the secretarial and clerical positions. The women who merited more than low-level appointments found themselves clustered in particular sections identified with "women's issues"—particularly the Fifth Committee, known as "La Commission Sentimentale," which dealt with social questions, including the traffic in women and children. As the official history of WILPF put it, women's voice rose to "no more than a whisper in the assembly of nations." But the connections between the international organizations and the women who did make it into the hallowed halls is notable. So pervasive was the affiliation that the male colleagues of women at the League perceived them as having dual loyalties to their countries and their groups. . . .

The history of women's participation at the League of Nations, then, had its ups and downs. Although women remained seriously underrepresented and likely to be segregated in areas considered feminine, they would not have made even the limited progress they did without the agitation of the international women's organizations. Organized women's assumptions about female tendencies to pacifism, as well as the interests of the major groups in certain "women's issues," reinforced men's tendencies to consider women for only certain appointments. But at the same time the claim of speaking for a "women's bloc" amplified women's voices. And in fact the League of Nations itself, on the larger world stage, took on a kind of "feminine" role, staking moral claims without any force to back them up. Perhaps the League's gendered role in world affairs helps to explain women's relatively greater participation there than in most national governments. . . .

Even as the stories of women in the ICW, Alliance, and WILPF give the contemporary international women's movement a history, the link between past and present also returns us to the question of the consequences of creating internationalism. Certainly we can see the ways that the limits to universalism that were embedded in the functioning of the transnational women's organization shaped collective identity. Euro-American assumptions, based on a specific history of sexual differentiation in industrialized societies, underlay both the conceptualization of difference between women and men and the tradition of separatist organizing. The notion of transcending nationalism assumed an independent, secure, and perhaps even powerful national existence. And the chance to partake of personal interaction depended heavily on the ability to travel, to speak and understand one of the three official languages, and to be accepted as part of the "international family."

But despite the echoes of Western domination that reverberated throughout the international women's movement, the international collective identity held the potential of wider appeal. Even though the extension of political rights to women in some parts of the world around the time of the First World War divided rather than united women, and though appeals based on women's social roles in the home struck no chords in societies where women played a central part in agriculture or trade, women's universal roles as potential mothers and the reality of worldwide violence against women might nevertheless unite them all. As we have seen, the perspectives of women from countries struggling for independence in the interwar period could shed fresh light on the meaning of internationalism. And the rituals of belonging, especially if congresses broke out of the narrow orbit of the traditional host cities (as they finally did after the Second World War), could pull in a far more varied group of women. Although universal participation without regard to economic resources was still far from a reality at Nairobi or Beijing [sites for United Nations Conferences on Women (1985 and 1995)], certainly the range of colors, nationalities, and classes of women at these two gatherings—especially at the non-governmental meetings—would have rendered many an earlier activist—say, Lady Aberdeen—speechless.

While the bases of gender solidarity have shifted since the early twentieth century—from the unity of political powerlessness to, I would argue, a recognition of women's universal economic disadvantage and the multifaceted manifestations of violence against women—the notion of commonality across differences of class, ethnicity, religion, and other fundamental cleavages lives on. Even the call for solidarity based on gender-specific violence, which seems a recent theme in the history of women's international organizing, can be traced to the pained protests of women during the First World War against the rape of women in wartime.

If we recognize that all ties among groups of people are constructed, not "natural," then we can contemplate ways that different transnational actors—organizations, institutions, and governments—can design means to facilitate the creation of a variety of international collective identities. . . .

Imagine, for a moment, a scenario in which individuals and groups across the world felt a sense of kinship, on the basis of occupation or religion or gender or politics or age or a whole host of other characteristics, with others who did not share the same nationality. The multitude of international organizations that sprung up, beginning (as with the women's groups) in the late nineteenth century but intensifying in the period between the world wars, gives witness to the myriad ways that people might feel a connection across national borders. Involvement in agriculture, common economic interests, concern with law or medicine, devotion to culture, participation in philanthropy, a career in science or education, love of sport—a vast array of commonalities served as the basis of transnational organizations. No one identity was necessarily primary; certainly none was exclusive of all others. And if the creation of such international ties has not yet shaken a world system based on national identity, that does not mean that the creation of alternative bonds is unimportant. A scientist whose worldview is more like that of a colleague halfway around the globe than a next-door neighbor's raises the same implicit challenges to national identity as the embrace of Lida Gustava Heymann and Jeanne Mélin [German and French feminists] at the 1919 Zurich congress [of the WILPF]. Yet this is an aspect of international organization that has been little attended to by existing scholarship.

The first steps in the direction of a more universal collective identity may in themselves have been insignificant, but their trailblazing role demands attention.

Furthermore, the construction of internationalism within the transnational women's organizations prompts us to rethink the notion of identity politics. In line with the postmodernist and feminist recognition of multiple identities and the search for commonalities among different identity communities, we see that women's international collective identity could coexist with their identities as Germans or Egyptians, pacifists or socialists or feminists, Christians or Jews, professional women or workers. If forging bonds across cultures can build on, rather than challenge, existing loyalties, the task of creating internationalism does not seem so impossible. . . .

[T]he particular construction of internationalism within transnational women's organizations did matter. Without the coalescing of discrete groups into a vibrant international women's movement, the history of intergovernmental relations at the League of Nations and United Nations would have taken a different course. Women's insistence on representation and attention to gender-specific questions did not dramatically transform those august bodies, but they did make a difference. And the dynamic and contentious process of forging bonds between women from different, even sometimes from warring, countries has consequences for both our understanding of history and our approach to contemporary identity politics. Despite its limitations, women's internationalism in the period before the Second World War points the way to one kind of global identity that we may add to the more parochial ways we view ourselves as we move into the twenty-first century.

 F U R T H E R   R E A D I N G

Harriet Hyman Alonso, *Peace as a Women's Issue* (1993)

Leroy Ashby, *The Spearless Leader: Senator Borah and the Progressive Movement in the 1920s* (1972)

John Braeman, "Power and Diplomacy: The 1920s Reappraised," *Review of Politics,* 44 (1982), 342–369

Thomas Buckley and Edwin B. Strong, *American Foreign and National Security Policies, 1914–1945* (1987)

Kathleen Burk, "The Lineaments of Foreign Policy: The United States and a 'New World Order,' 1919–39," *Journal of American Studies,* 26 (1992), 377–391

Bruce J. Calder, *The Impact of Intervention* (1984) (on the Dominican Republic)

Warren I. Cohen, *Empire Without Tears* (1987)

Caroline Daley and Melanie Nolan, eds., *Suffrage and Beyond: International Feminism* (1994)

Charles DeBenedetti, *Origins of the Modern American Peace Movement, 1915–1929* (1978)

Roger Dingman, *Power in the Pacific: The Origins of Naval Arms Limitations, 1914–1922* (1976)

Justus D. Doenecke, *When the Wicked Rise: American Opinion-Makers and the Manchurian Crisis of 1931–1933* (1984)

Richard W. Fanning, *Peace and Disarmament* (1995)

Martin L. Fausold, *The Presidency of Herbert C. Hoover* (1985)

Robert H. Ferrell, *Frank B. Kellogg and Henry L. Stimson* (1963)

David Fogelsong, *America's Secret War Against Bolshevism* (1995)

Carrie A. Foster, *The Women and the Warriors* (1995) (on the Women's International League for Peace and Freedom)

Betty Glad, *Charles Evans Hughes and the Illusions of Innocence* (1966)

Norman A. Graebner, *Ideas and Diplomacy* (1964)

Kenneth J. Grieb, *The Latin American Policy of Warren G. Harding* (1976)

Linda B. Hall, *Oil, Banks, and Politics* (1995) (Mexico)

Ellis W. Hawley, ed., *Herbert Hoover, Secretary of Commerce, 1921–1928* (1981)

Michael J. Hogan, *Informal Entente: The Private Structure of Cooperation in Anglo-American Economic Diplomacy* (1977)

Akira Iriye, *Cultural Internationalism and World Order* (1997)

———, *The Globalizing of America* (1993)

Jon Jacobson, "Is There a New International History of the 1920s?" *American Historical Review,* 88 (1983), 617–645

Robert D. Johnson, *The Peace Progressives and American Foreign Policy* (1995)

Harold Josephson, *James T. Shotwell and the Rise of Internationalism in America* (1976)

Robert G. Kaufman, *Arms Control in the Pre-Nuclear Era: The United States and Naval Limitation Between the Two World Wars* (1990)

Bruce Kent, *The Spoils of War* (1989) (on reparations)

Michael L. Krenn, *U. S. Policy Toward Economic Nationalism in Latin America, 1917–1929* (1990)

Walter LaFeber, *Inevitable Revolutions* (1993) (on Central America)

Melvyn P. Leffler, *The Elusive Quest: America's Pursuit of European Stability and French Security, 1919–1933* (1979)

David McFadden, *Alternative Paths* (1993) (on U.S.-U.S.S.R. relations)

Brian McKercher, ed., *Anglo-American Relations in the 1920s* (1991)

Charles S. Maier, *Recasting Bourgeois Europe* (1975)

Sally Marks, *The Illusion of Peace: International Relations, 1918–1933* (1976)

Williamson Murray and Allan R. Millet, *Military Innovation During the Interwar Period* (1998)

Louis A. Pérez, Jr., *Cuba Under the Platt Amendment, 1902–1934* (1986)

Stephen J. Randall, *United States Foreign Oil Policy, 1919–1948* (1986)

Emily S. Rosenberg, *Spreading the American Dream* (1982)

——— and Norman L. Rosenberg, "The Public-Private Dynamic in United States Foreign Financial Advising, 1898–1929," *Journal of American History,* 74 (1987), 59–82

Thomas J. Saunders, *Hollywood in Berlin: American Cinema and Weimar Germany* (1994)

David F. Schmitz, *Henry L. Stimson* (2000)

Stephen A. Schuker, *American "Reparations" to Germany, 1919–33* (1988)

Robert D. Schulzinger, *The Making of the Diplomatic Mind: The Training, Outlook, and Style of United States Foreign Service Officers, 1908–1931* (1975)

Michael S. Sherry, *The Rise of American Air Power* (1987)

Katherine A. S. Siegal, *Loans and Legitimacy* (1996) (U.S.-U.S.S.R. relations)

Robert F. Smith, "Republican Policy and Pax Americana, 1921–1932," in William Appleman Williams, ed., *From Colony to Empire* (1972), pp. 253–292

Marc Trachtenberg, *Reparation in World Politics* (1980)

John Trumbull, *Selling Hollywood to the World* (2002)

Christine A. White, *British and American Commercial Relations with Soviet Russia, 1918–1924* (1992)

John Hoff Wilson, *American Business and Foreign Policy, 1920–1933* (1971)

———, *Herbert Hoover* (1975)

———, *Ideology and Economics: U.S. Relations with the Soviet Union, 1918–1933* (1974)

U.S. Entry into World War II

German and Japanese aggression in the 1930s presented Americans once again with questions of war and peace, neutrality or alliance. The United States protested this aggression, but Americans sought to avoid entanglement in the cascading crises that engulfed Europe and Asia. Congress passed neutrality acts that banned arms sales and loans to belligerent nations in the event of war, and President Franklin D. Roosevelt publicly endorsed the United States's neutral stance. Recalling the horrors of World War I and beset by a demoralizing economic depression at home, many Americans embraced "isolationism," or what historians have called "independent internationalism." In Europe, France and Great Britain also remembered the horrors of the Great War and refrained from challenging German rearmament. They also acquiesced in Germany's remilitarization of the Rhineland, even though it violated the Versailles treaty, and subsequently the annexation of Austria. Most dramatically, they adopted a policy of "appeasement" whereby they responded to Hitler's bellicose threats toward Czechoslovakia by recognizing German sovereignty over the Sudetenland, a German-speaking region of the country, in September 1938. Their hope was that Hitler's expansionism was limited in scope, rather than continental or even global, and that the dictator could be satisfied with a small amount of territory immediately adjacent to Germany.

Allied appeasement did not deter Hitler's drive for territory and power. In March 1939 he occupied the rest of Czechoslovakia, and in September he brazenly ordered his armies into Poland. Britain and France now abandoned appeasement and honored their alliance with Poland, and World War II commenced in Europe. After a brief lull, Hitler's mechanized military launched a devastating "blitzkrieg" in the spring of 1940 through Holland, Belgium, Luxembourg, and France. Next came the Balkans and the Mediterranean. Increasingly alarmed by Hitler's aggression, Roosevelt and the nation gradually moved toward an interventionist posture, repealing the arms embargo portion of the Neutrality Acts in late 1939, arranging with British prime minister Winston S. Churchill to trade destroyers for bases in 1940, and gaining congressional approval to send Lend-Lease supplies to Britain in March 1941. Reluctant to challenge directly the nation's isolationist mood and perhaps not fully convinced of America's need to take up arms, Roosevelt also won an unprecedented third term in the White House by promising that American boys would not be sent to die in a foreign war. When Hitler turned his guns on Stalinist Russia in June 1941, Roosevelt worked to open the Lend-Lease spigot to the Soviet

The German Onslaught
1939—1942

Union. In the spring of 1941 the United States initiated naval patrols to assist British shipping across the Atlantic, and in September, following several hostile encounters with German submarines, U.S. naval convoys escorted cargo ships as far as Iceland. The country seemed to edge closer to war as its vessels traversed the submarine-infested waters of the North Atlantic.

When war came for the United States, however, it occurred six thousand miles away from Europe, in Asia. For most of the twentieth century the United States had opposed Japanese expansion into China. When the Japanese sought access to vital raw materials and markets to relieve their economic stress in the 1930s, taking Manchuria and renaming it Manchukuo, Americans viewed Japanese imperialism as a violation of the Open Door and a threat to world order. Later in the decade, as the Sino-Japanese war escalated, the United States gradually expanded its navy, granted loans to China, and did not invoke the neutrality acts—thereby permitting China to buy arms from the United States. Yet Washington protested Japanese aggression in a manner designed not to provoke war with the Empire of the Sun.

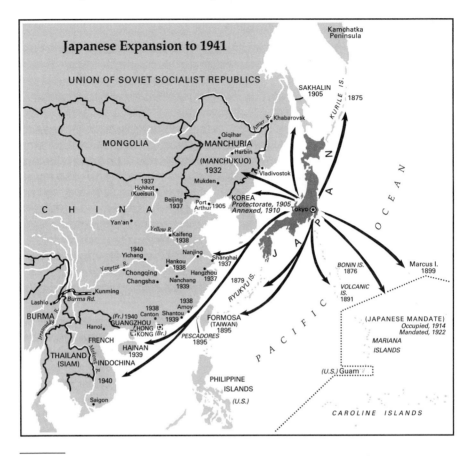

Japanese Expansion to 1941

Certain that America's strategic priorities lay across the Atlantic in Europe, the Roosevelt administration hoped to avoid a two-front war.

Following conclusion of the Tripartite Pact among Japan, Germany, and Italy in September 1940 and Japan's acquisition of bases in northern French Indochina, the administration embargoed shipments of scrap iron and steel to the island nation. The crisis in the Pacific reached a critical juncture when Japanese troops, in July 1941, occupied all of French Indochina. In response, the Roosevelt White House froze Japanese assets in the United States, thereby denying Japan essential petroleum shipments. Tokyo and Washington exchanged proposals and counterproposals for the rest of the year, but to no avail. On December 7, in a surprise attack, Japanese pilots bombed the U.S. naval base at Pearl Harbor in the Hawaiian islands, decimating the U.S. fleet and leaving over 2,400 American servicemen dead. One day later the United States declared war on Japan, and on December 11 Germany declared war on the United States. Americans braced for world war.

Historians have long debated the U.S. intervention in World War II. While most agree that German, Italian, and Japanese militarism threatened world peace, they disagree over the significance of that threat to the United States. They also debate President Franklin D. Roosevelt's handling of the crisis. The most widely shared view is that Nazi racial ideology, Germany's resources, and Hitler's personal ambition produced a hate-driven aggression that aimed at world domination. The danger heightened when Germany, Japan, and Italy joined in a military axis in September 1940. Some scholars praise the Roosevelt administration for recognizing the threat, preparing an isolationist public for action, and aiding the anti-Axis nations by all possible means—including, ultimately, U.S. military intervention following the Japanese attack on Pearl Harbor. Other writers agree that the United Stated faced imminent danger, but they criticize the Roosevelt White House for not acting earlier and more forcefully against both the aggressor states. Still others differentiate between German and Japanese aggression and argue that Hitler posed the most potent and immediate threat to U.S. interests. Thus, why didn't the United States negotiate a limited trade accord with Tokyo to dodge or delay a conflict in the Pacific, prepare for a military showdown in Europe, and avoid a resource-stretching, two-front war? Finally, although a distinct minority, some scholars have challenged their colleagues to consider the possibility that Hitler's capabilities have been exaggerated and that U.S. security might have been best protected by avoiding entry into the war and continuing FDR's pre–Pearl Harbor policy of sending large-scale assistance to Britain, the Soviet Union, and other anti-Axis nations.

What kind of threat did German and Japanese aggression pose to the United States? Did FDR deftly manage the crisis—or was he too forceful, or too timid, in confronting the danger? Did the United States realistically have any option other than full participation in the Second World War? Did the various policy options carry moral consequences—particularly in light of Hitler's racism and the Axis's disregard for human rights? These questions continue to hold meaning for a nation whose contemporary position as world leader is historically traceable to the events of the late 1930s and early 1940s.

 D O C U M E N T S

For Americans, the Japanese occupation of Manchuria in 1931, Italy's invasion of Ethiopia in 1935, the Spanish civil war in 1935–1937, and Germany's arms buildup and reoccupation of the Rhineland in 1936 all raised the ominous specter of a second world war. Adhering to the widespread belief that the U.S. entry into World War I had been a disaster and that U.S. trade and shipping to Britain had led the country to war in 1917, Congress passed the Neutrality Act of 1935, which banned arms exports to belligerents. At the same time, Senator Gerald P. Nye led congressional hearings to determine if munitions makers and bankers had lobbied President Wilson into war. Nye never proved the allegation, but he did expose the unsavory nature of war profiteering. In Document 1, a radio speech delivered on January 6, 1936, the North Dakota Republican recalls President Woodrow Wilson's "permissive neutrality" and urges passage of more restrictive legislation. In 1936 and 1937, Congress bolstered the neutrality laws by banning loans to belligerents and prohibiting U.S. travel on belligerent ships.

World events, however, overtook U.S. policy. Tension between the United States and Japan escalated following a clash between Japanese and Chinese troops at Marco

Polo bridge, south of Beijing, in July 1937 and after Japan's full-fledged invasion of China. In an obvious reference to what Japanese leaders called the "China incident," President Franklin D. Roosevelt told a Chicago audience on October 5, 1937, that aggressors should be "quarantined" (Document 2). Although FDR offered no concrete policies, the administration in the following months began to send modest amounts of aid to China. The Japanese were not deterred. Document 3, an official Japanese statement of November 3, 1938, following a string of military victories in China, proclaimed the establishment of a "new order" in Asia. Japan's bold actions sparked a debate among American policymakers over how to best halt and reverse the aggression. Hard-liners in the State Department urged the United States to punish Japan with economic measures, including the abrogation of the 1911 U.S.-Japan commercial treaty and sanctions on exports. Others, led by U.S. ambassador to Japan Joseph Grew, counseled that sanctions would only stiffen Japan's resolve for imperialism. The treaty lapsed in January 1940, but the Roosevelt administration for the moment refrained from implementing additional trade sanctions.

War broke out in Europe when Germany invaded Poland in September 1939 and Britain and France came to Poland's defense. Modifying his earlier endorsement of neutrality, Roosevelt now persuaded Congress to allow arms sales. Still, the rest of the Neutrality Acts survived, including those prohibiting loans and shipping. Thus the Allies were limited to purchasing arms on the basis of "cash and carry." The German military rapidly advanced through Europe, and in September 1940 Germany, Italy, and Japan concluded their Tripartite Pact alliance. Increasingly alarmed by the global crisis, Roosevelt devised new ways to assist the Allies without entering the war. Document 4 is FDR's December 1940 proposal for Lend-Lease, a program that allowed the United States to lease Britain massive amounts of military equipment, circumventing Britain's cash flow crisis and the Neutrality Acts' ban on monetary loans. The president's program won congressional approval in March 1941. The United States edged closer to war after FDR authorized U.S. naval patrols part way across the Atlantic to protect Lend-Lease shipping. In response to an attempted torpedoing of the U.S. destroyer *Greer* by a German U-boat submarine in September 1941—the *Greer* had been signaling submarine locations to British bombers—FDR denounced Hitler's "rattlesnakes of the Atlantic" and called for a new policy of "shoot on sight" to protect U.S. vessels. His speech of September 11, 1941, is reprinted here as Document 5.

Of course, the incident that led to U.S. entry into the war occurred on the other side of the world. On July 25, 1941, following Japan's invasion of the southern portion of French Indochina, the Roosevelt administration froze Japanese assets. Document 6, the final negotiating points adopted by the imperial government on November 5, 1941, sets forth two options for a settlement with the United States: Plan A, which called for a Japanese withdrawal from China only after a successful Sino-Japanese truce had been reached; and Plan B, a more limited and pragmatic understanding that skirted the China issue but pledged that Japan would advance no farther south than Indochina in exchange for an unfreezing of Japanese assets and resumption of normal trade with the United States. Document 7, a restatement of Washington's proposals to Japan dated November 26, 1941, rejected compromise and sought to roll back Japanese expansionism and revive Washington's cherished Open Door principle. The Japanese dismissed the final U.S. bargaining position, and on December 7, 1941, Japanese planes descended on Pearl Harbor. Document 8 is Roosevelt's war message delivered to Congress on December 8, 1941. Three days later Germany declared war against the United States.

1. Senator Gerald P. Nye Cites the Lessons of History and Advocates Neutrality, 1936

Neutrality is to be had if we are willing to pay the price of abandonment of expectation of profits from the blood of other nations at war. But it defies any man to write a neutrality program that would long endure and succeed in keeping us neutral if the policy contemplated a business boom or even "business as usual" in America while other nations are at war and wanting supplies from our mines, fields and factories. . . .

We saw the last European war until 1917 as one in no degree our business. . . . We rejoiced at the moment that leadership of our Government was showing greatest determination to keep America out of that war, a leadership affording a policy that was presumed to be a guarantee of our neutrality. That neutrality policy is now known as a permissive or a discretionary policy, with its administration in no degree mandatory upon the President. That the policy failed, and that miserably, is record. . . .

The [Woodrow] Wilson permissive neutrality policy held that it was not an unneutral act for America to sell munitions to nations at war so long as it was our policy to sell to both sides alike, and free trade in munitions was the result. Suddenly we became enraged, discovering that this permissive policy of neutrality was based upon international law defining our rights as a neutral upon the high seas, that Great Britain was not recognizing or abiding by that law. Britain, by her blockade, was interfering with our American commerce with Germany, writing new contraband definitions, searching and seizing the cargoes of American ships destined for Germany or even neutral ports which Great Britain suspicioned might be for ultimate German use. By reason of these practices we were losing even our normal trade with the Central Powers. We didn't like this interference with our trade and profits. President Wilson wrote notes of protest to Britain—notes which when now compared with those of protest later dispatched to Germany, sound like an apology. We were placated, however, with larger orders from the Allies which much more than offset our loss of trade with Germany. These Allied orders were tremendous and caused us to quite overlook the fact that our neutral policy was no longer one finding us furnishing munitions to both sides. It was our increasing commerce with the Allies upon which our prosperity now depended. Who doesn't remember how bitterly severe were our notes of protest to Germany when Germany, in retaliation of the British blockade, used the submarine to destroy commerce upon which the Allies were dependent. But, while this business with the Allies was maintaining a marvelous prosperity for us and while we were counting as a great thing so long as we kept out of it, we were nevertheless highly resolved to continue our neutrality "so called."

The Allies soon exhausted their own means of buying from us. They needed American credit. Our permissive neutrality policy of the hour forbade loans and credits, but it appears that such pressure was brought as caused the administrators

---

From Nye radio address 6 January 1936, Gerald P. Nye Papers, Herbert Hoover Library, West Branch, Iowa.

of that policy to turn their back upon it. It was concluded, by that administration, that while loans should be prohibited to any nation at war, credits would be countenanced. Our own economic well-being was so dependent upon the continuing boom market of war that we would only cut our own throats by refusing the credit that would let the Allies continue buying from us! So, for a time, the Allies bought upon credit furnished by Americans. But the time comes when individual credit is exhausted and the Allies need large loans if they are to continue buying American supplies. If these loans couldn't be had Europe couldn't continue buying from us! Somewhere the strings were pulled that caused our neutrality administrators to permit loans to the Allies contrary to our neutrality policy—a discretionary policy. To have insisted against loans would have ended the profits and the prosperity of Americans flowing from Europe's war!

Ah, business continues good; prosperity remains on every hand! War isn't such a bad thing when we don't have to be in it! "But," we said, "look at those Germans; they are destroying American cargoes going to England and France and sinking English passenger vessels with Americans on board! Maybe something ought to be done about it! But, whatever we do, let's not get into that war!" That was our reasoning at the hour. How childish it all was—this expectation of success in staying out of a war politically while economically we stayed in it; how childish this permissive flip-flop neutrality policy of ours and our belief that we could go on and on supplying the sinews of war to one or even both sides and avoid ourselves being ultimately drawn into the engagement with our lives and our fortunes at stake.

Well, to make a long story short, our prosperity, which at the moment was our commerce with the Allies, demanded a more and more warlike attitude on our part. Our rights on the high seas, our commerce is declared in jeopardy! . . .

After we had started stretching our permissive American neutrality policy to accommodate our commercial interests the Allied powers were never in doubt as to what America would ultimately do. They saw what we didn't seem to realize, namely, that where our pocketbook was there would we and our hearts ultimately be. . . .

Insistence now upon establishment of a mandatory policy of neutrality is no reflection upon any one man. It is only fair to say that the present [Franklin D.] Roosevelt determination to keep us out of war is no higher than was that expressed by Wilson. Yet . . . while the Wilson administration was declaring itself neutral, parts of that administration were actually contemplating the hour when we would ultimately get into the war without a doubt as to which side we would enter on. . . .

Based upon such facts and such experience Senator [Bennet Champ] Clark [D–Mo.] and I today introduced in the Senate a bill proposing a strict policy of neutrality, the enforcement of which shall at once be not permissive or at the discretion of the President, but mandatory upon him. The bill presents requirements and advantages roughly stated as follows:

First, at the outbreak of war between other nations the President shall by proclamation forbid the exportation of arms, ammunition and implements of war for the use of those nations, and that the President shall, not "may" but shall, extend this embargo to other nations if and when they may become engaged in such war.

Second, the bill proposes an embargo on other items of commerce which may be considered essential war materials, such as oil, and provides that the President shall forbid exportation to nations at war of these materials beyond what was the average annual exportation of these materials to those nations during the five-year period preceding the outbreak of war.

Third, the bill requires that the President shall upon the outbreak of war between foreign states proclaim that the buyer of any and all articles to or through the field of operations of belligerent states shall be at the risk solely of the buyer and the bill provides that the buyers shall be without redress in any court of the United States. Thus, it will be seen, there is provided a strict "cash and carry" basis with buyers taking their own risk in accomplishing delivery of supplies they buy from us in time of war.

Fourth, the bill requires that the President shall require American passengers to refrain from traveling on the vessels of belligerent states, and provides that passengers who ignore this requirement at once forfeit their right to protection of the United States. Thus we can avoid a repetition of the Lusitania experience.

Fifth, the bill introduced today does with loans and credits to time of war precisely what it does with war materials—it embargoes and limits them. . . .

There are those who will insist that this measure is too severe. We, who sponsor it, feel that in the light of experience, nothing short of those provisions is deserving of the title of a neutrality policy and we beg the confidence of the people of the land in it not as an instrument that will completely prevent war, but as one that will make it extremely difficult for the United States to be drawn into another foreign war that becomes our war only because of selfish interests that profit from the blood spilled in the wars of other lands.

2. President Franklin D. Roosevelt Proposes to "Quarantine" Aggressors, 1937

Some fifteen years ago the hopes of mankind for a continuing era of international peace were raised to great heights when more than sixty nations solemnly pledged themselves not to resort to arms in furtherance of their national aims and policies. The high aspirations expressed in the Briand-Kellogg Peace Pact and the hopes for peace thus raised have of late given way to a haunting fear of calamity. The present reign of terror and international lawlessness began a few years ago.

It began through unjustified interference in the internal affairs of other nations or the invasion of alien territory in violation of treaties; and has now reached a stage where the very foundations of civilization are seriously threatened. The landmarks and traditions which have marked the progress of civilization toward a condition of law, order and justice are being wiped away.

Without a declaration of war and without warning or justification of any kind, civilians, including vast numbers of women and children, are being ruthlessly murdered with bombs from the air. In times of so-called peace, ships are being attacked and sunk by submarines without cause or notice. Nations are fomenting and taking sides in civil warfare in nations that have never done them any harm. Nations claiming freedom for themselves deny it to others.

This document can be found in U.S. Department of State, *Papers Relating to the Foreign Relations of the United States, Japan: 1931–1941* (Washington, D.C.: Government Printing Office, 1943), I, 379–383.

Innocent peoples, innocent nations, are being cruelly sacrificed to a greed for power and supremacy which is devoid of all sense of justice and humane considerations. . . .

The peace-loving nations must make a concerted effort in opposition to those violations of treaties and those ignorings of humane instincts which today are creating a state of international anarchy and instability from which there is no escape through mere isolation or neutrality.

Those who cherish their freedom and recognize and respect the equal right of their neighbors to be free and live in peace must work together for the triumph of law and moral principles in order that peace, justice and confidence may prevail in the world. There must be a return to a belief in the pledged word, in the value of a signed treaty. There must be recognition of the fact that national morality is as vital as private morality. . . .

There is a solidarity and interdependence about the modern world, both technically and morally, which makes it impossible for any nation completely to isolate itself from economic and political upheavals in the rest of the world, especially when such upheavals appear to be spreading and not declining. There can be no stability or peace either within nations or between nations except under laws and moral standards adhered to by all. International anarchy destroys every foundation for peace. It jeopardizes either the immediate or the future security of every nation, large or small. It is, therefore, a matter of vital interest and concern to the people of the United States that the sanctity of international treaties and the maintenance of international morality be restored.

The overwhelming majority of the peoples and nations of the world today want to live in peace. They seek the removal of barriers against trade. They want to exert themselves in industry, in agriculture and in business, that they may increase their wealth through the production of wealth-producing goods rather than striving to produce military planes and bombs and machine guns and cannon for the destruction of human lives and useful property.

In those nations of the world which seem to be piling armament on armament for purposes of aggression, and those other nations which fear acts of aggression against them and their security, a very high proportion of their national income is being spent directly for armaments. It runs from thirty to as high as fifty percent. We are fortunate. The proportion that we in the United States spend is far less— eleven or twelve percent.

How happy we are that the circumstances of the moment permit us to put our money into bridges and boulevards, dams and reforestation, the conservation of our soil and many other kinds of useful works rather than into huge standing armies and vast supplies of implements of war.

I am compelled and you are compelled, nevertheless, to look ahead. The peace, the freedom and the security of ninety percent of the population of the world is being jeopardized by the remaining ten percent who are threatening a breakdown of all international order and law. Surely the ninety percent who want to live in peace under law and in accordance with moral standards that have received almost universal acceptance through the centuries, can and must find some way to make their will prevail.

The situation is definitely of universal concern. The questions involved relate not merely to violations of specific provisions of particular treaties; they are questions of war and of peace, of international law and especially of principles of humanity. It is true that they involve definite violations of agreements, and especially of the Covenant of the League of Nations, the Briand-Kellogg Pact and the Nine Power Treaty. But they also involve problems of world economy, world security and world humanity.

It is true that the moral consciousness of the world must recognize the importance of removing injustices and well-founded grievances; but at the same time it must be aroused to the cardinal necessity of honoring sanctity of treaties, of respecting the rights and liberties of others and of putting an end to acts of international aggression.

It seems to be unfortunately true that the epidemic of world lawlessness is spreading.

When an epidemic of physical disease starts to spread, the community approves and joins in a quarantine of the patients in order to protect the health of the community against the spread of the disease.

It is my determination to pursue a policy of peace. It is my determination to adopt every practicable measure to avoid involvement in war. It ought to be inconceivable that in this modern era, and in the face of experience, any nation could be so foolish and ruthless as to run the risk of plunging the whole world into war by invading and violating, in contravention of solemn treaties, the territory of other nations that have done them no real harm and are too weak to protect themselves adequately. Yet the peace of the world and the welfare and security of every nation, including our own, is today being threatened by that very thing.

3. Japan Envisions a "New Order" in Asia, 1938

What Japan seeks is the establishment of a new order which will insure the permanent stability of East Asia. In this lies the ultimate purpose of our present military campaign.

This new order has for its foundation a tripartite relationship of mutual aid and co-ordination between Japan, Manchoukuo [the name Japan gave to Manchuria in February 1932], and China in political, economic, cultural and other fields. Its object is to secure international justice, to perfect the joint defence against Communism, and to create a new culture and realize a close economic cohesion throughout East Asia. This indeed is the way to contribute toward the stabilization of East Asia and the progress of the world.

What Japan desires of China is that that country will share in the task of bringing about this new order in East Asia. She confidently expects that the people of China will fully comprehend her true intentions and that they will respond to the call of Japan for their co-operation. Even the participation of the Kuomintang Government would not be rejected, if, repudiating the policy which has guided it in the past and remolding its personnel, so as to translate its re-birth into fact, it were to come forward to join in the establishment of the new order.

This document can be found in U.S. Department of State, *Papers Relating to the Foreign Relations of the United States, Japan: 1931–1941* (Washington, D.C.: Government Printing Office, 1943), I, 477–478.

Japan is confident that other Powers will on their part correctly appreciate her aims and policy and adapt their attitude to the new conditions prevailing in East Asia. For the cordiality hitherto manifested by the nations which are in sympathy with us, Japan wishes to express her profound gratitude.

The establishment of a new order in East Asia is in complete conformity with the very spirit in which the Empire was founded; to achieve such a task is the exalted responsibility with which our present generation is entrusted. It is, therefore, imperative to carry out all necessary internal reforms, and with a full development of the aggregate national strength, material as well as moral, fulfill at all costs this duty incumbent upon our nation.

Such the Government declare to be the immutable policy and determination of Japan.

4. FDR Proposes Lend-Lease Aid to Great Britain, 1940

December 17, 1940, Press Conference

Now, what I am trying to do is to eliminate the dollar sign, and that is something brand new in the thoughts of practically everybody in this room, I think—get rid of the silly, foolish old dollar sign. All right!

Well, let me give you an illustration: Suppose my neighbor's home catches fire, and I have got a length of garden hose four or five hundred feet away; but, my Heaven, if he can take my garden hose and connect it up with his hydrant, I may help him to put out his fire. Now what do I do? I don't say to him before that operation, "Neighbor, my garden hose cost me $15; you have got to pay me $15 for it." What is the transaction that goes on? I don't want $15—I want my garden hose back after the fire is over. All right. If it goes through the fire all right, intact, without any damage to it, he gives it back to me and thanks me very much for the use of it. But suppose it gets smashed up—holes in it—during the fire; we don't have to have too much formality about it, but I say to him, "I was glad to lend you that hose; I see I can't use it any more, it's all smashed up." He says, "How many feet of it were there?" I tell him, "there were 150 feet of it." He said, "All right, I will replace it." Now, if I get a nice garden hose back, I am in pretty good shape. In other words, if you lend certain munitions and get the munitions back at the end of the war, if they are intact—haven't been hurt—you are all right; if they have been damaged or deteriorated or lost completely, it seems to me you come out pretty well if you have them replaced by the fellow that you have lent them to. . . .

December 29, 1940, Radio Address

This is not a fireside chat on war. It is a talk on national security; because the nub of the whole purpose of your President is to keep you now, and your children later,

Dec. 17 remarks from *Complete Presidential Press Conferences of Franklin D. Roosevelt,* vol. 15–16, 1940 (New York: DaCapo Press, 1972), 353–355. Dec. 29 radio address in State Department *Bulletin* 4 (1941): 3–8.

and your grandchildren much later, out of a last-ditch war for the preservation of American independence and all of the things that American independence means to you and to me and to ours. . . .

Never before since Jamestown and Plymouth Rock has our American civilization been in such danger as now.

For, on September 27, 1940, by an agreement signed in Berlin, three powerful nations, two in Europe and one in Asia, joined themselves together in the threat that if the United States interfered with or blocked the expansion program of these three nations—a program aimed at world control—they would unite in ultimate action against the United States.

The Nazi masters of Germany have made it clear that they intend not only to dominate all life and thought in their own country, but also to enslave the whole of Europe, and then to use the resources of Europe to dominate the rest of the world. . . .

Some of our people like to believe that wars in Europe and in Asia are of no concern to us. But it is a matter of most vital concern to us that European and Asiatic war-makers should not gain control of the oceans which lead to this hemisphere. . . .

Does anyone seriously believe that we need to fear attack while a free Britain remains our most powerful naval neighbor in the Atlantic? Does anyone seriously believe, on the other hand, that we could rest easy if the Axis powers were our neighbor there?

If Great Britain goes down, the Axis powers will control the continents of Europe, Asia, Africa, Australasia, and the high seas—and they will be in a position to bring enormous military and naval resources against this hemisphere. It is no exaggeration to say that all of us in the Americas would be living at the point of a gun—a gun loaded with explosive bullets, economic as well as military. . . .

There are those who say that the Axis powers would never have any desire to attack the Western Hemisphere. This is the same dangerous form of wishful thinking which has destroyed the powers of resistance of so many conquered peoples. The plain facts are that the Nazis have proclaimed, time and again, that all other races are their inferiors and therefore subject to their orders. And most important of all, the vast resources and wealth of this hemisphere constitute the most tempting loot in all the world. . . .

The experience of the past two years has proven beyond doubt that no nation can appease the Nazis. No man can tame a tiger into a kitten by stroking it. There can be no appeasement with ruthlessness. There can be no reasoning with an incendiary bomb. We know now that a nation can have peace with the Nazis only at the price of total surrender. . . .

The American appeasers ignore the warning to be found in the fate of Austria, Czechoslovakia, Poland, Norway, Belgium, the Netherlands, Denmark, and France. They tell you that the Axis powers are going to win anyway; that all this bloodshed in the world could be saved; and that the United States might just as well throw its influence into the scale of a dictated peace, and get the best out of it that we can.

They call it a "negotiated peace." Nonsense! Is it a negotiated peace if a gang of outlaws surrounds your community and on threat of extermination makes you pay tribute to save your own skins?

Such a dictated peace would be no peace at all. It would be only another armistice, leading to the most gigantic armament race and the most devastating trade wars in history. And in these contests the Americas would offer the only real resistance to the Axis powers. . . .

The proposed "new order" is the very opposite of a United States of Europe or a United States of Asia. It is not a government based upon the consent of the governed. It is not a union of ordinary, self-respecting men and women to protect themselves and their freedom and their dignity from oppression. It is an unholy alliance of power . . . to dominate and enslave the human race.

The British people are conducting an active war against this unholy alliance. Our own future security is greatly dependent on the outcome of that fight. Our ability to "keep out of war" is going to be affected by that outcome.

Thinking in terms of today and tomorrow, I make the direct statement to the American people that there is far less chance of the United States getting into war if we do all we can now to support the nations defending themselves against attack by the Axis than if we acquiesce in their defeat, submit tamely to an Axis victory, and wait our turn to be the object of attack in another war later on.

If we are to be completely honest with ourselves, we must admit there is risk in *any* course we may take. But I deeply believe that the great majority of our people agree that the course that I advocate involves the least risk now and the greatest hope for world peace in the future.

The people of Europe who are defending themselves do not ask us to do their fighting. They ask us for the implements of war, the planes, the tanks, the guns, the freighters, which will enable them to fight for their liberty and our security. Emphatically we must get these weapons to them in sufficient volume and quickly enough, so that we and our children will be saved the agony and suffering of war which others have had to endure.

Let not defeatists tell us that it is too late. It will never be earlier. Tomorrow will be later than today.

Certain facts are self-evident.

In a military sense Great Britain and the British Empire are today the spearhead of resistance to world conquest. They are putting up a fight which will live forever in the story of human gallantry.

There is no demand for sending an American Expeditionary Force outside our own borders. There is no intention by any member of your Government to send such a force. You can, therefore, nail any talk about sending armies to Europe as deliberate untruth.

Our national policy is not directed toward war. Its sole purpose is to keep war away from our country and our people.

Democracy's fight against world conquest is being greatly aided, and must be more greatly aided, by the rearmament of the United States and by sending every ounce and every ton of munitions and supplies that we can possibly spare to help the defenders who are in the front lines. It is no more unneutral for us to do that than it is for Sweden, Russia, and other nations near Germany to send steel and ore and oil and other war materials into Germany every day.

We are planning our own defense with the utmost urgency; and in its vast scale we must integrate the war needs of Britain and the other free nations resisting aggression. . . .

As planes and ships and guns and shells are produced, your Government, with its defense experts, can then determine how best to use them to defend this hemisphere. The decision as to how much shall be sent abroad and how much shall remain at home must be made on the basis of our over-all military necessities.

We must be the great arsenal of democracy. For us this is an emergency as serious as war itself. We must apply ourselves to our task with the same resolution, the same sense of urgency, the same spirit of patriotism and sacrifice, as we would show were we at war. . . .

5. Roosevelt Orders the U.S. Navy to "Shoot on Sight," 1941

The Navy Department of the United States has reported to me that on the morning of September fourth the United States destroyer *Greer,* proceeding in full daylight toward Iceland, had reached a point southeast of Greenland. She was carrying American mail to Iceland. She was flying the American flag. Her identity as an American ship was unmistakable.

She was then and there attacked by a submarine. Germany admits that it was a German submarine. The submarine deliberately fired a torpedo at the *Greer,* followed later by another torpedo attack. In spite of what Hitler's propaganda bureau has invented, and in spite of what any American obstructionist organization may prefer to believe, I tell you the blunt fact that the German submarine fired first upon this American destroyer without warning, and with deliberate design to sink her.

Our destroyer, at the time, was in waters which the Government of the United States had declared to be waters of self-defense—surrounding outposts of American protection in the Atlantic.

In the North of the Atlantic, outposts have been established by us in Iceland, in Greenland, in Labrador and in Newfoundland. Through these waters there pass many ships of many flags. They bear food and other supplies to civilians; and they bear matérial of war, for which the people of the United States are spending billions of dollars, and which, by Congressional action, they have declared to be essential for the defense of our own land.

The United States destroyer, when attacked, was proceeding on a legitimate mission. . . .

This was piracy—piracy legally and morally. It was not the first nor the last act of piracy which the Nazi Government has committed against the American flag in this war. For attack has followed attack.

A few months ago an American flag merchant ship, the *Robin Moor,* was sunk by a Nazi submarine in the middle of the South Atlantic, under circumstances violating long-established international law and violating every principle of humanity. The passengers and the crew were forced into open boats hundreds of miles from land, in direct violation of international agreements signed by nearly all Nations

---

This document can be found in *Public Papers and Addresses of Franklin D Roosevelt, 1941* (New York: Harper and Brothers, 1950), pp 384–392.

including the Government of Germany. No apology, no allegation of mistake, no offer of reparations has come from the Nazi Government. . . .

Five days ago a United States Navy ship on patrol picked up three survivors of an American-owned ship operating under the flag of our sister Republic of Panama—the *S.S. Sessa*. On August seventeenth, she had been first torpedoed without warning, and then shelled, near Greenland, while carrying civilian supplies to Iceland. It is feared that the other members of her crew have been drowned. In view of the established presence of German submarines in this vicinity, there can be no reasonable doubt as to the identity of the flag of the attacker.

Five days ago, another United States merchant ship, the *Steel Seafarer,* was sunk by a German aircraft in the Red Sea two hundred and twenty miles south of Suez. She was bound for an Egyptian port. . . .

In the face of all this, we Americans are keeping our feet on the ground. . . .

But it would be inexcusable folly to minimize such incidents in the face of evidence which makes it clear that the incident is not isolated, but is part of a general plan.

The important truth is that these acts of international lawlessness are a manifestation of a design which has been made clear to the American people for a long time. It is the Nazi design to abolish the freedom of the seas, and to acquire absolute control and domination of these seas for themselves.

For with control of the seas in their own hands, the way can obviously become clear for their next step—domination of the United States—domination of the Western Hemisphere by force of arms. Under Nazi control of the seas, no merchant ship of the United States or of any other American Republic would be free to carry on any peaceful commerce, except by the condescending grace of this foreign and tyrannical power. The Atlantic Ocean which has been, and which should always be, a free and friendly highway for us would then become a deadly menace to the commerce of the United States, to the coasts of the United States, and even to the inland cities of the United States. . . .

To be ultimately successful in world mastery, Hitler knows that he must get control of the seas. He must first destroy the bridge of ships which we are building across the Atlantic and over which we shall continue to roll the implements of war to help destroy him, to destroy all his works in the end. He must wipe out our patrol on sea and in the air if he is to do it. He must silence the British Navy.

I think it must be explained over and over again to people who like to think of the United States Navy as an invincible protection, that this can be true only if the British Navy survives. And that, my friends, is simple arithmetic.

For if the world outside of the Americas falls under Axis domination, the shipbuilding facilities which the Axis powers would then possess in all of Europe, in the British Isles, and in the Far East would be much greater than all the shipbuilding facilities and potentialities of all of the Americas—not only greater, but two or three times greater—enough to win. Even if the United States threw all its resources into such a situation, seeking to double and even redouble the size of our Navy, the Axis powers, in control of the rest of the world, would have the manpower and the physical resources to outbuild us several times over.

It is time for all Americans, Americans of all the Americas to stop being deluded by the romantic notion that the Americas can go on living happily and peacefully in a Nazi-dominated world. . . .

No tender whisperings of appeasers that Hitler is not interested in the Western Hemisphere, no soporific lullabies that a wide ocean protects us from him—can long have any effect on the hard-headed, far-sighted, and realistic American people.

Because of these episodes . . . we Americans are now face to face not with abstract theories but with cruel, relentless facts.

This attack on the *Greer* was no localized military operation in the North Atlantic. This was no mere episode in a struggle between two Nations. This was one determined step toward creating a permanent world system based on force, on terror, and on murder. . . .

There has now come a time when you and I must see the cold, inexorable necessity of saying to these inhuman, unrestrained seekers of world conquest and permanent world domination by the sword: "You seek to throw our children and our children's children into your form of terrorism and slavery. You have now attacked our own safety. You shall go no further."

Normal practices of diplomacy—note writing—are of no possible use in dealing with international outlaws who sink our ships and kill our citizens.

One peaceful Nation after another has met disaster because each refused to look the Nazi danger squarely in the eye until it actually had them by the throat.

The United States will not make that fatal mistake.

No act of violence, no act of intimidation will keep us from maintaining intact two bulwarks of American defense: First, our line of supply of matériel to the enemies of Hitler; and second, the freedom of our shipping on the high seas.

No matter what it takes, no matter what it costs, we will keep open the line of legitimate commerce in these defensive waters.

We have sought no shooting war with Hitler. We do not seek it now. But neither do we want peace so much, that we are willing to pay for it by permitting him to attack our naval and merchant ships while they are on legitimate business.

I assume that the German leaders are not deeply concerned, tonight or any other time, by what we Americans or the American Government say or publish about them. We cannot bring about the downfall of Nazism by the use of long-range invective.

But when you see a rattlesnake poised to strike, you do not wait until he has struck before you crush him.

These Nazi submarines and raiders are the rattlesnakes of the Atlantic. They are a menace to the free pathways of the high seas. They are a challenge to our sovereignty. They hammer at our most precious rights when they attack ships of the American flag—symbols of our independence, our freedom, our very life. . . .

In the waters which we deem necessary for defense, American naval vessels and American planes will no longer wait until Axis submarines lurking under the water, or Axis raiders on the surface of the sea, strike their deadly blow—first.

Upon our naval and air patrol—now operating in large number over a vast expanse of the Atlantic Ocean—falls the duty of maintaining the American policy of freedom of the seas—now. That means, very simply, very clearly, that our patrolling vessels and planes will protect all merchant ships—not only American ships but ships of any flag—engaged in commerce in our defensive waters. They will protect them from submarines; they will protect them from surface raiders. . . .

It is no act of war on our part when we decide to protect the seas that are vital to American defense. The aggression is not ours. Ours is solely defense. . . .

The orders which I have given as Commander in Chief of the United States Army and Navy are to carry out that policy—at once. . . .

I have no illusions about the gravity of this step. I have not taken it hurriedly or lightly. It is the result of months and months of constant thought and anxiety and prayer. In the protection of your Nation and mine it cannot be avoided.

The American people have faced other grave crises in their history—with American courage, and with American resolution. They will do no less today.

They know the actualities of the attacks upon us. They know the necessities of a bold defense against these attacks. They know that the times call for clear heads and fearless hearts.

And with that inner strength that comes to a free people conscious of their duty, and conscious of the righteousness of what they do, they will—with Divine help and guidance—stand their ground against this latest assault upon their democracy, their sovereignty, and their freedom.

6. Japan Proposes Two Diplomatic Options to the United States, November 1941

Plan A

The most important pending matters in negotiations between Japan and the United States are: 1) the stationing and withdrawal of troops in China and French Indochina; 2) nondiscriminatory trade in China; 3) interpretation and observance of the Tripartite Pact; and 4) the Four Principles [see Document 7]. These matters are to be moderated to the following extent:

1) The stationing and withdrawal of troops in China.

Setting aside for the moment our reasons for stationing troops, we shall moderate our stance to the following extent, considering that the United States has (a) attached great importance to the stationing of troops for an indeterminate period of time, (b) objected to the inclusion of this item in the terms for a peace settlement, and (c) called for a clearer expression of intent regarding the withdrawal of troops:

> Japanese forces dispatched to China because of the China Incident shall occupy designated areas of north China and Mongolia and Hainan island for as long as is necessary after peace is concluded between Japan and China. The evacuation of other forces shall commence the minute peace is concluded, in accordance with separate arrangements made between Japan and China, and shall be completed within two years.
>
> Note: Should the United States ask what "for as long as is necessary" means, we shall reply to the effect that our goal is roughly 25 years.

2) The stationing and withdrawal of troops in French Indochina.

The United States entertains misgivings that Japan has territorial ambitions in French Indochina and is attempting to make it into a base for military advances

Excerpts from *Japan's Decision for War: Records of the 1941 Policy Conferences.* Edited and translated by Nobutaka Ike. Copyright © 1967 by the Board of Trustees of the Leland Stanford Junior University, renewed 1995 by the author. Used with permission of Stanford University Press, www.sup.org.

into adjacent territories. In recognition of this, we shall moderate our stance to the following extent:

> The Japanese government respects the territorial sovereignty of French Indochina. Japanese troops currently dispatched to French Indochina will be immediately evacuated upon the settlement of the China Incident or upon the establishment of a just peace in the Far East.

3) Nondiscriminatory treatment in trade with China.

In the event that there is no prospect of securing complete agreement to our previous proposal of September 25, we shall deal with this issue on the basis of the following proposal:

> The Japanese government acknowledges that the principle of nondiscrimination will be applied in the entire Pacific region and China as well, insofar as that principle is applied throughout the world.

4) Interpretation and observance of the Tripartite Pact.

We shall respond on this matter by making it even clearer that we have no intention of unduly broadening our interpretation of the right of self defense; that as far as interpreting and observing the Tripartite Pact is concerned, the Japanese government will act on its own discretion, as we have frequently elaborated before; and that we think that the United States already understands this fully.

5) As for what the United States calls its four principles, we shall avoid with all our might their inclusion in anything formally agreed to between Japan and the United States (whether that be the Draft Understanding or other declarations).

Plan B

1) Both Japan and the United States shall promise not to make any advances by military force into Southeast Asia and the South Pacific region, other than French Indochina.

2) The governments of Japan and the United States shall cooperate together so as to guarantee the procurement of necessary resources from the Dutch East Indies.

3) The governments of Japan and the United States shall together restore trade relations to what they were prior to the freezing of assets, and the United States will promise to supply Japan with the petroleum it needs.

4) The United States government shall not engage in such actions as may hinder efforts toward peace by Japan and China

Notes

1) If it is necessary to do so, there is no objection to promising that if the present agreement is concluded, Japanese forces now stationed in southern Indochina are prepared, with the approval of the French government, to transfer to northern French Indochina, and that these Japanese forces will withdraw from French Indochina upon settlement of the China Incident or the establishment of a just peace in the Pacific region.

2) If it is also necessary to do so, additional insertions may be made to the provisions regarding nondiscriminatory treatment in trade and those regarding interpretation and observance of the Tripartite Pact in the existing proposals (last plans).

7. Washington Rejects Japan's Proposals and Reaffirms the Open Door, November 1941

Section I   Draft Mutual Declaration of Policy

The Government of the United States and the Government of Japan both being solicitous for the peace of the Pacific affirm that their national policies are directed toward lasting and extensive peace throughout the Pacific area, that they have no territorial designs in that area, that they have no intention of threatening other countries or of using military force aggressively against any neighboring nation, and that, accordingly, in their national policies they will actively support and give practical application to the following fundamental principles upon which their relations with each other and with all other governments are based:

1. The principle of inviolability of territorial integrity and sovereignty of each and all nations.
2. The principle of non-interference in the internal affairs of other countries.
3. The principle of equality, including equality of commercial opportunity and treatment.
4. The principle of reliance upon international cooperation and conciliation for the prevention and pacific settlement of controversies and for improvement of international conditions by peaceful methods and processes.

The Government of Japan and the Government of the United States have agreed that toward eliminating chronic political instability, preventing recurrent economic collapse, and providing a basis for peace, they will actively support and practically apply the following principles in their economic relations with each other and with other nations and peoples:

1. The principle of non-discrimination in international commercial relations.
2. The principle of international economic cooperation and abolition of extreme nationalism as expressed in excessive trade restrictions.
3. The principle of non-discriminatory access by all nations to raw material supplies.
4. The principle of full protection of the interests of consuming countries and populations as regards the operation of international commodity agreements.
5. The principle of establishment of such institutions and arrangements of international finance as may lend aid to the essential enterprises and the continuous development of all countries and may permit payments through processes of trade consonant with the welfare of all countries.

This document can be found in U.S. Department of State, *Papers Relating to the Foreign Relations of the United States, Japan: 1931–1941* (Washington, D.C.: Government Printing Office, 1943), II, 768–769.

Section II   Steps to Be Taken by the Government of the United States and by the Government of Japan

The Government of the United States and the Government of Japan propose to take steps as follows:

1. The Government of the United States and the Government of Japan will endeavor to conclude a multilateral non-aggression pact among the British Empire, China, Japan, the Netherlands, the Soviet Union, Thailand and the United States.
2. Both Governments will endeavor to conclude among the American, British, Chinese, Japanese, the Netherland and Thai Governments an agreement whereunder each of the Governments would pledge itself to respect the territorial integrity of French Indochina and, in the event that there should develop a threat to the territorial integrity of Indochina, to enter into immediate consultation with a view to taking such measures as may be deemed necessary and advisable to meet the threat in question. Such agreement would provide also that each of the Governments party to the agreement would not seek or accept preferential treatment in its trade or economic relations with Indochina and would use its influence to obtain for each of the signatories equality of treatment in trade and commerce with French Indochina.
3. The Government of Japan will withdraw all military, naval, air and police forces from China and from Indochina.
4. The Government of the United States and the Government of Japan will not support—militarily, politically, economically—any government or regime in China other than the National Government of the Republic of China with capital temporarily at Chungking.
5. Both Governments will give up all extraterritorial rights in China, including rights and interests in and with regard to international settlements and concessions, and rights under the Boxer Protocol of 1901.
    Both Governments will endeavor to obtain the agreement of the British and other governments to give up extraterritorial rights in China, including rights in international settlements and in concessions and under the Boxer Protocol of 1901.
6. The Government of the United States and the Government of Japan will enter into negotiations for the conclusion between the United States and Japan of a trade agreement, based upon reciprocal most-favored-nation treatment and reduction of trade barriers by both countries, including an undertaking by the United States to bind raw silk on the free list.
7. The Government of the United States and the Government of Japan will, respectively, remove the freezing restrictions on Japanese funds in the United States and on American funds in Japan.
8. Both Governments will agree upon a plan for the stabilization of the dollar-yen rate, with the allocation of funds adequate for this purpose, half to be supplied by Japan and half by the United States.
9. Both Governments will agree that no agreement which either has concluded with any third power or powers shall be interpreted by it in such a way as to conflict with the fundamental purpose of this agreement, the establishment and preservation of peace throughout the Pacific area.

10. Both Governments will use their influence to cause other governments to adhere to and to give practical application to the basic political and economic principles set forth in this agreement.

8. Roosevelt Delivers His War Message to Congress, 1941

Yesterday, December 7, 1941—a date which will live in infamy—the United States of America was suddenly and deliberately attacked by naval and air forces of the Empire of Japan.

The United States was at peace with that Nation and, at the solicitation of Japan, was still in conversation with its Government and its Emperor looking toward the maintenance of peace in the Pacific. Indeed, one hour after Japanese air squadrons had commenced bombing in Oahu, the Japanese Ambassador to the United States and his colleague delivered to the Secretary of State a formal reply to a recent American message. While this reply stated that it seemed useless to continue the existing diplomatic negotiations, it contained no threat or hint of war or armed attack.

It will be recorded that the distance of Hawaii from Japan makes it obvious that the attack was deliberately planned many days or even weeks ago. During the intervening time the Japanese Government has deliberately sought to deceive the United States by false statements and expressions of hope for continued peace.

The attack yesterday on the Hawaiian Islands has caused severe damage to American naval and military forces. Very many American lives have been lost. In addition American ships have been reported torpedoed on the high seas between San Francisco and Honolulu.

Yesterday the Japanese Government also launched an attack against Malaya.

Last night Japanese forces attacked Hong Kong.

Last night Japanese forces attacked Guam.

Last night Japanese forces attacked the Philippine Islands.

Last night the Japanese attacked Wake Island.

This morning the Japanese attacked Midway Island.

Japan has, therefore, undertaken a surprise offensive extending throughout the Pacific area. The facts of yesterday speak for themselves. The people of the United States have already formed their opinions and well understand the implications to the very life and safety of our Nation.

As Commander-in-Chief of the Army and Navy I have directed that all measures be taken for our defense.

Always will we remember the character of the onslaught against us.

No matter how long it may take us to overcome this premeditated invasion, the American people in their righteous might will win through to absolute victory.

I believe I interpret the will of the Congress and of the people when I assert that we will not only defend ourselves to the uttermost but will make very certain that this form of treachery shall never endanger us again.

This document can be found in U.S. Department of State, *Papers Relating to the Foreign Relations of the United States, Japan: 1931–1941* (Washington, D.C.: Government Printing Office, 1943), II, 793–794.

Hostilities exist. There is no blinking at the fact that our people, our territory, and our interests are in grave danger.

With confidence in our armed forces—with the unbounded determination of our people—we will gain the inevitable triumph—so help us God.

I ask that the Congress declare that since the unprovoked and dastardly attack by Japan on Sunday, December seventh, a state of war has existed between the United States and the Japanese Empire.

 E S S A Y S

In the first essay, Gerhard Weinberg, a noted World War II scholar from the University of North Carolina, lays out the case for U.S. military intervention in World War II. Weinberg, whose research unearthed a second book authored by Hitler after *Mein Kampf,* argues that the German dictator pursued a global agenda that included plans to conquer the United States. Wartime exigencies forced Hitler to delay, but never abandon, the development of naval and air capabilities for a trans-Atlantic attack. Germany's alliance with Japan in 1940 provided the Führer with a naval ally to help him advance his dream. According to Weinberg, President Roosevelt—unlike his isolationist critics—grasped the international dimensions of the threat, but still hoped to avoid war by aiding Britain, Russia, and China. Germany's relentless aggression, and Japan's determination to thrust southward across the Pacific, doomed any chance for peace. Weinberg concludes that U.S. entry into the war was both necessary and inevitable.

In the second essay, Bruce M. Russett of Yale University challenges conventional wisdom that the United States had little choice but to enter World War II. Russett argues that Hitler lacked the capability to achieve victory in Europe and posed no direct military threat to the United States. By late 1941 Britain's survival had already been assured by FDR's policy of providing assistance by all measures short of war, and Germany's imprudent invasion of the Soviet Union was doomed to end in a stalemate. As for Asia, Japan's conquest of China had reached a standstill by 1941, and until Washington slapped down a sweeping embargo on raw materials, including petroleum, Japan had been determined to avoid war with the United States. Thus, U.S. entry into the Second Word War was unnecessary and avoidable. First published in 1972, Russett explains in his updated preface in 1994 that the Vietnam War had moved him to ponder the legacies of World War II, including an exaggerated sense of power that has led postwar America to undertake military interventions globally.

The Global Threat and the Case for War

GERHARD WEINBERG

The initial reaction of both the leadership and the public in the United States to the outbreak of war in Europe was essentially similar and uniform. The overwhelming majority blamed Germany for starting the war; the overwhelming majority hoped that Britain and France would win; the overwhelming majority wanted to stay out

Gerhard Weinberg, *A World at Arms: A Global History of World War II* (Cambridge: Cambridge University Press, 1994), pp. 84–86, 178–180, 182, 239–241, 243–246, 249–252, 256–257, 261–263. Source notes in original text have been omitted. Copyright © 1994 by Cambridge University Press. Reprinted with the permission of Cambridge University Press.

of the war. The near unanimity on these three basic issues did not extend, however, to two other subsidiary but in practice critical matters: the real prospects of the Allies and the policy to be followed by the United States toward them.

There were those in the United States who thought it made no difference who won, but for many, the prospect of the victory of the Allies was not only the preferred but the most likely outcome of the conflict. As German victory in Poland was followed by a quiet winter, more of the public began to doubt the ability of Britain and France to defeat her; and their doubt, not surprisingly, increased with German victories in Scandinavia and the West in the spring of 1940. President Roosevelt's views on this subject appear to have been somewhat different—and in retrospect a great deal more far-sighted—than those of many others. He certainly always hoped for an Allied victory over Germany, but he was very skeptical of Western power. . . .

These perceptions of the President must be kept in mind in assessing and understanding the practical steps Roosevelt urged on Congress and the American people. He believed that Nazi Germany and its allies threatened the whole world, including the Western Hemisphere, and he very much hoped to keep the United States out of the war. Unlike, Stalin, who believed that the best way to avert war from the Soviet Union was to help the Germans fight the Western Powers, Roosevelt thought that the most likely prospect for continual avoidance of war was to assist Britain and France in defeating Germany. Because he believed, correctly as we now know, that the Western Powers were deficient in weapons of war, he considered the prohibition on the sale of weapons to them in the neutrality laws a bonus for the early rearmament of the aggressors and a major handicap for the Allies. He would, therefore, try again to have the neutrality laws changed.

Roosevelt hoped that this could be done on a non-partisan or bi-partisan basis, and in the initial stages tried to involve the 1936 Republican President and Vice-Presidential candidates, Alfred Landon, and Frank Knox, in the process. In the Congress, however, a bitter debate, largely though not entirely on partisan lines, ensued. The issue divided the country. What came to be a standard pattern over the next two years emerged. On the one side were those who believed that, both to stay out of war and to assist Britain and France, neutrality law revision was in the country's interest. A few took this side because they expected or wanted the United States to join the Allies. Against this position were those, generally called isolationists and later strongly identified with the America First Committee, who believed that the best way to stay out of the war was to do nothing to assist Britain and France or to help them to help themselves; and some took this side because they thought that it might be just as well if Germany won or at least that it made little difference to the United States if she did so.

In the weeks before the outbreak of war, the isolationists had won on the issue of allowing others to buy arms in the United States, when Roosevelt had proposed it as a way of warning Germany that American arsenals would be open to those certain to control the seas if Germany started a war. Now that the Germans had started it, the isolationists lost. After a lengthy and bitter struggle, during which Roosevelt, as he put it, was "walking on eggs," the Congress approved what had come to be called "cash and carry" early in November; the President signed the bill on November 4. . . .

Hitler's view of the United States was based on an assessment that this was a weak country, incapable because of its racial mixture and feeble democratic government of organizing and maintaining strong military forces. The antagonism of Americans, both in government and among the public, toward Germany was therefore no cause for worry. Certain that Allied victory in World War I was the result of Germany's having been stabbed in the back by the home front, he was never interested in the American military effort in that conflict or any possible renewal of it. He had long assumed that Germany would have to fight the United States after conquering Eurasia, and he had begun preparations toward that end both in airplane and naval construction. The outbreak of war in Europe in 1939, however, forced a temporary postponement in the program to construct a big navy of huge battleships and numerous other surface ships. . . .

For years Hitler [also] had been calling for an airplane capable of bombing the United States, and work on such a plane had been under way since 1937. The realization of this project, however, was still not imminent in 1940, and the Germans could only push forward with it in the hope that by the time the planes were ready, refueling in the Portuguese Azores would be possible and would increase the possible bomb load. The prerequisites for war with the United States were being worked on, but it was obvious that they would take time to complete. While the preparations went forward, a project which was thought to be much simpler and capable of completion long before the huge blue-water navy and swarms of four-engined bombers had been built was to be carried out by Germany's victorious army: the invasion of the Soviet Union and the defeat of that country so that huge portions of it could be annexed and settled by German farmers, and the area's metal and oil resources harnessed to the subsequent campaign against the United States.

The whole project of crushing France and England had, after all, been undertaken only as a necessary preliminary, in Hitler's eye, to the attack in the East which would enable Germany to take the living space, the *Lebensraum,* he believed she needed. And it is too often forgotten in retrospect that in his view the campaign in the West was always expected to be the harder one. If in World War I Germany had struggled unsuccessfully in the West though victorious in the East, the fortunate willingness of the Soviet Union to assist her in winning in the West this time could make it all the easier to win in the East against inferior Slavs ruled by incompetent Jews, as Hitler believed. . . .

In view of this background it should not be surprising that already in mid and late May of 1940, as soon as it became clear that the German offensive in the West was going forward as quickly and successfully as Hitler could possibly hope, he began to turn his thoughts to the attack on the Soviet Union. He was beginning to discuss this project with his military associates in late May, and in June had them starting on the first preparations of plans for such an operation. Initially conceived of as an offensive to be launched in the fall of 1940, the campaign was expected to last only a few weeks. If the mighty French army, which had stopped the Germans in the last war, could be crushed in six weeks and the British driven ignominiously from the continent, then victory in the East would take hardly any time at all. The concept of a "one-front" war always meant one *land* front to Hitler, so that the question of whether or not England remained in the war after the defeat of France was initially irrelevant to the timing of an attack in the East.

During the latter part of July, the preliminary discussion of the new offensive coincided with the recognition that Britain would not withdraw from the war. Far from discouraging Hitler, this had the opposite effect of making him all the more determined to attack the Soviet Union. In his eyes, the British were staying in the war in expectation of the Soviet Union and United States replacing France as Britain's continental ally, something he assumed the English invariably needed. This quick destruction of the Soviet Union would not only remove one of these two hopes but would indirectly eliminate the other as well. Once Japan was reassured by the German attack on the Soviet Union against any threat to her home islands from the Pacific territories of Russia, she could strike southwards into the areas she had long coveted, and such an action would necessarily draw American attention and resources into the Pacific. The destruction of Russia, accordingly, would serve as an indirect means of forcing Britain out of the war as well as opening up the agricultural land and raw materials of the Soviet Union for German settlement and exploitation.

In those same days, however, as the indirect fight against England was added to the original aims of the invasion of Russia, Hitler came to the conclusion that the attack in the East had best be launched in the early summer of 1941 rather than in the fall of 1940. Influenced it would seem by the arguments of his immediate military advisors that the transfer of German forces from the West to the East, their refitting for new operations, and the needed logistical preparations in an area of underdeveloped transportation facilities meant risking that the short campaign could not be completed victoriously before the onset of winter, Hitler had decided by the end of July that it made more sense to wait until the following year when the whole operation could be completed in one blow. . . .

The limited industrial resources of Germany at their relatively low level of mobilization were not, however, capable of coping simultaneously with the preparations for the new land campaign in the East and the construction of the great battleship navy. Once again—as in September 1939—these projects had to be postponed. Victory over the Soviet Union would release the necessary resources for a resumption of construction on the big ships; in the interim, Germany would concentrate at sea on the blockade of Great Britain by submarines and airplanes.

The postponement of fleet building, in turn, had immediate implications for Germany's direct and indirect relations with the United States. In the direct sense, it meant that the German submarines were instructed to be careful of incidents with the United States, and Hitler ordered restraint on a navy ever eager to strike at American shipping. Simultaneously, in the indirect sense the position and role of Japan with its great navy became more important in German eyes. As already mentioned, Hitler anticipated that an attack on the Soviet Union would help propel Japan forward in Asia, thus tying up the United States in the Pacific in the years that Germany was still building her own surface navy. Between the decision to attack Russia and the implementation of that decision, however, there were now the intervening months to consider.

It was in this context that lining up Japan with the Axis came to be seen as increasingly important, a process which met the interests of the new leadership which had come to power in Tokyo in the days of decision in Berlin. The Tripartite Pact of Germany, Italy and Japan was not signed until September 27, but the new impetus from Berlin, in spite of earlier German unhappiness with Japan, needs to be seen in the context of the decisions of late July. Furthermore, the slow dawning on Germany's leaders of the realization that England was not going to give in operated to reinforce the policy choice previously made. A Japanese attack on Britain's possessions in Southeast Asia, particularly on Singapore, could not help but assist Germany's own fight against the United Kingdom. . . .

The American President hoped to avoid open warfare with Germany altogether. He urged his people to aid Great Britain, and he devised and proposed, as we shall see, a whole variety of ways to do just that and to make sure that the aid actually reached its destination; but he hoped until literally the last minute that the United States could stay out of the war. There has been almost as much argument about Roosevelt's foreign policy in 1940–41 among historians as there was among contemporaries. Several types of recently available sources confirm dramatically the reliability of a number of long-known statements made by Roosevelt at the time but not always taken as accurate indications of his views.

On August 22, 1940, when trying to get the support of the chairman of the Senate Naval Affairs Commission for the destroyers for bases deal, Roosevelt engaged the argument that such a step might lead to war with Germany because of retaliatory acts by the latter. He argued that if the Germans wanted to go to war with the United States, they would always find an excuse to do so, but that the United States would not fight unless attacked. At the end of the year, when explaining his policy in detail to the American high commissioner in the Philippines, he stressed the global aspects of the aid to Britain policy but again asserted that the country could and should stay out of the war in both Europe and the Far East unless herself attacked. When recordings of press conferences made in the White House in the fall of 1940 became available recently, and it turned out that a machine had been inadvertently left turned on, extraordinarily similar remarks by Roosevelt in private conversation came to light. On October 4 and on October 8, he explained to political and administrative associates that the United States would not enter the war unless the Germans or Japanese actually attacked; even their considering themselves at war with the United States would not suffice. We know that in practice he would follow that approach in December 1941 towards Hungary, Romania, and Bulgaria, trying unsuccessfully for half a year to persuade those countries that they might find it wiser to withdraw their declarations of war on the United States.

The picture of Roosevelt trying and hoping to avoid war has been reinforced by what we now know about the breaking of German codes. Although the Americans told the British of their successes in breaking the major Japanese diplomatic code already in September 1940, and provided them with a machine for reading such messages themselves in January 1941, the British did not reciprocate with information on their breaking of German enigma machine codes until April 1941. Thereafter cooperation became more and more extensive. For the rest of 1941, the knowledge of German naval dispositions gained from the reading of naval messages was regularly and carefully utilized to *avoid* incidents, when it could very easily have been used to *provoke* them. The famous Presidential order to shoot at German submarines on sight, thus, was more to frighten them off than to provoke them. Aware of German orders to submarines to avoid incidents, the President could push forward with his program of aid to Britain knowing that at worst there might be isolated incidents in the Atlantic.

The general assumption of many that countries are either at war or at peace with each other was not shared by Roosevelt, who knew that the American navy had originated in the quasi-war with France at the turn of the eighteenth to the nineteenth century and that more recently Japan and the Soviet Union had engaged in bloody encounters at specific points in East Asia while continuing to have diplomatic relations and without entering into general hostilities with each other. Some of Roosevelt's advisors did think the United States should or would have to enter the war to assure the defeat of Hitler, but there is no evidence that the President himself abandoned his hope that the United States could stay out. He had been proved right in his belief that Britain could hold on in 1940—against the view of many; he would be proved right in his expectation that the Soviet Union could hold on in 1941— again against the view of many. In a way he would be proved right on the question of formal American entrance into the war. We now have his comments on October 8, 1940; "the time may be coming when the Germans and the Japs [sic] will do some fool thing that would put us in. That's the only real danger of our getting in . . ."

Lord Lothian, the British ambassador to the United States, was one of the few who understood the desire of Roosevelt to help England within the limits of the politically and legally feasible but to stay out of the war if at all possible. As Britain's ability to pay for supplies was nearing its end, he persuaded a reluctant Churchill to lay the financial facts openly before the President, and Lothian himself in public exposed the fact that England was running out of money. Out of this approach came Roosevelt's call for the Lend-Lease program, a massive system of Congressional appropriation for the purpose of providing assistance to Britain in wartime which was subsequently extended to other countries. Following great pressure by Roosevelt, [Secretary of State Cordell] Hull, and Secretary of the Treasury Henry Morgenthau—the administration's key figure on the issue—for Britain to come up with as much gold and dollars from the sale of investments as possible, and a very noisy debate in the public arena as well as in Congress, the bill, cleverly labeled H.R. 1776 to reassure House Majority Leader John McCormack's Irish constituents, became law on March 11, 1941. The first appropriation of seven billion dollars had been voted before the month was out.

Passage of this legislation in intense and widely reported debate signaled the American public's belief that the threat posed by Germany was great enough to merit drastic American support of Germany's enemies. Most still hoped to stay out of hostilities, but by contrast with the identical Soviet hopes of those months, the way to realize that hope was seen to be the massive shipment of supplies to Hitler's enemies rather than to Hitler. Simultaneously, this process assisted in the more efficient and effective building up of America's own rearmament program. . . .

The British [military] disasters in the Mediterranean in the spring of 1941 led to anguished debates in Washington as to what to do. The most important new step to aid Britain that the United States took was the result of Roosevelt's shift in favor of sending American troops to Iceland to replace the British garrison there, a step he had earlier refrained from taking in the face of a request from Iceland. The Americans, furthermore, drew for themselves the conclusion that part of the British military trouble had been caused by their divided command structure, with a resulting American emphasis on the power of theater commanders. In the immediate situation, they worried about what would happen if the Germans were now to seize the Spanish and Portuguese islands in the Atlantic the way they had taken Crete and thereby shift the battle in that theater decisively to their advantage. The Germans, however, moved east, not west, with the result that the new puzzle facing Washington was whether to extend aid to the Soviet Union and how to divide the scarce available supplies between the British and the Soviets while still building up America's own military power. . . .

The President quickly determined to send the Soviet Union whatever help could be provided; the fact that he placed his closest confidante, Harry Hopkins, in charge of this endeavor testifies to the importance he attached to it. Hopkins was sent to Moscow to get the whole project moving and took along Colonel Philip Faymonville, a strong believer in the ability of the Red Army to hold out, to handle aid at the Russian end. Knowing of popular opposition to aid to the Soviet Union, Roosevelt worked hard to try to have people see that this dictatorship was less threatening than the immediate menace of the German dictatorship, and he was especially concerned about calming the widespread concern over the lack of religious freedom in the Soviet Union. There were great worries and enormous difficulties, some growing out of the fact that there had been such vast differences between United States and Soviet policies in the preceding years. The Moscow conferences of early August 1941 produced an agreement on major shipments of military supplies in the face of the preference of United States and British military leaders who preferred to keep what weapons were coming off the assembly lines for their own forces. In the face of the German advances in the East, which if victorious would then free them for a renewed push in the Atlantic, Roosevelt pressed his associates to get the materials moving. In a way, he understood better than many contemporaries and most subsequent observers the anti-American component in Hitler's planning and hoped to preclude its success by making the German search for victory in the East as hard as possible. . . .

[Meanwhile,] [a]ll through 1940 and 1941 the Roosevelt administration tried to find ways to hold off Japan while the United States rearmed itself, aided Britain, and, after the German invasion of the Soviet Union, aided the latter. Concentrating primary attention on the Atlantic and the dangers there, the administration hoped to restrain Japan, possibly pry her loose from the Tripartite Pact, and figure out ways to keep her from expanding the war she had already started in China. The assistance provided to the Chinese Nationalists was one element in this policy. The end of the US–Japan trade agreement, which left the Japanese guessing as to the next American step, was another. Roosevelt did not want to take steps which might drive Japan to take radical action, but he was being pushed by a public opinion which objected to the United States selling Japan the materials it needed for the war against China; on this subject the same people who objected to aid for Britain for fear of war were among the most vociferous advocates of a forward policy in East Asia.

The hope of the administration that some accommodation could be reached with Japan which would restrain the latter by a combination of patient negotiations, continued American rearmament, and a passive stance in the Pacific, was dashed by the insistence of the Japanese government on a sweeping offensive in Southeast Asia; but for months there at least appeared to be a prospect of success. . . . On the Japanese side, the ambassador to the United States, Nomura Kichisaburo, really wanted peace with the United States. The Americans correctly believed this to be the case, and since several of the key figures in Washington, including the

President and Secretary of State, knew and respected him, they did their best to accommodate him. Nomura, however, was not an experienced and skillful diplomat, frequently failed to inform his government accurately, and never recognized that the whole negotiating project was a fraud. . . . The hopeless confusion within the Japanese government, in which some elements did indeed still want peace with the United States, only confirmed Nomura's mistaken impressions.

On the American side, the hope that some way of avoiding war with Japan could still be found encouraged the President and Secretary of State to meet time and again with the Japanese ambassador, and later the special envoy sent to assist him. . . . It was their hope, furthermore, that the negotiations themselves might enable them to win enough time to rearm to such an extent that eventually the Japanese would give up any projects of new conquests altogether. In this regard, the two-ocean navy program looked to the distant future; for the time immediately ahead, the anticipated delivery of the new B-17 Flying Fortress 4-engine bomber was thought to be a possible deterrent. Quite exaggerated expectations were attached to the small numbers of these planes becoming available in 1941 and 1942, and it was seriously believed that their presence in the Philippines would make it possible to deter a Japanese attack southward—by the implied threat of fire-bombing the cities of Japan—or, if worse came to worse, to defend those islands effectively. Since all prior American planning had been based on the assumption that the islands in the Western Pacific could not be defended in the years before they were to attain independence anyway, this new concept showed how greatly illusions about small numbers of planes affected thinking in Washington in 1941. . . .

For months, the Germans had weighed the advantages of Japan's attacking the British in Southeast Asia, even if that also meant war with the United States. Each time they looked at the prospect, it looked better to them. Time and again the Japanese had shown their caution to be both excessive and at Germany's expense. There were innumerable German grievances over the failure of the Japanese to assist Germany in moving raw materials she needed from East and Southeast Asia. Unfavorable comparisons were made between what the United States was doing for Britain and what Japan was doing for its German ally. Over and over the Germans urged the Japanese to strike at Singapore: the way to destroy the British empire was to attack it while it was vulnerable, and that time was obviously now. To reassure the Japanese that such a move would not be dangerous for them, they provided Tokyo with one of their great intelligence scoops of the war: the capture in November, 1940, of a British Cabinet report which showed that Britain could not and would not send major fleet units to East Asia in case of a Japanese attack.

From time to time, the Japanese would point out to the Germans that Japan would be ready to move in 1946, the year when the last United States forces were scheduled to leave the Philippines, to which the Germans responded by pointing out that by that time the war in Europe would be over and the American fleet doubled. Perhaps more important was the German assurance that if Japan could move against Singapore only if she struck the United States at the same time, then she could count on Germany to join her. . . .

[I]f the Japanese, who had hung back so long, took the plunge, then the naval deficit would automatically disappear. [Hitler] had thought of removing that discrepancy by a German sneak under-water attack on the United States navy in port.

Told by his navy that this was impossible, there was the obvious alternative of Japan providing a navy for his side of the war; that the Japanese would do from above the water what he had hoped to do from underneath was not known to him beforehand, but that made no difference. The key point was that Japan's joining openly on the Axis side would provide a big navy right away, not after years of building, and hence remove the main objection to going to war with the United States now rather than later. It was therefore entirely in accord with his perception of the issues that he promised [Foreign Minister Yosuke] Matsuoka on April 4 that if Japan believed that the only way for her to do what the Germans thought they should do, namely attack the British, was also to go to war at the same time with the United States, they could move in the knowledge that Germany would immediately join them. This policy was fully understood in German headquarters and would be voiced repeatedly thereafter.

Because they held this point of view, the Germans were seriously alarmed by what they learned of a possible Japanese–United States accommodation growing out of the negotiations between the two countries. The dangerous converse of tension in the Pacific leading to war and the tying up of the United States fleet there was the possibility of a United States–Japanese agreement freeing the United States fleet for even greater employment in the Atlantic. Like the immediately involved negotiators in Washington and Tokyo, the Germans did not understand that this was all shadow-boxing . . . and the German government did what it could to discourage any agreement from the sidelines. (Had the Germans actually wanted to avoid a war with the United States, an opposite policy would, of course have been followed by Berlin.) . . .

The definitive Japanese decision to shift from concentrating on war with China to war against the Western Powers came in early June 1941. The hinge of decision was the shift from occupying *northern* French Indo-China, which was part of the war against China because that country could then be blockaded more effectively, to occupying *southern* Indo-China, which pointed in the opposite direction, that is, to war against the British and Dutch to the south and against the Americans in the Philippines and on the Pacific flank of the southern advance. . . .

Because of the insistence of the United States government on continuing negotiations and the desire of the Japanese ambassador in the United States (who was not informed about his government's intention) to do so also, the authorities in Tokyo had to reexamine the issues several times in October and November, always coming back to the same conclusion: now was the time to fight. In the process, [Prime Minister Prince Fumimaro] Konoe became tired of the discussion of a policy he had himself launched and was replaced by War Minister Tojo Hideki, but there was no inclination within the government to reverse the course for war. The new Foreign Minister, Togo Shigenori, and Finance Minister Kaya Okinori had doubts but were overridden by the others. . . .

The Japanese had decided to provide a public explanation by making extensive demands on the United States which they expected to be refused and which could be increased if accepted. A lengthy memorandum was therefore sent to Washington following on earlier such demands. In between, they received and disregarded a restatement of the American position (which they afterwards for propaganda purposes called an ultimatum). All this was shadow-boxing. The Japanese government had decided on war; had kept this fact from their own diplomats in Washington so that these could appear to be negotiating in good faith; and instructed them to present a lengthy note in time for Japan to initiate hostilities. . . .

In reality, the Pearl Harbor attack proved a strategic and tactical disaster for Japan, though the Japanese did not recognize this. The ships were for the most part raised; by the end of December, two of the battleships [Admiral] Yamamoto [Isoroku] had imagined sunk were on their way to the West Coast for repairs. All but the *Arizona* returned to service, and several played a key role . . . in a great American naval victory in October 1944. Most of the crew members survived to man the rebuilding American navy. These tactical factors were outgrowths of the basic strategic miscalculation. As anyone familiar with American reactions to the explosion on the *Maine* or the sinking of the *Lusitania* could have predicted, an un-provoked attack in peacetime was guaranteed to unite the American people for war until Japan surrendered, thus destroying in the first minutes of war Japan's basic strategy. The hope that the American people would never expend the blood and treasure needed to reconquer from Japan all sorts of islands—most of which they had never heard of—so that these could be returned to others or made independent, became completely unrealistic with the attack on Pearl Harbor. The attainment of surprise guaranteed defeat, not victory, for Japan.

Others were eager to join Japan in war with the United States. The Germans and Italians had been asked by Japan to join in and enthusiastically agreed. Mussolini had already promised to join in on December 3 and now did so, an extraordinary sit-uation given Italy's string of defeats. Hitler had repeatedly urged the Japanese to move against Britain and was positively ecstatic that they had acted at last. The idea of a Sunday morning air attack in peacetime was especially attractive to him. He had started his campaign against Yugoslavia that way a few months earlier; here was an ally after his own heart. Now there would be a navy of battleships and aircraft carriers to deal with the Americans. His own navy had been straining at the leash for years and could now sink ships in the North Atlantic to its heart's content. Since the Japa-nese had not told Hitler precisely when they planned to move, he had just returned to East Prussia from the southern end of the Eastern Front, where he had dealt with a crisis caused by a Soviet counter-offensive, when the news of Pearl Harbor reached him. It would take a few days to organize the proper ceremonies in Berlin on Decem-ber 11, but that did not have to hold up the open hostilities he was eager to begin. In the night of December 8–9, at the earliest possible moment, orders were given to sink the ships of the United States and a string of countries in the Western Hemisphere. Two days later Hitler told an enthusiastic Reichstag the good news of war with America. Those who really believed that Germany had lost World War I because of a stab-in-the-back, not defeat at the front, were certain that it was American military power which was the legend. For once the unanimity in the Reichstag mirrored near unanimity in the government of the Third Reich. The German government's only worry was that the Americans might get their formal declaration of war in before they could deliver one themselves; they would get their way.

President Roosevelt asked and obtained declarations of war against Germany and Italy from Congress in response to the German and Italian declarations, steps which those countries had followed up by a treaty with Japan promising never to sign a separate peace. When Romania, Hungary, and Bulgaria also declared war on the United States, the President tried to get these declarations withdrawn. Perhaps the peoples of those countries could live quite happily without having a war with the United States. But the effort to persuade them of this truth failed, and in June the Congress reciprocated. The whole world was indeed aflame.

Stalemate and the Case Against U.S. Entry into the War

BRUCE M. RUSSETT

Whatever criticisms of twentieth-century American foreign policy are put forth, United States participation in World War II remains almost entirely immune. According to our national mythology, that was a "good war," one of the few for which the benefits clearly outweighed the costs. Except for a few books published shortly after the war and quickly forgotten, this orthodoxy has been essentially unchallenged. The isolationists stand discredited, and "isolationist" remains a useful pejorative with which to tar the opponents of American intervention in foreign land.

Such virtual unanimity on major policy matters is rare. World War I long ago came under the revisionists' scrutiny. The origins of the cold war have been challenged more recently, with many people asking whether the Soviet-American conflict was primarily the result of Russian aggressiveness or even whether it was the inevitable consequence of throwing together "two scorpions in a bottle." But all orthodoxy ought to be confronted occasionally, whether the result be to destroy, revise, or reincarnate old beliefs. Furthermore, this does seem an auspicious time to reexamine the standard credo about participation in World War II. Interventionism is again being questioned and Americans are groping toward a new set of principles to guide their foreign policy. Where should we intervene and where withdraw; where actively to support a "balance of power" and where husband our resources? A reexamination of the World War II experience is deliberately a look at a limiting case—an effort to decide whether, in the instance where the value of intervention is most widely accepted, the interventionist argument really is so persuasive. We should consider the World War II experience not because intervention was obvious folly, but indeed because the case for American action there is strong. . . .

American participation in World War II brought the country few gains; the United States was no more secure at the end than it could have been had it stayed out. First, let us look at the "might have beens" in Europe. The standard justification of American entry into the war is that otherwise Germany would have reigned supreme on the continent, victor over Russia and Britain. With all the resources of Europe at the disposal of his totalitarian government, plus perhaps parts of the British fleet, Hitler would have posed an intolerable threat to the security of the United States. He could have consolidated his winnings, built his war machine, established bridgeheads in South America, and ultimately could and likely would have moved against North America to achieve world domination.

From Bruce M. Russett, *No Clear and Present Danger: A Skeptical View of American Entry into World War II* (New York: Harper and Row, 1972, 1997), pp. 24–30, 41–48, 60–66, 88. Material has been retitled for this publication. Copyright © 1972 by Bruce M. Russett. Reprinted by permission of HarperCollins Publishers, Inc.

Several links in this argument might deserve scrutiny, but by far the critical one is the first, that Hitler would have won World War II. Such a view confuses the ability of Germany's enemies to *win* with their ability to achieve a *stalemate*. Also, it tends to look more at the military-political situation of June 1940 than at that of December 1941, and to confuse President Roosevelt's decision to aid Britain (and later Russia) by "all measure short of war" with an actual American declaration of war. Let me say clearly: I basically accept the proposition that German domination of all Europe, with Britain and Russia prostrate, would have been intolerable to the United States. By any of the classical conceptions of "power-balancing" and "national interest," the United States should indeed have intervened if necessary to prevent that outcome. . . .

I do not, therefore, argue that American nonbelligerent assistance to Britain was a mistake, quite the contrary. Yet that is just the point—by the end of 1941 Britain's survival was essentially assured. She might lose some colonies, her world position would be weakened, perhaps in the long run her independent existence would be threatened by the Germans in a second round of war. For the immediate future, nevertheless, Britain would live. Indeed, such a conclusion helps to make sense of Hitler's daring gamble in attacking Russia in the late spring of 1941. The British had made it through the worst patch, and only by a long and mutually-exhausting war could Germany hope to wear them down. At the least, German hopes for a quick end to the war had been irretrievably lost.

If British survival into 1941 raised the specter of deadlock or war of attrition to Hitler, the failure of his attack on Russia brought the specter to life. He had intended to invade the Soviet Union in mid-May 1941, but things had not gone well. His ally, Mussolini, had invaded Greece and met with repeated defeats. Hitler felt obliged to divert German troops from the Russian front to rescue the Italians and the German flank. His invasion of Russia, Operation Barbarossa, was thus delayed five weeks until June 22 when, without ultimatum or declaration of war, the troops moved east.

The attack itself was an admission that the war against Britain had gone badly. By some interpretations the German invasion of Russia was an attempt to secure the resources, especially oil, necessary to bring the British down in a long war of attrition; by others it was an effort to strike the Russians at a time of Hitler's choosing rather than wait for the Russians to come in on the British side later. Surely the prospect of being the weight in balance at the key moment would have been greatly tempting to Stalin. By either interpretation the attack accepted great risks, and was the last try with any hope of success to seize a clear victory.

With the onset of the Russian winter and Hitler's inability to take Moscow— Napoleon had at least managed that—the prospect of German failure was sharp. Looking back, we now can see that *this* was in fact the hinge of fate; the more visible turning a year later was more nearly the outward sign of a predetermined shift. . . .

The essential point is that the Russian success, like the British, occurred quite independently of American military action. . . .

Had America remained in the status of twilight belligerence Germany probably would not have been defeated, though as I have argued above, neither could it have won. Probably World War II would have ended in some sort of draw and negotiated settlement, or would have continued on for a decade or two with occasional truces for breathing spells—not unlike the Napoleonic Wars. Or perhaps most likely is some combination of the two, in which the negotiated peace was uneasy and soon broken. What I imagine, then, is a very long and bloody war, longer and even more bloody than the one that really was fought, with protracted savage fighting in east and central Europe. . . .

Some contemporaries of course took a more alarmist view, especially immediately after the fall of France. A *Fortune* magazine survey of Americans in July 1940 found that 63 percent expected that an Axis triumph would bring an immediate German attempt to seize territory in the Western Hemisphere; 43 percent expected an imminent attack on the United States. American army generals feared a Nazi invasion of South America, and to forestall it wanted a major base in Trinidad. The continued resistance of Britain calmed such alarm for a while, though it was to be revived in somewhat similar form in 1942 with the anticipation of German aerial attacks on American cities and towns. Seacoast areas were allotted major antiaircraft units. Blackout regulations were widely enforced. School children were taught how to crouch against basement walls clenching corks between their teeth in the event of bombardment. Fiorello LaGuardia, then head of the Office of Civilian Defense, wanted 50 million gas masks.

All of this of course seems more than a little absurd in light of known—then as well as now—German capabilities. Not a single German bomb ever did fall in North or South America. Any kind of troop landing required naval and logistic support utterly beyond Hitler's reach. After all, it was not until two and a half years of war, with vast shipping and naval superiority, and a base in Britain, that the Allies felt able to cross even the English Channel in an invasion the other way. The bogeyman of Nazi troops in America had no more substance than that, several years later, of Russian landings. . . .

Very possibly a stalemate would not have marked the end of Hitler's ambitions, but that is not really the point. For some time at least, Germany would not have been supreme as an immediate menace to the United States. One further step in still another war would first be required—the ultimate victory over Britain and/or Russia, and if that should in fact be threatened, the United States could still have intervened *then,* and done so while allies existed. By the end of 1941 the pressure for such intervention had really passed for *that* war. Even those who most heavily stress the dangers of Nazi subversion in North and South America grant that "There still would be ominous eddies, but by the summer of 1940 the Nazi cause was in retreat in the new world." . . .

Finally, we ought to confront the argument that sheer morality demanded American intervention against Hitler. I have deliberately left this issue aside, defining our concern to be only with the structure of the international system, the relative weight of power facing the United States and its potential allies. My argument has accepted the "realist" one that fears the concentration of great power in other hands regardless of the apparent goals, ideology, or morality of those wielding that power. Concern with the morality of others' domestic politics is an expensive luxury, and evaluations all too subject to rapid change. . . .

Yet some would maintain that Hitler was just too evil to tolerate, that the United States had a moral duty to exterminate him and free those under his rule. . . .

Still, in this context Hitler must be compared with Stalin, who was hardly a saint, and who as a result of the complete German collapse in 1945 emerged from the war with an immensely greater empire. We must remember the terror and para-noid purges of his rule, and such examples of Stalinist humanity as the starvation of millions of kulaks. The worst Nazi crimes emerged only in 1943 and later at Nuremberg. German "medical experiments" and extermination camps were un-known to the world in 1941. Though the Hitler regime had anything but a savory reputation then, the moral argument too is essentially one made in hindsight, not a primary motivation at the time war was declared. . . .

If one rejects the purely moral justification of American entry into the war against Hitler, no very effective moral brief can then be made for the war in the Pacific. True, the Japanese were often unkind conquerors, though this can easily be exag-gerated by American memories of the Bataan death march and other horrors in the treatment of prisoners. Japanese occupation was often welcomed in the former Euro-pean colonies of Southeast Asia, and Japan retains some reservoir of good will for its assistance, late in the war, of indigenous liberation movements. In any case it is Hitler, not Tojo, who is customarily presented as the personification of evil. Possibly Americans did have some vague obligation to defend Chinese independence, but more clearly than in Europe the basis for American participation has to be *realpolitik.* The case has to be founded on a conviction that Japan was too powerful, too dan-gerously expansionist without any apparent restraint, to have been left alone. An extreme but widely accepted version is given by an early chronicler of the war:

> Japan in the spring and summer of 1941 would accept no diplomatic arrangement which did not give it everything that it might win in the Far East by aggression, without the trouble and expense of military campaigns.

The evidence, however, shows quite a different picture both of intent and capa-bility. Nor is it enough simply to assert that, because Japan attacked the United States at Pearl Harbor, America took no action to begin hostilities. This is formally true, but very deceptive. The Japanese attack would not have come but for the Amer-ican, British, and Dutch embargo on shipment of strategic raw materials to Japan. Japan's strike against the American naval base merely climaxed a long series of mutually antagonistic acts. In initiating economic sanctions against Japan the United States undertook actions that were widely recognized in Washington as carrying grave risk of war. To understand this requires a retracing of the events of the pre-ceding years. . . .

[The Japanese] apparently believed that their Empire's status as an independent world power depended on military equality with Russia and the United States in the Far East; that in turn depended on a hegemonical position, preferably economic but achieved by force if necessary, in the area of China. Though this seems strange now, an adequate view of Japanese policy in its contemporary context has to remember Tokyo's position as a latecomer to colonialism, in a world where France, Britain, and the United States all had their own spheres of influence.

Japanese forces made important initial gains by occupying most of the Chinese coast and most of China's industrial capacity, but with a trickle of American aid the nationalist armies hung on in the interior. By 1941 the Japanese armies were bogged down, and their progress greatly impeded by raw material shortages. . . .

Following the July 1941 freeze on Japanese assets in America, and the conse-quent cessation of shipment of oil, scrap iron, and other goods from the United

States, Japan's economy was in most severe straits and her power to wage war directly threatened. Her military leaders estimated that her reserves of oil, painfully accumulated in the late 1930s when the risk of just such a squeeze became evident, would last at most two years. She was also short of rice, tin, bauxite, nickel, rubber and other raw materials normally imported from the Dutch East Indies and Malaya. Negotiations with the Dutch authorities to supply these goods, plus extraordinary amounts of oil from the wells of Sumatra, had failed, ostensibly on the grounds that the Dutch feared the material would be reexported to the Axis in Europe. The United States, and the British and Dutch, made it quite clear that the embargo would be relaxed only in exchange for Japanese withdrawal from air and naval bases in Indochina (seized in order to prosecute better the war against China) and an agreement which would have meant the end of the Japanese involvement in China and the *abandonment* of any right to station troops in that country, not just a halt to the fighting. The purpose of the Western economic blockade was to force a favorable solution to the "China incident."

Under these conditions, the High Command of the Japanese navy demanded a "settlement" of one sort or other that would restore Japan's access to essential raw materials, most particularly oil. Without restored imports of fuel the fleet could not very long remain an effective fighting force. While the navy might have been willing to abandon the China campaign, it was utterly opposed to indefinite continuation of the status quo. Either raw material supplies had to be restored by a peaceful settlement with the Western powers, or access to the resources in Thailand, Malaya, and the Indies would have to be secured by force while Japan still retained the capabilities to do so.

If the navy demanded either settlement or war, most members of the Japanese elite were opposed to any settlement which would in effect have meant withdrawal from China. No serious thought was given to the possibility of peace with Chiang's [Chinese leader Chiang Kai-shek's] government, for it would have meant the end of all hopes of empire in East Asia and even, it was thought, of influence on the continent of Asia. . . .

Having decided against withdrawal from China, failed to negotiate a settlement with America, and decided on the necessity of seizing supplies from Southeast Asia, [the Japanese] were faced with the need to blunt what they regarded as the inevitable American response. Thus they launched a surprise attack on Pearl Harbor to destroy any American capability for immediate naval offensive. For all the audacity of the strike at Hawaii, its aims were limited: to destroy existing United States offensive capabilities in the Pacific by tactical surprise. The Japanese High Command hoped only to give its forces time to occupy the islands of the Southwest Pacific, to extract those islands' raw materials, and to turn the whole area into a virtually impregnable line of defense which could long delay an American counteroffensive and mete out heavy casualties when the counterattack did come. . . .

[T]he Japanese attack on Pearl Harbor, and for that matter on Southeast Asia, [was] not evidence of any unlimited expansionist policy or capability by the Japanese government. It was the consequence only of a much less ambitious goal, centering on an unwillingness to surrender the position that the Japanese had fought for years to establish in China. When that refusal met an equal American determination that Japan should give up many of her gains in China, the result was war. Japanese expansion into Southeast Asia originated less in strength than in weakness; it was predominantly instrumental to the China campaign, not a reach for another slice of global salami. Of course there were Japanese political and military leaders with wider ambitions, but they were not predominant in policy-making.

Throughout the 1930s the United States government had done little to resist the Japanese advance on the Asian continent. There were verbal protests, but little more. Even in early 1941 Washington apparently would have settled for a *halt* in China, and saw little danger of a much wider move into Southeast Asia. But the application of economic sanctions against Tokyo was very successful; it was obviously hurting, and the moderate Premier Prince Konoye proposed a direct meeting with Roosevelt to try to reach an understanding. At about that point the American Government seems to have been so impressed with its success that it rebuffed Konoye's approach, demanding that he agree in advance on terms of a settlement. Konoye's cabinet fell, and American observers concluded—on the basis of untestable evidence that sounded a bit like sour grapes—that he could not have enforced a "reasonable" settlement in Japanese politics anyway. Washington then raised the ante, calling for a Japanese *withdrawal* from all occupied territory in China. Several officials in the State Department proposed settling for a halt, giving China a breathing spell that would have served it better for several more years of war while America made its main effort in the Atlantic. Hull considered and then rejected their plan for such a *modus vivendi,* which rather closely resembled the second of two Japanese proposals ("Plan B") that represented Tokyo's last efforts. Economic sanctions continued to provide a warm moral glow for those who disapproved of trading with an aggressor, but they then served to make inevitable an otherwise avoidable war which was peripheral to American vital interests and for which the country was ill-prepared. . . .

On purely strategic grounds some observers might argue that the danger was not from Germany, Italy, or Japan alone, but rather from their combination in an aggressive alliance encircling the Western Hemisphere. The rhetoric of the time could suggest such a threat, but in fact the Tripartite Pact of Germany and Italy with Japan had become quite fragile. As explained [previously] . . . it was designed to deter United States entry into either of the then still-separate conflicts. The Japanese foreign minister in early 1941, Yosuke Matsuoka, had negotiated the Pact and was by far its strongest supporter in the cabinet. He tried to persuade his colleagues to follow the German attack on Russia with a similar act by Japan, but failed and was deposed. Thereafter the Pact faded in importance to the Tokyo government. In considering their subsequent negotiations with the United States the Japanese leaders were fully willing to sacrifice the Pact in return for the necessary economic concessions. Had Hitler managed to get himself into war with America in the Atlantic he could not successfully have invoked the Pact unless the Japanese clearly had seen war to be in their own interests.

Moreover, this drift away from Germany was, it has been well argued, adequately known to American and British officials—Ambassadors Grew and [Britain's Sir Robert] Craigie, Cordell Hull, Roosevelt and Churchill—thanks in part to American ability to crack the codes used in all Japanese secret cables. "After Matsuoka's fall . . . no Axis leader was able even to keep up the pretense of expecting Japanese intervention in behalf of Germany and Italy." In the context of late 1941, therefore, the prospects of close cooperation among Germany, Italy and Japan were not very menacing. Given their very diverse long-run interests, and Hitler's racial notions, a "permanent" alliance surely does not seem very plausible. A special irony of the situation is that Roosevelt was particularly anxious to see Hitler beaten first, and that British and Dutch colonial possessions in Southeast Asia, which seemed essential to the European war, be unmolested. His belated insistence on Japanese evacuation from China then pushed the Axis back together and endangered his other goals. . . .

In retrospect, the fear that America would be left alone in the world against two great victorious empires in Europe and Asia seems terribly exaggerated. Clear-cut victory was not in prospect for either, nor does the assumption that they could long have maintained a close alliance seem especially plausible. The critical American mistake may well have been in backing the Japanese into a corner, for without war in the Pacific the American conflict with Germany very possibly could have been held to limited naval engagements, but no clash of ground troops. In short, we might at most have fought a limited war.

These conclusions are highly speculative; the situation of the time cannot be reproduced for another run, searching for an alternate future. Perhaps I underestimate the risks that an American determination to avoid war would have entailed. On the other hand, the proposition that the war was unnecessary—in a real sense premature, fought before the need was sufficiently clearly established, though the need might well have become apparent later—is worth considering. Just possibly the isolationists were right in their essential perspective. . . .

I do not imagine that the United States should have carried on blithely in 1941 as though nothing were happening elsewhere in the world. Complete isolation would have been much worse than intervention. All Americans would agree that American strategic interests required substantial assistance to the belligerents against Germany. Both Britain and Russia had to be preserved as independent and powerful states. With a little less certainty I would also grant the need to keep a significant portion of China viable.

It seems, however, that those goals could have been achieved by the belligerents themselves, with great American economic and noncombatant military aid. As insurance, American rearmament had to go on. A sustained defense effort not less than what was later accepted during the cold war would have been required. That would imply 10 percent of the American GNP devoted to military purposes, as compared with about that amount actually expended in 1941 and a mere one and one-half percent in 1939. That much, incidentally, would with Lend-Lease have been quite enough to revive the economy from the depression and assuredly does not imply idle resources.

With this prescription I find myself at odds with the extreme critics of Roosevelt's policy, men who spoke at that time and again, briefly, after the war. Most of the President's military and economic acts seem appropriate and, in deed, necessary. I have no quarrel with the decisions for rearmament or to institute Selective Service, with revision of the Neutrality Act to permit "cash-and-carry" by belligerents (effectively by the Allies only), with the destroyers-for-bases exchange, with Lend-Lease, or with the decision to convoy American vessels as far as Iceland. Even the famous "shoot-on-sight" order, even as interpreted to allow American destroyers to seek out the sight of U-boats, seems necessary if the convoys were to be protected on the first stage of the critical lifeline to Britain. I do have some

serious reservations about the way in which those decisions were publicly justified. . . . But the content of those decisions seems fully defensible. And irritating
as they surely were, Hitler would probably have continued to tolerate them in
preference to more active American involvement.

Only two major exceptions to the content of American policy in 1941 appear
worth registering. One is the vote by Congress in mid-November 1941, at the President's behest, removing nearly all the remaining restrictions of the Neutrality Act.
It permitted American ships to carry supplies all the way across the Atlantic, instead of merely as far as Iceland. This almost certainly would have been too much
for Hitler to bear. . . .

The other and still more serious exception I take is with President Roosevelt's
policy toward Japan as described [previously]. . . . It was neither necessary nor desirable for him to have insisted on a Japanese withdrawal from China. An agreement
for a standstill would have been enough, and he did not make an honest diplomatic
attempt to achieve it. He refused to meet Prince Konoye in the Pacific to work out a
compromise, and after Konye's fall he rejected, on Hull's advice, a draft proposal
that could have served as a basis for compromise with the Japanese. We have no
guarantee that agreement could have been reached, but here was at least some
chance and the effort was not made. . . .

It would of course be unfair and inaccurate to trace all the developments cited
in this chapter, and especially the adoption of interventionist policies, only back to
1940, just as it is wrong to think they emerged full-blown at the beginning of the
cold war. One can find roots in our earlier Caribbean policy, in Woodrow Wilson's
acts, in the war of 1898, and even earlier. But World War II, rather like mono-
sodium glutamate, made pungent a host of unsavory flavors that had until then
been relatively subdued. We cannot really extirpate contemporary "global policeman" conceptions from American thinking unless we understand how, in World
War II, they developed and became ingrained.

Preface to the Twenty-fifth Anniversary Edition

[W]here did the book come from in my personal history? As I stated clearly in the
original preface, it stemmed from my experience, as a scholar of American foreign
policy, of the Vietnam War. Published at the height of the war, it originated from my
disgust and represented my effort to understand why the war had happened and persisted. I believed then, and still do, that such standard interpretations as bureaucratic
inertia on Pennsylvania Avenue, economic interest on Wall Street, or anti-communist
ideology on Main Street, constitute at best partial explanations that missed a broader
kind of ideological underpinning. I would characterize that ideological underpinning
as a particular kind of "realist" view of international power politics that exaggerated
both the necessity and the possibility of effectively exerting American military power
all over the globe. A shorthand label for such a view now comes under the expression
"imperial overstretch." And I believe that view was, for many Americans, born out of
the experience of World War II. . . .

The fundamental problem with the World War II experience—rightly judged in
some degree to be a success—was, in my view, that it led to an exaggerated sense of

American power and wisdom; *hubris,* in effect. It seemed such a success that the limits and the particular circumstances of that success were ignored in subsequent policy. And that hubris led to the intervention in Vietnam, a military expedition for which the motivation and the need were far less clear than in World War II. Consequently, the national will for a total commitment in Vietnam was, properly, lacking, and thus the prospects for that intervention were poor. In other words, the construction put upon the World War II experience was an invitation to subsequent failure; to understand that failure, and to avoid repeating it, required some deconstruction of World War II's lessons. It required speculating about whether active American participation in the war could have been avoided, and if so, what the costs and benefits of such an alternative might have been. It was a task for historical evaluation as well as a practically oriented form of theoretical discussion.

FURTHER READING

Irvine H. Anderson, *The Standard-Vacuum Oil Company and United States East Asia Policy* (1975)
Michael Barnhart, *Japan Prepares for Total War* (1987)
———, "The Origins of the Second World War in Asia and the Pacific: Synthesis Impossible?" *Diplomatic History,* 20 (1996), 241–260
Charles A. Beard, *President Roosevelt and the Coming of the War, 1941* (1948)
Michael Beschloss, *Kennedy and Roosevelt* (1980)
Günter Bischof and Robert L. Dupont, eds., *The Pacific War Revisited* (1997)
Conrad Black, *Franklin Delano Roosevelt* (2003)
Dorothy Borg, *The United States and the Far Eastern Crisis of 1933–1938* (1964)
———and Shumpei Okamoto, eds., *Pearl Harbor as History* (1973)
Richard D. Burns and Edward M. Bennett, eds., *Diplomats in Crisis* (1974)
Robert J. C. Butow, *The John Doe Associates* (1974)
Steven Casey, *Cautious Crusade* (2001) (on FDR and public opinion)
Thurston Clarke, *Pearl Harbor Ghosts* (2000)
J. Garry Clifford and Samuel R. Spencer Jr., *The First Peacetime Draft* (1986)
Warren I. Cohen, *America's Response to China* (2000)
Wayne S. Cole, *Roosevelt and the Isolationists, 1932–1945* (1983)
Hilary Conroys and Harry Wray, eds., *Pearl Harbor Reexamined* (1990)
James Crowley, *Japan's Quest for Autonomy* (1966)
Robert Dallek, *Franklin D. Roosevelt and American Foreign Policy* (1979)
Kenneth R. Davis, *FDR* (1993)
Roger Dingman, *Power in the Pacific* (1976)
Robert A. Divine, *The Reluctant Belligerent* (1979)
——— and John E. Wilz, *From Isolation to War* (1991)
John Dower, *Japan in War and Peace* (1993)
Barbara Rearden Farnham, *Roosevelt and the Munich Crisis* (2000)
Herbert Feis, *The Road to Pearl Harbor* (1950)
Frank Freidel, *Franklin D. Roosevelt: A Rendezvous with Destiny* (1990)
Lloyd Gardner, *Economic Aspects of New Deal Diplomacy* (1964)
Martin Gilbert, *Winston S. Churchill: Finest Hour, 1939–1941* (1983)
Patrick Hearden, *Roosevelt Confronts Hitler* (1987)
Waldo H. Heinrichs Jr., *American Ambassador* (1966) (on Joseph Grew)
Saburō Ienaga, *The Pacific War* (1978)

Akira Iriye, *The Origins of the Second World War in Asia and the Pacific* (1987)
———, *Pearl Harbor and the Coming of the Pacific War* (1999)
——— and Warren Cohen, eds., *American, Chinese, and Japanese Perspectives on Wartime Asia, 1931–1949* (1990)
Manfred Jonas, *Isolationism in America* (1966)
Kenneth P. Jones, *U.S. Diplomats in Europe, 1919–1941* (1981)
Charles P. Kindleberger, *The World in Depression, 1929–1939* (1973)
Walter LaFeber, *The Clash* (1997) (on Japan)
Robert D. Lowe, ed., *Pearl Harbor Revisited* (1994)
Mark A. Lowenthal, *Leadership and Indecision* (1988) (on war planning)
Thomas R. Maddux, *Years of Estrangement* (1980) (on the Soviet Union)
Joseph A. Maiolo and Robert Boyce, eds., *The Origins of World War Two* (2003)
Frederick W. Marks III, *Wind over Sand* (1988) (on FDR)
Jonathan Marshall, *To Have and Have Not* (1995) (on raw materials and war)
Gorden Martel, ed., *The Origins of the Second World War Reconsidered* (1986)
James W. Morley, ed., *Japan's Road to the Pacific War: The Final Confrontation* (1994)
Norman Moss, *19 Weeks* (2003)
Charles Neu, *The Troubled Encounter* (1975)
Arnold Offner, *The Origins of the Second World War* (1975)
Stephen Pelz, *Race to Pearl Harbor* (1974)
John Prados, *Combined Fleet Decoded* (2001)
Gordon W. Prange, *At Dawn We Slept: The Untold Story of Pearl Harbor* (1981)
———, *Pearl Harbor* (1986)
David Reynolds, *The Creation of the Anglo-American Alliance, 1937–41* (1982)
———, *From Munich to Pearl Harbor* (2001)
Emily S. Rosenberg, *A Date Which Will Live: Pearl Harbor in American Memory* (2003)
Michael Schaller, *The U.S. Crusade in China, 1938–1945* (1978)
Arthur M. Schlesinger, Jr., "The Man of the Century," *American Heritage,* May/June 1994, 82–93 (on FDR)
David F. Schmitz, *The United States and Fascist Italy, 1922–1940* (1988)
Paul W. Schroeder, *Axis Alliance and Japanese-American Relations, 1941* (1958)
Raymond Sontag, *A Broken World, 1919–1939* (1971)
Richard Steele, *Propaganda in an Open Society* (1985) (on FDR and the media)
Youli Sun, *China and the Origins of the Pacific War* (1993)
Charles C. Tansill, *Back Door to War* (1952)
James C. Thomson Jr. et al., *Sentimental Imperialists* (1981)
John Toland, *Infamy: Pearl Harbor and Its Aftermath* (1982)
Cornelis A. Van Minnen and John F. Sears, eds., *FDR and His Contemporaries* (1992) (on foreign views)
D. C. Watt, *How War Came* (1989)
Lawrence Wittner, *Rebels Against War* (1984)
Roberta Wohlstetter, *Pearl Harbor: Warning and Decision* (1962)

Defeating the Axis, Planning the Peace: The Second World War

After American entry into the Second World War, Great Britain, the United States, and the Soviet Union formed the fifty-nation Grand Alliance, which in time forced the Axis to surrender. Through extensive correspondence and summit meetings, the Allied leaders Winston S. Churchill, Franklin D. Roosevelt, and Joseph Stalin not only plotted military strategy to defeat Germany, Italy, and Japan but also shaped plans for the postwar era. Big Three decisions about war and peace and the upending results of the war transformed the international system: power shifted from some states to others, wartime destruction battered economies, decolonization eroded empires, political instability in both defeated and victorious nations fractured, new world organizations emerged, and the atomic bomb terrified all. Soon after defeating the Axis, the Grand Alliance splintered, already having generated the Cold War.

Although the Allies cooperated sufficiently to win the war, they bickered over both war strategy and the postwar structure of international relations. Legacies of distrust from hostile prewar relations and opposing ideologies endured. Allied goals also differed: Britain sought to salvage its empire, to blunt Soviet expansionism, and to direct European affairs; the Soviet Union coveted the Baltic states and friendly communist governments in Eastern Europe; and the United States anticipated new influence, especially in the Pacific, worked for the expansion of capitalism, and viewed itself as first among what Roosevelt called the postwar world's "Four Policemen."

The Allies exchanged sharp views during the war on the opening of a second, western military front. They squabbled over the timely availability of U.S. supplies under the Lend-Lease program. They suspected each other of seeking separate peace arrangements. They jockeyed for political position in the countries liberated from Nazi and Japanese control, such as Poland and China. The Allies also debated the colonial question—what would become of French Indochina, for example? They created the United Nations, the World Bank, and the International Monetary Fund. Then they competed for influence in the new bodies, in the process shattering unity. All the while, three individuals of exceptional stature—Churchill, Roosevelt, and Stalin— alternately clashed and cooperated in extraordinary episodes of personal diplomacy.

The foreign policy of President Franklin D. Roosevelt stands at the center of any discussion of the Grand Alliance. Some scholars treat his record favorably, emphasizing his grasp of political realities, his understanding of power, his deft handling of Churchill and Stalin to keep the alliance together, his progressive anti-colonialism, and his skill in negotiating the unique complexities of conducting a global war. After all, the Allies did crush powerful enemies and sketched out the future international system. Some historians argue, furthermore, that the United States used the opportunity of war to weaken the British Empire, to expand American interests, including overseas bases and new markets, and to thwart a rising political left. Under Roosevelt's leadership, then, the United States developed a larger American sphere of influence while offering to honor the spheres of the other great powers. Without recognized spheres, some defenders of Roosevelt suggest, the world would have descended deeper into chaos than it in fact did.

Roosevelt's management of wartime and postwar issues has also drawn considerable criticism. Some writers believe that the president made military decisions without adequately weighing their long-term political impact. Some hold Roosevelt responsible for the postwar Soviet domination of Eastern Europe, faulting him for not using American power to stall Stalin's aggressive push into neighboring nations. The president's performance at summit conferences has also drawn fire, in part because many of the agreements did not hold, and in the case of the Yalta Conference, Roosevelt's deteriorating health may have hindered his decision making. Critics too challenge his spheres-of-influence approach to world politics, noting that it trampled on weaker nations. Others charge that the president, sensitive to isolationist opinion, failed to prepare the American people for the global role they would have to play after the war. Finally, some claim that Roosevelt deceived people and ignored his advisers, holding his cards close to his vest, thinking that he would eventually iron out the imperfections and compromises that wartime diplomacy momentarily required. But for Roosevelt, time ran out; he died in April 1945 just months before the war ended. Thus is prompted a perennial question in history. What if he had lived?

🌐 D O C U M E N T S

The timing of the opening of a second front in Europe troubled Allied relations until June 6, 1944, when British, American, and Canadian troops crossed the English Channel to attack German forces in France. Until that time, bearing the brunt of the European war, the Soviets pressed for action. In Document 1, a U.S. report on the Washington, D.C., meeting of May 30, 1942, between President Franklin D. Roosevelt and Soviet foreign minister V. M. Molotov, FDR promised a second front before year's end. But delays set in. Marshal Joseph Stalin's letter of June 24, 1943, to Churchill reveals the embittered Soviet leader's impatience. A Soviet record, it is reprinted here as Document 2. At the Allied conference held at Teheran, Iran, Roosevelt and Stalin discussed the president's concept of "Four Policemen." The American record of the Roosevelt-Stalin meeting on November 29, 1943, is reprinted as Document 3. Allied interest in spheres of influence is illustrated by Document 4—the Churchill-Stalin percentages agreement, which delineated British and Soviet roles in liberated nations. This account of the Moscow meeting of October 1944 is drawn from Churchill's memoirs.

Document 5 and Document 6—agreements struck at the Yalta Conference of February 4–11, 1945—demonstrate a high degree of Allied compromise and unity on many issues as the Big Three neared victory over Germany. In Document 7, a letter dated April 4, 1945, Roosevelt chided Stalin for charging that U.S. officials were negotiating with German authorities in Switzerland behind Soviet backs. Just before Roosevelt's death, in response to Churchill's warnings about Soviet manipulation of Polish politics, the president wrote the prime minister a reassuring letter of April 11, 1945, reprinted here as Document 8.

1. Roosevelt Promises a Second Front, 1942

Mr. [V. M.] Molotov . . . remarked that, though the problem of the second front was both military and political, it was predominantly political. There was an essential difference between the situation in 1942 and what it might be in 1943. In 1942 Hitler was the master of all Europe save a few minor countries. He was the chief enemy of everyone. To be sure, as was devoutly to be hoped, the Russians might hold and fight on all through 1942. But it was only right to look at the darker side of the picture. On the basis of his continental dominance, Hitler might throw in such reinforcements in manpower and material that the Red Army might *not* be able to hold out against the Nazis. Such a development would produce a serious situation which we must face. The Soviet front would become secondary, the Red Army would be weakened, and Hitler's strength would be correspondingly greater, since he would have at his disposal not only more troops, but also the foodstuffs and raw materials of the Ukraine and the oil-wells of the Caucasus. In such circumstances the outlook would be much less favorable for all hands, and he would not pretend that such developments were all outside the range of possibility. . . .

Mr. Molotov therefore put this question frankly: could we undertake such offensive action as would draw off 40 German divisions which would be, to tell the truth, distinctly second-rate outfits? If the answer should be in the affirmative, the war would be decided in 1942. If negative, the Soviets would fight on alone, doing their best, and no man would expect more from them than that. He had not, Mr. Molotov added, received any positive answer in London. Mr. [Winston] Churchill had proposed that he should return through London on his homeward journey from Washington, and had promised Mr. Molotov a more concrete answer on his second visit. Mr. Molotov admitted he realized that the British would have to bear the brunt of the action if a second front were created, but he also was cognizant of the role the United States plays and what influence this country exerts in questions of major strategy. . . .

The difficulties, Mr. Molotov urged, would not be any less in 1943. The chances of success were actually better at present while the Russians still have a solid front. "If you postpone your decision," he said, "you will have eventually to bear the brunt of the war, and if Hitler becomes the undisputed master of the continent, next year will unquestionably be tougher than this one."

The President then put to General [George C.] Marshall the query whether developments were clear enough so that we could say to Mr. Stalin that we are preparing a second front. "Yes," replied the General. The President then authorized Mr. Molotov to inform Mr. Stalin that we expect the formation of a second front this year.

This document can be found in U.S. Department of State, *Foreign Relations of the United States: Diplomatic Papers, 1942* (Washington D.C.: Government Printing Office, 1961), III, 576–577.

2. Marshal Joseph Stalin Conveys Impatience over a Second Front, 1943

From your [Winston Churchill's] messages of last year and this I gained the conviction that you and the President [FDR] were fully aware of the difficulties of organising such an operation and were preparing the invasion accordingly, with due regard to the difficulties and the necessary exertion of forces and means. Even last year you told me that a large-scale invasion of Europe by Anglo-American troops would be effected in 1943. In the Aide-Memoire handed to V. M. Molotov on June 10, 1942, you wrote:

> Finally, and most important of all, we are concentrating our maximum effort on the organization and preparation of a large-scale invasion of the Continent of Europe by British and American forces in 1943. We are setting no limit to the scope and objectives of this campaign, which will be carried out in the first instance by over a million men, British and American, with air forces of appropriate strength.

Early this year you twice informed me, on your own behalf and on behalf of the President, of decisions concerning an Anglo-American invasion of Western Europe intended to "divert strong German land and air forces from the Russian front." You had set yourself the task of bringing Germany to her knees as early as 1943, and named September as the latest date for the invasion.

In your message of January 26 you wrote:

> We have been in conference with our military advisers and have decided on the operations which are to be undertaken by the American and British forces in the first nine months of 1943. We wish to inform you of our intentions at once. We believe that these operations together with your powerful offensive, may well bring Germany to her knees in 1943.

In your next message, which I received on February 12, you wrote, specifying the date of the invasion of Western Europe, decided on by you and the President:

> We are also pushing preparations to the limit of our resources for a cross-Channel operation in August, in which British and United States units would participate. Here again, shipping and assault-landing craft will be the limiting factors. If the operation is delayed by the weather or other reasons, it will be prepared with stronger forces for September.

Last February, when you wrote to me about those plans and the date for invading Western Europe, the difficulties of that operation were greater than they are now. Since then the Germans have suffered more than one defeat: they were pushed back by our troops in the South, where they suffered appreciable loss; they were beaten in North Africa and expelled by the Anglo-American troops; in submarine warfare, too, the Germans found themselves in a bigger predicament than ever, while Anglo-American superiority increased substantially; it is also known that the Americans and British have won air superiority in Europe and that their navies and mercantile marines have grown in power.

It follows that the conditions for opening a second front in Western Europe during 1943, far from deteriorating, have, indeed, greatly improved.

This document can be found in Ministry of Foreign Affairs of the U.S.S.R., *Correspondence Between the Chairman of the Council of Ministers of the U.S.S.R. and the President of the U.S.A. and the Prime Minister of Great Britain During the Great Patriotic War of 1941–1945* (Moscow: Foreign Languages Publishing House, 1957), pp. 74–76.

That being so, the Soviet Government could not have imagined that the British and U.S. Governments would revise the decision to invade Western Europe, which they had adopted early this year. In fact, the Soviet Government was fully entitled to expect the Anglo-American decision would be carried out, that appropriate preparations were under way and that the second front in Western Europe would at last be opened in 1943. . . .

So when you now declare: "I cannot see how a great British defeat and slaughter would aid the Soviet armies," is it not clear that a statement of this kind in relation to the Soviet Union is utterly groundless and directly contradicts your previous and responsible decisions, listed above, about extensive and vigorous measures by the British and Americans to organise the invasion this year, measures on which the complete success of the operation should hinge.

I shall not enlarge on the fact that this [ir?]responsible decision, revoking your previous decisions on the invasion of Western Europe, was reached by you and the President without Soviet participation and without inviting its representatives to the Washington conference, although you cannot but be aware that the Soviet Union's role in the war against Germany and its interest in the problems of the second front are great enough.

There is no need to say that the Soviet Government cannot become reconciled to this disregard of vital Soviet interests in the war against the common enemy.

You say that you "quite understand" my disappointment. I must tell you that the point here is not just the disappointment of the Soviet Government, but the preservation of its confidence in its Allies, a confidence which is being subjected to severe stress. One should not forget that it is a question of saving millions of lives in the occupied areas of Western Europe and Russia and of reducing the enormous sacrifices of the Soviet armies, compared with which the sacrifices of the Anglo-American armies are insignificant.

3. Roosevelt and Stalin Discuss the "Four Policemen" at the Teheran Conference, 1943

The President then said the question of a post-war organization to preserve peace had not been fully explained and dealt with and he would like to discuss with the Marshal the prospect of some organization based on the United Nations.

The President then outlined the following general plan:

1. There would be a large organization composed of some 35 members of the United Nations which would meet periodically at different places, discuss and make recommendations to a smaller body.

Marshal Stalin inquired whether this organization was to be world-wide or European, to which the President replied, world-wide.

The President continued that there would be set up an executive committee composed of the Soviet Union, the United States, United Kingdom and China, together

This document can be found in U.S. Department of State, *Foreign Relations of the United States: Diplomatic Papers, The Conferences at Cairo and Teheran, 1943* (Washington, D.C.: Government Printing Office, 1961), pp. 530–532.

with two additional European states, one South American, one Near East, one Far Eastern country, and one British Dominion. He mentioned that Mr. Churchill did not like this proposal for the reason that the British Empire only had two votes. This Executive Committee would deal with all non-military questions such as agriculture, food, health, and economic questions, as well as the setting up of an International Committee. This Committee would likewise meet in various places.

Marshal Stalin inquired whether this body would have the right to make decisions binding on the nations of the world.

The President replied, yes and no. It could make recommendations for settling disputes with the hope that the nations concerned would be guided thereby, but that, for example, he did not believe the Congress of the United States would accept as binding a decision of such a body. The President then turned to the third organization which he termed "The Four Policemen," namely, the Soviet Union, United States, Great Britain, and China. This organization would have the power to deal immediately with any threat to the peace and any sudden emergency which requires this action. He went on to say that in 1935, when Italy attacked Ethiopia, the only machinery in existence was the League of Nations. He personally had begged France to close the Suez Canal, but they instead referred it to the League which disputed the question and in the end did nothing. The result was that the Italian Armies went through the Suez Canal and destroyed Ethiopia. The President pointed out that had the machinery of the Four Policemen, which he had in mind, been in existence, it would have been possible to close the Suez Canal. The President then summarized briefly the idea that he had in mind.

Marshal Stalin said that he did not think that the small nations of Europe would like the organization composed of the Four Policemen. He said, for example, that a European state would probably resent China having the right to apply certain machinery to it. And in any event, he did not think China would be very powerful at the end of the war. He suggested as a possible alternative, the creation of a European or a Far Eastern Committee and a European or a Worldwide organization. He said that in the European Commission there would be the United States, Great Britain, the Soviet Union and possibly one other European state.

The President said that the idea just expressed by Marshal Stalin was somewhat similar to Mr. Churchill's idea of a Regional Committee, one for Europe, one for the Far East, and one for the Americas. Mr. Churchill had also suggested that the United States be a member of the European Commission, but he doubted if the United States Congress would agree to the United States' participation in an exclusively European Committee which might be able to force the dispatch of American troops to Europe.

The President added that it would take a terrible crisis such as at present before Congress would ever agree to that step.

Marshal Stalin pointed out that the world organization suggested by the President, and in particular the Four Policemen, might also require the sending of American troops to Europe.

The President pointed out that he had only envisaged the sending of American planes and ships to Europe, and that England and the Soviet Union would have to handle the land armies in the event of any future threat to the peace. He went on to say that if the Japanese had not attacked the United States, he doubted very much if it would have been possible to send any American forces to Europe.

4. British Prime Minister Winston S. Churchill and Stalin Cut Their Percentages Deal, 1944

The moment was apt for business, so I [Churchill] said, "Let us settle about our affairs in the Balkans. Your armies are in Rumania and Bulgaria. We have interests, missions, and agents there. Don't let us get at cross-purposes in small ways. So far as Britain and Russia are concerned, how would it do for you to have ninety per cent predominance in Rumania, for us to have ninety per cent of the say in Greece, and go fifty-fifty about Yugoslavia?" While this was being translated I wrote out on a half-sheet of paper:

Rumania	
Russia	90%
The others	10%
Greece	
Great Britain (in accord with U.S.A.)	90%
Russia	10%
Yugoslavia	50–50%
Hungary	50–50%
Bulgaria	
Russia	75%
The others	25%

I pushed this across to Stalin, who had by then heard the translation. There was a slight pause. Then he took his blue pencil and made a large tick upon it, and passed it back to us. It was all settled in no more time than it takes to set down.

Of course, we had long and anxiously considered our point, and were only dealing with immediate war-time arrangements. All larger questions were reserved on both sides for what we then hoped would be a peace table when the war was won.

After this there was a long silence. The pencilled paper lay in the centre of the table. At length I said, "Might it not be thought rather cynical if it seemed we had disposed of these issues, so fateful to millions of people, in such an offhand manner? Let us burn the paper." "No, you keep it," said Stalin.

5. The Yalta Protocol of Proceedings, 1945

I. World Organization

It was decided:

1. that a United Nations Conference on the proposed world organization should be summoned for Wednesday, 25th April, 1945, and should be held in the United States of America.
2. the Nations to be invited to this Conference should be:
   a. the United Nations as they existed on the 8th February, 1945; and

---

Document 4 is an excerpt from *Triumph and Tragedy,* Volume VI of *The Second World War.* Copyright © 1953 by Houghton Mifflin Co., renewed 1981 by The Honourable Lady Sarah Audley and The Honourable Lady Soames. Reprinted by permission of Houghton Mifflin Co. All rights reserved.

Document 5 can be found in U.S. Department of State, *Foreign Relations of the United States: The Conferences at Malta and Yalta,* 1945 (Washington, D.C.: Government Printing Office, 1955), pp. 975–982.

b. such of the Associated Nations as have declared war on the common enemy by 1st March, 1945. (For this purpose by the term "Associated Nations" was meant the eight Associated Nations and Turkey). When the Conference on World Organization is held, the delegates of the United Kingdom and United States of America will support a proposal to admit to original membership two Soviet Socialist Republics, i.e. the Ukraine and White Russia.

3. that the United States Government on behalf of the Three Powers should consult the Government of China and the French Provisional Government in regard to decisions taken at the present Conference concerning the proposed World Organization.

4. that the text of the invitation to be issued to all the nations which would take part in the United Nations Conference should be as follows:

Invitation

The Government of the United States of America, on behalf of itself and of the Governments of the United Kingdom, the Union of Soviet Socialist Republics, and the Republic of China and the Provisional Government of the French Republic, invite the Government of ———— to send representatives to a Conference of the United Nations to be held on 25th April, 1945, or soon thereafter, at San Francisco in the United States of America to prepare a Charter for a General International Organization for the maintenance of international peace and security.

The above named governments suggest that the Conference consider as affording a basis for such a Charter the Proposals for the Establishment of a General International Organization, which were made public last October as a result of the Dumbarton Oaks Conference, and which have now been supplemented by the following provisions for Section C of Chapter VI:

C. Voting

1. Each member of the Security Council should have one vote.
2. Decisions of the Security Council on procedural matters should be made by an affirmative vote of seven members.
3. Decisions of the Security Council on all other matters should be made by an affirmative vote of seven members including the concurring votes of the permanent members; provided that, in decisions under Chapter VIII, Section A, and under the second sentence of paragraph 1 of Chapter VIII, Section C, a party to a dispute should abstain from voting.

Further information as to arrangements will be transmitted subsequently. In the event that the Government of ———— desires in advance of the Conference to present views or comments concerning the proposals, the Government of the United States of America will be pleased to transmit such views and comments to the other participating Governments.

Territorial Trusteeship.   It was agreed that the five Nations which will have permanent seats on the Security Council should consult each other prior to the United Nations Conference on the question of territorial trusteeship.

The acceptance of this recommendation is subject to its being made clear that territorial trusteeship will only apply to (a) existing mandates of the League of Nations; (b) territories detached from the enemy as a result of the present war; (c) any other territory which might voluntarily be placed under trusteeship; and (d) no discussion of actual territories is contemplated at the forthcoming United Nations Conference or in the preliminary consultations, and it will be a matter for subsequent agreement which territories within the above categories will be placed under trusteeship.

II. Declaration on Liberated Europe

The following declaration has been approved:

The Premier of the Union of Soviet Socialist Republics, the Prime Minister of the United Kingdom and the President of the United States of America have consulted with each other in the common interests of the peoples of their countries and those of liberated Europe. They jointly declare their mutual agreement to concert during the temporary period of instability in liberated Europe the policies of their three governments in assisting the peoples of the former Axis satellite states of Europe to solve by democratic means their pressing political and economic problems.

The establishment of order in Europe and the rebuilding of national economic life must be achieved by processes which will enable the liberated peoples to destroy the last vestiges of Nazism and Fascism and to create democratic institutions of their own choice. This is a principle of the Atlantic Charter—the right of all peoples to choose the form of government under which they will live—the restoration of sovereign rights and self-government to those peoples who have been forcibly deprived of them by the aggressor nations.

To foster the conditions in which the liberated peoples may exercise these rights, the three governments will jointly assist the people in any European liberated state or former Axis satellite state in Europe where in their judgment conditions require (a) to establish conditions of internal peace; (b) to carry out emergency measures for the relief of distressed peoples; (c) to form interim governmental authorities broadly representative of all democratic elements in the population and pledged to the earliest possible establishment through free elections of governments responsible to the will of the people; and (d) to facilitate where necessary the holding of such elections.

The three governments will consult the other United Nations and provisional authorities or other governments in Europe when matters of direct interest to them are under consideration.

When, in the opinion of the three governments, conditions in any European liberated state or any former Axis satellite state in Europe make such action necessary, they will immediately consult together on the measures necessary to discharge the joint responsibilities set forth in this declaration.

By this declaration we reaffirm our faith in the principles of the Atlantic Charter, our pledges in the Declaration by the United Nations, and our determination to build in cooperation with other peace-loving nations world order under law, dedicated to peace, security, freedom and general well-being of all mankind.

In issuing this declaration, the Three Powers express the hope that the Provisional Government of the French Republic may be associated with them in the procedure suggested.

III. Dismemberment of Germany

It was agreed that Article 12 (a) of the Surrender Terms for Germany should be amended as follows:

> The United Kingdom, the United States of America and the Union of Soviet Socialist Republics shall possess supreme authority with respect to Germany. In the exercise of such authority they will take such steps, including the complete disarmament demilitarization and dismemberment of Germany as they deem requisite for future peace and security. . . .

IV. Zone of Occupation for the French and Control Council for Germany

It was agreed that a zone in Germany, to be occupied by the French Forces, should be allocated to France. This zone would be formed out of the British and American zones and its extent would be settled by the British and Americans in consultation with the French Provisional Government.

It was also agreed that the French Provisional Government should be invited to become a member of the Allied Control Council of Germany.

V. Reparation

The heads of the three governments agreed as follows:

1. Germany must pay in kind for the losses caused by her to the Allied nations in the course of the war. Reparations are to be received in the first instance by those countries which have borne the main burden of the war, have suffered the heaviest losses and have organized victory over the enemy.
2. Reparation in kind to be exacted from Germany in three following forms:
   a. Removals within 2 years from the surrender of Germany or the cessation of organized resistance from the national wealth of Germany located on the territory of Germany herself as well as outside her territory (equipment, machine-tools, ships, rolling stock, German investments abroad, shares of industrial, transport and other enterprises in Germany etc.), these removals to be carried out chiefly for purpose of destroying the war potential of Germany.
   b. Annual deliveries of goods from current production for a period to be fixed.
   c. Use of German labor.
3. For the working out on the above principles of a detailed plan for exaction of reparation from Germany, an Allied Reparation Commission will be set up in Moscow. It will consist of three representatives—one from the Union of Soviet Socialist Republics, one from the United Kingdom and one from the United States of America.
4. With regard to the fixing of the total sum of the reparation as well as the distribution of it among the countries which suffered from the German aggression the Soviet and American delegations agreed as follows:

> The Moscow Reparation Commission should take in its initial studies as a basis for discussion the suggestion of the Soviet Government that the total sum of the reparation in accordance with the points (a) and (b) of the paragraph 2 should be 20 billion dollars and that 50% of it should go to the Union of Soviet Socialist Republics.

The British delegation was of the opinion that pending consideration of the reparation question by the Moscow Reparation Commission no figures of reparation should be mentioned.

The above Soviet-American proposal has been passed to the Moscow Reparation Commission as one of the proposals to be considered by the Commission.

VI. Major War Criminals

The Conference agreed that the question of the major war criminals should be the subject of enquiry by the three Foreign Secretaries for report in due course after the close of the Conference.

VII. Poland

The following Declaration on Poland was agreed by the Conference:

> A new situation has been created in Poland as a result of her complete liberation by the Red Army. This calls for the establishment of a Polish Provisional Government which can be more broadly based than was possible before the recent liberation of [the] Western part of Poland. The Provisional Government which is now functioning in Poland should therefore be reorganized on a broader democratic basis with the inclusion of democratic leaders from Poland itself and from Poles abroad. This new Government should then be called the Polish Provisional Government of National Unity.
>
> M. Molotov, Mr. Harriman and Sir A. Clark Kerr are authorized as a commission to consult in the first instance in Moscow with members of the present Provisional Government and with other Polish democratic leaders from within Poland and from abroad, with a view to the reorganization of the present Government along the above lines. This Polish Provisional Government of National Unity shall be pledged to the holding of free and unfettered elections as soon as possible on the basis of universal suffrage and secret ballot. In these elections all democratic and anti-Nazi parties shall have the right to take part and to put forward candidates.
>
> When a Polish Provisional Government of National Unity has been properly formed in conformity with the above, the Government of the U.S.S.R., which now maintains diplomatic relations with the present Provisional Government of Poland, and the Government of the United Kingdom and the Government of the United States of America will establish diplomatic relations with the new Polish Provisional Government of National Unity, and will exchange Ambassadors by whose reports the respective Governments will be kept informed about the situation in Poland.
>
> The three Heads of Government consider that the Eastern frontier of Poland should follow the Curzon Line with digressions from it in some regions of five to eight kilometers in favor of Poland. They recognize that Poland must receive substantial accession of territory in the North and West. They feel that the opinion of the new Polish Provisional Government of National Unity should be sought in due course on the extent of these accessions and that the final delimitation of the Western frontier of Poland should therefore await the Peace Conference.

[Following this declaration, but omitted here for reasons of space, are brief statements on Yugoslavia, the Italo-Yugoslav frontier and Italo-Austrian frontier, Yugoslav-Bulgarian relations, Southeastern Europe, Iran, meetings of the three foreign secretaries, and the Montreux Convention and the Straits.]

6. The Yalta Agreement on Soviet Entry into the War Against Japan, 1945

The leaders of the three Great Powers—the Soviet Union, the United States of America and Great Britain—have agreed that in two or three months after Germany has surrendered and the war in Europe has terminated the Soviet Union shall enter into the war against Japan on the side of the Allies on condition that:

1. The *status quo* in Outer-Mongolia (The Mongolian People's Republic) shall be preserved;
2. The former rights of Russia violated by the treacherous attack of Japan in 1904 shall be restored, viz:
   a. the southern part of Sakhalin as well as all the islands adjacent to it shall be returned to the Soviet Union,
   b. the commercial port of Dairen shall be internationalized, the preeminent interests of the Soviet Union in this port being safeguarded and the lease of Port Arthur as a naval base of the USSR restored,
   c. the Chinese-Eastern Railroad and the South-Manchurian Railroad which provides an outlet to Dairen shall be jointly operated by the establishment of a joint Soviet-Chinese Company; it being understood that the preeminent interests of the Soviet Union shall be safeguarded and that China shall retain full sovereignty in Manchuria;
3. The Kurile islands shall be handed over to the Soviet Union.

It is understood, that the agreement concerning Outer-Mongolia and the ports and railroads referred to above will require concurrence of Generalissimo Chiang Kai-shek. The President will take measures in order to obtain this concurrence on advice from Marshal Stalin.

The Heads of the three Great Powers have agreed that these claims of the Soviet Union shall be unquestionably fulfilled after Japan has been defeated.

For its part the Soviet Union expresses its readiness to conclude with the National Government of China a Pact of friendship and alliance between the USSR and China in order to render assistance to China with its armed forces for the purpose of liberating China from the Japanese yoke.

7. Roosevelt's Anger with Stalin, 1945

I have received with astonishment your message of April 3 containing an allegation that arrangements which were made between Field Marshals [Harold] Alexander and [Albert] Kesselring at Berne [Switzerland] "permitted the Anglo-American troops to advance to the East and the Anglo-Americans promised in return to ease for the Germans the peace terms."

In my previous messages to you in regard to the attempts made in Berne to arrange a conference to discuss a surrender of the German army in Italy I have told

---

Document 6 can be found in U.S. Department of State, *Foreign Relations of the United States: The Conferences at Malta and Yalta* (Washington, D.C.: Government Printing Office, 1955), p. 984.

Document 7 can be found in U.S. Department of State, *Foreign Relations of the United States, 1945* (Washington, D.C.: Government Printing Office, 1968), III, 745–746.

you that: (1) No negotiations were held in Berne, (2) The meeting had no political implications whatever, (3) In any surrender of the enemy army in Italy there would be no violation of our agreed principle of unconditional surrender, (4) Soviet officers would be welcomed at any meeting that might be arranged to discuss surrender.

For the advantage of our common war effort against Germany, which today gives excellent promise of an early success in a disintegration of the German armies, I must continue to assume that you have the same high confidence in my truthfulness and reliability that I have always had in yours.

I have also a full appreciation of the effect your gallant army has had in making possible a crossing of the Rhine by the forces under General [Dwight D.] Eisenhower and the effect that your forces will have hereafter on the eventual collapse of the German resistance to our combined attacks.

I have complete confidence in General Eisenhower and know that he certainly would inform me before entering into any agreement with the Germans. He is instructed to demand and will demand unconditional surrender of enemy troops that may be defeated on his front. Our advances on the Western Front are due to military action. Their speed has been attributable mainly to the terrific impact of our air power resulting in destruction of German communications, and to the fact that Eisenhower was able to cripple the bulk of the German forces on the Western Front while they were still west of the Rhine.

I am certain that there were no negotiations in Berne at any time and I feel that your information to that effect must have come from German sources which have made persistent efforts to create dissension between us in order to escape in some measure responsibility for their war crimes. If that was [General Karl] Wolff's purpose in Berne, your message proves that he has had some success.

With a confidence in your belief in my personal reliability and in my determination to bring about, together with you, an unconditional surrender of the Nazis, it is astonishing that a belief seems to have reached the Soviet Government that I have entered into an agreement with the enemy without first obtaining your full agreement.

Finally I would say this, it would be one of the great tragedies of history if at the very moment of the victory, now within our grasp, such distrust, such lack of faith should prejudice the entire undertaking after the colossal losses of life, material and treasure involved.

Frankly I cannot avoid a feeling of bitter resentment toward your informers, whoever they are, for such vile misrepresentations of my actions or those of my trusted subordinates.

8. Roosevelt's Last Letter to Churchill, 1945

I would minimize the general Soviet problem as much as possible because these problems, in one form or another, seem to arise every day and most of them straighten out as in the case of the Berne meeting.

We must be firm, however, and our course thus far is correct.

This document can be found in U.S. Department of State, *Foreign Relations of the United States, 1945* (Washington, D.C.: Government Printing Office, 1967), V, 210.

⊕ E S S A Y S

In the first essay, a positive appraisal of President Franklin D. Roosevelt's wartime diplomacy, the historian Warren F. Kimball of Rutgers University at Newark argues that Roosevelt possessed a coherent vision of America's role in the world and practiced considerable diplomatic skill in pursuing his goals. During the war, according to Kimball, the president won Allied backing to launch a second military front in France that eased pressures on the Soviet Union, contained British imperialism, and ensured an Anglo-American presence in postwar Europe. Although Roosevelt recognized that the Second World War presented an opportunity to restructure international politics, he did not advocate a Wilsonian League of Nations, but instead worked to negotiate a balance of power between the victorious states. At the same time, the president hoped that open rather than closed spheres of influence, gradual decolonization, and a United Nations that entrusted veto power to the alliance leaders would promote a liberal world order conducive to U.S. security and economic needs. Although the Yalta accords, signed in February 1945, were later criticized for sanctioning Soviet domination of Eastern Europe, Kimball concludes that the agreements struck by both Roosevelt and British Prime Minster Winston Churchill with Soviet Marshal Joseph Stalin were the best that could be had given the U.S.S.R.'s military presence in Poland and other states at the time.

The second essay, in contrast, attempts to deflate Roosevelt's reputation as an adept manager of Allied relations. Joseph L. Harper of The Johns Hopkins University School of Advanced International Studies portrays FDR as a narrow-minded American nationalist, whose Jeffersonian outlook made him contemptuous of Europe and eager to disengage the United States from the continent's postwar affairs. Harper maintains that Roosevelt planned to erect two regional pillars, Britain and the Soviet Union, in lieu of a continued U.S. presence on the continent. As evidence grew that Stalin would clamp down on Poland and other East European states, Roosevelt refused to alter his plans for U.S. withdrawal and ignored Churchill's advice to toughen his stance against Soviet expansionism. As the war drew to a close, discrepancies between Roosevelt's Wilsonian rhetoric and his cynical practice of power politics had diminished prospects for Allied cooperation and aroused a suspicious American public opinion. Harper concludes that Roosevelt's policies sowed the seeds of postwar instability.

Franklin D. Roosevelt's Successful Wartime Diplomacy

WARREN F. KIMBALL

[President Franklin D.] Roosevelt had come into the war with vague but what proved to be consistent views on how to restructure international relations. The United States had to work with other nations to preserve peace, but it also had to avoid commitments that would drag it into every little argument and local squabble. Woodrow Wilson's League of Nations concept had fallen into that trap, and the American public and Congress had rejected the scheme, insisting that the United States retain its freedom of action. That experience, and FDR's assessment of the causes of the two world wars, left him convinced that only the Great Powers could maintain the peace. As he had told one of [French leader Charles] De Gaulle's emissaries a few months earlier, "I am not a Wilsonian idealist, I have problems to resolve."

Like hereditary aristocrats throughout history, Roosevelt assumed that power and responsibility justified each other, a geopolitical version of noblesse oblige. During the Atlantic Conference in August 1941 he had suggested to [British prime minister] Churchill that the two Great Powers, the United States and Great Britain, would have to act as policemen after the war, although some sort of international organization might be possible later on. That same month he casually repeated the idea to dinner guests, saying that the two nations would "have to police the entire world—not on a sanction basis but in trust." Only the Great Powers would have arms, and there would be "complete economic and commercial and boundary liberty, but America and England would have to maintain the peace." Disarmament would be key—"the smaller powers might have rifles but nothing more dangerous," he once commented—though he had to make a virtue of vice by entrusting enforcement to the Great Powers, which would never accept disarmament. Small nations would have to trust in the Great Powers; "another League of Nations with 100 different signatories" would mean "simply too many nations to satisfy." He had spoken similarly to [Soviet foreign minister V. M.] Molotov in May–June 1942, and the concept received Stalin's strong endorsement. . . . [On another occasion,] Roosevelt wondered why smaller nations needed arms. "Will it be necessary for these states to defend themselves after this war?" he asked. . . .

FDR's four policemen would also act as trustees for colonial societies not ready for full independence. The Pacific islands held by the Japanese (usually old League of Nations mandates), Korea (despite its being independent for centuries before the United States existed), and Indochina were his favorite examples, but the idea tended to be Roosevelt's catchall answer for any difficult territorial problem, as in the case of the Croatians and Serbs. When he spoke to [Anthony] Eden of trusteeships for Japan's Pacific island empire, French Indochina, and Portuguese Timor, Eden knew the president meant all European empires. . . .

The Atlantic Charter and FDR's subsequent scheme for bringing the Soviets into his group of world policemen have routinely been dismissed as unrealistic "Wilsonian nonsense." And "Wilsonianism," that catchall term for anything less than untrammeled power politics, was supposedly dangerous daydreaming.

But the Americans saw it differently. The Atlantic Charter was more than mere moral posturing. It was a call for reform, for the new world order, a consistent theme in American foreign policy before and since. Economic liberalism may have promised tangible benefits for the United States, but Americans had pursued economic liberalism since their Revolution; was that merely two centuries of cynicism? The decolonization of European empires could, and sometimes did, enhance American power and interests. Shall we then conclude that Franklin Roosevelt and all his predecessors plotted to "succeed John Bull"? The United Nations organization became, for more than a decade after the Second World War, an instrument of American foreign policy. Does that mean internationalism in the United States was just a ploy? . . .

Roosevelt had assumed a great peace conference would come after the fighting, just as after the First World War, but it would be a meeting of the Great Powers, not all the United Nations. Like Wilson, Roosevelt was determined that "something 'big' will come out of this war: a new heaven and a new earth." The president was convinced that only the New World—the United States—offered any innovative thinking in international relations. . . .

The discussions [held between the three alliance leaders] at Teheran [in November and December 1943] had an air of cordiality. . . .

But a tension existed that is apparent even in the dry, printed records of the talks. FDR was expansive and optimistic, but he failed in his efforts to get Stalin to preserve at least the appearances of self-determination in Eastern Europe. Nor did the president trust his Soviet counterpart enough to mention the atomic bomb, despite knowing that the Soviet leader already knew about the Manhattan Project. Stalin pushed the Anglo-Americans politely but relentlessly on Overlord [the Anglo-American cross-channel invasion of northern France], dismissing [British-led] operations in the Aegean as a diversion, then baiting Churchill and the British during two supposedly festive dinners. Yet he was obviously aware of and uncomfortable with the Soviet Union's dependence on the Anglo-Americans. Churchill, fearful that Britain was being relegated to lesser status, later described "the poor little English donkey," caught between "the great Russian bear" on one side and the "Great American buffalo" on the other. . . .

The talks went quickly to the key issues. Overlord was the initial focus and produced the easiest decision of the conference. FDR gave Stalin an opportunity to endorse the British strategy [of concentrating Anglo-American forces in the Aegean area]. "One of the questions to be considered here," said the president, was how to use Allied forces in the Mediterranean "to bring the maximum aid to the Soviet armies on the Eastern front." Stalin, assuming that the Americans tied the second front to a commitment to enter the Pacific war, promised to create a "common front" against Japan once Germany surrendered. Next he exploited the advantage of having a victorious army by summarizing the situation on the Russian front. Only then did he casually dismiss the campaign in Italy, where it seemed to him that Hitler had succeeded in tying up a large number of Allied divisions. He was equally dismissive of a Balkans campaign. That would require Turkey's entry into the war, which Stalin repeatedly insisted would not happen. Moreover, "the Balkans were far from the heart of Germany." . . .

Churchill had done his best to look to Britain's postwar interests. Throughout the war he expressed little concern for, and even dislike of, formal postwar planning, but that did not mean he had no postwar goals. He paid little heed to structure but gave much attention to using the war to develop and maintain his nation's interests. Italy might not ever be Great Britain's satellite, but British-led campaigns in the Mediterranean offered one last opportunity to enhance the U.K.'s prestige and protect its influence in the region. It was one last chance to appear like a Great Power.

Because the Americans generally assumed Britain's Great Power status, particularly the opulence of its empire, they interpreted the motives for the Mediterranean option more narrowly. As FDR pointed out to his military chiefs, "the British look upon the Mediterranean as an area under British domination." One American naval attaché expressed the common sentiment: "Now 168 years later [after the American Revolution] we are again being taxed hundreds of thousands of lives and billions of dollars to save the British Empire. . . ."

But it was more than just formal empire. Perhaps the prime minister truly hoped that victory in Italy, military action in the Aegean and Adriatic, and Turkish entry into the war would stimulate uprisings in the Balkans against the Germans, uprisings that could also liberate those countries before Stalin could apply his axiom ["that everyone imposes his own system" on occupied territories] to their political reconstruction, though Churchill never said so by the time of the Teheran meeting. The Americans viewed Churchill's policy as power politics, not ideological conflict. . . .

The details of the postwar settlements were not agreed on at Teheran. The three leaders preferred to paper over the cracks rather than endanger the Grand Alliance, which all believed still necessary in order to defeat Germany and Japan. But the Teheran talks prefigured the decisions that would come, particularly at Yalta, although the devil was in the details, particularly for FDR, whose bureaucracy, already embarked on postwar planning, had little understanding of his thinking.

One of the papered-over cracks was the matter of France, which stood as a symbol for weakness in both Europe and in the colonial world. On the first day of the talks Stalin roundly condemned "the entire French ruling class" for being "rotten to the core" and for having "delivered over France to the Germans." FDR agreed, saying anyone over forty should be kept out of the postwar French government. When Stalin suggested that the Allies should not "shed blood to restore Indochina" to France, FDR agreed and then implied that China, which had forsworn any "designs" on Indochina, should act as a trustee while Indochina prepared for independence, which would take "20 to 30 years." No sense in talking to Churchill about India, Roosevelt commented privately to Stalin, but perhaps reform from the bottom up, "somewhat on the Soviet line," was the best solution. That would mean "revolution," was the candid reply. The president made no reply but then seized on Stalin's comment that the French should not control any strategic points to insist that Dakar, on the bulge of West Africa, had to be "under the trusteeship of the United Nations." . . .

The partitioning of Germany remained something that both Roosevelt and Stalin supported, though the Soviet leader's primary concern was with making Germany "impotent ever again to plunge the world into war." Churchill agreed that Prussia should be "detached" from the rest of Germany but backed away from much more than that. They could agree that the European Advisory Commission (EAC) had to deal with the details, but that led ineluctably to the question of postwar frontiers, and that brought the Polish question to the table.

Stalin's proposal, offered on the first day and never modified, was that Poland should have a western boundary on the Oder River [formerly within Germany's boundaries] and generally along the old Curzon Line in the east [which assured Soviet control over eastern Poland and the Balkan states]. Pounds of paper and gallons of ink have since been expended in arguments over just which Oder River line should apply and what adjustments were needed to the Curzon Line, which Churchill accurately but cantankerously insisted on calling the "Ribbentrop-Molotov Line." But the basic agreement was crystal clear. For the British prime minister's part, "he would like to see Poland moved westward in the same manner as soldiers at drill execute the drill 'left close' and illustrated his point with three matches representing the Soviet Union, Poland and Germany." His instinctive solution to the dangers of postwar confrontation was to establish clearly defined boundaries and spheres of influence. Churchill, whose sense of history underpinned his policies, reckoned that such arrangements had worked in the nineteenth century, why not again? . . .

Roosevelt was not assuming that the Red Army would liberate and occupy Eastern Europe all the way to Germany; that eventuality was, in December 1943, only a possibility. The reality for FDR was that the Soviet Union would be the major player in the politics of that region. The choice seemed clear: Try to work with that dominant power or adopt Churchill's approach of setting up clear, and exclusive, spheres of influence. But when FDR suggested that some sort of plebiscite in the Baltic states would be "helpful to him personally" and then expressed confidence that the people would vote to be part of the Soviet Union, Stalin seemed less confident and rejected any "international" role in the Baltic region. The president's attempt to separate security from ownership was either too subtle or too unthinkable for the Soviet leader.

FDR's concern for appearances underpinned his supposed concern for "'the Polish vote'—six to seven million Polish-Americans," he told Stalin. But that number was "evidently plucked from the air." There were less than half that number of Polish-Americans, many of whom were not voters. FDR's hyperbole was perhaps a bit more calculated and less casual than it appeared, for it allowed him to escape public responsibility for the political fact that he, Churchill, and Stalin's Red Army together ensured that in the short run Poland's independence would depend on Moscow's self-restraint, not on Anglo-American guarantees.

There were ways to push the Russians to exercise that self-restraint. The Anglo-Americans had long assumed that the Soviet Union would be dependent on postwar aid for economic reconstruction. In January 1942 Churchill had written of "the United States and the British Empire" being "the most powerfully armed and economic *bloc* the world has ever seen, and that the Soviet Union will need our aid," although by late 1943 Britain had begun to take its own place in line for such postwar assistance. FDR presumed that the Soviet Union's need for postwar economic aid would give the United States continued leverage, although perhaps thinking of the remarkable Soviet industrial performance, he seems not to have placed as much faith in that mechanism as some others. . . .

The next afternoon, during a tête-à-tête with Stalin, the president sketched out his concept of the four policemen. When the Soviet leader questioned having China play a role in European affairs, FDR warned that the United States could not participate in an exclusively European committee that might try to force the dispatch of American troops to Europe, a comment that suggests [British foreign secretary Anthony] Eden was correct when he surmised that the president was using the American public's "feeling for China" to "lead his people to accept international responsibilities." When Stalin pressed him about an American response to a request from the other policemen, FDR resorted to his prewar notion of sending only planes and ships from the United States to keep the peace in Europe. Then he slipped back another couple of years to 1937, suggesting that the "quarantine method" might be best. . . .

Stalin got the message and the next day agreed that any international organization should be worldwide, not regional, although FDR remained uncertain of Stalin's conversion. But trying to work out the details could derail the concept, and the four policemen then nearly disappeared from the American record of the conference. . . .

"We leave here friends in fact, in spirit, and in purpose," said Roosevelt at the closing dinner. Churchill used more relative terms when he cabled [labor leader and future prime minister Clement] Attlee that "relations between Britain, United

States and USSR have never been so cordial and intimate. All war plans are agreed and concerted." . . .

The Normandy invasion [the following June, 1944] was the largest amphibious attack in history, a logistical tour de force. Men and equipment were landed on the beaches, at adjacent small ports, and later using the Mulberries (floating harbors) constructed once the beachheads were secure. . . . Within three weeks the Allies managed to land more than 850,000 men, nearly 150,000 vehicles, and some 570,000 tons of supplies. . . .

What the cross-Channel invasion did ensure was an Anglo-American presence on the Continent at war's end, a presence that would provide stability, order, and the opportunity to exercise Stalin's axiom and determine the course of political (and hence economic and social) reconstruction in Western Europe. At the same time the invasion of Western Europe also preserved the Grand Alliance, at least for the rest of the war. The implication that Overlord aimed at getting into Western and Central Europe before the Russians writes Cold War thinking into World War II, since the decision to invade at Normandy came well before the Red Army began to roll inexorably across Central Europe. But fear of the Soviet Union was there. Roosevelt and Churchill hedged their bets by drawing up the Rankin plans [for an earlier invasion of France in the event of a sudden German collapse] and by keeping the atomic bomb secret from everyone else. Yet even while the president admitted that "he didn't know what to do about Russia," he pursued goals that went against a get-tough approach toward the Soviet Union. . . .

By mid-autumn 1944, as the Germans were crushing the Warsaw uprising, Churchill . . . found a spheres of influence arrangement more practical than confrontation, despite his intense dislike of bolshevism. In 1939 he had sought to limit German expansion by exploiting Nazi-Soviet rivalry. Now, in 1944, he sought to protect British interests in the Mediterranean and Central Europe; that necessitated limiting Soviet expansion. In each case he proposed diplomacy and compromise to accomplish what Britain could not achieve by arms. . . .

With Roosevelt not in Moscow to preach his own hybrid form of "open" spheres of influence, Churchill and Stalin got down to serious horse trading. The talks, code-named Tolstoy, were long (October 9–17, 1944), but the key discussions came early. Taking advantage of [U.S. ambassador Averell] Harriman's absence from the first meeting (Roosevelt had agreed that Churchill should conduct some private discussions), the prime minister offered his notorious "percentages" proposal—what he later called a "naughty document." The note, which he slid across the table to Stalin, seemed a callous return to an era when princes swapped chunks of territory like pieces on a chessboard. Ninety percent influence for the Soviets in Romania; the same for Britain in Greece. Seventy-five percent in Bulgaria went to Moscow, while Yugoslavia and Hungary were split fifty-fifty. Churchill warned that they should "express these things in diplomatic terms and not to use the phrase 'dividing into spheres,' because the Americans might be shocked" and suggested destroying the paper; Stalin "ticked" the proposal and told the prime minister to keep it. When Stalin agreed that "Britain must be the leading Mediterranean power," Churchill endorsed a request that the Soviet Union gain unrestricted access to the Mediterranean from the Black Sea, despite a long-standing British-sponsored international agreement that allowed Turkey to close the Dardanelles to warships.

Both the British and the Soviets took the percentages formula seriously, with Eden and Molotov subsequently haggling over 5 percent here and 10 percent there. . . .

Churchill found the combination of nationalism and Roosevelt's calls for Britain to grant independence to its empire as great a threat to British interests as was Soviet expansion into Eastern Europe. Britain's place in East Asia, specifically, China, deeply concerned the prime minister. Seeking Stalin's support, or at least neutrality, in a region of intensifying nationalism, he outlined concessions he thought should go to the Soviet Union in the Far East. The deal between Stalin and Churchill was implied, not the sort of explicit arrangement they had made over Greece and Romania, but the approach was the same. The Soviet Union should have "effective rights at Port Arthur," said Churchill. Why worry about Soviet naval power in the Far East? he told his chiefs of staff; the Soviet fleet was "vastly inferior" and would be "hostages to the stronger Naval Powers." More important, "any claim by Russia for indemnity at the expense of China, would be favourable to our resolve about Hong Kong." The Hong Kong issue led Churchill quickly to instruct that no agreements be reached with the United States to oppose a "restoration of Russia's position in the Far East."

Four months later, at Yalta, Roosevelt worked out a Far Eastern settlement with Stalin that paralleled the quid pro quo Churchill had floated at Moscow, but FDR's reasons were a bit different. First and foremost, the Soviet Union's entry into what all expected to be a long and bloody war against Japan had always been framed to include something for Russia. Roosevelt had no doubt Stalin would live up to his promise so long as the United States and Great Britain lived up to theirs. Beyond that, FDR was, like Churchill, concerned about China, although it was the impending conflict between Mao [Zedong] and Chiang [Kai-shek (Jiang Jieshi)], not the decolonization of Hong Kong, that worried him. Persuading Stalin not to throw in with the Chinese Communists and thus give the Kuomintang a chance to consolidate its rule was Roosevelt's goal. . . .

Eight years after the Yalta Conference, at the height of Cold War tensions, Churchill distanced himself from the Far Eastern settlement at Yalta. Since the State Department had released the Far Eastern protocol to the public in February 1946, Churchill could only pretend that Britain had played no role in the arrangement, claiming the matter was, for Britain, "remote and secondary." We signed the agreement, but "neither I nor Eden took any part in making it," Churchill wrote. "In the United States there have been many reproaches about the concessions made to Soviet Russia. The responsibility rests with their own representatives. To us the problem was remote and secondary." This was technically correct. Churchill had not helped draft the language adopted at Yalta. Why bother? He had cut his deal five months earlier. . . .

Although Churchill and Stalin saved their most sensitive conversations for the times Harriman was excluded, the American "observer," a confidant of the prime minister and a close friend of many of the Churchills (he and Randolph Churchill's wife, Pamela, had an affair while Harriman was in London), soon found out what was going on. When the ambassador accurately reported the spheres of influence arrangement that was developing for the Balkans, Roosevelt blandly replied that his concern was to take practical steps "to insure against the Balkans getting us into a future international war." Spheres of influence were neither endorsed nor rejected. Since Stalin's insistence on a "friendly" government in Poland meant that Poles in the West would be unhappy, FDR asked Churchill for a two-week delay in any announcement of an agreement, should one be reached. Roosevelt had no expectations of a change of heart on Stalin's part, but two weeks would take him past the presidential election. "I am delighted," he cabled Stalin, "to learn from your message and from reports by Ambassador Harriman of the success attained by you and Mr. Churchill. . . ." FDR reserved the right to disagree when the Big Three next met but gave no hint of concern about the results of the Churchill-Stalin talks. . . .

At the beginning of 1945 had the Anglo-Americans sought to redirect the thrust of the postwar settlement that had already emerged, they had very little military leverage. The Trinity test of the atomic bomb was five months away, a lifetime in the midst of frantic postwar peacemaking. As the [Yalta] conference opened, the Red Army stood on the Oder River, a mere 40 miles from Berlin, having rolled some 250 miles westward in only three weeks. Soviet forces had liberated almost all of Poland, and the Anglo-Americans assumed the final assault on Berlin was only a few days or weeks away. Meanwhile, Eisenhower's armies were still recovering from the disruption caused by the German offensive in the Ardennes (the Battle of the Bulge). Nervous American diplomats, unaware that the Red Army needed time to consolidate its positions and let its supply system catch up, advised Roosevelt to endorse the occupation zone boundaries for Germany worked out by the European Advisory Commission before Stalin could claim that no agreement existed and moved his forces into the western part of Germany. . . .

Roosevelt and Churchill tried during and after the Crimea talks [at the Black Sea resort of Yalta] to get Stalin to make concessions in Eastern Europe that would improve appearances rather than substance, an approach they had taken since autumn 1944. The Soviet leader, either hostile toward or unbelieving about their domestic political concerns, conceded a few words and phrases but not an inch of control. A vague promise to allow "all democratic and anti-Nazi parties" to participate in "free and unfettered elections" guaranteed nothing for the London Poles since those elections would be supervised by Soviet officials. A tripartite commission for Poland turned out to be just like the one in Italy, only this time the Anglo-Americans here excluded. Stalin was nothing if not a fast learner. Little wonder, then, that Roosevelt and Churchill admitted that implementation of the Yalta accords depended on Stalin's goodwill, for it did. . . .

Although most of the discussions at Yalta about Germany's future took place among the three foreign ministers—Molotov, Eden, and [Edward] Stettinius—the attitudes of the Big Three set the context. Unconditional surrender, agreed upon from the outset, remained tripartite policy. They all agreed that nazism had to be extirpated and that Germany must never again threaten the peace of Europe. But each had a different take on how best to accomplish that. Stalin's solution was a weak Germany, unable to threaten the Soviet Union. Roosevelt's was a reformed Germany, uninterested in threatening peace. Churchill seemed to see nazism as a veneer imposed by a powerful few. Fearful of the changing power relationships in Europe, he argued against any permanent partitioning of Germany and toyed with the idea of Germany's again acting as Prussia had in the eighteenth and nineteenth centuries: as a British-financed barrier to any powerful rival, this time against Soviet expansion.

Stalin remained quietly adamant that Germany must never be able to threaten Russia, but faced with the enormous task of rebuilding a devastated nation, he talked most about reparations, proposing a ten-year reparations-in-kind program and extensive removals of German industrial plants. Churchill considered the plan unreasonable and impractical. Roosevelt, uncertain about what policy to pursue, avoided specifics. Remembering the American experience following World War I, he rejected any notion that the United States should or would provide aid to assist the Germans in meeting reparations demands or to prevent the collapse of the German economy. He never brought up the issue of postwar reconstruction aid to the Soviet Union—despite, or perhaps because of, Harriman's arguments that the promise of loans could be used to pry concessions out of Stalin. Then, in typically contradictory Roosevelt fashion, he endorsed large short-term reparations from Germany, with half of an estimated twenty billion dollars' worth going to the Soviet Union. But even that agreement was vaguely labeled a "basis for discussion" by a "reparation commission." The tough decisions on German dismemberment and its economy were postponed. . . .

[The] Yalta agreement on the Far East, vilified later for "giving away" so much of China to Stalin, did little more than spell out what had been agreed to earlier. Territory and privilege Russia claimed it had lost in 1905 after the Russo-Japanese War were returned: the southern part of Sakhalin Island, the Kurile Islands, and control of railroads in Manchuria. The Big Three confirmed the status of Outer Mongolia, which had been a Soviet-sponsored "people's republic" since the 1920s. Stalin was guaranteed use of two ports, Dairen (Dalian) and Port Arthur (now Lushun), on the Liaotung Peninsula, just west of Korea. (Roosevelt understood the desire for naval bases, although he wanted both ports internationalized, which Stalin rejected in the case of Port Arthur.) All this was to be done with Chiang Kai-shek's approval, but getting that approval was Roosevelt's job. . . .

The only "new" agreement at Yalta was the Declaration on Liberated Europe, and it proved the most disillusioning agreement of all. Signed by the Big Three, it called for free elections. Yet it was not new, only a restatement of the Atlantic Charter principle: "the right of all people to choose the form of government under which they will live." But the persistent Soviet demand for a "friendly" government in Warsaw demonstrated that none of the anti-Soviet Poles in London would be acceptable in a new Polish government, elected or not, while British actions in Greece and American policy in Italy demonstrated that Stalin's axiom still governed. The declaration was put together with a minimum of time and bargaining, suggesting that all three leaders understood full well what it meant—or did not mean. "It was the best I could do," Roosevelt told one adviser. . . .

Stalin's performance following Yalta fell far short of the "responsible" behavior expected of one of the world's policemen, and Churchill had no more prepared his public for the gap between ideals and reality than did Roosevelt his. The Soviets took control in Romania, Hungary, and Bulgaria with speed and brutality—an impression strengthened by the growing controversy over Stalin's demands for forcible repatriation of German-held Soviet prisoners of war. Many of those POWs, often from the Baltic states and the Ukraine, refused to return to a homeland now dominated by a "foreign" power, the Soviet Union.

But Poland remained the litmus test. Molotov, who handled the "diplomacy" of the situation, had refused to allow the London Poles [non-Communist Poles who had established a government-in-exile in London] any role in the new government, leaving no alternative but the Lublin committee [Communist Poles]. Since Soviet control over all those areas had long been agreed to by the British, as well as the Americans, style rather than substance was the only cause for concern. Yet a mere two weeks after Yalta Churchill shifted from support of those agreements to arguing that he had been deceived by Stalin. With an election coming up the prime minister found an immediate reason to back away from agreements he could not change but did not like. . . .

For the next two months [February–April, 1945] Churchill repeatedly pushed the president to challenge Stalin, but FDR's responses were consistent: Let us not be hasty; give the Yalta accords a chance to work. "I cannot agree that we are confronted with a breakdown of the Yalta agreements until we have made the effort to overcome the obstacles," said Roosevelt in a message drafted in the State Department. He, and those drafting his messages, repeated that practical advice over and over, for the only other choice seemed confrontation and the collapse of any hope for postwar cooperation.

Nor could Churchill persuade FDR to enter the "race" for Berlin, even if the president had himself raised that possibility more than a year earlier. Roosevelt's refusal to order a dash for the German capital followed the recommendations of his military advisers who disliked the very idea of a president's interfering with the field commander. Moreover, American generals argued that there was little military advantage in attacking Berlin since the Red Army was in position to launch an offensive. Eisenhower, with Marshall's strong support, insisted on pursuing the military objective, the German Army. Rumors of a last-ditch stand by fanatical Nazis holed up in an strong redoubt somewhere in southern Germany made Ike even more cautious. . . .

Churchill later pretended to blame the [U.S.] decision[s] on Roosevelt's deteriorating health. "We can now see the deadly hiatus which existed between the fading of President Roosevelt's strength and the growth of President Truman's grip of the vast world problem. In this melancholy void one President could not act and the other could not know." . . .

But FDR's health was not why American policy remained constant. He did not have to make significant changes to the draft messages provided him by aides in the White House. The advisers who had been with Roosevelt at Yalta—[Harry] Hopkins, [James] Byrnes, Admiral [William D.] Leahy—had returned home believing the president's approach had been successful. Even Harriman in Moscow had not lost faith in Roosevelt's dream of Soviet cooperation, although he was cautious, telling FDR that if the United States was "definite and firm" the Soviets will "make substantial concessions." Avoiding tension and confrontation with the Soviets was the tactic. Within the context of the dispute over the makeup of the "new" Polish government and with the Soviets preparing for an assault on the German capital, a "race" for Berlin in spring 1945 would have had the wrong effect. Perhaps if the Arnhem operation [allied air attacks on the strategic Dutch town of Arnhem in October 1944] had worked, or if the German counterattack in the Ardennes [forest of Belgium in December 1944] had not delayed the Anglo-Americans, things would have been different. But in April 1945 it was too late—if it had ever mattered. . . .

Roosevelt's awkward, imprecise, poorly articulated distinction between "closed" or "exclusive" spheres of influence and what might be called "open" spheres was the bridge he tried to construct between the structure proposed by Churchill and Stalin and the one suggested twenty-five years earlier by Woodrow Wilson. FDR tried to make Wilsonian idealism practical. "Open spheres" would permit the flow of culture, trade, and the establishment of what he called "free ports of information." He seems casually to have assumed that such openness would, in the fullness of time, expand American-style political and economic liberalism since those concepts worked. He had seen Wilson's experiment collapse under the weight of nationalism and political insecurity. Why bother to re-create that system if it would only fail? . . .

[T]he structure that Churchill and Roosevelt helped create, even if it was not what either had in mind, what historians have come to call the Yalta system, lasted for nearly fifty years—until the early 1990s, when the Soviet Empire crumbled. During that time the old colonial empires collapsed only to be replaced by less formal ones, nationalism changed the maps time and again, and the Great Powers—the Anglo-Americans and the Soviets—confronted each other. But they never went to war directly, and Europe, the cockpit of war for the first half of the twentieth century, avoided that horror. In one sense Yalta firmed up a settlement that, like the Congress of Vienna, created an era of peace—or, more precisely, an era without war. . . .

Caught up in the celebratory atmosphere of the 1990s, Britons and Americans have focused on all that went wrong with the results of the Second World War, forgetting that few, if any, of those "mistakes" could have been made if Hitler's Germany and militaristic Japan had won or even survived the war intact. Winning the Second World War was the prerequisite to all the failures, and all the successes, that followed. Had Churchill and Roosevelt chosen to fight the war solely for postwar advantage against Russia, communism, and the left, they could not have won the struggle. But almost always, when faced with crucial choices about victory versus postwar political advantage, Roosevelt, Churchill, or both made the decision to keep the Grand Alliance together and to defeat the Axis. They could not solve all the political, social, and economic problems of the world, but they could lead their nations to victory and prevent a far worse set of problems.

And they did.

The Failure of Roosevelt's Wartime Diplomacy

JOSEPH L. HARPER

Roosevelt's solution—his mature vision of Europe—was Jeffersonian in its Europhobic spirit. . . . Like the Jefferson Memorial, which rose during the war at FDR's behest within view of the White House, the vision took definite shape over several years. Like Jefferson's, FDR's vision was inspired by a fundamental cynicism, compounded by the vexation of his failure to insulate America from Europe or to influence it from a distance. FDR sketched in the details, calling up concepts and sentiments that had accumulated over a lifetime and now became the brick and mortar of a culminating structure. To pursue the metaphor, FDR's eventual design for Europe consisted of three mutually reinforcing levels or components: a new political

From Joseph L. Harper, *American Visions of Europe: Franklin D. Roosevelt, George F. Kennan, and Dean G. Acheson.* © 1994 Cambridge University Press. Reprinted with the permission of Cambridge University Press.

and territorial groundwork, two regional pillars bearing direct responsibility for peace, and an overarching structure in which the United States would occupy the position of keystone or *primus inter pares.* The purpose of these arrangements was to bring about a radical reduction in the weight of Europe, in effect to preside over its indefinite retirement from the international scene. As such, it was conceived as a set of arrangements drastic and definitive enough to allow the United States to return to its natural Western Hemisphere and Pacific habitat and preoccupations— but with one eye cocked toward Europe and able to exercise long-range striking power. The trick, which had been beyond America's power in Jefferson's time, was to be able to arbitrate from afar. . . .

Like Jefferson, FDR was less interested in saving Europe from itself than in rescuing the rest of the world from Europe. "Fractionization" was the path to a weak and harmless Europe, and one subject to outside manipulation. Decentralization and renewal from below meant removal of the old forces that had pursued destructive foreign policies. The new political forces would be in no position to resist the restructuring of Europe's world position through disarmament and decolonization. FDR's ideal was an Indian Raj writ in European terms: a fragmented continent over which the two remaining powers, Britain and the Soviet Union, could conduct a game of *divide et impera* [divide and rule] without depending on the United States.

The logic of decentralization and territorial rearrangement pervades FDR's discussion of postwar problems. To [Britain's foreign secretary Anthony] Eden in March 1943 he expressed his "opinion that the Croats and Serbs had nothing in common" and that it was "ridiculous to try to force them to live together." Belgium was another "artificial bilingual state" that might share the fate of Yugoslavia. The same argument applied to the chief troublemakers, Germany and France. He considered detaching Alsace and Lorraine from both, perhaps incorporating the contested areas into a new entity including Belgium and Luxembourg. He also asked, "After Germany is disarmed, what is the reason for France having a big military establishment?" . . .

FDR's solution to the German problem was dismemberment of a kind that went well beyond the detachment of East Prussia and the restoration of Austria. He was encouraged by [Under Secretary of State Sumner] Welles, [Treasury Secretary Henry] Morgenthau, [presidential adviser Harry] Hopkins, and former ambassadors James Gerard and Hugh Wilson, but the notion was very much his own. In March 1943, he told Eden, "We should encourage the differences and ambitions that will spring up within Germany." Even if "that spontaneous desire [should] not spring up . . . Germany must be divided into several states." At [the wartime summit in] Tehran [in November and December 1943], FDR suggested a five-state Germany, with the Kiel Canal–Hamburg area, the Ruhr, and the Saar under international control. He privately accepted the cession to Poland of German territory up to the Oder River to compensate for Polish territory lost to the Soviet Union. FDR agreed with Stalin that most of the differences among the Germans had been eliminated by the experience of unity, but thought religious, dynastic, linguistic, and cultural divisions could be revived. According to [Secretary of the Interior Harold] Ickes, he toyed with the idea of a Roman Catholic southern German state under Archduke Otto of Austria. He believed the German people themselves were redeemable within a looser, pre-1870 political framework and did not lose sleep over the possibility that they would go communist "in the Russian manner." The important thing was "not to leave in the German mind the concept of the Reich." The word itself "should be stricken from the language." . . .

In 1943 [former U.S. ambassador to the Soviet Union] William Bullitt wrote Roosevelt several letters on the subject of Russia. They are of considerable interest because they are links in a chain connecting the turn-of-the-century protocontainment outlook with the post–World War II strategy of the United States. According to Bullitt, Stalin aimed to dominate all of Europe, but he put "out pseudopodia like an amoeba rather than leaping like a tiger. If the pseudopodia meet no obstacle, the Soviet Union flows in." What he tactfully referred to as British policy—it was actually FDR's—Bullitt called the "Balance of Impotence." "Europe cannot be made a military vacuum for the Soviet Union to flow into." FDR should try personal diplomacy with Stalin, but the best way to deal with him was the "prior arrival of American and British Armies in the Eastern Frontiers of Europe . . . by way of Salonika and Constantinople." In August, he repeated that "the first step toward preventing Soviet domination of Europe is the creation of a British–American line in Eastern Europe."

FDR's subsequent actions suggest that he was not converted by Bullitt's thesis but was alarmed by its appearance. In May, he tried to arrange a tête-à-tête with Stalin in Alaska (Stalin declined) and pledged his support—this time definite—to the plan for a cross-channel invasion in the spring of 1944. In August, he won a commitment to plan "Overlord" [the cross-channel invasion of France] from the British. Roosevelt said, "We could if necessary carry out the operation ourselves." He was "anxious to have American preponderance . . . starting from the first day of the assault." A second plan ("Rankin") was developed in case of sudden German collapse, reflecting Roosevelt's desire "to be ready to get to Berlin as soon as did the Russians" (and the British). These decisions indicate a sense of urgency about forging a direct relationship with Stalin while harnessing the British to his will. . . .

In May, [British prime minister Churchill] proposed a "Supreme World Council" including the United States, Russia, Britain (and, if the United States insisted, China) and regional councils for Europe, the Western Hemisphere, and Pacific. Members of the Supreme Council would "sit on the Regional Councils in which they were directly interested." Thus "in addition to being represented on the American Regional Council the United States would be represented on the European Regional Council." Churchill also wanted a strong France and thought Coudenhove-Kalergi's ideas "had much to recommend them." . . .

Such proposals created a basic dilemma for Roosevelt. On one hand, Theodore Roosevelt's notion of great-power regional hegemony was central to his vision. FDR said: "Russia would be charged with keeping peace in Europe. The United States would be charged with keeping peace in the Western Hemisphere." Pan-American and European councils might facilitate the regional policemen's work. In the first public airing of the four-policeman concept, [the journalist] Forrest Davis's April 1943 article in the *Saturday Evening Post,* FDR let it be known that his basic approach to foreign policy was closer to Theodore Roosevelt's than to Wilson's. He floated the idea of "a security commission" of Britain, the United States, and Russia "to police the peace of Europe . . . until the political reorganization of the Continent is completed." At the same time, Roosevelt feared Churchill's council as a device for tying the United States down in Europe. FDR did not foresee "the U.S.

forever embroiled in foreign quarrels and required to keep large military forces abroad." He was "very emphatic" that the United States could not join "any independent regional body such as a European Council." America's military assets were to be committed elsewhere; FDR had commissioned elaborate studies for an expanded chain of postwar U.S. bases in the Atlantic and Pacific. But a European council to which the United States did not belong presented a different set of problems: it might resist U.S. influence or evolve into an anti-Soviet combination. On balance, regional bodies were not a good idea.

FDR's shift away from regionalism, embodied in the Moscow Conference Four Power Declaration of October 1943, was also a victory for [Secretary of State Cordell] Hull and his advisers. They had argued, with regrettable accuracy from FDR's standpoint, that domestic and world opinion would support only a "general international organization based on the principle of sovereign equality"—as opposed to a cabal of the big powers. . . . FDR was obliged to juggle once again. If in his frank secret dealings with Churchill and Stalin he continued to think in terms of great-power regional hegemony, he henceforth had to cater to public and congressional support for an egalitarian United Nations. Such an organization, hatched by Hull's inner circle, would prove to be the secretary's fitting, if unintended, revenge for years of humiliation by the White House. . . .

Roosevelt's purpose at Tehran, and throughout 1944, was to put himself in an intermediary position between Great Britain and the Soviet Union. At Tehran, FDR played the card of the second front to the embarrassment of the British, who wanted to delay it once more in favor of Mediterranean operations. "The trip was *almost* a complete success," he wrote, "specially the Russians." He referred to the personal relationship established with Stalin, as well as the latter's pledge to enter the war against Japan.

Roosevelt was always on guard against what he saw as British efforts to entangle the United States in Europe. He flatly rejected the U.S. occupation zone—southern Germany, France, and Austria—contained in a plan that gave the British northwest Germany, Belgium, Holland, and Denmark. Since, according to the invasion plans, U.S. forces would occupy the right (south) side of the line and the British the left (north), FDR insisted that there would have to be a "cross-over" of U.S. and British armies after they entered Germany to allow the United States to occupy the northwest zone and channel ports. He cabled Churchill, "I am absolutely unwilling to police France and possibly Italy and the Balkans as well." He dismissed Churchill's answer that "the question of policing" France did not arise:

> "Do please don't" ask me to keep any American forces in France. I just cannot do it! . . . As I suggested before, I denounce and protest the paternity of Belgium, France and Italy. You really ought to bring up and discipline your own children. In view of the face that they may be your bulwark in future days, you should at least pay for their schooling now.

Roosevelt accepted an Anglo-Soviet proposal to settle the boundary between the Soviet occupation zone and the western zones in Germany, but he was adamant that the United States would take the northern zone.

There is little need to emphasize that 1944 was a presidential election year: "political considerations in the United States" made his decision final. But Roosevelt's aversion to entrapment in Europe went beyond electoral politics, as did his intention to force the British to accept the consequences of a rapid U.S. pullout. They would have no choice, as Churchill himself put it, except "to make friends with Stalin," and this was one of the purposes of forcing Churchill to face the nakedness of the British position at Tehran. FDR's reservations about Britain's 1944 approach to the Russians on Eastern Europe had to do with the possible domestic fallout and with his abiding suspicion of the British. Though the two were supposedly "95 percent together," FDR knew perfectly well that Eden opposed his plans for the weakening and fragmentation of Europe. Eden, in any case, was far too stereotypical a Tory creature to be trusted by FDR.

Roosevelt's relationship with Churchill himself has been "much romanticized." When Churchill took power in 1940, FDR reportedly considered him a "playboy and a drunkard." Churchill the nationalist, imperialist, Russophobe, and purveyor of Anglo-American brotherhood deeply irritated Roosevelt, even if the prime minister was too much of a "museum piece, a rare relic," to be taken altogether seriously. It is also true that Churchill's "un-English" exuberance—he was after all half-American—allowed for a kind of informality and companionship that FDR found impossible with most Britons. The only precedent was the young Nigel Law, whose rapt courtship of FDR during the First World War had won him a similar condescending warmth. Roosevelt remarked, "I have a feeling when I am with Winston that I am twenty years older than he is." Churchill recalled, "I always looked up to him as an older man, though he was eight years my junior." If there was a basic element of trust in the relationship, it was based on a tacit acceptance of Roosevelt's dominant position: in effect, FDR trusted Churchill as long as he thought he could control him.

In April 1944, Churchill began to explore an arrangement whereby the Russians would "take the lead" in Romania and the British in Greece. He asked FDR's "blessing" on May 31. Ostensibly temporary, the arrangement was supposed to formalize what FDR himself favored: the predominance of the British on the Mediterranean littoral and of the Russians in Eastern Europe. When Hull objected, FDR allowed the State Department to draft a disapproving cable, but the next day he unilaterally approved Churchill's suggestion that the arrangement be tried for three months. FDR complained that the Foreign Office had decided to tell the United States about its Balkan negotiations only after the Russians had broached the subject with the State Department, but he did not oppose the idea. FDR accepted Hopkin's suggestion that Stalin and Churchill be told that any decisions made during Churchill's visit to Moscow in October 1944 were subject to his approval, but his intuition told him that the mission was worthwhile. He soon knew the gist of the sphere-of-influence arrangements and there is little evidence that he objected. . . .

At Dumbarton Oaks [a private estate in Washington, D.C., where the first conference on the United Nations convened in August 1943], meanwhile, he tried to erect an overarching structure that would permit America to remain aloof from Europe while retaining a decisive voice in the determination of its fate. FDR's reluctant acceptance of a universal world organization had to do with the development of wide support for such a body in 1943. In deference to the claims of smaller countries, FDR also agreed that the organization's executive council would have three or more revolving as well as four permanent members. Still, FDR stuck to his conviction that only the "four policemen" would be armed and would enforce peace on the basis of regional assignments. The real problem was how to ensure collaboration among the great powers themselves. FDR had said, "The United States will have to *lead*" and use its "good offices always to conciliate, to help solve the differences which will arise between the others." . . .

The crucial problem at Dumbarton Oaks was whether the four policemen could veto decisions in cases where they were directly involved. If the big powers possessed an absolute veto, the kind of United States-led coalitions suggested by FDR's poker allusion could not materialize within the council. The organization would become a mere debating society, and "a poor one at that." There were obvious counterarguments: no country would accept restrictions when its vital interests were involved. The United States and Britain decided to support the principle that the big four should not vote on questions involving the peaceful settlement of a dispute to which they were a party, while retaining the right to veto enforcement measures. . . .

How should one interpret Roosevelt's decision in the same context to initial the secret aide-mémoire [in 1944 with British prime minister Winston Churchill] on atomic energy at Hyde Park? The agreement [which called for full atomic collaboration between Britain and the U.S.] is the chief exhibit in the case that far from being naive or too optimistic, FDR was now preparing to contain the Russians. According to [the historian] Martin Sherwin, FDR saw an atomic-armed Britain as "America's outpost on the European frontier." Sherwin and [the historian] Barton Bernstein emphasize the importance that the weapon had acquired: FDR was "reserving the option of using it in the future as a bargaining lever, threat, military counter-weight, or even as a weapon again the Soviets." . . .

In all likelihood, FDR's real preference was an American monopoly. As someone concerned to allay Soviet suspicion of Britain and of Anglo-American collusion, he probably saw exclusive American control as more palatable to Moscow than independent British possession of the bomb. In a more visceral way, he no doubt coveted the bomb as the symbol and instrument of American supremacy and independence. At this level, the bomb was the rod of yore that someday "we may shake . . . over the heads of all [the Europeans]," the means by which America could remain remote and secure from Europe, as well as the arbiter of its fate. The air-delivered atomic bomb was the ultimate Jeffersonian weapon. . . .

The Quebec agreement [reached by FDR and Churchill in August 1943, which called for a full exchange of atomic information], to which the Hyde Park aide-mémoire was essentially a codicil, came about after Churchill threatened to pursue the bomb on his own and in a way that might have negative consequences for the United States. FDR's choice was now a possibly serious delay in the Manhattan Project and crisis with Britain versus an agreement restoring a flow of information that would allow the British to build a bomb at some point in the future. Anglo-American atomic diplomacy is another instance in which FDR made a valiant effort to eat his cake and have it. . . .

The final meeting of Roosevelt and Churchill [at the Yalta Conference in February 1945], though it gave rise to a brief euphoria, did not reestablish trust. At the center of the negotiations were the questions of the future Polish regime and the United Nations voting formula. The Americans agreed to the mere broadening of the [Communist] Lublin cabinet, through the inclusion of additional democratic elements, rather than a genuinely new government. FDR's earlier resistance on this point melted away once Stalin had accepted the U.S. voting formula for the United Nations and dropped a demand for membership for all fifteen Soviet republics. The British, who held out for more concrete guarantees on Poland, had no choice but to go along. FDR approached the question, in his words, as the inhabitant "of another hemisphere" and once again reminded those present that U.S. troops would leave Europe within two years after the war. Stalin and FDR reiterated the Tehran decision to proceed with the dismemberment of Germany; the British were reluctant. On the question of German reparations, the U.S. and Soviet sides agreed to the figure of $20 billion as a basis of discussion, with the Russians to receive half. Churchill was appalled. FDR and Stalin conducted secret talks resulting in territorial gains by the Soviet Union in the Far East. . . .

Churchill later said of the president at Yalta, "He was a tragic figure." He was referring to FDR's shrunken, world-weary appearance, but the remark conveys the regret that he felt over the fading of a relationship based, at least for Churchill, on affection as well as self-interest. When it came in April, FDR's was "an enviable death." He "had brought his country through the worst of its perils and the heaviest of its toils." But it was enviable also because it prevented further estrangement and more violent disagreement. Churchill, with his sense of the drama of history, was suggesting that Roosevelt's decline had been tragic in the deeper, classical meaning of the term—a great figure brought down by a fatal flaw of character. Roosevelt's vision of America's relationship to the Old World was animated by a combination of animosity and hubris. Both impulses, along with a dose of sadism, were present in his personal relationships with Churchill and de Gaulle. At bay in 1944, the two exponents of old-fashioned European power politics turned and defied the New World. Their resistance opened cracks in Roosevelt's "monumental conception," even as the Soviet pillar seemed to be rising in its place. . . .

The unexpected controversy occurred during the two months between Yalta and Roosevelt's death. Stalin's mid-April remark ("Everyone imposes his own system. . . . It cannot be otherwise") was not a declaration of strategy but a reflection on what, willy-nilly, was actually taking place. It rings like an epitaph for Roosevelt and the Rooseveltian vision of Europe. What Stalin meant was, "From now on, it cannot be otherwise." Without Roosevelt, Rooseveltian policies were certainly doomed.

What went wrong? Who was responsible? [The historian] Robert Messer makes a convincing case that initial post-Yalta troubles had to do with the manner in which the agreements were presented to the public in the United States. James Byrnes, FDR's "Yalta salesman," returned from the conference, where, thanks to FDR, he had received a selective impression of what had happened and proceeded to portray the Declaration on Liberated Europe and the Polish settlement as the triumph of self-determination. FDR was pleased by the performance, at least by the positive public reaction to Yalta that resulted. In private remarks immediately after Yalta, Roosevelt denounced the U.S. Senate as incompetent and obstructionist, affirming that the only way to accomplish anything was to circumvent it. But the Russians were bound to take a dim view of the Wilsonian love feast being staged by FDR. Vice Foreign Minister [Andrei] Vishinsky's brutal ultimatum to the Romanian government on February 27 was a reminder that the Declaration on Liberated Europe was something less than an instrument to foster bourgeois democracy in Eastern Europe. Other historians argue that FDR was naive to assume that the Russians would behave in a way that would not create undue embarrassment for him at home, while his own vagueness at Yalta had only encouraged Stalin to make new demands. But if Soviet behavior after Yalta was partly a reaction to distorted public claims arising from FDR's domestic requirements, Roosevelt's responsibility appears in a somewhat different light. It is hard to avoid the conclusion that Roosevelt had been sincere with Stalin (with whom he had tended to deal as if he himself were a kind of absolute monarch) and was trying to deceive his Wilsonian public. The Russians appear not to have understood this and believed somebody was trying to deceive them.

FDR's, arguably, was another case of "useful deceit" and in any event unavoidable given his ambiguous, instrumental relationship to Wilson and the Wilsonians all along. By 1945, [the historian] William McNeill notes, "Roosevelt embodied a myth." Partly through his own doing, the myth was essentially Wilsonian. To be sure, FDR had occasionally tried to explain to the public . . . that his was a hardheaded and "partial internationalism," closer to Theodore Roosevelt than to Wilson. Privately he had said, "You can't invoke high moral principles when high moral principles don't exist." But since the twenties—and never more so than in 1944—he had prospered as a politician by wrapping himself in Wilson's mantle. While he shared Wilson's dream of abolishing the centrality of Europe, his postwar plans had little to do with the self-determination of nations. As the gap between right hand and left, between public expectations and the Eastern European reality, plainly widened after Yalta, the helpless juggler was hoist aloft on his Wilsonian petard.

Controversy erupted after the February 23 meeting of the "Moscow Commission" set up to consult the various Polish groups with a view to reorganizing the Polish government. While disturbed, Roosevelt recognized the predominance of the Communist Poles and was determined not to allow a secondary issue to destroy his foreign policy. For his part, however, Churchill asked Parliament on February 27:

> Are they [the Poles] to be free, as we in Britain and the United States or France are free? Are their sovereignty and independence to be untrammeled, or are they to become a mere projection of the Soviet State, forced against their will by an armed minority to adopt a command or totalitarian system. I am putting the case in all its bluntness.

Privately he said, "I have not the slightest intention of being cheated over Poland, not even if we go to the verge of war with Russia." Churchill was now in revolt against FDR's foreign policy. . . .

The laws of physics decreed that FDR's structure would not stand: his two telemones [supporting columns], Russia and Britain, emerged from the war profoundly inimical and disproportionate in stature. Britain and Russia did not believe that, even acting together, they had the strength to keep Europe in the reduced and fragmented condition that Roosevelt envisioned. "Give them [the Germans] twelve to fifteen years and they'll be on their feet again," Stalin told [the Yugoslav Communist Milovan] Djilas in April 1945. "We shall recover in fifteen or twenty years, and then we'll have another go at it." The prospect of the American withdrawal, brutally reiterated by Roosevelt at Yalta, the absence of an American pillar in Europe, weighed heavily in the calculations of both Churchill and Stalin in 1945. Every instinct drove Churchill to try to force the Americans to confront the dominant Continental power and re-create the Anglo-American intimacy of 1940–41. . . .

The progressive hardening of the British and Soviet positions in Europe weighed heavily on Roosevelt in the last days of his life. There could have been no more eloquent signal of the collapse of his design. Stalin's behavior was a bitter cup to swallow. . . . It is impossible to say whether with approaching death came self-knowledge, whether, in other words, Roosevelt recognized the Jeffersonian hubris and fatal ambivalence about entanglement in Europe that lay at the heart of his monumental failure. He had tried to concoct the transformation and retirement of Europe—a solution to the European Question—without American responsibility and entanglement. Only someone of Roosevelt's profoundly solipsistic nationalism and sense of American superiority—incorporating a turn-of-the-century certainty of the Old World's moral bankruptcy—could have seriously entertained the idea.

 F U R T H E R   R E A D I N G

Stephen E. Ambrose, *Eisenhower and Berlin, 1945* (1967)
——— and Douglas Brinkley, *Rise to Globalism* (1993)
Edward M. Bennett, *Franklin D. Roosevelt and the Search for Victory* (1990)
Michael Beschloss, *The Conquerers* (2003)
Robert Blake and Wm. Roger Louis, eds., *Churchill* (1993)
Richard Breitman and Alan M. Kraut, *American Refugee Policy and European Jewry, 1933–1945* (1987)
Susan Brewer, *To Win the Peace* (1997)
Douglas Brinkley and David Facey-Crowther, eds., *The Atlantic Charter* (1994)
Charles Brower, ed., *World War II in Europe* (1998)
Russell Buhite, *Decisions at Yalta* (1986)
Thomas M. Campbell, *Masquerade Peace: America's UN Policy, 1944–1945* (1973)
Diane Shaver Clemens, *Yalta* (1970)
Kenton J. Clymer, *Quest for Freedom* (1995) (on India)
Wayne S. Cole, *Roosevelt and the Isolationists, 1932–1945* (1983)
Mark J. Conversino, *Fighting with the Soviets* (1997)
Kenneth R. Crispell and Carlos F. Gomez, *Hidden Illness in the White House* (1988)
Robert Dallek, *Franklin D. Roosevelt and American Foreign Policy, 1933–1945* (1979)
Kenneth S. Davis, *FDR: The War President* (2001)
Robert A. Divine, *Roosevelt and World War II* (1969)
John W. Dower, *War Without Mercy* (1986)
Robin Edmonds, *The Big Three* (1991)
Carol Eisenberg, *Drawing the Line: The American Decision to Divide Germany, 1944–1949* (1996)
Herbert Feis, *Between War and Peace* (1960)
Robert H. Ferrell, *Ill-Advised* (1992)
Richard B. Frank, *Downfall: The End of the Imperial Japanese Empire* (2000)
Frank Freidel, *Franklin D. Roosevelt* (1990)
"The Future of World War II Studies: A Roundtable," *Diplomatic History,* 25 (2001), 347–499
Lloyd C. Gardner, *Spheres of Influence* (1993)
Martin Gilbert, *Winston S. Churchill* (1986)
Mary N. Hampton, *The Wilsonian Impulse* (1996) (on Germany)
Gary R. Hess, *America Encounters India, 1941–1947* (1971)
———, *The United States at War, 1941–1945* (1986)
———, *The United States' Emergence as a Southeast Asian Power, 1940–1950* (1987)
Robert C. Hilderbrand, *Dumbarton Oaks* (1990)
Townsend Hoopes and Douglas Brinkley, *FDR and the Creation of the UN* (1997)
Julian C. Hurstfield, *America and the French Nation, 1939–1945* (1986)
Akira Iriye, *Power and Culture* (1981)
Warren Kimball, *The Juggler* (1991)
Gabriel Kolko, *The Politics of War* (1968)

Eric Larrabee, *Commander in Chief* (1987)

Clayton D. Laurie, *The Propaganda Warriors* (1996)

Lloyd E. Lee, *World War II: Crucible of the Contemporary World* (1991)

Ralph B. Levering, *American Opinion and the Russian Alliance* (1976)

Judy Barrett Litoff and David C. Smith, eds., *What Kind of World Do We Want? American Women Plan for Peace* (2000)

Wm. R. Louis, *Imperialism at Bay* (1978) (on decolonization)

Richard Lukas, *The Strange Alliance* (1978) (on Poland)

Frederick W. Marks III, *Over Sand: The Diplomacy of Franklin Roosevelt* (1988)

Vojtech Mastny, *Russia's Road to the Cold War* (1979)

Jon Meacham, *Franklin and Winston* (2003)

Steven M. Miner, *Between Churchill and Stalin* (1988)

J. Robert Moskin, *Mr. Truman's War* (1996)

Robert Nisbet, *Roosevelt and Stalin* (1988)

Raymond G. O'Connor, *Diplomacy for Victory* (1971) (on unconditional surrender)

Arnold Offner and Theodore A. Wilson, *Victory in Europe 1945: From World War to Cold War* (2000)

William O'Neill, *A Democracy at War* (1993)

R. A. C. Parker, *The Second World War* (2002)

Joseph E. Persico, *Roosevelt's Secret War* (2001) (on espionage)

Forrest C. Pogue, *George C. Marshall* (1963–1987)

William A. Renzi and Mark D. Roehrs, *Never Look Back* (1991)

David Reynolds et al., eds., *Allies at War* (1994)

———, *Churchill and Roosevelt at War* (1994)

———, *Rich Relations: The American Occupation of Britain* (1995)

——— and David Dimbleby, *An Ocean Apart* (1989) (on Anglo-American relations)

David Ryan and Victor Pungong, eds., *The United States and Decolonization* (2000)

Keith Sainsbury, *Churchill and Roosevelt at War* (1994)

———, *The Turning Point* (1985)

John Sbrega, *Anglo-American Relations and Colonialism in East Asia* (1983)

Georg Schild, *Bretton Woods and Dumbarton Oaks* (1995)

Stephen C. Schlesinger, *Act of Creation* (2003) (on the United Nations)

Michael S. Sherry, *Preparing for the Next War* (1977)

———, *The Rise of American Air Power* (1987)

Bradley F. Smith, *Sharing Secrets with Stalin* (1996)

Gaddis Smith, *American Diplomacy During the Second World War, 1941–1945* (1985)

Neil Smith, *American Empire* (2003) (on geography)

Ronald H. Spector, *Eagle Against the Sun* (1984)

Mark A. Stoler, *Allies and Adversaries* (2000)

———, *George Marshall* (1989)

———, *The Politics of the Second Front* (1977)

Kenneth W. Thompson, *Winston Churchill's World View* (1983)

Christopher Thorne, *Allies of a Kind* (1978)

———, *The Issue of War* (1985)

Adam Ulam, *Expansion and Coexistence* (1974) (on Soviet foreign policy)

Cornelius Van Minnen and John F. Sears, eds., *FDR and His Contemporaries* (1992)

Gerhard L. Weinberg, *A World at Arms* (1993)

Randall Woods, *A Changing of the Guard* (1990)

David S. Wyman, *The Abandonment of the Jews* (1984)

CHAPTER
6

The Origins of the
Cold War

The Grand Alliance collapsed soon after the Second World War. Strife had developed during the war itself, and the scramble for postwar position accentuated differences of power, interests, and ideology, especially between the United States and the Soviet Union. As they defined their postwar goals, each side in the unfolding contest drew different lessons from the 1930s and pushed aside the plans devised at the Yalta and Potsdam conferences near the end of the war.

While Soviet leaders came to see the United States as an expansionist power seeking world supremacy, threatening USSR security, and manipulating weaker states, U.S. leaders increasingly read the Soviet Union as a bullying communist aggressor bent on grabbing territory, subjugating neighbors, and disturbing the postwar peace through subversion. The Kremlin charged the United States with trying to encircle the Soviet Union; Washington claimed that it was only trying to contain the Soviet Union. Each side saw offense when the other saw defense. Fearing the future, the adversaries competed to build and enlarge spheres of influence, to attract allies, to enhance military capabilities, and to gain economic advantage. Shortly after the Second World War, a new, long global war that would endure for more than four decades began—the Cold War.

Poland, Germany, Iran, Czechoslovakia, Greece, China, Korea, and many other nations became the diplomatic and military battlegrounds for the Cold War by midcentury. The Soviet Union and the United States never sent their troops into battle directly against one another. Instead, they started an expensive arms race, cultivated and at times intimidated client states, constructed overseas bases and intelligence posts, intervened in civil wars, launched covert operations, constructed rival alliance systems, sponsored exclusionist economic partnerships and foreign aid programs, and initiated propaganda campaigns in which they charged one another with conspiracy. Soon such designations as "West" and "East" and "Third World" (nonaligned nations in the developing world) reflected global divisions.

The end of the Cold War in the late 1980s and early 1990s, and the question of who won or lost it, are treated in a later chapter of this book. Here we strive to understand why and how the Cold War began. The scholarship on this subject continues to grow. In the past decade and a half, post–Cold War Russian, Eastern European, Chinese, and other archives have opened for the first time, providing illuminating but still limited new documentation. The Cold War International History Project Bulletin, published by the Woodrow Wilson International Center for Scholars in Washington, D.C., has since 1992 reprinted many declassified Soviet and communist documents. The new evidence, at times clarifying and at other times ambiguous (because Soviet leaders rarely stated their motives, even to one another, in unguarded terms), has by no means brought closure in debates about the Cold War. The documents of "the other side" nonetheless enable scholars to consider the interactive nature of Soviet-American relations, to understand better the impact of the superpower rivalry on client states, and to present new or revised perspectives on the origins of the Cold War.

Three areas of inquiry have intrigued scholars who explore the sources of the Cold War. First is the international context. The Second World War produced wrenching changes in the international system that increased the likelihood of postwar conflict. Power was redistributed, empires collapsed, and wartime destruction spawned social and economic dislocation. The United States and the Soviet Union each sought to influence the postwar world: to defend against threats, to exploit new opportunities, and to enhance their stature. Which of the two was more responsible for the Cold War—or must they share responsibility?

Second, scholars study the national context of the Soviet Union and the United States. What drove them to become international activists? Some analysts stress power and security concerns: the Soviet preoccupation with the borderlands of Eastern Europe and Washington's determination to plant air and naval bases around the globe to prevent a repetition of the infamous attack on Pearl Harbor. Other writers highlight the centrality of economics: America's appetite for capitalist markets and investment opportunities and Russia's desperate need for postwar reconstruction and reparations. Still others probe the role of ideology and the dramatic clash between democratic capitalism and authoritarian Marxism. In the United States, the influence of the Congress, political parties, and public opinion warrants close examination, while the dictatorial and secretive nature of Soviet communism also carried unique consequences for international relations. In addition to ideology, scholars deconstruct culture to divine how policymakers, the media, and the public in both countries may have fallen back on prevailing notions of race, ethnicity, class, gender, and national identity to decipher—as well as distort—the attitudes and behaviors of the other. At bottom, historians seek to explain why Americans came to see the Soviets as ruthless expansionists and an unparalleled menace to civilization, and why Soviet leaders so often thought of the United States as a reckless practitioner of atomic diplomacy and economic imperialism. Did the Cold War evolve because the two sides simply misunderstood one another, or because they understood each other very well, including their quite different national interests?

Third, historians assess the role of individuals, whose personalities, political ambitions, and styles of diplomacy influenced their nation's foreign relations. In the early Cold War, the personal imprints of President Harry S. Truman and Marshal Joseph Stalin stand out. Individual leaders usually define their nation's needs and goals, give voice to ideologies and cultural assumptions, and decide whether to negotiate or play politics with foreign policy. Some leaders are wise and patient, others shallow and impatient; some understand nuance and gray areas, while others see extreme blacks and whites; some decisionmakers are driven blindly by

ideology, entrenched interests, or ignorance, while others are more knowledgeable,
practical, and flexible. In an accounting of the origins of the Cold War, how much
weight should scholars give to Truman and Stalin as compared to systemic and
national sources of conflict? More precisely, to ask a counterfactual question in the
case of the United States, would Franklin D. Roosevelt have handled Soviet-American
relations differently?

While the sources of the early Cold War were numerous and varied, we end
with one overarching question: Was the Cold War inevitable, or were there viable
alternatives to a half century of mutual suspicion, militarization, and fear?

🌐 D O C U M E N T S

On June 11, 1945, a group of scientists in Chicago who had been secretly developing
an atomic bomb petitioned Secretary of War Henry L. Stimson to recognize the importance of future international (especially Soviet) agreement to prevent nuclear warfare.
Headed by James Franck, the scientists' committee recommended against a surprise
atomic attack on Japan and instead advocated a noncombatant use of the bomb on an
island or in a desert, with international observers. But President Truman and his advisers
rejected the Franck Committee's advice, presented as Document 1. On September 11,
1945, Stimson sent Truman a memorandum in which the secretary of war argued that
"the problem" of the atomic bomb "dominated" Soviet-American relations. Stimson
now urged that the United States approach the Soviet Union to discuss controls in order
to reduce distrust, as Document 2 indicates.

Document 3, written by George F. Kennan, is his "long telegram" sent to
Washington on February 22, 1946, from his post as attaché in the U.S. embassy in
Moscow. Kennan pessimistically speculated on the motivations for Soviet behavior.
His critique proved persuasive among Truman officials, and Kennan went on to
serve as head of the State Department's Policy Planning Staff, where he helped to
establish "containment" as U.S. Cold War doctrine. Document 4 is former British
Prime Minister Winston S. Churchill's "iron curtain" speech of March 5, 1946, delivered in Fulton, Missouri, with an approving President Truman present. Secretary
of Commerce Henry A. Wallace disapproved of the trend toward an American "get
tough" policy and appealed to Truman to seek accommodation, not confrontation,
with the Soviets. Wallace's memorandum of July 1946 is printed as Document 5.
When Wallace went public with his criticisms in September, Truman fired him
from the cabinet. On September 27, 1946, Nikolai Novikov, Soviet ambassador to
the United States, sent his own long telegram to his superiors in Moscow. Included
as Document 6, Novikov's report described the United States as an expansionist
power bent on world supremacy.

On March 12, 1947, the president addressed Congress to announce the "Truman
Doctrine," or containment doctrine, in conjunction with a request for aid to Greece and
Turkey. Much of the significant speech is reprinted here as Document 7. The Marshall
Plan for European reconstruction soon followed. Suggested by Secretary of State
George C. Marshall in June 1947, the aid program took form in the Economic Coopera-
tion Act of 1948, which the president signed on April 3; the introduction to this legislation
is included as Document 8. An excerpt from National Security Council Paper No. 68
(NSC-68), dated April 7, 1950, is reprinted as Document 9. Requested by the president,
this alarmist report represented high-level American thinking about the Cold War and
argued the need for a large military buildup.

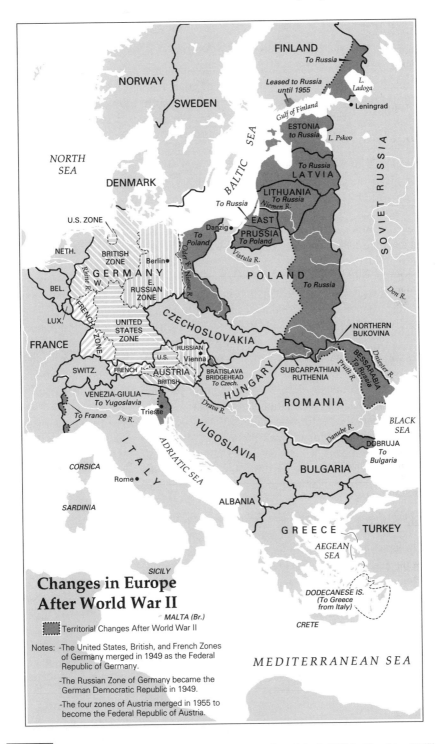

FINLAND
To Russia

Leased to Russia until 1955

NORWAY

SWEDEN

L. Ladoga

Gulf of Finland

• Leningrad

ESTONIA
to Russia   *L. Pskov*

NORTH
SEA

DENMARK

BALTIC SEA

To Russia
LATVIA

SOVIET RUSSIA

LITHUANIA
To Russia
Niemen R.

To Russia

U.S. ZONE

Danzig •
To Poland

EAST
PRUSSIA
To Poland

NETH.

BRITISH
ZONE
Berlin •

GERMANY
W.   E.
RUSSIAN
ZONE

Rhine R.

Oder R.

Neisse R.

Vistula R.

POLAND

To Russia

Don R.

BEL.

FRENCH
ZONE

CZECHOSLOVAKIA

LUX.

UNITED
STATES
ZONE

FRANCE

NORTHERN
BUKOVINA

SWITZ.

FRENCH

BRITISH

RUSSIAN
Vienna
U.S.
AUSTRIA

BRATISLAVA
BRIDGEHEAD
To Czech.

HUNGARY

SUBCARPATHIAN
RUTHENIA

BESSARABIA
to Russia

Dniester R.

Pruth R.

VENEZIA-GIULIA
To Yugoslavia

To France   *Po R.*

Trieste

Drava R.

ROMANIA

BLACK
SEA

ITALY

ADRIATIC SEA

YUGOSLAVIA

Danube R.

DOBRUJA
To Bulgaria

CORSICA

Rome •

BULGARIA

SARDINIA

ALBANIA

GREECE   TURKEY

*AEGEAN
SEA*

SICILY

Changes in Europe
After World War II

MALTA (Br.)

Territorial Changes After World War II

DODECANESE IS.
(To Greece
from Italy)

CRETE

Notes: -The United States, British, and French Zones
of Germany merged in 1949 as the Federal
Republic of Germany.

-The Russian Zone of Germany became the
German Democratic Republic in 1949.

-The four zones of Austria merged in 1955 to
become the Federal Republic of Austria.

MEDITERRANEAN SEA

1. The Franck Committee Predicts a Nuclear-Arms Race If the Atomic Bomb Is Dropped on Japan, 1945

The way in which the nuclear weapons, now secretly developed in this country, will first be revealed to the world appears of great, perhaps fateful importance.

One possible way—which may particularly appeal to those who consider the nuclear bombs primarily as a secret weapon developed to help win the present war—is to use it without warning on an appropriately selected object in Japan. It is doubtful whether the first available bombs, of comparatively low efficiency and small in size, will be sufficient to break the will or ability of Japan to resist, especially given the fact that the major cities like Tokyo, Nagoya, Osaka and Kobe already will largely be reduced to ashes by the slower process of ordinary aerial bombing. Certain and perhaps important tactical results undoubtedly can be achieved, but we nevertheless think that the question of the use of the very first available atomic bombs in the Japanese war should be weighed very carefully, not only by military authority, but by the highest political leadership of this country. If we consider international agreement on total prevention of nuclear warfare as the paramount objective, and believe that it can be achieved, this kind of introduction of atomic weapons to the world may easily destroy all our chances of success. Russia, and even allied countries which bear less mistrust of our ways and intentions, as well as neutral countries, will be deeply shocked. It will be very difficult to persuade the world that a nation which was capable of secretly preparing and suddenly releasing a weapon, as indiscriminate as the rocket bomb and a thousand times more destructive, is to be trusted in its proclaimed desire of having such weapons abolished by international agreement. . . .

Thus, from the "optimistic" point of view—looking forward to an international agreement on prevention of nuclear warfare—the military advantages and the saving of American lives, achieved by the sudden use of atomic bombs against Japan, may be outweighed by the ensuing loss of confidence and wave of horror and repulsion, sweeping over the rest of the world, and perhaps dividing even the public opinion at home.

From this point of view a demonstration of the new weapon may best be made before the eyes of representatives of all United Nations, on the desert or a barren island. The best possible atmosphere for the achievement of an international agreement could be achieved if America would be able to say to the world, "You see what weapon we had but did not use. We are ready to renounce its use in the future and to join other nations in working out adequate supervision of the use of this nuclear weapon."

This may sound fantastic, but then in nuclear weapons we have something entirely new in the order of magnitude of destructive power, and if we want to capitalize fully on the advantage which its possession gives us, we must use new and imaginative methods. After such a demonstration the weapon could be used against Japan if a sanction of the United Nations (and of the public opinion at home) could

---

This document can be found in "Political and Social Problems," June 11, 1945, Manhattan Engineering District Papers, National Archives, Washington, D.C. It can also be found in The Committee of Social and Political Implications, A Report to the Secretary of War, June 1945, *Bulletin of the Atomic Scientists*, I (May 1, 1946), 2–4, 16.

be obtained, perhaps after a preliminary ultimatum to Japan to surrender or at least to evacuate a certain region as an alternative to the total destruction of this target.

It must be stressed that if one takes a pessimistic point of view and discounts the possibilities of an effective international control of nuclear weapons, then the advisability of an early use of nuclear bombs against Japan becomes even more doubtful—quite independently of any humanitarian considerations. If no international agreement is concluded immediately after the first demonstration, this will mean a flying start of an unlimited armaments race.

2. Secretary of War Henry L. Stimson Appeals for Atomic Talks with the Soviets, 1945

In many quarters it [atomic bomb] has been interpreted as a substantial offset to the growth of Russian influence on the continent. We can be certain that the Soviet Government has sensed this tendency and the temptation will be strong for the Soviet political and military leaders to acquire this weapon in the shortest possible time. Britain in effect already has the status of a partner with us in the development of this weapon. Accordingly, unless the Soviets are voluntarily invited into the partnership upon a basis of cooperation and trust, we are going to maintain the Anglo-Saxon bloc over against the Soviet in the possession of this weapon. Such a condition will almost certainly stimulate feverish activity on the part of the Soviet toward the development of this bomb in what will in effect be a secret armament race of a rather desperate character. There is evidence to indicate that such activity may have already commenced. . . .

To put the matter concisely, I consider the problem of our satisfactory relations with Russia as not merely connected with but as virtually dominated by the problem of the atomic bomb. Except for the problem of the control of that bomb, those relations, while vitally important, might not be immediately pressing. The establishment of relations of mutual confidence between her and us could afford to await the slow progress of time. But with the discovery of the bomb, they became immediately emergent. Those relations may be perhaps irretrievably embittered by the way in which we approach the solution of the bomb with Russia. For if we fail to approach them now and merely continue to negotiate with them, having this weapon rather ostentatiously on our hip, their suspicions and their distrust of our purposes and motives will increase. . . .

If the atomic bomb were merely another though more devastating military weapon to be assimilated into our pattern of international relations, it would be one thing. We could then follow the old custom of secrecy and nationalistic military superiority relying on international caution to prescribe the future use of the weapon as we did with gas. But I think the bomb instead constitutes merely a first step in a new control by man over the forces of nature too revolutionary and dangerous to fit into

---

This document can be found in Henry L. Stimson, Memorandum for the President, 11 September 1945, "Proposed Actions for Control of Atomic Bombs," Harry S. Truman Papers, PSF: General File, Folder: Atomic Bomb, Box 112, Harry S. Truman Presidential Library, Independence, Mo. It can also be found in Henry L. Stimson and McGeorge Bundy, *On Active Service in Peace and War* (New York: Harper & Brothers, 1948), pp. 642–646.

the old concepts. I think it really caps the climax of the race between man's growing technical power for destructiveness and his psychological power of self-control and group control—his moral power. If so, our method of approach to the Russians is a question of the most vital importance in the evolution of human progress. . . .

My idea of an approach to the Soviets would be a direct proposal after discussion with the British that we would be prepared in effect to enter an arrangement with the Russians, the general purpose of which would be to control and limit the use of the atomic bomb as an instrument of war and so far as possible to direct and encourage the development of atomic power for peaceful and humanitarian purposes. Such an approach might more specifically lead to the proposal that we would stop work on the further improvement in, or manufacture of, the bomb as a military weapon, provided the Russians and the British would agree to do likewise. It might also provide that we would be willing to impound what bombs we now have in the United States provided the Russians and the British would agree with us that in no event will they or we use a bomb as an instrument of war unless all three Governments agree to that use. We might also consider including in the arrangement a covenant with the U.K. and the Soviets providing for the exchange of benefits of future developments whereby atomic energy may be applied on a mutually satisfactory basis for commercial or humanitarian purposes. . . .

I emphasize perhaps beyond all other considerations the importance of taking this action with Russia as a proposal of the United States—backed by Great Britain but peculiarly the proposal of the United States. Action of any international group of nations, including many small nations who have not demonstrated their potential power or responsibility in this war would not, in my opinion, be taken seriously by the Soviets. . . .

. . . The use of this bomb has been accepted by the world as the result of the initiative and productive capacity of the United States, and I think this factor is a most potent lever toward having our proposals accepted by the Soviets, whereas I am most skeptical of obtaining any tangible results by way of any international debate. I urge this method as the most realistic means of accomplishing this vitally important step in the history of the world.

3. Attaché George F. Kennan Critiques Soviet Foreign Policy in His "Long Telegram," 1946

At bottom of Kremlin's neurotic view of world affairs is traditional and instinctive Russian sense of insecurity. Originally, this was insecurity of a peaceful agricultural people trying to live on vast exposed plain in neighborhood of fierce nomadic peoples. To this was added, as Russia came into contact with economically advanced West, fear of more competent, more powerful, more highly organized societies in that area. But this latter type of insecurity was one which afflicted rather Russian rulers than Russian people; for Russian rulers have invariably sensed that their rule was relatively archaic in form, fragile and artificial in its psychological foundation,

---

This document can be found in U.S. Department of State, *Foreign Relations of the United States, 1946, Eastern Europe: The Soviet Union* (Washington, D.C.: Government Printing Office, 1969), VI, 699–701, 706–707.

unable to stand comparison or contact with political systems of Western countries. For this reason they have always feared foreign penetration, feared direct contact between Western world and their own, feared what would happen if Russians learned truth about world without or if foreigners learned truth about world within. And they had learned to seek security only in patient but deadly struggle for total destruction of rival power, never in compacts and compromises with it.

It was no coincidence that Marxism, which had smouldered ineffectively for half a century in Western Europe, caught hold and blazed for first time in Russia. Only in this land which had never known a friendly neighbor or indeed any tolerant equilibrium of separate powers, either internal or international, could a doctrine thrive which viewed economic conflicts of society as insoluble by peaceful means. After establishment of Bolshevist regime, Marxist dogma, rendered even more truculent and intolerant by Lenin's interpretation, became a perfect vehicle for sense of insecurity with which Bolsheviks, even more than previous Russian rulers, were afflicted. In this dogma, with its basic altruism of purpose, they found justification for their instinctive fear of outside world, for the dictatorship without which they did not know how to rule, for cruelties they did not dare not to inflict, for sacrifices they felt bound to demand. In the name of Marxism they sacrificed every single ethical value in their methods and tactics. Today they cannot dispense with it. It is fig leaf of their moral and intellectual respectability. Without it they would stand before history, at best, as only the last of that long succession of cruel and wasteful Russian rulers who have relentlessly forced country on to ever new heights of military power in order to guarantee external security of their internally weak regimes. This is why Soviet purposes must always be solemnly clothed in trappings of Marxism, and why no one should underrate importance of dogma in Soviet affairs. Thus Soviet leaders are driven [by?] necessities of their own past and present position to put forward a dogma which [apparent omission] outside world as evil, hostile and menacing, but as bearing within itself germs of creeping disease and destined to be wracked with growing internal convulsions until it is given final *coup de grace* by rising power of socialism and yields to new and better world. This thesis provides justification for the increase of military and police power of Russian state, for that isolation of Russian population from outside world, and for that fluid and constant pressure to extend limits of Russian police power which are together the natural and instinctive urges of Russian rulers. Basically this is only the steady advance of uneasy Russian nationalism, a centuries old movement in which conceptions of offense and defense are inextricably confused. But in new guise of international Marxism, with its honeyed promises to a desperate and war torn outside world, it is more dangerous and insidious than ever before.

It should not be thought from above that Soviet party line is necessarily disingenuous and insincere on part of all those who put it forward. Many of them are too ignorant of outside world and mentally too dependent to question [apparent omission] self-hypnotism, and who have no difficulty making themselves believe what they find it comforting and convenient to believe. Finally we have the unsolved mystery as to who, if anyone, in this great land actually receives accurate and unbiased information about outside world. In atmosphere of oriental secretiveness and conspiracy which pervades this Government, possibilities for distorting or poisoning sources and currents of information are infinite. The very disrespect of Russians for objective truth—indeed, their disbelief in its existence—leads them to view all stated facts as instruments for furtherance of one ulterior purpose or another. There is good reason to suspect that this Government is actually a conspiracy within a conspiracy; and I for one am reluctant to believe that Stalin himself receives anything like an objective picture of outside world. Here there is ample scope for the type of subtle intrigue at which Russians are past masters. Inability of foreign governments to place their case squarely before Russian policy makers—extent to which they are delivered up in their relations with Russia to good graces of obscure and unknown advisers who they never see and cannot influence—this to my mind is most disquieting feature of diplomacy in Moscow, and one which Western statesmen would do well to keep in mind if they would understand nature of difficulties encountered here. . . .

In summary, we have here a political force committed fanatically to the belief that with US there can be no permanent *modus vivendi,* that it is desirable and necessary that the internal harmony of our society be disrupted, our traditional way of life be destroyed, the international authority of our state be broken, if Soviet power is to be secure. This political force has complete power of disposition over energies of one of world's greatest peoples and resources of world's richest national territory, and is borne along by deep and powerful currents of Russian nationalism. In addition, it has an elaborate and far flung apparatus for exertion of its influence in other countries, an apparatus of amazing flexibility and versatility, managed by people whose experience and skill in underground methods are presumably without parallel in history. Finally, it is seemingly inaccessible to considerations of reality in its basic reactions. For it, the vast fund of objective fact about human society is not, as with us, the measure against which outlook is constantly being tested and reformed, but a grab bag from which individual items are selected arbitrarily and tendenciously to bolster an outlook already preconceived. This is admittedly not a pleasant picture. Problem of how to cope with this force [is] undoubtedly greatest task our diplomacy has ever faced and probably greatest it will ever have to face. It should be point of departure from which our political general staff work at present juncture should proceed. It should be approached with same thoroughness and care as solution of major strategic problem in war, and if necessary, with no smaller outlay in planning effort. I cannot attempt to suggest all answers here. But I would like to record my conviction that problem is within our power to solve—and that without recourse to any general military conflict. And in support of this conviction there are certain observations of a more encouraging nature I should like to make:

1. Soviet power, unlike that of Hitlerite Germany, is neither schematic nor adventuristic. It does not work by fixed plans. It does not take unnecessary risks. Impervious to logic of reason, and it is highly sensitive to logic of force. For this reason it can easily withdraw—and usually does—when strong resistance is encountered at any point. Thus, if the adversary has sufficient force and makes clear his readiness to use it, he rarely has to do so. If situations are properly handled there need be no prestige-engaging showdowns.
2. Gauged against Western World as a whole, Soviets are still by far the weaker force. Thus, their success will really depend on degree of cohesion, firmness and vigor which Western World can muster. And this is factor which it is within our power to influence.

3. Success of Soviet system, as form of internal power, is not yet finally proven. It has yet to be demonstrated that it can survive supreme test of successive transfer of power from one individual or group to another. Lenin's death was first such transfer, and its effects wracked Soviet state for 15 years. After Stalin's death or retirement will be second. But even this will not be final test. Soviet internal system will now be subjected, by virtue of recent territorial expansions, to series of additional strains which once proved severe tax on Tsardom. We here are convinced that never since termination of civil war have mass of Russian people been emotionally farther removed from doctrines of Communist Party than they are today. In Russia, party has now become a great and—for the moment—highly successful apparatus of dictatorial administration, but it has ceased to be a source of emotional inspiration. Thus, internal soundness and permanence of movement need not yet be regarded as assured.

4. All Soviet propaganda beyond Soviet security sphere is basically negative and destructive. It should therefore be relatively easy to combat it by any intelligent and really constructive program.

4. Former British Prime Minister Winston Churchill Declares an "Iron Curtain" Has Descended on Europe, 1946

A shadow has fallen upon the scenes so lately lighted by the Allied victory. Nobody knows what Soviet Russia and its Communist international organization intends to do in the immediate future, or what are the limits, if any, to their expansive and proselytizing tendencies. I have a strong admiration and regard for the valiant Russian people and for my wartime comrade, Marshal Stalin. There is sympathy and good will in Britain—and I doubt not here also—toward the peoples of all the Russias and a resolve to persevere through many differences and rebuffs in establishing lasting friendships.

We understand the Russian need to be secure on her western frontiers from all renewal of German aggression. We welcome her to her rightful place among the leading nations of the world. Above all, we welcome constant, frequent, and growing contacts between Russian people and our own people on both sides of the Atlantic. It is my duty, however, to place before you certain facts about the present position in Europe.

From Stettin in the Baltic to Trieste in the Adriatic, an iron curtain has descended across the continent. Behind that line lie all the capitals of the ancient states of Central and Eastern Europe. Warsaw, Berlin, Prague, Vienna, Budapest, Belgrade, Bucharest, and Sofia, all these famous cities and the populations around them lie in the Soviet sphere and all are subject, in one form or another, not only to Soviet influence but to a very high and increasing measure of control from Moscow. Athens alone, with its immortal glories, is free to decide its future at an election under British, American, and French observation.

This document can be found in *Congressional Record,* XCII (1946, Appendix), A1145–A1147.

The Russian-dominated Polish government has been encouraged to make enormous and wrongful inroads upon Germany, and mass expulsions of millions of Germans on a scale grievous and undreamed of are now taking place. The Communist parties, which were very small in all these eastern states of Europe, have been raised to preeminence and power far beyond their numbers and are seeking everywhere to obtain totalitarian control. Police governments are prevailing in nearly every case, and so far, except in Czechoslovakia, there is no true democracy.

Turkey and Persia are both profoundly alarmed and disturbed at the claims which are made upon them and at the pressure being exerted by the Moscow government. An attempt is being made by the Russians in Berlin to build up a quasi-Communist party in their zone of occupied Germany by showing special favors to groups of left-wing German leaders. At the end of the fighting last June, the American and British Armies withdrew westward, in accordance with an earlier agreement, to a depth at some points of 150 miles on a front of nearly 400 miles, to allow the Russians to occupy this vast expanse of territory which the Western democracies had conquered.

If now the Soviet government tries, by separate action, to build up a pro-Communist Germany in their areas, this will cause new serious difficulties in the British and American zones, and will give the defeated Germans the power of putting themselves up to auction between the Soviets and the Western democracies. Whatever conclusions may be drawn from these facts—and facts they are—this is certainly not the liberated Europe we fought to build up. Nor is it one which contains the essentials of permanent peace.

In front of the iron curtain which lies across Europe are other causes for anxiety. In Italy the Communist party is seriously hampered by having to support the Communist-trained Marshall Tito's claims to former Italian territory at the head of the Adriatic. Nevertheless, the future of Italy hangs in the balance. Again, one cannot imagine a regenerated Europe without a strong France. . . .

However, in a great number of countries, far from the Russian frontiers and throughout the world, Communist fifth columns are established and work in complete unity and absolute obedience to the directions they receive from the Communist center. Except in the British Commonwealth, and in the United States, where communism is in its infancy, the Communist parties or fifth columns constitute a growing challenge and peril to Christian civilization. These are somber facts for anyone to have to recite on the morrow of a victory gained by so much splendid comradeship in arms and in the cause of freedom and democracy, and we should be most unwise not to face them squarely while time remains.

The outlook is also anxious in the Far East and especially in Manchuria. The agreement which was made at Yalta, to which I was a party, was extremely favorable to Soviet Russia, but it was made at a time when no one could say that the German war might not extend all through the summer and autumn of 1945 and when the Japanese war was expected to last for a further eighteen months from the end of the German war. In this country you are all so well informed about the Far East and such devoted friends of China that I do not need to expatiate on the situation there. . . .

Our difficulties and dangers will not be removed by closing our eyes to them; they will not be removed by mere waiting to see what happens; nor will they be relieved by a policy of appeasement. What is needed is a settlement, and the longer this is delayed, the more difficult it will be and the greater our dangers will become. From what I have seen of our Russian friends and allies during the war, I am convinced that there is nothing they admire so much as strength, and there is nothing for which they have less respect than for military weakness. For that reason the old doctrine of a balance of power is unsound. We cannot afford, if we can help it, to work on narrow margins, offering temptations to a trial of strength. If the Western democracies stand together in strict adherence to the principles of the United Nations Charter, their influence for furthering these principles will be immense and no one is likely to molest them. If, however, they become divided or falter in their duty, and if these all-important years are allowed to slip away, then indeed catastrophe may overwhelm us all.

5. Secretary of Commerce Henry A. Wallace Questions the "Get Tough" Policy, 1946

How do American actions since V-J Day appear to other nations? I mean by actions the concrete things like $13 billion for the War and Navy Departments, the Bikini tests of the atomic bomb and continued production of bombs, the plan to arm Latin America with our weapons, production of B-29s and planned production of B-36s, and the effort to secure air bases spread over half the globe from which the other half of the globe can be bombed. I cannot but feel that these actions must make it look to the rest of the world as if we were only paying lip service to peace at the conference table. These facts rather make it appear either (1) that we are preparing ourselves to win the war which we regard as inevitable or (2) that we are trying to build up a predominance of force to intimidate the rest of mankind. How would it look to us if Russia had the atomic bomb and we did not, if Russia had ten thousand-mile bombers and air bases within a thousand miles of our coast lines and we did not?

Some of the military men and self-styled "realists" are saying: "What's wrong with trying to build up a predominance of force? The only way to preserve peace is for this country to be so well armed that no one will dare attack us. We know that America will never start a war."

The flaw in this policy is simply that it will not work. In a world of atomic bombs and other revolutionary new weapons, such as radioactive poison gases and biological warfare, a peace maintained by a predominance of force is no longer possible. . . .

Insistence on our part that the game must be played our way will only lead to a deadlock. The Russians will redouble their efforts to manufacture bombs, and they may also decide to expand their "security zone" in a serious way. Up to now, despite all our outcries against it, their efforts to develop a security zone in Eastern Europe and in the Middle East are small change from the point of view of military power as compared with our air bases in Greenland, Okinawa and many other places thousands of miles from our shores. We may feel very self-righteous if we

Henry A. Wallace, "The Path to Peace with Russia," *New Republic,* 115 (1946), 401–406.

refuse to budge on our plan and the Russians refuse to accept it, but that means only one thing—the atomic armament race is on in deadly earnest. . . .

I should list the factors which make for Russian distrust of the United States and of the Western world as follows: The first is Russian history, which we must take into account because it is the setting in which Russians see all actions and policies of the rest of the world. Russian history for over a thousand years has been a succession of attempts, often unsuccessful, to resist invasion and conquest—by the Mongols, the Turks, the Swedes, the Germans and the Poles. The scant thirty years of the existence of the Soviet government has in Russian eyes been a continuation of their historical struggle for national existence. The first four years of the new regime, from 1917 through 1921, were spent in resisting attempts at destruction by the Japanese, British and French, with some American assistance, and by the several White Russian armies encouraged and financed by the Western powers. Then, in 1941, the Soviet state was almost conquered by the Germans after a period during which the Western European powers had apparently acquiesced in the rearming of Germany in the belief that the Nazis would seek to expand eastward rather than westward. The Russians, therefore, obviously see themselves as fighting for their existence in a hostile world.

Second, it follows that to the Russians all of the defense and security measures of the Western powers seem to have an aggressive intent. Our actions to expand our military security system—such steps as extending the Monroe Doctrine to include the arming of the Western Hemisphere nations, our present monopoly of the atomic bomb, our interest in outlying bases and our general support of the British Empire—appear to them as going far beyond the requirements of defense. I think we might feel the same if the United States were the only capitalistic country in the world and the principal socialistic countries were creating a level of armed strength far exceeding anything in their previous history. From the Russian point of view, also, the granting of a loan to Britain and the lack of tangible results on their request to borrow for rehabilitation purposes may be regarded as another evidence of strengthening of an anti-Soviet bloc.

Finally, our resistance to her attempts to obtain warm water ports and her own security system in the form of "friendly" neighboring states seems, from the Russian point of view, to clinch the case. After twenty-five years of isolation and after having achieved the status of a major power, Russia believes that she is entitled to recognition of her new status. Our interest in establishing democracy in Eastern Europe, where democracy by and large has never existed, seems to her an attempt to reestablish the encirclement of unfriendly neighbors which was created after the last war and which might serve as a springboard of still another effort to destroy her.

If this analysis is correct, and there is ample evidence to support it, the action to improve the situation is clearly indicated. The fundamental objective of such action should be to allay any reasonable Russian grounds for fear, suspicions and distrust. We must recognize that the world has changed and that today there can be no "one world" unless the United States and Russia can find some way of living together. For example, most of us are firmly convinced of the soundness of our position when we suggest the internationalization and defortification of the Danube or of the Dardanelles, but we would be horrified and angered by any Russian counterproposal that would involve also the internationalizing and disarming of Suez or Panama. We must recognize that to the Russians these seem to be identical situations. . . .

It is of the greatest importance that we should discuss with the Russians in a friendly way their long-range economic problems and the future of our cooperation in matters of trade. The reconstruction program of the USSR and the plans for the full development of the Soviet Union offers tremendous opportunities for American goods and American technicians. . . .

Many of the problems relating to the countries bordering on Russia could more readily be solved once an atmosphere of mutual trust and confidence is established and some form of economic arrangements is worked out with Russia. These problems also might be helped by discussions of an economic nature. Russian economic penetration of the Danube area, for example, might be countered by concrete proposals for economic collaboration in the development of the resources of this area, rather than by insisting that the Russians should cease their unilateral penetration and offering no solution to the present economic chaos there.

This proposal admittedly calls for a shift in some of our thinking about international matters. It is imperative that we make this shift. We have little time to lose. Our postwar actions have not yet been adjusted to the lessons to be gained from experience of Allied cooperation during the war and the facts of the atomic age.

6. Soviet Ambassador Nikolai Novikov Identifies a U.S. Drive for World Supremacy, 1946

The foreign policy of the United States, which reflects the imperialist tendencies of American monopolistic capital, is characterized in the postwar period by a striving for world supremacy. This is the real meaning of the many statements by President Truman and other representatives of American ruling circles: that the United States has the right to lead the world. All the forces of American diplomacy—the army, the air force, the navy, industry and science—are enlisted in the service of this foreign policy. . . .

Europe has come out of the war with a completely dislocated economy, and the economic devastation that occurred in the course of the war cannot be overcome in a short time. All of the countries of Europe and Asia are experiencing a colossal need for consumer goods, industrial and transportation equipment, etc. Such a situation provides American monopolistic capital with prospects for enormous shipments of goods and the importation of capital into these countries—a circumstance that would permit it to infiltrate their national economies. . . .

At the same time, there has been a decline in the influence on foreign policy of those who follow Roosevelt's course for cooperation among peace-loving countries. Such persons in the government, in Congress, and in the leadership of the Democratic party are being pushed farther and farther into the background. The contradictions in the field of foreign policy existing between the followers of [Henry] Wallace and [Claude] Pepper, on the one hand, and the adherents of the reactionary "bi-partisan"

From *Origins of the Cold War: The Novikov, Kennan, and Roberts "Long Telegram" of 1946*, Kenneth M. Jensen, editor, Washington: United States Institute of Peace, 1991. Translated by Kenneth M. Jensen and John Glad.

policy, on the other, were manifested with great clarity recently in the speech by Wallace that led to his resignation from the post of Secretary of Commerce. . . .

In the summer of 1946, for the first time in the history of the country, Congress passed a law on the establishment of a peacetime army, not on a volunteer basis but on the basis of universal military service. The size of the army, which is supposed to amount to about one million persons as of July 1, 1947, was also increased significantly. The size of the navy at the conclusion of the war decreased quite insignificantly in comparison with wartime. At the present time, the American navy occupies first place in the world, leaving England's navy far behind, to say nothing of those of other countries.

Expenditures on the army and navy have risen colossally, amounting to 13 billion dollars according to the budget for 1946–47 (about 40 percent of the total budget of 36 billion dollars). This is more than ten times greater than corresponding expenditures in the budget for 1938, which did not amount to even one billion dollars.

Along with maintaining a large army, navy, and air force, the budget provides that these enormous amounts also will be spent on establishing a very extensive system of naval and air bases in the Atlantic and Pacific oceans. According to existing official plans, in the course of the next few years 228 bases, points of support, and radio stations are to be constructed in the Atlantic Ocean and 258 in the Pacific. . . .

One of the stages in the achievement of dominance over the world by the United States is its understanding with England concerning the partial division of the world on the basis of mutual concessions. The basic lines of the secret agreement between the United States and England regarding the division of the world consist, as shown by facts, in their agreement on the inclusion of Japan and China in the sphere of influence of the United States in the Far East, while the United States, for its part, has agreed not to hinder England either in resolving the Indian problem or in strengthening its influence in Siam and Indonesia.

In connection with this division, the United States at the present time is in control of China and Japan without any interference from England. . . .

In recent years American capital has penetrated very intensively into the economy of the Near Eastern countries, in particular into the oil industry. At present there are American oil concessions in all of the Near Eastern countries that have oil deposits (Iraq, Bahrain, Kuwait, Egypt, and Saudi Arabia). American capital, which made its first appearance in the oil industry of the Near East only in 1927, now controls about 42 percent of all proven reserves in the Near East, excluding Iran. Of the total proven reserves of 26.8 billion barrels, over 11 billion barrels are owned by U.S. concessions. . . .

The current relations between England and the United States, despite the temporary attainment of agreements on very important questions, are plagued with great internal contradictions and cannot be lasting.

The economic assistance from the United States conceals within itself a danger for England in many respects. First of all, in accepting the [U.S.] loan, England finds herself in a certain financial dependence on the United States from which it will not be easy to free herself. Second, it should be kept in mind that the conditions created by the loan for the penetration by American capital of the British Empire can entail serious political consequences. The countries included in the British Empire or dependent on it may—under economic pressure from powerful American capital—reorient themselves toward the United States, following in this respect the example of Canada, which more and more is moving away from the influence of England and orienting itself toward the United States. The strengthening of American positions in the Far East could stimulate a similar process in Australia and New Zealand. In the Arabic countries of the Near East, which are striving to emancipate themselves from the British Empire, there are groups within the ruling circles that would not be averse to working out a deal with the United States. It is quite possible that the Near East will become a center of Anglo-American contradictions that will explode the agreements now reached between the United States and England.

The "hard-line" policy with regard to the USSR announced by [Secretary of State James F.] Byrnes after the rapprochement of the reactionary Democrats with the Republicans is at present the main obstacle on the road to cooperation of the Great Powers. It consists mainly of the fact that in the postwar period the United States no longer follows a policy of strengthening cooperation among the Big Three (or Four) but rather has striven to undermine the unity of these countries. The objective has been to impose the will of other countries on the Soviet Union. This is precisely the tenor of the policy of certain countries, which is being carried out with the blessing of the United States, to undermine or completely abolish the principle of the veto in the Security Council of the United Nations. This would give the United States opportunities to form among the Great Powers narrow groupings and blocs directed primarily against the Soviet Union, and thus to split the United Nations. Rejection of the veto by the Great Powers would transform the United Nations into an Anglo-Saxon domain in which the United States would play the leading role.

The present policy of the American government with regard to the USSR is also directed at limiting or dislodging the influence of the Soviet Union from neighboring countries. In implementing this policy in former enemy or Allied countries adjacent to the USSR, the United States attempts, at various international conferences or directly in these countries themselves, to support reactionary forces with the purpose of creating obstacles to the process of democratization of these countries. In so doing, it also attempts to secure positions for the penetration of American capital into their economies. . . .

The American occupation policy [in Germany] does not have the objective of eliminating the remnants of German Fascism and rebuilding German political life on a democratic basis, so that Germany might cease to exist as an aggressive force. The United States is not taking measures to eliminate the monopolistic associations of German industrialists on which German Fascism depended in preparing aggression and waging war. Neither is any agrarian reform being conducted to eliminate large landholders, who were also a reliable support for the Hitlerites. Instead, the United States is considering the possibility of terminating the Allied occupation of German territory before the main tasks of the occupation—the demilitarization and democratization of Germany—have been implemented. This would create the prerequisites for the revival of an imperialist Germany, which the United States plans to use in a future war on its side. One cannot help seeing that such a policy has clearly outlined anti-Soviet edge and constitutes a serious danger to the cause of peace.

The numerous and extremely hostile statements by American government, political, and military figures with regard to the Soviet Union and its foreign policy are very characteristic of the current relationship between the ruling circles of the

United States and the USSR. These statements are echoed in an even more unrestrained tone by the overwhelming majority of the American press organs. Talk about a "third war," meaning a war against the Soviet Union, and even a direct call for this war—with the threat of using the atomic bomb—such is the content of the statements on relations with the Soviet Union by reactionaries at public meetings and in the press. . . .

Careful note should be taken of the fact that the preparation by the United States for a future war is being conducted with the prospect of war against the Soviet Union, which in the eyes of American imperialists is the main obstacle in the path of the United States to world domination. This is indicated by facts such as the tactical training of the American army for war with the Soviet Union as the future opponent, the siting of American strategic bases in regions from which it is possible to launch strikes on Soviet territory, intensified training and strengthening of Arctic regions as close approaches to the USSR, and attempts to prepare Germany and Japan to use those countries in a war against the USSR.

7. The Truman Doctrine Calls for Aid to Greece and Turkey to Contain Totalitarianism, 1947

The gravity of the situation which confronts the world today necessitates my appearance before a joint session of the Congress.

The foreign policy and the national security of this country are involved.

One aspect of the present situation, which I present to you at this time for your consideration and decision, concerns Greece and Turkey.

The United States has received from the Greek Government an urgent appeal for financial and economic assistance. Preliminary reports from the American Economic Mission now in Greece and reports from the American Ambassador in Greece corroborate the statement of the Greek Government that assistance is imperative if Greece is to survive as a free nation. . . .

The British Government has informed us that, owing to its own difficulties, it can no longer extend financial or economic aid to Turkey.

As in the case of Greece, if Turkey is to have the assistance it needs, the United States must supply it. We are the only country able to provide that help. . . .

The peoples of a number of countries of the world have recently had totalitarian regimes forced upon them against their will. The Government of the United States has made frequent protests against coercion and intimidation, in violation of the Yalta agreement, in Poland, Rumania, and Bulgaria. I must also state that in a number of other countries there have been similar developments.

At the present moment in world history nearly every nation must choose between alternative ways of life. The choice is too often not a free one.

One way of life is based upon the will of the majority, and is distinguished by free institutions, representative government, free elections, guarantees of individual liberty, freedom of speech and religion, and freedom from political oppression.

This document can be found in *Public Papers of the Presidents of the United States, Harry S. Truman, 1947* (Washington, D.C.: U.S. Government Printing Office, 1963), pp. 176–180.

The second way of life is based upon the will of a minority forcibly imposed upon the majority. It relies upon terror and oppression, a controlled press and radio, fixed elections, and the suppression of personal freedoms.

I believe that it must be the policy of the United States to support free peoples who are resisting attempted subjugation by armed minorities or by outside pressures.

I believe that we must assist free peoples to work out their own destinies in their own way.

I believe that our help should be primarily through economic and financial aid which is essential to economic stability and orderly political processes.

The world is not static, and the *status quo* is not sacred. But we cannot allow changes in the *status quo* in violation of the Charter of the United Nations by such methods as coercion, or by such subterfuges as political infiltration. In helping free and independent nations to maintain their freedom, the United States will be giving effect to the principles of the Charter of the United Nations.

It is necessary only to glance at a map to realize that the survival and integrity of the Greek nation are of grave importance in a much wider situation. If Greece should fall under the control of an armed minority, the effect upon its neighbor, Turkey, would be immediate and serious. Confusion and disorder might well spread throughout the entire Middle East.

Moreover, the disappearance of Greece as an independent state would have a profound effect upon those countries in Europe whose peoples are struggling against great difficulties to maintain their freedoms and their independence while they repair the damages of war. . . .

Should we fail to aid Greece and Turkey in this fateful hour, the effect will be far reaching to the West as well as to the East.

We must take immediate and resolute action.

I therefore ask the Congress to provide authority for assistance to Greece and Turkey in the amount of $400,000,000 for the period ending June 30, 1948. In requesting these funds, I have taken into consideration the maximum amount of relief assistance which would be furnished to Greece out of the $350,000,000 which I recently requested that the Congress authorize for the prevention of starvation and suffering in countries devastated by the war.

In addition to funds, I ask the Congress to authorize the detail of American civilian and military personnel to Greece and Turkey, at the request of those countries, to assist in the tasks of reconstruction, and for the purpose of supervising the use of such financial and material assistance as may be furnished. I recommend that authority also be provided for the instruction and training of selected Greek and Turkish personnel. . . .

This is a serious course upon which we embark.

I would not recommend it except that the alternative is much more serious. The United States contributed $341,000,000,000 toward winning World War II. This is an investment in world freedom and world peace.

The assistance that I am recommending for Greece and Turkey amounts to little more than 1/10 of 1 percent of this investment. It is only common sense that we should safeguard this investment and make sure that it was not in vain.

The seeds of totalitarian regimes are nurtured by misery and want. They spread and grow in the evil soil of poverty and strife. They reach their full growth when the hope of a people for a better life has died.

We must keep that hope alive.

The free peoples of the world look to us for support in maintaining their freedoms.

If we falter in our leadership, we may endanger the peace of the world—and we shall surely endanger the welfare of this Nation.

Great responsibilities have been placed upon us by the swift movement of events.

I am confident that the Congress will face these responsibilities squarely.

8. The Marshall Plan (Economic Cooperation Act) Provides Aid for European Reconstruction, 1948

Recognizing the intimate economic and other relationships between the United States and the nations of Europe, and recognizing that disruption following in the wake of war is not contained by national frontiers, the Congress finds that the existing situation in Europe endangers the establishment of a lasting peace, the general welfare and national interest of the United States, and the attainment of the objectives of the United Nations. The restoration or maintenance in European countries of principles of individual liberty, free institutions, and genuine independence rests largely upon the establishment of sound economic conditions, stable international economic relationships, and the achievement by the countries of Europe of a healthy economy independent of extraordinary outside assistance. The accomplishment of these objectives calls for a plan of European recovery, open to all such nations which cooperate in such plan, based upon a strong production effort, the expansion of foreign trade, the creation and maintenance of internal financial stability, and the development of economic cooperation, including all possible steps to establish and maintain equitable rates of exchange and to bring about the progressive elimination of trade barriers. Mindful of the advantages which the United States has enjoyed through the existence of a large domestic market with no internal trade barriers, and believing that similar advantages can accrue to the countries of Europe, it is declared to be the policy of the people of the United States to encourage these countries through a joint organization to exert sustained common efforts as set forth in the report of the Committee of European Economic Cooperation signed at Paris on September 22, 1947, which will speedily achieve that economic cooperation in Europe which is essential for lasting peace and prosperity. It is further declared to be the policy of the people of the United States to sustain and strengthen principles of individual liberty, free institutions, and genuine independence in Europe through assistance to those countries of Europe which participate in a joint recovery program based upon self-help and mutual cooperation: *Provided,* That no assistance to the participating countries herein contemplated shall seriously impair the economic stability of the United States. It is further declared to be the policy of the United States that continuity of assistance provided by the United States should, at all times, be dependent upon continuity of cooperation among countries participating in the program.

This document can be found in *United States Statutes at Large, 1948* (Washington, D.C.: Government Printing Office, 1949), Vol. 62, p. 137.

9. The National Security Council Paper No. 68 (NSC-68) Reassesses the Soviet Threat and Recommends a Military Buildup, 1950

Within the past thirty-five years the world has experienced two global wars of tremendous violence. It has witnessed two revolutions—the Russian and the Chinese—of extreme scope and intensity. It has also seen the collapse of five empires—the Ottoman, the Austro-Hungarian, German, Italian, and Japanese—and the drastic decline of two major imperial systems, the British and the French. During the span of one generation, the international distribution of power has been fundamentally altered. For several centuries it had proved impossible for any one nation to gain such preponderant strength that a coalition of other nations could not in time face it with greater strength. The international scene was marked by recurring periods of violence and war, but a system of sovereign and independent states was maintained, over which no state was able to achieve hegemony.

Two complex sets of factors have now basically altered this historical distribution of power. First, the defeat of Germany and Japan and the decline of the British and French Empires have interacted with the development of the United States and the Soviet Union in such a way that power has increasingly gravitated to these two centers. Second, the Soviet Union, unlike previous aspirants to hegemony, is animated by a new fanatic faith, antithetical to our own, and seeks to impose its absolute authority over the rest of the world. Conflict has, therefore, become endemic and is waged, on the part of the Soviet Union, by violent or non-violent methods in accordance with the dictates of expediency. With the development of increasingly terrifying weapons of mass destruction, every individual faces the ever-present possibility of annihilation should the conflict enter the phase of total war. . . .

Our overall policy at the present time may be described as one designed to foster a world environment in which the American system can survive and flourish. It therefore rejects the concept of isolation and affirms the necessity of our positive participation in the world community.

This broad intention embraces two subsidiary policies. One is a policy which we would probably pursue even if there were no Soviet threat. It is a policy of attempting to develop a healthy international community. The other is the policy of "containing" the Soviet system. These two policies are closely interrelated and interact on one another. Nevertheless, the distinction between them is basically valid and contributes to a clearer understanding of what we are trying to do. . . .

As for the policy of "containment," it is one which seeks by all means short of war to (1) block further expansion of Soviet power, (2) expose the falsities of Soviet pretentions, (3) induce a retraction of the Kremlin's control and influence and (4) in general, so foster the seeds of destruction within the Soviet system that the Kremlin is brought at least to the point of modifying its behavior to conform to generally accepted international standards.

This document can be found in U.S. Department of State, *Foreign Relations of the United States, 1950, National Security Affairs; Foreign Economic Policy* (Washington, D.C.: Government Printing Office, 1977), I, 237, 252–253, 262–263, 264, 282, 290.

It was and continues to be cardinal in this policy that we possess superior overall power in ourselves or in dependable combination with other like-minded nations. One of the most important ingredients of power is military strength. In the concept of "containment," the maintenance of a strong military posture is deemed to be essential for two reasons: (1) as an ultimate guarantee of our national security and (2) as an indispensable backdrop to the conduct of the policy of "containment." Without superior aggregate military strength, in being and readily mobilizable, a policy of "containment"—which is in effect a policy of calculated and gradual coercion—is no more than a policy of bluff.

At the same time, it is essential to the successful conduct of a policy of "containment" that we always leave open the possibility of negotiation with the U.S.S.R. A diplomatic freeze—and we are in one now—tends to defeat the very purposes of "containment" because it raises tensions at the same time that it makes Soviet retractions and adjustments in the direction of moderated behavior more difficult. It also tends to inhibit our initiative and deprives us of opportunities for maintaining a moral ascendancy in our struggle with the Soviet system.

In "containment" it is desirable to exert pressure in a fashion which will avoid so far as possible directly challenging Soviet prestige, to keep open the possibility for the U.S.S.R. to retreat before pressure with a minimum loss of face and to secure political advantage from the failure of the Kremlin to yield or take advantage of the openings we leave it.

We have failed to implement adequately these two fundamental aspects of "containment." In the face of obviously mounting Soviet military strength ours has declined relatively. Partly as a byproduct of this, but also for other reasons, we now find ourselves at a diplomatic impasse with the Soviet Union, with the Kremlin growing bolder, with both of us holding on grimly to what we have and with ourselves facing difficult decisions. . . .

It is apparent from the preceding sections that the integrity and vitality of our system is in greater jeopardy than ever before in our history. Even if there were no Soviet Union we would face the great problem of the free society, accentuated many fold in this industrial age, of reconciling order, security, the need for participation, with the requirements of freedom. . . .

It is quite clear from Soviet theory and practice that the Kremlin seeks to bring the free world under its dominion by the methods of the cold war. The preferred technique is to subvert by infiltration and intimidation. Every institution of our society is an instrument which it is sought to stultify and turn against our purposes. Those that touch most closely our material and moral strength are obviously the prime targets, labor unions, civic enterprises, schools, churches, and all media for influencing opinion. . . .

At the same time the Soviet Union is seeking to create overwhelming military force, in order to back up infiltration with intimidation. In the only terms in which it understands strength, it is seeking to demonstrate to the free world that force and the will to use it are on the side of the Kremlin, that those who lack it are decadent and doomed. In local incidents it threatens and encroaches both for the sake of local gains and to increase anxiety and defeatism in all the free world.

The possession of atomic weapons at each of the opposite poles of power, and the inability (for different reasons) of either side to place any trust in the other, puts a premium on a surprise attack against us. It equally puts a premium on a more violent and ruthless prosecution of its design by cold war, especially if the Kremlin is sufficiently objective to realize the improbability of our prosecuting a preventive war. It also puts a premium on piecemeal aggression against others, counting on our unwillingness to engage in atomic war unless we are directly attacked. . . .

A more rapid build-up of political, economic, and military strength and thereby of confidence in the free world than is now contemplated is the only course which is consistent with progress toward achieving our fundamental purpose. The frustration of the Kremlin design requires the free world to develop a successfully functioning political and economic system and a vigorous political offensive against the Soviet Union. These, in turn, require an adequate military shield under which they can develop. It is necessary to have the military power to deter, if possible, Soviet expansion, and to defeat, if necessary, aggressive Soviet or Soviet-directed actions of a limited or total character. The potential strength of the free world is great; its ability to develop these military capabilities and its will to resist Soviet expansion will be determined by the wisdom and will with which it undertakes to meet its political and economic problems. . . .

Our position as the center of power in the free world places a heavy responsibility upon the United States for leadership. We must organize and enlist the energies and resources of the free world in a positive program for peace which will frustrate the Kremlin design for world domination by creating a situation in the free world to which the Kremlin will be compelled to adjust. Without such a cooperative effort, led by the United States, we will have to make gradual withdrawals under pressure until we discover one day that we have sacrificed positions of vital interest.

It is imperative that this trend be reversed by a much more rapid and concerted build-up of the actual strength of both the United States and the other nations of the free world. The analysis shows that this will be costly and will involve significant domestic financial and economic adjustments.

 E S S A Y S

In the opening essay, Barton J. Bernstein, a professor of history at Stanford University, analyzes the Roosevelt and Truman administrations' thinking about the atomic bomb's place both as a weapon to defeat Japan and as a lever to pry diplomatic concessions from the Soviet Union. Bernstein agrees with most historians that Truman ordered the use of the atomic bomb against Japanese civilians primarily to end the war quickly and to save American lives. But he also explores the bomb as a diplomatic "bonus" that American leaders believed would enhance U.S. bargaining power in the Cold War, and he explains the detrimental effects of the bomb and atomic diplomacy on Soviet-American relations. In the second essay, Arnold A. Offner of Lafayette College critically assesses President Harry S. Truman's role in the coming of the Cold War. Offner acknowledges that Stalin's ruthless dictatorship and the deep ideological differences between the Soviet Union and the United States contributed to Cold War conflict. But he emphasizes how Truman's own insecurity, parochialism, and nationalism led the president to oversimplify complex issues, exaggerate the Soviet threat, and rely on military preparedness to contain Soviet expansionism. The administration's atomic diplomacy, its insistence on making West Germany the cornerstone for Europe's reconstruction, and deployment of U.S. naval power in the Mediterranean, according to Offner, unnecessarily antagonized Moscow. And while the Marshall Plan helped ensure Western Europe's economic health, it also precluded Soviet participation and further divided the world. Thus Truman's confrontational policies helped provoke the Cold War.

In the last selection, John Lewis Gaddis of Yale University takes issue with those who view the United States and the Soviet Union as equally responsible for the Cold War. Relying partly on newly released materials from Russian archives, Gaddis observes that World War II produced two distinctively different Cold War empires, and he highlights the Soviet Union's thirst for security through territorial expansion, motivated both by traditional Russian nationalism and Joseph Stalin's authoritarian Marxism-Leninism. The U.S. empire, by contrast, reflected America's democratic traditions and allowed multilateral give and take between the imperial power and its clients. Whereas Stalin used military force to impose the Soviet Union's will on occupied Eastern Europe, Washington negotiated with its West European allies, compromised on differences, and extended its influence primarily with its partners' approval. Therefore, according to Gaddis, the Soviet empire was the more dangerous and destabilizing of the two, and more directly culpable for the onset of the Cold War.

Secrets and Threats: Atomic Diplomacy and Soviet-American Antagonism

BARTON J. BERNSTEIN

When Harry S. Truman became president on April 12, 1945, he was only dimly aware of the existence of the Manhattan Project and unaware that it was an atomic-bomb project. Left uninformed of foreign affairs and generally ignored by Roosevelt in the three months since the inaugural, the new president inherited a set of policies and a group of advisers from his predecessor. While Truman was legally free to reverse Roosevelt's foreign policies and to choose new advisers on foreign policy, in fact he was quite restricted for personal and political reasons. Because Truman was following a very prestigious president whom he, like a great many Americans, loved and admired, the new president was not free psychologically or politically to strike out on a clearly new course. Only a bolder man, with more self-confidence, might have tried critically to assess the legacy and to act independently. But Truman lacked the confidence and the incentive. When, in fact, he did modify policy—for example, on Eastern Europe—he still believed sincerely, as some advisers told him, that he was adhering to his predecessor's agreements and wishes. . . .

In the case of the international-diplomatic policy on the bomb, Truman was even more restricted by Roosevelt's decisions, for the new president inherited a set of reasonably clear wartime policies. Because Roosevelt had already decided to exclude the Soviets from a partnership on the bomb, his successor could not *comfortably* reverse this policy during the war—unless the late president's advisers pleaded for such a reversal or claimed that he had been about to change his policy. They did neither. Consider, then, the massive personal and political deterrents that

From Barton J. Bernstein, "Roosevelt, Truman, and the Atomic Bomb, 1941–1945: A Reinterpretation," *Political Science Quarterly* 90 (Spring 1975), 23–69. Reprinted by permission.

blocked Truman from even reassessing this legacy. What price might he have paid at home if Americans learned later that he had reversed Roosevelt's policy and had launched a bold new departure of sharing with the Soviets a great weapon that cost the United States $2 billion? Truman, in fact, was careful to follow Roosevelt's strategy of concealing from Congress even the dimensions of the secret partnership on atomic energy with Britain. . . .

During his first weeks in office, Truman learned about the project from [Secretary of War Henry] Stimson and from James F. Byrnes, Roosevelt's former director of the Office of War Mobilization and Reconversion who was to become Truman's secretary of state. Byrnes, despite his recent suspicions that the project might be a scientific boondoggle, told Truman, in the president's words, that "the bomb might well put us in a position to dictate our own terms at the end of the war." On April 25, Stimson discussed issues about the bomb more fully with Truman, especially the "political aspects of the S-1 [atomic bomb's] performance." The bomb, the secretary of war explained in a substantial memorandum, would probably be ready in four months and "would be the most terrible weapon ever known in human history [for it] . . . could destroy a whole city." . . .

The entire discussion, judging from Stimson's daily record and [Manhattan Project director General Leslie R.] Groves's memorandum, assumed that the bomb was a legitimate weapon and that it would be used against Japan. The questions they discussed were not *whether* to use the bomb, but its relationship to the Soviet Union and the need to establish postwar atomic policies. Neither Stimson nor Truman sought then to resolve these outstanding issues, and Truman agreed to his secretary's proposal for the establishment of a high-level committee to recommend "action to the executive and legislative branches of our government when secrecy is no longer in full effect." At no time did they conclude that the committee would also consider the issue of whether to use the bomb as a combat weapon. For policy makers, that was not a question; it was an operating assumption.

Nor did Stimson, in his own charge to the Interim Committee, ever *raise* this issue. Throughout the committee's meetings, as various members later noted, all operated on the assumption that the bomb would be used against Japan. They talked, for example, about drafting public statements that would be issued after the bomb's use. They did not discuss *whether* but how to use it. Only one member ultimately endorsed an explicit advance warning to Japan, and none was prepared to suggest that the administration should take any serious risks to avoid using the bomb. At lunch between the two formal meetings on May 31, some members, perhaps only at one table, briefly discussed the possibility of a noncombat demonstration as a warning to Japan but rejected the tactic on the grounds that the bomb might not explode and the failure might stiffen Japanese resistance, or that Japan might move prisoners of war to the target area. . . .

Two weeks later, after the Franck Committee [a scientific advisory group] recommended a noncombat demonstration, Stimson's assistant submitted this proposal to the four-member scientific advisory panel for advice. The panel promptly rejected the Franck Committee proposal: "we can propose no technical demonstration likely to bring an end to the war; we see no acceptable alternative to direct military use." Had the four scientists known that an invasion was not scheduled until November, or had they even offered their judgment after the unexpectedly impressive Alamogordo test on July 16, perhaps they would have given different counsel. But in June, they were not sure that the bomb explosion would be so dramatic, and, like many others in government, they were wary of pushing for a change in tactics if they might be held responsible for the failure of those tactics—especially if that failure could mean the loss of American lives.

A few days after the panel's report, the issue of giving Japan an advance warning about the bomb was raised at a White House meeting with the president, the military chiefs, and the civilian secretaries. On June 18, after they agreed upon a two-stage invasion of Japan, beginning on about November 1, Assistant Secretary of War John J. McCloy became clearly troubled by the omission of the bomb from the discussion and planning. When Truman invited him to speak, the assistant secretary argued that the bomb would make the invasion unnecessary. Why not warn the emperor that the United States had the bomb and would use it unless Japan surrendered? "McCloy's suggestion had appeal," the official history of the AEC [Atomic Energy Commission] later recorded, "but a strong objection developed" to warning Japan in advance, "which no one could refute—there was no assurance the bomb would work." Presumably, like the Interim Committee, they too feared that a warning, followed by a "dud," might stiffen Japan's morale. There was no reason, policy makers concluded, to take this risk.

Though the Interim Committee and high administration officials found no reason not to use the bomb against Japan, many were concerned about the bomb's impact, and its later value, in Soviet-American relations. "[I]t was already apparent," Stimson later wrote, "that the critical questions in American policy toward atomic energy would be directly connected with Soviet Russia." At a few meetings of the Interim Committee, for example, members discussed informing the Soviets of the bomb before its use against Japan. When the issue first arose, [the scientists] Vannevar Bush and [James B.] Conant estimated that the Soviet Union could develop the bomb in about four years and argued for informing the Soviets before combat use as a preliminary to moving toward international control and thereby avoiding a postwar nuclear arms race. Conant and Bush had been promoting this strategy since the preceding September. Even though Roosevelt had cast them to the side in 1943, when he cemented the Anglo-American alliance, the two scientist-administrators had not abandoned hope for their notions. They even circulated to the Interim Committee one of their memoranda on the subject. But at the meetings of May 18 and 31 they again met defeat. General Groves, assuming that America was far more advanced technologically and scientifically and also that the Soviet Union lacked uranium, argued that the Soviets could not build a bomb for about twenty years. He contributed to the appealing "myth" of the atomic secret—that there was a secret and it would long remain America's monopoly. James Byrnes, with special authority as secretary of state–designate and Truman's representative on the committee, accepted Groves's analysis and argued for maintaining the policy of secrecy— which the committee endorsed. Byrnes was apparently very pleased, and Stimson agreed, as he told Truman on June 6, "There should be no revelation to Russia or anyone else of our work on S-1 [the atomic bomb] until the first bomb has been laid successfully on Japan."

At a later meeting on June 21, the Interim Committee, including Byrnes, reversed itself. Yielding to the pleas of Bush and Conant, who were strengthened by the scientific panel's recommendations, the Interim Committee advised Truman to inform the Soviets about the bomb before using it in combat. Like the Franck Committee, the Interim Committee concluded (as the minutes record):

> In the hope of securing effective future control and in view of the fact that general information concerning the project would be made public shortly after the [Potsdam] conference, the Committee *agreed* that there would be considerable advantage, if suitable opportunity arose, in having the President advise the Russians that we were working on this weapon with every prospect of success and that we expected to use it against Japan.
>
> The president might say further that he hoped this matter might be discussed some time in the future in terms of insuring that the weapon would become an aid to peace.

Because of this recommendation, and perhaps also because of the continuing prodding of Bush and Conant, Stimson reversed his own position. He concluded that if the United States dropped the bomb on Japan without first informing the Soviet Union, that act might gravely strain Soviet-American relations. Explaining the committee's position to Truman, Stimson proposed that if the President "thought that Stalin was on good terms with him" at the forthcoming Potsdam conference, he would inform Stalin that the United States had developed the bomb, planned to use it against Japan, knew the Soviets were working on the bomb, and looked forward to discussing international control later. . . .

The issues of the bomb and the Soviet Union had already intruded in other ways upon policy and planning. Awaiting the bomb, Truman had postponed the Potsdam conference, delayed negotiations with Russia, and hoped that atomic energy would pry some concessions from Russia. Truman explained in late May to Joseph Davies, an advocate of Soviet-American friendship, and in early June to Stimson that he was delaying the forthcoming Potsdam conference until the Alamogordo test, when he would know whether the United States had a workable atomic bomb—what Stimson repeatedly called the "mastercard." . . .

For the administration, the atomic bomb, if it worked, had great potential value. It could reduce the importance of early Soviet entry into the war and make American concessions unnecessary. It could also be a lever for extracting concessions from the Soviet Union. On June 6, for example, Stimson discussed with Truman "quid pro quos which should be established for our taking them [Russia] into [a nuclear] partnership. He [Truman] said that he had been thinking of the same things that I was thinking of, namely the settlement of the Polish, Rumanian, Yugoslavian, and Manchurian problems." There is no evidence that they were planning explicitly to threaten the Soviets to gain these concessions, but, obviously, they realized that the Soviets would regard an American nuclear monopoly as threatening and would yield on some issues in order to terminate that monopoly and thereby reduce, or eliminate, the threat. . . .

At Yalta, Roosevelt had granted the Soviet Union concessions in China in order to secure Soviet entry into the Pacific war, which Stalin promised, within two to three months after V-E Day (May 8). Stalin made it clear that Soviet entry would await a Sino-Soviet pact ratifying these concessions. At the time of Yalta, American military planners were counting on a Soviet attack in Manchuria to pin down the Kwantung army there and hence stop Japan from shifting these forces to her homeland to meet an American invasion.

But by April, war conditions changed and military planners revised their analysis: Japan no longer controlled the seas and therefore could not shift her army, so Soviet entry was not essential. In May, the State Department asked Stimson whether

Soviet participation "at the earliest possible moment" was so necessary that the United States should abide by the Far East section of the Yalta agreement. Stimson concluded that the Soviets would enter the war for their own reasons, at their schedule, and with little regard to any American action, that the Yalta concessions would be largely within the grasp of Soviet military power, and that Soviet assistance would be useful, but not essential, if an American invasion was necessary. If there is an invasion, "Russian entry," he wrote, "will have a profound military effect in that almost certainly it will materially shorten the war and thus save American lives." But if the bomb worked, he implied in other discussions, then an invasion would probably not be necessary and Soviet help would be less important. As a result, he urged a delay in settling matters with Russia on the Far East until after the Alamogordo test, and the President apparently followed this counsel. . . .

Could the United States keep the Soviet Union out of the war? Did policy makers try to do this? In mid-July Soviet troops were stationed on the Manchurian border and would soon be ready to intervene. [General George C.] Marshall concluded that even if Japan surrendered on American terms before Soviet entry, Russia could still march into Manchuria and take virtually whatever she wanted there in the surrender terms. Truman, if he believed Marshall's analysis, had nothing to gain politically from deterring Soviet entry, unless he feared, as did Stimson, that the Soviets might try to reach the Japanese homeland and put in a "claim to occupy and help rule it." Perhaps Truman followed the counsel of Stimson and Byrnes, who, for slightly different reasons, were eager to restrain the Soviets. . . .

Why didn't Truman invite Stalin to sign the Potsdam Proclamation of July 26 calling for Japan's surrender? Some analysts argued later that this omission was part of a devious strategy: that Truman wanted to use the bomb and feared that Stalin's signature, tantamount to a declaration of war, might catapult Japan to surrender, thereby making a nuclear attack impossible. The major difficulty with this interpretation is that it exaggerates occasional, sometimes ambiguous, statements about the *possible* impact of Soviet entry and ignores the fact that this possible shock was not a persistent or important theme in American planning. Truman did not exclude the Soviets from the Proclamation in order to use the bomb. The skimpy, often oblique evidence *suggests* a more plausible explanation and a less devious pattern: he wanted to avoid requesting favors from the Soviets. As a result, he did not try this one possible, but not very likely, way of ending the war without using atomic weapons.

At Potsdam, on July 24, Truman told Stalin casually that the United States had developed "a new weapon of unusual destructive force" for use against Japan but did not specify an atomic weapon. Why didn't Truman explicitly inform Stalin about the atomic bomb? Was Truman, as some have suggested, afraid that the news would prompt Stalin to hasten Soviet intervention and therefore end the war and make combat use of the bomb impossible? Did Truman simply want to delay Soviet entry and did he, like Byrnes, fear that his news would have the opposite effect? Did Truman think that the destruction wrought by the bomb would not impress the Soviets as forcefully if they were informed in advance? Why did Truman reject the counsel of the Interim Committee, of Stimson, and even of [British prime minister Winston S.] Churchill, who, after the glowing news of the Alamogordo test, "was not worried about giving the Russians information on the matter but was rather inclined to use it as an argument in our favor in the negotiations"?

Many of these questions cannot be definitively answered on the basis of the presently available evidence, but there is enough evidence to refute one popular interpretation: that Truman's tactic was part of an elaborate strategy to prevent or retard Soviet entry *in order* to delay Japan's surrender and *thereby* make combat use of the bomb possible. That interpretation claims too much. Only the first part can be supported by some, albeit indirect, evidence: that he was probably seeking to delay or prevent Soviet entry. Byrnes later said that he feared that Stalin would order an immediate Soviet declaration of war if he realized the importance of this "new weapon"—advice Truman dubiously claimed he never received. Truman was not trying to postpone Japan's surrender *in order* to use the bomb. In addition to the reasonable theory that he was seeking to prevent or retard Soviet entry, there are two other plausible, complementary interpretations of Truman's behavior. First, he believed, as had some of his advisers earlier, that a combat demonstration would be more impressive to Russia without an advance warning and therefore he concealed the news. Second, he was also ill-prepared to discuss atomic energy with Stalin, for the president had not made a decision about postwar atomic policy and how to exploit the bomb, and probably did not want to be pressed by Stalin about sharing nuclear secrets. Perhaps all three theories collectively explained Truman's evasive tactics.

Even without explicit disclosure, the bomb strengthened American policy at Potsdam. The Alamogordo test stiffened Truman's resolve, as Churchill told Stimson after the meeting of the Big Three on July 22: "Truman was evidently much fortified . . . and . . . he stood up to the Russians in a most emphatic and decisive manner, telling them as to certain demands that they absolutely could not have." Probably, also, the bomb explains why Truman pushed more forcefully at Potsdam for the Soviets to open up Eastern Europe. It is less clear whether the bomb changed the substance of American policy at Potsdam. Probably Byrnes endorsed a reparations policy allowing the division of Germany because the bomb replaced Germany as a potential counterweight to possible Soviet expansion. . . .

Scholars and laymen have criticized the combat use of the atomic bomb. They have contended, among other points, that the bombs were not necessary to end the war, that the administration knew or should have known this, that the administration knew that Japan was on the verge of defeat and *therefore* close to surrender, and that the administration was either short-sighted or had other controlling international-political motives (besides ending the war) for using the bomb. These varying contentions usually focus on the alleged failure of the United States to pursue five alternatives, individually or in combination, in order to achieve Japanese surrender before using the bomb: (1) awaiting Soviet entry, a declaration of war, or a public statement of intent (already discussed); (2) providing a warning and/or a noncombat demonstration (already discussed); (3) redefining unconditional surrender to guarantee the Imperial institution; (4) pursuing Japan's "peace feelers"; or (5) relying upon conventional warfare for a longer period. These contentions assume that policy makers were trying, or should have tried, to avoid using atomic bombs—precisely what they were not trying to do. . . .

There were powerful reasons why the fifth alternative—the use of conventional weapons for a longer period *before* using atomic bombs—seemed undesirable to policy makers. The loss of American lives, while perhaps not great, would have been unconscionable and politically risky. How could policy makers have justified to themselves or to other Americans delaying the use of this great weapon and squandering American lives? Consider the potential political cost at home. In contrast, few Americans were then troubled by the mass killing of enemy citizens, especially if they were yellow. The firebombings of Tokyo, of other Japanese cities, and even of Dresden had produced few cries of outrage in the United States. There was no evidence that most citizens would care that the atomic bomb was as lethal as the raids on Dresden or Tokyo. It was unlikely that there would be popular support for relying upon conventional warfare and not using the atomic bomb. For citizens and policy makers, there were few, if any, moral restraints on what weapons were acceptable in war.

Nor were there any powerful advocates within the high councils of the administration who wanted to delay or not use the bomb and rely instead upon conventional warfare—a naval blockade, continued aerial bombings, or both. The advocates of conventional warfare were not powerful, and they did not directly oppose the use of the bomb. Admiral Ernest L. King, chief of Naval Operations, did believe that the invasion and the atomic bomb were not the only alternative tactics likely to achieve unconditional surrender. A naval blockade, he insisted, would be successful. The army, however, he complained, had little faith in sea power and, hence, Truman did not accept his proposal. [Admiral William] Leahy had serious doubts about using the bomb, but as an old explosives expert who had long claimed that the bomb would never work, he carried little weight on this matter. Surprisingly, perhaps, he did not forcefully press his doubts on the president. . . .

For policy makers, the danger was not simply the loss of a few hundred American lives *prior* to the slightly delayed use of the bombs if the United States relied upon conventional warfare for a few more weeks. Rather the risk was that, if the nuclear attacks were even slightly delayed, the scheduled invasion of Kyushu, with perhaps 30,000 casualties in the first month, would be necessary. After the war, it became fashionable to assume that policy makers clearly foresaw and comfortably expected that an atomic bomb or two would shock Japan into a speedy surrender. But the evidence does not support this view. "The abrupt surrender of Japan came more or less as a surprise," Henry H. Arnold, commanding general of the air force, later explained. Policy makers were planning, if necessary, to drop at least three atomic bombs in August, with the last on about August 24, and more in September. . . .

There have been criticisms of the administration for failing to pursue two other alleged opportunities: (1) redefining the unconditional surrender demands before Hiroshima to guarantee the Imperial institution; (2) responding to Japan's "peace feelers," which stressed the need for this guarantee. Byrnes and apparently Truman, however, were fearful at times that concessions might strengthen, not weaken, the Japanese military and thereby prolong, not shorten, the war. Some critics imply that Byrnes and Truman were not sincere in presenting this analysis and that they rejected concessions consciously in order to use the bomb. That is incorrect. Other critics believe that these policy makers were sincere but disagree with their assessment—especially since some intelligence studies implied the need for concessions on peace terms to shorten the war. Probably the administration was wrong, and these latter critics right, but either policy involved risks and some were very unattractive to Truman.

Truman, as a new president, was not comfortable in openly challenging Roosevelt's policy of unconditional surrender and modifying the terms. That was risky. It could fail and politically injure him at home. Demanding unconditional surrender meant fewer risks at home and, according to his most trusted advisers at times, fewer risks in ending the war speedily. . . . After August 10, when Japan made the guarantee the only additional condition, Truman yielded on the issue. He deemed it a tactical problem, not a substantive one. But even then, Byrnes was wary of offering this concession, despite evidence that it would probably end the war promptly—precisely what he wanted in order to forestall Soviet gains in the Far East. . . .

Let us look at the remaining, but connected, alternative—pursuing Japan's "peace feelers." Japan's so-called peace feelers were primarily a series of messages from the foreign minister to his nation's ambassador in Moscow, who was asked to investigate the possibility of having the Soviets serve as intermediaries in negotiating a peace. American intelligence intercepted and decoded all the messages. Most, if not all, were sent on to Potsdam, where Truman and Byrnes had access to them. Both men showed little interest in them, and may not even have read all of them, apparently because the proposed concessions were insufficient to meet American demands and because Truman and Byrnes had already decided that the peace party in Japan could not succeed until American attacks—including atomic bombs—crushed the military's hopes. The intercepted and decoded messages fell short of American expectations. Not only did Japan's foreign minister want to retain the Imperial institution, which was acceptable to some policy makers, but he also wanted a peace that would maintain his nation's "honor and existence," a phrase that remained vague. As late as July 27, the day after the Potsdam Proclamation, when Japan's foreign minister was planning a special peace mission to Russia, he was still unwilling or unable to present a "concrete proposal" for negotiations. . . .

Looking back upon these years, Americans may well lament the unwillingness of their leaders to make some concessions at this time and to rely upon negotiations before using the bombs. That lament, however, is logically separable from the unfounded charges that policy makers consciously avoided the "peace feelers" *because* they wanted to drop the bombs in order to intimidate the Soviets. It is true that American leaders did not cast policy in order to avoid using the atomic bombs. Given their analysis, they had no reason to avoid using these weapons. As a result, their analysis provokes ethical revulsion among many critics, who believe that policy makers should have been reluctant to use atomic weapons and should have sought, perhaps even at some cost in American lives, to avoid using them. . . .

[One can also suggest that the bomb was used as] retribution against Japan. A few days after Nagasaki, Truman hinted at this theme in a private letter justifying the combat use of the bombs:

> Nobody is more disturbed over the use of Atomic bombs than I am but I was greatly disturbed over the unwarranted attack by the Japanese on Pearl Harbor. The only language they seem to understand is the one that we have been using to bombard them. When you have to deal with a beast you have to treat him as a beast. It is most regrettable but nevertheless true.

In this letter, one can detect strains of the quest for retribution (the reference to Pearl Harbor), and some might even find subtle strains of racism (Japan was "a beast"). The enemy was a beast and deserved to be destroyed. War, as some critics would stress, dehumanized victors and vanquished, and justified inhumanity in the name of nationalism, of justice, and even humanity.

In assessing the administration's failure to challenge the assumption that the bomb was a legitimate weapon to be used against Japan, we may conclude that Truman found no reason to reconsider, that it would have been difficult for him to challenge the assumption, and that there were also various likely benefits deterring a reassessment. For the administration, in short, there was no reason to avoid using the bomb and many reasons making it feasible and even attractive. The bomb was used primarily to end the war *promptly* and thereby to save American lives. There were other ways to end the war, but none of them seemed as effective. They would not produce victory as promptly and seemed to have greater risks. Even if Russia had not existed, the bombs would have been used in the same way. How could Truman, in the absence of overriding contrary reasons, justify not using the bombs, or even delaying their use, and thereby prolonging the war sacrificing American lives? . . .

On August 9, the day that Nagasaki was bombed, the president delivered a national address on the Potsdam meeting. The United States, he declared, "would maintain military bases necessary for the complete protection of our interests and of world peace." The secret of the bomb, he promised, would be retained until the world ceased being "lawless." "We must constitute ourselves trustees of this new force—to prevent its misuse, and to turn it into the channels of service to mankind." He also emphasized that the Balkan nations "are not to be the spheres of influence of any one power"—a direct warning to the Soviet Union. Here was the first, albeit muted, statement of atomic diplomacy: the implicit threat that the bomb could roll back Soviet influence from Eastern Europe.

"In many quarters," Stimson lamented in late August and early September, the bomb is "interpreted as a substantial offset to the growth of Russian influence on the continent." He complained that Byrnes was wearing the bomb ostentatiously on his hip and hoping to use the weapon to secure his program at the September Conference of Foreign Ministers in London. "His mind is full of his problems," Stimson wrote in his diary. Byrnes "looks to having the presence of the bomb in his pocket, so to speak, as a great weapon to get through the thing. . . . " Assistant Secretary of War John J. McCloy concluded, after a long discussion with Byrnes, that he "wished to have the implied threat of the bomb in his pocket during the conference . . . [in London]." This evidence is unambiguous as to Byrnes's intent, and it cannot be ignored or interpreted as misleading. Byrnes had no reason to seek to deceive Stimson and McCloy about his hopes and tactics. Byrnes had no incentive to posture with them or to appear militant, since they opposed his vigorous tactics and instead counseled moderation and international control of atomic energy. . . .

At the [postwar] London Conference [of Foreign Ministers], an uneasy Vyacheslav Molotov, the Soviet foreign minister, twitted Byrnes about America's nuclear monopoly and tried uneasily to minimize its importance. Molotov's humor betrayed Soviet fears. On September 13, three days into the conference, "Molotov asks JFB if he has an atomic bomb in his side pocket. 'You don't know Southerners,' Byrnes replied. 'We carry our artillery in our hip pocket. If you don't cut out all this stalling and let us get down to work I am going to pull an atomic bomb out of my hip pocket and let you have it.' " In response to this veiled threat, according to the informal notes, "Molotov laughed as did the interpreter." Byrnes's barb emphasized American power. A few nights later, after a stormy session during the day, Molotov commented once more, with strained jocularity, that Byrnes had two advantages that the Soviet minister could not match—eloquence and the atomic bomb. . . .

Though the bomb strengthened American policy and partly compensated for reductions in conventional forces, Truman had private doubts about whether he could use atomic weapons against the Soviet Union. On October 5, in talking with Harold Smith, his budget director, the president worried about the international situation and that the United States might be demobilizing too fast. "There are some people in the world who do not seem to understand anything except the number of divisions you have," he complained. Smith replied, "You have the atomic bomb up your sleeve." "Yes," Truman acknowledged, "but I am not sure it can ever be used." He did not explain his thinking, but presumably he meant that, short of a Soviet attack on Western Europe or on the United States, the American people, given the prevailing sentiments of late 1945, would not tolerate dropping atomic bombs on the Soviet Union. Certainly, they would not then countenance the military use of the bomb to roll back the Soviets from Eastern Europe. Few Americans then cared enough about Eastern Europe or were willing to endorse war against the Soviet Union. The bomb, rather than conferring omnipotence on the United States, had a more restricted role: it was a limited threat. . . .

Did the bomb make a critical difference in shaping the early Cold War? Roosevelt's repeated decisions to bar the Soviets from the nuclear project and Truman's decision to use the bomb in combat without explicitly informing the Soviet Union and inviting her to join in postwar control of atomic energy undoubtedly contributed to the Cold War and helped shape the form that it took. Yet, in view of the great strains in the fragile wartime Soviet-American alliance, historians should not regard America's *wartime* policy on the bomb as *the* cause, but only as one of the causes, of the Cold War. The wartime policy on atomic energy represented one of a number of missed opportunities at achieving limited agreements and at testing the prospects for Soviet-American cooperation on a vital matter.

The atomic bomb, first as prospect and then as reality, did influence American policy. The bomb reduced the incentives for compromise and even stiffened demands by the time of the Potsdam meeting in July 1945 because the weapon gave the United States enhanced power. Without the bomb, policy makers probably would have been more conciliatory after V-J Day in dealing with the Soviet Union, especially about Eastern Europe. The president certainly would have been unable to try to use atomic diplomacy (implied threats) to push the Soviets out of Eastern Europe. Rather, he might have speedily, though reluctantly, agreed to the dominance of Soviet power and to the closed door in that sector of the world. The bomb, as potential or actual weapon, did *not* alter the administration's conception of an ideal world, but possession of the weapon did strengthen the belief of policy makers in their capacity to move toward establishing their goal: an "open door" world with the Soviets acceding to American demands. This ideal world included free elections, an open economic door, and the reduction of Soviet influence in Eastern Europe. Without the bomb, the Truman administration would not have surrendered these ultimate aims, but policy makers would have had to rely primarily on economic power as a bargaining card to secure concessions from the Soviet Union. And economic power, taken alone, would probably have seemed insufficient—as the record of lend-lease and the Russian loan suggests. . . .

Without the bomb, in summary, American policy after V-J Day would have been more cautious, less demanding, less optimistic. Such restraint would not have prevented the breakdown of the Soviet-American alliance, but probably the cold war would not have taken the form that it did, and an uneasy truce, with less fear and antagonism, might have been possible.

Provincialism and Confrontation: President Harry S. Truman and the Origins of the Cold War

ARNOLD A. OFFNER

As the twenty-first century nears, Present Harry S. Truman's reputation stands high. This is especially true regarding his stewardship of foreign policy although, ironically, he entered the Oval Office in 1945 untutored in world affairs, and during his last year in the White House Republicans accused his administration of having surrendered fifteen countries and five hundred million people to communism and sending twenty thousand Americans to their "burial ground" in Korea. Near the end of his term, Truman's public "favorable" rating had plummeted to 23 percent.

Within a decade, however, historians rated Truman a "near great" president, crediting his administration with reconstructing Western Europe and Japan, resisting Soviet or Communist aggression from Greece to Korea, and forging collective security through NATO. In the 1970s the "plain speaking" Truman became a popular culture hero. Recently, biographers have depicted him as the allegory of American life, an ordinary man whose extraordinary character led him to triumph over adversity from childhood through the presidency, and even posited a symbiotic relationship between "His Odyssey" from Independence to the White House and America's rise to triumphant superpower status. . . .

Collapse of the Soviet Union and Europe's other Communist states, whose archives have confirmed Truman's belief in 1945 that their regimes governed largely by "clubs, pistols and concentration camps," has further raised the former president's standing. This has encouraged John Lewis Gaddis and others to shift their focus to Stalin's murderous domestic rule as the key determinant of Soviet foreign policy and the Cold War. As Gaddis has contended, Stalin was heir to Ivan the Terrible and Peter the Great, responsible for more state-sanctioned murders than Adolf Hitler, and treated world politics as an extension of domestic politics: a zero sum game in which his gaining security meant depriving all others of it. For Gaddis and others, that is largely the answer to the question of whether Stalin sought or caused the Cold War.

But as Walter LaFeber has said, to dismiss Stalin's policies as the work of a paranoid is greatly to oversimplify the Cold War. Indeed, historians of Stalin's era

Arnold A. Offner, "'Another Such Victory': President Truman, American Foreign Policy, and the Cold War," *Diplomatic History,* 23 (Spring 1999), 127–142, 153–155. Reprinted with permission of Blackwell Publishing Ltd.

seem to be of the preponderant view that he pursued a cautious but brutal realpolitik. He aimed to restore Russia's 1941 boundaries, establish a sphere of influence in border states, provide security against a recovered Germany or Japan or hostile capitalist states, and gain compensation, notably reparations, for the ravages of war. Stalin calculated forces, recognized America's superior industrial and military power, put Soviet state interests ahead of Marxist-Leninist ideology, and pursued pragmatic or opportunistic policies in critical areas such as Germany, China, and Korea.

Thus, the time seems ripe, given our increased knowledge of Soviet policies, to reconsider President Truman's role in the Cold War. As Thomas G. Paterson has written, the president stands as the pinnacle of the diplomatic-military establishment, has great capacity to set the foreign policy agenda and to mold public opinion, and his importance, especially in Truman's case, cannot be denied. But contrary to prevailing views, I believe that his policymaking was shaped by his parochial and nationalistic heritage. This was reflected in his uncritical belief in the superiority of American values and political-economic interests and his conviction that the Soviet Union and communism were the root cause of international strife. Truman's parochialism also caused him to disregard contrary views, to engage in simplistic analogizing, and to show little ability to comprehend the basis for other nations' policies. Consequently, his foreign policy leadership intensified Soviet-American conflict, hastened the division of Europe, and brought tragic intervention in Asian civil wars. . . .

Truman's parochialism and nationalism, and significant insecurity, were rooted in his background, despite his claim to have had a bucolic childhood of happy family, farm life, and Baptist religiosity. In fact, young Harry's poor eyesight, extended illness, and "sissy" piano playing alienated him from both his peers and his feisty father and fostered ambivalence in him toward powerful men. On the one hand, Truman deferred to "Boss" Thomas Pendergast, his dishonest political benefactor, and to Secretaries of State George Marshall and Dean Acheson, whose manner and firm viewpoints he found reassuring. On the other hand, he denounced those whose style or ways of thinking were unfamiliar. This included the State Department's "striped pants boys," the military's "brass hats" and "prima donnas," political "fakirs" [*sic*] such as Teddy and Franklin Roosevelt, and "professional liberals." For Truman, Charles de Gaulle, Josef Stalin, Ernest Bevin, and Douglas MacArthur were each, at one time or another, a "son of a bitch." . . .

Truman's self-tutelage in history derived largely from didactic biographies of "great men" and empires. This enhanced his vision of the globe but provided little sense of complexity or ambiguity and instilled exaggerated belief that current events had exact historical analogues that provided the key to contemporary policy. The new president was "amazed" that the Yalta accords were so "hazy" and fraught with "new meanings" at every reading, which probably contributed to his "lackluster" adherence to them. Shortly, Truman uncritically applied analogues about 1930s appeasement of Nazi Germany to diplomacy with the Soviet Union and crises in Iran, Greece, Turkey, and Korea.

Further, young Harry's Bible reading and church going did not inspire an abiding religiosity or system of morals so much as a conviction that the world was filled with "liars and hypocrites," terms he readily applied to his presidential critics, and a stern belief, as he wrote in 1945, that "punishment always followed transgression," a maxim that he applied to North Korea and the People's Republic of China (PRC).

Truman's early writings disdained non-Americans and minorities ("Chink doctor," "dago," "nigger," "Jew clerk," and "bohunks and Rooshans"), and in 1940 he proposed to deport "disloyal inhabitants." As president in 1945 he questioned the loyalty of "hyphenate" Americans, and in 1947 he signed Executive Order 9835, creating an unprecedented "loyalty" program that jettisoned basic legal procedural safeguards and virtually included a presumption of guilt.

Truman's command of men and bravery under fire in World War I were exemplary but not broadening. He deplored Europe's politics, mores, and food and sought only to return to "God's country." He intended never to revisit Europe: "I've nearly promised old Miss Liberty that she'll have to turn around to see me again," he wrote in 1918, and in 1945 he went reluctantly to Potsdam to his first and only European summit.

Nonetheless, Truman identified with Wilsonian internationalism, especially the League of Nations, and as a senator he supported President Franklin Roosevelt on the World Court, neutrality revision, rearmament, and Lend Lease for Britain and Russia. He rightfully said "I am no appeaser." But his internationalism reflected unquestioned faith in American moral superiority, and his foreign policy proposals largely comprised military preparedness. He was indifferent to the plight of Republican Spain and too quickly blamed international conflict on "outlaws," "savages," and "totalitarians." After Germany invaded the Soviet Union in 1941, he hastily remarked that they should be left to destroy one another—although he opposed Germany's winning—and he likened Russian leaders to "Hitler and Al Capone" and soon inveighed against the "twin blights—atheism and communism." Hence, while Truman supported the fledgling United Nations and the liberalization of world trade, the man who became president in April 1945 was less an incipient internationalist than a parochial nationalist given to excessive fear that appeasement, lack of preparedness, and enemies at home and abroad would thwart America's mission (the "Lord's will") to "win the peace" on its terms.

President Truman inherited an expedient wartime alliance that stood on shaky ground at Yalta in February 1945 and grew more strained over Soviet control in Romania and Poland and U.S. surrender talks with German officials at Bern that aroused Stalin's fears of a separate peace. Truman lamented that "they didn't tell me anything about what was going on." He also had to depend on advisers whose views ranged from Ambassador Averell Harriman's belief that it was time to halt the Russians' "barbarian invasion" of Europe to counsel from FDR emissaries Joseph Davies and Harry Hopkins to try to preserve long-term accord. Truman's desire to appear decisive by making quick decisions and his instinct to be "tough" spurred his belief that he could get "85 percent" from the Russians on important matters and that they could go along or "go to hell."

Initially, the president's abrupt style and conflicting advice produced inconsistent policy. His mid-April call for a "new" government in Poland and his "one-two to the jaw" interview with [Soviet foreign minister Vyacheslav] Molotov brought only a sharp reply from Stalin, after which the United States recognized a predominantly Communist Polish government. In May, Truman approved "getting tough" with the Russians by suddenly curtailing Lend Lease shipments, but Anglo-Soviet protests caused him to countermand the cutoffs. He then refused Prime Minister Winston Churchill's proposal to keep Anglo-American troops advanced beyond their agreed occupation zones to bargain in Germany and soon wrote that he was "anxious to keep all my engagements with the Russians because they are touchy and suspicious of us."

Still, Truman determined to have his way with the Russians, especially in Germany. Tutored in part by Secretary of War Henry L. Stimson, he embraced the emergent War-State Department position that Germany was key to the balance of power in Europe and required some reconstruction because a "poor house" standard of living there meant the same for Europe, and might cause a repeat of the tragic Treaty of Versailles history. Truman replaced Roosevelt's reparations negotiator, Isador Lubin, with conservative oil entrepreneur Edwin Pauley, who brushed off both Soviet claims to Yalta's $20 billion in reparations and State Department estimates that Germany could pay $12–14 billion. Truman also said that when he met with Churchill and Stalin he wanted "all the bargaining power—all the cards in my hands, and the plan on Germany is one of them."

The other card was the atomic bomb, which inspired Truman and [Secretary of State] Byrnes to think that they could win their way in Europe and Asia. Byrnes told the president in April that the bomb might allow them to "dictate our terms" at the war's end and in May indicated his belief that it would make the Russians more "manageable." Stimson counseled Truman that America's industrial strength and unique weapon comprised a "royal straight flush and we mustn't be a fool about how we play it," that it would be "dominant" in any dispute with Russia over Manchuria, and a "weapon" or "master card" in America's hand in its "big stakes" diplomacy with the Russians. . . .

After meeting Stalin [at Potsdam, Germany,] on 17 July Truman wrote that he was unfazed by the Russian's "dynamite" agenda because "I have some dynamite too which I'm not exploding now." The following day he asserted that the "Japs will fold up" before Russia entered the Pacific war, specifically "when Manhattan appears over their homeland." Truman agreed with Byrnes that use of the bomb would permit them to "out maneuver Stalin on China," that is, negate the Yalta concessions in Manchuria and guarantee that Russia would "not get in so much on the kill" of Japan or its occupation. . . .

News of the bomb's power also greatly reinforced Truman's confidence to allow Byrnes to press European negotiations to impasse by refusing the Russians access to the Ruhr, rejecting even their low bid for $4 billion in industrial reparations, and withdrawing the Yalta accords. Convinced that the New Mexico atomic test would allow the United States to "control" events, Byrnes pushed his famous 30 July tripartite ultimatum on German zonal reparations [limiting Soviet reparations mainly to the Soviet occupational zone and reducing the amounts discussed by FDR and Stalin at Yalta], Poland's de facto control over its new western border (including Silesia) with Germany, and Italy's membership in the UN "Mr. Stalin is stallin'," Truman wrote hours before the American-set deadline on 31 July, but that was useless because "I have an ace in the hole and another one showing," aces that he knew would soon fall upon Japan.

Truman won his hand, as Stalin acceded to zonal reparations. But Truman's victory was fraught with more long-term consequences than he envisioned. He had not only equated his desire to prevent use of taxpayer dollars to help sustain occupied Germany with the Russians' vital need for reparations but also given them reason to think, as Norman Naimark has written, that the Americans were deaf to their question for a "paltry" $10 billion or less to compensate for Germany's having ravaged their nation. Further, America's insistence on zonal reparations would impeded development of common economic policy for all of Germany and increase likelihood of its East-West division. . . .

Truman backed Byrnes's [hard-headed] diplomacy at the London CFM [Council of Foreign Ministers], which deadlocked over Russian control in Eastern Europe and American control in Japan. Truman told Byrnes to "stick to his guns" and tell the Russians "to go to hell." The president then agreed with "ultranationalist" advisers who opposed international atomic accord by drawing misleading analogies about interwar disarmament and "appeasement" and by insisting that America's technological-industrial genius assured permanent atomic supremacy. Truman held that America was the world's atomic "trustee"; that it had to preserve the bomb's "secret"; and that no nation would give up the "locks and bolts" necessary to protect its "house" from "outlaws." The atomic arms race was on, he said in the fall of 1945, and other nations had to "catch up on their own hook."

In the spring of 1946, Truman undercut the Dean Acheson-David Lilienthal plan for international control and development of atomic resources by appointing as chief negotiator Bernard Baruch, whose emphasis on close inspections, sanctions, no veto, and indefinite American atomic monopoly virtually assured Russian refusal. Despite Acheson's protests, Truman analogized that "if Harry Stimson had been back up in Manchuria [in 1931] there would have been no war." And as deadlock neared in July 1946, the president told Baruch to "stand pat."

Ultimately the UN commission weighing the Baruch Plan approved it on 31 December 1946. But the prospect of a Soviet veto in the Security Council precluded its adoption. Admittedly, Stalin's belief that he could not deal with the United States on an equal basis until he had the bomb and Soviet insistence on retention of their veto power and national control of resources and facilities may have precluded atomic accord in 1946. Still, Baruch insisted that the United States could get its way because it had an atomic monopoly, and American military officials sought to preserve a nuclear monopoly as long as possible and to develop a strategy based on air power and atomic weapons. . . .

Meanwhile, Byrnes's diplomacy in Moscow in December 1945 had produced Yalta-style accords on a European peace treaty process, Russian predominance in Bulgaria and Romania and American primacy in China and Japan, and compromise over Korea, with Soviet disputes with Iran and Turkey set aside. But conservative critics cried "appeasement," and in his famous but disputed letter of 5 January 1946, an anxious president charged that Byrnes had kept him "completely in the dark"; denounced Russian "outrage[s]" in the Baltic, Germany, Poland, and Iran and intent to invade Turkey; and said that the Russians understood only an "iron fist" and "divisions" and that he was tired of "babying" them. In fact, Truman knew of most of Byrnes's positions; they had hardly "babied" Russia since Potsdam; and no Russian attack was imminent. The letter reflected Truman's new "get tough" policy, or personal cold war declaration, which, it must be emphasized, came six weeks before George Kennan's Long Telegram and Churchill's Iron Curtain speech.

Strong American protests in 1946 caused the Russians to withdraw their troops from Iran and their claims to joint defense of the Turkish Straits. In the latter case, Truman said he was ready to follow his policy of military response "to the end" to determine if Russia intended "world conquest." Once again he had taken an exaggerated, nationalist stance. No one expected a Russian military advance; America's action rested on its plans to integrate Turkey into its strategic planning and to use it as a base of operations against Russia in event of war. And in September Truman approved announcement of a Mediterranean command that led to the United States becoming the dominant naval power there by year's end.

Meanwhile, Truman ignored Secretary of Commerce Henry Wallace's lengthy memoranda during March–September 1946 that sought to promote economic ties with Russia and questioned America's atomic policies and global military expansiveness. The president then fired Wallace after he publicly challenged Byrnes's speech on 6 September in Stuttgart propounding West German reconstruction and continued American military presence there. The firing was reasonable, but not the rage at Wallace as "a real Commy" and at "parlor pinks and soprano-voiced men" as a "national danger" and "sabotage front" for Stalin.

Equally without reason was Truman's face value acceptance of White House special counsel Clark Clifford's "Russian Report" of September 1946 and accompanying "Last Will of Peter the Great." Clifford's report rested on a hasty compilation of apocalyptic projections of Soviet aim to conquer the world by military force and subversion, and he argued that the United States had to prepare for total war. He wrote in the "black and white" terms that he knew Truman would like and aimed to justify a vast global military upgrade and silence political critics on the left and right. Tsar Peter's will was an old forgery purporting to show that he had a similar design to conquer Eurasia. Truman may have found the report so "hot" that he confined it to his White House safe, but he believed the report and the will and soon was persisting that the governments of the czars, Stalin, and Hitler were all the same. Later he told a mild critic of American policy to read Tsar Peter's will to learn where Russian leaders got their "fixed ideas."

It was a short step, Clifford recalled, from the Russian Report to Truman's epochal request in March 1947 for military aid to Greece and Turkey to help "free peoples" fight totalitarianism. Truman vastly overstated the global-ideological aspects of Soviet-American conflict. Perhaps he sought to fire "the opening gun" to rouse the public and a fiscally conservative Republican Congress to national security expenditures. But he also said that this was "only the beginning" of the "U.S. going into European politics," that the Russians had broken every agreement since Potsdam and would now get only "one language" from him. He added in the fall of 1947 that "if Russia gets Greece and Turkey," it would get Italy and France, the iron curtain would extend to western Ireland, and the United States would have to "come home and prepare for war."

Truman's fears were excessive. Stalin never challenged the Truman Doctrine or Western primacy in Turkey, now under U.S. military tutelage, and Greece. He provided almost no aid to the Greek rebels and told Yugoslavia's leaders in early 1948 to halt their aid because the United States would never allow the Greek Communists to win and break Anglo-American control in the Mediterranean. When Marshal Josip Broz Tito balked, Stalin withdrew his advisers from Yugoslavia and expelled that nation from the Cominform. Tito finally closed his borders to the Greek rebels in July 1949.

Perhaps U.S. officials feared that Britain's retreat from Greece might allow Russia to penetrate the Mediterranean, or that if Greek Communists overthrew the reactionary Greek regime (Turkey was not threatened) they might align Athens with

Moscow. Still, the Truman administration's costly policy never addressed the causes of Greece's civil war; instead, it substituted military "annihilation of the enemy for the reform of the social and economic conditions" that had brought civil war. Equally important, Truman's rhetorical division of the world into "free" versus "totalitarian" states . . . created . . . an unfortunate model for later interventions, such as in Korea— "the Greece of the Far East," as Truman would say—and in French Indochina.

The Truman Doctrine led to the Marshall Plan in June 1947, but they were not "two halves of the same walnut," as Truman claimed. State Department officials who drew up the European Recovery Plan (ERP) differentiated it from what they viewed as his doctrine's implications for "economic and ultimately military warfare." The Soviets likened the Truman Doctrine to retail purchase of separate nations and the Marshall Plan to wholesale purchase of Europe.

The Soviet view was narrow, although initially they had interest in participating and perhaps even harbored dreams that the United States would proffer a generous Lend Lease-style arrangement. But as the British quickly saw, Soviet participation was precluded by American-imposed financial and economic controls and, as Michael J. Hogan has written, by the integrated, continental approach to aid rather than a nation-by-nation basis that would have benefited war-devastated Russia. Indeed, in direct talks in Paris, U.S. officials refused concessions, focused on resources to come from Russia and East Europe, and insisted on German contributions to the ERP ahead of reparations payments or a peace treaty—and then expressed widespread relief when the Soviets rejected the ERP for themselves and East Europe.

The Marshall Plan proved to be a very successful geostrategic venture. It helped to spur American-European trade and Western European recovery, bring France into camp with Germany and satisfy French economic and security claims, and revive western Germany industrially without unleashing the 1930s-style "German colossus" that Truman's aides feared. The Marshall Plan was also intended to contain the Soviets economically, forestall German-Soviet bilateral deals, and provide America with access to its allies' domestic and colonial resources. Finally, as the British said, the Truman administration sought an integrated Europe resembling the United States, "God's own country."

The Marshall Plan's excellent return on investment, however, may have cost far more than the $13 billion expended. "The world is definitely split in two," Undersecretary of State Robert Lovett said in August 1947, while Kennan forewarned that for defensive reasons the Soviets would "clamp down completely on Czechoslovakia" to strengthen their hold on Eastern Europe. Indeed, the most recent evidence indicates that Stalin viewed the Marshall Plan as a "watershed" event, signaling an American effort to predominate over all of Europe. This spurred the Soviets into a comprehensive strategy shift. They now rigged the elections in Hungary, proffered [Politburo spokesman] Andrei Zhdanov's "two camps" approach to world policy, created the Cominform, and blessed the Communist coup in Czechoslovakia in February 1948. Truman, in turn, concluded that the Western world confronted the same situation it had a decade earlier with Nazi Germany, and his bristling St. Patrick's Day speeches in March 1948 placed sole onus for the Cold War on the Soviet Union. Subsequently, Anglo-American talks at the Pentagon would culminate in NATO in April 1949.

Meanwhile, The U.S. decision to make western Germany the cornerstone of the ERP virtually precluded negotiations to reunify the country. In fact, when Secretary of State Marshall proposed during a CFM meeting in the spring of 1947 to offer current production reparations to the Russians to induce agreement to unify Germany, the president sternly refused. Marshall complained of lack of "elbow room" to negotiate. But Truman would not yield, and by the time of the next CFM in late 1947 the secretary showed no interest in Russian reparations or Ruhr access. Despite America's public position, Ambassador to Moscow Walter Bedell Smith wrote, "we really do not want nor intend to accept German unification on any terms that the Russians might agree to, even though they seemed to meet most of our requirements."

The Americans were by then onto their London Conference program to create a West German state and, as Stalin said in February 1948, "The West will make Western Germany their own, and we shall turn Eastern Germany into our own state." In June the Soviet dictator initiated the Berlin blockade to try to forestall the West's program, but Truman determined to "stay period." He believed that to withdraw from Berlin would seriously undermine U.S. influence in Europe and the ERP and destroy his presidential standing, and he remained determined to avert military confrontation.

But Truman saw no connection between the London program and the blockade, as Carolyn Eisenberg has written. Further, his belief that "there is nothing to negotiate" and accord with General Lucius Clay's view that to withdraw from Berlin meant "we have lost everything we are fighting for" exaggerated the intent of Stalin's maneuver and diminished even slim chances for compromise on Germany, including Kennan's "Plan A" for a unified, neutralized state with American and Soviet forces withdrawn to its periphery. As Marshall said in August 1948, there would be "no abandonment of our position" on West Germany.

Eventually, Truman and the airlift prevailed over Stalin, who gave in to a face-saving CFM in May 1949 that ended the blockade, with nothing else agreed. The new secretary of state, Acheson, said that the United States intended to create a West German government "come hell or high water" and that Germany could be unified only by consolidating the East into the West on the basis of its incipient Bonn Constitution. Likewise Truman said in June 1949 that he would not sacrifice West Germany's basic freedoms to gain "nominal political unity." . . .

No one leader or nation caused the Cold War. The Second World War generated inevitable Soviet-American conflict as two nations with entirely different political-economic systems confronted each other on two war-torn continents. The Truman administration would seek to fashion a world order friendly to American political and economic interests, to achieve maximum national security by preventing any nation from severing U.S. ties to its traditional allies and vital areas of trade and resources, and to avoid 1930s-style "appeasement." Truman creditably favored creation of the UN, fostered foreign aid and reconstruction, and wished to avert war. . . .

Nonetheless, from the Potsdam Conference through the Korean War, the president contributed significantly to the growing Cold War and militarization of American foreign policy. He assumed that America's economic-military-moral superiority assured that he could order the world on its terms, and he ascribed only dark motives to nations or leaders who resisted America's will. . . .

It is clear that Truman's insecurity with regard to diplomacy and world politics led him to seek to give the appearance of acting decisively and reinforced his penchant to view conflict in black and white terms and to divide nations into free or totalitarian societies. He shied from weighing the complexities of historic national conflicts and local or regional politics. Instead, he attributed nearly every diplomatic crisis or civil war—in Germany, Iran, Turkey, Greece, and Czechoslovakia—to Soviet machination and insisted that the Russians had broken every agreement and were bent on "world conquest." To determine his response he was quick to reach for an analogy, usually the failure of the Western powers to resist Germany and Japan in the 1930s, and to conclude that henceforth he would speak to the Russians in the only language that he thought they understood: "divisions." This style of leadership and diplomacy closed off both advocates and prospects for more patiently negotiated and more nuanced or creative courses of action. . . .

In conclusion, it seems clear that despite Truman's pride in his knowledge of the past, he lacked insight into the history unfolding around him. He often could not see beyond his immediate decision or visualize alternatives, and he seemed oblivious to the implications of his words or actions. More often than not he narrowed rather than broadened the options that he presented to the American citizenry, the environment of American politics, and the channels through which Cold War politics flowed. Throughout his presidency, Truman remained a parochial nationalist who lacked the leadership to move America away from conflict and toward détente. Instead, he promoted an ideology and politics of Cold War confrontation that became the modus operandi of successor administrations and the United States for the next two generations.

Two Cold War Empires: Imposition vs. Multilaterialism

JOHN LEWIS GADDIS

Leaders of both the United States and the Soviet Union would have bristled at having the appellation "imperial" affixed to what they were doing after 1945. But one need not send out ships, seize territories, and hoist flags to construct an empire: "informal" empires are considerably older than, and continued to exist alongside, the more "formal" ones Europeans imposed on so much of the rest of the world from the fifteenth through the nineteenth centuries. During the Cold War years Washington and Moscow took on much of the character, if never quite the charm, of old imperial capitals like London, Paris, and Vienna. And surely American and Soviet influence, throughout most of the second half of the twentieth century, was at least as ubiquitous as that of any earlier empire the world had ever seen.

Ubiquity never ensured unchallenged authority, though, and that fact provides yet another reason for applying an imperial analogy to Cold War history. For contrary to popular impressions, empires have always involved a two-way flow of influence. Imperializers have never simply acted upon the imperialized; the imperialized have also had a surprising amount of influence over the imperializers. The Cold War was no exception to this pattern, and an awareness of it too will help us to see how that rivalry emerged, evolved, and eventually ended in the way that it did.

From John Lewis Gaddis, *We Now Know: Rethinking Cold War History* (New York: Oxford University Press, 1997), pp. 27–46. © 1997 by John Lewis Gaddis. Reprinted by permission of Oxford University Press.

Let us begin with the structure of the Soviet empire, for the simple reason that it was, much more than the American, deliberately designed. It has long been clear that, in addition to having had an authoritarian vision, Stalin also had an imperial one, which he proceeded to implement in at least as single-minded a way. No comparably influential builder of empire came close to wielding power for so long, or with such striking results, on the Western side.

It was, of course, a matter of some awkwardness that Stalin came out of a revolutionary movement that had vowed to smash, not just tsarist imperialism, but all forms of imperialism throughout the world. The Soviet leader constructed his own logic, though, and throughout his career he devoted a surprising amount of attention to showing how a revolution and an empire might coexist. Bolsheviks could never be imperialists, Stalin acknowledged in one of his earliest public pronouncements on this subject, made in April 1917. But surely in a *revolutionary* Russia nine-tenths of the non-Russian nationalities would not *want* their independence. Few among those minorities found Stalin's reasoning persuasive after the Bolsheviks did seize power later that year, however, and one of the first problems Lenin's new government faced was a disintegration of the old Russian empire not unlike what happened to the Soviet Union after communist authority finally collapsed in 1991.

Whether because of Lenin's own opposition to imperialism or, just as plausibly, because of Soviet Russia's weakness at the time, Finns, Estonians, Latvians, Lithuanians, Poles, and Moldavians were allowed to depart. Others who tried to do so—Ukrainians, Belorussians, Caucasians, Central Asians—were not so fortunate, and in 1922 Stalin proposed incorporating these remaining (and reacquired) nationalities into the Russian republic, only to have Lenin as one of his last acts override this recommendation and establish the multi-ethnic Union of Soviet Socialist Republics. After Lenin died and Stalin took his place it quickly became clear, though, that whatever its founding principles the USSR was to be no federation of equals. Rather, it would function as an updated form of empire even more tightly centralized than that of the Russian tsars.

Lenin and Stalin differed most significantly, not over authoritarianism or even terror, but on the legitimacy of Great Russian nationalism. The founder of Bolshevism had warned with characteristic pungency of "that truly Russian man, the Great-Russian chauvinist," and of the dangers of sinking into a "sea of chauvinistic Great-Russian filth, like flies in milk." Such temptations, he insisted, might ruin the prospects of revolution spreading elsewhere in the world. But Stalin—the implied target of Lenin's invective—was himself a Great Russian nationalist, with all the intensity transplanted nationals can sometimes attain. "The leaders of the revolutionary workers of all countries are avidly studying the most instructive history of the working class of Russia, its past, the past of Russia," he would write in a revealing private letter in 1930, shortly after consolidating his position as Lenin's successor. "All this instills (cannot but instill!) in the hearts of the Russian workers a feeling of revolutionary national pride, capable of moving mountains and working miracles."

The "Stalin constitution" of 1936, which formally specified the right of non-Russian nationalities to secede from the Soviet Union, coincided with the great purges and an officially sanctioned upsurge in Russian nationalism that would persist as a prominent feature of Stalin's regime until his death. It was as if the great authoritarian had set out to validate his own flawed prediction of 1917 by creating a set of circumstances in which non-Russian nationalities would not even *think* of seceding, even though the hypothetical authority to do so remained. The pattern resembled that of the purge trials themselves: one maintained a framework of legality—even, within the non-Russian republics, a toleration of local languages and cultures considerably greater than under the tsars. But Stalin then went to extraordinary lengths to deter anyone from exercising these rights or promoting those cultures in such a way as to challenge his own rule. He appears to have concluded, from his own study of the Russian past, that it was not "reactionary" to seek territorial expansion. His principal ideological innovation may well have been to impose the ambitions of the old princes of Muscovy, especially their determination to "gather in" and dominate all of the lands that surrounded them, upon the anti-imperial spirit of proletarian international- ism that had emanated from, if not actually inspired, the Bolshevik Revolution.

Stalin's fusion of Marxist internationalism with tsarist imperialism could only reinforce his tendency, in place well before World War II, to equate the advance of world revolution with the expanding influence of the Soviet state. He applied that linkage quite impartially: a major benefit of the 1939 pact with Hitler had been that it regained territories lost as a result of the Bolshevik Revolution and the World War I settlement. But Stalin's conflation of imperialism with ideology also ex- plains the importance he attached, following the German attack in 1941, to having his new Anglo-American allies confirm these arrangements. He had similar goals in East Asia when he insisted on bringing the Soviet Union back to the position Russia had occupied in Manchuria prior to the Russo-Japanese War: this he finally achieved at the 1945 Yalta Conference in return for promising to enter the war against Japan. "My task as minister of foreign affairs was to expand the borders of our Fatherland," Molotov recalled proudly many years later. "And it seems that Stalin and I coped with this task quite well."

From the West's standpoint, the critical question was how far Moscow's in- fluence would extend *beyond* whatever Soviet frontiers turned out to be at the end of the war. Stalin had suggested to Milovan Djilas that the Soviet Union would im- pose its own social system as far as its armies could reach, but he was also very cautious. Keenly aware of the military power the United States and its allies had accumulated, Stalin was determined to do nothing that might involve the USSR in another devastating war until it had recovered sufficiently to be certain of winning it. "I do not wish to begin the Third World War over the Trieste question," he ex- plained to disappointed Yugoslavs, whom he ordered to evacuate that territory in June 1945. Five years later, he would justify his decision not to intervene in the Korean War on the grounds that "the Second World War ended not long ago, and we are not ready for the Third World War." Just how far the expansion of Soviet in- fluence would proceed depended, therefore, upon a careful balancing of opportuni- ties against risks. "[W]e were on the offensive," Molotov acknowledged:

> They [presumably the West] certainly hardened their line against us, but we had to con- solidate our conquests. We made our own socialist Germany out of our part of Ger- many, and restored order in Czechoslovakia, Poland, Hungary, and Yugoslavia, where the situations were fluid. To squeeze out capitalist order. This was the cold war.

But, "of course," Molotov added, "you had to know when to stop. I believe in this respect Stalin kept well within the limits."

Who or what was it, though, that set the limits? Did Stalin have a fixed list of countries he thought it necessary to dominate? Was he prepared to stop in the face of resistance within those countries to "squeezing out the capitalist order"? Or would expansion cease only when confronted with opposition from the remaining capitalist states, so that further advances risked war at a time when the Soviet Union was ill-prepared for it?

Stalin had been very precise about where he wanted Soviet boundaries changed; he was much less so on how far Moscow's sphere of influence was to extend. He insisted on having "friendly" countries around the periphery of the USSR, but he failed to specify how many would have to meet this standard. He called during the war for dismembering Germany, but by the end of it was denying that he had ever done so: that country would be temporarily divided, he told leading German communists in June 1945, and they themselves would eventually bring about its reunification. He never gave up on the idea of an eventual world revolution, but he expected this to result—as his comments to the Germans suggested—from an expansion of influence emanating from the Soviet Union itself. "[F]or the Kremlin," a well-placed spymaster recalled, "the mission of communism was primarily to consolidate the might of the Soviet state. Only military strength and domination of the countries on our borders could ensure us a superpower role."

But Stalin provided no indication—surely because he himself did not know—of how rapidly, or under what circumstances, this process would take place. He was certainly prepared to stop in the face of resistance from the West: at no point was he willing to challenge the Americans or even the British where they made their interests clear. Churchill acknowledged his scrupulous adherence to the famous 1944 "percentages" agreement confirming British authority in Greece, and Yugoslav sources have revealed Stalin's warnings that the United States and Great Britain would never allow their lines of communication in the Mediterranean to be broken. He quickly backed down when confronted with Anglo-American objections to his ambitions in Iran in the spring of 1946, as he did later that year after demanding Soviet bases in the Turkish Straits. This pattern of advance followed by retreat had shown up in the purges of the 1930s, which Stalin halted when the external threat from Germany became too great to ignore, and it would reappear with the Berlin Blockade and the Korean War, both situations in which the Soviet Union would show great caution after provoking an unexpectedly strong American response.

What all of this suggests, though, is not that Stalin had limited ambitions, only that he had no timetable for achieving them. Molotov retrospectively confirmed this: "Our ideology stands for offensive operations when possible, and if not, we wait." Given this combination of appetite with aversion to risk, one cannot help but wonder what would have happened had the West tried containment earlier. To the extent that it bears partial responsibility for the coming of the Cold War, the historian Vojtech Mastny has argued, that responsibility lies in its failure to do just that.

Where Western resistance was unlikely, as in Eastern Europe, Stalin would in time attempt to replicate the regime he had already established inside the Soviet Union. Authority extended out from Moscow by way of government and party structures whose officials had been selected for their obedience, then down within each of these countries through the management of the economy, social and political institutions, intellectuals, even family-relationships. The differentiation of public and private spheres that exists in most societies disappeared as all aspects of life were fused with, and then subordinated to, the interests of the Soviet Union as Stalin himself had determined them. Those who could not or would not go along encountered the same sequence of intimidation, terror, and ultimately even purges, show trials, and executions that his real and imagined domestic opponents had gone through during the 1930s. "Stalin's understanding of friendship with other countries was that the Soviet Union would lead and they would follow," Khrushchev recalled. "[He] waged the struggle against the enemies of the people there in the same way that he did in the Soviet Union. He had one demand: absolute subordination."

Stalin's policy, then, was one of imperial expansion and consolidation differing from that of earlier empires only in the determination with which he pursued it, in the instruments of coercion with which he maintained it, and in the ostensibly anti-imperial justifications he put forward in support of it. It is a testimony to his skill, if not to his morality, that he was able to achieve so many of his imperial ambitions at a time when the tides of history were running against the idea of imperial domination—as colonial offices in London, Paris, Lisbon, and The Hague were finding out—and when his own country was recovering from one of the most brutal invasions in recorded history. The fact that Stalin was able to *expand* his empire when others were contracting and while the Soviet Union was as weak as it was requires explanation. Why did opposition to this process, within and outside Europe, take so long to develop?

One reason was that the colossal sacrifices the Soviet Union had made during the war against the Axis had, in effect, "purified" its reputation: the USSR and its leader had "earned" the right to throw their weight around, or so it seemed. Western governments found it difficult to switch quickly from viewing the Soviet Union as a glorious wartime ally to portraying it as a new and dangerous adversary. President Harry S. Truman and his future Secretary of State Dean Acheson—neither of them sympathetic in the slightest to communism—nonetheless tended to give the Soviet Union the benefit of the doubt well into the early postwar era. A similar pattern developed within the United States occupation zone in Germany, where General Lucius D. Clay worked out a cooperative relationship with his Soviet counterparts and resisted demands to "get tough" with the Russians, even after they had become commonplace in Washington.

Resistance to Stalin's imperialism also developed slowly because Marxism-Leninism at the time had such widespread appeal. It is difficult now to recapture the admiration revolutionaries outside the Soviet Union felt for that country before they came to know it well. "[Communism] was the most rational and most intoxicating, all-embracing ideology for me and for those in my disunited and desperate land who so desired to skip over centuries of slavery and backwardness and to bypass reality itself," Djilas recalled, in a comment that could have been echoed throughout much of what came to be called the "third world." Because the Bolsheviks themselves had overcome one empire and had made a career of condemning others, it would take decades for people who were struggling to overthrow British, French, Dutch, or Portuguese colonialism to see that there could also be such a thing as Soviet imperialism. European communists—notably the Yugoslavs—saw this much earlier, but even to most of them it had not been apparent at the end of the war.

Still another explanation for the initial lack of resistance to Soviet expansionism was the fact that its repressive character did not become immediately apparent to all who were subjected to it. With regimes on the left taking power in Eastern and Central Europe, groups long denied advancement could now expect it. For many who remembered the 1930s, autarchy within a Soviet bloc could seem preferable to exposure once again to international capitalism, with its periodic cycles of boom and bust. Nor did Moscow impose harsh controls everywhere at the same time. Simple administrative incompetence may partially account for this: one Russian historian has pointed out that "[d]isorganization, mismanagement and rivalry among many branches of the gigantic Stalinist state in Eastern Europe were enormous." But it is also possible, at least in some areas, that Stalin did not expect to *need* tight controls; that he anticipated no serious challenge and perhaps even spontaneous support. Why did he promise free elections after the war? Maybe he thought the communists would win them.

One has the impression that Stalin and the Eastern Europeans got to know one another only gradually. The Kremlin leader was slow to recognize that Soviet authority would not be welcomed everywhere beyond Soviet borders; but as he did come to see this he became all the more determined to impose it everywhere. The Eastern Europeans were slow to recognize how confining incorporation within a Soviet sphere was going to be; but as they did come to see this they became all the more determined to resist it, even if only by withholding, in a passive but sullen manner, the consent any regime needs to establish itself by means other than coercion. Stalin's efforts to consolidate his empire therefore made it at once more repressive and less secure. Meanwhile, an alternative vision of postwar Europe was emerging from the other great empire that established itself in the wake of World War II, that of the United States, and this too gave Stalin grounds for concern.

The first point worth noting, when comparing the American empire to its Soviet counterpart, is a striking reversal in the sequence of events. Stalin's determination to create his empire preceded by some years the conditions that made it possible: he had first to consolidate power at home and then defeat Nazi Germany, while at the same time seeing to it that his allies in that enterprise did not thwart his long-term objectives. With the United States, it was the other way around: the conditions for establishing an empire were in place long before there was any clear intention on the part of its leaders to do so. Even then, they required the support of a skeptical electorate, something that could never quite be taken for granted.

The United States had been poised for global hegemony at the end of World War I. Its military forces played a decisive role in bringing that conflict to an end. Its economic predominance was such that it could control both the manner and the rate of European recovery. Its ideology commanded enormous respect, as Woodrow Wilson found when he arrived on the Continent late in 1918 to a series of rapturous public receptions. The Versailles Treaty fell well short of Wilson's principles, to be sure, but the League of Nations followed closely his own design, providing an explicit legal basis for an international order that was to have drawn, as much as anything else, upon the example of the American constitution itself. If there was ever a point at which the world seemed receptive to an expansion of United States influence, this was it.

Americans themselves, however, were not receptive. The Senate's rejection of membership in the League reflected the public's distinct lack of enthusiasm for international peace-keeping responsibilities. Despite the interests certain business, labor, and agricultural groups had in seeking overseas markets and investment opportunities, most Americans saw few benefits to be derived from integrating their economy with that of the rest of the world. Efforts to rehabilitate Europe during the 1920s, therefore, could only take the form of private initiatives, quietly coordinated with the government. Protective tariffs hung on well into the 1930s—having actually increased with the onset of the Great Depression—and exports as a percentage of gross national product remained low in comparison to other nations, averaging only 4.2 per cent between 1921 and 1940. Investments abroad had doubled between 1914 and 1919 while foreign investment in the United States had been cut in half; but this shift was hardly sufficient to overcome old instincts within the majority of the public who held no investments at all that it was better to stand apart from, rather than to attempt to dominate, international politics outside of the Western hemisphere.

This isolationist consensus broke down only as Americans began to realize that a potentially hostile power was once again threatening Europe: even their own hemisphere, it appeared, might not escape the consequences this time around. After September 1939, the Roosevelt administration moved as quickly as public and Congressional opinion would allow to aid Great Britain and France by means short of war; it also chose to challenge the Japanese over their occupation of China and later French Indochina, thereby setting in motion a sequence of events that would lead to the attack on Pearl Harbor. Historians ever since have puzzled over this: why, after two decades of relative inactivity on the world scene, did the United States suddenly become hyperactive? Might the administration have realized that it would never generate public support for the empire American elites had long desired without a clear and present danger to national security, and did it not then proceed to generate one? Can one not understand the origins and evolution of the Cold War in similar terms?

There are several problems with such interpretations, one of which is that they confuse contingency with conspiracy. Even if Roosevelt had hoped to maneuver the Japanese into "firing the first shot," he could not have known that Hitler would seize this opportunity to declare war and thereby make possible American military intervention in Europe. The Pacific, where the United States would have deployed most of its strength in the absence of Hitler's declaration, would hardly have been the platform from which to mount a bid for global hegemony. These explanations also allow little room for the autonomy of others: they assume that Hitler and the Japanese militarists acted *only* in response to what the United States did, and that other possible motives for their behavior—personal, bureaucratic, cultural, ideological, geopolitical—were insignificant. Finally, these arguments fail to meet the test of proximate versus distant causation. The historian Marc Bloch once pointed out that one could, in principle, account for a climber's fall from a precipice by invoking physics and geology: had it not been for the law of gravity and the existence of the mountain, the accidents surely could not have occurred. But would it follow that all who ascend mountains must plummet from them? Just because Roosevelt *wanted* the United States to enter the war and to become a world power afterwards does not mean that his actions made these things happen.

A better explanation for the collapse of isolationism is a simpler one: it had to do with a resurgence of authoritarianism. Americans had begun to suspect, late in the nineteenth century, that the internal behavior of states determined their external behavior; certainly it is easy to see how the actions of Germany, Italy, and Japan during the 1930s could have caused this view to surface once again, much as it had in relations with tsarist Russia and imperial Germany during World War I. Once that happened, the Americans, not given to making subtle distinctions, began to oppose authoritarianism everywhere, and that could account for their sudden willingness to take on several authoritarians at once in 1941. But that interpretation, too, is not entirely adequate. It fails to explain how the United States could have coexisted as comfortably as it did with authoritarianism in the past—especially in Latin America—and as it would continue to do for some time to come. It certainly does not account for the American willingness during the war to embrace, as an ally, the greatest authoritarian of this century, Stalin himself.

The best explanation for the decline of isolationism and the rise of the American empire, I suspect, has to do with a distinction Americans tended to make—perhaps they were more subtle than one might think—between what we might call benign and malignant authoritarianism. Regimes like those of Somoza in Nicaragua or Trujillo in the Dominican Republic might be unsavory, but they fell into the benign category because they posed no serious threat to United States interests and in some cases even promoted them. Regimes like those of Nazi Germany and imperial Japan, because of their military capabilities, were quite another matter. Stalin's authoritarianism had appeared malignant when linked to that of Hitler, as it was between 1939 and 1941; but when directed against Hitler, it could come to appear quite benign. What it would look like once Germany had been defeated remained to be seen.

With all this, the possibility that even malignant authoritarianism might harm the United States remained hypothetical until 7 December 1941, when it suddenly became very real. Americans are only now, after more than half a century, getting over the shock: they became so accustomed to a Pearl Harbor mentality—to the idea that there really are deadly enemies out there—that they find it a strange new world, instead of an old familiar one, now that there are not. Pearl Harbor was, then, the defining event for the American empire, because it was only at this point that the most plausible potential justification for the United States becoming and remaining a global power as far as the American people were concerned—an endangered national security—became an actual one. Isolationism had thrived right up to this moment; but once it became apparent that isolationism could leave the nation open to military attack, it suffered a blow from which it never recovered. The critical date was not 1945, or 1947, but 1941.

It did not automatically follow, though, that the Soviet Union would inherit the title of "first enemy" once Germany and Japan had been defeated. A sense of vulnerability preceded the identification of a source of threat in the thinking of American strategists: innovations in military technology—long-range bombers, the prospect of even longer-range missiles—created visions of future Pearl Harbors before it had become clear from where such an attack might come. Neither in the military nor the political-economic planning that went on in Washington during the war was there consistent concern with the USSR as a potential future adversary. The threat, rather, appeared to arise from war itself, whoever might cause it, and the most likely candidates were thought to be resurgent enemies from World War II.

The preferred solution was to maintain preponderant power for the United States, which meant a substantial peacetime military establishment and a string of bases around the world from which to resist aggression if it should ever occur. But equally important, a revived international community would seek to remove the fundamental causes of war through the United Nations, a less ambitious version of Wilson's League, and through new economic institutions like the International Monetary Fund and the World Bank, whose task it would be to prevent another global depression and thereby ensure prosperity. The Americans and the British assumed that the Soviet Union would want to participate in these multilateral efforts to achieve military and economic security. The Cold War developed when it became clear that Stalin either could not or would not accept this framework.

Did the Americans attempt to impose their vision of the postwar world upon the USSR? No doubt it looked that way from Moscow: both the Roosevelt and Truman administrations stressed political self-determination and economic integration with sufficient persistence to arouse Stalin's suspicions—easily aroused, in any event—as to their ultimate intentions. But what the Soviet leader saw as a challenge to his hegemony the Americans meant as an effort to salvage multilateralism. At no point prior to 1947 did the United States and its Western European allies abandon the hope that the Russians might eventually come around; and indeed negotiations aimed at bringing them around would continue at the foreign ministers' level, without much hope of success, through the end of that year. The American attitude was less that of expecting to impose a system than one of puzzlement as to why its merits were not universally self-evident. It differed significantly, therefore, from Stalin's point of view, which allowed for the possibility that socialists in other countries might come to see the advantages of Marxism-Leninism as practiced in the Soviet Union, but never capitalists. They were there, in the end, to be overthrown, not convinced.

The emergence of an opposing great power bloc posed serious difficulties for the principle of multilateralism, based as it had been on the expectation of cooperation with Moscow. But with a good deal of ingenuity the Americans managed to *merge* their original vision of a single international order built around common security with a second and more hastily improvised concept that sought to counter the expanding power and influence of the Soviet Union. That concept was, of course, containment, and its chief instrument was the Marshall Plan.

The idea of containment proceeded from the proposition that if there was not to be one world, then there must not be another world war either. It would be necessary to keep the peace while preserving the balance of power: the gap that had developed during the 1930s between the perceived requirements of peace and power was not to happen again. If geopolitical stability could be restored in Europe, time would work against the Soviet Union and in favor of the Western democracies. Authoritarianism need not be the "wave of the future"; sooner or later even Kremlin authoritarians would realize this fact and change their policies. "[T]he Soviet leaders are prepared to recognize *situations,* if not arguments," George F. Kennan wrote in 1948. "If, therefore, situations can be created in which it is clearly not to the advantage of their power to emphasize the elements of conflict in their relations with the outside world, then their actions, and even the tenor of their propaganda to their own people, *can* be modified."

This idea of time being on the side of the West came—at least as far as Kennan was concerned—from studying the history of empires. Edward Gibbon had written in *The Decline and Fall of the Roman Empire* that "there is nothing more contrary to nature than the attempt to hold in obedience distant provinces," and few things Kennan ever read made a greater or more lasting impression on him. He had concluded during the early days of World War II that Hitler's empire could not last, and in the months after the war, he applied similar logic to the empire Stalin was setting out to construct in Easter Europe. The territorial acquisitions and spheres of influence the Soviet Union had obtained would ultimately become a source of *insecurity* for it, both because of the resistance to Moscow's control that was sure to grow within those regions and because of the outrage the nature of that control was certain to provoke in the rest of the world. "Soviet power, like the capitalist world of its own conception, bears within it the seeds of its own decay," Kennan insisted in the most famous of all Cold War texts, his anonymously published 1947 article on the "The Sources of Soviet Conduct." He added, "the sprouting of those seeds is well advanced."

All of this would do the Europeans little good, though, if the new and immediate Soviet presence in their midst should so intimidate them that their own morale collapsed. The danger here came not from the prospect that the Red Army would invade and occupy the rest of the continent, as Hitler had tried to do; rather, its demoralized and exhausted inhabitants might simply vote in communist parties who would then do Moscow's bidding. The initial steps in the strategy of containment—stopgap military and economic aid to Greece and Turkey, the more carefully designed and ambitious Marshall Plan—took place within this context: the idea was to produce instant intangible reassurance as well as eventual tangible reinforcement. Two things had to happen in order for intimidation to occur, Kennan liked to argue: the intimidator had to make the effort, but, equally important, the target of those efforts had to agree to be intimidated. The initiatives of 1947 sought to generate sufficient self-confidence to prevent such acquiescence in intimidation from taking place.

Some historians have asserted that these fears of collapse were exaggerated: that economic recovery on the continent was already underway, and that the Europeans themselves were never as psychologically demoralized as the Americans made them out to be. Others have added that the real crisis at the time was within an American economy that could hardly expect to function hegemonically if Europeans lacked the dollars to purchase its products. Still others have suggested that the Marshall Plan was the means by which American officials sought to project overseas the mutually-beneficial relationship between business, labor, and government they had worked out at home: the point was not to make Wilsonian values a model for the rest of the world, but rather the politics of productivity that had grown out of American corporate capitalism. All of these arguments have merit: at a minimum they have forced historians to place the Marshall Plan in a wider economic, social, and historical context; more broadly they suggest that the American empire had its own distinctive internal roots, and was not solely and simply a response to the Soviet external challenge.

At the same time, though, it is difficult to see how a strategy of containment could have developed—with the Marshall Plan as its centerpiece—had there been nothing to contain. One need only recall the early 1920s, when similar conditions of European demoralization, Anglo-French exhaustion, and American economic predominance had existed; yet no American empire arose as after World War II. The critical difference, of course, was national security: Pearl Harbor created an atmosphere of vulnerability Americans had not known since the earliest days of the republic, and the Soviet Union by 1947 had become the most plausible source of threat. The American empire arose *primarily,* therefore, not from internal causes, as had the Soviet empire, but from a perceived external danger powerful enough to overcome American isolationism.

Washington's wartime vision of a postwar international order had been premised on the concepts of political self-determination and economic integration. It was intended to work by assuming a set of *common* interests that would cause other countries to *want* to be affiliated with it rather than to resist it. The Marshall Plan, to a considerable extent, met those criteria: although it operated on a regional rather than a global scale, it did seek to promote democracy through an economic recovery that would proceed along international and not nationalist lines. Its purpose was to create an American sphere of influence, to be sure, but one that would allow those within it considerable freedom. The principles of democracy and open markets required nothing less, but there were two additional and more practical reasons for encouraging such autonomy. First, the United States itself lacked the capability to administer a large empire: the difficulties of running occupied Germany and Japan were proving daunting enough. Second, the idea of autonomy was implicit in the task of restoring Europeans self-confidence; for who, if not Europeans themselves, was to say when the self-confidence of Europeans had been restored?

Finally, it is worth noting that even though Kennan and the other early architects of containment made use of imperial analogies, they did not see themselves as creating an empire, but rather a restored balance of power. Painfully—perhaps excessively—aware of limited American resources, fearful that the domestic political consensus in favor of internationalism might not hold, they set out to reconstitute *independent* centers of power in Europe and Asia. These would be integrated into the world capitalist system, and as a result they would certainly fall under the influence of its new hegemonic manager, the United States. But there was no intention here of creating satellites in anything like the sense that Stalin understood that term; rather, the idea was that "third forces" would resist Soviet expansionism while preserving as much as possible of the multilateralist agenda American officials had framed during World War II. What the United States really wanted, State Department official John D. Hickerson commented in 1948, was "not merely an extension of US influence but a real European organization strong enough to say 'no' both to the Soviet Union and to the United States, if our actions should seem so to require."

The American empire, therefore, reflected little imperial consciousness or design. An anti-imperial tradition dating back to the American Revolution partially accounted for this: departures from that tradition, as in the Spanish–American War of 1898 and the Philippine insurrection that followed, had only reinforced its relevance—outside the Western hemisphere. So too did a constitutional structure that forced even imperially minded leaders like Wilson and the two Roosevelts to accommodate domestic attitudes that discouraged imperial behavior long after national capabilities had made it possible. And even as those internal constraints diminished dramatically in World War II—they never entirely dropped away—Americans still found it difficult to think of themselves as an imperial power. The idea of remaking the international system in such a way as to transcend empires altogether still lingered, but so too did doubts as to whether the United States was up to the task. In the end it was again external circumstances—the manner in which Stalin managed his own empire and the way in which this pushed Europeans into preferring its American alternative—that brought the self-confidence necessary to administer imperial responsibilities into line with Washington's awareness of their existence.

The test of any empire comes in administering it, for even the most repressive tyranny requires a certain amount of acquiescence among its subjects. Coercion and terror cannot everywhere and indefinitely prop up authority: sooner or later the social, economic, and psychological costs of such measures begin to outweigh the benefits. Empires that can accommodate dissent, defuse it, and perhaps even reorient themselves to reflect certain aspects of it, are more likely to survive than those that simply try to suppress it. Resilience is as important as rigidity in designing buildings, bridges, and baseball bats: the world of politics is not all that different.

It is apparent now, even if it was not always at the time, that the Soviet Union did not manage its empire particularly well. Because of his personality and the structure of government he built around it, Stalin was—shall we say—less than receptive to the wishes of those nations that fell within the Soviet sphere. He viewed departures from his instructions with deep suspicion, but he also objected to manifestations of independent behavior where instructions had not yet been given. As a result, he put his European followers in an impossible position: they could satisfy him only by seeking his approval for whatever he had decided they should do—even, at times, before he had decided that they should do it.

An example occurred late in 1944 when the Yugoslavs—then the most powerful but also the most loyal of Stalin's East European allies—complained politely to Soviet commanders that their troops had been raping local women in the northern corner of the country through which they were passing. Stalin himself took note of this matter, accusing the Yugoslavs—at one point tearfully—of showing insufficient respect for Soviet military sacrifices and for failing to sympathize when "a soldier who has crossed thousands of kilometers through blood and fire and death has fun with a woman or takes some trifle." The issue was not an insignificant one: the Red Army's behavior was a problem throughout the territories it occupied, and did much to alienate those who lived there. Stalin's only concern, though, seems to have been that the Yugoslavs were failing to meet the standards of deference and obedience he expected from allies; for their part, the Yugoslavs began to wonder, apparently for the first time, just whose interests international communism as directed from Moscow was supposed to serve.

Similar questions arose regarding Yugoslav plans for a postwar Balkan federation. Stalin had initially supported this idea, perhaps as an excuse for removing American and British military representatives from former enemy states like Romania, but he soon developed reservations. The Yugoslavs themselves might become too powerful; and their propensity for hot-headedness—evident in their claims to Trieste and their shooting down of two American Air Force planes in 1946—might provoke the West. Orders went out that the Yugoslavs were to proceed slowly in their plans to take over Albania, and were to stop assisting the Greek guerrillas altogether. Within the context of the Cold War, these actions reflected Stalin's caution about confronting the British and the Americans; to that extent, they defused tensions. But to the militant Yugoslavs, they suggested the arrogance of an imperial authority determined to subordinate their interests—which they had defined largely in ideological terms—to those of the Soviet state.

Stalin did little better managing Western European communists, despite the fact that they still regarded themselves as his loyal supporters. In May 1947, the French Communist Party voted no confidence in the government of Premier Paul Ramadier, only to have him expel their representatives from his cabinet. The Italians, with strong American encouragement, threw out their own communists later that month. Andrei Zhdanov, who managed the Soviet Communist Party's relations with its foreign counterparts, sharply reprimanded the French comrades for acting without Moscow's authorization and therefore arousing concerns in the minds of "Soviet workers." He then passed on this communication to all other European communist parties. The implication seemed to be that none of them should do anything without consulting Moscow first, a requirement that would obviously be difficult to meet for communists who had responsibilities within national governments and therefore some obligation to consider national interests.

The Americans' unexpected offer of Marshall Plan aid to the Soviet Union and Eastern Europe in June 1947, caused even greater difficulties for Stalin's management of empire—which is precisely what Kennan hoped for when he recommended making it. In one of the stranger illusions arising from their ideology, Soviet leaders had always anticipated United States economic assistance in some form. Lenin himself expected American capitalists, ever in search of foreign markets, to invest eagerly in the newly formed USSR, despite its official antipathy toward them. Stalin hoped for a massive American reconstruction loan after World War II, and even authorized Molotov early in 1945 to offer acceptance of such assistance in order to help the United States stave off the economic crisis that Marxists analysis showed must be approaching. When the Marshall Plan was announced Stalin's first reaction was that the capitalists must be desperate. He concluded, therefore, that the Soviet Union and its East European allies should indeed participate in the plan, and quickly dispatched Molotov and a large delegation of economic experts to Paris to take part in the conference that was to determine the nature and extent of European needs.

But then Stalin began to reconsider. His ambassador in Washington, Nikolai Novikov, warned that the American offer to the Soviet Union could not be sincere: "A careful analysis of the Marshall Plan shows that ultimately it comes down to forming a West European bloc as a tool of US policy. All the good wishes accompanying the plan are demagogic official propaganda serving as a smokescreen." Soviet intelligence picked up reports—accurate enough—that American Under-Secretary of State William Clayton had been conspiring with British officials on using the Marshall Plan to reintegrate Germany into the West European economy and to deny further reparations shipments to the Soviet Union. This information, together with indications at Paris that the Americans would require a coordinated European response, caused Stalin to change his mind and order his own representatives to walk out. "The Soviet delegation saw those claims as a bid to interfere in the internal affairs of European countries," Molotov explained lamely, "thus making the economies of these countries dependent on US interests."

Curiously, though, Stalin did not at first demand that the East Europeans follow the Soviet example. Instead he instructed their delegations to attend follow-up sessions of the Paris conference, but to "show . . . that the Anglo-French plan is unacceptable, prevent its unanimous approval and then . . . withdraw from the meeting, taking with them as many delegates of other countries as possible." These orders stood for only three days, however, because Stalin then considered again: what if the East Europeans—especially the Czechs, whose communists did not yet completely control the government—chose not to follow the script and proceeded to accept Marshall Plan aid? Accordingly, a new message went out stating awkwardly that the Soviet Communist Party Central Committee "proposes refusing to participate in the meeting, that is, sending no delegations to it. Each country may give the reasons for its refusal as it sees fit."

Unfortunately, the Czechs and the Poles, following the earlier instructions, had already announced their intention to attend. The Poles quickly changed their mind but the Czechs procrastinated, more because of confusion than determined resistance. Stalin responded by peremptorily summoning their leaders to Moscow. He had been persuaded "on the basis of material reasons," he told them, that the Americans were using the Marshall Plan to consolidate a Western coalition hostile to the Soviet Union:

> The Soviet government has therefore been surprised by your decision to accept this invitation. For us it is a matter of friendship. . . . If you go to Paris you shall demonstrate your will to cooperate in the action of isolating the Soviet Union. All the Slavonic states have refused, not even Albania feared to refuse, and therefore, we think you should reverse your decision.

Stalin's intentions were now clear to all including himself: there would be no East European participation in the Marshall Plan, or in any other American scheme for the rehabilitation of Europe. "I went to Moscow as the Foreign Minister of an independent sovereign state," Czech Foreign Minister Jan Masaryk commented bitterly. "I returned as a lackey of the Soviet government."

But the Kremlin boss too had shed some illusions. Marxist-Leninist analyses had long predicted, not just a postwar economic collapse in the West, but eventual conflict between the British and the Americans. In a September 1946 report from Washington which Molotov had carefully annotated, Ambassador Novikov had insisted that "the United States regards England as its greatest potential competitor." The Anglo-American relationship "despite the temporary attainment of agreements on very important questions, [is] plagued with great internal contradictions and cannot be lasting." By early 1947, Stalin was even offering the British a military alliance: as one report to Molotov put it, "Soviet diplomacy has in England practically unlimited possibilities." What the Marshall Plan showed was how wrong these assessments were. Capitalists, it now appeared, could indeed reconcile their differences; they considered the Soviet Union a greater threat to all than each posed to the other; time was not on Moscow's side. Ideology again had led Stalin into romanticism and away from reality. Once he realized this—in Europe at least—he never quite recovered from the shock.

The United States, in contrast, proved surprisingly adept at managing an empire. Having attained their authority through democratic processes, its leaders were experienced—as their counterparts in Moscow were not—in the arts of persuasion, negotiation and compromise. Applying domestic political insights to foreign policy could produce embarrassing results, as when President Truman likened Stalin to his old Kansas City political mentor, Tom Pendergast, or when Secretary of State James F. Byrnes compared the Russians to the US Senate: "You build a post office in their state, and they'll build a post office in our state." But the habits of democracy had served the nation well during World War II: its strategists had assumed that their ideas would have to reflect the interests and capabilities of allies; it was also possible for allies to advance proposals of their own and have them taken seriously. That same pattern of mutual accommodation persisted after the war, despite the fact that all sides acknowledged—as they had during most of the war itself—the disproportionate power the United States could ultimately bring to bear.

Americans so often deferred to the wishes of allies during the early Cold War that some historians have seen the Europeans—especially the British—as having managed *them.* The new Labour government in London did encourage the Truman administration to toughen its policy toward the Soviet Union; Churchill—by then out of office—was only reinforcing these efforts with his March 1946 "Iron Curtain" speech. The British were ahead of the Americans in pressing for a consolidation of Western occupation zones in Germany, even if this jeopardized prospects for an overall settlement with the Russians. Foreign Secretary Ernest Bevin determined the timing of the February 1947 crisis over Greece and Turkey when he ended British military and economic assistance to those countries, leaving the United States little choice but to involve itself in the eastern Mediterranean and providing the occasion for the Truman Doctrine. And it was the desperate economic plight of the West Europeans generally that persuaded newly appointed Secretary of State George C. Marshall, in June 1947, to announce the comprehensive program of American assistance that came to bear his name.

But one can easily make too much of this argument. Truman and his advisers were not babes in the woods. They knew what they were doing at each stage, and did it only because they were convinced their actions would advance American interests. They never left initiatives entirely up to the Europeans: they insisted on an integrated plan for economic recovery and quite forcefully reined in prospective recipients when it appeared that their requests would exceed what Congress would approve. "[I]n the end we would not *ask* them," Kennan noted, "we would just *tell* them, what they would get." The Americans were flexible enough, though, to accept and build upon ideas that came from allies; they also frequently let allies determine the timing of actions taken. As a consequence, the British, French, and other West Europeans came to feel that they had a stake in what Washington was doing, despite the fact that it amounted to their own incorporation within an American sphere of influence.

One might argue, to be sure, that European elites agreed to all of this for their own self-interested reasons; that the European "masses" were never consulted. It is worth remembering, however, that free elections ultimately ratified alignment with the United States in every country where that took place. The newly-formed Central Intelligence Agency, not always confident of such outcomes, did take it upon itself at times to manipulate democratic processes, most conspicuously in the Italian elections of April 1948. But these convert efforts—together with clandestine CIA support for anti-communist labor unions and intellectual organizations—could hardly have succeeded had there not already existed in Europe a widespread predisposition to see the Americans as the lesser of two evils, and perhaps even as a force for good. "I am entirely convinced," the French political theorist Raymond Aron insisted, "that for an anti-Stalinist there is no escape from the acceptance of American leadership." French peasants did not see it all that differently.

The habits of democracy were no less significant when it came to defeated adversaries. The Roosevelt administration had planned to treat Germany harshly after the war; and even after the President himself backed away from the punitive Morgenthau Plan in late 1944, its spirit lingered in the occupation directive for American forces, JCS 1067, which prohibited doing anything to advance economic rehabilitation beyond the minimum necessary to avoid disease or disorder. The American design for a postwar world based on economic integration and political self-determination seemed not to apply, or so at first it appeared, to occupied Germany.

Uneasiness about this inconsistency soon developed, though; and in any event Americans far from Washington customarily maintained a certain irreverence toward orders emanating from it. General Clay concluded almost at once that his instructions were unworkable and that he would either get them changed, sabotage them, or ignore them. Here he followed the lead of his own troops who, having found prohibitions against fraternizing with the Germans to be ridiculous, quickly devised ways of circumventing them. Confronted with inappropriate directives in a difficult situation, the American occupiers—with a breezy audacity that seems remarkable in retrospect—fell back upon domestic instincts and set about transplanting democracy into the part of Germany they controlled.

Soviet occupation authorities too, we now know, found themselves hampered by unclear directives ill-suited to the problems they faced; some of them managed to carve out a fair amount of autonomy, at times in defiance of Moscow's wishes. But it was what was done with autonomy that made the difference. The Red Army, repeating its practices elsewhere in Eastern Europe, indulged in looting and physical assaults on so massive a scale that the full extent of it is only now becoming known: reparations extractions removed about a third of the Soviet zone's industrial capacity and Russian troops raped as many as *two million* German women in 1945 and 1946. As the historian Norman Naimark has emphasized,

> women in the Eastern zone—both refugees from further east and inhabitants of the towns, villages, and cities of the Soviet zone—shared an experience for the most part unknown in the West, the ubiquitous threat and the reality of rape, over a prolonged period of time.

Whereas the American occupation authorities at first forbade fraternization but quickly reversed that policy, their Soviet counterparts initially encouraged such contacts but eventually had to prohibit them altogether because of the hostility they generated. Certainly the Russians did little to evolve practices or build institutions that promised Germans within their zone—apart from Communist Party functionaries—a stake in their success.

The United States could of course hold out the prospect of economic recovery and the Soviet Union could not: this certainly made the advantages of democracy more evident than they might otherwise have been. But democratization, under Clay's leadership, was well under way before there was any assurance that Germans would receive Marshall Plan aid or anything comparable. Authoritarianism, which was all Moscow would or could provide, was by far the less attractive alternative. "Soviet officers bolshevized their zone," Naimark has concluded, "not because there was a plan to do so, but because that was the only way they knew to organize society. . . . By their own actions, the Soviet authorities created enemies out of potential friends." Or, as General Clay recalled years afterwards: "We began to look like angels, not because we were angels, but we looked [like] that in comparison to what was going on in Eastern Europe."

The Americans simply did not find it necessary, in building a sphere of influence, to impose unrepresentative governments or brutal treatment upon the peoples that fell within it. Where repressive regimes already existed, as in Greece, Turkey, and Spain, serious doubts arose in Washington as to whether the United States should be supporting them at all, however useful they might be in containing Soviet expansionism. Nor, having constructed their empire, did Americans follow the ancient imperial practice of "divide and rule." Rather, they used economic leverage to overcome nationalist tendencies, thereby encouraging the Europeans' emergence as a "third force" whose obedience could not always be assumed. It was as if the Americans were projecting abroad a tradition they had long taken for granted at home: that civility made sense; that spontaneity, within a framework of minimal constraint, was the path to political and economic robustness; that to intimidate or to overmanage was to stifle. The contrast to Stalin's methods of imperial administration could hardly have been sharper.

 # *F U R T H E R   R E A D I N G*

Gar Alperovitz, *Atomic Diplomacy* (1965 and 1985)
———, *The Decision to Use the Atomic Bomb* (1995)
———, "Why the U.S. Dropped the Atomic Bomb," *Technology Review,* 93 (1990), 22–34
Stephen Ambrose and Douglas Brinkley, *Rise to Globalism* (1997)
Terry H. Anderson, *The United States, Great Britain, and the Cold War* (1981)
Christopher Appy, *Cold War Constructions* (2000)
Volker Berghahn, *America and the Intellectual Cold Wars in Europe* (2001)
Barton J. Bernstein, ed., *The Atomic Bomb* (1975)
———, "The Atomic Bombings Reconsidered," *Foreign Affairs,* 74 (1995), 135–142
Kai Bird and Lawrence Lifschultz, *Hiroshima Shadows* (1998)
Paul Boyer, *By the Bomb's Early Light* (1986)
H. W. Brands, *The Devil We Knew* (1993)
Douglas Brinkley, ed., *Dean Acheson and the Making of U.S. Foreign Policy* (1993)
Bulletin of the Atomic Scientists, 41 (1985), entire issue for August
McGeorge Bundy, *Danger and Survival* (1990) (on the nuclear-arms race)
David Callahan, *Dangerous Capabilities* (1990) (on Paul Nitze)
James Chace, *Acheson* (1998)
Warren I. Cohen, *America in the Age of Soviet Power* (1995)
Committee for the Compilation of Materials on Damage Caused by the Atomic Bombs in
     Hiroshima and Nagasaki, *Hiroshima and Nagasaki* (1981)
Frank Costigliola, "Unceasing Pressure for Penetration: Gender, Pathology, and Emotion in
     George Kennan's Formation of the Cold War," *Journal of American History,* 83
     (1997), 1309–1338
Richard Crockatt, *The Fifty Years War* (1995)
James E. Cronin, *The World the Cold War Made* (1996)
Robert Dean, *Imperial Brotherhood* (2001) (on gender)
Jeffrey M. Diefendorf et al., eds., *American Policy and the Reconstruction of West
     Germany* (1993)
Robert J. Donovan, *Conflict and Crisis* (1977)
———, *Tumultuous Years* (1982)
John W. Dower, "The Most Terrible Bomb in the History of the World," in James M.
     McPherson and Alan Brinkely, eds., *Days of Destiny* (2001)

Christopher Duggan and Christopher Wagstaff, eds., *Italy in the Cold War* (1996)

Carol Eisenberg, *Drawing the Line* (1996) (on Germany)

David Ellwood, *Rebuilding Europe* (1992)

Robert H. Ferrell, *Harry S. Truman* (1994)

John Fousek, *To Lead the Free World* (2000)

John Lewis Gaddis, *The Long Peace* (1987)

———, *Russia, the Soviet Union, and the United States* (1990)

———, *Strategies of Containment* (1982)

Lloyd C. Gardner, *Architects of Illusion* (1970)

Richard Gardner, *Sterling-Dollar Diplomacy* (1969)

John Gimbel, *The American Occupation of Germany* (1968)

———, *The Origins of the Marshall Plan* (1976)

———, *Science, Technology, and Reparations* (1990)

James L. Gormly, *The Collapse of the Grand Alliance, 1945–1948* (1987)

Alonzo Hamby, *Man of the People* (1995) (Truman biography)

Fraser J. Harbutt, *The Iron Curtain* (1986)

John L. Harper, *American Visions of Europe* (1994)

———, *America and the Reconstruction of Italy* (1986)

Robert M. Hathaway, *Ambiguous Partnership: Britain and America, 1944–1947* (1981)

Gregg Herken, *The Winning Weapon* (1981)

George Herring, *Aid to Russia, 1941–1946* (1973)

James Hershberg, *James B. Conant and the Birth of the Nuclear Age* (1994)

Walter Hixson, *George F. Kennan* (1990)

———, *Parting the Curtain: Propaganda, Culture, and the Cold War* (1997)

Michael J. Hogan, *A Cross of Iron: Harry S. Truman and the Origins of the National Security State* (1998)

———, ed., *Hiroshima in History and Memory* (1996)

———, *The Marshall Plan* (1987)

David Holloway, *The Soviet Union and the Arms Race* (1984)

———, *Stalin and the Bomb* (1994)

Michael Hopkins, *Oliver Franks and the Truman Administration* (2003)

Jeff Hughes, *The Manhattan Project* (2003)

John O. Iatrides, *Revolt in Athens* (1972)

——— and Linda Wrigley, eds., *Greece at the Crossroads* (1995)

Walter Isaacson and Evan Thomas, *The Wise Men* (1986)

Howard Jones, *"A New Kind of War"* (1989)

Lawrence S. Kaplan, *The United States and NATO* (1984)

Frank Kofsky, *Harry S. Truman and the War Scare of 1948* (1993)

Gabriel Kolko and Joyce Kolko, *The Limits of Power* (1972)

Richard Kuisel, *Seducing the French* (1993) (on cultural relations)

Bruce Kuniholm, *The Origins of the Cold War in the Near East* (1980)

Peter J. Kuznik and James Gilbert, eds., *Rethinking Cold War Culture* (2001)

Walter LaFeber, *America, Russia, and the Cold War* (1997)

Deborah Larson, *Anatomy of Distrust* (1997)

Melvyn Leffler, *A Preponderance of Power* (1992)

———, *The Specter of Communism* (1994)

——— and David S. Painter, eds., *Origins of the Cold War* (1994)

Ralph Levering, *The Cold War* (1994)

Scott Lucas, *Freedom's War* (1999)

Gier Lundestad, *Empire by Integration* (1998)

Robert J. McMahon, *The Cold War* (2003)

David McLellan, *Dean Acheson* (1976)

Robert J. McMahon, *The Cold War* (2003)

———, *The Cold War on the Periphery* (1994) (on India and Pakistan)

——— and Thomas G. Paterson, eds., *The Origins of the Cold War* (1999)

Robert H. McNeal, *Stalin* (1988)

Robert J. Maddox, *Weapons for Victory* (1995) (on atomic bombings)

Michael Mandlebaum, *The Fate of Nations* (1988)

Vojtech Mastny, *The Cold War and Soviet Insecurity* (1996)

David Mayers, *The Ambassadors and America's Soviet Policy* (1995)

Richard L. Merritt, *Democracy Imposed* (1995) (on Germany)

Robert L. Messer, *The End of an Alliance* (1982)

James E. Miller, *The United States and Italy, 1940–1950* (1986)

Wilson D. Miscamble, *George F. Kennan and the Making of American Foreign Policy* (1992)

Robert P. Newman, "Ending the War with Japan: Paul Nitze's Early Surrender Counter-factual," *Pacific Historical Review,* 64 (1995), 167–194

Frank Ninkovich, *Modernity and Power* (1994)

Robert S. Norris, *Racing for the Bomb* (2002) (on General Leslie Groves)

Arnold A. Offner, *Another Such Victory* (2002)

David S. Painter, *The Cold War* (1999)

Thomas G. Paterson, ed., *Cold War Critics* (1971)

———, *Meeting the Communist Threat* (1988)

———, *On Every Front: The Making and Unmaking of the Cold War* (1992)

———, *Soviet-American Confrontation* (1973)

Richard Pells, *Not Like US* (1997) (on U.S.-European cultural relations)

Edvard Radzinsky, *Stalin* (1996)

David Reynolds, ed., *The Origins of the Cold War in Europe* (1994)

T. Michael Ruddy, *The Cautious Diplomat* (1986) (on Bohlen)

Thomas A. Schwartz, *America's Germany* (1991)

Martin Sherwin, *A World Destroyed* (1975)

E. Timothy Smith, *The United States, Italy, and NATO* (1991)

Gaddis Smith, *Dean Acheson* (1972)

Joseph Smith, ed., *The Origins of NATO* (1990)

John Spanier, *American Foreign Policy Since World War II* (1997)

Ronald Steel, *Walter Lippmann and the American Century* (1980)

"Symposium: Soviet Archives: Recent Revelations and Cold War Historiography," *Diplomatic History,* 21 (1997), 215–305

Ronald Takaki, *Hiroshima* (1995)

William Taubman, *Stalin's American Policy* (1982)

Athan G. Theoharis, *The Yalta Myths* (1970)

Hugh Thomas, *Armed Truce* (1987)

Kenneth W. Thompson, *Cold War Theories* (1981)

Adam Ulam, *The Rivals* (1971)

Dimitri Volkogonov, *Stalin* (1991)

J. Samuel Walker, "The Decision to Use the Bomb: A Historiographical Update," *Diplomatic History,* 14 (1993), 97–114

———, *Henry A. Wallace and American Foreign Policy* (1976)

———, *Prompt and Utter Destruction* (1997) (on atomic bombings)

Irwin M. Wall, *The United States and the Making of Postwar France* (1991)

Piotr S. Wandycz, *The United States and Poland* (1980)

Imanuel Wexler, *The Marshall Plan Revisited* (1983)

Graham White and John Maze, *Henry A. Wallace* (1995)

Allan M. Winkler, *Life Under a Cloud* (1993)

Lawrence S. Wittner, *American Intervention in Greece, 1943–1949* (1982)

Daniel Yergin, *Shattered Peace* (1977)

Thomas W. Zeiller, *Unconditional Defeat* (2003)

Vladislav Zubok and Constantine Pleshakov, *Inside the Kremlin's Cold War* (1996)

The Korean War and Containment in Asia

Although postwar Soviet-American tensions initially flared in Europe and the Middle East, the Cold War soon spread to Asia. U.S. troops first engaged in Cold War combat on the Korean peninsula in the summer of 1950, following Communist North Korea's invasion of U.S.-backed South Korea. But the decision to intervene in Korea grew out of a broader regional context. Following years of bloody civil war, the Chinese revolution in October 1949 overthrew the U.S.-backed Guomindang (GMD) or Nationalist regime of Jiang Jieshi (Chiang Kai-shek) and established the People's Republic of China (PRC) led by Communist Mao Zedong (Mao Tse-tung). Having funneled more than $3 billion in military and economic aid to the GMD from 1945 to 1949, the Truman White House blamed Jiang's rampant corruption for the defeat. Administration critics, however, charged that Washington had not adequately supported Jiang's regime. Faced with both domestic and international constraints, Truman delayed diplomatic recognition of the PRC in late 1949 and early 1950 and reluctantly stuck by Jiang, who had retreated to the island of Formosa (Taiwan). As China's capacity to play a stabilizing role in the Far East dimmed, Washington increasingly looked upon Japan as its stalwart ally in the region. Beginning in 1947, U.S. occupation authorities moderated their economic reform and democratization agendas and targeted aid dollars to establish Japan as Asia's industrial powerhouse. The Asian drama deepened as a series of nationalist insurgencies, some with a Marxist tinge, pressed the area's colonial powers for independence. In response, Washington in early 1950 provided economic and military assistance to anticommunist regimes in Burma, French Indochina, Indonesia, the Philippines, and Thailand. In this atmosphere, the Korean War erupted in June 1950 and the Truman administration opted to apply the containment doctrine to the Korean peninsula.

U.S. intervention in Korea had actually begun in 1945, during the closing days of the Second World War, when Washington and Moscow drew a line at the thirty-eighth parallel and occupied the former Japanese colony. The two superpowers had agreed to a temporary division, but Korea soon became an arena where the Soviets and the Americans competed to establish client states. In South Korea the United States threw its support behind the conservative government of Syngman Rhee, and in North Korea the Soviets backed Kim Il Sung's Communist regime. Both Korean leaders considered themselves devout nationalists, and each envisioned himself as the head of a unified, independent Korea. As American and Soviet forces pulled back from the peninsula in 1949 and 1950, the two Koreas clashed in frequent border skirmishes and headed for a showdown. War came on June 25, 1950, when seventy-five thousand Soviet-equipped North Korean troops punched through the thirty-eighth parallel and invaded South Korea.

The Korean War significantly altered the Cold War's course. In addition to dispatching U.S forces to Korea, the Truman administration redoubled its efforts to contain communism around the globe, and increasingly relied on military power to do the job. At home the administration raised annual defense expenditures from some $17 billion in 1950 to more than $50 billion in 1953, implementing the buildup envisioned by the authors of NSC-68. In Europe military aid outpaced economic aid as Washington sought to give NATO more muscle. U.S. officials also laid plans for regional defense alliances in the Middle East and Asia, increased military aid to noncommunist forces in French Indochina (deepening U.S. intervention in Vietnam's struggle for independence), and deployed U.S. naval power to block the Taiwan Strait. Following China's entrance into the war in November 1950, Washington reaffirmed its nonrecognition of the PRC, and in September 1951 it signed a peace treaty and mutual defense pact with Japan.

Since then, a number of complex questions have challenged historians. First, how does one account for the origins of the war? Bolstered by the opening of Soviet, Chinese, and Korean documents since the end of the Cold War in the early 1990s, some scholars highlight the international aspects of the conflict, that is, the decisive roles played by external Communist powers. According to this perspective, Soviet marshal Joseph Stalin and China's Mao Zedong set events in motion in April 1950 when they endorsed and pledged support for Kim Il Sing's war plans. The Truman administration may have erred by not previously indicating its resolve to defend South Korea, but it responded effectively once combat commenced by utilizing the United Nations and U.S. military power to repel Communist aggression. Another school of thought, noting significant gaps in the new records and divisions within the Communist alliance, posits that the war's sources lie primarily in Korean social and political conditions. Like much of the unrest sweeping Asia at the time, Korea's torment was a legacy of colonial rule, which left the country economically dependent and politically divided. When the superpowers descended on Korea in 1945, they became enmeshed in an emerging civil war that eventually pitted two highly nationalistic Korean governments against one another. According to this perspective, the United States shares with the Soviets and the Chinese responsibility for escalating a local, civil war into a dangerous and costly global confrontation.

A second basic question, put simply, is: Why did the conflict in Korea lead to a shooting war between the United States and the PRC? Some scholars argue that Mao's ideological fervor and the Communist alliance system dictated Chinese entry into the war. Others view Mao's intervention as defensive, provoked by Truman's decision to order United Nations troops across the thirty-eighth parallel in October 1950. Indeed, scholars have debated whether the opening of diplomatic relations with the PRC in 1949 and 1950, or at least a limited dialogue, might have allowed leaders to read better each other's intentions and avoid war by miscalculation.

A third area of inquiry addresses the issue of limited war. Although President Truman won United Nations approval for his actions in Korea, he did not seek a congressional declaration of war. The administration portrayed the conflict as a police action to contain communism rather than an all-out war against the communist world. It rejected the advice of the head of the UN command, General Douglas MacArthur,

to expand the war to Manchuria and to use atomic weapons. Was the Truman
administration wise to contain the fighting? The controversy led to Truman's firing
of MacArthur in April 1951 and stoked heated debate in Congress and the press,
foreshadowing a similar controversy during the Vietnam War a decade late.

Although the Korean War was a limited war, the final casualty rate proved
staggering. An estimated 3 million Koreans, nine hundred thousand Chinese, and
thirty-five thousand Americans perished. The fighting dragged on until July 1953,
when lengthy negotiations finally produced a cease-fire and peace terms that estab-
lished the status quo that had existed before June 25, 1950. The belligerents never
formally ended hostilities and Korea remained a divided nation, each side heavily
armed and destined to live in a constant state of readiness and alert. The danger has
outlasted the Cold War itself, and in recent years North Korea's nuclear programs
and weapons exports have alarmed the United States. Thus the Korean peninsula
remains one of the world's potential crisis spots, and the history of the Korean War
carries enduring relevance.

 ## D O C U M E N T S

The Chinese Communist revolution of October 1949 initiated a new phase in the Cold
War, and set the stage for the Korean War, by establishing Asia as a hotly contested
territory between communism and capitalism. Yet it remains unclear whether armed
conflict between the United States and revolutionary China was inevitable or if the two
could have lived in peaceful coexistence. Document 1 consists of two telegrams sent
from the U.S. ambassador in China, John Leighton Stuart, in May and June 1949 to
Washington. Stuart reported conversations with Huang Hua, a Chinese foreign affairs
official, during which the latter tendered an "invitation" to meet and conduct discussions
with Mao and his foreign policy adviser Zhou Enlai. Zhou Enlai indirectly approached
the U.S. consulate in Beijing at about the same time regarding Sino-U.S. relations. The
Truman administration, nonetheless, discouraged any softening toward the Communists.
In December 1949 the National Security Council completed NSC 48, "The Position
of the United States with Respect to Asia" (Document 2). The policy statement declared
the reduction of Soviet influence in the region to be a fundamental U.S. objective. It
reaffirmed Washington's nonrecognition policy toward the Chinese Communists but did
not rule out future ties and did not recommend using American military force to defend
Chiang's regime on Taiwan in the event of attack. The NSC also urged promoting
regional trade and collective security; strengthening the security of Japan, the Ryukyus
(an island chain just north of Japan and east of the Soviet Union), and the Philippines;
and giving special U.S. assistance to South Korea. NSC 48 also recommended dispensing $75 million in aid to noncommunist governments "in the general area of China,"
including French Indochina.

As Mao consolidated his rule in China, political tensions remained high on the
divided Korean peninsula. On January 12, 1950, Secretary of State Dean Acheson delivered a major speech, Document 3, defining the American defense perimeter in Asia,
from which he excluded Korea. Critics later charged that his omission gave the Soviet
Union the incentive to use its North Korean allies to attack South Korea. Recently available Soviet sources, however, suggest that the Kremlin remained cautious. In Document 4, a telegram of January 19, 1950, the Soviet ambassador in the North Korean
capital Pyongyang, Terenti Shtykov, relays to Moscow the intent of Kim Il Sung to use
force to "liberate" South Korea and unify the two Koreas. Shtykov at the time warned
Kim that an attack would not be advisable but that the matter could be taken up again

with Marshal Joseph Stalin. Kim visited Moscow in April, where Stalin finally endorsed his plan, pending the cooperation of the PRC.

Immediately following the North Korean attack of June 25, 1950, President Harry S. Truman met with key advisers at Blair House, a building near the White House. Document 5 is a record of the June 26, 1950, meeting in which Secretary of State Dean Acheson recommended several important policies, not only for Korea but also for the Philippines, Formosa, and French Indochina. In August 1950, the Truman administration approved military plans to send UN troops above the thirty-eighth parallel into North Korea. On September 15, American marines landed at Inchon on the west coast of South Korea and soon marched north.

Meanwhile, in Beijing, Chinese authorities watched the United States's advance northward with deep concern. They decided to launch a counteroffensive. On October 2, 1950, Mao Zedong sent a cable, Document 6, to Stalin in Moscow. Describing the danger posed by the American "invaders," Mao informed the Soviet leader of China's decision for war and asked for the USSR's support. Yet around the same time, at a meeting with Truman on Wake Island on October 15, 1950, General Douglas MacArthur, supremely confident of U.S. power, assured the president that the Chinese would not enter the war. The official account of this conversation is printed below as Document 7. Six weeks later, UN and U.S. troops frantically retreated down the Korean peninsula following China's entry into the war.

On November 30, 1950, President Truman told a press conference that the United States had not ruled out the use of atomic weapons in the Korean theater. Washington nonetheless avoided further escalation and limited its goals to the reestablishment of a noncommunist South Korea. When MacArthur publicly questioned the strategy of limited war, the president relieved the outspoken general of his command on April 11, 1951. Document 8 is MacArthur's rebuttal of April 19, delivered as a speech to Congress.

1. U.S. Ambassador John Leighton Stuart
Reports Mao's Overture, 1949
Telegram of May 14, 1949

Huang [Hua] called my residence last evening remaining almost 2 hours. Our conversation was friendly and informal. I refrained from political remarks until he opened way which he did after few personal exchanges. I then spoke earnestly of great desire that peoples of all countries had for peace, including, emphatically, my own, of dangerous situation developing despite this universal popular will; of indescribable horrors of next war; of my conviction that much, but not all, present tension due to misunderstandings, fears, suspicions which could be cleared away by mutual frankness; of fears Americans and other non-Communists had of Marxist-Leninist doctrine, subscribed to by CCP [Chinese Communist party], that world revolution and overthrow of capitalistic governments necessary, thus proclaiming subversive interference or armed invasion as fixed policy. Huang spoke of Chinese people's resentment at American aid to Kmt [Kuomintang, or Nationalist party] and other "mistakes" of US Policy to which I briefly replied.

Huang asked about my plans and I told him of my instructions, adding that I was glad to stay long enough for symbolic purpose of demonstrating American

This document can be found in U.S. Department of State, *Foreign Relations of the United States, 1949* (Washington, D.C.: Government Printing Office, 1978), VIII, 745–746.

people's interest in welfare of Chinese people as whole; that I wished to maintain friendly relations of past; that being near end of my active life I hoped to be able somewhat to help restore these relations as I knew my Government and people desired; that my aim was unity, peace, truly democratic government and international good will for which Huang knew I had worked all my life in China.

Huang expressed much interest in recognition of Communist China by USA on terms of equality and mutual benefit. I replied that such terms together with accepted international practice with respect to treaties would be only proper basis. He was greatly surprised at my explanation of status of armed forces in China particularly Marines in Shanghai. Our side of story, that is desire to protect American lives during civil disturbances and chaotic conditions brought on by war, appeared never to have occurred to him. He was obviously impressed. I explained question of national government was internal; that Communists themselves at present had none; that it was customary to recognize whatever government clearly had support of people of country and was able and willing to perform its international obligations; that therefore USA and other countries could do nothing but await developments in China. I hinted that most other nations would tend to follow our lead. I explained functions of foreign consulates in maintaining informal relations with *de facto* regional authorities.

Huang expounded upon needs of China for commercial and other relations with foreign countries. He said instructions had been issued to all military units to protect safety and interests of foreigners. Intrusion into my bedroom [by Communist soldiers] was discussed and he promised to do his best in constantly shifting military situation to trace offenders. He explained that first Communist troops in city had not been prepared or properly instructed on treatment of foreigners.

Telegram of June 30, 1949

Huang Hua called on me by appointment June 28. He reported that he had received message from Mao Tse-tung and Chou En-lai assuring me that they would welcome me to Peiping if I wished to visit Yenching University. Background of this suggestion is as follows:

In early June Philip Fugh, in one of his conversations with Huang, asked casually, and not under instructions from me, if it would be possible for me to travel to Peiping to visit my old University as had been my habit in previous years on my birthday and Commencement. At that time Huang made no comment. However, 2 weeks later, June 18 to be precise, in discussing my return to Washington for consultation, Huang himself raised question with Fugh of whether time permitted my making trip to Peiping. Fugh made no commitment, commenting only that he himself had made this suggestion 2 weeks earlier. Neither Fugh nor I followed up this suggestion but apparently Huang did. Present message (almost an invitation) is reply.

Regardless whether initiation of this suggestion is considered [by] Peiping to have come from me or from Communists, I can only regard Huang's message as veiled invitation from Mao and Chou to talk with them while ostensibly visiting Yenching. To accept would undoubtedly be gratifying to them, would give me chance to describe American policy; its anxieties regarding Communism and world

This document can be found in U.S. Department of State, *Foreign Relations of the United States, 1949* (Washington, D.C.: Government Printing Office, 1978), VIII, 766–767.

revolution; its desires for China's future; and would enable me to carry to Washington most authoritative information regarding CCP intentions. Such trip would be step toward better mutual understanding and should strengthen more liberal anti-Soviet element in CCP. It would provide unique opportunity for American official to talk to top Chinese Communists in informal manner which may not again present itself. It would be imaginative, adventurous indication of US open-minded attitude towards changing political trends in China and would probably have beneficial effect on future Sino-American relations.

On negative side, trip to Peiping before my return to US on consultation would undoubtedly start rumors and speculations in China and might conceivably embarrass Department because of American criticism. It would probably be misunderstood by my colleagues in Diplomatic Corps who might feel that US representative was first to break united front policy which we have sponsored toward Communist regime and might prove beginning of trek of chiefs of mission to Peiping on one pretext or another. Trip to Peiping at this time invariably suggests idea of making similar one to Canton [temporary Nationalist capital] before my return to US.

While visiting both capitals might effectively dramatize American interest in Chinese people as a whole, it might also appear as peace-making gesture, unwarranted interference in China's internal affairs, and would probably be misunderstood by Chinese Communists, thus undoing any beneficial effects of visit north. Finally, trip of US Ambassador to Peiping at this time would enhance greatly prestige, national and international, of Chinese Communists and Mao himself and in a sense would be second step on our part (first having been my remaining Nanking) toward recognition of Communist regime.

I received clear impression that Mao, Chou and Huang are very much hoping that I make this trip, whatever their motives. I, of course, gave Huang no answer to Mao's message. . . .

I have made this rather full statement of case for Department's consideration and decision. I am, of course, ready to make journey by either means should Department consider it desirable, and should be grateful for instructions earliest and nature of reply to Huang.

2. The National Security Council Extends Containment to Asia, December 1949

Our basic security objectives with respect to Asia are:

a. Development of the nations and peoples of Asia on a stable and self-sustaining basis in conformity with the purposes and principles of the United Nations Charter.

b. Development of sufficient military power in selected non-Communist nations of Asia to maintain internal security and to prevent further encroachment by communism.

This document, "A Report to the President by the National Security Council, NSC 48/2," 30 December 1949, can be found in U.S. Department of State, *Foreign Relations of the United States, 1949* (Washington, D.C.: Government Printing Office, 1983), VII, 1215–1220.

c. Gradual reduction and eventual elimination of the preponderant power and influence of the USSR in Asia to such a degree that the Soviet Union will not be capable of threatening from that area the security of the United States or its friends and that the Soviet Union would encounter serious obstacles should it attempt to threaten the peace, national independence and stability of the Asiatic nations.

d. Prevention of power relationships in Asia which would enable any other nation or alliance to threaten the security of the United States from that area, or the peace, national independence and stability of the Asiatic nations.

2. In pursuit of these objectives, the United States should act to:

a. Support non-Communist forces in taking the initiative in Asia;

b. Exert an influence to advance its own national interests; and

c. Initiate action in such a manner as will appeal to the Asiatic nations as being compatible with their national interests and worthy of their support.

3. As the basis for realization of its objectives, the United States should pursue a policy toward Asia containing the following components:

a. The United States should make known its sympathy with the efforts of Asian leaders to form regional associations of non-Communist states of the various Asian areas, and if in due course associations eventuate, the United States should be prepared, if invited, to assist such associations to fulfill their purposes under conditions which would be to our interest. . . .

b. The United States should act to develop and strength the security of the area from Communist external aggression or internal subversion. These steps should take into account any benefits to the security of Asia which may flow from the development of one or more regional groupings. The United States on its own initiative should now:

(1) Improve the United States position with respect to Japan, the Ryukyus and the Philippines.

(2) Scrutinize closely the development of threats from Communist aggression, direct or indirect, and be prepared to help within our means to meet such threats by providing political, economic, and military assistance and advice where clearly needed to supplement the resistance of the other governments in and out of the area which are more directly concerned.

(3) Develop cooperative measures through multilateral or bilateral arrangements to combat Communist internal subversion.

(4) Appraise the desirability and the means of developing in Asia some form of collective security arrangements. . . .

c. The United States should encourage the creation of an atmosphere favorable to economic recovery and development in non-Communist Asia, and to the revival of trade along multilateral, non-discriminatory lines. The economic policies of the United States should be adapted to promote, where possible, economic conditions that will contribute to political stability in friendly countries of Asia, but the United States should carefully avoid assuming responsibility for the economic welfare and development of that continent. Such policies might be projected along the following lines:

(1) Vigorous prosecution of the Point IV [foreign aid] program in friendly countries of Asia, in an endeavor to assist them, by providing technical assistance, to make a start toward the solution of some of their long-range economic problems.

(2) Maintenance of a liberal United States trade policy with Asia and stimulation of imports from Asia. . . .

(3) Execution of a stockpiling program for strategic materials, based upon United States needs for strategic reserves and upon immediate and long-range economic effects in the supplying countries.

(4) Negotiation of treaties of friendship, commerce and navigation with non-Communist countries of Asia. . . .

(5) Encouragement of private United States investment in non-Communist countries and support of the early extension of credits by the International Bank and the Export–Import Bank for specific key economic projects of a self-liquidating nature, especially those directed towards increasing production of food in this area.

(6) Efforts to obtain the adherence of Asiatic countries to the principles of multilateral, non-discriminatory trade as embodied in the General Agreements on Tariffs and Trade, as a means of reducing trade barriers and expanding the international and intra-regional trade of the region on an economic basis. This would include, for example, further efforts to secure the benefits of most-favored-nation treatment for Japan.

d. The question of a peace settlement with Japan, now receiving separate consideration, will be presented for the consideration of the National Security Council at a later date. . . .

e. (1) The United States should continue to provide for the extension of political support and economic, technical, military and other assistance to the democratically-elected Government of the Republic of Korea.

(2) The United States should therefore press forward with the implementation of the ECA [Economic Cooperation Administration], MDAP [Military Defense Assistance Program], USIE [United States Information and Educational Exchange Program]and related programs for Korea, and should continue to accord political support to the Republic of Korea, both within and without the framework of the United Nations.

f. (1) The United States should continue to recognize the National Government of China until the situation is further clarified. The United States should avoid recognizing the Chinese Communist regime until it is clearly in the United States interest to do so. The United States should continue to express to friendly governments its own views concerning the dangers of hasty recognition of the Chinese Communist regime but should not take a stand which would engage the prestige of the United States in an attempt to prevent such recognition. In general, however, it should be realized that it would be inappropriate for the United States to adopt a posture more hostile or policies more harsh towards a Communist China than towards the USSR itself. It should also be realized that the according of recognition by other friendly countries would affect the bargaining position of the United States in the absence of United States recognition and would affect United States private and national interests in China. In the event that recognition of the Chinese Communists is anticipated, appropriate steps should be taken to make it clear that recognition should not be construed as approval of the Chinese Communist regime, or abatement of our hostility to Soviet efforts to exercise control in China.

(2) The United States should continue the policies of avoiding military and political support of any non-Communist elements in China unless such elements are willing actively to resist Communism with or without United States aid and unless such support would mean reasonable resistance to the Communists and contribute to the over-all national interests of the United States. . . .

(3) The United States should exploit, through appropriate political, psychological and economic means, any rifts between the Chinese Communists and the USSR and between the Stalinists and other elements in China, while scrupulously avoiding the appearance of intervention. Where appropriate, covert as well as overt means should be utilized to achieve these objects.

(4) The United States should, as a security measure, seek to prevent the USSR, its European satellites, and North Korea from obtaining from abroad through China supplies of strategic materials and equipment which are currently denied them by the United States and its European allies through direct channels. The United States should also use every effort to prevent the Chinese Communists from obtaining from non-Soviet sources supplies of materials and equipment of direct military utility. . . .

g. (1) The United States should continue the policy . . . of attempting to deny Formosa and the Pescadores [offshore islands] to the Chinese Communists through diplomatic and economic means. . . .

(2) Since the United States may not be able to achieve its objectives through political and economic means, and in view of the opinion of the Joint Chiefs of Staff . . . that, while Formosa is strategically important to the United States, "the strategic importance of Formosa does not justify overt military action . . . so long as the present disparity between our military strength and our global obligations exists," the United States should make every effort to strengthen the over-all U.S. position with respect to the Philippines, the Ryukyus, and Japan. . . .

h. The United States should continue to use its influence in Asia toward resolving the colonial-nationalist conflict in such a way as to satisfy the fundamental demands of the nationalist movement while at the same time minimizing the strain on the colonial powers who are our Western allies. Particular attention should be given to the problem of French Indo-China and action should be taken to bring home to the French the urgency of removing the barriers to the obtaining by Bao Dai or other non-Communist nationalist leaders of the support of a substantial proportion of the Vietnamese. . . . [T]he United States should give immediate consideration to the problems confronting the new Republic of United Indonesia and how best it can be aided in maintaining its freedom in the face of internal and external Communist pressures. . . .

m. The sum of $75,000,000 for assistance to the general area of China, which was made available under Section 303 of the Mutual Defense Assistance Act of 1949, should be programmed as a matter of urgency.

3. Secretary of State Dean Acheson Defines the Defense Perimeter in Asia, 1950

What is the situation in regard to the military security of the Pacific area, and what is our policy in regard to it?

In the first place, the defeat and the disarmament of Japan has placed upon the United States the necessity of assuming the military defense of Japan so long as that is required, both in the interest of our security and in the interests of the security of the entire Pacific area and, in all honor, in the interest of Japanese security. We have American—and there are Australian—troops in Japan. I am not in a position to speak for the Australians, but I can assure you that there is no intention of any sort of abandoning or weakening the defenses of Japan and that whatever arrangements are to be made either through permanent settlement or otherwise, that defense must and shall be maintained.

This defensive perimeter runs along the Aleutians to Japan and then goes to the Ryukyus. We hold important defense positions in the Ryukyu Islands, and those we will continue to hold. In the interest of the population of the Ryukyu Islands, we will at an appropriate time offer to hold these islands under trusteeship of the United Nations. But they are essential parts of the defensive perimeter of the Pacific, and they must and will be held.

The defensive perimeter runs from the Ryukyus to the Philippine Islands. Our relations, our defensive relations with the Philippines are contained in agreements between us. Those agreements are being loyally carried out and will be loyally carried out. Both peoples have learned by bitter experience the vital connections between our mutual defense requirements. We are in no doubt about that, and it is hardly necessary for me to say an attack on the Philippines could not and would not be tolerated by the United States. But I hasten to add that no one perceives the imminence of any such attack.

So far as the military security of other areas in the Pacific is concerned, it must be clear that no person can guarantee these areas against military attack. But it must also be clear that such a guarantee is hardly sensible or necessary within the realm of practical relationship.

Should such an attack occur—one hesitates to say where such an armed attack could come from—the initial reliance must be on the people attacked to resist it and then upon the commitments of the entire civilized world under the Charter of the United Nations which so far has not proved a weak reed to lean on by any people who are determined to protect their independence against outside aggression. But it is a mistake, I think, in considering Pacific and Far Eastern problems to become obsessed with military considerations. Important as they are, there are other problems that press, and these other problems are not capable of solution through military means. These other problems arise out of the susceptibility of many areas, and many countries in the Pacific area, to subversion and penetration. That cannot be stopped by military means. . . .

This document can be found in *Department of State Bulletin*, XXII (January 23, 1950), 115–116.

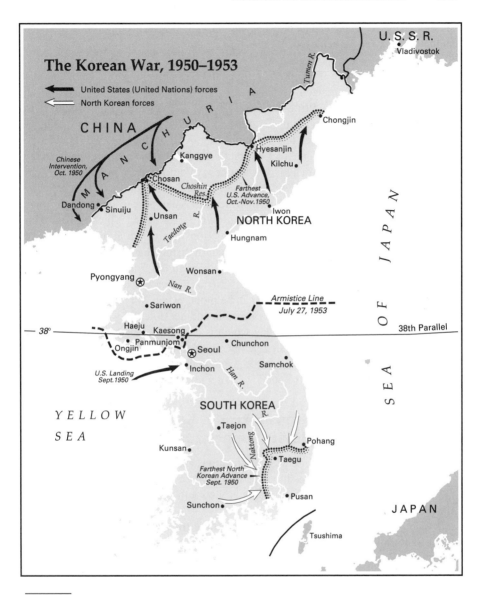

The Korean War, 1950–1953

Thomas G. Paterson et al., *American Foreign Relations,* 6/e. Copyright © 2005 by Houghton Mifflin Company. Used with permission.

That leads me to the other thing that I wanted to point out, and that is the limitation of effective American assistance. American assistance can be effective when it is the missing component in a situation which might otherwise be solved. The United States cannot furnish all these components to solve the question. It can not furnish determination, it can not furnish will, and it can not furnish the loyalty of a people to its government. But if the will and if the determination exists and if the people are behind their government, then, and not always then, is there a very good chance. In that situation, American help can be effective and it can lead to an accomplishment which could not otherwise be achieved. . . .

In Korea, we have taken great steps which have ended our military occupation, and in cooperation with the United Nations, have established an independent and sovereign country recognized by nearly all the rest of the world. We have given that nation great help in getting itself established. We are asking the Congress to continue that help until it is firmly established, and that legislation is now pending before the Congress. The idea that we should scrap all of that, that we should stop half way through the achievement of the establishment of this country, seems to me to be the most utter defeatism and utter madness of our interests in Asia. . . .

So after this survey, what we conclude, I believe, is that there is a new day which has dawned in Asia. It is a day in which the Asian peoples are on their own, and know it, and intend to continue on their own. It is a day in which the old relationships between east and west are gone, relationships which at their worst were exploitation, and which at their best were paternalism. That relationship is over, and the relationship of east and west must now be in the Far East one of mutual respect and mutual helpfulness. We are their friends. Others are their friends. We and those others are willing to help, but we can help only where we are wanted and only where the conditions of help are really sensible and possible. So what we can see is that this new day in Asia, this new day which is dawning, may go on to a glorious noon or it may darken and it may drizzle out. But that decision lies within the countries of Asia and within the power of the Asian people. It is not a decision which a friend or even an enemy from the outside can decide for them.

4. North Korean Leader Kim Il Sung Pleads for Soviet Support, January 1950

[On January 17, 1950,] Kim, addressing the advisers Ignatiev and Pelishenko in an excited manner, began to speak about how now, when China is completing its liberation, the liberation of the Korean people in the south of the country is next in line. In connection with this he said:

"The people of the southern portion of Korea trust me and rely on our armed might. Partisans will not decide the question. The people of the south know that we have a good army. Lately I do not sleep at night, thinking about how to resolve the question of the unification of the whole country. If the matter of the liberation of the people of the southern portion of Korea and the unification of the country is drawn out, then I can lose the trust of the people of Korea." Further Kim stated that when he was in Moscow, Comrade Stalin said to him that it was not necessary to attack the south, in case of an attack on the north of the country by the army of Rhee Syngman [South Korean leader Syngman Rhee], then it is possible to go on the counteroffensive to the south of Korea. But since Rhee Syngman is still not instigating an attack, it means that the liberation of the people of the southern part of the country and the unification of the country are being drawn out, that he (Kim Il Sung) thinks that he

This document can be found in *Cold War International History Project Bulletin*, Woodrow Wilson International Center for Scholars, Washington, D.C., No. 5 (Spring 1995), 8.

needs again to visit Comrade Stalin and receive an order and permission for offensive action by the Peoples' Army for the purpose of the liberation of the people of Southern Korea. Further Kim said that he himself cannot begin an attack, because he is a communist, a disciplined person and for him the order of Comrade Stalin is law. Then he stated that if it is [not] possible to meet with Comrade Stalin, then he will try to meet with Mao Zedong, after his return from Moscow. Kim underscored that Mao Zedong promised to render him assistance after the conclusion of the war in China. (Apparently Kim Il Sung has in mind the conversation of his representative Kim Il with Mao Zedong in June 1949, about which I reported by ciphered telegram.) Kim said that he also has other questions for Mao Zedong, in particular the question of the possibility of the creation of an eastern bureau of the Cominform. He further stated that on all these questions he will try to meet with Comrade Shtykov and to secure through him a meeting with Comrade Stalin.

The advisers of the embassy Ignatiev and Pelishenko, avoiding discussing these questions, tried to switch the discussion to a general theme, then Kim Il Sung came toward me, took me aside and began the following conversation: can he meet with Comrade Stalin and discuss the question of the position in the south and the question of aggressive actions against the army of Rhee Syngman, that their people's army now is significantly stronger than the army of Rhee Syngman. Here he stated that if it is impossible to meet with Comrade Stalin, then he wants to meet with Mao Zedong, since Mao after his visit to Moscow will have orders on all questions.

Then Kim Il Sung placed before me the question, why don't I allow him to attack the Ongjin peninsula, which the People's Army could take in three days, and with a general attack the People's Army could be in Seoul in several days.

I answered Kim that he has not raised the question of a meeting with Comrade Stalin and if he raises such a question, then it is possible that Comrade Stalin will receive him. On the question of an attack on the Ongjin peninsula I answered him that it is impossible to do this. Then I tried to conclude the conversation on these questions and, alluding to a later time, proposed to go home. With that the conversation was concluded. . . .

In the process of this conversation Kim Il Sung repeatedly underscored his wish to get the advice of Comrade Stalin on the question of the situation in the south of Korea, since [Kim Il Sung] is constantly nurturing his idea about an attack.

5. President Harry S. Truman and His Advisers Confer at the "Blair House Meeting," June 26, 1950

GENERAL [HOYT S.] VANDENBERG reported that the First Yak [North Korean] plane had been shot down.

THE PRESIDENT remarked that he hoped that it was not the last.

GENERAL VANDENBERG read the text of the orders which had been issued to our Air Forces calling on them to take "aggressive action" against any planes interfering with their mission or operating in a manner unfriendly to the South Korean forces.

This document can be found in U.S. Department of State, *Foreign Relations of the United States, 1950, Korea* (Washington, D.C.: Government Printing Office, 1976), VII, 179–183.

He indicated, however, that they had been avoiding combat where the direct carrying-out of their mission was not involved.

MR. [DEAN] ACHESON suggested that an all-out order be issued to the Navy and Air Force to waive all restrictions on their operations in Korea and to offer the fullest possible support to the South Korean forces, attacking tanks, guns, columns, etc., of the North Korean forces in order to give a chance to the South Koreans to reform.

THE PRESIDENT said he approved this.

MR. [FRANK] PACE inquired whether this meant action only south of the thirty-eighth parallel.

MR. ACHESON said this was correct. He was making no suggestion for any action across the line.

GENERAL VANDENBERG asked whether this meant also that they should not fly over the line.

MR. ACHESON said they should not.

THE PRESIDENT said this was correct; that no action should be taken north of the thirty-eighth parallel. He added "not yet.". . .

MR. ACHESON said that the second point he wished to bring up was that orders should be issued to the Seventh Fleet to prevent an attack on Formosa.

THE PRESIDENT said he agreed.

MR. ACHESON continued that at the same time the National Government of China should be told to desist from operations against the mainland and that the Seventh Fleet should be ordered to see that those operations would cease.

MR. ACHESON said his third point was an increase in the United States military forces in the Philippines and an acceleration of aid to the Philippines in order that we might have a firm base there.

THE PRESIDENT said he agreed.

MR. ACHESON said his fourth point was that aid to Indochina should be stepped up and that a strong military mission should be sent. . . .

THE PRESIDENT said that he had a letter from the Generalissimo [Jiang Jieshi] about one month (?) ago to the effect that the Generalissimo might step out of the situation if that would help. He said this was a private letter and he had kept it secret. He said that we might want to proceed along those lines in order to get Chinese forces helping us. He thought that the Generalissimo might step out if MacArthur were put in.

MR. ACHESON said that the Generalissimo was unpredictable and that it was possible that he might resist and "throw the ball game." He said that it might be well to do this later.

THE PRESIDENT said that was alright. He himself thought that it was the next step. . . .

MR. ACHESON added in regard to the Formosan situation that he thought it undesirable that we should get mixed up in the question of the Chinese administration of the Island.

THE PRESIDENT said that we were not going to give the Chinese "a nickel" for any purpose whatever. He said that all the money we had given them is now invested in United States real estate. . . .

MR. [JOHN D.] HICKERSON read the draft of the Security Council resolution recommending that UN members render such assistance as was needed to Korea to repel the attack.

THE PRESIDENT said that was right. He said we wanted everyone in on this, including Hong Kong.

GENERAL [OMAR] BRADLEY reported that British Air Marshall Tedder had come to see him, was generally in accord with our taking the firm position, and gave General Bradley a full report of the forces which the British have in that area.

MR. [DEAN] RUSK pointed out that it was possible the Russians would come to the Security Council meeting and cast a veto. In that case we would still take the position that we could act in support of the Charter.

THE PRESIDENT said that was right. He rather wished they would veto. He said we needed to lay a base for our action in Formosa. He said that he would work on the draft of his statement tonight and would talk to the Defense and State Departments in the morning regarding the final text.

MR. RUSK pointed out that it was Mr. [George F.] Kennan's estimate that Formosa would be the next likely spot for a Communist move.

SECRETARY [LOUIS A.] JOHNSON reported that SCAP's [Supreme Commander to the Allied Powers] guess was that the next move would be on Iran. He thought there should be a check on this.

GENERAL [J. LAWTON] COLLINS said that SCAP did not have as much global information as they have in Washington. He and Mr. Pace stated that they have asked for full reports all over the world in regard to any developments, particularly of Soviet preparations.

SECRETARY JOHNSON suggested to Mr. Acheson that it would be advisable to have some talks with the UK regarding possible action in Iran.

MR. ACHESON said he would talk with both the British and French. . . .

MR. ACHESON suggested that the President might wish to get in Senator [Tom] Connally and other members of the Senate and House and tell them what had been decided.

THE PRESIDENT said that he had a meeting scheduled for 10:00 tomorrow morning with the Big Four [congressional leaders] and that he would get in any others that the Secretary thought should be added. He suggested that Secretaries Acheson and Johnson should also be there. . . .

GENERAL COLLINS stated that the military situation in Korea was bad. It was impossible to say how much our air can do. The Korean Chief of Staff has no fight left in him.

MR. ACHESON stated that it was important for us to do something even if the effort were not successful.

MR. JOHNSON said that even if we lose Korea this action would save the situation. He said this action "suits me." He then asked whether any of the military representatives had any objection to the course of action which had been outlined. There was no objection.

GENERAL VANDENBERG, in response to a question that Mr. [Thomas] Finletter, said that he bet a tank would be knocked out before dark.

THE PRESIDENT said he had done everything he could for five years to prevent this kind of situation. Now the situation is here and we must do what we can to meet it. He had been wondering about the mobilization of the National Guard and asked General Bradley if that was necessary now. If it was he must go to Congress and ask for funds. He was merely putting the subject on the table for discussion. He repeated we must do everything we can for the Korean situation—"for the United Nations."

GENERAL BRADLEY said that if we commit our ground forces in Korea we cannot at the same time carry out our other commitments without mobilization. He wondered if it was better to wait now on the question of mobilization of the National Guard. He thought it would be preferable to wait a few days.

THE PRESIDENT said he wished the Joint Chiefs to think about this and to let him know in a few days time. He said "I don't want to go to war."

GENERAL COLLINS stated that if we were going to commit ground forces in Korea we must mobilize.

MR. ACHESON suggested that we should hold mobilization in reserve. . . .

GENERAL COLLINS remarked that if we had had standing orders we could have stopped this. We must consider this problem for the future.

THE PRESIDENT said he agreed.

6. Chinese Leader Mao Zedong Informs Joseph Stalin of China's Decision to Enter the Korean War, 1950

(1) We have decided to send a portion of our troops, under the name of [the Chinese] Volunteers, to Korea, assisting the Korean comrades in fighting the troops of the United States and its running dog Syngman Rhee. We regarded the mission as necessary. If Korea were completely occupied by the Americans and the Korean revolutionary forces were substantially destroyed, the American invaders would be more rampant, and such a situation would be very unfavorable to the whole East.

(2) We realize that since we have decided to send Chinese troops to Korea to fight the Americans, we must first be able to solve the problem, that is, that we are prepared to annihilate the invaders from the United States and from other countries, and to drive them out [of Korea]; second, since Chinese troops will fight American troops in Korea (although we will use the name the Chinese Volunteers), we must be prepared for an American declaration of war on China. We must be prepared for the possible bombardments by American air forces of many Chinese cities and industrial bases, and for attacks by American naval forces on China's coastal areas.

(3) Of the two issues, the first one is whether the Chinese troops would be able to defeat American troops in Korea, thus effectively resolving the Korean problem. If our troops could annihilate American troops in Korea, especially the Eighth Army (a competent veteran U.S. army), the whole situation would become favorable to the revolutionary front and China, even though the second question ([the possibility] that the United States would declare war on China) would still remain as a serious issue. In other words, the Korean problem will end in fact with the defeat of American troops (although the war might not end in name, because the United States would not recognize the victory of Korea for a long period). If this occurs, even though the United States had declared war on China, the ongoing confrontation would not be on a large-scale, nor would it last very long. We consider that the most unfavorable situation would be that the Chinese forces fail to destroy American troops in large numbers in Korea, thus resulting in a stalemate, and that,

From *Chinese Historians* 5 (Spring 1992), 67–68, translated by Li Xiaobing, Wang Xi, and Jian Chen. Reprinted with the permission of Chinese Historians of the United States, Inc.

at the same time, the United States openly declares war on China, which would be detrimental to China's economic reconstruction already under way, and would cause dissatisfaction among the national bourgeoisie and some other sectors of the people (who are absolutely afraid of war).

(4) Under the current situation, we have decided, starting on October 15, to move the twelve divisions, which have been earlier transferred to southern Manchuria, into suitable areas in North Korea (not necessarily close to the thirty-eighth parallel); these troops will only fight the enemy that venture to attack areas north of the thirty-eighth parallel; our troops will employ defensive tactics, while engaging small groups of enemies and learning about the situation in every respect. Meanwhile, our troops will be awaiting the arrival of Soviet weapons and being equipped with those weapons. Only then will our troops, in cooperation with the Korean comrades, launch a counter-offensive to destroy the invading American forces.

(5) According to our information, every U.S. army (two infantry divisions and one mechanized division) is armed with 1500 pieces of artillery of various calibers ranging from 70mm to 240mm, including tank guns and anti-aircraft guns, while each of our armies (three divisions) is equipped with only 36 pieces of artillery. The enemy would control the air while our air force, which has just started its training, will not be able to enter the war with some 300 planes until February 1951. Therefore, at present, we are not assured that our troops will be able to annihilate an entire U.S. army once and for all. But since we have decided to go into the war against the Americans, we should be prepared that, when the U.S. high command musters up one complete army to fight us in a campaign, we should be able to concentrate our forces four times greater than those of the enemy (that is, to use four of our armies to fight against one enemy army) and to marshal firing power one and a half to two times stronger than that of the enemy (that is, to use 2200 to 3000 pieces of artillery of 70mm calibre and upward to deal with the enemy's 1500 pieces of artilleries of the same calibers), so that we can guarantee a complete and thorough destruction of one enemy army.

(6) In addition to the above-mentioned twelve divisions, we are transferring another twenty-four divisions, as the second and third echelons to assist Korea, from south of the Yangzi River and the Shaanxi-Ganshu areas to the Long-hai, Tianjin-Pukuo, and Beijing–Southern Manchuria railways; we expect to gradually employ these divisions next spring and summer in accordance with the situation at the time.

7. General Douglas MacArthur Dismisses the Likelihood of Chinese Intervention, 1950

The President: What are the chances for Chinese or Soviet interference?

General MacArthur: Very little. Had they interfered in the first or second months it would have been decisive. We are no longer fearful of their intervention. We no longer stand hat in hand. The Chinese have 300,000 men in Manchuria. Of these probably not more than 100/125,000 are distributed along the Yalu River.

This document can be found in U.S. Department of State, *Foreign Relations of the United States, 1950, Korea* (Washington, D.C.: U.S. Government Printing Office, 1976), VII, 179–183.

Only 50/60,000 could be gotten across the Yalu River. They have no Air Force. Now that we have bases for our Air Force in Korea, if the Chinese tried to get down to Pyongyang there would be the greatest slaughter.

With the Russians it is a little different. They have an Air Force in Siberia and a fairly good one, with excellent pilots equipped with some jets and B-25 and B-29 planes. They can put 1,000 planes in the air with some 2/300 more from the Fifth and Seventh Soviet Fleets. They are probably no match for our Air Force. The Russians have no ground troops available for North Korea. They would have difficulty in putting troops into the field. It would take six weeks to get a division across and six weeks brings the winter. The only other combination would be Russian air support of Chinese ground troops. Russian air is deployed in a semicircle through Mukden and Harbin, but the coordination between the Russian air and the Chinese ground would be so flimsy that I believe Russian air would bomb the Chinese as often as they would bomb us. Ground support is a very difficult thing to do. Our Marines do it perfectly. They have been trained for it. Our own Air and Ground Forces are not as good as the Marines but they are effective. Between untrained Air and Ground Forces an air umbrella is impossible without a lot of joint training. I believe it just wouldn't work with Chinese Communist ground and Russian air. We are the best.

8. MacArthur's "No Substitute for Victory" Speech, 1951

While I was not consulted prior to the President's decision to intervene in the support of the Republic of Korea, that decision from a military standpoint proved a sound one. As I say, a brief and sound one as we hurled back the invaders and decimated his forces. Our victory was complete and our objectives within reach when Red China intervened with numerically superior ground forces. This created a new war and an entirely new situation, a situation not contemplated when our forces were committed against the North Korean invaders, a situation which called for new decisions in the diplomatic sphere to permit the realistic adjustment of military strategy. Such decisions have not been forthcoming.

While no man in his right mind would advocate sending our ground forces into continental China—and such was never given a thought—the new situation did urgently demand a drastic revision of strategic planning if our political aim was to defeat this new enemy as we had defeated the old.

Apart from the military need as I saw it to neutralize sanctuary, protection given to the enemy north of the Yalu, I felt that military necessity in the conduct of the war made necessary:

First, the intensification of our economic blockade against China.

Second, the imposition of a naval blockade against the China coast.

Third, removal of restrictions on air reconnaissance of China's coastal areas and of Manchuria.

Fourth, removal of restrictions on the forces of the Republic of China on Formosa with logistical support to contribute to their effective operation against the Chinese mainland.

This document can be found in *Congressional Record*, XCVII (April 19, 1951), 4124–4125.

For entertaining these views all professionally designed to support our forces committed to Korea and bring hostilities to an end with the least possible delay and at a saving of countless American and Allied lives, I have been severely criticized in lay circles, principally abroad, despite my understanding that from a military standpoint the above views have been fully shared in the past by practically every military leader concerned with the Korean campaign, including our own Joint Chiefs of Staff.

I called for reinforcements, but was informed that reinforcements were not available. I made clear that if not permitted to utilize the friendly Chinese force of some 600,000 men on Formosa; if not permitted to blockade the China coast to prevent the Chinese Reds from getting succor from without; and if there were to be no hope of major reinforcements, the position of the command from the military standpoint forbade victory. We could hold in Korea by constant maneuver and at an approximate area where our supply advantages were in balance with the supply line disadvantages of the enemy, but we could hope at best for only an indecisive campaign, with its terrible and constant attrition upon our forces if the enemy utilized his full military potential. I have constantly called for the new political decisions essential to a solution. Efforts have been made to distort my position. It has been said in effect that I was a warmonger. Nothing could be further from the truth. I know war as few other men now living know it, and nothing to me is more revolting. . . .

But once war is forced upon us, there is no other alternative than to apply every available means to bring it to a swift end. War's very object is victory—not prolonged indecision. In war, indeed, there can be no substitute for victory.

There are some who for varying reasons would appease Red China. They are blind to history's clear lesson. For history teaches with unmistakable emphasis that appeasement but begets new and bloodier war. . . .

The tragedy of Korea is further heightened by the fact that as military action is confined to its territorial limits, it condemns that nation, which it is our purpose to save, to suffer the devastating impact of full naval and air bombardment, while the enemy's sanctuaries are fully protected from such attack and devastation. Of the nations of the world, Korea alone, up to now, is the sole one which has risked its all against communism. . . .

I am closing my 52 years of military service. When I joined the Army even before the turn of the century, it was the fulfillment of all my boyish hopes and dreams. The world has turned over many times since I took the oath on the plain at West Point, and the hopes and dreams have long since vanished. But I since remember the refrain of one of the most popular barrack ballads of that day which proclaimed most proudly that—

"Old soldiers never die; they just fade away." And like the old soldier of that ballad, I now close my military career and just fade away—an old soldier who tried to do his duty as God gave him the light to see that duty.

 E S S A Y S

In the first essay, Professor Bruce Cumings of the University of Chicago analyzes the origins of the Korean War and the roots of U.S. intervention. He challenges Cold War interpretations that blame the Soviet Union exclusively for igniting the war, and he concludes that the conflict began as a civil war between rival Korean governments, north and south, both of which sought to unify their country following its arbitrary division in 1945. Cumings attributes U.S. interest in Korea to both Cold War politics and Korea's economic importance to Japan's postwar recovery. He faults the Truman administration for supporting an oppressive regime in South Korea and then leading the United Nations to contain a monolithic Communist threat that did not exist. In the second essay, two Russian scholars, Vladislov Zubok, a senior fellow at the National Security Archive in Washington, D.C., and Constantine Pleshakov, a writer who lives in Moscow, use recently declassified Communist sources to probe Russian, Chinese, and North Korean policies. They place responsibility for the war on Soviet leader Joseph Stalin. Zubok and Pleshakov argue that Stalin gave his backing to Kim Il Sung's war plans hoping to demonstrate Moscow's leadership among Communist states. Stalin, they observe, was surprised by Washington's strong response and, in order to avoid direct confrontation with the United States, pressed his Communist Chinese ally Mao Zedong to intervene on Kim's behalf. In the end, Zubok and Pleshakov suggest, the Truman administration's astute countermeasures foiled Stalin's expansionist gamble.

In the last selection, Thomas J. Christensen of Cornell University examines U.S. relations with China's Communist leadership in 1949 and 1950, and he detects a link between Washington's nonrecognition policy and Chinese intervention in Korea in the fall of 1950. He concedes that U.S. support for Jiang Jieshi and the Chinese Communist Party's (CCP) ideological zeal generated deep hostility in Beijing and undermined the chance for amicable relations. He emphasizes, however, that Mao Zedong and the CCP held out the possibility of normal diplomatic ties and initiated high-level contacts with U.S. officials in the spring of 1949. Christensen argues that the Truman administration's continued support for Jiang, reinforced by the stationing of the Seventh Fleet in the Taiwan Strait at the start of the Korean War, increased tensions with the People's Republic of China and hindered reliable lines of communication with Beijing that might have prevented the escalation of the Korean conflict.

Korea's Civil War and the Roots of U.S. Intervention

BRUCE CUMINGS

A Cold War narrative is all too imbedded in American histories of the liberation period (Koreans call August 15, 1945, *haebang,* meaning liberation from Japan). The accounts begin with Japan's surrender, move quickly to the December 1945 agreements on Korea with the Soviets and the two U.S.-Soviet "joint commissions" of 1946 and 1947 that followed them; they then detail the United Nations's role in sponsoring elections that established the Republic of Korea in 1948, and conclude with the war in 1950. The literature lays most of the problems in these five years at the door of Soviet obstructionism or Korean political immaturity. In fact, Koreans were the prime historical actors in this period, shaping American and Soviet power to their ends and generally ignoring all the "externals" I have just mentioned, unless they appeared to serve Korean purposes. The national division, however, was not their doing: it is Americans who bear the lion's share of the responsibility for the thirty-eighth parallel.

In the days just before Koreans heard the voice of Emperor Hirohito for the first time, broadcasting Japan's surrender and Korea's liberation on August 15, 1945, John J. McCloy of the State-War-Navy Coordinating Committee (SWNCC) directed two young colonels, Dean Rusk and Charles H. Bonesteel, to withdraw to an adjoining room and find a place to divide Korea. It was around midnight on August 10–11, the atomic bombs had been dropped, the Soviet Red Army had entered the Pacific War, and American planners were rushing to arrange the Japanese surrender throughout the region. Given thirty minutes to do so, Rusk and Bonesteel looked at a map and chose the thirty-eighth parallel because it "would place the capital city in the American zone"; although the line was "further north than could be realistically reached . . . in the event of Soviet disagreement," the Soviets made no objections—which "somewhat surprised" Rusk. General Douglas MacArthur, the hero of the Pacific campaigns, issued General Order Number One for the Japanese surrender on August 15, including in it (and thus making public) the thirty-eighth parallel decision. The Russians accepted in silence this division into spheres, while demanding a Russian occupation of the northern part of Hokkaido in Japan (which MacArthur refused).

American officials consulted no Koreans in coming to this decision, nor did they ask the opinions of the British or the Chinese, both of whom were to take part in a planned "trusteeship" for Korea. Instead, the decision was unilateral and hasty. Still, it grew out of previous American planning. The United States had taken the initiative in great-power deliberations on Korea during the war, suggesting a multilateral trusteeship for postwar Korea to the British in March 1943, and to the Soviets at the end of the same year. President Franklin D. Roosevelt worried about the disposition of enemy-held colonial territories and aware of colonial demands for independence, sought a gradualist, tutelary policy of preparing colonials (like the Koreans) for self-government and independence. He knew that since Korea touched the Soviet border, the Russians would want to be involved in the fate of postwar Korea; he hoped to get a Soviet commitment to a multilateral administration, to forestall unilateral solutions and provide an entry for American interests in Korea. Korean independence would come only at an appropriate time, or "in due course." . . .

The United States gained Soviet adherence to a modified version of the trusteeship idea at the foreign ministers' conference in December 1945, an important agreement that eliminated irrelevant British and Chinese influence, while suggesting that the two powers might ultimately come to terms on how to reunify Korea. Roosevelt, basing himself on the experience of American colonialism in the Philippines, had argued that a Korean trusteeship might last as long as forty or fifty years, but the December 1945 agreement shortened the period of great-power involvement in Korean affairs to no more than five years and called for a unified provisional government of Korea. But even by that early date the agreement was still too late, because the de facto policies of the two occupations had identified the Soviets with Kim Il Sung and the people's committees [leftist governing units organized at the local level in both North Korea and South Korea], while the Americans backed [the conservative] Syngman Rhee and opposed the committees and widespread Korean demands for a thorough renovation of colonial legacies. . . .

The American military command, along with such high-ranking emissaries dispatched from Washington as John J. McCloy, tended to interpret resistance to U.S.

desires in the South as radical and pro-Soviet. In particular the United States saw the [indigenously organized] "People's Republic" as part of a Soviet master plan to dominate all of Korea. Radical activity, such as the ousting of landlords and attacks on Koreans in the colonial police, was usually a matter of settling scores left over from the colonial period, or of demands by Koreans to run their own affairs. But it immediately became wrapped up with Soviet-American rivalry, such that the Cold War arrived in Korea in the last months of 1945. . . .

The problem was that Korean society had no base for either a liberal or a democratic party as Americans understood it; it had a population the vast majority of which consisted of poor peasants, and a tiny minority of which held most of the wealth: landowners, who formed the real base of the KDP [South Korea's noncommunist political power structure]. The elite of Korean society during the colonial period, nearly all of them were widely perceived to have fattened under colonial rule while everybody else suffered. The historical documentation could not be clearer: the United States intervened on behalf of the smallest group in Korea. . . .

With fifty years of hindsight—or even five, in 1950—we can imagine a cauterizing fire that would have settled Korea's multitude of social and political problems caused by the pressure cooker of colonial rule and instant "liberation," a purifying upheaval that might have been pretty awful, but nothing like the millions of lives lost in 1950–53. . . .

Had the Americans and the Russians quit Korea, a leftist regime would have taken over quickly, and it would have been a revolutionary nationalist government that, over time, would have moderated and rejoined the world community—as did China, as Vietnam is doing today. But we have to imagine this, because Americans do not understand the point of social revolutions, never having had one themselves; to allow this to happen would have meant that [U.S. commanding general John Reed] Hodge and many other Americans would have occupied Korea only to "turn it over to the communists." . . . The Americans would not turn Korea over to the Koreans, and so they got on with the "positive action" necessary to create an anticommunist South Korea. Korea thus became a harbinger of policies later followed throughout the world—in Greece, Indochina, Iran, Guatemala, Cuba, Nicaragua—where Americans came to defend any group calling itself anticommunist, because the alternative was thought to be worse. And fifty years later the Korean problem remains unsolved.

The establishment of official organizations for the South alone went on apace. The ROK was not proclaimed until August 15, 1948, but the southern political system was built in the first few months of the occupation, and did not substantially change until the 1960s. In November and December 1945 Hodge and his advisers chose to take four steps: first, to build up an army to defend the thirty-eighth parallel; second, to buttress the Korean National Police (KNP) as the primary political weapon for pacifying the South; third, to strengthen the alliance with rightist parties; and fourth, to suppress Koreans who didn't like such policies. An army that occupied Korea to disarm the Japanese was now intensively shaping a containment bulwark in South Korea. . . .

The effective opposition to the developing southern system was almost wholly on the left, mainly because Japanese policies had left Korea with such a tiny middle class. A mass popular resistance from 1945 to 1950 mingled raw peasant protest with organized labor union activity and, finally, armed guerrilla resistance. . . .

American policy, of course, never set out to create one of the worst police states in Asia. The Korean problem was what we would now call a Third World problem or a North-South problem, a conflict over how best to overcome the debilities of colonial rule and comparative backwardness. In the Cold War milieu of the time, however, it was always seen by Americans as an East-West problem. The Soviets, we might say, pushed the North-South angle as a way of besting the United States in the East-West conflict on the peninsula. That is, they stayed in the background and let Koreans run the government, they put anti-Japanese resistance leaders out front, and they supported radical reforms of the land system, labor conditions, and women's rights—all of which were pushed through by the end of 1946. Although very active behind the scenes, the Russians made it seem that Kim Il Sung was in charge— especially after they withdrew their troops from Korea in late 1948.

The Americans could not withdraw their troops so easily, because they were worried about the viability of the southern regime, its dictatorial tendencies, and its oft-stated bluster about marching north. But much more important was Korea's growing importance to American global policy, as part of a new, dual strategy of containing communism and reviving the Japanese industrial economy as a motor of the world economy, but one now shorn of its previous political and military clout. In early 1947 officials in Washington decided to revive Japanese heavy industries and end the purges of wartime leaders, a policy long known as the reverse course. They all thought the solution to the sluggish European and Japanese recovery lay in lifting restrictions on heavy industry and finding ways to combine Germany and Japan with their old providers of raw materials and markets. [The historian] William Borden wrote that Germany and Japan thus formed "the key to the balance of power," and shrewdly observed that whereas Germany was merely "the pivot" of the larger Marshall Plan program, "the Japanese recovery program formed the sole large-scale American effort in Asia."

Secretary of State George Marshall scribbled a note to Dean Acheson in late January 1947 that said, "Please have plan drafted of policy to organize a definite government of So. Korea and *connect up [sic]* its economy with that of Japan," a stunning mouthful. A few months later Secretary of the Army William Draper said that Japanese influence may again develop in Korea, "since Korea and Japan form a natural area for trade and commerce." Acting Secretary of State Dean Acheson remarked in secret congressional testimony in early 1947 that the United States had drawn the line in Korea, and sought funding for a major program to turn back communism there on the model of "Truman Doctrine" aid to Greece and Turkey. Acheson understood containment to be primarily a political and economic problem, of positioning self-supporting, viable regimes around the Soviet periphery; he thought the truncated Korean economy could still serve Japan's recovery, as part of what he called a "great crescent" linking Japan with Korea, Taiwan, Southeast Asia, and ultimately the oil of the Persian Gulf. Congress and the Pentagon balked at a major commitment to Korea, however, and so Acheson and his advisers took the problem to the United Nations, in order to reposition and contain Korea through collective security mechanisms. . . .

The United Nations, dominated by the United States at the time, agreed to form a committee (the United Nations Temporary Commission on Korea, or UNTCOK) to observe democratic elections in Korea. Its members included representatives of the Philippines and Nationalist China, who could be counted on to follow American directions, and representatives from Australia and Canada, who, although more recalcitrant once they got a taste of South Korean politics, came from allied governments subject to American influence and pressure. The North Koreans and Soviets opposed UNTCOK and refused to participate in such elections. . . .

The UNTCOK-observed elections in May 1948 presaged the final emergence of a separate southern government and thus raised the issue of Korea's permanent division. For that reason, and because of the right-wing cast of the Rhee government, virtually all the major politicians and political parties to the right of Rhee refused to participate—including Kim Kyu-sik, a rare Korean centrist, and Kim Ku, a man probably to the right of Rhee. The election went forward even though the outcome, according to several members of UNTCOK, was a foregone conclusion. The National Police and associated right-wing auxiliaries organized the voting, requiring that peasants have their food ration cards stamped at the polls (if they did not vote, they would lose their rations). On May 10, 1948, the ROK's first National Assembly was elected, composed mostly of supporters of Rhee or Kim Sŏng-su.

The ROK was inaugurated on August 15, 1948, with General MacArthur on the podium—it was only the second time he had left Japan since September 1945. Soon the Truman administration replaced the military government with the 500-man Korean Military Advisory Group (KMAG), established an aid mission (known as the Economic Cooperation Administration, or ECA), pushed big aid bills through Congress to get the Korean economy moving and to equip an army capable of defending South Korea, and arranged for KMAG to retain operational control of the Korean police and military as long as American combat troops remained. The State Department successfully delayed the final withdrawal of American troops until June 30, 1949, mainly because of worries about South Korean security. . . .

Americans knew they had a volatile charge in the new president, Syngman Rhee, and his relations with the embassy were often tempestuous. In small doses, Rhee came off as a handsome, warm, charming gentleman; he was a past master of flattery and disarming, endearing use of the democratic symbolism that stirs American hearts. It took a measure of experience with Rhee to disabuse Americans of their first impressions of him. Hodge knew him best, and by 1948 Hodge thought of Rhee about what "Vinegar Joe" Stilwell thought of Chiang Kai-shek. . . . Within a year of his arrival in Korea, if not earlier, he developed a profound disgust with and distrust for Rhee; it is the measure of his bonehard pragmatic anticommunism that he backed him anyway, having no alternative. . . .

North Korea was never simply a Soviet satellite in the 1940s, but evolved from a coalition regime based on widespread people's committees in 1945–46 to one under relative Soviet dominance in 1947–48, thence in 1949 to one with important links to China, which in turn enabled the DPRK to maneuver between the two communist giants. Kim Il Sung was not a handpicked Soviet puppet, but maneuvered politically first to establish his leadership, then to isolate and defeat the communists who had remained in Korea during the colonial period, then to ally with Soviet-aligned Koreans for a time, then to create a powerful army under his own leadership (in February 1948) that melded Koreans who had fought together in Manchuria and China proper with those who remained at home. . . .

[T]he North Koreans soon eliminated all nonleftist political opposition with a draconian thoroughness. A couple of united-front noncommunist parties were still allowed to exist, but they had no power. The intent was the same as that of the right wing in the South, to squash alternative centers of power. But the northerners did it much more thoroughly, because of their superior organization and the general weakness of the opposition. . . .

The Korean War did not begin on June 25, 1950, much special pleading and argument to the contrary. If it did not begin then, Kim Il Sung could not have "started" it then, either, but only at some earlier point. As we search backward for that point, we slowly grope toward the truth that civil wars do not start: they come. They originate in multiple causes, with blame enough to go around for everyone. . . .

Organized guerrilla warfare on the Korean mainland dates from November 1948. . . . This movement began the armed conflict on the peninsula, carrying the urban political turmoil and rural peasant protest of 1945–47 to the level of unconventional warfare. In early 1949 the CIA estimated that the total number of guerrillas in the South was somewhere between 3,500 and 6,000, not counting several thousand more on Cheju Island [off Korea's southeast coast]. Some were armed with rifles, mostly Japanese and American, but many just carried clubs and bamboo spears. Food and other supplies came from foraging, contributions in villages, or theft of rice stocks. KMAG advisers thought overall strategy was in North Korean hands, passed through the South Korean Labor Party headquarters in Haeju, just across the thirty-eighth parallel. One team of 60 guerrillas was known to have been dispatched from the North, and defectors estimated that another 1,000 or so were undergoing training for missions in the South. . . .

There was little evidence [, however,] of [large-scale] Soviet or North Korean support for the southern guerrillas. . . . No Soviet weapons had ever been authenticated in South Korea, except near the parallel; most guerrillas had Japanese and American arms. Another report found that the guerrillas "apparently receive little more than moral support from North Korea." . . .

The war that came in June 1950 followed on the guerrilla fighting and nine months of battles along the thirty-eighth parallel in 1949. Border conflict lasted from early May until late December, taking hundreds of lives and embroiling thousands of troops. . . .

[T]he important border battles began at Kaesŏng on May 4, 1949, in an engagement that the South started. It lasted about four days and took an official toll of 400 North Korean and 22 South Korean soldiers, as well as upwards of 100 civilian deaths in Kaesŏng, according to American and South Korean figures. The South committed six infantry companies and several battalions, and two of the companies defected to the North. . . .

On the last Sunday in June 1949, heavy fighting opened up in the dawn hours on the Ongjin peninsula; three days later the South sent about 150 "Horim" (forest tiger) guerrillas on a long foray across the parallel . . . but [they] were wiped out by July 5. The Sunday, June 26, battle bears some scrutiny because the UN Commission on Korea (UNCOK) sent a delegation to Ongjin after hearing reports of "heavy fighting." It arrived courtesy of an ROK naval vessel and was guided around by ROKA personnel. UNCOK members remained on the peninsula for a day or so and then returned on Monday evening to Seoul, from which they then filed a report to the UN blaming "northern invaders" for the trouble. It is probable that the North was to blame, but what is remarkable is UNCOK's failure to investigate and report upon provocations by the South as well. . . .

When we now look at both sides of the parallel with the help of some new (if scattered and selective) Soviet materials, we learn that Kim Il Sung's basic conception of a Korean War was quite similar to Rhee's and was influenced deeply by the August 1949 fighting: namely, attack the cul de sac of Ongjin, move eastward and grab Kaesŏng, and then see what happens. At a minimum, this would establish a much more secure defense of P'yŏngyang, which was quite vulnerable from Ongjin and Kaesŏng. At a maximum, it might open Seoul to his forces. That is, if the southern army collapses, move on to Seoul and occupy it in a few days. . . .

The critical issue in the Soviet documents is a military operation to seize the Ongjin peninsula. According to these documents, Kim Il Sung first broached the idea of an operation against Ongjin to the Soviet ambassador to P'yŏngyang, Terenti Shtykov, on August 12, 1949, right on the heels of the August 4 battle. Like southern leaders, Kim Il Sung wanted to bite off a chunk of exposed territory or grab a small city—all of Kaesŏng, for example, or Haeju just above the parallel on Ongjin, which southern commanders wanted to occupy in 1949–50. We also see how similar the Russians were in seeking to restrain hotheaded Korean leaders, including the chief of state. When Kim spoke about an invasion of Ongjin, two key Russian embassy officials "tried to switch the discussion to a general theme." The Soviet documents also demonstrate the hard-won, *learned* logic of this civil war by late 1949, namely, that both sides understood that their big-power guarantors would not help them if they launched an unprovoked general attack. . . . A telegram from Shtykov to Moscow in January 1950 has Kim Il Sung impatient that *the South* "is still not instigating an attack" (thus to justify his own), and the Russians in P'yŏngyang tell him once again that he cannot attack Ongjin without risking general civil war.

Thus the 1950 logic for both sides was to see who would be stupid enough to move first, with Kim itching to invade and hoping for a clear southern provocation, and hotheads in the South hoping to provoke an "unprovoked" assault, in order to get American help—for that was the only way the South could hope to win. Kim already had begun playing Moscow off against Beijing, too; for example, he let Shtykov overhear him say, at an apparently drunken luncheon on January 19, 1950, that if the Russians would not help him unify the country, "Mao Zedong is his friend and will always help Korea." In general these materials underline that the victory of the Chinese revolution had a great influence on North Korea and that the latter's China connection was a trump card Kim could play to create some breathing room for his regime between the two communist giants. . . .

In late February 1949, Kim Il Sung left P'yŏngyang for his only official, publicized visit to the Soviet Union before the Korean War. When he returned in March, Kim brought with him an economic and cultural agreement and, intelligence rumor had it, a secret military agreement. In 1948 the Soviets left quite a bit of surplus military equipment behind for the North Koreans (as did the Americans when their troops pulled out), but in 1949 the Soviets made the Koreans pay for everything, including a 220 million-ruble loan at 2 percent interest, which was about what mortgages returned to American banks in 1949—that is, there was profit in it. A January 1950 document shows Stalin appearing to be more interested than at any previous point in Kim Il Sung's invasion plans for South Korea, without a hint of what Stalin's own strategic thinking might be. Meanwhile, the North engaged in public bond drives to buy more and more equipment from Moscow. . . .

At this time South Korea was getting more than $100 million a year from the United States, most of it in the form of outright grants. (The entire southern national budget for 1951 was $120 million.) The ECA aid mission and the KMAG contingent were the biggest of their type in the world. The U.S. Information Service had, by its own testimony, "one of the most extensive country programs that we are operating anywhere," with nine centers in Korea, parlaying libraries, mobile units, a variety of publications, films, and Americanism before the Korean people. American officials ran Kimp'o International Airport, controlling the entry and exit of American citizens. Besides the official presence, private Americans often advised or directed private industry. . . .

[In May] the South . . . held its second National Assembly elections. The result was a disastrous loss for the Rhee regime, bringing into the assembly a strong collection of middle-of-the-roaders and moderate leftists, several of them associated with Yŏ Un-hyŏng's political lineage, and most of them hoping for unification with the North. The Korean ambassador to the United States, John Chang, informed American officials of a resulting crisis in his regime in early June, prompting John Foster Dulles (then an adviser to Truman) to decide to visit Korea on his way to see MacArthur in Tokyo.

During Dulles's visit to Seoul (which began on June 18), Rhee not only pushed for a direct American defense but advocated an attack on the North. Dulles invited along with him a favorite reporter, William Mathews, editor of the *Arizona Daily Star;* Mathews wrote just after the meeting between Rhee and Dulles, "He is militantly for the unification of Korea. Openly says it must be brought about soon . . . Rhee pleads justice of going into North country. Thinks it could succeed in a few days. . . . [I]f he can do it with our help, he will do it." And Mathews noted that Rhee said he would "do it," even if "it brought on a general war." All this is yet more proof of Rhee's provocative behavior, but it is not different from his threats to march North made many times before. Rhee hoped that a military alliance with the United States would come out of his meetings with Dulles, but got only some pro forma reassurances of U.S. support. In P'yŏngyang, Dulles's long-standing pro-Japan positions raised the gravest suspicions. But the Dulles visit merely brought out the vintage Rhee: there is no evidence that Dulles was in collusion with him, as the North Koreans have always claimed—while featuring a famous photo of Dulles peering into the North, across the thirty-eighth parallel.

It may be, however, that Chinese Nationalists on Taiwan were willing to collude with Rhee. Taiwan was a hotbed of intrigue in June 1950. From New Year's Day onward, American and British intelligence agencies predicted that the "last battle" of the Chinese civil war would come in June 1950. In January, British Foreign Office sources predicted an invasion of Taiwan "by the end of June." Interestingly enough, Guy Burgess, infamous spy for Moscow and director of the Far Eastern Office of Britain's Foreign Office in 1950, watched this situation closely. In April, Burgess said the invasion would come in May–June or September–October. Some Americans wanted to defend Chiang's regime, while others were hoping to say good riddance— President Truman among them, or so the newspapers said. MacArthur hoped that Dulles's visit would bring a change in U.S. policy in the Far East, especially in regard to Taiwan (which he thought should be defended). Chiang Kai-shek hoped that the high-level talks in Tokyo would herald an American commitment to his regime. In

Moscow, the Kremlin would monitor the journey to the East of the very personification of the "Wall Street master." . . .

In an interview the late Dean Rusk said that some elements of the Nationalist military were preparing to move against Chiang on the last weekend in June 1950, but then the Korean War intervened. In fact, Rusk was a key mover in this coup attempt and met with several important Chinese figures at the Plaza Hotel in New York on June 23, seeking to get them to form a government to replace the Kuomintang. Just after the war broke out, Kennan told a top-secret NSC meeting that "Chiang might be overthrown at any time." Guy Burgess read everything coming in from Taiwan in May and June 1950, it would appear, including unclassified press reports. The British chancery in Moscow had earlier noted that Soviet newspapers took an inordinate interest in any scraps of information on the Taiwan question. Burgess's judgment on June 24, 1950, was that "the Soviets seem to have made up their minds that the U.S.A. have a finally decided policy [not to defend Taiwan]. This *we [sic]* have never quite come to believe."

For over a decade I have been trying to get documents on this episode and various others through the Freedom of Information Act. . . . We still lack critical documents on the coup against Chiang, on American intelligence-gathering overflights of North Korean and Chinese territory that began before June 1950, and the signals intelligence that the United States collected on North Korea, China, and the USSR. We still do not know why the Pentagon approved and distributed in the week of June 19, 1950, a war plan known as SL-17, which assumed a KPA invasion, a quick retreat to and defense of a perimeter at Pusan, and then an amphibious landing at Inch'ŏn.

With all this bubbling activity, the last weekend in June 1950 nonetheless dawned on a torpid, somnolent, and very empty Washington. Harry Truman was back home in Independence. Acheson was at his Sandy Spring country farm, Rusk was in New York, Kennan had disappeared to a remote summer cottage without so much as a telephone, Paul Nitze was salmon fishing, the Joint Chiefs of Staff were occupied elsewhere, and even the United Nations representative, Warren Austin, was not at his post.

Most accounts of the outbreak of fighting in June 1950 leave the impression that a North Korean attack began all along the parallel at dawn, against an enemy taken completely unawares. But the war began in the same, remote locus of much of the 1949 fighting, the Ongjin peninsula, and some hours later spread along the parallel eastward, to Kaesŏng, Ch'unch'ŏn, and the east coast. As an official American history put it,

> On the Ongjin Peninsula, cut off from the rest of South Korea, soldiers of the 17th Regiment stood watch on the quiet summer night of 24–25 June 1950. For more than a week, there had been no serious incident along the 38th parallel. . . . Then at 0400, with devastating suddenness . . . [artillery and mortar fire] crashed into the ROK lines. . . .

The official American position has always been that the Soviets and the North Koreans stealthily prepared an attack that was completely unprovoked, one that constituted an all-out invasion. On June 26, Kim Il Sung, on the contrary, accused the South of making "a general attack" across the parallel. Rhee had long sought to touch off a fratricidal civil war, he said, having "incessantly provoked clashes" at the front line; in preparing a "northern expedition," he had "even gone so far as to collude with our sworn enemy, Japanese militarism." Some of these charges were true, but the charge of making a general attack across the parallel is false: the North attacked, and all along the parallel, by 6 A.M. at the latest. The book still cannot be closed on the possibility that the South opened the fighting on Ongjin, with an eye to seizing Haeju, but there is no evidence that it intended a general invasion of the North on June 25.

The evidence that scholars now have (there is much more to come from un-opened archives) is compatible both with an unprovoked North Korean invasion (one prefigured in North Korean and Soviet planning as we have seen) and with an interpretation linking the summer of 1949 to June 1950: that the North, like the South, wanted to seize the Ongjin peninsula and Kaesŏng and then see what hap-pened next, but waited until it had the majority of its crack soldiers back from China, and the support or acquiescence of Stalin and Mao. It positioned its troops to take advantage of the first southern provocation in June 1950 or merely to attack and claim a direct provocation. (As we saw, new Soviet documents show Kim anx-ious for the South to make a move.) Kim Il Sung bears the grave responsibility for raising the civil conflict in Korea to the level of general war, with intended and un-intended consequences that no one could have predicted. To say that this was the culmination of previous struggles and that Rhee wanted to do the same thing is true, but does not gainsay Kim's responsibility for the horrible consequences.

Scattered Soviet materials have shown that Soviet involvement in preparing and planning an invasion after Stalin gave his reluctant endorsement in January 1950 was higher than previous writers had thought, but we still know too little to determine the respective North Korean, Soviet, and Chinese roles in initiating the June fighting. Even when we have every document the Soviets ever produced, we will still need the South Korean archives, the North Korean archives, the Chinese archives on both sides of the Taiwan Strait, and the American intelligence, signals, and cryptography archives before we will be able to argue on truly solid ground the question we ought all try to forget, namely, "Who started the Korean civil war?"

Whatever happened on or before June 25, it was immediately clear that this war was a matter of "Koreans invading Korea"; it was not aggression across gener-ally accepted international lines. Nor was this the point at which the civil conflict began. The question pregnant with ideological dynamite "Who started the Korean War?" is the wrong question. It is not a civil war question; it only holds the viscera in its grasp for the generations immediately afflicted by fratricidal conflict. Ameri-cans do not care any more that the South fired first on Fort Sumter; they do still care about slavery and secession. No one wants to know who started the Vietnam War. Someday Koreans in North and South will reconcile as Americans eventually did, with the wisdom that civil wars have no single authors. It took Americans about a century to do so; it is therefore not surprising that Korean reconciliation is still pending after fifty years.

Word of fighting in Korea arrived in Washington on Saturday night, June 24. In succeeding days Dean Acheson dominated the decision making that soon committed American air and ground forces to the fight. Acheson, along with Dean Rusk, made the decision to take the Korean question to the UN, before he had notified President Truman of the fighting (Acheson told Truman there was no need to have him back in Washington until the next day); at the famous Blair House meetings on the evening of June 25, Acheson argued for increased military aid to the ROK, American air cover for the evacuation, and the interposition of the Seventh Fleet between Taiwan and the mainland; and on the afternoon of June 26 Acheson labored alone on the fundamental decisions committing American air and naval power to the Korean War, approved that evening at Blair House. Thus the decision to intervene was Acheson's decision, supported by the president but taken before United Nations, Pentagon, or congressional approval.

The military representatives at Blair House offered the only serious opposition to American intervention. General Omar Bradley supported Acheson's containment policy at the first Blair House meeting, remarking, "We must draw the line somewhere." But he questioned "the advisability" of introducing American ground troops in large numbers, as did Secretary of the Army Frank Pace and Defense Secretary Louis Johnson. At the second meeting on June 26, Generals Bradley and Lawton Collins again expressed the view that committing ground troops would strain American combat troop limits, unless a general mobilization was undertaken.

The United Nations merely ratified American decisions. In 1950 the General Assembly was a legislature more amenable to Truman's policies than the U.S. Congress was, so he got his war resolution out of the former. As an official Joint Chiefs of Staff study later put it, "Having resolved upon armed intervention for itself, the U.S. Government the next day sought the approval and the assistance of the United Nations." Truman called his intervention in Korea a "police action" so that he would not have to get a declaration of war; this inaugurated the pattern for the subsequent conflicts in Vietnam and the Persian Gulf, of war by executive decision rather than through proper constitutional procedure.

Korea: Stalin's Expansionist Gamble

VLADISLOV ZUBOK AND CONSTANTINE PLESHAKOV

During their fateful meeting in Moscow in April 1950, [Soviet marshal Joseph] Stalin agreed with Kim [Il Sung] that, though he had opposed a "reunification" of Korea before, now it could be accomplished "in light of the changed international situation." Earlier, Stalin had feared that the Americans would intervene. What, then, caused him to reassess the situation?

The new alliance with Communist China must have been the biggest cause for reassessment. From Stalin's viewpoint, this treaty was a watershed: the Yalta-Potsdam agreement on the spheres of influence had been broken. The world was now open for a redivision of spheres of influence on the basis of new, ideologically drawn alliances. As a Leninist, Stalin knew that this redivision meant global war. He said to Mao [Zedong]: "If we make a decision to revise treaties, we must go all the way." This phrase, in a nutshell, contained the origins of the Korean War. As the world headed for its third global confrontation, the Korean peninsula acquired new strategic meaning. Stalin worried that should the United States rearm Japan in the future, South Korea could become a dangerous beachhead for enemy forces. Therefore, it had to be captured before Japan could get back on its feet.

Several factors made the Soviet leader believe that the United States might not defend South Korea. On August 29, 1949, the Soviet Union broke the American monopoly on atomic weapons. At about the same time, the last American troops withdrew from South Korea—a development that was closely watched from Moscow. Early in 1950 some key figures in U.S. governmental circles, particularly Secretary of State Dean Acheson, made statements that excluded South Korea from the American "defense perimeter" in the Pacific arena and even hinted that the regime of Syngman Rhee was expendable. On January 28 intelligence sources reported to Stalin that the South Korean government had "little hope of American assistance" and expected that "President Truman would leave Formosa as he had left China." The report quoted Syngman Rhee as saying that "America has shown from the very beginning that it does not intend to fight for the interests of South Korea." Stalin must have felt that the Truman leadership was in disarray, incapable of mobilizing domestically. In this view, the United States failed to make use of its atomic diplomacy, could not prevent the collapse of the Guomindang, its primary ally in Asia, and now it was withdrawing from the Asian mainland altogether, returning to its traditional role of defending the islands.

Another consideration had never been spoken. Had Stalin said no to North Korea, it would have looked as if again, as during the civil war in China, he were putting the brakes on the revolutionary process in the Far East. And Mao Zedong was autonomous and unpredictable. The Chinese could start supporting Kim without the sanction of Moscow, in the same way [Josip] Tito's Yugoslavia had supported the Albanians and the Greek guerrillas, ignoring Moscow's objections. Taking issue with the PRC just months after the much-trumpeted conclusion of the Sino-Soviet treaty in Moscow would be unacceptable and ruinous. Equally so would be the recognition of Mao's revolutionary supremacy in Asia. That could lead the Chinese comrades to think too much about their international role, and to revive their nationalist ambitions. Stalin knew that Korea, before it was occupied by Japan in the late nineteenth century, had been a traditional sphere of Chinese imperial influence.

When, in early April 1950, Stalin supported Kim's invasion plan, he believed that he was preventing both of these developments, while maintaining the appearance of parity with Mao. He told Kim that North Korea could "get down to action" only after their plans were cleared "with Comrade Mao Zedong personally." The North Korean offensive could be postponed if the Chinese leadership objected. Kim then returned to Pyongyang and made another trip, this time to Beijing. On May 13 Mao sent [Foreign Minister] Zhou Enlai to the Soviet ambassador N. V. Roshchin, asking urgently for the "personal clarifications of Comrade Filippov [a pseudonym of Stalin in correspondence among Communist leaders] on this question." Stalin's answer, a masterpiece of political astuteness, was that "the question should ultimately be decided by the Chinese and Korean comrades together, and in the event the Chinese comrades should disagree, the decision on the question should be postponed until a new discussion can take place." Never secure about communications, Stalin refused to be specific about his talks with Kim in Moscow. "The Korean comrades," he wrote, "can relay to you the details of the conversation."

Stalin protected his credentials as the pontiff of world Communist revolution, responsive to the aspirations of the Korean people. At the same time he shared with Mao the burden of responsibility for the risky enterprise. Mao complained later that when he was in Moscow signing the Sino-Soviet treaty, Stalin "did not say a word about the conquest of South Korea." When Stalin invited Kim to Moscow, "nobody took pains to ask [Mao's] advice in advance."

Stalin's logic provides an explanation as to why he recalled the Soviet representative from the United Nations in the spring of 1950. Stalin boycotted the United Nations because it refused to recognize the PRC as a legitimate successor to the Chinese seat on the Security Council. In Stalin's view, the risk of the Soviets' absence was less than the strategic advantages of stressing the Sino-Soviet alliance and unmasking the United Nations as a "voting machine" obedient to America. It bears repeating that Stalin's reading of the United States' withdrawal from South Korea led him to believe that the Americans would not intervene in the Korean civil war.

Stalin and Mao were completely surprised when the Truman administration took advantage of the Soviet absence in the United Nations to obtain international approval for U.S. intervention in Korea. It was, ironically, the desire in the Kremlin to make a quick and victorious war, which the Western allies "so feared would happen in Europe," that "prompted the United States to respond with precisely the intervention in Korea that Moscow wanted above all to avoid." After the successful U.N. counterattack at Inchon in September 1950 and the resulting collapse of the North Korean army, American troops advanced to the Sino-Korean border.

Very soon the Kremlin leader concluded that the Inchon operation was a "strategic breakthrough by the U.N. forces fraught with fatal consequences." But he and his Soviet advisors had no control over the distant war. Kim's army got stuck south of the Korean peninsula, was cut off by enemy troops, and eventually disintegrated. Despite the gathering thunder in the Far East, Stalin took a train to his dacha at Sochi, on the Black Sea. As in June 1941, when developments went against his expectations, he took a time-out. What's more, the Generalissimo's physical condition necessitated a long rest. At Sochi, on October 1, after midnight, Stalin received an urgent cable from Pyongyang with a panicky letter from Kim Il Sung and the second-ranked man in the North Korean leadership, Pak Hong-yong. The letter informed him that the U.S.-led forces had taken Seoul and would probably capture North Korea, and that the North Korean army ceased to exist and thus would not be able to offer serious resistance. "The moment enemy troops cross the 38th parallel," Kim and Pak wrote, "we will desperately need immediate military assistance from the Soviet Union. If, for some reason, this help is not possible, then [would you] assist us in organizing international volunteer units in China and other people's democracies to provide military assistance in our struggle?"

This must have been a hard moment for Stalin: Kim turned out to be a bad military leader, but he was a loyal puppet who vowed to continue a protracted war to prevent, in the name of the strategic interests of the USSR and the whole Communist camp, the emergence of an American military springboard on the Korean peninsula. In the event of defeat, Stalin faced the ultimate responsibility for the deterioration of Sino-Soviet strategic positions and, as the Communist pontiff, the blame for losing the Korean "revolutionary" regime. His whole crafty strategy in the Far East had backfired. Nevertheless, Stalin must have been expecting this moment, for he had made his tactical decision in advance. It took him only a few minutes to dictate a telegram to Mao Zedong and Zhou Enlai, advising the Chinese to "move immediately at least five or six divisions to the 38th parallel" to shield Kim's regime from the advancing U.N. troops and enable him to mobilize a new army. Stalin mentioned almost elegiacally that he was "far from Moscow and somewhat cut off from the events in Korea." He wrote that the Chinese troops "could pose as volunteers [but], of course, with the Chinese command at the helm." He left it to the discretion of the leadership in Beijing to tell "the Korean comrades" about their decision on this question. In a matter of minutes, Stalin passed the buck to the Chinese, making them responsible for Kim's regime and the war.

Stalin's real "master plan" at that time was not a counterattack in Europe, as many in the West had thought, but postponement of a head-on collision with the West. He had taken precautions: his cables to Kim and Mao were all in military intelligence codes (considered to be "safe"), and he signed them with the Chinese alias Pheng Xi. He also had forbidden Soviet advisors to travel south of the 38th parallel, and Soviet pilots, flying over Korea, to speak Russian! He now refused to send Soviet troops back to North Korea, because that would lead to direct war with the Americans. Let the brave Chinese fight, with Soviet arms and Soviet air cover.

Some Chinese politicians, particularly the Communist boss of Manchuria, Gao Gang, had spoken in favor of Chinese intervention, to prevent the return of the United States (and, potentially, a remilitarized Japan) to the Asian mainland. There were, however, serious reservations in Beijing about starting another war barely a year after the end of the civil war. Mao's position was ambiguous, to say the least. He argued for intervention before his colleagues at home. At the same time, on October 2, he wrote back to Stalin that the PRC could not enter the war because several Chinese divisions would not be enough to stop the Americans. Always careful to appear Stalin's loyal ally, Mao also expressed his fear that the United States might declare war on China, which would mean a Soviet-American war as well. Feeling the urgency of the moment, Stalin stopped mincing words and, on October 5, dispatched to Mao the most remarkable cable in their whole correspondence, displaying the full force of his realpolitik logic.

The United States, Stalin wrote, "was not prepared at the present time for a big war," and Japan was still incapable of rendering any military assistance to the Americans. Therefore, if the United States faced the threat of such a war, they would "have to give in to China, backed by its Soviet ally, in [the settlement] of the Korean question." They would also be forced to leave Taiwan and renounce "a separate peace with Japanese reactionaries." Stalin warned that "without serious struggle and a new impressive display of its strength, China would not obtain all these concessions" from the Americans.

Stalin finished his seduction of the Chinese comrades with a stunning passage: "Of course I had to reckon with the fact that, despite its unpreparedness, the United States still may pull itself into a big war, [acting] out of prestige; consequently, China would be dragged into the war, and the USSR, which is bound to China by the pact of mutual assistance, would be dragged into the war as well. Should we fear this? In my opinion, we should not, since together we will be stronger than the United States and Great Britain. Other European capitalist states do not possess any serious military power, save Germany, which cannot provide assistance to the United States now. If war is inevitable, let it happen now, and not in a few years, when Japanese militarism will be restored as a U.S. ally, and when the United States and Japan will have a beach-head on the continent ready, in the form of Syngman Rhee's Korea."

Arguably, deep down Stalin hoped for just the opposite: that the Sino-Soviet treaty would be a sufficient deterrent and that the United States would hesitate to declare war on the PRC, knowing it would automatically bring in the Soviet Union. But he made a point of demonstrating to Mao that the Kremlin "father" of the Communist world had a sober vision of World War III and was not afraid of it. In this way, also, Stalin denied Mao his strongest argument against China's intervention.

Mao seemed to have surrendered to Stalin's logic: he agreed to send nine divisions to fight in Korea. Zhou Enlai flew by Soviet military plane to Sochi, allegedly to discuss with Stalin the terms under which the Soviets would supply armaments, ammunition, and particularly air cover for the Chinese "volunteers" in North Korea. The Stalin-Zhou meeting took place on October 9–10, and here again, as in the case of the Sino-Soviet treaty, the existing Chinese versions differ significantly from the newly available Soviet documents. According to Chinese sources, including Mao himself, at some point Stalin changed his mind: he would *not* supply military equipment and provide air cover. The Chinese leadership in Beijing was stunned by this act of perfidy but, *despite* it, decided to enter the war. According to Soviet records, however, Zhou told Stalin that the Politburo of the Chinese Communist party's Central Committee had decided not to send troops to Korea, restating the same old arguments. It is not clear what happened in Beijing: was Mao really facing strong opposition, or was Zhou deliberately playing the role of "bad messenger" assigned to him by Mao? One analyst of the Chinese evidence concludes that Mao and Zhou deliberately played "games" with Stalin. They were determined to send volunteers to Korea, but at the same time they were seeking the best possible deal from him. Yet another dramatic scenario is likely: the majority of Chinese leaders at that time strongly opposed the war and still hoped that Stalin was bluffing and would come to Kim's rescue once U.S. troops moved to the Soviet borders. Stalin, at least, interpreted the Chinese "game" in this light.

Stalin decided to call the Chinese bluff. The Soviet Union, he told Zhou, was not ready to fight a large-scale war in the Far East so soon after the Second World War. Besides, the Soviet–North Korean border was too narrow to allow massive troop transfers. If the U.S. actions were to jeopardize the fate of world socialism, however, the Soviet Union would be ready to take up the American challenge. Stalin began to lose his temper. The Chinese comrades should know, he said, that should they refuse to intervene, "socialism in Korea would collapse within a very short period of time." What Stalin in fact did was directly challenge the PRC's self-legitimacy from the high ground of the Soviet revolutionary-imperial paradigm. The USSR, he implied, should save itself for an ultimate battle with the forces of imperialism, whereas it is the duty of the PRC, as the major Soviet ally in Asia and the hegemon of the Asian revolutionary process, to fend off a regional imperialist offensive. In the light of the PRC's failure to perform its historic role, all Stalin could suggest was that the Soviet Union and China should work out specific plans to help the Korean comrades and their forces withdraw from North Korea and move to shelters in Manchuria and the Soviet Far East. When the stunned Zhou asked Stalin if China could count on Soviet air cover should it decide to fight in Korea, Stalin answered yes, and assured him that the Soviet Union would take care of all supplies of arms and equipment as soon as the PRC defined its actual needs. Despite all this, the Sino-Soviet talks ended without the establishment of any joint policy.

This episode showed Stalin displaying, under duress, the best of his realpolitik side. He was willing to swallow a serious regional defeat and even the loss of a "Socialist" regime on the Soviet borders rather than risk a military clash with U.N. forces. He saw to it that this policy would be shared by all his lieutenants by passing several Politiburo decisions. In [Nikita] Khrushchev's [future premier of the Soviet Union] presence he once said, "So what? If Kim Il Sung fails, we are not going to intervene with our troops. Let the Americans be our neighbors in the Far East." On October 12, Stalin surprised Kim, who expected Soviet military assistance, with a letter advising evacuation of the rest of Kim's forces to the Soviet and Chinese sanctuaries. Interestingly, Stalin referred to the "recommendations" of the "conference of the Chinese [and] Soviet leading comrades" (that is, to his talks with Zhou in Sochi). He didn't forget to blame Mao for what was solely his decision! At that moment, argues one Russian historian, the Korean War could have ended in a victory for the West.

The Chinese opposition to war crumbled under the weight of Stalin's stand, however. Within hours, on October 13, Mao informed the Kremlin leader that the CCP Politburo had decided to fight. Stalin, barely concealing his delight, sent another message to Kim, ordering him "to postpone temporarily" the evacuation, in expectation of "detailed reports from Mao Zedong about this matter." The next day Stalin announced to Kim that "after hesitation and a series of provisional decisions, the Chinese comrades at last made a final decision to render assistance to Korea with troops." He had quite a nerve to wish the Korean leader "luck." Less than a week later, on October 19, 1950, Chinese troops crossed the Yalu River. One week later they fought their first battle with U.S. troops. This seemed to many Western observers to be the prelude to a third world war.

Soviet documents dispel the myth that Stalin had allegedly been moved to the point of tears by how "good the Chinese comrades were." They reveal not a trace of revolutionary romanticism in the Soviet leader and show that, as in 1941–1945, he was even ready to act as a hard-nosed realist. The Chinese intervention, however, bore out Stalin's revolutionarism in a different way. Cynical as the Stalin-Mao bargaining may look today, its outcome was a great victory from the viewpoint of the revolutionary-imperial paradigm embraced by Stalin. The war helped wash away the ambiguity in Stalin-Mao relations: the Soviet leader accepted Mao without reservations, as long as the latter fought American power and depended on Soviet aid.

But the price of that new friendship and the continuation of the Korean War was high and tragic; it resulted in a huge setback for the USSR. The U.S. leadership adopted the view that the Sino-Soviet bloc was bent on global conquest. In turn, it was determined to destroy the aggressor and, if necessary, to embark on a large-scale campaign of mobilization and armament. The military budget of the United States quadrupled, and the arms race on the Western side did not slow down until the late 1980s.

The Korean War allowed the United States to exclude the Soviet Union from a peace settlement with Japan. Incensed by the conditions insisted upon by the Americans and careful to foil Western attempts to ruin the Sino-Soviet alliance, Stalin boycotted a final peace treaty with Japan. Immediately, the United States signed a treaty of defense and alliance with Japan—Stalin's prophecy fulfilled. With Stalin's refusal to sign the Japanese peace treaty in San Francisco, Soviet territorial acquisitions did not acquire international recognition de jure. Therefore, the ground remained for controversy over four tiny islands in the Kuriles—Shikotan, Kunashiri, Iturup, and Habomai, which to this day poison relations between Moscow and Tokyo.

Another of Stalin's worst nightmares came true. The hostilities in the Far East gave a decisive impulse to the rearmament of West Germany, with the help of some of Hitler's former generals—an idea unthinkable not long before. With the Bundeswehr, a new West German army, NATO was on the way to becoming a full-fledged military force in Europe. And the U.S. government, through the CIA and other means, intensified covert operations to assist the anti-Communist underground in Eastern Europe, the Baltic states, and Ukraine. In a word, the Americans began to wage the Cold War in earnest, with all available means short of outright attack on the USSR.

Did Stalin acknowledge these setbacks? He never gave any indication that he did. Several times after June 1951, when the frontline in Korea stabilized along the 38th parallel, the North Koreans, suffering mounting casualties from U.S. air strikes, begged Stalin for peace. Kim Il Sung told Stalin that the protracted war allowed "the enemy, who suffers almost no casualties, to cause continuous and terrible damage" to North Korea. Yet each time Stalin advised Kim to hold on, because the enemy, according to him, would capitulate first and soon. In fact, Stalin must have believed that the war of attrition would best serve the USSR's interests: it would tie down the United States in the Far East, and it would make both North Korea and the PRC even more dependent on Soviet economic and military power, which would guarantee the Kremlin a monolithic bloc and undisputed hegemony in the Communist universe. . . .

The Korean War proved to be the same for Stalin as the Crimean War had been for Czar Nicholas I a century earlier. The reign of Nicholas had started when Russia was an unquestionable great power, respected and envied in all European capitals. It ended in a shameful defeat for the czar's empire on its own territory, the Crimea, from the technologically superior coalition of Great Britain, France, and Turkey. Nicholas, however, refused to recognize defeat: only after the sudden death of the czar (suicide was suspected) did his successor end the war. Stalin had a similar decline from the Great Victory of 1945 to the deadlock on the Korean peninsula, virtually at the Soviets' doorstep.

The Lost Chance for Peace: Washington Rejected Chinese Communist Overtures

THOMAS J. CHRISTENSEN

In light of the documentary evidence from China and the United States, we can detect a causal link between two key American China policies of 1949–50—nonrecognition of Beijing and the blocking of the Taiwan Straits—and the disastrous escalation of the Korean War that occurred when China crossed the Yalu in

Thomas J. Christensen, *Useful Adversaries: Grand Strategy, Domestic Mobilization, and Sino-American Conflict, 1947–1958.* Copyright © 1996 by Princeton University Press. Reprinted by permission of Princeton University Press.

the fall of 1950. To demonstrate this link, below I offer a new version of the "lost chance" in China thesis, arguing that while friendship between China and the United States was precluded by their ideological differences, peace between the two nations was not. A plausible argument can be made that Sino-American combat in Korea could have been avoided if the United States had recognized Beijing and had honored Truman's January pledge to stay out of the Chinese Civil War. . . .

The original lost-chance debate too often focused on Washington's ability to replace the Soviets as a friend and benefactor. In the early 1980s scholars began to address the lost-chance question more subtly, asking whether Sino-American relations could not have been somewhat better, even if they could not have been friendly. But despite these contributions, there has not been enough exploration of just how American policies, if different, might have reduced conflict between the two sides. This is not coincidental. The lack of documentary evidence on the Chinese side rendered speculation highly problematic. Using such evidence—including Mao's military and diplomatic manuscripts—below I analyze Mao's attitudes toward the United States in order to determine whether there was a lost chance for peace between the United States and China in 1949–50. I conclude that, while Mao viewed the United States as unquestionably hostile to the CCP in this period, he believed that American hostility might manifest itself in more or less threatening ways. American recognition of Beijing and abandonment of Chiang Kai-shek would not have provided a panacea for the many ills facing Sino-American relations. Still, those policies might have prevented the escalation of the Korean War in fall 1950.

In January 1949 Mao advised the Central Committee of its responsibilities in bringing the civil war to a successful conclusion. Mao's assessment of the American threat was a central element in his presentation. His view of America's future policies toward China was complex. On the level of intentionality, Mao saw the United States as unalterably hostile to his revolution. He saw no chance for friendship with Washington. On the other hand, he viewed the United States as a somewhat rational actor that eventually would recognize the futility of armed intervention in China. He went so far as to speculate that the United States might end direct military assistance to the KMT [Chiang's non-Communist Kuomintang] and then recognize the CCP regime. Still, Mao believed that even if the United States withdrew entirely from the civil war and recognized the Communists, Washington would still support covertly all available domestic opponents to his regime.

Despite intermittent notes of caution, Mao's talk was generally quite optimistic. He believed that American leaders, relative newcomers to "imperialism," were becoming wiser, recognizing the futility of significant assistance to Chiang Kai-shek. Therefore, in the future, Mao believed the United States would likely limit its activities to subversion. Mao said:

> In our strategic planning, we have always calculated in the possibility that the United States would directly send troops, occupying several coastal cities and engaging in warfare with us. We still must not dismiss this type of possibility. . . . *But, as the Chinese people's revolutionary strength increases and becomes more resolute, the possibility that the United States will carry out a direct military intervention also decreases, and moreover, in the same vein, the American involvement in financial and military assistance to the KMT may also decrease.* In the past year, especially in the past three months, the multiple changes in and unsteadiness of the American government's attitudes prove this point. *Among the Chinese people and in the Party there still exists*

a mistaken viewpoint which overestimates the power of American imperialism. It is essential [that we] continue to uncover and overcome [this tendency]. . . .

The acquiescence of the U.S. Pacific Command to Chinese victories in Shanghai and Tianjin in spring 1949 demonstrated that Mao's first and most important prediction about the United States was basically correct: the United States was not going to involve itself directly in defending the remaining KMT forces on the mainland. The historical importance of Mao's predictions should not be underestimated. In April 1949 Mao decided to cross the Yangzi despite the warnings of Stalin's emissary, Anastas Mikoyan, that such an action should not be taken hastily lest the United States enter the Chinese Civil War. It was the crossing of the Yangzi that drove Chiang's government to Taiwan and ended the KMT's reign on the mainland.

After seizing Nanjing, Mao was impressed that the American embassy did not flee to Canton along with the KMT government. Mao stated on April 28:

> We should educate our troops to protect British and American residents . . . as well as foreign ambassadors, ministers, consuls, and other diplomats, especially those from the United States and Britain. Now the American side is asking a third party to contact us for the purpose of establishing diplomatic relations. We think that, if the United States and Britain can cut off their relations with the KMT, we can consider the question of establishing diplomatic relations with them. . . . The old U.S. policy of assisting the KMT and opposing the CCP is bankrupt. It seems that its policy is turning to one of establishing diplomatic relations with us.

Mao was actively considering the establishment of relations with the United States and, on April 30, he stated that the CCP would establish diplomatic relations with any country that broke with the KMT, removed its forces from China, and treated China "fairly."

Various Communist Party actions were in accord with these statements. . . . [I]n April, [a leading Chinese Communist official] Yao Yilin sought trade ties through [U.S. General Consul O. Edmund] Clubb's offices in Shanghai. In May and June, [Zhou Enlai's assistant] Huang Hua responded positively to the overture from Ambassador [John Leighton] Stuart's office. These policies were not a sign of CCP factionalism, as was previously believed by many foreign analysts. It is clear that Mao directly controlled Huang's mission to the American embassy in Nanjing. In fact, a May 10 telegram from Mao to the Nanjing Municipal Bureau gives specific instructions to Huang Hua about what issues were to be raised with Stuart regarding the establishing of diplomatic relations with a CCP government. Huang was ordered to be firm and to emphasize that American support for the KMT, not the lack of American aid to CCP-held areas, was the main stumbling block to improved relations. . . .

The events of April through July convinced the CCP leadership that, while Mao may have been right that the United States would not enter the Chinese Civil war directly, in the near term American distancing from the KMT was likely to be extremely limited. Despite the Huang mission and the CCP's July dispatch of Chen Mingshu, the United States rejected rapprochement with the CCP. Stuart did more than refuse to meet with Mao in Beijing, he also failed to respond satisfactorily to Huang Hua's main criticism of American behavior: that the United States was still actively involved in the civil war on the side of the KMT. Despite Stuart's assurances that American aid to Chiang was small and decreasing, Chinese Communist leaders believed that American involvement with Chiang Kai-shek was even greater than it actually was. For example, a leading Chinese Communist, Bo Yibo, reports that in July 1949 Chinese leaders believed (falsely) that the American and British navies were participating directly in the KMT naval blockade of China's southern and eastern ports. . . . .

Some authors argue that Mao did not seek recognition from the United States in 1949 and that he did not plan to do so for years to come. This is correct if, by this, we mean that Mao was not going to revise the goals of his revolution in order to persuade the Americans to recognize the PRC. But the CCP was willing to accept, and in fact formally requested, recognition from the Western powers. The CCP's actions, party documents, and leaders' memoirs all suggest that Mao would have accepted recognition from all countries, including the United States, albeit with suspicion and on China's terms.

Mao's metaphor for China's policy toward foreign powers in 1949–50 was to "sweep China clean before inviting guests." The CCP was to eliminate all imperialist power in China before allowing real foreign influence to return to the mainland. But despite the image of foreigners flying out of China like swept dust and a virulent anti-American propaganda campaign, Mao's strategy did not preclude direct relations with Western powers. . . . [W]hile Mao was preparing to announce the founding of the People's Republic, the CCP sent an emissary to the American consul general, O. Edmund Clubb, in order to explain again the CCP's attitude toward establishing relations with outside countries. On October 1, 1949, Clubb was given the same request for the establishment of relations as other foreign representatives in China.

The Chinese conditions for accepting recognition and beginning a dialogue that would lead to diplomatic relations were not extremely arduous. In a December 1949 telegram regarding the establishment of relations with Burma, Mao laid out the two conditions for establishing relations with nonsocialist countries. The recognizing country must be willing to break diplomatic relations with the KMT and to enter a negotiation process to hammer out the terms of diplomatic exchanges. In his memoirs, Bo Yibo states that in late 1949 Mao had consistent criteria for the establishment of relations with any country: the recognition of the sole legitimacy of the PRC and respect for Chinese sovereignty. Bo emphasizes that "it is self-evident that Western countries were included under this principle." Huang Hua made similar statements about CCP preconditions in midyear. . . .

For practical purposes, a nation could establish high-level contacts merely by recognizing the CCP as the sole legitimate government, halting assistance to Chiang, and sending a team of representatives to negotiate the formalizing of relations. The British did this successfully in January. Although Britain fell far short of meeting Mao's terms for the exchange of ambassadors, the British still were able to dispatch a team of representatives to Beijing and to undertake long-term negotiations over the details of "unequal treaties" and other matters. These types of contacts, while not ideal, still provide direct channels of communication, which are critical in times of crisis.

But even if such contacts had been possible between Washington and Beijing, there is no reason to believe that friendship and significant economic relations would have flowed from them. Given what we now know about his deep-seated caution about the United States, Mao would have been extremely suspicious of the motives behind American recognition. But these concerns apparently would not have led him to denounce American attempts to establish more normal relations. While in Moscow, rather than worrying about the possible negative effects of recognition by nonsocialist countries, Mao seemingly welcomed the possibility, decreeing that, when nonsocialist countries agree to recognize China, the Chinese media should announce the news promptly. Three days later, Mao discussed plans for increased trade with the West, including the United States, although in no sense did he believe that the West would or should supplant the Soviet Union as China's main economic partner. Even after Mao made his decision to enter the Korean War and troops had begun crossing the Yalu, Mao still held some outside hope that a major blow to UN forces (the killing of tens of thousands of troops) might compel the Americans to open diplomatic talks with the PRC. In 1949–50, Mao saw no contradiction between diplomatic contacts and severe forms of mutual hostility. . . .

Even though American recognition of China in the period December 1949– January 1950 would not have made Mao view the United States as a friendly power, it may have indirectly damaged Sino-Soviet relations. Stalin almost certainly would have objected vigorously to Chinese contacts with Washington. Fearing Chinese Titoism, the Soviets put a great deal of pressure on Mao to shun any overtures from the United States. They pointed to American support for the KMT as a reason to reject any such overtures. Interestingly, [U.S. Secretary of State Dean] Acheson was well aware of this problem. On January 23, American intelligence officers informed Acheson of the potentially divisive effects of American recognition on Sino-Soviet relations, concluding that the "Soviets could not brook American recognition."

Stalin's protestations and pressure would have appeared to Mao as increased Soviet interference in China's sovereign affairs, particularly if the United States had already broken relations with the KMT. Mao, however, clearly did want to prove to Stalin that he was no Tito. Although the Chinese evidence suggests otherwise, it is possible that Mao would have denounced American attempts at recognition in order to curry favor with Stalin. But even in the event that Mao decided to buckle to Soviet pressure and react belligerently to such an American overture, this episode would have exacerbated existing tensions between the two sides, tensions that an internal CCP history chalks up to Stalin's "great power chauvinism." . . .

The only chance of avoiding significant Sino-American conflict in Korea was missed in late September and early October [1950], before American troops crossed the 38th parallel [into North Korea]. This failure was at least partially due to the poor communication channels available to leaders in Beijing and Washington. . . .

The standard interpretations of the Chinese failure to deter the United States from crossing the 38th parallel in October are straightforward and stand up well to the documentary evidence. The tragedy was based both in American misperceptions about how Chinese weakness would affect Beijing's calculations and in poor communication channels between the two capitals. In calling for the unconditional surrender of North Korean troops (on October 1) and crossing the 38th parallel (on October 7), the Americans believed that China's vulnerability would probably preclude Chinese entrance into the war. However, as Allen Whiting argued, it was China's vulnerability that precipitated its October 19 crossing of the Yalu. Although the Chinese attempted to deter the American crossing, the lack of direct communications meant that their warnings were both too weak and too late to reverse the American decisions. In September and October the United States was emboldened in Korea both by MacArthur's stunning success at Inchon [where he staged a successful amphibious landing of UN troops on the South Korean coast] and by China's military, economic and political weakness. In late September, Marshal Nie Rongzhen and Premier Zhou Enlai voiced deterrent warnings. These statements were accompanied by movements of Chinese troops in and around Manchuria. On the night of October 2, Zhou called Indian ambassador K. M. Panikkar to a midnight meeting. Zhou gave him a message to pass to Washington: if U.S. forces crossed the 38th parallel, China would enter the war. Considering these warnings to be bluffs, Americans crossed the parallel on October 7.

The Chinese faced several serious problems in their effort to deter the Americans. First, the United States had solid realpolitik incentives to cross the parallel. Second, without direct diplomatic relations it was difficult for Beijing to communicate a message strong and authoritative enough to deter implementation of the American strategy. Third, the clearest Chinese warning came only after the American decision to cross the 38th parallel had been made. . . .

Given the importance of . . . American goals in Korea, only a strong and clear warning from China might have reversed Truman's course. The Zhou-Panikkar communique did not meet this criterion. Washington lacked direct contacts in Beijing and had received unreliable messages from mainland sources before, so it questioned Zhou's authority. In addition, Washington questioned the credibility of the messenger, Panikkar, viewing him as a gullible Communist sympathizer. The October 3 communique was the most direct Chinese deterrent threat, but it came only after Truman had authorized MacArthur's crossing of the parallel (September 27) and the UN had called for Pyongyang's capitulation (October 1). . . .

There is evidence that suggests some possibility for successful deterrence if Chinese threats had been better communicated. Before Inchon, civilian and military leaders wanted to avoid actions in Korea that might cause a Chinese or Soviet entry and sap America's strategic reserves in an area of little geostrategic value. On September 8 the NSC viewed favorably the crossing of the 38th parallel, "provided MacArthur's plans could be carried out without risk of a major war with the Chinese Communists or the Soviet Union." Even after Inchon, on September 27 Truman authorized MacArthur to proceed north only if he was certain that there would be no significant Soviet or Chinese intervention in Korea. The qualifications in Truman's September 27 orders demonstrate that his willingness to go north was not unconditional. Moreover, in his memoirs Truman himself recalled that the lack of direct and reliable communication channels caused him to discount [indirect warnings issued by Beijing]. . . .

It is, however, impossible to determine with certainty whether better communications would have prevented the disaster in North Korea. Given the American incentives to end the Korean problem once and for all, Truman might very well have ignored even the most direct Chinese warnings. By deciding to discount the weak and indirect October . . . warnings from Beijing, Washington squandered the last chance for peace. Once Americans crossed the 38th parallel on October 7, no coercive or reassuring acts by Truman or MacArthur could have prevented a wider war.

The history of Mao's Korean War decision making demonstrates the vital importance of the two American policy problems, . . . Truman's inability to abandon Chiang Kai-shek and his related failure to establish working relations with Beijing. For both political and strategic reasons, Truman's June [1950] decision to protect Chiang [by positioning the U.S. Seventh fleet in the Taiwan Strait] intensified Mao's sense that any long-term American presence in North Korea would threaten his new nation's security. The possibility of a future two-front war against the United States not only led Mao to fight but also counseled him to adopt an extremely offensive strategy designed to drive the Americans completely off the Korean peninsula. Finally, the lack of direct government-to-government channels complicated China's last genuine attempt to deter an expansion of the Korean conflict. . . . Truman's assistance to Chiang and his lack of contacts in Beijing were rooted in the American domestic politics of Cold War mobilization. These two policies played a more important role in Korean War escalation than the details of American military operations or the nuances of Truman's coercive threats and assurance in fall and winter 1950.

🌐 *F U R T H E R   R E A D I N G*

Barton J. Bernstein, "The Truman Administration and the Korean War," in Michael Lacey, ed., *The Truman Presidency* (1989), 410–444

Clay Blair, *The Forgotten War* (1988)

Robert M. Blum, *Drawing the Line* (1982)

William S. Borden, *The Pacific Alliance* (1984) (on the U.S. and Japan)

Dorothy Borg and Waldo Heinrichs, eds., *Uncertain Years: Chinese-American Relations, 1947–1950* (1980)

William B. Breuer, *Shadow Warriors: The Covert War in Korea* (1996)

Russell Buhite, *Soviet-American Relations in Asia, 1945–1954* (1982)

Gordon H. Chang, *Friends and Enemies* (1990)

Jongsuk Chay, *Unequal Partners* (2002) (on the U.S. and South Korea)

Jian Chen, *China's Road to the Korean War* (1994)

———, *Mao's China and the Cold War* (2001)

Warren I. Cohen, *America's Response to China* (2000)

Bruce Cumings, *The Origins of the Korean War,* 2 vols. (1981–1990)

Roger Dingman, "Atomic Diplomacy During the Korean War," *International Security,* 13 (1988–1989), 50–91

Charles Dobbs, *The Unwanted Symbol* (1981)

John W. Dower, *Embracing Defeat* (2000) (on Japan)

Rosemary J. Foot, *A Substitute for Victory* (1990)

Marc S. Gallicchio, *The Cold War Begins in Asia* (1988)

Sergei N. Goncharov et al., *Uncertain Partners: Stalin, Mao, and the Korean War* (1993)

Harry Harding and Yuan Ming, eds., *Sino-American Relations* (1989)

Gary R. Hess, *Presidential Decisions for War* (2001)

———, *The United States's Emergence as a Southeast Asian Power* (1989)

Michael H. Hunt, *The Genesis of Chinese Communist Foreign Policy* (1996)

Akira Iriye, *The Cold War in Asia* (1974)

———, and Warren Cohen, eds., *American, Chinese, and Japanese Perspectives on Wartime Asia 1931–1949* (1990)

D. Clayton James, *Refighting the Last War* (1992)

Richard Jensen and Jon Davidan, *Trans-Pacific Relations* (2003)

Christopher T. Jesperson, *American Images of China* (1996)

Burton I. Kaufman, *The Korean War* (1986)

Yuen Foong Khong, *Analogies at War* (1992)

Nam G. Kim, *From Enemies to Allies* (1997) (on Japan)

Yukiko Koshiro, *Trans-Pacific Racism* (1999) (on the U.S. and Japan)

Peter Lowe, *The Korean War* (2000)

Callum A. MacDonald, *Korea* (1987)

Ronald L. McGlothlen, *Controlling the Waves: Dean Acheson and U.S. Foreign Policy in Asia* (1993)

Robert J. McMahon, *The Limits of Empire* (1999) (on Southeast Asia)

James I. Matray, *The Reluctant Crusade* (1985)

David Mayers, *Cracking the Monolith: U.S. Policy Against the Sino-Soviet Alliance* (1986)

John Merrill, *Korea: The Peninsular Origins of the War* (1989)

Alan R. Millet, "The Korean War: A 50-Year Critical Historiography," *The Journal of Strategic Studies* 24: 1 (March 2001), 184–224

Katherine H. S. Moon, *Sex Among Allies* (1997) (on the U.S. and Korea)

Brian Murray, "Stalin, the Cold War, and the Division of China," Working Paper 12 (June 1995), Cold War International History Project, Woodrow Wilson International Center for Scholars

Bonnie B. C. Oh, ed., *Korea Under the American Military Government* (2002)

Mark A. Ryan, *Chinese Attitudes Toward Nuclear Weapons: China and the United States During the Korean War* (1989)

Michael Schaller, *The American Occupation of Japan* (1985)

———, *Douglas MacArthur* (1989)

———, *The United States and China in the Twentieth Century* (1990)

Yu-Ming Shaw, *John Leighton Stuart* (1992)

Michael Sheng, *Battling Western Imperialism: Mao, Stalin, and the United States* (1998)

Russell Spurr, *Enter the Dragon: China's Involvement in the Korean War* (1988)

William Steuck Jr., *The Korean War* (1995)

———, *Rethinking the Korean War* (2000)

"Symposium: Rethinking the Lost Chance in China," *Diplomatic History,* 21 (1997), 71–115

Richard Thorton, *Odd Man Out: Truman, Stalin, Mao, and the Origins of the Korean War* (2000)

John Tolland, *In Mortal Combat* (1991)

Rudy Tomedi, *No Bugle, No Drums* (1993)

Nancy B. Tucker, "Continuing Controversies in the Literature of US-Chinese Relations Since 1945," in Warren I. Cohen, ed., *Pacific Passages* (1996)

———, *Patterns in the Dust* (1983) (on the U.S. and China)

———, *Taiwan, Hong Kong, and the United States* (1994)

Arthur N. Waldron, *The Chinese Civil Wars, 1911–1949* (1995)

Kathryn Weathersby, "To Attack, or Not to Attack? Stalin, Kim Il Sung, and the Prelude to War," *Cold War International History Bulletin,* 5 (1995), 1–9

Arne O. Westad, *Brothers in Arms* (1998) (on the Sino-Soviet Alliance)

Richard Whelan, *Drawing the Line* (1990)

Shu Guang Zhang, *Economic Cold War: America's Economic Embargo Against China and the Sino-Soviet Alliance, 1949–1963* (2001)

———, *Mao's Military Romanticism* (1995)

CHAPTER
8

Dwight D. Eisenhower
and Nuclear Arms

In 1952 Americans elected Dwight D. Eisenhower president. The popular World War II hero, known to many simply as Ike, named John Foster Dulles his secretary of state and promised to oppose communism vigorously and to assert American leadership around the globe. Yet in line with his conservative, Republican principles, the president also pledged to keep taxes low and to contain spiraling military costs.

Eisenhower found a way to realize his twin goals in the doctrine of "massive retaliation." Buttressed by America's overwhelming superiority in nuclear arms at the time, Eisenhower and Dulles proclaimed that the United States reserved the right to counter communist aggression wherever it occurred with a swift, decisive nuclear response. Massive retaliation, they hoped, would allow the United States to block aggressive nations, defend its interests, and at the same time cut back on expensive conventional weapons and troops. The "New Look" for the American armed forces, sloganeers concluded, would provide the United States with "more bang for the buck," or, as the Soviets put it, "more rubble for the ruble."

As the Eisenhower administration's policies took shape, the world witnessed an ever accelerating nuclear arms race. The United States had enjoyed an atomic monopoly until September 1949, when Moscow had detonated its first atomic bomb. The Truman administration had responded by immediately speeding up development of the hydrogen bomb, a nuclear weapon that packed nearly eight hundred times the destructive force of the original atom bomb dropped on Hiroshima, Japan. But the successful test of that awesome weapon on November 1, 1952, was duplicated by the Soviet Union in less than a year's time.

Technological innovations during the 1950s further fueled the arms race. U.S. scientists and military officials engineered more powerful warheads and produced and deployed sophisticated intercontinental jet bombers such as the B-52 to serve as "delivery vehicles." Also in the early 1950s, the U.S. Army began to develop and deploy nuclear weapons for battlefield use. Then, in 1957, the Soviet Union stunned the world when it used a ballistic missile to lift an artificial satellite, Sputnik, into outer space. The achievement revealed that Moscow had developed the ability to place a nuclear warhead atop a long-range missile and strike targets as far away as the United States. Meanwhile, atmospheric nuclear tests conducted by both sides showered poisonous, radioactive fallout on the Earth. When U.S. tests at Bikini atoll in the western Pacific in March 1954 infected unsuspecting Japanese fishermen with radiation poisoning, pressure mounted for a nuclear test ban. Cities and towns rushed to construct shelters for civil defense, but arms race critics believed that few people would survive a nuclear war. By the time Eisenhower left office in 1961, the two superpowers together possessed more than twenty thousand nuclear weapons with enough firepower to inflict millions of casualties and incalculable damage.

Cold War politics during the Eisenhower era heightened tensions. In the Soviet Union, Joseph Stalin died, and eventually Nikita Khrushchev took command. Although the new regime in Moscow hinted at improved relations with the West, the two superpowers continued to quarrel over familiar problems: Korea, Indochina, Berlin, and Eastern Europe. Challenges also arose in the Third World, or non-Western world, where emerging nations asserted their independence. The Middle East, Asia, Africa, and Latin America became more politically volatile, and hence more dangerous, to international stability. The people of the world shuddered during Cold War crises—Korea (1953), the Taiwan Strait (1954 and 1958), and Berlin (1959)—when leaders careened toward the nuclear brink.

Eisenhower and Khrushchev tried to ease tensions by participating in summit conferences at Geneva (1955) and Camp David (1959), and they evidently shared a profound unease with reliance on nuclear weapons and the numbing consequences of nuclear competition. In 1955 the Soviets proposed a step-by-step disarmament. Eisenhower countered with a program called "Open Skies" to allow air surveillance and inspection of nuclear facilities as a first step toward arms control. The concrete results of summit diplomacy, however, proved meager and the arms race continued to gain a frightening momentum. In the United States, a group of antinuclear activists formed the Committee for a Sane Nuclear Policy (SANE) in 1957 to press the United Nations to oversee a cessation of nuclear testing and to initiate disarmament negotiations, but they carried little weight. Meanwhile, in another development of the Eisenhower fifties, both the United States and the Soviet Union initiated programs for the "controlled export" of electricity-generating nuclear reactors to developing countries; Ike named the U.S. program "Atoms for Peace." The International Atomic Energy Agency (IAEA), the UN's nuclear watchdog, instituted on-site inspections to prevent the diversion of fissionable materials to weapons development. But post–Cold War nuclear proliferation and inspection crises in Iraq, North Korea, and elsewhere have raised questions about the reliability of monitoring procedures.

The place of nuclear weapons in international relations remains a matter of scholarly and political debate. Some analysts have concluded that nuclear weapons stabilized world politics during the Cold War by making the consequences of a super-power clash so costly that neither side dared to provoke the other. Other writers note that the nuclear threat did not prevent violent Cold War conflicts—client-state wars, civil wars, and interventions—that proliferated among smaller allied states such as Korea, Vietnam, and Afghanistan. Historians, moreover, continue to ponder whether the Eisenhower administration's massive retaliation policy actually deterred superpower confrontation. Skeptics posit that Ike's strategy simply encouraged the Soviets to try to match American capabilities and thus fed an increasingly dangerous arms race. Others defend Eisenhower's policy, doubting the seriousness of Moscow's disarmament proposals and noting that the Soviet's development of the Sputnik *missile heightened the threat of a surprise first strike against the United States. Still others argue that the arms race was primarily a product of defense contractors and military hawks, what Eisenhower called the "military industrial complex," whose tireless lobbying for larger defense budgets proved politically effective. Scientists and*

*universities, eager for federal grant dollars, undoubtedy participated in the spiral—
as did partisan Democrats, who cried "missile gap" in the wake of Soviet advances
and pressed the administration and Congress to take action.*

*The impact of the arms race went beyond Soviet-American relations. Critics of
Eisenhower's nuclear saber rattling worried that the United States might use nuclear
weapons to win limited wars in non-Western areas, or perhaps to resolve thorny
political problems better suited to diplomacy. The administration's face-off with the
People's Republic of China in the Taiwan Strait in the fall of 1954 is a case in point.
When Ike and Dulles publicly advanced the nuclear threat to counter China's bombardment of several offshore islands held by Jiang Jieshi's noncommunist Republic
of China, domestic critics and European allies expressed concern. Many maintained
that the doctrine of massive retaliation might escalate a small localized conflict into
a nuclear crisis, fought over issues of secondary strategic importance. Democrats such
as Senator John F. Kennedy of Massachusetts argued that Eisenhower's reliance on
nuclear weapons left the United States ill-prepared to fight limited wars, especially
against communist insurgencies in former colonial areas.*

*While Eisenhower's massive retaliation strategy and the history of the nuclear
arms race raise a host of debatable issues, one major question hung over the era:
Why could not American and Soviet leaders find a way to halt, slow, or at least
control the arms race? Had Cold War politics and the march of technology made
them prisoners of a headlong race they could not stop?*

 # D O C U M E N T S

The Eisenhower administration struggled to balance the nation's need for military
defense with budgetary constraints. Document 1, tagged NSC 162/2, approved by the
president and adopted on October 30, 1953, concluded that the United States should
rely on cost-effective nuclear weapons to safeguard its interests.

The Eisenhower administration publicly threatened to use nuclear weapons during
the Taiwan Strait crisis of late 1954 and early 1955. Document 2 consists of two parts:
an official account of Secretary of State John Foster Dulles's press conference on
March 15, 1955, in which the secretary discussed the possible use of tactical nuclear
weapons to resolve the Taiwan Strait crisis; and an excerpt from a press conference the
next day in which President Eisenhower reiterated the nuclear threat. Some of the tensions of the times temporarily dissipated in 1955 when U.S. and Soviet leaders agreed
to hold their first summit meeting since World War II.

Despite a thaw in the Cold War tensions following the Geneva Conference, the
superpowers' stockpiling and testing of nuclear weapons went on apace. On October 4,
1957, the Soviet Union placed its *Sputnik* satellite into outer space, a feat that intensified
Cold War fears and generated charges that Eisenhower's conservative spending policies
had caused the country to lag behind in missile and satellite development. The National
Security Council met on October 10, 1957, to discuss the political, scientific, and military
ramifications of the Soviet achievement. Document 3 is an excerpt from that discussion.
Document 4 is a public proclamation, published by the National Committee for a Sane
Nuclear Policy (SANE) in the *New York Times* on November 15, 1957, that questioned
the rationality and morality of the nuclear arms race and called for an immediate halt to
nuclear testing and United Nations efforts to promote arms control and disarmament.

In Document 5, an excerpt from Nikita Khrushchev's memoirs, the former Soviet
premier explains how he came to depend on nuclear-tipped ballistic missiles to implement
a Soviet version of massive retaliation. Khrushchev also recalls his conversations with
Eisenhower and their mutual lament over how both the Soviet and American military

establishments continually lobbied for more weapons. Domestic politics also increased the pressure for a buildup. In a speech delivered on February 29, 1960, Document 6, Democratic senator and presidential hopeful John F. Kennedy charged that the Eisenhower administration's tight-fisted budgets had made the nation vulnerable to Soviet attack. Kennedy's criticisms echoed those of others who decried the existence of a missile gap in the Soviets' favor at the end of the Eisenhower era. (The "gap" actually favored the United States.) Document 7 is Eisenhower's farewell address of January 17, 1961, whose warning against a "military-industrial complex" aroused wide interest.

1. National Security Council Paper No. 162/2 (NSC-162/2) Promotes Atomic Power, 1953

The capability of the USSR to attack the United States with atomic weapons has been continuously growing and will be materially enhanced by hydrogen weapons. The USSR has sufficient bombs and aircraft, using one-way missions, to inflict serious damage on the United States, especially by surprise attack. The USSR soon may have the capability of dealing a crippling blow to our industrial base and our continued ability to prosecute a war. Effective defense could reduce the likelihood and intensity of a hostile attack but not eliminate the chance of a crippling blow. . . .

The USSR does not seem likely deliberately to launch a general war against the United States during the period covered by current estimates (through mid-1955). The uncertain prospects for Soviet victory in a general war, the change in leadership, satellite unrest, and the U.S. capability to retaliate massively, make such a course improbable. Similarly, an attack on NATO [North Atlantic Treaty Organization] countries or other areas which would be almost certain to bring on general war in view of U.S. commitments or intentions would be unlikely. The Soviets will not, however, be deterred by fear of general war from taking the measures they consider necessary to counter Western actions which they view as a serious threat to their security. . . .

Although Soviet fear of atomic reaction should still inhibit local aggression, increasing Soviet atomic capability may tend to diminish the deterrent effect of U.S. atomic power against peripheral Soviet aggression. It may also sharpen the reaction of the USSR to what it considers provocative acts of the United States. If either side should miscalculate the strength of the other's reaction, such local conflicts could grow into general war, even though neither seeks nor desires it. To avoid this, it will in general be desirable for the United States to make clear to the USSR the kind of actions which will be almost certain to lead to this result, recognizing, however, that as general war becomes more devastating for both sides the threat to resort to it becomes less available as a sanction against local aggression. . . .

Within the free world, only the United States can provide and maintain, for a period of years to come, the atomic capability to counterbalance Soviet atomic power. Thus, sufficient atomic weapons and effective means of delivery are indispensable for U.S. security. Moreover, in the face of Soviet atomic power, defense of the continental United States becomes vital to effective security: to protect our striking force, our mobilization base, and our people. Such atomic capability is also a major contribution to the security of our allies, as well as of this country.

This document can be found in U.S. Department of State, *Foreign Relations of the United States, 1952–1954* (Washington, D.C: Government Printing Office, 1984), II, 579, 580–581, 583, 588, 589, 593.

The United States cannot, however, meet its defense needs, even at exorbitant cost, without the support of allies. . . .

The United States must maintain a sound economy based on free private enterprise as a basis both for high defense productivity and for the maintenance of its living standards and free institutions. Not only the world position of the United States, but the security of the whole free world, is dependent on the avoidance of recession and on the long-term expansion of the U.S. economy. Threats to its stability or growth, therefore, constitute a danger to the security of the United States and of the coalition which it leads. Expenditures for national security, in fact all federal, state and local governmental expenditures, must be carefully scrutinized with a view to measuring their impact on the national economy. . . .

The requirements for funds to maintain our national security must thus be considered in the light of these dangers to our economic system, including the danger to industrial productivity necessary to support military programs, arising from excessive levels of total Government spending, taxing and borrowing. . . .

In specific situations where a warning appears desirable and feasible as an added deterrent, the United States should make clear to the USSR and Communist China, in general terms or with reference to specific areas as the situation requires, its intention to react with military force against any aggression by Soviet bloc armed forces.

In the event of hostilities, the United States will consider nuclear weapons to be as available for use as other munitions. Where the consent of an ally is required for the use of these weapons from U.S. bases on the territory of such ally, the United States should promptly obtain the advance consent of such ally for such use. The United States should also seek, as and when feasible, the understanding and approval of this policy by free nations.

This policy should not be made public without further consideration by the National Security Council.

2. Secretary of State John Foster Dulles and President Dwight D. Eisenhower Threaten to Use Nuclear Weapons: The Taiwan Strait Crisis, 1955

Dulles Statement, March 15, 1955

A correspondent said that in his speech, the secretary had referred to the existence in the hands of our forces in the Far East of new and powerful weapons which he had indicated would be used if necessary under other conditions or conditions of war out there. Asked if he could tell them anything about the nature of those weapons or the circumstances under which they might be used, the secretary replied that he thought it was generally known that certain types of atomic missiles were becoming conventional in the United States armed services. He stated that those were weapons of relatively small dimensions with considerably more explosive power than was contained in the conventional weapons. He added that, however, they were weapons of precision.

The Dulles statement can be found as Secretary of State John F. Dulles Press Conference, 15 March, 1955: Charles McCardle Papers, Box 7, Folder "1955 Secretary's Press Conferences," Dwight D. Eisenhower Presidential Library, Abilene, Kansas.

Mr. Dulles continued that he imagined that if the United States became engaged in a major military activity anywhere in the world that those weapons would come into use because, as he had said, they were more and more becoming conventional and replacing what used to be called conventional weapons. He commented that they might recall that at the meeting of the NATO Council, which had been held in Paris last December, there had been pretty much agreement at that time that atomic missiles would be treated as a conventional and normal means for the defense of Europe. He explained that what he was speaking of was merely another application of that basic policy.

Asked if he would regard United States defense of Quemoy and Matsu a major military effort in that context, Mr. Dulles answered that he could not tell that in advance because it depended upon what the effort was which we had to meet. He added that if that was a major effort on the part of the Chinese Communists, it might take a major effort on our part to counter it.

A correspondent inquired if in the case of these atomic weapons which the secretary had described as having become or in the state of becoming conventional, he was referring to what we ordinarily called tactical atomic weapons. The secretary responded that that was right.

Eisenhower Statement, March 16, 1955

Q. Mr. President, yesterday at his news conference, Secretary of State Dulles indicated that in the event of general war in the Far East, we would probably make use of some tactical small atomic weapons. Would you care to comment on this and, possibly, explain it further?

The President. I wouldn't comment in the sense that I would pretend to foresee the conditions of any particular conflict in which you might engage; but we have been, as you know, active in producing various types of weapons that feature nuclear fission ever since World War II.

Now, in any combat where these things can be used on strictly military targets and for strictly military purposes, I see no reason why they shouldn't be used just exactly as you would use a bullet or anything else.

I believe the great question about these things comes when you begin to get into those areas where you cannot make sure that you are operating merely against military targets. But with that one qualification, I would say, yes, of course they would be used.

3. The National Security Council Discusses the Ramifications of *Sputnik*, 1957

Mr. Allen Dulles [director of the Central Intelligence Agency] stated that . . . on October 4 the Soviets had fired their earth satellite from the Tyura Tam range. Its initial path followed the range, crossing approximately over the range's other end at

---

The Eisenhower Statement can be found in *Public Papers of the Presidents, Dwight D. Eisenhower, 1955* (Washington, D.C.: U.S. Government Printing Office, 1950), 332.

Document 3 can be found in U.S. Department of State, *Foreign Relations of the United States, 1955–1957* (Washington, D.C.: U.S. Government Printing Office, 1958), XI, 757–758, 759, 761–762.

Klyuchi. . . . [A]fter the successful orbiting of the earth satellite and after the second circuit of the earth by the satellite, the Soviets announced their achievement. This delay in the announcement was in line with the previous statements of the Soviet Union that they would not announce an attempt to orbit their satellite until they had been assured that the orbiting had been successful. . . .

Mr. Dulles then turned to the world reaction to the Soviet achievement. He first pointed out that Khrushchev had moved all his propaganda guns into place. The launching of an earth satellite was one of a trilogy of propaganda moves, the other two being the announcement of the successful testing of an ICBM [intercontinental ballistic missile] and the recent test of a large-scale hydrogen bomb at Novaya Zemlya. . . .

Larded in with Khrushchev's propaganda statements had been a number of interesting remarks, such as the one in which Khrushchev consigned military aircraft to museums in the future. With respect to this remark, Mr. Dulles pointed out that U.S. intelligence had not observed as many Soviet heavy bombers on airfields as had been expected. This raised the question as to whether the Soviets are in the process of de-emphasizing the role of the heavy bomber. There had been no clear verdict yet by the intelligence community on this question.

Mr. Dulles thought that there was no doubt that in gearing up all this propaganda of recent days and weeks, the Soviets had had an eye to the situation in the Middle East, and wished to exert the maximum influence they could summon on that situation. Much of the Soviet propaganda comment is following closely the original Soviet boast relating their scientific accomplishments to the effectiveness of the Communist social system. The target for this particular thrust, thought Mr. Dulles, was evidently the underdeveloped nations in the world. . . .

At the conclusion of Mr. Allen Dulles' briefing, [National Security Affairs Advisor] Mr. [Robert] Cutler asked [Deputy Defense] Secretary [Donald] Quarles to speak. Secretary Quarles began by stating that much of what he was going to say would be familiar to the President and other members of the Council. The President quipped that this was indeed the case, and he was beginning to feel somewhat numb on the subject of the earth satellite. Thereafter, Secretary Quarles outlined briefly the development of satellite programs beginning with the period of World War II. . . .

As to the implications of the Soviet achievement, Secretary Quarles said he would not comment on the [C]old [W]ar aspects, since they had been dealt with by the Director of Central Intelligence. Beyond this, it was clear that the Soviets possess a competence in long-range rocketry and in auxiliary fields which is even more advanced than the competence with which we had credited them; although, of course, we had always given them the capability of orbiting an earth satellite. Finally, said Secretary Quarles, the outer space implications of the launching of this satellite were of very great significance, especially in relation to the development of reconnaissance satellites. . . .

Mr. Cutler then called on Dr. [Detlev W.] Bronk [president of the U.S. National Academy of Sciences], who stated initially that there was one thing about which he was very greatly concerned—that is, that we avoid getting our whole scientific community into a race to accomplish everything before the Russians do. He therefore thought we should adhere strictly to our stated earth satellite program and not be deflected from our course merely by the fact that the Russians had been the first to launch an earth satellite.

The President pointed out that all those around the table and others could anticipate before very long being obliged to testify before Congressional committees, to talk to the press, and the like. In the circumstances, he could imagine nothing more important than that anybody so involved should stand firmly by the existing earth satellite program which was, after all, adopted by the Council after due deliberation as a reasonable program. In short, we should answer inquiries by stating that we have a plan—a good plan—and that we are going to stick to it.

Mr. Cutler then called on Secretary [of State Christian] Herter for an appraisal of the foreign policy implications for U.S. security of the successful launching of the Soviet satellite. Secretary Herter initially stated that it was extremely difficult to make such an assessment because there was such a mass of information pouring into the Department of State. While there had been insufficient time to analyze this intake, there were already some indications of the serious effects of the Soviet success which we hope to be able to counteract.

Thereafter, Secretary Herter read selected quotations to illustrate his point, with particular reference to Turkey, Morocco, and the Philippines. He also pointed out the probable repercussions of the Soviet success in the United Nations. The United States may now encounter much greater difficulty in defending its disarmament position.

By and large, continued Secretary Herter, the reaction of our allies had been pretty firm and good, though even the best of them require assurance that we have not been surpassed scientifically and militarily by the USSR. The neutralist countries are chiefly engaged in patting themselves on the back and insisting that the Soviet feat proves the value and the wisdom of the neutralism which these countries have adopted.

Summing up, Secretary Herter described the first foreign policy reactions as "pretty somber." The United States will have to do a great deal to counteract them and, particularly, to confirm the existence of our own real military and scientific strength. . . .

Mr. Cutler then called on Mr. [Arthur] Larson [director of the U.S. Information Agency], who said that he was hesitant to say what he was going to say because he was not sure that he really believed it. He then went on to say that while we could not permit ourselves to be panicked by the Soviet achievement, he did wonder whether our U.S. plans were now adequate with regard to the next great break-through. If we lose repeatedly to the Russians as we have lost with the earth satellite, the accumulated damage would be tremendous. We should accordingly plan, ourselves, to accomplish some of the next great break-throughs first—for example, the achievement of a manned satellite, or getting to the moon. Do we have any such plans, asked Mr. Larson. If not, our people should begin to think about them.

The President replied to Mr. Larson by stating that while he could hardly quarrel with Mr. Larson's conclusions if the Soviets were to win every time, the fact remained that the United States couldn't possibly set up a whole vast scientific program of basic research in areas about which we don't know anything, and then attempt to outdo the Russians in each aspect of such a program. We must, above all, still seek a military posture that the Russians will respect.

4. The National Committee for a Sane Nuclear Policy (SANE) Protests the Nuclear Arms Race, 1957

A deep uneasiness exists inside Americans as we look out on the world. . . .

We are facing a danger unlike any danger that has ever existed. In our possession and in the possession of the Russians are more than enough nuclear explosives to put an end to the life of man on earth.

Our uneasiness is the result of the fact that our approach to the danger is unequal to the danger. Our response to the challenge of today's world seems out of joint. The slogans and arguments that belong to the world of competitive national sovereignties—a world of plot and counter-plot—no longer fit the world of today or tomorrow.

Just in front of us opens a grand human adventure into outer space. But within us and all around us is the need to make this world whole before we set out for other ones. We can earn the right to explore other planets only as we make this one safe and fit for human habitation.

The sovereignty of the human community comes before all others—before the sovereignty of groups, tribes, or nations. In that community, man has natural rights. He has the right to live and to grow, to breathe unpoisoned air, to work on uncontaminated soil. He has the right to his sacred nature.

If what nations are dong has the effect of destroying these natural rights, whether by upsetting the delicate balances on which life depends, or fouling the air, or devitalizing the land, or tampering with the genetic integrity of man himself; then it becomes necessary for people to restrain and tame the nations.

Indeed, the test of a nation's right to survive today is measured not by the size of its bombs or the range of its missiles, but by the size and range of its concern for the human community as a whole.

There can be no true security for America unless we can exert leadership in these terms, unless we become advocates of a grand design that is directed to the large cause of human destiny.

There can be no true security for America unless we can establish and keep vital connections with the world's people, unless there is some moral grandeur to our purposes, unless what we do is direct to the cause of human life and the free man.

There is much that America has said to the world. But the world is still waiting for us to say and do the things that will in deed and in truth represent our greatest strength.

What are these things?

That we pledge ourselves to the cause of peace with justice on earth, and that there is no sacrifice that we are not prepared to make, nothing we will not do to create such a just peace for all peoples;

That we are prepared to support the concept of a United Nations with adequate authority under law to prevent aggression, adequate authority to compel and enforce disarmament, adequate authority to settle disputes among nations according to principles of justice;

That the earth is too small for intercontinental ballistic missiles and nuclear bombs, and that the first order of business for the world is to bring both under control;

That the development of satellites or rocket stations and the exploration of outer space must be carried on in the interests of the entire human community through a pooling of world science;

That because of the grave unanswered questions with respect to nuclear test explosions—especially as it concerns the contamination of air and water and food, and the injury to man himself—we are calling upon all nations to suspend such explosions at once;

That while the abolition of testing will not by itself solve the problem of peace or the problem of armaments, it enables the world to eliminate immediately at least one real and specific danger. Also, that the abolition of testing gives us a place to begin on the larger question of armaments control, for the problems in monitoring such tests are relatively uncomplicated;

That none of the differences separating the governments of the world are as important as the membership of all peoples in the human family;

That the big challenge of the age is to develop the concept of a higher loyalty—loyalty by man to the human community;

That the greatest era of human history on earth is within reach of all mankind, that there is no area that cannot be made fertile or habitable, no disease that cannot be fought, no scarcity that cannot be conquered;

That all that is required for this is to re-direct our energies, re-discover our moral strength, re-define our purposes.

5. Soviet Premier Nikita Khrushchev Reflects on the Nuclear Arms Race, 1970

Even honest people who want to avoid the use of atomic and hydrogen weapons can't ignore the question of how many such arms are available to us in case a global war should break out. That's why we must decide realistically on priorities for the allocation of funds.

When I was the leader of the Party and the Government, I decided that we had to economize drastically in the building of homes, the construction of communal services, and even in the development of agriculture in order to build up our defenses. I even suspended the construction of subways in Kiev, Baku, and Tblisi so that we could redirect those funds into strengthening our defense and attack forces. We also built fewer athletic stadiums, swimming pools, and cultural facilities. I think I was right to concentrate on military spending, even at the expense of all but the most essential investments in other areas. If I hadn't put such a high priority on our military needs, we couldn't have survived. I devoted all my strength to the rearmament of the Soviet Union. It was a challenging and important stage of our lives. . . .

Our potential enemy—our principal, our most powerful, our most dangerous enemy—was so far away from us that we couldn't have reached him with our air force. Only by building up a nuclear missile force could we keep the enemy from unleashing war against us. As life has already confirmed, if we had given the West a chance, war would have been declared while Dulles was alive. But we were the first to launch rockets into space; we exploded the most powerful nuclear devices; we accomplished those feats first, ahead of the United States, England, and France. Our accomplishments and our obvious might had a sobering effect on the aggressive forces in the United States, England, France, and, of course, inside the Bonn [West German] government. They knew that they had lost their chance to strike at us with impunity.

Now that it's the size of our nuclear missile arsenal and not the size of our army that counts, I think the army should be reduced to an absolute minimum. There's no question in my mind that we have indeed reached the stage where that's possible. When I led the Government and had final authority over our military allocations, our theoreticians calculated that we had the nuclear capacity to grind our enemies into dust, and since that time our nuclear capacity has been greatly intensified. During my leadership we accumulated enough weapons to destroy the principal cities of the United States, not to mention our potential enemies in Europe. . . .

I have always been against war, but at the same time I've always realized full well that the fear of nuclear war in a country's leader can paralyze that country's defenses. And if a country's defenses are paralyzed, then war really is inevitable: the enemy is sure to sense your fright and try to take advantage of it. . . .

However, we must also keep in mind the true character of all imperialists, capitalists, monopolists, and militarists who are interested in making money out of the political tension between nations. We must make sure that we don't allow ourselves to get involved in a lot of senseless competition with the West over military spending. If we try to compete with America in any but the most essential areas of military preparedness, we will be doing two harmful things. First, we will be further enriching wealthy aggressive capitalist circles in the United States who use our own military buildups as a pretext for overloading their own country's arms budget. Second, we will be exhausting our material resources without raising the living standard of our people. We must remember that the fewer people we have in the army, the more people we will have available for other, more productive kinds of work. This realization would be a good common point of departure for the progressive forces of the world in their struggle for peaceful coexistence. If one side were to curtail its accumulation of military means, it would be easier for the other side to do the same. We must be prepared to strike back against our enemy, but we must also ask, "Where is the end to this spiraling competition?"

I know from experience that the leaders of the armed forces can be very persistent in claiming their share when it comes time to allocate funds. Every commander has all sorts of very convincing arguments why he should get more than anyone else. Unfortunately there's a tendency for people who run the armed forces to be greedy and self-seeking. They're always ready to throw in your face the slogan "If you try to economize on the country's defenses today, you'll pay in blood when war breaks out tomorrow." I'm not denying that these men have a huge responsibility, and I'm not impugning their moral qualities. But the fact remains that the living standard of the country suffers when the budget is overloaded with allocations to unproductive branches of consumption. And today as yesterday, the most unproductive expenditures are all of those made on the armed forces. That's why I think that military leaders can't be reminded too often that it is the government which must allocate funds, and it is the government which must decide how much the armed forces can spend.

Apparently the control of military spending is a universal problem. I remember a conversation I once had with President Eisenhower when I was a guest at his dacha at Camp David [in September 1959]. We went for walks together and had some useful informal talks. During one of these talks, he asked, "Tell me, Mr. Khrushchev, how did you decide the question of funds for military expenses?" Then, before I had a chance to say anything, he said, "Perhaps first I should tell you how it is with us."

"Well, how is it with you?"

He smiled, and I smiled back at him. I had a feeling what he was going to say. "It's like this. My military leaders come to me and say, 'Mr. President, we need such and such a sum for such and such a program.' I say, 'Sorry, we don't have the funds.' They say, 'We have reliable information that the Soviet Union has already allocated funds for their own such program. Therefore if we don't get the funds we need, we'll fall behind the Soviet Union.' So I give in. That's how they wring money out of me. They keep grabbing for more and I keep giving it to them. Now tell me, how is it with you?"

"It's just the same. Some people from our military department come and say, 'Comrade Khrushchev, look at this! The Americans are developing such and such a system. We could develop the same system, but it would cost such and such.' I tell them there's no money; it's all been allotted already. So they say, 'If we don't get the money we need and if there's a war, then the enemy will have superiority over us.' So we discuss it some more, and I end up by giving them the money they ask for."

"Yes," he said, "that's what I thought. You know, we really should come to some sort of an agreement in order to stop this fruitless, really wasteful rivalry."

"I'd like to do that. Part of my reason for coming here was to see if some sort of an agreement would come out of these meetings and conversations."

But we couldn't agree then, and we can't agree now. I don't know. Maybe it's impossible for us to agree.

6. Senator John F. Kennedy Presses for More Military Spending to Close the Missile Gap, 1960

Winston Churchill said: "We arm—to parley." We prepare for war—in order to deter war. We depend on the strength of armaments, to enable us to bargain for disarmament. It is my intention, later this week, to make a second address on what positive preparations for disarmament we can make now. We compare our military strength with the Soviets, not to determine whether we should use it, but to determine whether we can persuade them that to use theirs would be futile and disastrous, and to determine whether we can back up our own pledges in Berlin, Formosa, and around the world.

This document can be found in *Congressional Record,* CVI (February 29, 1960), 3801–3803.

In short, peace, not politics, is at the heart of the current debate—peace, not war, is the objective of our military policy. But peace would have no meaning if the time ever came when the deterrent ratio shifted so heavily in favor of the Soviet Union that they could destroy most of our retaliatory capacity in a single blow. It would then be irrelevant as to whether the Soviets achieved our demise through massive attack, through the threat of such attack, or through nibbling away gradually at our security.

Will such a time come?

The current debate has too often centered on how our retaliatory capacity compares today with that of the Soviets. Our striking force, the President said one week ago Sunday night, is "ample for today—far superior to any other" and large enough to deter any aggressor. But the real issue is not how we stand today but tomorrow—not in 1960 but in 1961, 1962 and particularly 1963 and thereafter. Nineteen hundred and sixty is critical because this is the year that the money must be appropriated—by this session of this Congress—if we are to obtain initial results in subsequent years. . . .

Whether the missile gap—that everyone agrees now exists—will become critical in 1961, 1962, or 1963—whether during the critical years of the gap the Russian lead will be 2 to 1, 3 to 1, or 5 to 1—whether the gap can be brought to a close—by the availability in quantity of Polaris and Minuteman missiles—in 1964 or in 1965 or ever—on all these questions experts may sincerely differ. I do not challenge the accuracy of our intelligence reports—I do not charge anyone with intentionally misleading the public for purposes of deception. For whichever figures are accurate, the point is that we are facing a gap on which we are gambling with our survival— and this year's defense budget is our last real chance to do something about it. . . .

Unless immediate steps are taken, failure to maintain our relative power of retaliation may in the near future expose the United States to a nuclear missile attack. Until our own mobile solid-fuel missiles are available in sufficient quantities to make it unwise for an enemy to consider an attack we must scrape through with what we can most quickly make available. At the present time there are no Polaris submarines on station ready for an emergency. There are no hardened missile bases. There is no adequate air defense. There is no capacity for an airborne alert in anything like the numbers admittedly needed. . . .

Time is short. This situation should never have been permitted to arise. But if we move now, if we are willing to gamble with our money instead of our survival, we have, I am sure, the wit and resource to maintain the minimum conditions for our survival, for our alliances, and for the active pursuit of peace.

7. Eisenhower Warns Against the "Military-Industrial Complex," 1961

A vital element in keeping the peace is our military establishment. Our arms must be mighty, ready for instant action, so that no potential aggressor may be tempted to risk his own destruction.

Our military organization today bears little relation to that known by any of my predecessors in peacetime, or indeed by the fighting men of World War II or Korea.

This document can be found in *Public Papers of the Presidents, Dwight D. Eisenhower, 1960–1961* (Washington, D.C.: U.S. Government Printing Office, 1961), pp. 1037–1040.

Until the latest of our world conflicts, the United States had no armaments industry. American makers of plowshares could, with time and as required, make swords as well. But now we can no longer risk emergency improvisation of national defense; we have been compelled to create a permanent armaments industry of vast proportions. Added to this, three and a half million men and women are directly engaged in the defense establishment. We annually spend on military security more than the net income of all United States corporations.

This conjunction of an immense military establishment and a large arms industry is new in the American experience. The total influence—economic, political, even spiritual—is felt in every city, every State house, every office of the Federal government. We recognize the imperative need for this development. Yet we must not fail to comprehend its grave implications. Our toil, resources and livelihood are all involved; so is the very structure of our society.

In the councils of government, we must guard against the acquisition of unwarranted influence, whether sought or unsought, by the military-industrial complex. The potential for the disastrous rise of misplaced power exists and will persist.

We must never let the weight of this combination endanger our liberties or democratic processes. We should take nothing for granted. Only an alert and knowledgeable citizenry can compel the proper meshing of the huge industrial and military machinery of defense with our peaceful methods and goals, so that security and liberty may prosper together.

Akin to, and largely responsible for the sweeping changes in our industrial-military posture, has been the technological revolution during recent decades.

In this revolution, research has become central; it also becomes more formalized, complex, and costly. A steadily increasing share is conducted for, by, or at the direction of, the Federal government.

Today, the solitary inventor, tinkering in his shop, has been overshadowed by task forces of scientists in laboratories and testing fields. In the same fashion, the free university, historically the fountainhead of free ideas and scientific discovery, has experienced a revolution in the conduct of research. Partly because of the huge costs involved, a government contract becomes virtually a substitute for intellectual curiosity. For every old blackboard there are now hundreds of new electronic computers.

The prospect of domination of the nation's scholars by Federal employment, project allocations, and the power of money is ever present—and is gravely to be regarded.

Yet, in holding scientific research and discovery in respect, as we should, we must also be alert to the equal and opposite danger that public policy could itself become the captive of a scientific-technological elite.

It is the task of statesmanship to mold, to balance, and to integrate these and other forces, new and old, within the principles of our democratic system—ever aiming toward the supreme goals of our free society. . . .

Down the long lane of the history yet to be written America knows that this world of ours, ever growing smaller, must avoid becoming a community of dreadful fear and hate, and be, instead, a proud confederation of mutual trust and respect.

Such a confederation must be one of equals. The weakest must come to the conference table with the same confidence as do we, protected as we are by our moral, economic, and military strength. That table, though scarred by many past frustrations, cannot be abandoned for the certain agony of the battlefield.

⊕ E S S A Y S

In the first essay, Michael S. Sherry, a professor of history at Northwestern University, renders a sympathetic portrayal of President Dwight D. Eisenhower's struggle to avoid war and contain Cold War militarization. Sherry argues that Eisenhower's "New Look" strategy, which relied on nuclear weapons and the threat of "massive retaliation" to prevent Communist aggression, balanced the nation's long-term security needs with its budgetary constraints. More compelling, according to Sherry, the "New Look" grew from Eisenhower's conviction that a more expansive military buildup would ultimately create a garrison state that undermined democracy at home and threatened the world with nuclear annihilation. Sherry maintains that even at the time of the Taiwan Strait crises in 1954–1955 and 1958, during which the administration exaggerated the Communist threat and threatened massive retaliation against the People's Republic of China, Eisenhower ultimately backed away from a dangerous gamble. Yet in the end, Eisenhower slowed but could not reverse the trend toward militarism. Sherry concludes that America's political culture and domestic insecurities, the march of technology, and Eisenhower's own failure to articulate an alternative to Cold War containment and nuclear security fed the Soviet-American arms race and accounted for the president's failure to rein in the swelling military industrial complex.

In the second essay, Gordon H. Chang of Stanford University and He Di of the Institute of American Studies, Chinese Academy of Social Sciences in Beijing, use both American and Chinese sources to explore in depth the Taiwan Strait crisis of 1954–1955 and advance a more critical analysis of Eisenhower's policies. They assert that the administration's strategy of threatening massive retaliation without clarifying what the United States would and would not defend ("deterrence through uncertainty") led the People's Republic of China to conclude that its controlled military campaign against Jinmen (Quemoy), Mazu (Matsu), and other offshore islands would not draw a U.S. military response. When Mao Zedong subsequently launched an invasion of the island of Yijiangshan in the Tachens, Eisenhower and Secretary of State John Foster Dulles misinterpreted the action as likely to lead to an offensive against Taiwan itself. Rather than defusing the Taiwan Strait crisis, Eisenhower's threat to use nuclear weapons and his plans for a naval blockade of China's coast carried the United States to the nuclear brink over relatively insignificant territories and spurred China's nuclear program.

Eisenhower's Heroic but Failed Crusade Against Militarization

MICHAEL S. SHERRY

Eisenhower faced sharply different options for national security [from those faced by Harry S. Truman]. Truman's ambitious policy, laid out in NSC-68 and implemented during the Korean War, presumed protracted struggle with communism, posited abundant American resources to wage it, and prized American ability to respond symmetrically to any aggression. Nuclear intimidation or attack, conventional war and covert action, economic and political pressure—each would be met by similar forms of American power. An alternative, advanced mostly by conservative

Michael S. Sherry, *In the Shadow of War: The United States Since the 1930s.* Copyright © 1995 Yale University press. Reprinted with permission.

Republicans who recoiled at the costs and compromises of protracted struggle, prized asymmetry: the United States should not meet the enemy gun for gun but instead rely on those forms of power, above all atomic and aerial, at which it excelled and which might provide quick victory.

As in many areas of policy, Ike chose a "middle way" between conflicting options, grafting his limited view of resources to the Truman administration's assumptions about global struggle. For him, too, the Cold War was a protracted conflict promising no quick victory (campaign rhetoric aside), but precisely for that reason the United States had to hoard its resources, limit its efforts, and spread its burdens, or else exhaust itself over the long haul. "To amass military power without regard to our economic capacity would be to defend ourselves against one kind of disaster by inviting another," his 1953 State of the Union message declared. "We can't afford to let the negative actions of the Communists force us into world-wide deployment," he argued in 1954. "We need to be free to decide where we can strike most effectively."

The result was the much-touted "New Look," an effort to limit defense spending by relying on enhanced nuclear forces, as well as alliances and covert action, rather than on costly conventional forces to counter enemy initiatives. Confrontation with the enemy was to be selective, focused on conflicts in which American power was superior and available at limited cost. At times Eisenhower still echoed the previous administration's expansive view: "As there is no weapon too small, no arena too remote, to be ignored, there is no free nation too humble to be forgotten." But the emphasis was on American freedom "to respond vigorously at places and with means of its own choosing," in Dulles's famous phrasing, or in the National Security Council's words, it was "on the capability of inflicting massive retaliatory damage by offensive striking power." Truman's programs to mass-produce nuclear weapons and bombers created the means for this strategy—so abundantly "that the margin of American superiority seemed if anything greater than it had been in the days of the American atomic monopoly."

Why did Eisenhower take this approach? Critics once singled out his fear of deficit spending and bloated government, but many considerations were at play, their weight varying among members of the administration. For Ike, those considerations all reflected his anxiety about militarization, which defined his outlook as much as the Cold War itself. He was perilously alone in that anxiety. Dulles talked of Cold War and diplomacy; Treasury Secretary George Humphrey of budgets and fiscal prudence; Defense Secretary Charles Wilson of preparedness and efficiency. Eisenhower too spoke in those terms, but also transcended them. No unbending aversion to war guided him—he had waged war and never ruled out doing so again—but a complex aversion to militarization did sustain him. . . .

Eisenhower feared strategic disaster less through communist victory, about which his warnings were few, than through nuclear war. No President worried more about the dangers of initiating or stumbling into nuclear conflict. His concern drew in part on his doubts as an army man about air power. Already "damn tired of Air Force sales programs" in his first months in office, he lectured congressmen: "We pulverized Germany . . . but their actual rate of production was as big at the end as at the beginning." Even if—especially if—bombers could destroy the Soviet Union, he could see no real victory, as he told senior officers: "Gain such a victory, and what do you do with it? Here would be a great area from the Elbe to Vladivostok and down through Southeast Asia torn up and destroyed without government, without its communications, just an area of starvation and disaster. I ask you what would the civilized world do about it? I repeat there is no victory in any war except through our imaginations, through our dedication and through our work to avoid it." . . .

Ike's resistance to militarization probably drew most on his fear of its consequences even if war were avoided. He was reasonably confident that war would be avoided, at least on his watch—his view of himself in such matters was not modest. He was less confident of resisting a broader political process that nurtured anxiety, swollen budgets, economic stagnation, and constraints on freedom—the evils of the "garrison state." His resounding statement of those dangers came in an April 16, 1953, address. Though blaming communists for the Cold War, he warned that even if atomic war were averted, the arms race offered "a life of perpetual fear and tension; a burden of arms draining the wealth and labor of all peoples. . . . Every gun that is made, every warship launched, every rocket fired, signifies, in the final sense, a theft from those who hunger and are not fed, those who are cold and not clothed. This world in arms is not spending money alone. It is spending the sweat of its laborers, the genius of its scientists, the hopes of its children." As he eloquently concluded: "This is not a way of life at all, in any true sense. Under the cloud of threatening war, it is humanity hanging from a cross of iron." Proposing what a post–Cold War generation would call a "peace dividend," he promised to devote "a substantial percentage of the savings achieved by disarmament to a fund for world aid and reconstruction." The savings would be used for "a new kind of war . . . a declared total war, not upon any human enemy but upon the brute forces of poverty and need."

Critics often applauded these broad sentiments but attacked the strategy that flowed from them, above all its reliance on threats of massive retaliation. They decried the creation of a technologically muscle-bound America so dependent on nuclear weapons that it had no choice between capitulation and catastrophe in the face of communist aggression—a strategy at once helpless and horrifying. As the 1950s wore on, the New Look seemed a feeble bulwark against the limited wars and subversive efforts waged by communist and leftist forces in the Third World. Ike himself acknowledged the force of this criticism even before becoming President. "What should we do if Soviet *political* aggression, as in Czechoslovakia, successively chips away exposed positions in the free world?" he wrote Dulles in 1952. "To my mind this is the case where the theory of 'retaliation' falls down." He never devised a satisfactory solution to the problem.

Still, critics of the New Look also tended to caricature it—it hardly denied the administration a non-nuclear capability. Between 1954 and 1958, the army fell from 1,404,598 to 898,925 personnel, but remained 50 percent larger than at its low point in the late 1940s. Other "conventional" forces, the navy and marines, shrank only by 10 percent, as did the air force. The 2.6 million personnel of 1958 marked a 30 percent decline from the Korean War peak, but the military reserves had grown and the nation was no longer at war. This force was far more capable of limited war than any previous peacetime force. It was backed up by the CIA's enhanced capacity for paramilitary and covert action, and by military resources given allies and clients (Ike insisted on foreign military and economic aid in the face of conservatives furious about fiscal imprudence and liberals suspicious of aiding despots). . . .

In addition to force levels, budgets measured Eisenhower's approach to national security. Defense spending fell 20 percent between fiscal 1953 and 1955 and, though rising later in the 1950s, continued to move within a narrow range. It also declined as a fraction of the national budget (from two-thirds to one-half by 1960) and as percentage of GNP (from 13.8 to 9.1 percent). Taft wanted sharper cuts, but Eisenhower did not listen, "partly because the clamor from the other side—demanding more spending on the military—was so much louder." Indeed, Ike sustained his defense budgets in the face of heated protests from the armed forces and, after 1957, widespread pressure to spend more. . . .

As other situations showed, no refusal to use power guided Eisenhower, only a shrewd determination to act when the odds were favorable and the costs low—unless misjudged. In the nail-biting crises of 1955 and 1958 over Quemoy and Matsu—small islands near China's coast held by Taiwan's Nationalist government—the administration threatened a nuclear response if Mao's government attacked, while Dulles equated Mao's "aggressive fanaticism" with that of Hitler. Ike gained apparent victory for brinkmanship, but also "thoroughly discredited it in the eyes of the American public and allies overseas by revealing how little it would take to push the administration into a war with China," by showing the administration's "bland self-confidence that it could use nuclear weapons without setting off an all-out nuclear war," and by doing so in a crisis over real estate of purely symbolic value (although Dulles later boasted that "his most brilliant" achievement had been "to save Quemoy and Matsu").

Moreover, the outcome seemed to rest on one man whose judgment, however assessed, would have to falter on occasion. The Formosa crises showed the administration's penchant for recklessness in small matters as against restraint in larger ones. Only when the 1955 crisis threatened to explode did Ike show caution. . . .

Eisenhower also maintained, as public reactions confirmed, that the United States now valued diplomacy with the enemy, though diplomacy rarely yielded concrete results. A 1955 treaty made Austria a permanent neutral and required withdrawal of occupying Soviet and Western forces, a significant precedent not followed for solving the weightier problem of divided Germany. The United States did not even sign the 1954 Geneva Accords on Indochina. Eisenhower offered a much-touted "Atoms for Peace" program and later an imaginative "Open Skies" proposal—foreshadowing the spirit of later mutual surveillance—whereby the superpowers would give each other "a complete blueprint of our military establishments" and allow each to photograph the other from the air. Every such proposal led to a nasty round of public posturing, Soviet and American leaders blaming each other for the arms race. Even more ballyhoo, but no agreements, accompanied the 1955 Geneva "Big Four" meeting of Ike and the Soviet, French, and British leaders. Eisenhower, and sometimes his counterparts elsewhere, were duly criticized for performing empty rituals that masked growing perils.

There was something to be said for ritual, however. Reminiscent of FDR's summit diplomacy, Eisenhower's version, undertaken in the face of shrill prophecies of "appeasement," established expectations and processes for superpower consultation that no later President could ignore. The lavish media attention given the Geneva summit reflected the substantive shallowness of the event, but also the hopes it aroused. As Eisenhower aide Emmet John Hughes said, Geneva "was widely understood to signalize, without articulating, the acceptance by the major powers of the common necessity to shun recourse to nuclear war." A similar signal arose from lofty and now-forgotten aspirations, earnestly supported by Eisenhower among others, that the United Nations become an effective instrument of world peace and prosperity.

Nonetheless, beneath the surface of international crisis and consultation ran currents that undermined Eisenhower's hopes to contain militarization. In the sprawling national security apparatus, pressure kept mounting to develop new weapons and to subvert arms control. Through the budget process, Ike exercised general control over defense policy but not over its qualitative shift toward new, expensive weapons. By bringing scientists into the White House, he gained access to experts skeptical about new programs, but also subjected himself to more direct pressure from scientists championing an aggressive course. The administration, complained Treasury Secretary Humphrey in 1957, had been "led astray by scientists and by vested interests." By denunciations of nuclear overkill or sheer explosions of temper, Eisenhower could interrupt the momentum. He could not or would not stop it. Nuclear warheads swelled in numbers and power, their megatonnage (destructive power) soaring from 150 in 1953 to 19,000 in 1960, the historic peak. By mid-decade the United States was plunging into the next stage of the arms race, intercontinental rockets for delivering nuclear weapons. A nuclear arms race whose logic had "no connection to experience or reality" was taking over. Eisenhower and the American people insisted on "clear American superiority. How they would use that lead—except to insure deterrence, which could be assured with one hundred bombs anyway—they did not know."

Historians [such as H. W. Brands] have faulted "the inadequacy of [Eisenhower's] leadership, combined with the intractable problems he faced" and his administration's "overblown rhetoric," for creating "an atmosphere in which consideration of defense issues became nearly impossible." Beyond that was a dilemma that Eisenhower barely grasped. The New Look involved a resort to technology to contain militarization—new weapons were to cut costs by minimizing force levels and averting limited wars. Drawing on an American tradition of seeking technological solutions to problems created in part by technology, it aggravated the very militarization that Ike hoped to arrest. Militarization was a qualitative phenomenon, not just a quantitative one measurable by the size of budgets or armies. The New Look accelerated it at its most technically exquisite, and exquisitely dangerous, nuclear core. Any other President might have done worse in that regard, but the higher standard of success Eisenhower set for himself makes the judgment on him more severe—as he soon felt.

Since his successors rarely did better in these matters, however, he alone was obviously not the problem. Beyond him lay a political culture hardly his to control. Humphrey's private complaint about "scientists" and "vested interests" suggested one facet of the problem. Ike could claim greater wisdom than generals and admirals, but for him to complain publicly about the pressures of scientists and other experts was virtually impossible—it would have smacked of the anti-intellectualism and cramped vision already imputed to Eisenhower and his associates too often for their political comfort. To challenge Gen. Maxwell Taylor was one thing; to dispute Edward Teller was another at a time when so much wisdom and objectivity were attributed to scientists.

One controversy over nuclear weapons did give Ike a chance to challenge the scientists' authority. A test in the Pacific of an American hydrogen bomb in 1954 stirred alarm about its sheer explosive power, but even more about the fallout that contaminated Americans, area natives, and nearby Japanese fishermen (their fate ominously resonant with August 1945). Eisenhower publicly doubted scientists' infallibility, announcing that "this time something must have happened that we have never experienced before, and must have surprised and astonished the scientists." Privately, he said that after the current American tests he would be "willing to have a moratorium on all further experimentation" with nuclear weapons.

Instead he vacillated, then drifted with the tide of experts seeking more tests, more bombs, and more vehicles to carry them. His New Look strategy was one reason, but also his desire for elite control, which public debate now threatened to erode. Dissident scientists and grass-roots activists formed new organizations. Books— Nevil Shute's *On the Beach* (1957), Walter Miller's *A Canticle for Leibowitz* (1959), Mordecai Roshwald's *Level 7* (1959)—widened debate. The Soviets grandstanded with new proposals to end the arms race. Neutrals like India, hardly wishing to bathe in the fallout of Soviet and American tests, enlivened a global debate. Charged cultural symbols were at play—Strontium-90 was entering the food chain, poisoning the milk mothers fed babies.

Eisenhower was not immune to the anxieties expressed in this widening debate. Had a strong challenge to nuclear policy emerged within his policy apparatus, he might have acted forcefully: in that arena, similar to the one he knew as a commander, he could be confident and courageous. But insiders critical of the arms race were few—Eisenhower as much as anyone, and he discouraged the criticism he also sought by his choice of scientific advisors and by his willingness to see [the Manhattan Project physicist and H-bomb opponent J. Robert] Oppenheimer forced out. A lifetime's habits made him distrust the unpredictable anxieties of outsiders. Repeatedly he considered blunt efforts to inform Americans of the nuclear danger. Repeatedly he backed away, sensing that public alarm was as likely to undermine efforts at disarmament as to strengthen them. Already in 1953, when the scientist Vannevar Bush had taken up "the case for scaring the people into a big tax program to build bomb defenses," Ike had seen "the dangers in telling too much of the truth." His distrust of public candor was not unfounded, but his chosen course served him no better. . . .

Earth's first artificial satellite went into orbit on October 4, 1957, on a Soviet rocket. Weighing less than two hundred pounds, it had no practical utility, although larger Soviet satellites and canine cosmonauts soon followed, but its symbolic import seemed incalculable, as Soviet premier Nikita Khrushchev appreciated, so eager was he to change the perception of Soviet backwardness.

If Sputnik was bait in a propaganda war, leading Americans swallowed it whole, naively or for calculated purposes. A cascade of dire warnings, expressions of humiliation, and calls for action flowed. Sen. Henry Jackson called for a "national week of shame and danger." Congressman Daniel Flood, rejecting fiscal limits on national action, cried, "I would rather have red ink in the books than red blood on the streets of America." Senate Majority Leader Lyndon Johnson proclaimed that "control of space means control of the world," with its possessor able to impose "tyranny" or "freedom." Foreseeing the miraculous developments Americans often have expected of technological change, Johnson argued that the winners in space would be "masters of infinity" able to "control the earth's water, to cause drought and flood, to change the tides and raise the levels of the sea, to divert the gulf stream and change the climates to frigid." . . .

Hard issues of power and survival were ostensibly at stake. If Soviet rockets were powerful enough to launch satellites, it was reasoned, they could strike the United States: massive retaliation seemed hollow, Khrushchev's boasts about his rockets irrefutable, Eisenhower's defense policy bankrupt. Given that dire situation, some members of the Eisenhower-appointed Gaither committee saw as the only recourse an attack on the Soviet Union before its lead in rocketry became insurmountable. Less trigger-happy Cold Warriors rejected that option, only to see a different danger. The Soviets, John Kennedy warned, now had a "shield" of bombs and rockets "behind which they will slowly, but surely, advance—through Sputnik diplomacy, limited brush-fire wars, indirect nonovert aggression, intimidation and subversion, internal revolution, increased prestige or influence, and the vicious blackmail of our allies. The periphery of the Free World will slowly be nibbled away. The balance of power will gradually shift against us." The United States, argued politicians like Kennedy, could only return to the principles of NSC-68, building up both strategic forces and conventional ones capable of "flexible response." . . .

Old worries that the United States was becoming an empty, hedonistic nation also surfaced again, yielding calls to recapture the frontier spirit and jeremiads against complacency and materialism that Puritan divines might have admired. Once emblems of its superiority, the nation's cars and television sets now seemed tokens of its rot. "If America ever crashes, it will be in a two-tone convertible," the venerable financier-politician Bernard Baruch predicted; the United States had to worry less about the "height of the tail fin in the new car and be more prepared to shed blood, sweat, and tears if this country and the free world are to survive," argued one senator. Although the space program was later sold as a fountainhead of technological abundance, unease about that abundance deepened the Sputnik panic.

Like most panics, this one was not a reaction to a single event but a state of mind built over time. That was evident in an array of proposed crash programs for fallout shelters, new weapons, and new strategies. Scientists aggravated and exploited the panic, as when one group approached Eisenhower with a plan to reach the moon by using "elegant little [nuclear] bombs to drive an elegant little spaceship around the solar system," as one scientist later put it. Reworking fears of a closed society and world-system that had haunted Americans for decades, scientists promoting new ventures in space thought it "essential to the growth of any new and high civilization that small groups of people can escape from their neighbors and from their governments, to go and live as they please in the wilderness." Panic also sanctioned lavish military schemes, as [the journalist] I. F. Stone discovered in the congressional testimony of an air force general who proposed that warheads "could be catapulted from shafts sunk deep into the moon's surface" and argued that if a lunar balance of terror then developed between the superpowers, stations could be built "on planets far more distant, from which control over the moon might then be exercised." Such schemes hardly enjoyed unanimous military support, but Stone could be excused for concluding: "Thus, as the Pentagon maps it, peace by mutual terror would spread outward toward the far stars." The Sputnik panic seemed to have no boundaries.

Eisenhower tried mightily to reestablish them. The psychology of the panic should not have shocked him, insofar as his strategy of massive retaliation already had rested on the psychological mysteries of deterrence and the symbolic import of new technology. Nonetheless, he was baffled by the Sputnik scare, partly because of his attachment to elite control and his reluctance to admit its erosion. His inability to articulate a visionary alternative to Cold War and militarization compounded his problems. For all its banality and hysteria, reactions to Sputnik did reveal a broad yearning for something more daring than he could provide. For good reasons, he would not embrace a race to the moon, agreeing with his first National Aeronautics and Space Administration director that if the nation's prestige rested on "'When do we get a man on the moon?'" then "all sense of perspective has gone out the window." But Ike offered no substitute. . . . Four years later, Ike was still uncomprehending, contemptuous of JFK's decision to stake national prestige on a race to the moon.

Uncomprehending he may have been, uncertain he was not. His effort to dampen hysteria and restrain militarization dominated the rest of his presidency. His primary asset was the enormous authority in military matters he still commanded. A general abandoned by most of his lieutenants (though not by Dulles and the CIA), he still gained a tactical victory in a losing campaign against the forces of militarization. "It was one of his finest hours," writes [the Eisenhower biographer] Stephen Ambrose. "The demands for shelters, for more bombers, for more bombs, for more research and development of missiles and satellites, [were] nearly irresistible," but Eisenhower rejected them. "He thereby saved his country untold billions of dollars and no one knows how many war scares."

A cold calculation of strategic realities guided him. Khrushchev might threaten the United States with extinction, but Ike knew it was a bluff. Secret flights by American U-2 aircraft—the evidence Ike would not make public, lest it infuriate the Soviets or terminate the reconnaissance—revealed that the Soviets were deploying few long-range rockets and could not match America's formidable heavy bombers. Knowing that, Eisenhower decided to leapfrog large-scale production of costly and combustible first-generation rockets in favor of advanced solid-fuel rockets (land-based Minuteman and sub-based Polaris missiles). Tied to that decision was a broader acceptance shared by Dulles of rough strategic parity with the Soviets, a heresy that helped prompt the strident charges of appeasement. Hardly neglecting America's military might, he was keen to maintain its qualitative lead, but numbers alone, nuclear "overkill" as it was now called, counted for little with him as he questioned, "How many times do we have to destroy Russia?" The armed forces were getting "into an incredible position—of having enough to destroy every conceivable target all over the world, plus a three-fold reserve," he complained. Even if the United States escaped direct attack and won a nuclear war, "there just might be nothing left of the Northern Hemisphere" because of fallout (atmospheric tests alone, he worried, might produce that result). . . .

Sometimes grudgingly, Eisenhower did agree to changes: a new National Aeronautics and Space Administration (NASA); a presidential science advisor (James Killian and then George Kistiakowsky, who helped offset science hawks like Teller); modest increases in weapons and space programs; reorganization of the Department of Defense. But, as he commented on one supplemental budget he accepted, two-thirds of it went "more to stabilize public opinion than to meet any real need." As before Sputnik, he supported space programs meeting scientific curiosity and military needs—the reconnaissance capacities of satellites were especially alluring—but scorned the prestige-driven race in space.

Despite his effort to restrain militarization—and because of the exceptions he allowed in order to placate public opinion and meet his own test of vigilant defense— his success was only rearguard and temporary. By one standard it was considerable: defense budgets rose only modestly in Ike's last years. Pressure kept building for more money, programs, and forceful action, however, its power emerging more sharply under his successors.

Defense-related spending on science and technology measured those forces. Such spending remained hard to calculate because much of it was buried in non-defense budgets, went to technologies with both civilian and military uses, or had little military payoff. Moreover, the share of federal research and development spending devoted to defense was declining (the National Institutes of Health budget increased tenfold over the decade). But since total R&D budgets increased dramatically (to 15.6 percent of the budget by 1965), defense-related spending still swelled: the Defense Department's R&D budget nearly doubled between 1958 and 1961, while NASA's multiplied tenfold. . . .

Some progress in Soviet-American negotiations was made, but it was bedeviled by many obstacles. Britain and France, eager to develop their own nuclear weapons (and, in the French case, to aid Israel's development as well), threw up roadblocks. Leaders vacillated: Eisenhower worried that a unilateral suspension of American tests would prompt Democrats to say, "This is our Munich"; Khrushchev worried that on-site inspections would expose Soviet weakness and bluster. . . .

Strategic doctrine mirrored and exacerbated the pressures involved, as theorists, officers, and policymakers scrambled to impart rationality and equilibrium to a system spinning out of control. From one vantage point, stability seemed foreseeable. Prevailing American doctrine assumed a balance of terror in which each superpower deterred the other's initiation of nuclear war with its threat of a devastating response. Refined as "mutual assured destruction" (MAD), this doctrine implied that once superpowers gained rough parity, they would have powerful incentives to stabilize the competition—money would be saved, worried constituencies reassured, and the dangers of surprise minimized. Superiority might even be dangerous if it led the weaker power, fearful it could never survive a first strike, to launch such a strike itself.

Despite that finely spun argument, stability was unattainable: external pressures disrupted it, logical inconsistencies arose within it, and logic never fully governed strategy anyway. Given the Soviet rocket capability supposedly revealed by Sputnik, American strategists argued for a "second-strike" force able to survive an enemy first strike and still respond devastatingly. Building such a force, however, required missiles on submarines and in hardened silos, cost billions, drove the Soviets to reply in kind, and further ratcheted up the arms race. Costs went still higher as strategy shifted from "city-busting" to destroying enemy military forces. It seemed more humane and effective to target those forces, but since they were far more numerous, scattered, and protected than cities, "counterforce" strategy required far more missiles with far more sophisticated guidance systems. . . .

Still, the balance of terror held, and perhaps underwrote what [the historian] John Gaddis has called the "long peace" of the Cold War. The symbolic value of nuclear weapons certainly implied a kind of functional restraint: they were there for show, not for use, it often seemed. Did peace endure because of the balance of terror or despite it? The answer may be both: the terror that stayed the nuclear powers from plunging into the abyss also drove them to its edge. It also encouraged them to tolerate, promote, or enter non-nuclear wars that scared many other nations; this was a "long peace" only by the essential but singular standard of avoiding nuclear war. And what restrained the superpowers was less some *balance* of terror than mutual terror at the prospect of nuclear war, regardless of whether one side had an edge in it. They were, that is, deterred as much by their own weapons as by the enemy's, not because Americans were restrained while Soviets were reckless, or because American superiority forced a truculent enemy to back away from war. A psychological more than a military construct, the balance of terror rested less on forces than on attitudes, ones shared by superpower elites who proclaimed hatred of each other.

And it barely did hold, never more precarious than in the late 1950s and early 1960s. No episode demonstrated its fragility more than the Berlin crisis of the winter of 1958–1959. Berlin itself still stood oddly close to 1945: even in West Berlin the rubble of wartime bombing remained evident; no border guards stopped traffic between the east and west sectors; and both sectors still seemed "the pets of the occupation powers." But the dazzle of the West's Kurfurstendamm [West Berlin's commercial shopping area] mocked the drabness of Communist East Berlin, however prosperous it was by East European standards. Khrushchev, for various possible reasons—frustration and embarrassment over the drain of population and talent out of East Berlin into the West, or fear that West Germany might soon gain control of NATO nuclear weapons—precipitated the crisis, issuing a stream of menacing metaphors: "West Berlin has become a sort of malignant tumor" and "we have decided to do some surgery"; Berlin was "a bone in my throat" and "the testicles of the West. Every time I give them a yank, they holler." Many did holler when he demanded an agreement to end the Allied occupation of Berlin, make West Berlin a demilitarized free city, and establish East Berlin as East Germany's capital—and when he hinted at another Berlin blockade if he did not get his way.

Eisenhower's response was measured in the face of formidable pressures. Most NATO allies supported his cautious response, but not so many Americans. A dying Dulles spoke bitterly of spending billions on defense only to have "appeasement and partial surrender" threaten "to be our attitude." The armed forces pressed Ike to plan a military effort to break any blockade. Congressional leaders renewed their calls to increase the defense budget. Journalists asked about using NATO forces or nuclear weapons in the event of blockade. In all cases, Eisenhower rejected the pressures outright or sharply scaled back the plans urged on him. Keen to ease "pressures at home for precipitous action," he responded to questions about liberating Berlin with nuclear weapons in his typically flat style: "Well, I don't know how you could free anything with nuclear weapons." . . . Publicly he held fast to Allied rights and privately he weighed the nuclear option, but Khrushchev's ultimatum passed without incident in May. Essentially, Eisenhower talked his way out of the crisis—indeed, refused to treat it as crisis—but not before many Americans thought a nuclear war might begin. Stability, and peace itself, again seemed to pivot on him.

Berlin was only one tilt in the see-saw of events that sent hopes for detente alternately soaring and sinking. Nixon's visit to Moscow in July 1959 yielded the Kitchen Debate and a stream of vulgarities: Khrushchev likened one recent congressional action to "fresh horse shit, and nothing smells worse than that!"; Nixon retorted that "the Chairman is mistaken. There is something that smells worse than horse shit—and that is pig shit." A visit by Khrushchev to the United States produced the celebrated "spirit of Camp David," plus fury on the American right (William F. Buckley, Jr., condemned having a visitor who "profanes the nation"). Eisenhower embarked on globe-trotting diplomacy to round up allies for detente, but just as hopes for a breakthrough peaked in the spring of 1960, the Soviets shot down an American U-2 spy plane. When Khrushchev and Eisenhower bungled into a loud exchange of lies, accusations, and threats about the incident, the fragile process of summit diplomacy shattered. . . .

With his inauguration [in January 1961], John Kennedy said, the torch "passed to a new generation of Americans," those "tempered by war" and "disciplined by a hard and bitter peace." But the generational change JFK proclaimed was unclear. His youth was striking, but he also drew for advice on elders like [former High Commissioner to West Germany] John McCloy and [former Secretary of State] Dean Acheson. Both generations had experienced World War II, but older men like Eisenhower had held high rank in it and were familiar with prewar suspicions of militarism, while men like Kennedy knew little of those suspicions, waged war from lesser positions, and had their outlook more decisively shaped by the war. Proud of their ability to break from their elders, they were nonetheless more the prisoners of World War II than Eisenhower's generation.

Moreover, the very notion of a torch passed also presumed continuity: the newcomers stood in Eisenhower's shadow and sought his blessing. When Eisenhower and Kennedy discussed Southeast Asia on January 19, complex political and generational relationships were at play. Kennedy insiders later recalled that Eisenhower's insistence on Laos as "the most important problem facing the United States" had done "a disservice to the incoming Administration," in Clark Clifford's summary. "You might have to go in there and fight it out," perhaps "'unilaterally,'" Ike warned, according to Ted Sorensen and Arthur Schlesinger, Jr. But other accounts show that Eisenhower used such phrases to more ambiguous effect. Unilateral intervention, while not ruled out, "would be very bad for our relations" in Asia, he said, at best "a last desperate effort" in a region where communists had many advantages. . . .

Whatever the thrust of Eisenhower's advice on the 19th, his televised farewell address to the nation two days earlier had a different focus. Ike told Americans they were in a global conflict that "absorbs our very beings" and—again urging the long view—"promises to be of indefinite duration." As a result, the United States had been "compelled to create a permanent armaments industry of vast proportions," along with huge, costly armed forces. "The total influence" of this new system—"economic, political, even spiritual—is felt in every city, every State house, every office of the Federal government." He enjoined Americans to "guard against the acquisition of unwarranted influence, whether sought or unsought, by the military-industrial complex. The potential for the disastrous rise of misplaced power exists and will persist." Alarming also was "the prospect of domination of the nation's scholars by Federal employment, project allocations, and the power of money" and "the equal and opposite danger that public policy could itself become the captive of a scientific-technological elite." And as he had before, he linked these dangers to ecological perils, warning against "the impulse to live only for today, plundering, for our own ease and convenience, the precious resources of tomorrow."

What did he mean? In one way, his comments were shrewdly exculpatory. Militarization had been forced on America by dangerous enemies and technologies—it was not *his* nation's fault. What happened on his watch was "compelled," while avoidable dangers (the "*potential* for the disastrous *rise* of misplaced power") lay ahead. *He* had held the line; lesser men might not.

Yet his farewell address also held a darker view of militarization and his own role in it. By describing its influence as "economic, political, even spiritual," he suggested that whatever its origins, militarization was taking on a life of its own apart from the world scene, becoming woven into the fabric of American life. Moreover, "the conjunction of an immense military establishment and a large arms industry" had already occurred, while *he* was President, whatever abuses lay in the future. And regarding disarmament, acknowledged Eisenhower, "I confess that I lay down my official responsibilities in this field with a definite sense of disappointment." Just as striking were the omissions in the address—no summons to greater vigilance against the enemy, no recitation of trouble spots in the world, and little talk of the enemy's evil. The address was remarkably inward-looking, calling for Americans to be vigilant not against enemies but themselves. Just as the Cold War was reaching a new intensity, he directed attention away from it. . . .

Yet unwittingly Eisenhower had also aggravated that problem. By skillfully balancing conflicting needs and by keeping cold war from erupting into hot war, he had made the pursuit of national security congruent with dominant aspirations for peace and prosperity. His successors could turn his success against him: if power abroad and prosperity at home were compatible, how much more could be—had to be—achieved regarding both if greater efforts were made? The Kennedy administration was just as keen to balance "the defense effort against the other demands of the economy," wrote Schlesinger in 1965, but like many liberals who saw national resources as expansive, "it believed—correctly—that the balance could be achieved at a much higher level." Ike's message about limited resources and balancing goals ("balance" appeared seven times in one sentence of his farewell) was undercut by his own success in juggling peace, prosperity, and power.

Eisenhower's Reckless Nuclear Gamble over the Taiwan Strait

GORDON H. CHANG AND HE DI

Eisenhower and most American historians have given September 3, 1954, when Chinese Communist shore batteries opened fire on the Nationalist-held offshore island of Quemoy, as the beginning of a crisis that lasted for almost nine months. Most Western accounts have assumed that the Communist leadership ordered the shelling as part of a centrally directed military campaign that was at least a probe of

Reprinted by permission of the authors from Gordon H. Chang and He Di, "The Absence of War in the U.S.-China Confrontation Over Quemoy and Matsu in 1954–1955; Contingency, Luck, Deterrence?" *American Historical Review* 98 (December 1993), 1502, 1504–1505, 1507–1523.

the strength of the U.S. security commitment to Quemoy, if not the beginning of an actual effort to seize the island. Washington reacted to the shelling by dramatically increasing the U.S. military presence in the Taiwan Strait, strengthening Nationalist defenses, and issuing increasingly stern warnings to Beijing over the following months. To bolster its commitment to the Nationalists, the Eisenhower administration completed negotiation of a mutual defense treaty and received a blank check from Congress in early 1955, the so-called Formosa Resolution, for the use of American forces to defend Taiwan island and the nearby Pescadores.

The Chinese documentary record of high-level decision making at that time, however, does not indicate that Beijing considered September 3 shelling a precipitant event or even an unintentional initiation of a confrontation with the United States. Furthermore, the Chinese documentary record does not show that China's leaders considered the period from September 1954 to late April 1955 to be especially tense. In contrast to former U.S. officials who vividly recollected the main events, high-level Communist officials and advisers active during the 1950s and interviewed for this essay did not recall the September 3 bombardment or consider the time one of sharp conflict with America. . . .

Other observers at the time, including forces friendly to the United States, also evaluated the September 3 shelling of Quemoy, and the subsequent events in the offshore island area, in a different light than did Washington. The British government saw the activity as part of the latest round of feuding between the Nationalists and the Communists that had broken out during the summer of 1954, and it was not convinced that the Communists intended to attack Quemoy or were even principally interested in the island. The Nationalist military high command also expressed in private its belief that the Communists were only probing U.S. intentions with the shelling and were not about to launch an all-out assault on Quemoy. On September 10, the Chinese Nationalist Party organ, *Central Daily News,* dismissed the mainland's "Liberate Taiwan" campaign, which began in late July 1954, as simple propaganda and the Quemoy shelling as part of a political, rather than military, campaign.

Why, then, did the Eisenhower administration mistakenly assess the situation and consider the shelling the start of a deliberate military confrontation? In September 1954, U.S. antipathy toward the Chinese Communists and fear of their international ambitions ran high in the aftermath of the Korean War and the Vietnamese Communist defeat of the French in Indochina during the spring of 1954. The United States had steadily increased its attention to the South China Sea and China mainland offshore area for some time before September 3. U.S. ambassador to the Nationalists, Karl Rankin, and military intelligence had both warned of the possibility of trouble, including the danger of a Communist attack on Quemoy months earlier. And two U.S. men in uniform, members of the Military Assistance Advisory Group, had been killed in the Communist bombardment, which was more serious than previous sporadic shelling.

In addition, and perhaps more important, the Eisenhower administration became alarmed because the September 3 attack apparently demonstrated the failure of previous U.S. efforts at deterrence. In the spring and summer of 1954, the United States had twice sent ships of the Seventh Fleet to the Dachens (offshore islands along the Zhejiang coast) in a show of force to impress the Communists. As late as

August 20, less than two weeks before the Quemoy shelling, Secretary of State John Foster Dulles sent a strong message of reassurance to the U.S. ambassador to Japan, who had communicated to Washington his own and the Japanese government's worries about possible Communist military activity in the offshore area. Dulles pointed out that because of his recent article in *Foreign Affairs,* which advanced the doctrine that later became known as "massive retaliation," he was certain that Beijing and Moscow fully appreciated the U.S. resolve to oppose Communist aggression. . . .

What was the actual purpose of the shelling that so disturbed U.S. officials? The memoir of General Ye Fei, the Communist commander of the Fujian forces responsible for the bombardment of Quemoy, reveals that orders Beijing sent on August 25 instructed Ye Fei to shell Quemoy, not as a preliminary to an assault on the island but as a specific and limited response to what was perceived as an increase in U.S. and Nationalist military provocations in the area and the rumored negotiation of a mutual defense treaty between Washington and Taibei [Taipei, capital city of the Republic of China (ROC)]. It was Ye Fei personally, not the central authorities, who recommended September 3 for the shelling for the simple reason, General Ye believed, that the Nationalists planned to supply the island by ship on that day. Communist shelling of Quemoy after September 3 in 1954 and 1955 was, in fact, infrequent and light. . . .

The order to Ye Fei reflected the thinking of Mao Zedong, China's commander-in-chief, about the Taiwan Strait. Convinced that the United States fully endorsed the Nationalist harassment of the mainland, Mao held Washington responsible for the mounting tensions in the area before September 1954 and firmly believed that Beijing was the defender, not the aggressor, in the Strait. Isolated in the international community, with relatively limited information, and with Leninist assumptions about the relationship of imperialism and semi-colonies, Mao could not know that there were serious strains in the U.S.-Nationalist relationship or that Washington, uneasy about the Nationalist activities, wanted to limit Chiang Kai-shek's attacks on mainland forces. He mistakenly assumed that Chiang was little more than a puppet of the United States. In addition, Mao questioned the sincerity of Washington's professed desire to reduce tensions with the Communist world after the 1954 Geneva Conference. As a result, he concluded that China had to respond to the perceived U.S.-Nationalist provocations that occurred in late 1953 and early 1954.

Mao was especially worried that a U.S.-Nationalist mutual defense treaty, reports of which began to circulate in China in mid-1954, would play a role similar to that of the cease-fire in Korea and the Geneva agreement on Vietnam, which had formalized the division of those two close neighbors of China. He had no idea that substantial differences existed between the Eisenhower administration and Chiang over the proposed treaty. Thus, on July 23, Mao sent a telegram to Zhou Enlai, who was en route from Geneva to Beijing, which admonished,

> in order to break up the collaboration between the United States and Chiang and to keep them from joining military and political forces, we must announce to our country and the world the slogan of the Liberation of Taiwan. It was improper of us not to raise the slogan in a timely manner after the cease-fire in Korea. If we were to continue dragging our heels now, we would be making a serious political mistake.

After Zhou's return to China, Mao convened a political bureau meeting at the leadership retreat at Beidaihe, where he presented, in his typically grand style, general guidelines for a propaganda campaign for the Liberation of Taiwan, the first such campaign against Taiwan in the history of the People's Republic.

In Mao's view, the conflict with the Nationalists in the Strait occurred on political, diplomatic, and propaganda fronts. Politically, acquisition of Taiwan was central to the unification of Chinese territory, and China could not accept any treaty arrangement between the United States and the Nationalists that formally separated Taiwan from the mainland or established an independent status for Taiwan. Diplomatically, the conflict was part of the struggle with the United States and a test of whether Washington's announced intention to relax tensions with the socialist camp was real. Militarily, the People's Liberation Army could respond to Taiwan's military harassment, gain control over the Dachen offshore islands, and use the opportunity to train its forces. In terms of domestic propaganda, the campaign for Taiwan would help rekindle the enthusiasm of the Chinese people for New China after the conclusion of the Korean and Vietnam conflicts. The country would have the slogan "We Must Liberate Taiwan" to rally around, providing both a goal for which to strive and a new external enemy to oppose. . . .

Over the years, [Mao] had accumulated much experience in using controlled military action for discrete political purposes. He often used his armed forces to raise tensions and to dramatize his political position, such as in the offensives of the People's Liberation Army in northeast China during George C. Marshall's mission to China in 1945–1946 and during the armistice negotiations in Korea. The bombardment of Quemoy was exactly such a political-military demonstration, as the Chinese Nationalist observers on Taiwan had correctly surmised in the *Central Daily News*. Large-scale "armed propaganda" might be another description of the effort. The shelling was part of Mao's attempt to focus world attention on the Taiwan issue and what he believed was U.S. interference in Chinese internal affairs.

In contrast to the shelling of Quemoy for political purposes, Mao saw the campaign to take the Dachen Islands as essentially a military operation. To be clear, Mao saw the two theaters, Quemoy and the Dachens (which were under two separate military commands), in very different ways. He considered the shelling of Quemoy to be essentially political and low risk, since he believed he could easily control the action and avoid widescale conflict in the region, as there would be no direct military contact between Communist and U.S. personnel. The assault on the Dachens was another matter. Mao estimated that it carried a higher risk, since the possibility of direct clashes with U.S. armed forces was much greater. Thus Mao and the Chinese central command, unlike the Eisenhower administration, paid almost no attention to Quemoy but closely followed the Dachens campaign. The Central Committee's confidential instruction on the Liberate Taiwan campaign, circulated on July 24, stated, "At present, the direct target of our military struggle is Chiang Kai-shek [Jiang Jieshi] and his cohorts in Taiwan. The United States should not be treated as our direct target; we should confine the conflicts with the United States to the diplomatic arena only."

As for the relationship of the activities directed against the offshore islands to the military liberation of Taiwan, China's leaders were under no illusion that they could soon successfully assault Chiang's main island fortress. In a leadership directive on September 25, the CCP Central Committee observed that the capture of Taiwan was a "long-term and complex struggle" and was a strategic rather than immediate task. "We are not able to liberate Taiwan without a powerful navy and air force and need time to build them up." . . .

Eisenhower, assuming that the Communists did present a military challenge, described his own policy in the offshore area after the September 3 shelling as one of "keeping the enemy guessing" whether the United States would actually involve itself in a battle over Quemoy and Matsu. Dulles later aptly described this policy in private as deterrence through uncertainty. This strategy was adopted for several reasons, which included Washington's own questions about overall Communist objectives, Eisenhower's insistence on avoiding rigid commitments and maintaining flexibility of action, and administration concern about the lack of domestic and international support for further U.S. involvement in the offshore island area. At the heart of the matter, though, was the U.S. dilemma that the president, while supporting Chiang on Taiwan, did not want to be pinned down to a commitment of indefinite length to any of the offshore islands, over a hundred miles away from Taiwan and insignificant militarily in his eyes. . . .

If Washington, instead of avoiding explicit commitments to the defense of the offshore islands, had consistently demonstrated its determination to defend the islands, Mao would not have been likely to approve the assault on the Dachens. For example, in the middle of July 1954, the Central Military Commission ordered the Yijiangshan campaign to begin in September or October, and on August 10, the East Military Headquarters approved preparations for the actual attack on Yijiangshan. On August 20, the Headquarters asked the Central Military Commission to approve the assault for sometime between September 1 and 5. But, on August 21, when Mao learned of the high level of American attention to the area, he ordered that the campaign start only when there were no U.S. ships and aircraft present. In this instance, U.S. military deterrence was successful; its naval presence raised the strong possibility of direct American involvement and made the Communists pause. The attack was delayed for several months.

But U.S. deterrent efforts were not consistent. In early December, release of the terms of the Mutual Defense Treaty revealed that its provisions expressly covered only Taiwan and the Pescadores, not the Dachens and other offshore islands. Before the treaty's provisions were known and because of the vagueness of the Eisenhower administration's position, Mao had wondered whether Washington would directly involve itself in combat over the offshore islands; after the disclosure of the treaty terms, he and his military commanders concluded that the United States would not join in active defense, since the treaty omitted specific mention of the offshore islands. He therefore allowed the commanders to go ahead with their military campaign. Mao drew conclusions directly opposite to those Eisenhower and Dulles had hoped to encourage with the treaty.

Mao nevertheless proceeded cautiously. On November 30, just before the release of the terms of the Mutual Defense Treaty, Su Yu, the chief of staff of the People's Liberation Army, ordered the Yijiangshan attack to start around December 20. But, on December 11, because of a new U.S. naval maneuver in the Dachens, Mao countermanded Su Yu's order and again postponed the campaign for a month. Even on the eve of the assault on Yijiangshan, the central leaders in Beijing considered further delaying the operation, as they worried about U.S. intervention if the campaign did not end quickly. Beijing asked General Zhang Aiping if he could guarantee success in the operation, and if he could not, he was to wait longer. Zhang, however, argued that "the arrow was in the bow" and had to be shot. He maintained that the United States, according to his intelligence sources, would not become involved; that technical and morale considerations required action; that it would not be possible to keep the plan to take Yijiangshan secret much longer; and that he had the "right" to select the specific timing for a local campaign. His insistence moved Mao to compromise and, thus, he deferred to Peng Dehuai, head of the army, to make the final decision. Peng approved Zhang's request, and the assault took place the next day. On January 18, 10,000 PLA troops in the People's Republic's first large-scale coordinated air, sea, and land operation overwhelmed 1,086 Kuomingtang soldiers on Yijiangshan, inflicting heavy losses.

On February 8, Chiang, under mounting pressure from the United States, announced he would withdraw from the vulnerable Dachens, which he did with U.S. help on February 12. In a major operation, U.S. ships evacuated 14,000 civilians and 10,000 Nationalist troops with their equipment from the islands; and People's Liberation Army troops, without firing a single shot, then occupied them and the Nanji, the last of the Zhejiang offshore islands. While the quick and smooth military victories achieved by the People's Liberation Army greatly encouraged and emboldened some local commanders (they wanted to continue and expand the campaign to include bombing Taiwan itself), Mao stopped such thinking and criticized their proposals as adventurist. What is more, he came to conclude that while the Zhejiang coastal operations had been military successes, they had been political failures, since they attracted more U.S. attention than expected and raised the danger of direct military conflict with the United States. Mao decided it was time to try to reduce tensions in the region; he did not want military operations to press any further.

Mao was right about the adverse consequences of the Dachens campaign. The capture of the Zhejiang islands by the People's Liberation Army led Washington to conclude that the Communists, rather than ending their "Liberate Taiwan" campaign, were intent on escalating the crisis and perhaps even assaulting Taiwan itself. The subsequent dramatic U.S. response, in turn, increased tensions. Ironically, Mao believed that he had taken a cautious and restrained path, while U.S. leaders concluded that China's leaders were aggressive and bent on war. As Eisenhower wrote in his diary on March 26, "the Red Chinese appear to be completely reckless, arrogant, possibly overconfident, and completely indifferent as to human losses."

Rather than deterring Communist action, Eisenhower's policy of keeping the enemy guessing had sent mixed signals to Beijing, which contributed to the Communist decision to assault Yijiangshan. For his part, Mao had underestimated the effect Beijing's actions and propaganda would have on Washington. Although attentive to the U.S. reaction, he had little sense of the extreme measures Eisenhower officials were then discussing (such as widespread bombing of Chinese industrial and military facilities and the use of nuclear weapons) as a response to what Washington believed was China's preparation for large-scale hostilities in the Strait. By misinterpreting each other's intentions and signals, both sides, in taking what each considered to be prudent and justifiable actions, contributed to an increasingly dangerous situation.

In addition to displaying military support for the Nationalists and making other deterrent efforts, the United States also energetically explored diplomatic means of negotiating an end to the crisis. . . .

But factors on the Chinese Communist side, of which Eisenhower was apparently not aware or to which he was not entirely sensitive, also made efforts at a negotiated approach problematic, if not virtually impossible. Washington had taken what it considered were serious measures to meet what it perceived as China's military challenge in the Strait, such as making shows of force there, strengthening the Nationalist defenses on the offshore islands, and issuing repeated warnings to the Communists. Nevertheless, by February 1955, Mao concluded that Washington would not go to war over the offshore islands, and therefore the enhanced U.S. military posture was primarily for psychological purposes. . . .

Beijing also concluded that the non-coercive efforts pursued by Washington indicated it was not ready to engage again in direct, widespread military conflict with China. These efforts included having third parties such as Britain, Sweden, and India urge China and Taiwan to take their dispute to the UN; having Nationalists withdraw from the Dachens with U.S. help; and urging China through the UN and various other channels to accept a cease-fire proposal. Not only Mao interpreted Washington's behavior as contradictory and as sending mixed signals; U.S. ambassador Karl Rankin also made this point in a personal note to assistant secretary [of state] Walter Robertson after the Nationalists withdrew from the Dachens. "It is almost impossible," he wrote, "to overestimate the danger of confirming the Reds in a belief that, despite recent strong statements by the Secretary and others, we are for peace at any price. Withdrawal from the Dachens undoubtedly strengthened them in this belief." To correct this misimpression, Rankin advocated a military engagement with the Communists to convince "the enemy that we mean business." Rankin had accurately anticipated Mao's reaction—U.S. diplomatic efforts were undercutting the credibility of its coercive efforts.

Since the United States did not pose a genuine threat to China in Mao's eyes, Beijing could continue to keep pressure on to split the allied camp and weaken the main enemy, the United States, without risking widespread conflict. As a Central Committee comment on British-Chinese relations put it, maintaining the campaign against Taiwan would "enlarge the contradiction between England and the United States."

The effort to divide the enemy camp was part of Mao's version of "brinksmanship," what Dulles described as his own policy of averting war by going to the edge of war to intimidate one's adversary. Mao had a similar view of war and war avoidance, reflected in the CCP's instruction titled "U.S. Interference in the Question of Our Liberation of Taiwan," issued on February 21, while Dulles was on tour in Asia. "Regarding Washington's call for a 'cease-fire' and its threat to start a war," the instruction pointed out, "if we show any fear, the enemy will consider us weak and easy to bully. In other words, if we give them an inch, they will take a mile and intensify their military expansion. Only by adopting an unyielding, resolute, and calm stance can we force the enemy to retreat." In its interpretation of the lessons of history, the Chinese Communist Party observed that the September 18th Incident, when Japan invaded Manchuria in 1931, and the 1938 Munich compromise showed that peace cannot be obtained through appeasement: "Therefore, we must adopt an intransigent stance against the United States." As part of that stance, Beijing rejected Washington's diplomatic efforts, advanced formal diplomatic proposals that it knew were unacceptable to the United States (although, at the same time, Zhou Enlai quietly suggested direct bilateral talks between the United States and China; his initiative will be discussed below), and persisted with a strident anti-U.S. campaign and a "Liberate Taiwan" campaign at home, which was one of Mao's main interests in the first place.

Thus Mao's own brinksmanship and China's inflexible declared position had little to do with "maintaining face," as Eisenhower once argued in an effort to explain Chiang's and "Oriental" behavior during the crisis. Instead, the perceived absence of a fully credible U.S. threat, Beijing's own tactical considerations, and concern for Chinese domestic politics all contributed to frustrating the diplomatic efforts of the United States. Eisenhower's dismissal of the diplomatic stalemate as being a result of Chinese preoccupation with "face" and of fanaticism was obviously too simple and avoided confronting the political complexity of the dispute between the Nationalists and Communists and the sophistication of the tactics each Chinese side employed.

After the People's Liberation Army ended its large-scale military operations off the Zhejiang coast with the taking of the Dachens, the situation in the Taiwan Strait should have stabilized. Dulles himself observed on March 9 that there was a "lull" in activity in the Strait, and some U.S. intelligence reports noted that the amount of belligerent Communist propaganda in late February and early March had fallen to its lowest point since the summer of 1954. The Eisenhower administration, however, again misjudged the situation and concluded that the Communists were continuing their preparation for aggression. Dulles saw the lull not as Beijing's effort to lessen tensions but as just the opposite. He concluded that the Communists were engaged in "a large-scale build up." It was this misassessment that led the United States to escalate tensions in mid-March, and the crisis lurched toward open hostilities. . . .

The administration began to think increasingly about preemptive military options to end the threat, including the use of nuclear weapons against Communist capabilities in the offshore area. The administration's alarm was reflected in dramatic White House discussions on March 10 and 11 during which the use of military force, including nuclear weapons, was extensively discussed and in the administration's repeated public warnings that it was prepared to use nuclear weapons against China. On March 16, Eisenhower himself frightened an American public by stating at a press conference that he saw no reason why nuclear weapons could not be used "as you use a bullet or anything else," in the event of war in the Taiwan Strait. . . .

The administration's belief that the situation required decisive steps led to the formulation of a secret Eisenhower-Dulles plan that included Chiang's withdrawal from Quemoy and Matsu, a U.S. blockage of five hundred miles of China's coastal waters opposite Taiwan, and the stationing of nuclear weapons on Taiwan so long as Beijing called for the "liberation" of the island. At the climax of the crisis, Eisenhower sent [Chairman of the Joint Chiefs of Staff Admiral Arthur] Radford and Robertson to present the proposal to Chiang in mid-April, but Chiang, not wanting to surrender any further territory and not fully trusting Washington, rejected it.

Neither Beijing nor Washington had wanted direct conflict, and Chiang's acceptance of the evacuation and blockade plan would have brought the situation

precipitously close to inadvertent war. As a provocative "fait accompli," the blockade would have invited Communist retaliation, including clashes between U.S. and
Chinese forces. Even Radford himself anticipated such a turn of events. The proposal "meant war," the U.S. ambassador to Taiwan remarked when he heard the
details of the plan, just before it was presented to Chiang.

American specialists suggest that Chinese Premier Zhou Enlai delivered his
famous statement at the Bandung Conference [of nonaligned nations in Indonesia]
in late April 1955 about China's peaceful intentions as a direct response to Washington's coercive efforts and that it constitutes evidence of the effectiveness of
Dulles's threat of "massive retaliation." It hardly seemed coincidental that Zhou
spoke at virtually the same moment that Radford and Robertson, known to be hard-
liners against China, were in Taiwan talking with Chiang. Soon after Zhou offered
his remarks, however, Dulles confidentially told associates that "diplomacy and not
merely force" had played a large part in producing Zhou's statement. Dulles claimed
that U.S. political work with Asian allies had led China to "follow a pacific rather
than belligerent course." It appears that Dulles's surmise was right, at least partly.
Zhou's speech was an impromptu response to discussion he had had with Asian delegates at Bandung, but it was neither specifically planned by the Beijing leadership
before Bandung nor presented as a response to U.S. nuclear threats.

In early April 1955, before Zhou Enlai's departure for Bandung, Indonesia, the
political bureau of the Chinese Communist Party met to discuss general policy
toward the conference. Party leaders at this meeting decided that China's delegation
was to seek common ground between China and other Asian countries and keep
differences to a minimum. Zhou was to try to establish new relationships with
China's neighbors [such as nonaligned India and Indonesia] based on the recently
formulated five principles of peaceful coexistence. In order to achieve this goal, the
Chinese delegation decided that they would not raise controversial issues, including
the Taiwan question, at the conference. Zhou was given full power to handle the situation during the meeting, which was held from April 18 to 24.

Despite Zhou's desire to avoid discussing Taiwan, and although he barely mentioned the issue publicly at the conference, many Asian leaders privately asked Zhou
about the situation in the Strait. Finally, the day before the meeting's conclusion,
toward the end of a luncheon with a number of Asian delegation leaders at the residence of the Indonesian prime minister, Zhou was again asked about the tensions in
the offshore area. Zhou responded that China distinguished the conflict between the
mainland and Taiwan from that between China and the United States. Taiwan was an
internal question and linked to the Chinese civil war, he stressed, but the tension
between China and the United States was an international matter, which China was
willing to discuss with Washington. Zhou's off-the-cuff conciliatory comments surprised many of those present, who were urged not to speak publicly about them to
avoid creating misunderstandings. Zhou was also asked, however, if he would make
a general public statement, and later in the afternoon of the same day, China's delegation issued a brief press release containing his views. The haphazard manner by
which Zhou's comments were delivered indicate that the presentation of his proposal
was unplanned. Zhou himself believed his statement reflected general policy that had
already been expressed, that adhered to Mao's point of view, and that was not a departure from China's previous position.

Upon learning of Zhou's remarks, the Eisenhower administration responded positively to what it considered to be a significant step on China's part, and tensions quickly subsided in the offshore island area. Although the build-up of military capabilities by both the Nationalists and Communists continued, direct talks between Washington and Beijing soon began. . . .

Zhou's conciliatory statement appeared to the Eisenhower administration by late April to be the last possible way off the "horns of the dilemma," as Dulles had put it. The Radford-Robertson mission to Chiang had failed, military tensions were high, European and Asian allies of the United States were deeply fearful of war, and Zhou's comments had won widespread support among Asian nations. The Eisenhower administration, under tremendous domestic and international pressure, finally had to respond positively.

With the material now available from the Chinese side, it is possible to advance a number of revised or new historical evaluations of the crisis. Beijing was partially successful in conducting a controlled military campaign to achieve political ends (bringing world attention to the Taiwan issue) and limited territorial objectives (the capture of Yijiangshan, the Dachens, and other Zhejiang offshore islands). The campaign also resulted in direct discussions between China and the United States, something in which Beijing had been interested for some time.

However, it could also be said, as Mao himself acknowledged, that the campaign set back China's interests in certain respects. Mao had been mistaken about U.S.-Nationalist relations and did not anticipate that his campaign would help push ahead the conclusion of the Mutual Defense Treaty or the Formosa Resolution that gave the president unrestricted authority to deploy U.S. forces in the defense of Taiwan. The treaty became a major political link between Washington and Taibei and later was one of the last obstacles to the eventual rapprochement between China and the United States in the 1970s. (The Formosa Resolution also formed a historical precedent for the 1964 Gulf of Tonkin Resolution that handed over war-making powers to President Lyndon Johnson in Vietnam.) Moreover, the Strait campaign contradicted Mao's wish to reduce tensions in the Southeast Asia region and damaged China's prestige with some of its Asian neighbors. . . .

As for the Eisenhower administration, it, too, made mistakes during the crisis. It fundamentally misunderstood the political nature of China's "Liberate Taiwan" campaign and thus played into it. It was the U.S. escalation of the crisis that helped bring world attention to the Strait, as well as dangerously exacerbated tensions there, especially in April 1955. But, most important, the Eisenhower administration erred in its belief that its effort at deterring China from assaulting Quemoy and Matsu was effective. The Quemoy-Matsu crisis of 1954–1955 is not an example of successful deterrence, since there was not an immediate, specific threat to these two island groups. (While it could be said that the United States succeeded in a general effort at deterrence of Chinese military activity in the Strait, since the U.S. presence did make Beijing cautious in its plans toward Taiwan island, this is another matter.) In addition, the Eisenhower administration made important concessions to both the Nationalists (namely, the Mutual Defense Treaty) and the Communists (bilateral talks). Its nuclear threats against the mainland not only stiffened Communist resolve, they also helped convince Beijing to launch its own nuclear weapons program. And through it all, the status of Quemoy and Matsu remained contested, ready to draw the United States into other highly charged confrontations with the mainland, as eventually happened in 1958 and in 1962.

 # F U R T H E R   R E A D I N G

Robert Accinelli, *Crisis and Commitment* (1996) (on Taiwan)

Stephen E. Ambrose, *Eisenhower: The President* (1984)

Robert Axelrod, *The Evolution of Cooperation* (1984)

Howard Ball, *Justice Downwind: America's Atomic Testing Program in the 1950s* (1986)

Michael R. Beschloss, *Mayday: Eisenhower, Khrushchev, and the U-2 Affair* (1986)

Timothy J. Botti, *Ace in the Hole* (1996)

Robert Bowie and Richard H. Immerman, *Waging Peace* (1998)

H. W. Brands, "The Age of Vulnerability: Eisenhower and the National Insecurity State," *American Historical Review,* 94 (1989), 963–989

McGeorge Bundy, *Danger and Survival* (1988)

Craig Campbell, *Destroying the Village: Eisenhower and Thermonuclear War* (1998)

Gordon H. Chang, *Friends and Enemies* (1992) (on China)

Ira Chernus, *Eisenhower's Atoms for Peace* (2002)

Ian Clark, *Nuclear Diplomacy and the Special Relationship* (1994)

Blanche Weisen Cook, *The Declassified Eisenhower* (1981)

Frank Costigliola, "The Nuclear Family: Tropes of Gender and Pathology in the Western Alliance," *Diplomatic History,* 21 (1997), 163–184

Richard Damms, *The Eisenhower Presidency* (2003)

Robert A. Divine, *Blowing on the Wind: The Nuclear Test Ban Debate* (1978)

———, *Eisenhower and the Cold War* (1981)

———, *The Sputnik Challenge* (1993)

Saki Dockrill, *Eisenhower's New Look National Security Policy* (1996)

Michael Evangelista, "Cooperation Theory and Disarmament Negotiations in the 1950s," *World Politics*, 42 (1990), 502–528

———, *Innovation and the Arms Race* (1988)

Lawrence Freedman, *The Evolution of Nuclear Strategy* (1981)

Aaron L. Friedberg, *In the Shadow of the Garrison State* (2000)

John Lewis Gaddis, *The Long Peace* (1987)

——— et al., *Cold War Statesmen Confront the Bomb* (1999)

Alexander L. George and Richard Smoke, *Deterrence in American Foreign Policy* (1974)

Alexander L. George et al., eds., *U.S.-Soviet Security Cooperation* (1988)

Fred I. Greenstein, *The Hidden-Hand Presidency* (1982)

Morton H. Halperin, *Nuclear Fallacy* (1987)

Margot Henriksen, *Dr. Strangelove's America: Society and Culture in the Atomic Age* (1997)

Greg Herken, *Counsels of War* (1985)

Richard G. Hewlett and Jack M. Holl, *Atoms for Peace and War* (1989)

David Holloway, *The Soviet Union and the Arms Race* (1983)

Townsend Hoopes, *The Devil and John Foster Dulles* (1973)

Richard H. Immerman, "Confessions of an Eisenhower Revisionist," *Diplomatic History,* 14 (1990), 319–342

———, *John Foster Dulles* (1998)

Robert Jervis, *The Meaning of the Nuclear Revolution* (1989)

Robert H. Johnson, *Improbable Dangers* (1994)

Fred Kaplan, *The Wizards of Armageddon* (1983)

Milton S. Katz, *Ban the Bomb: A History of SANE* (1986)

Douglas Kinnard, *President Eisenhower and Strategy Management* (1977)

Henry Kissinger, *Nuclear Weapons and Foreign Policy* (1957)

Stewart W. Leslie, *The Cold War and American Science* (1992)

Walter A. McDougall, *The Heavens and the Earth* (1985)

Laura McEnany, *Civil Defense Begins at Home* (2000)

Shane J. Maddock, ed., *The Nuclear Age* (2001)

Michael Mandlebaum, *The Nuclear Revolution* (1981)

Frederick W. Marks III, *Power and Peace* (1993)

George T. Mazuzan, "American Nuclear Policy," in John M. Carroll and George C. Herring, eds., *Modern American Diplomacy* (1986), pp. 147–163

Richard A. Melanson and David Mayer, eds., *Reevaluating Eisenhower* (1987)

Charles R. Morris, *Iron Destinies, Lost Opportunities* (1988)

John Newhouse, *War and Peace in the Nuclear Age* (1988)

Frank A. Ninkovich, *Modernity and Power* (1994)

Chester J. Pach, Jr., and Elmo Richardson, *The Presidency of Dwight D. Eisenhower* (1991)

Herbert S. Parmet, *Eisenhower and the Great Crusades* (1972)

Richard Pfau, *No Sacrifice Too Great: The Life of Lewis L. Strauss* (1984)

William B. Pickett, *Dwight David Eisenhower and American Power* (1995)

Joseph E. Pilate et al., *Atoms for Peace* (1986)

Ronald E. Powaski, *March to Armageddon* (1987)

Ronald W. Pruessen, *John Foster Dulles* (1982)

Stephen G. Rabe, "Eisenhower Revisionism: A Decade of Scholarship," *Diplomatic History,* 17 (1993), 97–115

Ron Robin, *The Making of the Cold War Enemy* (2001) (on the military industrial complex)

Peter J. Roman, *Eisenhower and the Missile Gap* (1995)

David Alan Rosenberg, "The Origins of Overkill," *International Security,* 7 (1983), 3–71

———, "Reality and Responsibility: Power and Process in the Making of United States Nuclear Strategy, 1945–68," *Journal of Strategic Studies,* 9 (1986), 35–52

Walt W. Rostow, *Open Skies* (1982)

Gerard Smith, *Disarming Diplomat* (1996)

David L. Snead, *The Gaither Committee, Eisenhower, and the Cold War* (1999)

Thomas F. Soapes, "A Cold Warrior Seeks Peace: Eisenhower's Strategy for Nuclear Disarmament," *Diplomatic History,* 4 (1980), 55–71

"Symposium: The Soviet Threat to Western Europe: A Roundtable," *Diplomatic History,* 22 (1998), 399–449

Strobe Talbott, *The Master of the Game: Paul Nitze and the Nuclear Peace* (1988)

Philip Taubman, *Secret Empire* (2003) (on space espionage)

William Taubman, *Khrushchev* (2003)

Marc Trachtenberg, *History and Strategy* (1991)

———, "A 'Wasting Asset': American Strategy and Shifting Nuclear Balance, 1949–1954," *International Security* (1988–1989), 5–49

Sheldon Ungar, *The Rise and Fall of Nuclearism* (1992)

J. Samuel Walker, *Containing the Atom* (1992) (on proliferation)

Robert J. Watson, *Into the Missile Age, 1956–1960* (1997)

Samuel F. Wells, "The Origins of Massive Retaliation," *Political Science Quarterly,* 96 (1981), 31–52

Andreas Wenger, *Living with Peril: Eisenhower, Kennedy, and Nuclear Weapons* (1997)

Samuel Williamson and Steven L. Rearden, eds., *The Origins of U.S. Nuclear Strategy* (1993)

Pascaline Winand, *Eisenhower, Kennedy and the United States of Europe* (1993)

Lawrence Wittner, *The Struggle Against the Bomb* (1998)

———, *Toward Nuclear Abolition* (2003)

Cold War Culture and
the "Third World"

*As several of the selections and documents in previous chapters demonstrate,
historians of American foreign relations in recent years have become increasingly
interested in the cultural aspects of international relations. The word* culture *is
difficult to define. Anthropologists and cultural theorists have advanced a working
definition that describes culture as a constellation of values, beliefs, symbols, and
language around which a society develops and maintains a sense of identity and a
means of interpreting the outside world. Since the eighteenth century, cultural
identity has usually intersected with national identity or, in the words of the international studies scholar Benedict Anderson, the imagined community in which
modern men and women feel a sense of commonality and communion. The history
of international relations lends itself to analysis of cultural and national identities.
We live in an age of globalization, where economic, technological, environmental,
political, cultural, and other developments have connected people, nations, and
regions in distant parts of the world. With roots that reach back to the age of European exploration and expansion, globalization accelerated during the twentieth
century. Breathtaking developments in aviation and rocketry seemed to shrink the
planet. Modern communications, long-distance telephone, television, and most
recently computers revolutionized business, politics, entertainment, and news
reporting. Accelerating world trade and investment stepped up the international
exchange of goods, services, and ideas. Global integration brought together the
world's peoples and nations as never before—sometimes producing culture clash
and at other times spawning intercultural cooperation. This chapter explores the
cultural dynamics of U.S. relations with the "Third World," or non-Western World,
during the early post–World War II years.*

    *The era of intensified globalization was also the era of the Cold War and de-
colonization in Asia, the Middle East, and Africa. The decline of colonialism transformed international politics—creating thirty-seven new nations between 1945
and 1960. U.S. officials and the American public at times sympathized with the
anticolonial movements, which reminded them of their own break from the British
Empire in 1776. But national security officials refrained from embracing the new
states when doing so undermined the position of colony-holding allies, unleashed*

unrest that threatened U.S. economic and strategic interests, or created opportunities for Soviet expansion. They assigned the label Third World *to the emerging nations and Latin America, a Cold War term that signified their geopolitical location outside of U.S. and Soviet spheres in Europe, their "undeveloped" or "underdeveloped" economies and their political instability. But the terminology lent a misleading coherence to the rich mosaic of regions, peoples, and cultures that constituted the non-Western world. To influence the new states, Washington relied on a number of mechanisms: trade agreements and cultural exchanges; military aid and economic assistance; diplomatic nonrecognition—China (1949) and Cuba (1961); covert operations and coup attempts—Iran (1953), Guatemala (1954), British Guiana (1959), and Cuba (1961); and military interventions—Korea (1950–1953), Lebanon (1958), the Dominican Republic (1965), and South Vietnam (1954–1975). Regardless of tactics, non-Western societies often resisted management by outsiders.*

Historians of American foreign relations examine several manifestations of cultural interaction. First, they explore the many ways in which cultural perceptions of self and of "others" can affect foreign policy decisionmaking. Although national security experts pride themselves on their ability to rationally assess power, interests, and threats, cultural analysis suggests that policymakers can be swayed by nonrational or irrational factors. Societies engage in what theorists call cultural discourses or, more simply put, ongoing conversations about shared beliefs and assumptions, such as notions of class, race, and gender; attitudes toward sexuality; or perhaps the meaning of nationhood and civilization itself. The discourse is dominated by society's most powerful people, and in twentieth-century America that usually meant upper-class white males. When U.S. policymakers during the early Cold War confronted inscrutable non-Western leaders, they no doubt viewed the "other" through an American cultural prism. At times, officials fell back on popular constructions of race and gender and considered Third World friends and foes alike to be backward and inferior, unmanly, or annoyingly obstinate. Fiery nationalists, such as Prime Minister Mohammed Mossadeq of Iran or President Kwame Nkrumah of Ghana, might be written off as childlike or effeminate. Deciphering nationalists from communists often challenged U.S. officials, in part because the Soviets did cultivate Third World friends and allies, but more often because the cultural and linguistic terrain was unfamiliar. This does not necessarily mean that cultural perceptions were more important than political, strategic, or economic considerations in policymaking, but they provided context that significantly shaped U.S. attitudes and actions.

A second arena of cultural interaction that is increasingly the object of study is the internationalization of culture itself. Whether it be the widespread popularity of rock 'n roll, the status of English as an international language, or the worldwide love affair with the cell phone, peoples of the world increasingly show evidence of building a common culture. The immigration and emigration of peoples encourage the sharing of customs and traditions. International travel and tourism, student exchange programs, and multinational business transactions blur boundaries and national identities. Peace movements, the women's rights lobby, and human rights organizations operate globally. Following World War II, the international struggle for decolonization by people of color dovetailed with the African-American struggle for civil rights in the United States. In the early 1960s, just before the United States geared up for a domestic War on Poverty, President John F. Kennedy launched the Peace Corps, a program that sent thousands of young, idealistic volunteers to rural villages in Africa, Asia, Latin America, and the Middle East to promote education and economic development. European, Soviet, and Canadian youth participated in

similar humanitarian efforts, sponsored either by governmental or private agencies.
Thus societies are capable of intercultural cooperation as well as culture clash.
Indeed, some analysts speculate that, for better or worse, the world's cultures are
becoming less distinct and more homogeneous. Others disagree and point to enduring
ethnic and religious conflicts, the continuing power of nationalism, and contrasting
codes of etiquette, gender relations, and family structure as evidence that cultural
differences survive and thrive. Skeptics are quick to observe, moreover, that even the
most noble American overseas undertakings, including the Peace Corps, have usually
contributed to Washington's self-interested global agenda.

   How do cultural perceptions, and misperceptions, influence the conduct of
American foreign policy and relations? How important is culture to the making
of U.S. diplomacy? To what extent is culture becoming globalized? These questions
are essential to an understanding of modern international relations.

 # D O C U M E N T S

Although the subject of U.S. relations with the non-Western world is expansive, three
examples illustrate key themes in Cold War cultural interactions. First, Iran's nationalist
prime minister Mohammed Mossadeq struck a blow against British imperialism in
June 1951 when he nationalized the Anglo-Iranian Oil Company. Concerned that the
flow of Middle East oil to postwar Europe and Japan might be disrupted, the Truman
administration worked to arbitrate the dispute between Tehran and London. Both the
British and the Iranians beseeched Washington for its support. Document 1 is a letter
from Prime Minister Mohammed Mossadeq to President Truman, dated June 11, 1951,
in which the Iranian leader denounces the exploitative practices of the British-owned
oil firm, offers to consider any proposal that is not contrary to the principle of nationalization, and assures the president that oil supplies will not be affected. As the crisis
dragged on, American sympathy for Iran dwindled, and U.S. officials became annoyed
by Mossadeq's tough bargaining posture. On July 28, 1952, U.S. ambassador Loy Henderson vented his frustration in a telegram to the State Department in Washington, D.C.,
reprinted here as Document 2. The cable lamented Mossadeq's anti-Americanism
and questioned the prime minister's mental stability. Scholars have noted the Western
tendency to dismiss non-Western adversaries by racially stereotyping them as "emotional" and "unstable." When the administration of Dwight D. Eisenhower took command in early 1953, Washington became alarmed by Mossadeq's contacts with Iran's
Communist Tudeh party, and CIA operatives worked covertly with Iranian supporters
of the Shah Reza Pahlavi to depose the prime minister. The new regime reversed the
nationalization of the oil industry, and U.S. oil companies received lucrative concessions. In the decades that followed, the United States became a stalwart ally of the
Shah's pro-Western regime—until its overthrow by Islamic followers of the Ayatollah
Khomeni in 1979.

   A second example of cultural relations, President John F. Kennedy's Peace Corps,
generated a very different kind of interaction. First proposed on the presidential campaign trail in the fall of 1960, the program resembled overseas development work
carried on by a number of European and Canadian volunteer agencies. Concerned that
congressional debate would delay the program, Kennedy launched the Peace Corps by
executive order on March 1, 1961, and named his brother in-law Sargent Shriver as
director. The president's statement upon signing the order appears here as Document 3.
As a U.S. senator and presidential candidate, Kennedy had voiced support for Third

World nationalism and economic development, both of which he viewed as antidotes to communism. After becoming president, he took a special personal interest in the Peace Corps. Document 4 is a photograph of Kennedy meeting with some of the program's earliest recruits. Soon thousands of youthful volunteers fanned out across the globe—assisting economic development and educational projects, representing America abroad, and learning firsthand about non-Western cultures and peoples. Of course, volunteers' experiences varied widely, but although many governments distanced themselves from U.S. Cold War policies, relations between Peace Corps volunteers and local populations tended to be warm. In a letter written to Peace Corps headquarters, Document 5, one of the first volunteers stationed in the African nation of Ghana offered advice to future volunteers. Knowledge of the local language, an acceptance of hard work, and a sense of humor seemed to win Ghanaian approval.

A third example of cultural interaction, the rising tide of North American tourism in the only partially autonomous U.S.-sponsored Commonwealth of Puerto Rico during the 1950s and 1960s, illustrates that cultural relations also occur on a people-to-people basis. During the 1920s developers popularized Miami, Havana, Bermuda, and the Bahamas as Caribbean-Atlantic retreats, but during the early Cold War years American affluence, efficient air travel, and modern advertising ushered in the age of mass tourism, and the competition stiffened. The Commonwealth of Puerto Rico used its newly acquired authority to invest public funds, subsidies, and tax breaks to jumpstart its tourism industry. Document 6 is a memo from Esteban A. Bird, a Puerto Rican tourism official, to Governor Luis Muñoz Marín, dated January 17, 1949, that lays out the Commonwealth's carefully planned strategy to woo North American visitors. Over the next decade the island's tourism boomed—especially after Fidel Castro's Communist revolution in late 1958 discouraged travel to Cuba, and advertisers portrayed Puerto Rico as a Cold War paradise. Document 7 is a photograph of the Caribe Hilton Hotel shortly after its opening in December 1949. The luxurious ocean-front resort captured the essence of modernity that appealed to U.S. travelers, yet it was owned and built by the Commonwealth government. Although many Puerto Ricans welcomed the tourists as a source of income and prestige, others viewed the influx of vacationers as a second Yankee invasion. Document 8 is a political cartoon that appeared in San Juan's Spanish-language independentista newspaper *Claridad*. It pokes fun at American tourists who blame the omnipresence of American street names in Puerto Rico on the island's unimaginative natives. The rickshaw image symbolizes the exploitative nature of the tourist trade.

1. Iranian Prime Minister Mohammed Mossadeq Defends the Nationalization of Oil, 1951

Concerning the nationalization of the oil industry in Iran I have to assure you, Mr. President, that the Government and Parliament of Iran, like yourself desire that the interests of the countries, which hitherto have used the Iranian oil should not suffer in the slightest degree. As, however, you have expressed the apprehension of

This document can be found in Text of Message from Prime Minister Mosadeq to President Truman, June 11, 1951, Papers of Harry S. Truman, President's Secretary Files, Harry S. Truman Library, Independence, Missouri. It can also be found in Dennis Merrill, ed., *Documentary History of the Truman Presidency, Vol. 29* (Bethesda, MD.: University Publications of America, 2000), 55–59.

the United States and it would seem that the matter is not fully clear to you, I ask permission to avail myself of the opportunity to put before you a cursory history of the case of the measures which have now been adopted.

For many years the Iranian Government have been dissatisfied with the activities of the former Anglo-Iranian Oil Company, but I feel it would be beyond the scope of this letter and would cause you undue trouble if I attempted to set forth in detail the exactions of that company and to prove with unshakable documentary evidence that the accounts of the company have not corresponded with the true facts and that even in their disclosed accounts, the share they have earmarked for the Iranian people, the sole owners of the oil, has been so meagre as to rouse the indignation of all fair-minded persons.

The Iranian people have suffered these events for a good many years, with the result that they are now in the clutches of terrible poverty and acute distress, and it has become impossible to continue this tolerance, especially with the situation brought into existence in this country by the second world war.

No doubt you will recall, Mr. President, that during the war Iran collaborated fully and most sincerely with the Allies for the ultimate triumph of right, justice and world freedom, and that she suffered untold hardships and made many sacrifices. During the war all our productive resources were directed day and night to carrying out large-scale plans for the transfer of ammunitions, the supply of foodstuffs and other requirements of the Allied armies. These heavy burdens, borne for several years, disorganized and weakened our finance and economy and brought us up against a series of very grave economic problems, with the result that the labouring classes of this country who had toiled for the Allies throughout the war, were faced with an unbearable rise in prices and wide-spread unemployment.

Had we been left alone, after the termination of war, we could have dealt with the situation brought about by the war, restored normal conditions and managed to move back to the depopulated villages the peasants who had been drawn to war work on roads and in factories, thus improving agriculture.

Had we been given outside help like other countries which suffered from war, we could soon have revived our economy, and even without that help, could have succeeded in our efforts had we not been hampered by the greed of the company and by the activities of its agents.

The company, however, always strove by restricting our income to put us under heavy financial pressure, and by disrupting our organizations to force us to ask its help and, as a consequence, to submit to whatever it desired to force upon us.

Secret agents on the one hand paralysed our reform movements by economic pressure, and on the other hand, on the contention that the country had enormous sources of wealth and oil, prevented us from enjoying the help which was given to other countries suffering from the effects of war.

I ask you in fairness, Mr. President, whether the tolerant Iranian people, who, whilst suffering from all these hardships and desperate privations, have so far withstood all kinds of strong and revolutionary propaganda, without causing any anxiety to the world, are not worthy of praise and appreciation, and whether they had any other alternative but recourse to the nationalization of the oil industry, which will enable them to utilize the natural wealth of their country and will put an end to the unfair activities of the company.

Having thus given a short summary of the motives which have led to nationalization of the oil industry in Iran, I wish to refer you, Mr. President, to the text of the law, and I hope you will agree that the two Houses of the Iranian Parliament have not deviated from the path of right and justice, and that the law, as repeatedly announced from the tribunes of both Houses and in various interviews, does not authorize the confiscation and seizure of property, but on the contrary envisages and gives security for the repayment of damages and losses, and that furthermore, it gives special consideration to the continuation of oil supplies to those countries hitherto using Iranian oil, and explicitly safeguards the viewpoints of former customers.

It is now a month since the law and the method of execution of the principle of the nationalization of the oil industry in Iran were ratified by both Houses of Parliament and received the Royal signature, and, although the law has decreed an immediate dispossession, and the government is under extraordinary pressure from public opinion impatiently demanding the dispossession of the former oil company, the government and the mixed committee appointed by the two Houses of Parliament have given careful study to the means of putting the law into force in the best possible way so that no disruption may occur in the exploitation of oil from the various centers and in the continuity of the flow of export.

The first evidence of the truth of this contention and the good-will of the Imperial Iranian Government is to be found in the provisions which have been communicated to the representatives of the former oil company, the most important of which are mentioned below:

1. So long as the status of the National Iranian Oil Company is not approved by the two Houses of the Iranian Parliament, the basis of operations of the temporary board of directors shall be the regulation devised by the former oil company (except insofar as such regulation [*sic*] are contrary to the law of nationalization of the oil industry).
2. The foreign and Iranian experts, employees and labourers of the former oil company shall remain in service as before, and shall henceforth be recognized as employees of the National Iranian Oil Company.
3. The temporary board of directors will take the utmost care to execute existing programmes and to increase the production of oil so that the level of production and exploitation shall be raised above the present level. . . .

Lastly the former oil company has been given the opportunity to submit immediate proposals, provided they are not contrary to the principle of the nationalization of the oil industry, and the government has promised to consider these proposals.

The aim of the Iranian Government and the mixed committee in adopting the above measures has been the continuation of the flow of oil to the consumer countries—an aim which has been your immediate concern.

You may rest assured, Mr. President, that the Iranian people are desirous of maintaining their friendship with all nations and especially with those, like the British nation, which have had age-long relations with them. . . .

I avail myself of this opportunity to offer to you, Mr. President, the expressions of my highest and most sincere regards and to wish the continuous progress and prosperity of the great American nation.

2. U.S. Ambassador Loy Henderson Questions Mossadeq's Mental Stability, 1952

During last two days I have recd various hints, including one from son, that Mosadeq was ready for me to call. Accordingly, I visited him yesterday evening. Our conversation, which lasted nearly two and half hours, was both exhausting and depressing. As I listened to him I cld not but be discouraged at thought that person so lacking in stability and clearly dominated by emotions and prejudices shld represent only bulwark left between Iran and communism. As during several previous conversations, I had feeling at times that I was talking with someone not quite sane and that therefore he shld be humored rather than reasoned with. On occasions he resorted to such silly exaggerations and extravagances it seemed almost useless to talk further. At one point I almost decided to abandon our conv when he rptd again and again in monotone that "Iran wld never, never want UK and US to have any differences over it. Iran wld prefer go Communist than cause any trouble between US and UK." There were periods during our talk when he seemed lucid and sensible. Gen impression which he left was however one of deterioration. I have noticed in past that in evenings he is likely to be more tired and to have less control over his emotions. I can only hope his behavior last evening was due to strain of recent events and fatigue and does not indicate serious degeneration.

I shall not attempt to outline conversation but will merely touch on those portions which seem to me to be more important and which may enable Dept have better understanding his present frame of mind. . . .

Mosadeq launched into bitter attack upon US foreign policy. He said US had no diplomacy. US in Mid-East was merely agent Brit. Manifestations of anti-Americans as witnessed during recent days had shown how great had been failure so-called US diplomacy in Iran. US had given billion dollars aid to Turkey and yet when Iran was bankrupt and on verge communism, it had refused finan assistance first because it feared that if Iran shld be able operate its own oil industry US oil interests in Saudi Arabia and elsewhere might suffer and, secondly, because it as afraid of Brit displeasure. I told Mosadeq that American interests in internatl oil were really of secondary nature and did not govern our policies re Iran.

Mosadeq said even certain Brit were charging that US, because of fear of effect of US oil concessions in other countries, did not wish Brit to compromise in oil dispute with Iran. I again emphasized that effects of possible settlement on US oil concessions in various parts world did not play major role in our policies re Iran. I added that in any event it did not seem likely that countries in which there were Amer oil concessions wld be tempted follow Iran's example. I had already on various occasions tried to make clear to him it wld not be in interest free world for us to give Iran finan aid in circumstances which might cause Brit and Amer public opinion to believe that US was subsidizing Iran's position re oil dispute. At this point Mosadeq began to chant that Iran wld prefer to go Communist that for US and UN [*UK*] to have differences of opinion with regard to it. Eventually, I was able to tell

This document can be found in The Ambassador in Iran (Henderson) to the Department of State, 28 July 1952, *Foreign Relations of the United States 1952–1954* (Washington, D.C.: Government Printing Office, 1989), X, 416–421.

him that US choice was not merely between US–UK friction and Iran going Communist. I stressed that if serious misunderstandings shld develop in present world situation between US and UK, Iran wld go Communist anyway. . . .

Mosadeq placed great stress on Communist danger facing Iran. He said Iranian army was no longer stabilizing factor. It was now hated by all Iranians. Iranian army, under orders [of former prime minister Ahmad] Qavam, who was Brit agent, had fired on and killed hundreds Iranians. Iranian people, therefore, considered army as tool Brit. I asked Mosadeq if he as MinWar, wld not be able by certain measures restore prestige army. He insisted too late. Nothing cld save army now. In fact, army was now danger to country since many officers and men, humiliated at their present unpopularity, might at any moment try to get back into public favor by taking leadership in revolt of Communist character. This revolt might not be fomented gradually. It might break out at any moment.

I asked Mosadeq if there was anything he cld tell me re future mil aid and mil missions. Various kinds rumors were afloat re his attitude on these subjects. He replied he not prepared to talk to me at present. He wld take matter up later. Any recommendations which might be circulated had no basis. He had not discussed his intention re mil missions and aid with anyone. . . .

Reverting to oil problem Mosadeq described briefly suggestion which he had made to Middleton. He made no request of me and I stated that I was glad that direct conversation on subject had been opened with Brit.

As I was preparing depart, Mosadeq said he hoped I wld not take amiss frankness his comments to me. It had been his practice to talk on personal basis rather than that of PriMin addressing Amb. He believed his country and govt were in great danger and he cld not understand why US, which was supposed to be so friendly to Iran shld not show friendship by action. I told Mosadeq that US was in many ways trying to help Iran. He laughed and said if we were really trying assist by other than words, we were certainly succeeding in hiding our helpful activities.

3. President John F. Kennedy Launches the Peace Corps, 1961

I have today signed an Executive Order providing for the establishment of a Peace Corps on a temporary pilot basis. I am also sending to Congress a message proposing authorization of a permanent Peace Corps. This Corps will be a pool of trained American men and women sent overseas by the U.S. Government or through private institutions and organizations to help foreign countries meet their urgent needs for skilled manpower.

It is our hope to have 500 or more people in the field by the end of the year.

The initial reactions to the Peace Corps proposal are convincing proof that we have, in this country, an immense reservoir of such men and women—anxious to sacrifice their energies and time and toil to the cause of world peace and human progress.

This document can be found in Statement by the President upon Signing Order Establishing Peace Corps, 1 March 1961, *Public Papers of the President: John F. Kennedy, 1961* (Washington, D.C.: Government Printing Office, 1962), pp. 134–135.

In establishing our Peace Corps we intend to make full use of the resources and talents of private institutions and groups. Universities, voluntary agencies, labor unions and industry will be asked to share in this effort—contributing diverse sources of energy and imagination—making it clear that the responsibility for peace is the responsibility of our entire society.

We will only send abroad Americans who are wanted by the host country—who have a real job to do—and who are qualified to do that job. Programs will be developed with care, and after full negotiation, in order to make sure that the Peace Corps is wanted and will contribute to the welfare of other people. Our Peace Corps is not designed as an instrument of diplomacy or propaganda or ideological conflict. It is designed to permit our people to exercise more fully their responsibilities in the great common cause of world development.

Life in the Peace Corps will not be easy. There will be no salary and allowances will be at a level sufficient only to maintain health and meet basic needs. Men and women will be expected to work and live alongside the nationals of the country in which they are stationed—doing the same work, eating the same food, talking the same language.

But if the life will not be easy, it will be rich and satisfying. For every young American who participates in the Peace Corps—who works in a foreign land—will know that he or she is sharing in the great common task of bringing to man that decent way of life which is the foundation of freedom and a condition of peace.

4. JFK Enlists Youth and Idealism in the Peace Corps, 1961

Photo from John F. Kennedy Library, Boston, Massachusetts.

5. A Peace Corps Volunteer Describes
Life in Ghana, 1964

What is the reaction of different groups to the Peace Corps volunteers? The students tend to be very much in favor of the volunteers. I have heard of no instances of trouble with anti-American students. On the contrary, they try to emulate you in every way possible. This may manifest itself in a broad American accent, or in an attempt to copy the teacher's mannerisms. They are also interested in any and all things American. American music is extremely popular, especially rock and roll and the twist.

The great majority of Ghanaians also show a great liking for the Americans. I leave the newspapers out of this, because the two party newspapers, the *Evening News* (C.P.P. paper) and the *Ghana Times* (official government paper), tend to take a neutral to pro-Eastern stand on most matters. However, you will find, I think, a great well of good feeling for us here. I must say that the Peace Corps has not hurt this feeling. It certainly has not hurt for us to know some of the Twi language.

The knowledge of their language has a profound effect on the villagers. You don't have to know too much, but if you have the proper answer to a greeting, it raises your prestige a great deal. They will laugh at you but they are proud that you are making the attempt to speak their language. Oh yes, the proper answer to '*Broni*' when it is yelled at you, is '*Bibini.*' This seems to make a big hit, in my area anyway.

As for the British and American communities in Ghana, for the most part you will find them to be very friendly and helpful people. Of course, there is bound to be the individual who makes your hackles rise. There is one Englishman who makes me angry every time I see him, but he has the same effect on the British, so I am not too worried. You will find that this type of person is in a distinct minority. The British tend to be a little distrustful of most Americans, because they tend to raise the cost of living by paying exorbitant prices to workers and traders. This cannot be said of the volunteers, though, as we don't get the salaries other Americans do and have to watch our money fairly carefully.

The Americans have been willing to give us any help we may desire. They are generally a pleasant bunch of people, again with the occasional exception to the rule, and will bend over backwards to make you comfortable. The only people who are hard to get to know are the Russians. There are a great many here, and more are coming. At present, most of them are up north, or in Accra. They travel in groups and talk little, if at all, with anyone outside the group. They are the closest thing I have seen to the so-called Ugly American image.

They are even somber when they go to the Lido. The Lido is a local nightspot which has a bad reputation as a place for pickups. Naturally, this is where all the Peace Corps volunteers go for an evening of high life. Actually, they have a

This document can be found in Iris Luce, ed., *Letters from the Peace Corps* (Washington, D.C.: Robert B. Luce, Inc., 1964), pp. 108–110, 112–113.

fine band, and the drinks are not too expensive. A few other places that are nice to go for drinks and good food are the Star Hotel and the Ambassador. The Glamour gives you fine Indian curry, while the Casanova gives you belly-dancers with your meal.

The biggest dance here is the 'high-life.' Everyone who comes here must learn it. It is akin to West Indian Calypso and entails a mass of bodies shuffling around a cement dance floor. It ruins shoes, but it is fun. If you like, you may learn classical high-life but if you are like me, you learn bush high-life. This is a no-holds-barred type of dance, where you may use any step you like, as long as you remain relatively in step and don't knock anyone down. Oh yes, we also have the twist here. The Ghanaians do it very well, as do most volunteers. Typically, I managed to hurt myself doing the twist, but that will come under the medical section, so I shan't say anymore along that line here. . . .

For those of you who think you are escaping the nine-to-five grind; you are! You work from seven to two. Life does not change as much as you think it will. You are doing a job that requires that you do the same type of work, day after day, through the months that you are here. Life will not be very exotic after the first excitement wears off. There will be the occasional exciting events, but it runs about the same as home.

Looking back over the last eight months, I find that my taste has dulled considerably. Movies that I wouldn't be caught dead seeing in the States help to kill an evening once a week. You also lose contact with all the new trends in books, plays, etc. Then there are the women. In eight months I have seen some remarkable changes in the expatriate and African women nearby. They seem to change for the better every month.

Before I start crying over the typewriter, though, I will move on to the running of your home. If you live alone, in a Ghana Trust house, life is not bad. My house has two bedrooms, a living room, dining room, den, kitchen, bathroom, and toilet.

As far as running the house is concerned, mine seems to run itself. My pay covers the electric bill, water bill, conservancy fees, rent, and a few nonessential luxuries such as food and tobacco. Clothing is no great problem and doesn't cost a great deal. Medical fees are virtually nonexistent.

This leads into the matter of health in Ghana. With all the shots you will be getting, you will probably think that you are entering the nearest thing to the Black Hole of Calcutta. This just does not prove true. I have heard of very few volunteers who have been very sick. Of course, you have your cases of malaria, dengue fever, dysentery, and sand fly fever, but strict adherence to the major rules will make life relatively illness-free.

If you do get sick, Bill C——, the Peace Corps doctor, usually has the remedy. If he doesn't, he at least smiles as he tells you. Seriously, there have been only a few things that have warranted any real notice. One fellow came down with hepatitis—he drank bad water—and was hospitalized for a while, and I have the distinction of having the Ghana Peace Corps' first and second operations. The first one removed a cyst, and the second patched me up after I tore myself open again doing the twist in the Lido.

6. The Commonwealth of Puerto Rico Plans for Tourism, 1949

Puerto Rico has all the basic requirements for a large scale tourist industry.

Climate   Close to ideal. Sunshine all but four or five days a year. Winter temperatures 68° to 78°, summer 70° to 88° and always cooled by the trade winds. . . .

Beauty   The island has great natural beauty varying from the coastal belt to the mountainous areas, including the two national forests with heights to nearly 5,000 feet. The scenic variety delights visitors and encourages their stay in Puerto Rico. Tropical flowers and fruits abound throughout the year.

Interest   The island is large, 100 miles by 35 miles. The old city of San Juan is outstanding with its 400 year old walls and fortifications. There are numerous old towns and cities around the island with their typical Spanish plazas; the town of San German with Porta Coeli—one of the oldest churches in the Western Hemisphere—is exceptionally interesting; Phosphorescent Bay near La Parguera has been called "unrivalled"; the many activities of the people are of great interest—sugar plantations; coffee fincas, tobacco farms, the salt evaporation marshes, handicrafts. . . .

Activities and Attractions   Attractions and activities suitable to the semi-tropics all exist or can be started. Puerto Rico is ringed by beaches, many of them superlative. There are literally hundreds of miles of beaches. There is good golf; there is tennis; there is magnificent swimming; Puerto Rico is superb for horseback riding; boating is good; and fishing is potentially excellent. There is first class baseball; horse racing on three tracks, cockfighting. Gambling has been legalized for tourist development; there are night clubs, bars and restaurants. Shopping—magnificent embroidered articles and handicrafts.

Transportation   In San Juan—taxis all metered; ample bus service at 5¢ fare. The island has an excellent system of roads, the best in the Caribbean. . . .

Geographical Location   The air hub of the Eastern Caribbean—8–9 hours from New York by DC4; 6–7 hours by Constellation; 5 hours by DC4 from Miami; 4–4½ by Constellation; the easiest point to get to in the Caribbean from main population centers of United States with possible exception of Havana; the nearest place from the New York area where warm winter climate can be assured. . . .

People   The people of Puerto Rico are naturally kind and anxious to assist the visitor. Mayor O'Dwyer, of New York, said: "Puerto Rico is alive with historic interest, beautiful climates from seacoast to mountain tops, pleasant vistas and a hospitable

This document can be found in "Puerto Rico's Tourist & Business," Estebán A. Bird (Tourist Advisory Board) to Governor," 17 January 1949, Oficina del Gobernador, Archivo General de Puerto Rico, San Juan, Puerto Rico.

people. The tourist looking for a combination of the romantic past and the serious business of modern living will find them both in Puerto Rico." . . .

The Government's Commitment

The Government of Puerto Rico is committed to a policy of developing a major tourist industry. This is part of its program of economic betterment of the island. It is also intended to improve understanding with, and to promote closer cultured ties with the Mainland of the United States.

It has taken positive steps to implement this policy. Among these are:

1. It has created the Tourist Advisory Board which is a part of the Puerto Rico Industrial Development Company. The Board operates through the Office of Tourism. . . .
2. The Government has appropriated $200,000 for the development and promotion expenses of the Board and Office of Tourism during the fiscal year 1948–1949.
3. The present legislature has legalized gambling to promote tourism.
4. Resort hotels are listed among the businesses entitled to 15 year tax exemption in the tax exemption law passed to encourage the industrialization of Puerto Rico. Commercial hotels receive 50% tax exemption on the same basis. . . .

The [Tourism Advisory] Board Has a Long Range and a Short Range Program

There follows here a partial listing of these programs particularly those that are already under way.

1. STAFF—It employed April 1, 1948, J. Stanton Robbins, who has an international reputation in the transportation and travel field extending over the last 25 years. Mr. Robbins has a staff of assistants in the Office of Tourism to implement the Board's program.
2. ACCOMMODATIONS—Places to stay in San Juan and in Puerto Rico are inadequate both in quantity and quality for a large tourist industry. This has been and is one of the Board's chief preoccupations. Here is what has been done.
   a) In cooperation with the Puerto Rico Industrial Development Company the Caribe-Hilton Hotel is being built—300 rooms—all air conditioned—in an ideal location with its own beach and sea-side swimming pool—twelve acres of grounds—in the middle of San Juan. It will open in late 1949 under Hilton management at [the government's] cost of over $5,000,000. It will be the finest hotel in the Caribbean.
   b) The Board has approved a short range program which includes the improvement and enlargement of existing hotels in Puerto Rico. . . .
      The Board's longer range programs envisions 3,500 hotel rooms in Puerto Rico by 1960 (2,500 in San Juan) accommodating over 6,000 visitors at one time. For projects approved by the Board financial assistance in the form of loans or participation by local capital are [*sic*] often possible. . . .

   i) The Board has cooperated with Eastern Air Lines and Tramp Trips in developing a special all expense trip covering Puerto Rico, the Dominican Republic and the Virgin Islands.

   j) The Transportation Authority and the Board are working together to make the new passenger terminal at the Isla Grande airport an attractive "front door" to Puerto Rico.

7. Modernity Goes on Display: San Juan's Caribe Hilton Hotel, 1949

Photo from Conrad N. Hilton Collection, Hospitality Industry Archives, University of Houston, Houston, Texas.

8. A Puerto Rican Cartoon Satirizes U.S. Tourists, 1960

 E S S A Y S

In the first essay, Mary Ann Heiss of Kent State University examines how cultural perceptions, especially gender-based views of Iran's prime minister Mohammed Mossadeq, influenced the U.S. response to the Anglo-Iranian oil controversy, 1951–1953. According to Heiss, the Iranian's manner of attire (especially his practice of wearing pajamas in daytime), his political passion, and his public display of tears marked the prime minister as effeminate and unstable by Western standards. U.S. and British officials also used gender-coded language that described Mossadeq with words commonly associated with females in masculine Western culture: *moody, impractical,* and *unrealistic.* Heiss concludes that gendered perceptions of Mossadeq buttressed claims of Western superiority over Iranian and other Middle East peoples, undergirded Washington's pro-British stand in the oil dispute, and justified the Anglo-American overthrow of Mossadeq in 1953.

Whereas Heiss's study highlights the perils of culture clash, the second essay by Elizabeth Cobbs Hoffman of the University of California, San Diego, concludes that President Kennedy's Peace Corps promoted cross-cultural cooperation. Her examination of the Peace Corps in Ghana, an excerpt from her book *All You Need Is Love: The Peace Corps and the Spirit of the 1960s,* concludes that the innovative program overcame the political reservations of Ghana's left-leaning nationalist president, Kwame Nkrumah, and fostered a positive image of the United States. The Peace Corps proved successful in Ghana because Nkrumah's government prioritized education, as did Peace Corps leaders and volunteers. Ghanaian culture, moreover, prized community-wide cooperation and did not shun outside aid. Peace Corps volunteers derived satisfaction from the effort because they were assigned well-structured responsibilities as teachers and demonstrated a willingness to know and respect another culture.

In the final selection, Dennis Merrill of the University of Missouri-Kansas City, explores how international tourists and their hosts negotiate cultural differences. Focusing on the Commonwealth of Puerto Rico, Merrill depicts the travel boom of the early Cold War as a manifestation of modernity, which he defines as the main cultural direction for global development. While visitors and hosts clashed over their cultural differences—class, language, race, and sexuality—each group negotiated benefits from tourism. The commonwealth government planned and regulated the trade to serve Puerto Rico's economic and cultural interests. U.S. officials and tourists perceived Puerto Rico not only as a tourist mecca but as a model for noncommunist development and modernization in the tumultuous Caribbean region.

Culture Clash: Gender, Oil, and Iranian Nationalism

MARY ANN HEISS

Between 1951 and 1953, Iran struggled to gain control of its oil industry—and the considerable wealth it generated—from the British-owned Anglo-Iranian Oil Company (AIOC). The AIOC and its predecessor, the Anglo-Persian Oil Company (APOC), had run Iran's oil industry since the first decade of the twentieth century. During the First World War, the British government had purchased a large amount of APOC stock, and by the time of the oil crisis it held slightly more than half—or a controlling interest—in that company's successor. The relationship between the Iranian government and the oil company was never particularly harmonious. Financial arrangements, especially the relatively low level of royalties the company paid to Iran, the almost total lack of Iranians in high-ranking positions within the company, and the overall aura of secrecy that pervaded the company's operations, led to Iranian discontent. Added to these practical complaints was the growing sense of Iranian nationalism after the Second World War. Nationalism, rather than simply a desire for greater oil revenues, motivated Iranian policy and sustained that policy when its fruits proved bitter. It helps to explain why Iran wanted Britain to abandon its exclusive control of the Iranian oil industry and why the Iranians persisted in spite of tremendous economic hardship. . . .

The Anglo-Iranian oil dispute seemed irresolvable from the start. Each side saw the conflict through the prism of its own history and perspective, and neither showed much willingness to compromise. The AIOC and the British Foreign Office emphasized legal issues, denied that Iran had the right to nationalize its oil industry, and sought to protect the considerable British financial stake in Iranian oil. Between

1945 and 1950, the AIOC earned £250 million from its Iranian operations. Iran's oil fields provided Britain with twenty-two million tons of oil products and seven million tons of crude oil annually, including 85 percent of the fuel needed by the British Admiralty. In other words, the British position stressed the company's value as an economic asset of great importance and the contribution that the AIOC made to Britain's overall Middle Eastern and world position. For British officials, this last consideration was paramount, as the crux of the matter for them was the danger that Iranian nationalization posed to their nation's status as a great power. As Britain's largest overseas investment, the refinery at Abadan and the AIOC's Iranian operations symbolized Britain's power in the Middle East. Losing control of these assets would be a deadly blow to British prestige the world over, especially considering Britain's recent withdrawals from India and Palestine. It might also imperil other British holdings around the world, foremost among them the Suez Canal. At a time when British policy makers were keenly aware of their diminishing status as a global power, it is not surprising that they were sensitive to anything that might undermine their position in Iran, particularly surrendering control of the nation's oil industry to the Iranians. . . .

By way of contrast, the Iranian stance during the oil dispute stressed politics and national independence. Although Iranian nationalists complained bitterly about the relatively small profits they received from the AIOC's Iranian operations—their royalties between 1945 and 1950 totaled only £90 million, slightly more than one-third of what the AIOC earned from its Iranian operations—what most galled them was the imperious way the company used its oil concession to dominate and control their nation almost as a colony. Convinced that the AIOC and the British government had interfered in Iran's internal affairs for decades by bribing legislators, influencing elections, and essentially holding the country hostage financially, nationalists like Prime Minister Mohammed Mossadeq asserted that such interference would stop only after Iran had gained control of its rich oil holdings. Mossadeq was ultimately willing to make concessions on price, production levels, and other technical details, but he would not budge on the central point that operational control of the oil industry had to rest in Iranian hands. Unless British officials were willing to concede that point, the prime minister was prepared to see his nation's oil industry shut down. "Tant pis pour nous. Too bad for us," was his usual response when Anglo-American officials warned him that his refusal to reach a resolution of the oil dispute might shut down the industry. . . .

It was the inability of the British and the Iranians to resolve the oil dispute on their own that ultimately brought the United States into the conflict. U.S. officials saw the oil crisis as potentially destabilizing force in Iran—and perhaps throughout the entire Middle East—that could lead to communist advances and provide the Soviets with an inroad to the oil-rich Persian Gulf. As the only direct land barrier between the Soviet Union and the Persian Gulf, Iran served as a vital link in the Western security chain; Soviet control of its territory would make the defense of Greece, Turkey, and the eastern Mediterranean all but impossible. Compounding Iran's importance were its rich oil reserves, which U.S. officials considered crucial to the reconstruction and rearmament of Western Europe. Loss of these resources would have dire consequences. In the short term, it would create serious shortages of aviation gasoline and other fuels needed for the military effort in Korea and would raise the specter of civilian rationing in the United States and throughout the West. In the long term it might compromise the West's ability to fight a protracted war with the Soviets, force augmentation of its military establishments, and result in an expansion of Soviet military bases in the Middle East.

Initially, the Truman administration acted as an honest broker in the search for a settlement that paid lip service to the idea of nationalization but also recognized the contractual rights of the AIOC. On the one hand, U.S. policy makers called for a firm, commercially acceptable agreement that did not set a dangerous precedent or encourage nationalization elsewhere. On the other, they advocated a flexible approach to the nationalization dispute that would make a settlement possible before Iran collapsed internally or succumbed to Soviet penetration. To this end, President Harry S. Truman and his secretary of state, Dean Acheson, lobbied for concessions from both sides, warning that "too much 'take'" on the part of the Iranians was as dangerous as "too little 'give'" on the part of the British.

As the dispute dragged on, however, and as the chance of destabilization in Iran became increasingly likely, officials in the Truman administration abandoned their middle-of-the-road stance and decided to prop up the British position in Iran, just as they were doing in Egypt and would soon do for the French in Indochina. By the summer of 1952, Truman went so far as to join British Prime Minister Winston S. Churchill in a joint Anglo-American proposal to Mossadeq that wedded the U.S. government to the British position in Iran. President Dwight D. Eisenhower and Secretary of State John Foster Dulles continued this pro-British position when they assumed office in January 1953, ultimately joining the British in a covert operation against Mossadeq late that summer. Administration officials justified this coup as necessary to save Iran from communism. The prolonged oil crisis was beginning to take its toll on the Iranian economy, and economic dislocation was spawning mass demonstrations that U.S. officials feared would grow into full-scale revolution. Making matters worse, Mossadeq was forging closer ties with the Communist Tudeh Party and moving his country closer to the Soviet Union through new trade agreements. He was even threatening to sell Iranian oil to the Soviet Union and its satellites. In truth, Mossadeq was a staunch anticommunist who hoped such moves would win U.S. assistance for his financially strapped government. Given the anticommunist hysteria of the early 1950s, however, officials in Washington could not easily dismiss the prime minister's apparent flirtation with communism. . . .

In addition to collaborating to remove Mossadeq from office, over the course of the oil dispute, Anglo-American officials came to a common way of looking at Mossadeq that used many of his personal characteristics, habits, and negotiating tactics, as well as some of his policy positions themselves, to justify a view of him as unmanly and unfit for office. Because Anglo-American officials did not view Mossadeq as their equal, they found it easy to dismiss him as an unworthy adversary whose position did not matter. Although these Anglo-American conceptions and descriptions of Mossadeq were not the sole, or even the most important, factor influencing policy, they deserve scholarly consideration because they helped to shape the context within which officials formulated policy. They buttressed claims of Western superiority over Iranian and other Middle Eastern peoples by perpetuating the idea that those peoples were weak and incapable. And their cumulative effect was to paint Mossadeq and others like him in unfavorable ways that rationalized and justified Western control. . . .

The analysis presented in this essay . . . postulates that Anglo-American officials joined to formulate a gender-based view of Mossadeq that denigrated him for departing from what they considered to be acceptable Western norms and that worked against their stated goal of seeking a resolution to the vexing oil imbroglio. It should not be construed as a complete picture of the Iranian oil crisis, and it certainly does not purport to be the only way of looking at what happened in Iran during the early 1950s. On the contrary, it utilizes the concepts of gender and culture as tools for examining the oil crisis in new ways.

When *Time* magazine designated Mossadeq as its 1951 Man of the Year, it proclaimed the Iranian prime minister to be "by Western standards an appalling caricature of a statesman." "His tears, his tantrums," and "his grotesque antics" led the magazine to dub Mossadeq a "dizzy old wizard" who "put Scheherazade in the petroleum business" by nationalizing the Anglo-Iranian Oil Company in the spring of 1951. *Time*'s editors accurately reflected the prevailing sentiment in the West and unknowingly echoed what British and U.S. government officials had been telling each other for quite some time. Influenced by long-standing stereotypes that justified Western superiority and sought to maintain Western control, Anglo-American policy makers consistently employed what Edward Said has termed "Orientalism" when dealing with Mossadeq, whom they considered inferior, childlike, and feminine. They often referred to him with gendered language that revealed their conviction that he was neither manly enough for international politics nor fit to hold the office of prime minister. They condemned as unacceptable examples of Mossadeq's unmanliness what were accepted forms of behavior in Iran, failed to see Mossadeq as their equal, and dismissed him as an unworthy adversary whose position did not matter. . . . The end result of the Orientalization of Mossadeq was an increasingly rigid Anglo-American position on the oil crisis that eschewed compromise or concessions and ultimately saw removing him from office as the only acceptable course of action.

Anglo-American officials found Mossadeq different from themselves in many ways, and these differences affected the way they dealt with him during his premiership. One startling difference concerned the way the prime minister dressed and his preferred place of conducting business. Because of his age and poor health, Mossadeq usually worked from his bed while dressed in pajamas, thereby presenting Anglo-American officials with a situation so strange that they took to including the color of his pajamas in their reports home. Some days, in fact, they noted that the prime minister wore two sets of pajamas on top of each other—khaki and green one day, blue and khaki another. Officials also thought it significant to note, sometimes with veiled sarcasm, those occasions when Mossadeq was up and about. U.S. ambassador Loy Henderson, for example, described one meeting in which Mossadeq "received me fully dressed (not pajama clad) as though for [a] ceremonial occasion." Officials from the International Bank for Reconstruction and Development, who went to Iran seeking to arrange an oil settlement in 1952, made the same point by expressing shock one day to find the prime minister "alert" and "on his feet." On another occasion they were astonished that Mossadeq actually "got out of bed, put on his slippers, and escorted us to the hall," as if the prime minister and his iron-framed bed had somehow become conjoined. The cultural assumptions behind such remarks are clear: Real leaders are expected to wear suits or other professional attire when conducting business, not pajamas, and they are expected to conduct their business from an upright position, not while reclining in their beds. Never mind that Winston Churchill often wore pajamas and worked from his bed. That Mossadeq did so marked him as an "eccentric" at best, a "lunatic" at worst, and contributed to a mounting Anglo-American conviction that what Mossadeq had to say from his bed was unimportant.

Another thing that U.S. and British officials had difficulty dealing with was what they termed Mossadeq's "fragile" and "emotional" temperament. On many occasions throughout his premiership, Mossadeq became teary eyed when speaking of the plight of the Iranian people, sometimes during private discussions, sometimes during public appearances. In part, these outbursts were genuine reflections of his outrage at the sufferings wrought upon the Iranians by the "evil" Anglo-Iranian Oil Company. In part, though, these episodes were carefully choreographed plays to the balcony designed to garner important popular support for the prime minister during the long and economically devastating oil crisis. Anglo-American officials did not give enough credence to the possibility that Mossadeq's tears might have stemmed from something other than uncontrolled emotionalism. To them, they were signs of weakness and effeminacy that diminished Mossadeq's standing as a statesman and absolved them of the responsibility of dealing with him as an equal.

Mossadeq's tears were not the only thing that made him feminine in Western eyes. The prime minister also displayed a host of other traits that earned him the opprobrium of officials in the Foreign Office and State Department and that yielded descriptions thick with gender-coded language. He was "moody," "impractical", and "unrealistic," they said. He lacked the capacity "to carry on complicated negotiations for any length of time in a single direction." He had a tendency "to change his mind, to forget, to become confused." He approached "international politics from [an] emotional point of view" rather than from a "rational" one. All of these descriptions painted Mossadeq in feminine terms and seemed to brand him unworthy of playing the role of an international statesman. Sometimes Anglo-American officials even went beyond simply gender-coded language to explicit and obvious characterization, as when they railed against the prime minister's "negative and feminine [negotiating] tactics." This description came during the failed mission of British Lord Privy Seal Sir Richard Stokes to arrange an oil settlement during the summer of 1952 and apparently meant that like most women, Mossadeq had trouble making up his mind, sought to avoid final decisions, and always wanted something better. The cumulative result of such characterizations was the conclusion that Mossadeq was an irrational and fickle adversary who was prone to emotional outbursts, often changed his mind, and could not be trusted. It seemed to follow that any permanent, realistic settlement required his removal from office and the appointment of a more reasonable and reliable prime minister.

Many of Mossadeq's policies contributed to Western descriptions of him as weak and incapable. By eschewing the economic gains that would come from a compromise settlement and insisting on total Iranian control of the oil industry, even if that meant operating at a reduced output, Mossadeq saw himself as safeguarding his nation's independence against the rapacious imperialism of the West. Anglo-American officials, however, saw things differently. For them, such a stance was further proof of Mossadeq's simple mind and unfitness for office. . . .

Mossadeq's effort to steer a middle course in the Cold War, which at the time took the name of "negative equilibrium," also made him look weak in Western eyes. Such a course turned the traditional Iranian policy of playing the Great Powers against each other on its head by proclaiming instead that no foreign power should have influence in Iran. As the prime minister saw it, what would later come to be called "nonalignment" was the only way to protect Iran from the kind of interference that the AIOC had practiced throughout Iran and thereby to ensure the attainment of the nation's true independence. For U.S. officials, though, refusing to stand with the West against the communist menace was unmanly, even perfidious. In the "if you're not with us you're against us" climate that characterized the early 1950s, especially once the Republicans returned to power in 1953. Mossadeq's neutralism only further confirmed suspicions that his regime was leading Iran toward disaster.

Also telling were the frequent Anglo-American references to Mosasdeq's child-ishness and immaturity and the attendant assumption that the West needed to save Iran from his unrealistic and naive policies. The prime minister was called "insolent" and "intransigent" when he refused to accept British and U.S. plans for resolving the oil crisis, and during negotiations he allegedly had to be "humored" like "a frac-tious child." In contrast to the British, who had been "'saints'" throughout the oil crisis, Mossadeq had "'been the naughty boy'" who needed to be disciplined. Such descriptions were dripping with the arrogance and superiority of Western colonialism and are perfect examples of the Orientalist thinking that pervaded Western policy-making circles. . . .

Anglo-American officials used yet another category of descriptors to denigrate and dismiss Mossadeq: the language of psychology and mental illness. The docu-mentary record on the oil crisis is replete with references to Mossadeq as "crazy," "sick," "mad," "hysterical," "neurotic," "demented," "periodically unstable," and "not quite sane." Because he was "suspicious" and "entirely impervious to reason," the ordinary rules [of] logic" were useless when dealing him. In the discourse of the 1950s, terms like *hysterical* and *neurotic* were usually reserved for females, and their use in this context reflects an Anglo-American proclivity to see Mossadeq as femi-nine as well as demented—and indeed to link the two, to consider Mossadeq's sup-posed effeminacy and his apparent mental illness as part and parcel of the same problem and to see both as reasons for dismissing him and what he had to say. Anglo-American references to Mossadeq's mental state also reflected a tendency by British and U.S. officials to practice pop psychology on the prime minister, to ascribe to him medical conditions they were certainly not qualified to diagnose, and to use those diagnoses to justify their refusal to take what he said seriously. "If Mr. Mossadiq is as mad as he seems," they concluded, talking and reasoning with him were futile. These characterizations of Mossadeq as mentally ill continued through the planning for the coup that ultimately overthrew him: Secretary of State John Foster Dulles reportedly exclaimed, "So this is how we get rid of that madman Mossadegh" when the opera-tion was laid out for him in June 1953. Mossadeq's "madness," it seemed, truly was grounds for the Anglo-American operation against him.

Finally, Anglo-American officials revealed their cultural biases when describ-ing Iranian society and the Iranian people in general. Mossadeq's supporters were termed little more than "mad and suicidal . . . lemmings" who needed to be saved from their folly by Western benevolence. It was difficult to negotiate an agreement with Tehran because of "characteristic defects in the Persian mode of conducting business." And any thought that the Iranians could operate the Abadan refinery in the absence of British technicians was roundly dismissed by Averell Harriman, sent by President Truman to arrange an oil settlement in the summer of 1951, as "lunacy." Anglo-American officials also wrote often about the "Iranian mentality" and the "Oriental mind," vague, undefined terms that became all-too-easy rationalizations for the failure to reach an acceptable oil agreement and prevented Western officials from searching for the real root of the impasse in oil talks. Blaming the inability to reach a settlement on inherent differences between the Iranians and themselves offered Anglo-American officials what they considered an honorable way to escape responsibility for the continued stalemate. It wasn't their fault there was no oil agreement; the fault lay with the Iranians, whose way of thinking was so different from the Anglo-American one that no settlement was possible. . . .

In characterizing Mossadeq as feminine and incapable, Anglo-American officials made two serious mistakes. One was their failure to recognize that Iranian standards of acceptable and normal behavior differed greatly from those that prevailed in the West. Whereas Mossadeq's tears symbolized weakness and emotionalism to them, for the Iranian people they were proof of Mossadeq's deep concern for the welfare of the country, concern that was so strong that he was driven to tears when he thought about the plight of his fellow countrymen. Whereas his proclivity to conduct business from his bed while dressed in pajamas proved his quirkiness to Westerners, for the Iranians these things were, as Andrew F. Westwood has noted, "deeply symbolic . . . of their personal plight and that of their nation, symbolic of the frailty of righteousness beset by powerful forces of evil." And whereas his fainting spells were for the Anglo-Americans something to mock and laugh about, they were the kinds of public displays of emotion and feeling that Iranians expected from a leader. In other words, the Iranian people found nothing wrong with Mossadeq's behavior. On the contrary, they respected and admired him for being so concerned about the plight of his nation that he was driven to faint and cry about it.

Anglo-American officials also erred by not giving enough weight to the possibility that Mossadeq's emotionalism might have been intentional, something he employed to serve his own ends: Maybe he fainted and cried on purpose. In fact, there is evidence to suggest that this is precisely what the prime minister did. The best example of the depth of Mossadeq's theatrical talent came from a Majlis depute who related the following personal experience. One day during an emotional speech on the floor of the Majlis, Mossadeq collapsed in a heap. Fearing that the elderly premier had suffered a heart attack, the deputy, who also happened to be a medical doctor, rushed to check Mossadeq's pulse, when he expected to find weak and fluttering. He was quite surprised when it was strong and regular, and even more surprised when the prime minister opened one eye and winked at him, as if to say, "My trick has worked. You were taken in, and so were the others. I have won you over." . . .

Like all of us, policy makers in London and Washington judged others, including Mossadeq, in relation to how they saw themselves. They developed in their own minds standards of acceptable behavior, action, and appearance and used these standards as a yardstick to measure others. Those who met the minimum were respected as equals; those who did not were denigrated and dismissed. As scholars such as Carol Cohn and Emily Rosenberg have noted, these standards consisted largely of opposing pairs of traits and behaviors with the positive element of each pair denoting acceptable (or Western) norms and the negative element signifying unacceptable (or Other) norms. For Westerners, the positive traits were coded as male, the negative traits as female. Thus, in the pairs "strong and weak," rational and irrational," and "realistic and emotional," "strong," "rational," and "realistic" were seen as male, and therefore desirable, traits, while "weak," "irrational," and "emotional" were seen as female, and therefore undesirable, traits.

In the case of Mossadeq, everything he did fed Western perceptions of him as weak and unmanly, which in turn made it much easier for Anglo-American officials to discount his position—and that of his country. Because Mossadeq neither looked nor acted like a Western leader and refused to kow-tow to Western pressures for continued control of Iran's oil industry, he was described as an irrational lunatic unfit to hold the office of prime minister. . . .

Assessing the immediate influence of Western characterizations of Mossadeq on the formulation of Anglo-American policy is tricky because it is not possible to determine a direct causal relationship between Anglo-American perceptions and prejudices and specific events. We cannot say, for example, that Western stereotypes led linearly to the coup that removed Mossadeq from office in the summer of 1953. But this does not mean that these stereotypes were unimportant. On the contrary, by shaping the mind-set of Anglo-American officials, they were part of the context within which those officials formulated policy. They buttressed claims of Western superiority over Iranian and other Middle Eastern peoples by perpetuating the idea that those peoples were weak and incapable. And their cumulative effect was to paint Mossadeq and others like him in unfavorable ways that rationalized and justified Western control.

The British and U.S. officials charged with negotiating an oil settlement with Mossadeq were probably not aware of the role cultural perceptions played in circumscribing their ability to reach such a settlement. But as this essay has demonstrated, those perceptions did constitute important obstacles to a negotiated resolution of the oil crisis on terms that Western officials would have considered acceptable. To be sure, there were many other contexts surrounding the oil crisis besides gender and culture—the East-West Cold War, Anglo-American relations, and decolonization and the rise of Third World nationalism, to name only three—and each of these contexts provided its own obstacles to an acceptable oil agreement. But in seeking a complete understanding of the Anglo-Iranian oil crisis, and especially the reasons why resolution proved so difficult, scholars should not discount the role of cultural perceptions. . . .

Without question, Mossadeq committed his own errors of perception. He misread the willingness of U.S. officials to come to Iran's assistance in its struggle against Britain, the difficulties of selling nationalized oil on the open market, and the degree of British opposition to surrendering control of Iranian oil. He also miscalculated the usefulness of communism as a way to win U.S. support. But of much greater consequence were the misperceptions of British and U.S. officials about Mossadeq—that he was senile, mentally unbalanced, and unfit for office. Because key U.S. Foreign Service officers had little understanding of Iranian history, culture, or tradition, they did not appreciate the role that emotion or public tears played in the political culture of Iran or why Mossadeq might have worn pajamas and worked from his bed. Instead of taking Mossadeq on his own terms, Western leaders chose to judge him according to their own standards and to dismiss him when he failed to measure up to expectations. This tendency was not unique to Iran, of course, but applied throughout the world's developing countries. It reflected an Anglo-American sense of cultural superiority over developing world leaders who sought to maintain their nations' independence and helps to explain why the Anglo-Iranian oil crisis, which was at its heart a North-South conflict, ultimately proved so difficult to resolve.

Cultural Cooperation: The Peace Corps in Ghana

ELIZABETH COBBS HOFFMAN

Beginning in 1958, Ghanaians requested help with a national commitment of their own: to make better use of their own human resources and to diminish through a national system of education the kinds of tribal rivalries that in the past had fed the slave trade and that thirty years later would make Rwanda a symbol of genocide. In the four decades since independence this commitment has been imperfectly realized, but the extent to which it has been is due to important part to the convergence of the free world and African goals that brought [President] Kwame Nkrumah together with the Peace Corps. . . .

Since winning its independence peacefully in 1957, the government of the former Gold Coast had promoted the slogan it used against the British, "Self Government Now," throughout colonial Africa. More than a dozen new nations emerged in the following three years, and they looked admiringly to Ghana as a model. Recognized by the United States as "the then leading spokesman for African nationalism," President Kwame Nkrumah also headed the continental movement for African unity, confering regularly with other independence leaders such as Sekou Touré of Guinea, Julius Nyerere of Tanganyika, and Patrice Lumumba of the Congo. . . .

The ten years he had spent as a student in the United States, from 1935 to 1945, gave Nkrumah a unique perspective. His first-hand experience of American segregation encouraged a race-consciousness (including exposure to the ideas of Marcus Gavey and W. E. B. Du Bois) he might otherwise not have attained. But while certain experiences rankled (such as being shown to the garden hose when he asked for a drink in a restaurant), others inspired him. Nkrumah, like many other Ghanaians, admired what the United States had made of itself since independence from Britain. "Forget about slavery," one early education officer later said; "we knew that Americans had struggled to achieve." Ghanaians also recognized America's historic resistance to Britain. . . .

Nkrumah also admired the American schooling system, in which he had studied for his bachelor's and doctoral degrees in education. Nkrumah was unusual in this respect, since at the time most Ghanaians considered the British school system far superior to the American. His close companion Kojo Botsio later attested that Nkrumah believed that when it came to practical training, "You couldn't beat America." Nkrumah himself wrote in an article for the Penn State University journal of education in 1943 that "the colonial school program of Africa . . . should give way to a new process of training and educating in life and current social, political, technical, and economic ideals now in vogue in progressive schools in America, China, and Russia."

This reference to the trio of "America, China, and Russia," then allies in World War II, foreshadowed the most important source of conflict between Ghana and the United States following independence. From the start, when Nkrumah with British approval invited China to attend Ghana's independence day celebrations instead of Taiwan, the United States objected to the sympathies of his government, which formally adopted socialism in 1962. Nkrumah, however, wanted to be free to pick and choose what he thought best in each system: for example, American education and technology and Russian economic planning. In the context of the cold war, however, that meant playing the Americans against the Russians and vice versa to obtain aid from both. . . .

When the first Peace Corps volunteers stepped off the Pan Am prop jet on August 30, 1961, wearing summer suits and light cotton dresses, the steamy, wood-smoke-tinged air of Accra signaled their arrival in a place far, far from home. The . . . minister of education . . . waited on the sizzling black tarmac with other dignitaries to greet them. Quietly forming themselves into a group, the volunteers sang as best they could the Ghanaian national anthem "Yen Ara Asaasa Ni" (This Is Our Homeland) in Twi, the local language they had studied. A gesture that appeared corny and inept to a later, more bruised generation of Americans struck Ghanaians as original and heart-felt—which is undoubtedly how it was meant at the time. Radio Ghana taped the performance and aired it repeatedly. Years later a Ghanaian associate of the Peace Corps program called it "a singular gesture of friendship, goodwill and understanding which . . . more than any official statement could convey, signaled to Ghanaians and to the world the deep respect and concern that the very first group of volunteers had for the people of the first country it was to serve." . . .

By American standards, and by the British standards that Ghana's Ministry of Education struggled to maintain, the majority of Peace Corps teachers were not qualified for the job. Most were neither education majors nor majors in the fields they were assigned to teach. But by the standards of Ghana's secondary schools, the volunteers were far better qualified than the local peer instructor alternative. The teachers were needed, and their willingness to try scaling the cultural barrier—to sing in Twi, as it were—was deeply appreciated. But perhaps the strongest proof of the value that members of the government placed on Peace Corps volunteers was the fact that Kwame Nkrumah never asked them to leave.

The government of Ghana had accepted word for word the Peace Corps contract presented by the American ambassador, with one amendment: "The Peace Corps program in Ghana may be terminated by either government ninety days after the date of written notification of such intent." Nkrumah made it clear that the Peace Corps would not be tolerated if volunteers sought to have a political effect or tried to "propagandize or spy or . . . subvert the Ghanaian system." The minister of Nigeria commented, when pressed by U.S. officials to commit to the program, that it was "naive to assume that for a government to invite the Peace Corps into its country was not a political act." For Kwame Nkrumah, under whom 93 percent of the National Assembly voted for socialism and one-party rule in 1962, this "political act" contradicted his economic policy at the same time that it moved forward his educational policy. It contradicted as well the trend of his foreign policy, which became increasingly cool toward the United States.

Answerable only to himself once "insults" of the "Osagyefo" were outlawed in 1961, Nkrumah never had to resolve these contradictions to anyone's satisfaction but his own. The result was that he kept the Peace Corps, even praised it, while taking steps to minimize its potential to stir dissent. At first, Nkrumah welcomed the volunteers enthusiastically. He gave them a party on arrival at which, one volunteer later recalled, "he danced with us and taught us the 'high life,'" then a popular dance step. On the following New Year's Day, without mentioning the Peace Corps by name, the president broadcast to the nation his expectation that Ghanaians would embrace volunteers who had "left homes and friends to come work among us." Ghana, he noted, had "invited [them] here to assist us to develop our country. . . . Those who have such a spirit deserve our co-operation and support in all they do for the good of the nation, and we should do nothing to discourage them." . . .

Nkrumah's satisfaction with the Peace Corps could also be seen through the press, controlled by the government. Yaw Agyeman-Badu has noted in his research comparing attitudes toward the United States in Ghana and Nigeria from 1960 to 1977 that Nkrumah's pan-African, socialist policies constantly "put him at variance" with American policies toward Africa. The only aspect of U.S. policy toward either Africa or third world development given even "neutral" press coverage in the Nkrumah years was the Peace Corps.

Agyeman-Badu's assessment of the press coverage as generally "neutral," rather than actually "favorable" up until the president's overthrow in 1966, reflects Nkrumah's growing suspicion after 1962 that the Peace Corps was a front for the Central Intelligence Agency. "Nkrumah was made to believe," according to K. B. Asante, "that many of them were CIA agents. Therefore he became very cool." Rumors of a link between the CIA and Peace Corps persisted for decades in many countries, and could at times approach the absurd—as when soldiers in Zaire confiscated one volunteer's maps of Africa and then examined a tampon from another one's suitcase. ("They dropped it like a hot potato when they found out what it was for," a compatriot wryly noted.) Such misgivings were natural considering the infamy of the agency's covert techniques. In the pursuit of victory in the cold war, the United States would stop at nothing to beat the Soviet Union, third world countries well understood. Even though the Ghanaian government never uncovered any evidence of CIA infiltration of the Peace Corps, and members of the regime later concluded that it had likely never occurred, in 1963 a suspicious Nkrumah took steps to counter the volunteers' influence.

One step was to bar the Peace Corps from teaching English and history. Nkrumah pointedly did not extend the restriction to Canadian volunteers. According to George Ayi-Bonte, an associate director of the Ghana Peace Corps program for twenty years, some of the Americans had been using George Orwell's *Animal Farm* in their classes and members of the government got wind of it. Peace Corps country director George Carter never knew, however, what precisely made Nkrumah believe that the volunteers had overstepped the bounds of math, science, and "neutral" English language instruction. . . .

Why did Kwame Nkrumah never expel the Peace Corps, which he thought might be CIA-infiltrated, as neighboring Guinea did when it was annoyed with U.S. policies? Perhaps because, as one of the volunteers suspended from teaching English said, "If it were really thought we were 'agents' of the C.I.A. type, I don't think we would be in Ghana at all." But the most important reason was probably just that the Peace Corps was too helpful. . . .

A Peace Corps proverb in the sixties, often repeated by veterans, was that volunteers who went to Asia came back meditating, volunteers who went to Latin America came back as revolutionaries, and volunteers who went to Africa came back laughing. Volunteers in Africa left "laughing" for various reasons, and one of them is the attitude expressed by the proverbs of the Africans themselves. As the scholar Kwame Gyekye has observed, the philosophy of the Akan (a collection of tribes encompassing the Ashanti, among others) has been handed down to each generation through proverbs that are both spoken and printed. The proverbs are guides to personal and collective behavior, reinforcing the values esteemed by the Akan. Chief among them is care of the family and the community. This value led many African villages to embrace young volunteers as one of their own turning odd-looking "obroni" (whites) into members of the community addressed as "brother" and "sister." . . .

The cultural traditions of Ghana, in particular, made for a hospitable environment. "Within the framework of Akan social and humanistic ethics," according to Gyekye, "what is morally good is generally that which promotes social welfare, solidarity, and harmony in human relationships." This emphasis on collectivity and reciprocity, rather than individuality and autonomy, was expressed in proverbs such as "the left arm washes the right arm and the right arm washes the left arm," and "man is not a palm tree that he should be . . . self-sufficient." For volunteers, this meant entering into a society that welcomed, accepted, and cared for them as members of a community quite unlike the industrialized societies from which they had come. One volunteer later summed up an experience common to many: "I was well looked after by concerned Ghanaian friends. One of the most remarkable and wonderful characteristics of the Ghanaian people is the way they look after their guests."

The other aspect of Ghanaian communalism that enhanced the volunteer experience was the cultural openness to "help." Ironically, the volunteers themselves came from a cultural context where the need to be helped was frequently interpreted as a sign of weakness or insufficiency. Symbols like the frontiersman bespoke a cultural admiration for "going it alone," for helping others, perhaps, but not needing help oneself—for being, in the words of Ralph Waldo Emerson, "self-reliant." Fortunately for the Peace Corps, the cultural ethos in Ghana was nearly the opposite.

Akan philosophy, while recognizing that not everyone contributed equally to society, still asserted the necessity, dignity, and rights of each member. "The fingers of the hand are not equal in length," one proverb said, complemented by the related saying, "One finger cannot lift up a thing." In Ghanaian society, gift giving and mutual aid were customary. And when a gift was given, it was considered rude to reciprocate too quickly, lest one appear to be trying to "pay off" the obligation of friendship. Thus aid that might have been resented in other cultures seemed natural to many African villagers who, having welcomed volunteers into their midst, accepted and appreciated the Americans' contributions to the life of the group. . . .

Volunteers raised on stories of hardy pioneers and frontier heroes also admired, as they frequently reported, the extraordinary work ethic of West Africans. Teachers noted that students worked in the fields before and after class. Community development workers were often amazed at the Herculean efforts of those students' parents to wrest sustenance from the sea or soil. Mike Tidwell, who advised the local chief on building his own fish pond, later said: "I knew that no man would ever command more respect from me than one who, to better feed his children, moves 4,000 cubic feet of dirt with a shovel."

One result was a significantly lower early termination rate in Ghana than in many other countries. Worldwide, the rate of early termination for Peace Corps volunteers, including those who did not make it through training, averaged 30 percent by the mid-1990s, whereas in Ghana the rate hovered around 20 percent. The reason for this, in addition to Ghanaian hospitality, was the placement itself, usually in teaching. According to Charles Peters, the happiest, least frustrated volunteers on average were teachers—"most were in Africa"—who had "structured jobs with a clear set of tasks to perform." In Africa, work usually consisted of six periods of high school English, algebra, or chemistry—enough to satisfy the passion of almost any idealistic college graduate.

Reasonable living conditions also helped ease the path of the Peace Corps in Ghana. For most Americans, far away and with almost no history of trade or mission-ary work there, Africa was truly *terra incognita* in 1961. Tarzan movies, museum ex-hibits, and *National Geographic* photos displays of bare-breasted villagers were as close as most Americans had ever come to the mysterious "dark continent." Volun-teers and their terrified parents knew somewhat more, much in the form of medical horror stories told by trainers determined to lose as few young Americans as possible. In addition to prescriptions on how to minimize the risk of cholera, malaria, yellow fever, typhoid, rabies, dysentery, meningitis, and giardia, which one could catch in any third world country, Peace Corps staff warned volunteers going to Africa of the even stranger maladies and dangers to be found there: the guinea worm, which could grow up to a meter long in the body before emerging from a skin blister (through which it could then be extracted by wrapping the worm around a matchstick and carefully pulling on it for a month, wrapping a little more of its length each time); or "schisto" worms, which burrowed into the skin in five minutes but stayed thirty years, rapidly aging the unlucky host; or "oncho," also called river blindness, whereby one could lose one's sight forever by taking an ill-considered dip in a lake or river. Going to Africa in the early 1960s "took a bunch of guts," in the words of George Carter, whose number one concern was "that I come back with [the same] 52 kids." And not all volunteers to Africa did return. The worst that usually happened was a case of malaria or severe dysentery. But over the years a number died in motorcycle or car crashes, and one twenty-five-year-old volunteer in Ethiopia even suffered the gruesome fate of being eaten by a crocodile.

Thus when daily conditions for teachers in Africa turned out to be relatively "civilized"—bungalows built for British teachers and other expatriates—volunteers gained confidence in their ability to endure the experience. "What they found when they got there was such a relief!" Carter recalled. Although some had to dig their own latrines, most volunteers were issued small gas-powered refrigators, kerosene lamps, and rooms complete with screens against mosquitoes. Food was simple and strange, but plentiful and often wonderfully tasty—pineapples so sweet that they smelled like coconut, chicken stewed with red peppers and peanuts, platains fried until the natural sugar in them crystallized, bland cassava pounded into gelatinous "fufu" and served with steaming palm fruit soup. . . .

For many volunteers, the physical pleasures they experienced were sometimes tinged with guilt or at least uneasiness. Throughout the 1960s volunteers battled within themselves and with Washington over the expectation that being in the Peace Corps meant living in mud huts, being best friends with the natives, and generally changing the world single-handedly. Physical comfort did not fit in the Peace Corps self-image. . . . Sargent Shriver made his first trip to inspect the volunteers' assignment in 1962, and he challenged the volunteers to reject the amenities offered by the Ghanaian community. . . .

[O]ver the next several years Peace Corps administrators gradually fine-tuned policy by . . . reducing volunteer living stipends and taking away jeep privileges from the few volunteers who had them.

Beyond the occasional defensiveness over "Sarge's" disappointment that they were not really roughing it, many volunteers were disturbed by the sense that the Peace Corps administration did not value teachers nearly as much as the heroes of community development. Both the American media and the Peace Corps newsletter, *The Volunteer,* tended to highlight those volunteers who either were in unusual or daring placements, or who—quite aside from their demanding jobs as teachers—had also managed to start so-called secondary projects such as libraries, craft cooperatives, adult literacy programs, or community gardens. From the attention these projects received, many volunteers drew the conclusion that the Peace Corps considered these projects not secondary but, rather, as the primary justification for placing young Americans in what otherwise seemed rather staid jobs. The volunteers felt that the newsletter "was implicitly critizing them," George Carter wrote to Washington headquarters in 1962, "because they were not involved in a project which involved hacking one's way though the bush with a bolo knife." . . .

The Peace Corps stayed in education because African governments requested it and because Sargent Shriver himself strongly supported the Peace Corps role in education. A former chairman of Chicago's Board of Education, Shriver had a natural compatibility with the emphasis of the Kennedy family and the Kennedy administration on achievement through education. Joseph and Rose Kennedy had sent their sons to the best schools money could buy and, having attained the presidency, John Kennedy built his Cabinet with professors from the Ivy League. In the United States as a whole, this was the post-Sputnik era of the "new math" and the "new physics," the era of the president's Commission on Physical Fitness and of growing federal aid to colleges, universities, and medical schools. Indeed, free compulsory education was the oldest of Yankee traditions. . . .

One result was a program in which, by the end of the 1960s, 90 percent of volunteers reported that they were "moderately" or "very" satisfied with their Peace Corps experience. Clearly structured jobs in response to a clear need, plus the support of the local culture, made the experience a good one in spite of occasional guilt about not doing enough, or loving enough, or sacrificing enough. One volunteer who taught high school English and ran an enormously popular Shakespeare festival in the nearby Nigerian bush said decades later: "My Peace Corps assignment was so perfect I hesitate to talk about it even now, fearing that someone will yet take it away." One woman wrote home from Ghana in 1962, "I'm more pleased with the world and humans and myself than previously." From Africa, volunteers came back laughing. . . .

Canada and Britain also . . . [sent] volunteers to Ghana, and their experiences in many ways paralleled those of the Americans. Indeed, what was perhaps most remarkable about the overlap among the Peace Corps, [the British] Voluntary Service

Overseas, and Canadian University Service Overseas was how similar they were, quite unintentionally, in their placements, organizational cultures, and political outlook. At the same time, the programs had differences. Those differences place in perspective the sometimes hypercritical treatment of the Peace Corps by scholars who wish to demythologize Kennedy's Camelot or to show the essential flaws of all U.S. foreign policy during the Vietnam era. Comparing the Peace Corps with its Anglo counterparts alters the significance of some of these complaints.

The historian Gary May, for example, says that Peace Corps language instruction "was almost legendary for its poor quality" and that "Peace Corps incompetence and ignorance" in the field of volunteer health created a "nightmare." In comparison with other programs, however, the Peace Corps not only gave volunteers extensive training on safety and hygiene (too much, some volunteers protested), but also innovated the practice of preventive gamma globulin shots (later adopted by the Canadians) and sent medical personnel to each country to attend to the volunteers. CUSO and VSO volunteers received relatively little of this kind of staff support, with the result that they suffered from a much higher incidence of potentially deadly hepatitis, dysentery, and malaria in the early 1960s than did Peace Corps volunteers. VSO volunteers thirty years later still complained about the lack of medical support compared with that given to American volunteers. . . .

Still, in fundamental ways, the experience of American, Canadian, and British volunteers in Ghana paralleled one another remarkably, and they generally got what they came for: a chance to know the existentialist "Other" and to deny his or her essential differentness: a chance to express the individual initiative central to their own Anglo-derived cultures yet seemingly threatened by mass society; a chance to try on preindustrial life and the values of communalism often associated with it; and, last but not least, a chance for old-fashioned adventure and heroism. . . .

For their part, Ghanaians welcomed the assistance of VSO in 1958 and the Peace Corps and CUSO in 1961. They continued to welcome volunteers decades later. The contributions in education stood out especially to Africans. "The importance of the Peace Corps programme to Ghana cannot be over-emphasized," the national director of secondary education told volunteers in 1995, echoing the assessment of other officials. Sheer numbers told part of the story: approximately 675,000 Ghanaians had American teachers between 1961 and 1991. Out of a population of 14 million, this equaled roughly 5 percent of all Ghanaians. Indeed, in Ghana it was difficult to find a person who had achieved white-collar status who had not had a Peace Corps teacher at some point.

Peace Corps also helped introduce educational innovations, such as the "new math" and learning by reasoning rather than by rote. These innovations did not all spread, however. Lacking books that could serve as an aid to memory, Ghanaian students continued to rely on copying down and memorizing the facts necessary to pass state exams. Julius Amin, a former Peace Corps student in nearby Cameroon, later wrote: "Memorization provided the . . . [village] student with a feeling of being knowledgeable" in an environment that was otherwise unfamiliar and intimidating. Still, he noted in in-depth research on Cameroon, the volunteers designed both textbooks and curricula more attuned to the needs of the rural students than those of the British system they helped transform, and laid the foundation for a national testing center that replaced the London-based exam board in 1977. Throughout West Africa, volunteers also started libraries, equipped rudimentary science labs and technical workshops, built school latrines, initiated athletic programs, conducted science fairs, and organized academic clubs. Even though many Peace Corps teachers taught subjects for which they had not prepared in college, "they made a difficult job look easy," according to Julius Amin. "Whatever the weaknesses of the volunteers, it remains true that their services were essential." . . .

Perhaps the most compelling contribution of the Peace Corps, however, was indeed its simple existence. As one Cameroonian later expressed it, "these Americans had their weaknesses but just the fact that these Kennedy boys came to struggle with us, I think, is the most important thing." Ghanaians often characterized the Peace Corps meaning to Ghana as one of morale. From the first singing of the national anthem in Twi to the volunteers in the 1990s who still reported to village chiefs before starting their assignments, the Peace Corps continuously impressed West Africans with its willingness to enter into the life of the villages "under all sort of conditions."

To K. B. Asante and Kojo Botsio, the individual, intangible effect had enriched particular lives as well as the life of the nation. Ghana, in its totality, may not have become measurably different, but many Ghanaians had. "The individual's effort seeps into society," according to Asante. Asante himself served a stint as Ghana's education minister in the 1970s and was "so impressed" with the American Peace Corps volunteers—working in remote places "where Ghanaians wouldn't go"—who came to his office to ask for supplies for their schools. To Kojo Botsio, who had weathered every political and economic crisis between 1951 and 1991 (from imprisonment by the British to a death sentence by a post-Nkrumah regime), the final judgment on the Peace Corps' thirty years in his country was simple: "We wanted to bring up the standard of education of the people and it contributed quite a lot . . . no doubt about it." . . .

In Ghana, the Peace Corps had not changed the world, but it had met its own stated goals: to serve the needs of another country, to promote local understanding of America, and to foster Americans' understanding of other people. Indeed, it had triumphed.

Cultural Negotiation: U.S. Tourism in Puerto Rico

DENNIS MERRILL

In May 1958, following his highly publicized tussle with the anti-American mobs of Caracas, Venezuela, Vice President Richard Nixon beat a hasty retreat to sunny Puerto Rico. The night of his arrival he spent forty minutes wading through four blocks of historic Old San Juan amidst throngs of people who cheered "Arriba Nixon!" Later that evening, in the candlelit dining room of the four-hundred-year-old governor's mansion, La Fortaleza, Governor Luis Muñoz Marín hosted a state dinner. Declared Nixon: "I couldn't think of a better place to be." To which a buoyant Muñoz replied: "Mr. Vice-President, está en su casa."

Although set apart by his celebrity, Richard Nixon was only one of approximately 250,000 U.S. citizens who annually made the trek to Puerto Rico in the late 1950s. By the mid-1960s, following the Cuban Revolution, the annual count swelled

Adapted from Dennis Merrill, "Negotiating Cold War Paradise: U.S. Tourism, Economic Planning, and Cultural Modernity in Twentieth Century Puerto Rico," *Diplomatic History,* 25 (Spring 2001), 179–214. Reprinted with permission of Blackwell Publishing Ltd.

to more than 500,000, making Puerto Rico the Caribbean's most visited island. Some came on business, a few like Nixon arrived in an official capacity, but most came as tourists.

The postwar era witnessed an unprecedented boom in international tourism. Pushed along by American affluence, liberalized employee vacation benefits, easy credit, affordable air travel, and growing communications links, tourism—once the privilege of an elite few—became a crucial element in the global economy and a component of international relations. During the early 1960s Americans alone spent $3 billion per year traveling overseas. By the mid-1990s, international tourism generated as much as $3.4 trillion annually, vying with oil as the world's largest industry.

Although U.S. visitors traveled to Puerto Rico in pursuit of fun and relaxation, they unavoidably became participants in a Cold War cultural experience. Commonwealth Puerto Rico, the advertising read, was a postcolonial territory tutored in democratic capitalism by the United States and generously granted autonomy. It had forsworn the turbulence that swept much of the Third World, denounced Castroism, and peacefully pursued private investment and economic development. The image juxtaposed the island's tropical allure and its material progress, its yearning for change and its stability. In short, Pueto Rico shone as a Cold War paradise, an outpost for liberal capitalism in a world seemingly tempted by the promises of communism.

Depicting tourism as a one-way street, where visitors bestowed progress upon hosts, the advertising hype oversimplified the give-and-take inherent to tourism. Local communities, in fact, are not static and often seize upon tourism as a means to display their existence and establish their power. Travel narratives and popular discourses of tourism illuminate how governments, media, businesses, workers, and consumers ultimately engage in the globalization of cultural modernity—a consciousness, or value system, that elevates urbanism, science, consumerism, and mastery over nature. To be modern, the theorist Marshall Berman has posited, is to find ourselves in an environment that promises economic and technological advance, yet to feel threatened by the loss of revered customs and life ways. Modernity is not simply imposed from the outside, but rather represents "the main cultural direction for global development." It is transmitted through many channels: trade, communications, diplomacy, and the migration of people. Tourism serves as a battleground on which hosts and visitors contest and negotiate their modern identities.

Acquired and awarded colonial status following the U.S. victory over Spain in 1898, Puerto Rico ranked with Cuba, Haiti, Jamaica, and the Dominican Republic as a featured tropical attraction for an affluent and adventurous leisure class. In the days before mass tourism, most who traveled to Puerto Rico went by steamship from New York, a four-day voyage by the 1920s that cost about $75. The early guidebooks, what the scholar Edward Said has termed a literature of exploration and discovery, highlighted Puerto Rico's natural beauty and colonial charm.

Early travel writers also paid homage to the United State's civilizing and modernizing powers. Philip Marsden's *Sailing South* explained to readers that the United States had acquired Puerto Rico as an afterthought following the crusade to free Cuba, but had brought to it modern health care, highways, civil administration, and English-language education. Tourism would enhance these benefits by promising an influx of capital, technology, and travel conveniences. By the early 1930s the beachfront capital city of San Juan boasted two foreign-owned tourist hotels, a handful of restaurants, and several nightclubs and casinos. The tourist, John Jennings noted in *Our American Tropics,* "takes nothing out of the country except a few souvenirs for which he pays extremely well, to say the least, and a coat of tan." He is "the modern goose that lays the golden egg and as such he should be treated with respect."

Meanwhile, colonialism and tourism made the island a meeting ground for distinctive cultures. A few American visitors during these years developed an appreciation for Puerto Rico. Most of the travel literature, however, advanced a derogatory set of perceptions. Guidebooks disparaged the island's poverty, illiteracy, and health problems, and depicted a helpless, dependent people, a foreign "other," who lived outside the boundaries of the civilized world. U.S. travel writers, reflecting the mores of the Jim Crow era, typically portrayed Puerto Ricans as a "mongrel race," among whom the Iberian tradition of mañana obstructed reform and progress.

The 1930s witnessed the first effort by U.S. officials to package Puerto Rico for mass tourism. It was a colonial enterprise, imposed on the island. The U.S. governor Blanton Winship viewed the industry as the centerpiece of a new economy—to replace the island's declining sugar plantations. In addition to launching a road beautification program, and expanding accommodations, Winship hired a public relations firm to churn out travel brochures highlighting Puerto Rico's beaches, golf courses, and deep sea fishing. The campaign portrayed Puerto Rico in condescending terms: a poverty stricken land whose simple people awaited the opportunity to serve their benefactors. It accented popular constructions of gender, with posters featuring attractive female models posed in swimsuits: "beautiful señoritas at the Canto de Piedras," one caption read. Colonial tourism literature commonly depicted Puerto Rico as a generous hostess, accepting of male domination, and eager to pamper her paying guests.

Winship's campaign failed to take hold, in part because of the depression-plagued 1930s economy, but also due to the rising nationalism that shaped Puerto Rican politics during the decade. The nationalist movement was associated with the name Pedro Albizu Campos, a graduate of Harvard Law School, a former U.S. Army officer, and leader of the Nationalist party. In the harsh depression atmosphere, compounded by punishing hurricanes in 1928 and 1932, Albizu's denunciation of U.S. colonial rule and call to arms found a receptive audience. At the same time, the "1930s generation" of Puerto Rican intellectuals decried the forced instruction of English in public schools and celebrated the island's Spanish-American, "hispanidad" culture. Winship's tourism activities, particularly his imposition of a subservient identity on the island, won the wrath of both political and cultural nationalists.

In this context, Puerto Rico first experienced the innovative leadership of Luis Muñoz Marín. The son of Luis Muñoz Rivera, Puerto Rico's resident commissioner in Washington, the younger Muñoz had been educated in the United States. After a stint as an independentista, Muñoz's pragmatism led him to champion commonwealth status, an ill-defined middle ground between independence and colonialism. In 1938 he organized the Popular Democratic party (Partido Populare Democratica, or PPD), which melded his moderate commonwealth cause with a leftist economic program, promising land redistribution and new, job-producing, state-owned industries. A talented politician, Muñoz echoed others during the 1940 legislative elections in denouncing Winship's tourism initiatives. When charges of casino corruption arose, he even demanded that San Juan's slot machines be tossed into the sea.

The PPD's smashing victory at the polls in 1940 foreshadowed Muñoz's domination of Puerto Rican politics for nearly three decades, and set the stage for a locally based, planned tourist industry. Prerequisite to the effort was a redefinition of Puerto Rico's political status. After becoming the island's first elected governor in 1948, Muñoz negotiated with Washington Public Law 600, which conferred on Puerto Rico limited self-government. Washington kept control of the island's judiciary and military, but San Juan gained the power to tax and regulate Puerto Rico's economy. Puerto Ricans maintained U.S. citizenship (first granted by the Jones Act of 1917), but did not receive the right to vote in U.S. elections. The legislation won popular approval in a 1951 plebiscite that offered a choice only between commonwealth or colonial status, much to the dismay of statehood and independence advocates. Nationalism remained a central impulse on the island, and profoundly shaped future tourism, but the independence party (Partido Independentista Puertorriqueño, or PIP) steadily lost ground in elections over the next decade—overtaken by Muñoz's populism and victimized by repression enforced by Commonwealth and U.S. authorities alike.

As he reshaped Puerto Rico's political identity, Muñoz also refined his economic agenda. Again, he sought greater self-reliance for the island without severing ties to the United States. With his American-educated economic adviser, Teodoro Moscoso, Muñoz established Puerto Rico's Economic Planning Board, or "Fomento." The two abandoned their preference for state-owned enterprises, and used their newly acquired taxing authority to offer exemptions to private investors undertaking new ventures. The goal was to transform Puerto Rico from a sugar-producing, colonial entity to a job-producing industrial workshop. Muñoz's modernist vision included public-private collaboration, state subsidies for key industries, and access to U.S. federal welfare programs for the poor. The strategy became known as "Operation Bootstrap."

Muñoz delegated to Fomento's Teodoro Moscoso the restructuring of the tourist industry. The effort would not be left solely to private, foreign investors, but instead draw on government subsidies and local capital. Planners estimated in 1949 that a modest, public investment of $1.7 million annually for staff, advertising, and subsidies would generate roughly $15,600,000 in revenue and create four thousand new jobs. In contrast to the colonial authority's earlier efforts to make tourism the island's economic mainstay, Fomento officials envisioned the industry's share of gross product topping off at 5 to 10 percent. That figure contrasted with other Atlantic-Caribbean retreats, such as the Bahamas and the U.S. Virgin Islands, which relied on travel for up to 80 percent of their national incomes. Manufacturing constituted the core of Operation Bootstrap.

The effort first required a tourism infrastructure. It was the availability of affordable air travel that made modern, mass tourism possible. Pan American Airlines inaugurated daily nonstop flights between New York and San Juan in 1946. Three years later, construction commenced on San Juan's $15 million Isla Verde airport, capable of handling more than five hundred flights per day. Then, a breakthrough came in 1951 when the U.S. Bureau of Civil Aviation granted authorization to Eastern Airlines to land in San Juan, breaking PanAm's monopoly and spurring lower airfares. By 1952 the Puerto Rico advertised six- to eight-hour flights from New York for $128 roundtrip; and ten-hour flights from Chicago for $275. Daily jet service, commencing in late 1959, reduced travel time from New York to three and one-half hours.

Another turning point came in 1949 when Moscoso hired J. Stanton Robbins, an American who had worked on Virginia's colonial Williamsburg, to head Fomento's Office of Tourism. Soon, the office was publishing *Qué Pasa in Puerto Rico,* a glossy magazine, still in print today, that featured photographs and articles on leading attractions. Equally important, the bureau established schools for hotel and restaurant employees and developed a survey system for departing tourists that helped fine-tune its promotional efforts. Tourism officials also prepared the island for legalized gambling, citing the nineteen-year-old Nevada experiment to argue that regulation countered infiltration by organized crime. Puerto Rico legalized casino gambling in late 1948, created a gambling division within the Tourism Office, and hired a corps of inspectors. Despite protests from smaller hotels, the government licensed only establishments larger than two hundred rooms. Consistent with Muñoz's antigambling posture in the 1940 elections, the government refused to sanction slot machines.

Infrastructure alone could not spark mass tourism. Critical to the undertaking, and a pivotal component of cultural modernity, was the refashioning of Puerto Rico's image. For more than a half century the island's people had been portrayed in narratives as dependent and subservient "others." Stereotypes had been reinforced by the migration of roughly fifty thousand Puerto Ricans annually, mainly to New York and the urban northeast, during the late 1940s and 1950s. A 1947 pictorial essay in *Life* magazine described the migration and dramatized the health, housing, and employment problems of the immigrants. In popular culture, the 1958 Broadway musical *West Side Story* reinforced these images by choreographing its characters as hot-tempered, knife-wielding juvenile delinquents. The musical drew an even less flattering image of Puerto Rico itself, a place, according to song, devoid of modern symbols such as washing machines, highways, and Buicks.

In 1948 the commonwealth contracted the New York public relations firm Hamilton Wright to engineer a media blitz. An army of journalists descended upon the island, where they were chauffeured about, given access to the governor, and fed a steady diet of government press releases. Publications such as *Travel, Saturday Review,* and the travel page of the *New York Times* filled with articles that accented Puerto Rico's climate, architecture, and natural beauty. Tropical images had been central to earlier advertising, but commonwealth officials also conveyed an image of an island in the throes of modernity. An array of publications told the story of "Operation Bootstrap," the name itself a powerful metaphor in Yankee culture for self-reliance. Under Muñoz annual earnings had risen from $125 per capita in 1940 to $514 by 1960, second only to Venezuela in Latin America. In the years 1958–59 alone 237 firms had signed contracts with Fomento.

The reinvention of Puerto Rico required above all the construction and advertisement of a glamorous tourist zone. At the end of World War II, Moscoso and Fomento surveyed the city for hotel sites, and targeted the Condado area, along the city's northern beach-lined coast, as the island's primary tourist district. The Condado's first new hotel, the stunning $7.2 million Caribe Hilton, was entirely government financed, built, and owned. The entrepreneur Conrad Hilton accepted a joint venture with the commonwealth government that placed management in company hands, reserved ownership for the government, and arranged a sharing of profits. When completed in late 1949, the ten-story, three-hundred-room, Caribe Hilton stood out on Old San Juan peninsula. Its dazzling white facade contrasted with the sparkling blue sea, and its modernity juxtaposed the centuries old San Gerónimo fort nearby. A testimony to technology, it had a swimming pool carved out of coral stone that held salt water replaced by attendants every four hours. The beachfront was also human-engineered, of powdery, coral sand so as not to stick uncomfortably to sunbathers. The hotel's open-air entrance took visitors through a manicured garden, signifying the taming of the tropics, and the interior's controlled environment, air-conditioned throughout, consisted of a collage of stone, glass, and stainless steel.

The Caribe Hilton inaugurated San Juan's tourism make-over. Soon after its opening, the World War I era Condado Beach hotel, only a few blocks from the Caribe, received a government-assisted $1.3 million facelift. Then other hotel projects followed and the landscape of Ashford Avenue, the Condado's main thoroughfare, filled with shops, restaurants, and clubs. For the commonwealth government, the Condado represented a source of revenue and an important symbol of Puerto Rican modernity. For affluent, Cold War Americans, the Caribe and other high-rises seemed to demonstrate that the American Dream had universal application. "San Juan is a new Miami with a Spanish accent," gloated the *Saturday Review* in 1952.

Puerto Rico's lunge toward modernity did not go uncontested. The editors of the influential Spanish-language daily *El Mundo* decried the Caribe Hilton as a sellout to foreigners. Even some members of Muñoz's PPD denounced casino gambling and questioned the allocation of public funds to the leisure industry. Muñoz and Moscoso defended both the Hilton deal and tourism as a whole. "How do you expect to pay for public education and social welfare," Moscoso chided his critics, "if the commonwealth is barred from earning revenue?" The journal *Architectural Forum* emphasized the role of New York consultants Warner Leeds and Associates in overseeing the project, commenting that the hotel had "the color, texture, and finish demanded by Americans off to the semi-tropics." But Moscoso and others emphasized that the Caribe had been designed by a local San Juan firm, headed by architects Osvaldo Toto and Miguel Ferrer, and reflected a unique Puerto Rican style—functional, clean, and modern.

Antitourism sentiment would intensify as the industry grew, but during the early 1950s it remained only an undercurrent in Puerto Rican cultural discourse. After all, the PPD easily captured majorities in the island's first several elections, and its main competitor, the Republican Statehood party (PER), favored close ties to the United States and applauded tourism. Commonwealth officials, moreover, eased the transition to modernity by promoting the island's rustic and traditional attractions—for both foreign and local tourists. Drawing on European bed and breakfast model, Fomento extended tax breaks to smaller, more affordable inns outside of San Juan, and travel publications began to emphasize that three thousand miles of road allowed visitors to escape the city and discover the less heavy touristed, more authentic "outer island."

To tap the tourist's thirst for authenticity, the government also initiated the restoration of Old San Juan, consisting of eight blocks of Spanish colonial residences, churches, and fortresses. In the spring of 1949 Tourist Bureau Director Stanton Robbins invited a group of former colleagues from colonial Williamsburg to San Juan to advise the project. The legislature designated Old San Juan an "ancient and historical zone," and in 1955 the government created the Institute of Puerto Rican Culture, which advised property owners on structural design and decor. Fomento granted tax incentives and loans to building owners who undertook restorations. By 1962 twenty-five major structures, dating to the sixteenth, seventeenth, and eighteenth centuries, had been rehabilitated and the ancient city bustled with restaurants, gift shops, and tourists. The traveler's taste for the elemental and the exotic did not conflict with the worship of modernity. As the anthropologist Grant MacCannell has put it: "the best indication of the final victory of modernity over other sociocultural arrangements is not the disappearance of the nonmodern world, but its artificial preservation and reconstruction in modern society." The maintenance of a reconstructed past, or "staged authenticity," reaffirmed rather than denied the march of progress.

History and modernity converged with Cold War politics as neighboring Cuba descended into revolution. While Havana had nurtured a tourist boom for over three decades, it had accumulated massive problems during the 1950s. The authoritarian government of Fulgencio Batista had adopted a free-wheeling, laissez faire policy toward the industry, content to leave matters to private interests, as long as it received its share of casino revenue. Cuba's capital had become synonymous with the darker side of tourism: mob-controlled gambling, drunkenness, and prostitution. The incongruities of tourism intensified domestic discontent, fed anti-Yankee sentiment, and contributed to Fidel Castro's communist revolution. In June 1960 Castro's government seized the landmark Havana Hilton, and relations with the tourist industry disintegrated.

As Castro's shadow stretched across the Caribbean, U.S. officials and the press heaped more praise than ever on Puerto Rico's "peaceful revolution." The *Saturday Review* editorialized in 1962 that the commonwealth had no revolutionary past—the island was managed pragmatically and democratically. "Under way here is an American-style revolution that really works," observed *U.S. News and World Report,* that stood "in sharp contrast to the violent revolution in nearby Cuba." At the center of it all was Muñoz Marín, whose picture graced the cover of *Time* in June 1958. Guidebooks and articles praised Puerto Rico's "success story," and Muñoz's Tourist Bureau made the island's economic progress, and the contrast to Cuba, a selling point.

Puerto Rico also won support from U.S. politicians. Richard Nixon found refuge there in 1958. The following year presidential hopeful Senator Hubert Humphrey (D-MN) visited the island and lauded it as a model for liberal development in the Third World. President Dwight D. Eisenhower made Puerto Rico the first stop on his Latin American tour in February 1960, and captured headlines when he took to the fairways of the recently opened, Rockefeller-owned Dorado Beach Club, east of San Juan. John F. Kennedy forged the strongest bond. In December 1958 he visited the island and made his first major speech on Latin America as a presidential candidate. Following his election he picked two of Muñoz's closest associates, Teodoro Moscoso and Arturo Morales Carrión, to serve on a task force on Latin American affairs and later appointed each to high-ranking administration positions. When the young president made his first trip to Latin America in December 1961, Puerto Rico topped the itinerary.

Cuba's turmoil also catapulted Puerto Rico into a leadership position among Caribbean vacation retreats. The Condado underwent another spurt of hotel construction, and the island's beach hotels booked for months ahead. Wrote *Time* magazine in December 1958, Puerto Rico is aimed to please the crowd "bored with Miami and scared of going to Havana because of the Cuban revolution." By 1964 the number of American tourists reached five hundred thousand; and five years later it surpassed the one million mark, second only to Mexico in Latin America.

The tourist binge received mixed reviews on the island. Part of the misgivings arose from economic inequalities. In a less developed country, where the technicalities of commonwealth status did not veil continued colonial power, the prospect of using tourism to attain economic progress encountered skepticism. Operation Bootstrap's accomplishments notwithstanding, much of Puerto Rico remained desperately poor. U.S.-based companies that took advantage of tax-free inducements often pulled up stakes when moratorium periods ended, and unemployment hovered at 10 to 12 percent, figures that did not consider the added problem of partial employment.

No issue better illustrated the intersection between tourism and class structure than the continuous effort to remove the inhabitants and demolish the slum dwellings of "La Perla." Perched along the rockbound shore, adjacent to Old San Juan, the neighborhood was immortalized by the sociologist Oscar Lewis's study of Puerto Rican poverty *La Vida*. In 1949 government tourist planners recommended clearance of the area, but community organizers mobilized and political pressure prevented action. The prostitute Soledad in *La Vida* related how her work and travels took her back and forth from ghetto to the stylish Condado and spoke of "the pain one feels after being in a nice hotel and walking past the Caribe Hilton" only to return home to the nearby slum. "They live in separate worlds, the poor and the rich," she observed.

Economic disparities constituted only one irritant. As the flood of tourists mounted, charges of "cultural imperialism" echoed across the island. Particularly abrasive was the tourist's disregard for the Spanish language. "The trouble with you Americans," one reader addressed the English-language *Puerto Rico World Journal*, "is that when you come to Puerto Rico you want to be understood in your own language, but don't give a damn to learn our language." Governor Muñoz wrote Hilton executives about a trip to the Castellano Hilton in Spain where menus were printed in Spanish and English. Could a similar practice be implemented in San Juan? Such a menu, he suggested, would be handy in a bilingual society, and provide tourists a point of interest. Hilton menus, however, remained English-only. Responding to the *World Journal,* an indignant American observed that the island's use of U.S. currency accorded him special rights. Until the commonwealth minted its own coins, he lectured, you "better damn well learn the language of the country that feeds you."

Of all the affronts that accompanied tourism, few touched as sensitive a chord as racism. Although Puerto Rican society had never been free of racial prejudice, the island had no history of rigid, racial separation until U.S. military units instituted the practice. In late 1949 rumors swirled that the Caribe Hilton would implement the color bar. The Caribe in fact shunned segregation, but reports surfaced throughout the 1950s that San Juan's hotel beaches prohibited black sunbathers and swimmers. Racism, moreover, manifested itself in other ways. Shortly after the Caribe's opening, Carl Hilton penned a letter to his brother Conrad decrying the work habits of the labor force. The hired "peons," he wrote, were "child-like or even dog-like; it is not what you say when directing their efforts it is your tone of voice that counts."

Gender and sexual relations also stirred tension. Although travel literature historically depicted Puerto Rico as an alluring woman, female tourists frequently encountered the island's patriarchy. Most common were complaints of sexual harassment, assaults, and rapes. The Condado beachfront, one letter to an island newspaper complained, had become a gathering place for "degenerates" who "are exposing themselves, masturbating, and saying ugly, filthy things to women." Of course, male sexism was a frequently cited problem at beachside in the United States as well. Still, a Puerto Rican woman wrote back to the paper and expressed contempt for the American women who walk the beaches in "tight bathing suits," and then complain of being harassed: "Do the Puerto Rican gentlemen let their women walk on the beaches alone?" she asked. Then a lecture: "Remember, you are a guest and a foreigner in this country and therefore abide with the customs and culture."

Other commentators turned their sights on the sexual prerogatives exercised by male vacationers. Puerto Rico never achieved the fame accorded Cuba as a zone for sexual license. Government surveys indicated that most tourists were married and came to the island as couples. North American men—businessmen, tourists, and sailors—were nonetheless often observed in the company of prostitutes. The Condado became a well-known meeting ground, and Puerto Ricans and tourists alike complained of overt solicitation outside bars and casinos. Other writers noted with alarm the presence of homosexuals. Old San Juan developed one of the few gay scenes in the Caribbean in the fifties, and as tourism flourished, a small homosexual subculture of hotels, restaurants, and clubs arose. Although most Puerto Ricans seemed willing to tolerate the subculture, it upset traditionalists. One concerned citizen lamented the turning of the capital into a "slum, a haven for all kinds of undesirable characters," including "the tight pant wiggle-walking homosexuals."

While tourism at times seemed a predatory force, the reality was more complex. The industry unleashed unease across the island, but antitourism sentiment never boiled over into organized protest. Hosts and tourists struggled to adapt to modernity, all the while sensing the discomfort of traditions lost. But the difference between cultural loss and cultural imposition is critical because it speaks to the difference between the globalization of culture and coercive colonialism. Puerto Ricans resented their subjugated past, and expressed uncertainty about the globalized future, but found in cultural modernity a reality that might be regulated, manipulated, and negotiated. As agents of change they both accepted and resisted tourism.

For its part, the Muñoz administration never abandoned state planning, and cited the Caribe Hilton as an example of its benefits. The joint venture handed over day-to-day operation of the hotel to Hilton, but secured ownership for the commonwealth government. The contract, moreover, specified that Hilton purchase the resort's furnishings and equipment, cover losses incurred in the first year's operation, and be barred from opening a competing hotel on the island. Finally, the arrangements guaranteed the government 66⅔ percent of the operating profit. Hilton Corporation certainly felt that Fomento had driven a hard bargain. Predicting success for the hotel, Caribe manager Frank Wangeman wrote to Conrad Hilton six months after the opening: "I think we have a gold mine here. Let's buy this hotel before they [the commonwealth] realize how prosperous it is going to be." Muñoz and Moscoso would have nothing of it. By 1953 the enterprise netted $1 million annually for the government.

Tourism workers also wrung concessions from the industry. A strike at two San Juan hotels, including the Caribe Hilton, erupted in January 1955 when negotiations with an American Federation of Labor affiliate collapsed due to disputes over wages, medical and vacation benefits, and overtime compensation. Five hundred workers, including maids, waiters and waitresses, bartenders, and kitchen workers, walked off the job. Tensions mounted as hotel managers accused the strikers, a majority of whom were female in this traditionally sex-segregated industry, of sabotaging company cars suspected of transporting strikebreakers. The strike organizers, in turn, accused police of siding with the hoteliers and trying to intimidate them away from the picket lines. The Muñoz administration first interceded with the police and then arbitrated the impasse, persuading Hilton to provide a 2 percent pay raise, a 4 percent increase in medical and insurance benefits, and liberalized overtime pay. After the settlement, strikers wrote to express their gratitude, informing Muñoz they were willing "morir por nuestro Gobernador" [to die for our Governor].

As tourism flourished, Puerto Ricans found countless ways to assert themselves. Although exit surveys showed a high level of tourist satisfaction, complaints about slow service in restaurants and hotels became commonplace. And while the petty crime that swept the island may have had no particular cultural significance, it rattled the nerves of some tourists. The English-language *Island Times* filled with letters decrying the island's "crime wave" from Yankee travelers and expatriots. Humor also registered as a form of resistance. The independentista organ *Claridad* regularly featured satirical cartoons with Yankees in tourist attire (bermuda shorts, flowered dresses, straw hats, and cameras) demanding royal treatment. One Spanish-language cartoon depicted a tour group, ignorant of imperial history, making disparaging remarks about Puerto Rico's Americanized street names while being pulled by a human-drawn rickshaw.

While the commonwealth tried to steer tourism to its economic advantage, it also grappled with the industry's cultural consequences. The most significant initiatives were undertaken by the Institute of Puerto Rican Culture, the agency that coordinated the reconstruction of Old San Juan. The institute's initial projects showcased the island's European heritage, especially its Spanish-built fortresses, residences, and churches. But by the later 1950s, it shifted focus and promoted indigenous Taíno-Indian art forms and Afro-Caribbean traditions. In the township of Loíza Aldea, the institute's scholars traced the origins of the popular drum-driven dance rhythms known as the "bomba" to the area's runaway African slave population. Archeological digs elsewhere recovered artifacts of the long-since decimated native Taíno people. The recovery of the island's distant past facilitated the representation of Puerto Rican culture as a harmonious blending of European, African, and Indian influences.

Thus PPD not only preserved, but manufactured a national identity—no small feat for a commonwealth denied full national sovereignty. The institute's programs, of course, generated a contentious dialogue between advocates of commonwealth status, statehood, and independence. During the legislative debate over its establishment, advocates of statehood and their recently reconstituted New Progressive party (PNP) denounced the institute's "incipient nationalism," dismissed the panning off of peasant handicrafts as art, and belittled the promotion of an "invented" past. Independentistas also opposed the bill, not because they imbibed Anglo-Saxon culture, but because they feared the institute would become a powerful propaganda organ for the ruling party.

Once passed, however, the programs proved popular with Puerto Ricans and tourists alike. Academics and university students, particularly those associated with the Federation of Pro-Independence Students, found in the institute's projects employment opportunities and a means to resist U.S. colonialism. Muñoz appointed independentistas to administrative positions in the organization, co-opting advocates of nationhood and outflanking statehood proponents. Meanwhile, premodern peasant music, folk dances, and village art became the backbone of the institute's activities, culminating in 1969 with the launching of the "National Indigenous Festival." Old San Juan's shops filled with wood-carved "santos" (likenesses of the saints) and handsewn needlework destined to be carted off by bargain-hunting Yankees and islanders alike.

Ambivalence toward tourism remained a fixture of Puerto Rican life. Still, by 1969 Fomento estimated that tourism contributed $200 million annually to the gross national product, and that hotels alone created nearly ten thousand jobs. Nor had the industry became a controlling factor in the Puerto Rican economy, ranking below both manufacturing and agriculture as a producer of wealth. Puerto Ricans and Yankees continued to grate on one another, but few could take issue with Teodoro Moscoso, who told a conference in April 1961: "In the jargon of the advertising trade, an image has been created; we have emerged from anonymity. That, for a tiny island halfway across the Atlantic, is no mean accomplishment."

In many ways mass tourism is theater, a dramatic and comedic play in which hosts and guests choreograph their responses to cultural modernity. Americans who traveled to Puerto Rico during the early Cold War years found in the island's hotels and restaurants confirmation that global uplift could best be achieved through U.S. consumerism rather than Soviet communism. By the late 1960s Puerto Rico had become synonymous with beachfront luxury, bootstrap capitalism, anticommunism, and old world charm: a mix of old and new, material and spiritual, the mythic and the trivial. Puerto Ricans also placed on stage an idealized self, at once rooted in a glorified past, and looking toward a capitalist future. In fact, tourism both reinforced and undermined U.S. and Puerto Rican identities. It globalized culture, blurred the line between inside and outside, and demonstrated the fragility of national identity in a mobile world.

FURTHER READING

Benedict Anderson, *Imagined Communities: Reflections of the Origins and Spread of Nationalism* (1991)

Ali Ansari, *A History of Modern Iran* (2003)

James A. Bill, *The Eagle and the Lion* (1988) (on Iran)

Scott L. Bills, *Empire and Cold War* (1990)

H. W. Brands, *The Specter of Neutralism* (1988)

D. Clayton Brown, *Globalization and America Since 1945* (2003)

Arturo Morales Carrión, *Puerto Rico* (1983)

Nick Cullather, *Secret History* (1999) (on Guatemala)

———, "Development? It's History," *Diplomatic History* 24 (Fall 2000), 641–654

Andrew DeRoche, *Black, White, and Chrome* (2001) (on Zimbabwe)

David Engerman, "Research Agenda for the History of Tourism," *American Studies International,* 32 (1994), 3–31

——— et al., *Staging Growth* (2003)

Arturo Escobar, *Encountering Development* (1995)

Ronald Fernandez, *The Disenchanted Island* (1992) (on Puerto Rico)

Max Paul Friedman, "Retiring Puppets, Bringing Latin America Back In: Recent Scholarship on United States-Latin American Relations," *Diplomatic History* 5 (November 2003), 621–636

Michael D. Gambone, *Eisenhower, Samoza, and the Cold War* (1997)

Mark Gasiorowski, *U.S. Foreign Policy and the Shah* (1991)

Irene L. Gendzier, *Notes from the Minefield* (1997) (on the Middle East)

Jessica C.E. Gienow-Hecht and Frank Schumacher, *Culture and International History* (2003)

Piero Gleijeses, *Conflicting Missions* (2002) (on Cuba and Africa)

———, *Shattered Hope* (1991) (on Guatemala)

James Goode, *The United States and Iran* (1997)

Mary Ann Heiss, *Empire and Nationhood* (1997) (on Iran)

Gerald C. Horne, *From the Barrel of a Gun* (2001) (on Zimbabwe)

Richard I. Immerman, *The C.I.A. in Guatemala* (1982)

Stephen Kinzer, *All the Shah's Men* (2003)

Christina Klein, *Cold War Orientalism* (2003) (on Asia)

Gabriel Kolko, *Confronting the Third World* (1988)

Peter Kuznik, *Rethinking Cold War Culture*

Marie-Francois Lanfant et al., eds., *International Tourism* (1995)

Michael Latham, *Modernization and Ideology* (2000)

Douglas Little, *American Orientalism* (2002) (on the Middle East)

Kyle Longley, *The Sparrow and the Hawk* (1997) (on Costa Rica)

Mark Hamilton Lytle, *The Origins of the Iranian-American Alliance* (1987)

Dean MacCannell, *The Tourist* (1999)

Robert J. McMahon, *Cold War on the Periphery* (1994) (on India and Pakistan)

Alan McPherson, *Yankee No! Anti-Americanism in U.S.–Latin American Relations* (2003)

Gary May, "Passing the Torch and Lighting Fires: The Peace Corps," in Thomas G. Paterson, ed., *Kennedy's Quest for Victory* (1989), 284–316

Dennis Merrill, *Bread and the Ballot* (1990) (on India)

Stephen R. Niblo, *War, Diplomacy, and Development* (1995) (on Mexico)

Louis A. Pérez Jr., *On Becoming Cuban* (1999)

Frederick B. Pike, *The United States and Latin America* (1992)

Stephen G. Rabe, *Eisenhower and Latin America* (1989)

———, *The Most Dangerous Area of the World* (1999) (on JFK and Latin America)

T. Zane Reeves, *The Politics of the Peace Corps and Vista* (1988)

Yale Richmond, *Cultural Exchange and the Cold War* (2003)

Darlene Rivas, *Missionary Capitalist* (2002) (on Nelson Rockefeller)

Eric Paul Roorda, *The Dictator Next Door* (1998) (on the Dominican Republic)

Andrew J. Rotter, *Comrades at Odds* (2000)

Edward Said, *Culture and Imperialism* (1993)

———, *Orientalism* (1978)

Frances Saunders, *The Cultural Cold War* (2000)

Stephen C. Schlesinger and Stephen Kinzer, *Bitter Fruit* (1983) (on Guatemala)

David E. Schmitz, *Thank God They're on Our Side* (1999) (on the U.S. and dictators)

Rosalie Schwartz, *Pleasure Island* (1997) (on Cuban tourism)

James F. Seikmeir, *Aid, Nationalism, and InterAmerican Relations* (2001)

Amy L.S. Staples, "Seeing Diplomacy Through Bankers' Eyes: The World Bank, the Anglo-Iranian Oil Crisis, and the Aswan High Dam," *Diplomatic History,* 26 (2002), 397–418

Joseph E. Stiglitz, *Globalization and Its Discontents* (2002)

Stephen M. Streeter, *Managing the Counterrevolution* (2000) (on Guatemala)

John A. Tomlinson, *Globalization and Culture* (1999)

J. Urry, *The Tourist Gaze in Contemporary Society* (1990)

Reinhold Wagnleitner and Elaine Tyler May, eds., *"Here, There, and Everywhere"* (2000)

Thomas Zeiller and Alfred Eckes Jr., *Globalization and the American Century* (2003)

Cuba and the Missile Crisis

In October 1962, American U-2 reconnaissance planes photographed missile sites installed by the Soviets on the Caribbean island of Cuba. The missiles could carry nuclear weapons, and they could reach the United States. After meeting with his advisers and deciding to announce U.S. policy in a television address, President John F. Kennedy demanded withdrawal of the missiles and imposed a blockade around Cuba. A chilling war scare gripped Moscow, Havana, and Washington— and terrified the world. This was the closest the United States and the Soviet Union had ever come to nuclear war. Exchanges of diplomatic letters, rallying of allies, exhausting meetings, military preparations, and operational accidents soon followed.

In the end, deeply frightened by the prospect of nuclear disaster, Premier Nikita Khrushchev and President Kennedy settled the crisis without consulting Cuban premier Fidel Castro. The United States promised not to invade Cuba (as it had done using Cuban exiles in April 1961, at the Bay of Pigs) and assented to the removal of its Jupiter missiles from Turkey. In return, the Soviet Union agreed to withdraw its missiles from Cuba. The U.S. no-invasion pledge in fact never took effect because Castro refused to permit U.S.-stipulated United Nations follow-up inspections. But the Soviets dismantled their missiles and sent them home, and the Jupiters in Turkey also came down.

Beneath the Cuban missile crisis—or the "Caribbean crisis," as Soviet leaders called it—lay years of Cuban-American antagonism. On taking power in 1959, Fidel Castro launched a revolution that challenged major U.S. interests on the island, including mob-run casinos, U.S. military missions, and investments worth a billion dollars. Castro decried U.S. hegemony and Cuban dependency, and he vowed a restructuring of economic and political life to reduce U.S. influence that had grown especially since the interventionist Platt Amendment at the start of the century. Washington became alarmed, too, because the Cuban Revolution gained popularity throughout the Western Hemisphere and because Castro declared as one of his missions the spread of revolution across Latin America. In 1960, economic relations deteriorated severely when the United States instituted trade sanctions. The Cubans increasingly turned for help to the Soviet Union, which became the island's economic and military partner. In January 1961 the United States broke diplomatic relations with Havana. In 1961–1962 came the Bay of Pigs expedition, covert operations designed to cripple the Cuban economy through sabotage, Central Intelligence Agency (CIA) assassination plots against Castro, diplomatic efforts to isolate Cuba, and military maneuvers and plans that seemed to portend a U.S.

invasion. Because these regional events occurred during a particularly tense time in the Cold War, the U.S.-Cuba contest held international consequences.

In recent years a greater proportion of the documentary record on the missile crisis in the archives of the United States, Russia, and Cuba has opened for research, and crisis participants have gathered in meetings to reexamine the 1962 confrontation. As a result, we have a more textured, nuanced, and international perspective on the nuclear showdown. Yet the expanding record has not dulled the thoughtfulness or intensity of the scholarly debate surrounding the events. Explaining the origins of the Soviet-American face-off, some analysts emphasize the importance of Moscow's global strategic goals: obtaining nuclear parity, or the appearance of parity, with the United States; or perhaps creating an atmosphere conducive to a favorable settlement of the Berlin crisis. Others accent the importance of the Cuban setting, especially the bad blood that ran between Washington and Havana in light of Castro's anti-Americanism and Washington's repeated efforts to snuff out the Communist regime. The interpretive differences are important. From one perspective the missile crisis stemmed from Soviet Cold War expansionism. The other side contends that the incident arose primarily from a long history of U.S. hegemony in the Caribbean and Latin America. Which imperialism triggered the dangerous drama—Soviet or American? Or both?

Scholars also disagree in assessing how the crisis was handled. Some writers have lavished praise on the Kennedy team for its "crisis management" skills. At the outset, the young president surrounded himself with a small group of talented advisers, the Executive Committee of the National Security Council, or ExComm, that according to analysts carefully weighed options and consequences. In the end the administration deployed a mix of diplomacy and military force designed to coerce peacefully an outcome favorable to the United States—the removal of the Soviet missiles. Critics, however, charge that Kennedy, a Cold War hawk eager to prove his mettle, shunned quiet, behind-the-scenes diplomacy in favor of televised oratory, a provocative naval blockade, and a highly publicized military buildup that heightened tensions. Instead of cool-headed, calibrated deliberation, ExComm operated under heavy stress and emotion, and on several occasions it nearly lost control of policy to subordinates. The critics contend that the crisis eased not when the Kremlin decided to submit to Washington's demands, but when Kennedy belatedly agreed to a secret removal of U.S. Jupiter missiles from Turkey—following a string of near misses involving both Soviet and American military mishaps. Castro, apparently left in the dark during the final negotiations, had little praise for either superpower by the time the impasse had been resolved.

What exactly brought about this very near human catastrophe? Did American and Soviet leaders realize the magnitude of the crisis and rise to the occasion with forceful but effective diplomacy? Or did they overact, misjudge, and in the end simply luck out? What lessons about international behavior can be drawn from the Cuban missile crisis?

🌐 D O C U M E N T S

Document 1 is drawn from a November 1975 report by the U.S. Senate Select Committee to Study Governmental Operations with Respect to Intelligence Activities. Chaired by Senator Frank Church of Idaho, this committee detailed CIA assassination plots against Fidel Castro. Document 2, dated March 14, 1962, constitutes the initial guidelines for Operation Mongoose, the CIA's conspiracy to overthrow the Castro government through "indigenous sources" and possibly U.S. military intervention. President Kennedy apparently approved this secret document, and his brother, Attorney General Robert F. Kennedy, became the primary overseer of the spoiling operation.

Document 3 includes significant parts of the transcribed record of Kennedy's first two meetings with his high-level advisers on October 16, 1962, the day intelligence officials presented him with photographs showing Soviet missile sites under construction in Cuba. Document 4 is Kennedy's October 22 television address to the nation and the world. The president insisted on removal of the missiles and announced the U.S. "quarantine" of Cuba. On October 26 Premier Khrushchev replied to a Kennedy letter of the preceding day that had reiterated the U.S. case against the missile bases. The Khrushchev letter, reprinted here as Document 5, denounces the blockade and claims that the Soviet weapons had been sent to defend Cuba against a U.S. invasion. The Soviet leader also offered a deal: He would remove the "armaments" from Cuba if the United States pledged not to invade Cuba.

On October 27 Khrushchev sent another letter to Kennedy, included here as Document 6. Adding to his earlier request for a no-invasion promise, Khrushchev asked for the removal of American Jupiter missiles from Turkey. President Kennedy again convened his advisers—now called the Executive Committee (ExComm)—to discuss this new request. A record of part of their meeting of October 27 is found in Document 7. Kennedy decided to pull the Jupiters out of Turkey; Robert Kennedy soon privately conveyed this concession to the Soviets, and the crisis dissipated. Document 8, from Russian archives, reports conversations between the high-ranking Soviet official Anastas I. Mikoyan and Fidel Castro in Havana on November 4 and 5. Standing out in these intense exchanges are Soviet claims of victory and Cuban protests against both superpowers for their ending the crisis without consulting the Cuban government.

1. CIA Assassination Plots Against Cuban Leader Fidel Castro (1960–1965), 1975

Efforts against Castro did not begin with assassination attempts.

From March through August 1960, during the last year of the Eisenhower Administration, the CIA considered plans to undermine Castro's charismatic appeal by sabotaging his speeches. According to the 1967 Report of the CIA's Inspector General, an official in the Technical Services Division (TSD) recalled discussing a scheme to spray Castro's broadcasting studio with a chemical which produced effects similar to LSD, but the scheme was rejected because the chemical was unreliable. During this period, TSD impregnated a box of cigars with a chemical which produced temporary disorientation, hoping to induce Castro to smoke one of the cigars before delivering a speech. The Inspector General also reported a plan to destroy Castro's image as "The Beard" by dusting his shoes with thallium salts, a strong depilatory that would cause his beard to fall out. The depilatory was to be administered during a trip outside Cuba, when it was anticipated Castro would leave his shoes outside the door of his hotel room to be shined. TSD procured the chemical and tested it on animals, but apparently abandoned the scheme because Castro cancelled his trip. . . .

A notation in the records of the Operations Division, CIA's Office of Medical Services, indicates that on August 16, 1960, an official was given a box of Castro's

This document can be found in U.S. Senate, Select Committee to Study Governmental Operations with Respect to Intelligence Activities, *Alleged Assassination Plots Involving Foreign Leaders: An Interim Report* (Washington, D.C.: Government Printing Office, November 1975), pp. 71–77, 79–80, 83–85, 148.

favorite cigars with instructions to treat them with lethal poison. The cigars were contaminated with a botulinum toxin so potent that a person would die after putting one in his mouth. The official reported that the cigars were ready on October 7, 1960; TSD notes indicate that they were delivered to an unidentified person on February 13, 1961. The record does not disclose whether an attempt was made to pass the cigars to Castro.

In August 1960, the CIA took steps to enlist members of the criminal underworld with gambling syndicate contacts to aid in assassinating Castro. . . .

The earliest concrete evidence of the operation is a conversation between DDP [Deputy Director for Plans Richard] Bissell and Colonel Sheffield Edwards, Director of the Office of Security. Edwards recalled that Bissell asked him to locate someone who could assassinate Castro. Bissell confirmed that he requested Edwards to find someone to assassinate Castro and believed that Edwards raised the idea of contacting members of a gambling syndicate operating in Cuba. . . .

Edwards and the Support Chief [of the Office of Security] decided to rely on Robert A. Maheu to recruit someone "tough enough" to handle the job. Maheu was an ex-FBI agent who had entered into a career as a private investigator in 1954. A former FBI associate of Maheu's was employed in the CIA's Office of Security and had arranged for the CIA to use Maheu in several sensitive covert operations in which "he didn't want to have an Agency person or a government person get caught.". . .

Sometime in late August or early September 1960, the Support Chief approached Maheu about the proposed operation. As Maheu recalls the conversation, the Support Chief asked him to contact John Rosselli, an underworld figure with possible gambling contacts in Las Vegas, to determine if he would participate in a plan to "dispose" of Castro. The Support Chief testified, on the other hand, that it was Maheu who raised the idea of using Rosselli. . . .

According to Rosselli, he and Maheu met at the Brown Derby Restaurant in Beverly Hills in early September 1960. Rosselli testified that Maheu told him that "high government officials" needed his cooperation in getting rid of Castro, and that he asked him to help recruit Cubans to do the job. Maheu's recollection of that meeting was that "I informed him that I had been asked by my Government to solicit his cooperation in this particular venture." . . .

A meeting was arranged for Maheu and Rosselli with the Support Chief at the Plaza Hotel in New York. The Inspector General's Report placed the meeting on September 14, 1960. Rosselli testified that he could not recall the precise date of the meeting, but that it had occurred during Castro's visit to the United Nations, which the New York Times Index places from September 18 through September 28, 1960. . . .

It was arranged that Rosselli would go to Florida and recruit Cubans for the operation. Edwards informed Bissell that contact had been made with the gambling syndicate. . . .

Maheu handled the details of setting up the operation and keeping the Support Chief informed of developments. After Rosselli and Maheu had been in Miami for a short time, and certainly prior to October 18, Rosselli introduced Maheu to two individuals on whom Rosselli intended to rely: "Sam Gold," who would serve as a "back-up man," or "key" man and "Joe," whom "Gold" said would serve as a courier to Cuba and make arrangements there. The Support Chief, who was using the name "Jim Olds," said he had met "Sam" and "Joe" once, and then only briefly.

The Support Chief testified that he learned the true identities of his associates one morning when Maheu called and asked him to examine the "Parade" supplement to the *Miami Times*. An article on the Attorney General's ten-most-wanted criminals list revealed that "Sam Gold" was Momo Salvatore Giancana, a Chicago-based gangster, and "Joe" was Santos Trafficante, the Cosa Nostra chieftain in Cuba. The Support Chief reported his discovery to Edwards, but did not know whether Edwards reported this fact to his superiors. The Support Chief testified that this incident occurred after "we were up to our ears in it," a month or so after Giancana had been brought into the operation, but prior to giving the poison pills to Rosselli. . . .

The Inspector General's Report described conversations among Bissell, Edwards, and the Chief of the Technical Services Division (TSD), concerning the most effective method of poisoning Castro. There is some evidence that Giancana or Rosselli originated the idea of depositing a poison pill in Castro's drink to give the "asset" a chance to escape. The Support Chief recalled Rosselli's request for something "nice and clean, without getting into any kind of out and out ambushing," preferably a poison that would disappear without a trace. . . .

Edwards rejected the first batch of pills prepared by TSD because they would not dissolve in water. A second batch, containing botulinum toxin, "did the job expected of them" when tested on monkeys. The Support Chief received the pills from TSD, probably in February 1961, with assurances that they were lethal, and then gave them to Rosselli.

The record clearly establishes that the pills were given to a Cuban for delivery to the island some time prior to the Bay of Pigs invasion in mid-April 1961. There are discrepancies in the record, however, concerning whether one or two attempts were made during that period, and the precise date on which the passage[s] occurred. The Inspector General's Report states that in late February or March 1961, Rosselli reported to the Support Chief that the pills had been delivered to an official close to Castro who may have received kickbacks from the gambling interests. The Report states that the official returned the pills after a few weeks, perhaps because he had lost his position in the Cuban Government, and thus access to Castro, before he received the pills. The Report concludes that yet another attempt was made in April 1961, with the aid of a leading figure in the Cuban exile movement. . . .

In early April 1962, Harvey, who testified that he was acting on "explicit orders" from [Director of Operations Richard] Helms, requested Edwards to put him in touch with Rosselli. The Support Chief first introduced [Operation Mongoose task force chief William K.] Harvey to Rosselli in Miami, where Harvey told Rosselli to maintain his Cuban contacts, but not to deal with Maheu or Giancana, whom he had decided were "untrustworthy" and "surplus." The Support Chief recalled that initially Rosselli did not trust Harvey although they subsequently developed a close friendship.

Harvey, the Support Chief and Rosselli met for a second time in New York on April 8–9, 1962. A notation made during this time in the files of the Technical Services Division indicates that four poison pills were given to the Support Chief on April 18, 1962. The pills were passed to Harvey, who arrived in Miami on April 21, and found Rosselli already in touch with the same Cuban who had been involved in the pre–Bay of Pigs pill passage. He gave the pills to Rosselli, explaining that "these would work anywhere and at any time with anything." Rosselli testified that he told Harvey that the Cubans intended to use the pills to assassinate Che Guevara as well as Fidel and Raul Castro. According to Rosselli's testimony, Harvey approved of the targets, stating "everything is all right, what they want to do."

The Cuban requested arms and equipment as a *quid pro quo* for carrying out the assassination operation. With the help of the CIA's Miami station which ran covert operations against Cuba (JM/WAVE), Harvey procured explosives, detonators, rifles, handguns, radios, and boat radar costing about $5,000. . . .

Harvey met Rosselli in Miami on September 7 and 11, 1962. The Cuban was reported to be preparing to send in another three-man team to penetrate Castro's bodyguard. Harvey was told that the pills, referred to as "the medicine," were still "safe" in Cuba.

Harvey testified that by this time he had grave doubts about whether the operation would ever take place, and told Rosselli that "there's not much likelihood that this is going anyplace, or that it should be continued." The second team never left for Cuba, claiming that "conditions" in Cuba were not right. During early January 1963, Harvey paid Rosselli $2,700 to defray the Cuban's expenses. Harvey terminated the operation in mid-February 1963. . . .

As [for the question of authorization], both Helms and the high Kennedy Administration officials who testified agreed that no direct order was ever given for Castro's assassination and that no senior Administration officials, including [CIA head John A.] McCone, were informed about the assassination activity. Helms testified, however, that he believed the assassination activity was permissible and that it was within the scope of authority given to the Agency. McCone and other Kennedy Administration officials disagreed, testifying that assassination was impermissible without a direct order and that Castro's assassination was not within the bounds of the MONGOOSE operation [the covert U.S. operation designed to undermine the Castro government].

As DDP, Helms was in charge of covert operations when the poison pills were given to Rosselli in Miami in April 1962. Helms had succeeded to this post following Bissell's retirement in February 1962. He testified that after the Bay of Pigs:

> Those of us who were still [in the agency] were enormously anxious to try and be successful at what we were being asked to do by what was then a relatively new Administration. We wanted to earn our spurs with the President and with other officers of the Kennedy Administration.

2. Guidelines for Operation Mongoose, 1962

1. Operation Mongoose will be developed on the following assumptions:
   a. In undertaking to cause the overthrow of the target government, the U.S. will make maximum use of indigenous resources, internal and external, but recognizes that final success will require decisive U.S. military intervention.
   b. Such indigenous resources as are developed will be used to prepare for and justify this intervention, and thereafter to facilitate and support it.

This document can be found in Document 6, Guidelines for *Operation Mongoose,* 14 March 1962; Alleged Assassination Plots Involving Foreign Leaders, 20 November 1975, pp. 145–147, 159, "The Cuban Missile Crisis: The Making of U.S. Policy," National Security Archive Microfiche Collection, National Security Archives, Washington, D.C. It can also be found in Lawrence Chang and Peter Kornbluh, eds., *The Cuban Missile Crisis: A National Security Archive Documents Reader* (New York: The New Press, 1992), pp. 38–39.

2. The immediate priority objective of U.S. efforts during the coming months will be the acquisition of hard intelligence on the target area. Concurrently, all other political, economic and covert actions will be undertaken short of those reasonably calculated to inspire a revolt within the target area, or other development which would require armed U.S. intervention. These actions, insofar as possible, will be consistent with overt policies of isolating the [two words illegible on the document but probably are "Cuban leader"] and of neutralizing his influence in the Western Hemisphere.

3. Missiles Photographed in Cuba: President John F. Kennedy Meets with His Advisers, October 16, 1962

Meeting of 11:50 A.M.–12:57 P.M.

Lundahl*: This is a result of the photography taken Sunday, sir.

JFK: Yeah.

Lundahl: There's a medium-range ballistic missile launch site and two new military encampments on the southern edge of Sierra del Rosario in west central Cuba.

JFK: Where would that be?

Lundahl: Uh, west central, sir. That. . . .

JFK: Yeah. . . .

Lundahl: Well, one site on one of the encampments contains a total of at least fourteen canvas-covered missile trailers measuring 67 feet in length, 9 feet in width. The overall length of the trailers plus the tow-bars is approximately 80 feet. The other encampment contains vehicles and tents but with no missile trailers. . . .

JFK: How far advanced is this? . . . How do you know this is a medium-range ballistic missile?

Lundahl: The length, sir. . . .

JFK: Is this ready to be fired?

Graybeal**: No, sir.

JFK: How long have we got. . . . We can't tell, I take it . . .

Graybeal: No, sir.

JFK: . . . how long before it can be fired?

Graybeal: That depends on how ready the . . .

JFK: But, what does it have to be fired from?

Graybeal: It would have to be fired from a stable hard surface. This could be packed dirt; it could be concrete or, or asphalt. The surface has to be hard, then you put a flame deflect-, a deflector plate on there to direct the missile.

This document can be found in Presidential Records, Transcripts, President's Office Files, John F. Kennedy Presidential Papers, John F. Kennedy Library, Boston, MA. It can also be found in U.S. Department of State, *Foreign Relations of the United States, 1961–1963, Cuban Missile Crisis and Aftermath* (Washington, D.C.: Government Printing Office, 1996), XI, 31–45, 49–93.

*Art Lundahl, National Photograhic Interpretation Center.

**Sidney Graybeal.

McNamara*: Would you care to comment on the position of nuclear warheads—this is in relation to the question from the president—explain when these can be fired?

Graybeal: Sir, we've looked very hard. We can find nothing that would spell nuclear warhead in terms of any isolated area or unique security in this particular area. The mating of the nuclear warhead to the missile from some of the other short range missiles there would take about, uh, a couple of hours to do this.

McNamara: This is not defensed, I believe, at the moment?

Lundahl: Not yet, sir. . . .

Rusk**: Don't you have to assume these are nuclear? . . .

McNamara: There's no question about that. The question is one of readiness of the, to fire and—and this is highly critical in forming our plans—that the time between today and the time when the readiness to fire capability develops is a very important thing. To estimate that we need to know where these warheads are, and we have not yet found any probable storage of warheads and hence it seems extremely unlikely that they are now ready to fire or may be ready to fire within a matter of hours or even a day or two. . . .

JFK: Secretary Rusk?

Rusk: Yes. [Well?], Mr. President, this is a, of course, a [widely?] serious development. It's one that we, all of us, had not really believed the Soviets could, uh, carry this far. . . . Now, uhm, I do think we have to set in motion a chain of events that will eliminate this base. I don't think we [can?] sit still. . . . The thing that I'm, of course, very conscious of is that there is no such thing, I think, as unilateral action by the United States. It's so [eminently or heavily?] involved with 2 allies and confrontation in many places, that any action that we take, uh, will greatly increase the risks of direct action involving, uh, our other alliances and our other forces in other parts of the world. Uhm, so I think we, we have to think very hard about two major, uh, courses of action as alternatives. One is the quick strike. The point where we [make or think?], that is the, uh, overwhelming, overriding necessity to take all the risks that are involved doing that. I don't think this in itself would require an invasion of Cuba. I think that with or without such an invasion, in other words if we make it clear that, uh, what we're doing is eliminating this particular base or any other such base that is established. We ourselves are not moved to general war, we're simply doing what we said we would do if they took certain action. Uh, or we're going to decide that this is the time to eliminate the Cuban problem by actually eliminating the island.

The other would be, if we have a few days—from the military point of view, if we have the whole time—uh, then I would think that, uh, there would be another course of action, a combination of things that, uh, we might wish to consider. Uhm, first, uh, that we, uh, stimulate the OAS [Organization of American States] procedure immediately for prompt action to make it quite clear that the entire hemisphere considers that the Rio Pact [the hemispheric Cold War military alliance] has been violated [and actually?] what acts should [we take or be taken?] in, under the terms of the Rio Pact. . . .

I think also that we ought to consider getting some word to Castro, perhaps through the Canadian ambassador in Havana or through, uh, his representative at

---

*Robert McNamara, secretary of defense.

**Dean Rusk, secretary of state.

the U.N. Uh, I think perhaps the Canadian ambassador would be best, the better channel to get to Castro [apart?] privately and tell him that, uh, this is no longer support for Cuba, that Cuba is being victimized here, and that, uh, the Soviets are preparing Cuba for destruction or betrayal. . . .

And I think there are certain military, uhm, uh, actions that we could, we might well want to take straight away. First, to, uh, to call up, uh, highly selective units [no more than?] 150,000. Unless we feel that it's better, more desirable to go to a general national emergency so that we have complete freedom of action. If we announce, at the time that we announce this development—and I think we do have to announce this development some time this week—uh, we announce that, uh, we are conducting a surveillance of Cuba, over Cuba, and we will enforce our right to do so. We reject the mission of secrecy in this hemisphere in any matters of this sort. We, we reinforce our forces in Guantánamo. We reinforce our forces in the southeastern part of the United States—whatever is necessary from the military point of view to be able to give, to deliver an overwhelming strike at any of these installations, including the SAM [surface-to-air missile] sites. And, uh, also, to take care of any, uh, MiGs or bombers that might make a pass at Miami or at the United States. Build up heavy forces, uh, if those are not already in position. . . .

I think also that we need a few days, uhm, to alert our other allies, for consultation with NATO [North Atlantic Treaty Organization]. I'll assume that we can move on this line at the same time to interrupt all air traffic from free world countries going into Cuba, insist to the Mexicans, the Dutch, that they stop their planes from coming in. Tell the British, who, and anyone else who's involved at this point, that, uh, if they're interested in peace, that they've got to stop their ships from Cuban trade at this point. Uh, in other words, isolate Cuba completely without at this particular moment a, uh, a forceful blockade. . . .

But I think that, by and large, there are, there are these two broad alternatives: one, the quick strike; the other, to alert our allies and Mr. Khrushchev that there is utterly serious crisis in the making here, and that, uh. . . . Mr. Khrushchev may not himself really understand that or believe that at this point. I think we'll be facing a situation that could well lead to general war. . . .

McNamara: Mr. President, there are a number of unknowns in this situation I want to comment upon, and, in relation to them, I would like to outline very briefly some possible military alternatives and ask General Taylor to expand upon them.

But before commenting on either the unknowns or outlining some military alternatives, there are two propositions I would suggest that we ought to accept as, uh, foundations for our further thinking. My first is that if we are to conduct an air strike against these installations, or against any part of Cuba, we must agree now that we will schedule that prior to the time these missile sites become operational. I'm not prepared to say when that will be, but I think it is extremely important that our talk and our discussion be founded on this premise: that any air strike will be planned to take place prior to the time they become operational. Because, if they become operational before the air strike, I do not believe we can state we can knock them out before they can be launched; and if they're launched there is almost certain to be, uh, chaos in part of the east coast or the area, uh, in a radius of six hundred to a thousand miles from Cuba.

Uh, secondly, I, I would submit the proposition that any air strike must be directed not solely against the missile sites, but against the missile sites plus the airfields plus the aircraft which may not be on the airfields but hidden by that time plus all potential nuclear storage sites. . . .

Taylor*: Uh, we're impressed, Mr. President, with the great importance of getting a, a strike with all the benefits of surprise, uh, which would mean *ideally* that we would have all the missiles that are in Cuba above ground where we can take them out. Uh, that, that desire runs counter to the strong point the secretary made if the other optimum would be to get every missile before it could, becomes operational. Uh, practically, I think the, our knowledge of the timing of the readiness is going to be so, so, uh, difficult that we'll never have the, the exact permanent, uh, the perfect timing. . . .

I would also mention among the, the military actions we should take that once we have destroyed as many of these offensive weapons as possible, we should, should prevent any more coming in, which means a naval blockade. . . .

JFK: What is the, uh, advant-. . . . Must be some major reason for the Russians to, uh, set this up as a. . . . Must be that they're not satisfied with their ICBMs [Intercontinental Ballistic Missiles]. What'd be the reason that they would, uh. . . .

Taylor: What it'd give 'em is primary, it makes the launching base, uh, for short range missiles against the United States to supplement their rather [deceptive?] ICBM system, for example. . . .

Rusk: Still, about why the Soviets are doing this, uhm, Mr. McCone** suggested some weeks ago that one thing Mr. Khrushchev may have in mind is that, uh, uh, he knows that we have a substantial nuclear superiority, but he also knows that we don't really live under fear of his nuclear weapons to the extent that, uh, he has to live under fear of ours. Also we have nuclear weapons nearby, in Turkey and places like that.

JFK: How many weapons do we have in Turkey?

Taylor?: We have Jupiter missiles. . . .

McNamara?: About fifteen, I believe it is. . . .

Rusk: . . . I think also that, uh, Berlin is, uh, very much involved in this. Uhm, for the first time, I'm beginning really to wonder whether maybe Mr. Khrushchev is entirely rational about Berlin. We've [hardly?] talked about his obsession with it. And I think we have to, uh, keep our eye on that element. But, uh, they may be thinking that they can either bargain Berlin and Cuba against each other, or that they could provoke us into a kind of action in Cuba which would give an umbrella for them to take action with respect to Berlin. . . .

JFK: Uh, eh, well, this, which . . . What you're really talking about are two or three different, uh, [tense?] operations. One is the strike just on this, these three bases. One, the second is the broader one that Secretary McNamara was talking about, which is on the airfields and on the SAM sites and on anything else connected with, uh, missiles. Third is doing both of those things and also at the same time launching a blockade, which requires really the, uh, the, uh, third and which is a larger step. And then, as I take it, the fourth question is the, uh, degree of consultation.

RFK***: Mr. President.

JFK: Yes.

---

*General Maxwell Taylor, chairman of the Joint Chiefs of Staff.
**John A. McCone, director of the Central Intelligence Agency.
***Robert F. Kennedy.

RFK: We have the fifth one, really, which is the invasion. I would say that, uh, you're dropping bombs all over Cuba if you do the second, uh, air, the airports, knocking out their planes, dropping it on all their missiles. You're covering most of Cuba. You're going to kill an awful lot of people, and, uh, we're going to take an awful lot of heat on it . . .

JFK: I don't believe it takes us, at least, uh. . . . How long did it take to get in a position where we can invade Cuba? Almost a month? Two months?

McNamara: No, sir. . . .

JFK: I think we ought to, what we ought to do is, is, uh, after this meeting this afternoon, we ought to meet tonight again at six, consider these various, uh, proposals. In the meanwhile, we'll go ahead with this maximum, whatever is needed from the flights, and, in addition, we will. . . . I don't think we got much time on these missiles. They may be. . . . So it may be that we just have to, we can't wait two weeks while we're getting ready to, to roll. Maybe just have to just take *them out,* and continue our other preparations if we decide to do that. That may be where we end up. I think we ought to, beginning right now, be preparing to. . . . Because that's what we're going to do *anyway.* We're certainly going to do number one; we're going to take out these, uh, missiles. Uh, the questions will be whether, which, what I would describe as number two, which would be a general air strike. That we're not ready to say, but we should be in preparation for it. The third is the, is the, uh, the general invasion. At least we're going to do number one, so it seems to me that we don't have to wait very long. We, we ought to be making *those* preparations.

Bundy*: You want to be clear, Mr. President, whether we have *definitely* decided *against* a political [i.e., diplomatic] track. I, myself, think we ought . . .

Taylor?: Well, we'll have . . .

Bundy: . . . to work out a contingency on that.

Taylor?: We, we'll develop both tracks.

Meeting of 6:30–7:55 P.M.

McNamara: Mr. President, could I outline three courses of action we have considered and speak very briefly on each one? The first is what I would call the political course of action, in which we, uh, follow some of the possibilities that Secretary Rusk mentioned this morning by approaching Castro, by approaching Khrushchev, by discussing with our allies. An overt and open approach politically to the problem [attempting, or in order?] to solve it. This seemed to me likely to lead to no satisfactory result, and it almost stops subsequent military action. . . .

A second course of action we haven't discussed but lies in between the military course we began discussing a moment ago and the political course of action is a course of action that would involve declaration of open surveillance; a statement that we would immediately impose an, uh, a blockade against *offensive* weapons entering Cuba in the future; and an indication that with our open-surveillance reconnaissance which we would plan to maintain indefinitely for the future. . . .

---

*McGeorge Bundy, assistant for national security affairs.

But the third course of action is any one of these variants of military action directed against Cuba, starting with an air attack against the missiles. The Chiefs are strongly opposed to so limited an air attack. But even so limited an air attack is a very extensive air attack. It's not twenty sorties or fifty sorties or a hundred sorties, but probably several hundred sorties. Uh, we haven't worked out the details. It's very difficult to do so when we lack certain intelligence that we hope to have tomorrow or the next day. But it's a substantial air attack. . . . I don't believe we have considered the consequences of any of these actions satisfactorily, and because we haven't considered the consequences, I'm not sure we're taking all the action we ought to take now to minimize those. I, I don't know quite what kind of a world we live in after we've struck Cuba, and we, we've started it. . . .

Taylor: And you'll miss some [missiles].

McNamara: And you'll miss some. That's right. Now after we've launched sorties, what kind of a world do we live in? How, how do we stop at that point? I don't know the answer to this. I think tonight State and we ought to work on the consequences of any one of these courses of actions, consequences which I don't believe are entirely clear. . . .

JFK: If the, uh, it doesn't increase very much their strategic, uh, strength, why is it, uh, can any Russian expert tell us why they. . . . After all Khrushchev demonstrated a sense of caution [thousands?] . . .

Speaker?: Well, there are several, several possible . . .

JFK: . . . Berlin, he's been cautious, I mean, he hasn't been, uh . . .

Ball:* Several possibilities, Mr. President. One of them is that he has given us word now that he's coming over in November to, to the UN. If, he may be proceeding on the assumption, and this lack of a sense of *apparent* urgency would seem to, to support this, that this *isn't* going to be discovered at the moment and that, uh, when he comes over this is something he can do, a ploy. That here is Cuba armed against the United States, or possibly use it to try to trade something in Berlin, saying he'll disarm Cuba, if, uh, if we'll yield some of our interests in Berlin and some arrangement for it. I mean, that this is a, it's a trading ploy.

Bundy: I would think one thing that I would still cling to is that he's not likely to give Fidel Castro nuclear warheads. I don't believe that has happened or is likely to happen.

JFK: Why does he put these in there though?

Bundy: Soviet-controlled nuclear warheads [of the kind?] . . .

JFK: That's right, but what is the advantage of that? It's just as if we suddenly began to put a major number of MRBMs [Medium-Range Ballistic Missiles] in Turkey. Now that'd be goddam dangerous, I would think.

Bundy: Well, we *did,* Mr. President. . . .

JFK: Yeah, but that was five years ago. . . .

Ball: Yes, I think, I think you, you look at this possibility that this is an attempt to, to add to his strategic capabilities. A second consideration is that it is simply a trading ploy, that he, he wants this in so that he could, he could [words unintelligible]. . . .

---

*George W. Ball, undersecretary of state.

JFK: Well, it's a goddam mystery to me. I don't know enough about the Soviet Union, but if anybody can tell me any other time since the Berlin blockade where the Russians have given us so clear provocation, I don't know when it's been, because they've been awfully cautious really. The Russians, I never. . . . Now, maybe our mistake was in not saying some time *before* this summer that if they do this we're [word unintelligible] to act.

4. Kennedy Addresses the Nation, October 22, 1962

This urgent transformation of Cuba into an important strategic base—by the presence of these large, long-range, and clearly offensive weapons of sudden mass destruction—constitutes an explicit threat to the peace and security of all the Americas, in flagrant and deliberate defiance of the Rio Pact of 1947, the traditions of this nation and hemisphere, the Joint Resolution of the 87th Congress, the Charter of the United Nations, and my own public warnings to the Soviets on September 4 and 13.

This action also contradicts the repeated assurances of Soviet spokesmen, both publicly and privately delivered, that the arms buildup in Cuba would retain its original defensive character and that the Soviet Union had no need or desire to station strategic missiles on the territory of any other nation.

The size of this undertaking makes clear that it has been planned for some months. Yet only last month, after I had made clear the distinction between any introduction of ground-to-ground missiles and the existence of defensive antiaircraft missiles, the Soviet Government publicly stated on September 11 that, and I quote, "The armaments and military equipment sent to Cuba are designed exclusively for defensive purposes," and, and I quote the Soviet Government, "There is no need for the Soviet Government to shift its weapons for a retaliatory blow to any other country, for instance Cuba," and that, and I quote the Government, "The Soviet Union has no powerful rockets to carry these nuclear warheads that there is no need to search for sites for them beyond the boundaries of the Soviet Union." That statement was false.

Only last Thursday, as evidence of this rapid offensive buildup was already in my hand, Soviet Foreign Minister Gromyko told me in my office that he was instructed to make it clear once again, as he said his Government had already done, that Soviet assistance to Cuba, and I quote, "pursued solely the purpose of contributing to the defense capabilities of Cuba," that, and I quote him, "training by Soviet specialists of Cuban nationals in handling defensive armaments was by no means offensive," and that "if it were otherwise," Mr. Gromyko went on, "the Soviet Government would never become involved in rendering such assistance." That statement also was false.

Neither the United States of America nor the world community of nations can tolerate deliberate deception and offensive threats on the part of any nation, large or small. We no longer live in a world where only the actual firing of weapons represents a sufficient challenge to a nation's security to constitute maximum peril.

This document can be found in *Department of State Bulletin,* XLVII (November 12, 1962), 715–720.

Nuclear weapons are so destructive and ballistic missiles are so swift that any substantially increased possibility of their use or any sudden change in their deployment may well be regarded as a definite threat to peace. . . .

[T]his secret, swift, and extraordinary buildup of Communist missiles—in an area well known to have a special and historical relationship to the United States and the nations of the Western Hemisphere, in violation of Soviet assurances, and in defiance of American and hemispheric policy—this sudden, clandestine decision to station strategic weapons for the first time outside of Soviet soil—is a deliberately provocative and unjustified change in the *status quo* which cannot be accepted by this country if our courage and our commitments are ever to be trusted again by either friend or foe.

The 1930's taught us a clear lesson: Aggressive conduct, if allowed to grow unchecked and unchallenged, ultimately leads to war. This nation is opposed to war. We are also true to our word. Our unswerving objective, therefore, must be to prevent the use of these missiles against this or any other country and to secure their withdrawal or elimination from the Western Hemisphere. . . .

I have directed that the following *initial* steps be taken immediately:

First: To halt this offensive buildup, a strict quarantine on all offensive military equipment under shipment to Cuba is being initiated. All ships of any kind bound for Cuba from whatever nation or port will, if found to contain cargoes of offensive weapons, be turned back. This quarantine will be extended, if needed, to other types of cargo and carriers. We are not at this time, however, denying the necessities of life as the Soviets attempted to do in their Berlin blockade of 1948.

Second: I have directed the continued and increased close surveillance of Cuba and its military buildup. The Foreign Ministers of the OAS in their communiqué of October 3 rejected secrecy on such matters in this hemisphere. Should these offensive military preparations continue, thus increasing the threat to the hemisphere, further action will be justified. I have directed the Armed Forces to prepare for any eventualities; and I trust that, in the interest of both the Cuban people and the Soviet technicians at the sites, the hazards to all concerned of continuing this threat will be recognized.

Third: It shall be the policy of this nation to regard any nuclear missile launched from Cuba against any nation in the Western Hemisphere as an attack by the Soviet Union on the United States, requiring a full retaliatory response upon the Soviet Union.

Fourth: As a necessary military precaution I have reinforced our base at Guantánamo, evacuated today the dependents of our personnel there, and ordered additional military units to be on a standby alert basis.

Fifth: We are calling tonight for an immediate meeting of the Organ of Consultation, under the Organization of American States, to consider this threat to hemispheric security and to invoke articles 6 and 8 of the Rio Treaty in support of all necessary action. The United Nations Charter allows for regional security arrangements—and the nations of this hemisphere decided long ago against the military presence of outside powers. Our other allies around the world have also been alerted.

Sixth: Under the Charter of the United Nations, we are asking tonight that an emergency meeting of the Security Council be convoked without delay to take action against this latest Soviet threat to world peace. Our resolution will call for the prompt dismantling and withdrawal of all offensive weapons in Cuba, under the supervision of U.N. observers, before the quarantine can be lifted.

Seventh and finally: I call upon Chairman Khrushchev to halt and eliminate this clandestine, reckless, and provocative threat to world peace and to stable relations between our two nations. I call upon him further to abandon this course of world domination and to join in an historic effort to end the perilous arms race and transform the history of man. He has an opportunity now to move the world back from the abyss of destruction—by returning to his Government's own words that it had no need to station missiles outside its own territory, and withdrawing these weapons from Cuba—by refraining from any action which will widen or deepen the present crisis—and then by participating in a search for peaceful and permanent solutions.

This nation is prepared to present its case against the Soviet threat to peace, and our own proposals for a peaceful world, at any time and in any forum—in the OAS, in the United Nations, or in any other meeting that could be useful—without limiting our freedom of action. . . .

But it is difficult to settle or even discuss these problems in an atmosphere of intimidation. That is why this latest Soviet threat—or any other threat which is made either independently or in response to our actions this week—must and will be met with determination. Any hostile move anywhere in the world against the safety and freedom of peoples to whom we are committed—including in particular the brave people of West Berlin—will be met by whatever action is needed.

Finally, I want to say a few words to the captive people of Cuba, to whom this speech is being directly carried by special radio facilities. I speak to you as a friend, as one who knows of your deep attachment to your fatherland, as one who shares your aspirations for liberty and justice for all. And I have watched and the American people have watched with deep sorrow how your nationalist revolution was betrayed and how your fatherland fell under foreign domination. Now your leaders are no longer Cuban leaders inspired by Cuban ideals. They are puppets and agents of an international conspiracy which has turned Cuba against your friends and neighbors in the Americas. . . .

Many times in the past the Cuban people have risen to throw out tyrants who destroyed their liberty. And I have no doubt that most Cubans today look forward to the time when they will be truly free—free from foreign domination, free to choose their own leaders, free to select their own system, free to own their own land, free to speak and write and worship without fear or degradation. And then shall Cuba be welcomed back to the society of free nations and to the associations of this hemisphere.

My fellow citizens, let no one doubt that this is a difficult and dangerous effort on which we have set out. No one can foresee precisely what course it will take or what costs or casualties will be incurred. Many months of sacrifice and self-discipline lie ahead—months in which both our patience and our will will be tested, months in which many threats and denunciations will keep us aware of our dangers. But the greatest danger of all would be to do nothing.

5. Soviet Premier Nikita Khrushchev Asks for a U.S. No-Invasion Pledge, October 26, 1962

I see, Mr. President, that you too are not devoid of a sense of anxiety for the fate of the world, [not without an] understanding . . . of what war entails. What would a war give you? You are threatening us with war. But you well know that the very least which you would receive in reply would be that you would experience the same consequences as those which you sent us. And that must be clear to us, people invested with authority, trust, and responsibility. We must not succumb to intoxication and petty passions, regardless of whether elections are impending in this or that country, or not impending. These are all transient things, but if indeed war should break out, then it would not be in our power to stop it, for such is the logic of war. I have participated in two wars and know that war ends when it has rolled through cities and villages, everywhere sowing death and destruction.

In the name of the Soviet Government and the Soviet people, I assure you that your conclusions regarding offensive weapons on Cuba are groundless. It is apparent from what you have written me that our conceptions are different on this score, or rather, we have different estimates of these or those military means. Indeed, in reality, the same forms of weapons can have different interpretations.

You are a military man and, I hope, will understand me. Let us take for example a simple cannon. What sort of means is this: offensive or defensive? A cannon is a defensive means if it is set up to defend boundaries or a fortified area. But if one concentrates artillery, and adds to it the necessary number of troops, then the same cannons do become an offensive means, because they prepare and clear the way for infantry to attack. The same happens with missile-nuclear weapons as well, with any type of this weapon. . . .

You have now proclaimed piratical measures, which were employed in the Middle Ages, when ships proceeding in international waters were attacked, and you have called this "a quarantine" around Cuba. Our vessels, apparently, will soon enter the zone which your Navy is patrolling. I assure you that these vessels, now bound for Cuba, are carrying the most innocent peaceful cargoes. Do you really think that we only occupy ourselves with the carriage of so-called offensive weapons, atomic and hydrogen bombs? Although perhaps your military people imagine that these [cargoes] are some sort of special type of weapon, I assure you that they are the most ordinary peaceful products.

Consequently, Mr. President, let us show good sense. I assure you that on those ships, which are bound for Cuba, there are no weapons at all. The weapons

---

This document can be found in *Problems of Communism,* Special Issue: "Back from the Brink," XLI (Spring 1992), 37–45. It can also be found in U.S. Department of State, *Foreign Relations of the United States, 1961–1963, Cuban Missile Crisis and Aftermath* (Washington, D.C.: Government Printing Office, 1996), XL, 235–240.

which were necessary for the defense of Cuba are already there. I do not want to say that there were not any shipments of weapons at all. No, there were such shipments. But now Cuba has already received the necessary means of defense. . . .

Let us normalize relations. We have received an appeal from the Acting Secretary General of the UN, U Thant, with his proposals. I have already answered him. His proposals come to this, that our side should not transport armaments of any kind to Cuba during a certain period of time, while negotiations are being conducted—and we are ready to enter such negotiations—and the other side should not undertake any sort of piratical actions against vessels engaged in navigation on the high seas. I consider these proposals reasonable. This would be a way out of the situation which has been created, which would give the peoples the possibility of breathing calmly.

You have asked what happened, what evoked the delivery of weapons to Cuba? You have spoken about this to our Minister of Foreign Affairs. I will tell you frankly, Mr. President, what evoked it.

We were very grieved by the fact—I spoke about it in Vienna [at the 1961 summit meeting]—that a landing took place [Bay of Pigs], that an attack on Cuba was committed, as a result of which many Cubans perished. You yourself told me then that this had been a mistake. . . .

Why have we proceeded to assist Cuba with military and economic aid? The answer is: we have proceeded to do so only for reasons of humanitarianism. At one time, our people itself had a revolution, when Russia was still a backward country. We were attacked then. We were the target of attack by many countries. The USA participated in that adventure. . . .

You once said that the United States was not preparing an invasion. But you also declared that you sympathized with the Cuban counterrevolutionary emigrants, that you support them and would help them to realize their plans against the present government of Cuba. It is also not a secret to anyone that the threat of armed attack, aggression, has constantly hung, and continues to hang over Cuba. It was only this which impelled us to respond to the request of the Cuban government to furnish it aid for the strengthening of the defensive capacity of this country.

If assurance were given by the President and the government of the United States that the USA itself would not participate in an attack on Cuba and would restrain others from actions of this sort, if you would recall your fleet, this would immediately change everything. I am not speaking for Fidel Castro, but I think that he and the government of Cuba, evidently, would declare demobilization and would appeal to the people to get down to peaceful labor. Then, too, the question of armaments would disappear, since, if there is no threat, then armaments are a burden for every people. Then, too, the question of the destruction, not only of the armaments which you call offensive, but of all other armaments as well, would look different. . . .

Let us therefore show statesmanlike wisdom. I propose: we, for our part, will declare that our ships, bound for Cuba, will not carry any kind of armaments. You would declare that the United States will not invade Cuba with its forces and will not support any sort of forces which might intend to carry out an invasion of Cuba. Then the necessity for the presence of our military specialists in Cuba would disappear.

Mr. President, I appeal to you to weigh well what the aggressive, piratical actions, which you have declared the USA intends to carry out in international waters, would lead to. You yourself know that any sensible man simply cannot agree with this, cannot recognize your right to such actions.

If you did this as the first step towards the unleashing of war, well then, it is evident that nothing else is left to us but to accept this challenge of yours. If, however, you have not lost your self-control and sensibly conceive what this might lead to, then, Mr. President, we and you ought not now to pull on the ends of the rope in which you have tied the knot of war, because the more the two of us pull, the tighter that knot will be tied. And a moment may come when that knot will be tied so tight that even he who tied it will not have the strength to untie it, and then it will be necessary to cut that knot. And what that would mean is not for me to explain to you, because you yourself understand perfectly of what terrible forces our countries dispose.

Consequently, if there is no intention to tighten that knot and thereby to doom the world to the catastrophe of thermonuclear war, then let us not only relax the forces pulling on the ends of the rope, let us take measures to untie that knot. We are ready for this.

6. Khrushchev Requests U.S. Removal of Jupiter Missiles from Turkey, October 27, 1962

You are worried over Cuba. You say that it worries you because it lies at a distance of 90 miles across the sea from the shores of the United States. However, Turkey lies next to us. Our sentinels are pacing up and down and watching each other. Do you believe that you have the right to demand security for your country and the removal of such weapons that you qualify as offensive, while not recognizing this right for us?

You have stationed devastating rocket weapons, which you call offensive, in Turkey literally right next to us. How then does recognition of our equal military possibilities tally with such unequal relations between our great states? This does not tally at all. . . .

This is why I make this proposal: We agree to remove those weapons from Cuba which you regard as offensive weapons. We agree to do this and to state this commitment in the United Nations. Your representatives will make a statement to the effect that the United States, on its part, bearing in mind the anxiety and concern of the Soviet state, will evacuate its analogous weapons from Turkey. . . .

The U.S. Government will . . . declare that the United States will respect the integrity of the frontiers of Cuba, its sovereignty, undertakes not to intervene in its domestic affairs, not to invade and not to make its territory available as place d'armes for the invasion of Cuba, and also will restrain those who would think of launching an aggression against Cuba either from U.S. territory or from the territory of other states bordering on Cuba.

This document can be found in *Problems of Communism,* Special Issue: "Back from the Brink," XLI (Spring 1992), 45–50. It can also be found in U.S. Department of State, *Foreign Relations of the United States, 1961–1963, Cuban Missile Crisis and Aftermath* (Washington, D.C.: Government Printing Office, 1996), XI, 257–260.

7. Kennedy and ExComm Consider Trading the Jupiter Missiles in Turkey, October 27, 1962

JFK (reading): "Premier Khrushchev told President Kennedy yesterday he would withdraw offensive missiles from Cuba if the United States withdrew its rockets from Turkey."

Speaker?: He didn't really say that, did he? . . .

JFK: That wasn't in the letter [of October 26] we received, was it?

Speaker?: No. . . .

JFK: We're going to be in an insupportable position on this matter if this becomes his proposal. In the first place, we last year tried to get the [Jupiter] missiles out of there [Turkey] because they're not militarily useful, number one. Number two, it's going to—to any man at the United Nations or any other rational man it will look like a very fair trade. . . .

I think you're going to find it very difficult to explain why we are going to take hostile military action in Cuba, against these [missile] sites—what we've been thinking about—the thing that he's saying is, if you'll get yours out of Turkey, we'll get ours out of Cuba. I think we've got a very tough one here. . . .

He's put this out in a way that's caused maximum tension and embarrassment. It's not as if it was a private proposal, which would give us an opportunity to negotiate with the Turks. He's put it out in a way that the Turks are bound to say they don't agree to this. . . .

They've got a very good card. This one is going to be very tough, I think, for us. It's going to be tough in England, I'm sure—as well as other places on the continent—we're going to be forced to take action, that might seem, in my opinion, not a blank check but a pretty good check to take action in Berlin on the grounds that we were wholly unreasonable. Most think—people think that if you're allowed an even trade you ought to take *advantage* of it. Therefore it makes it much more difficult for us to move with world support. These are all the things that—uh—why this is a pretty good play of his. . . .

I'm just thinking about what—what we're going to have to do in a day or so, which is [deleted] sorties and [deleted] days, and possibly an invasion, all because we wouldn't take missiles out of Turkey, and we all know how quickly everybody's courage goes when the blood starts to flow, and that's what's going to happen in NATO, when they—we start these things, and they grab Berlin, and everybody's going to say, "Well that was a pretty good proposition." Let's not kid ourselves that we've got—that's the difficulty. Today it sounds great to reject it, but it's not going to, after we do something. . . .

Thompson*: The important thing for Khrushchev, it seems to me, is to be able to say, I saved Cuba, I stopped an invasion—and he can get away with this, if he wants to, and he's had a go at this Turkey thing, and that we'll discuss later. . . .

This document can be found in Presidential Recordings, Transcripts, President's Office Files, John F. Kennedy Presidential Papers, John F. Kennedy Library, Boston, MA. It can also be found in David A. Welch and James G. Blight, "October 27, 1962: Transcript of the Meetings of the ExComm," *International Security*, XII (Winter 1987–1988), 30–92.

*Llewellyn E. Thompson, U.S. ambassador to the Soviet Union, July 16, 1957–July 27, 1962; U.S. ambassador-at-large, October 3, 1962–1966.

LBJ*: Bob [McNamara], if you're willing to give up your missiles in Turkey, you think you ought to [words unclear] why don't you say that to him and say we're cutting a trade—make the trade there? [mixed voices] save all the invasion, lives and—

Speaker?: The State Department, they invite them—we talked about this, and they said they'd be *delighted* to trade those missiles in Turkey for the things in Cuba.

McNamara: I said I thought it was the realistic solution to the problem.

LBJ: Sure. What we were afraid of was he'd never offer this, but what he'd want to do was trade [mixed voices] *Berlin.* . . .

JFK: We can't very well invade Cuba with all its toil, and long as it's going to be, when we could have gotten them out by making a deal on the same missiles in Turkey. If that's part of the record I don't see how we'll have a very good war. . . .

Well, let's see—uh—let's give him [Khrushchev] an explanation of what we're trying to do. We're trying to get it back on the original proposition of last night, and—because we don't want to get into this trade. If we're unsuccessful, then we—it's *possible* that we may have to get back on the Jupiter thing.

8. Soviet Official Anastas I. Mikoyan and Fidel Castro Debate and Review the Crisis, November 4–5, 1962

Mikoyan-Castro Meeting in Havana, November 4, 1962

[Mikoyan:] I remember that after visiting Bulgaria [in May 1962], Nikita Khrushchev told you that all through his stay in that country he had been thinking of Cuba, fearing that the Americans might mount armed intervention with the aid of reactionary Latin American governments or commit outright aggression. They refuse to allow Cuba to grow stronger, Nikita Khrushchev told us, and if Cuba were defeated, the whole world revolutionary movement would suffer a heavy blow. We must thwart the American imperialists' plans, he said. . . .

The only purpose of shipping Soviet troops and strategic arms to Cuba was to strengthen your defences. Ours was a containment plan, a plan intended to discourage the imperialists from playing with fire in regard to Cuba. Had we developed strategic arms in secrecy, with America knowing nothing about those arms' presence in Cuba, they would have served as a strong deterrent. That was the assumption we started from. Our military told us that Cuba's palm forests made it possible to dependably camouflage strategic missiles against detection from the air. . . .

[Despite the U.S. detection of the missiles] Kennedy agreed to Soviet troops being left in Cuba and as the Cubans kept powerful weapons and anti-aircraft missiles, we may consider that he made a concession for his part.

Kennedy's statement about nonaggression against Cuba by the United States and Latin American countries is another concession. If we take these reciprocal concessions and all other factors into account, we will see that we've won a big victory. Never before have the Americans made such statements. This is why we

This document can be found in "Documents: Dialogue in Havana. The Caribbean Crisis," *International Affairs* (Moscow). No. 10 (1992), pp. 109–111, 114, 115, 116, 117, 122, 123.

*Lyndon B. Johnson, vice president.

came to the conclusion that we were achieving the main goal, which is to preserve Cuba. There will be no attack on Cuba. Nor will there be any war. We are winning more favourable positions.

Of course, we should have sent our draft decision to Cuba, should have consulted you and secured your consent before publishing it. We would actually have done so in a normal situation. Fidel Castro wrote us in his letter [of October 26] that aggression within the next 24 hours was imminent. When we received the letter and discussed the situation, the start of aggression was only 10 to 12 hours away.

Let us compare the situation today with what it was before the crisis. At that time the Americans were planning armed intervention against Cuba. But now they have committed themselves not to attack Cuba. This is a great achievement. . . .

Frankly speaking, we had not at all been thinking about the bases in Turkey. But when discussing the dangerous situation that had developed, we received information from the United States saying that, from what [the journalist Walter] Lippmann wrote in his column, the Russians might raise the question of abolishing the US bases in Turkey. The possibility of our putting forward such a demand was discussed among Americans. The idea was debated in the United States. That was how that demand came to be advanced. Subsequently, however, we stopped insisting on it because the US bases in that country are no problem for us. The Turkish bases are of little significance as we see it. They will be destroyed in case of war. Of course, they have some political significance but we don't pay them any particular attention although we plan to press for their elimination.

Mikoyan-Castro Meeting in Havana, November 5, 1962

[*Castro:*] We have no doubt that had the siting of the strategic weapon been completed in secret, we would have obtained in that way a powerful deterrent against American plans for attack on our country. That would have meant achieving goals pursued by both the Soviet government and the government of the Republic of Cuba. We consider, however, that the deployment of Soviet missiles in Cuba was important in that it served the interests of the whole socialist camp. Even assuming that their deployment provided no military advantage, it was important politically and psychologically for the effort to contain imperialism and prevent it from implementing its plans for aggression. It follows that the strategic weapon was deployed in Cuba in the interest of defending not only Cuba but the socialist camp as a whole. It was a move made with our full consent.

We were well aware of the significance of that move and consider that it was the right thing to do.

We fully agree that war is inadmissible. We are not against the fact that the measures adopted had a twofold purpose, namely, preventing an attack on Cuba and staving off a world war. We fully subscribe to these aims pursued by the Soviet Union.

What gave rise to misunderstanding was the form in which the matter was discussed. We realise, however, that there were circumstances demanding prompt action and that the situation was not normal. . . .

The United States could have been told that the Soviet Union was ready to dismantle the facility but wanted to discuss the matter with the Cuban government. We believe you should have decided the question that way rather than issuing instructions at once on the removal of the strategic weapon. Such an approach would have eased international tension and made it possible to discuss the problem with the Americans in a more favourable context. It would have enabled us not only to bring about a lessening of international tension and discuss the matter in more favourable conditions but to secure the signing of a declaration.

 E S S A Y S

The first essay is by Robert Dallek of Boston University, an eminent presidential historian and a recent biographer of John F. Kennedy. Dallek acknowledges that the Kennedy administration's attempts to overthrow Fidel Castro soured Cuban-American relations, but he assigns primary responsibility for the Cuban missile crisis to Soviet leader Nikita Khrushchev. According to Dallek, Khrushchev recklessly used Cuban-American hostilities as an opportunity to place medium-range nuclear missiles in Cuba, redress the global balance of power with the United States, and increase Moscow's bargaining leverage on Cold War issues such as Berlin. Examining the administration's decisionmaking, Dallek exalts President Kennedy as a model for wise statesmanship by highlighting the president's role in the Executive Committee of the National Security Council, where he sidetracked calls for immediate military action and forged a consensus in favor of patient diplomacy and measured pressure. The president's determination and America's nuclear superiority, Dallek concludes, convinced Khrushchev to remove the missiles.

Thomas G. Paterson, who taught for many years at the University of Connecticut, disagrees. In the second essay, Paterson emphasizes the centrality of Cuban-American relations to the Cold War missile crisis. Conspicuous, repeated, and threatening U.S. actions incited Cuban fears of an invasion. Cuba's quest for defense joined with Soviet objectives to prompt the mid-1962 Cuban-Soviet agreement to deploy missiles on the island. Paterson next explores the management of the crisis. Noting the near misses and accidents, the severe stress experienced by administration officials, and the Executive Committee's inflated record, Paterson questions the thesis that Kennedy's leadership represents a superb example of crisis management. Rather, fear of events spinning out of control—of a nuclear doomsday—mattered as much as anything else in bringing the crisis to a close. Paterson concludes that the near miss did little to chasten Kennedy, whose fixation with Cuba quickly reasserted itself after the Soviet-American crisis had passed.

Patient Diplomacy and Measured Pressure: JFK's Finest Hour

ROBERT DALLEK

In the spring and summer of 1962, [Soviet leader Nikita] Khrushchev's renewed threats against Germany and Berlin were tied to his belief that Washington was planning an invasion to topple [Cuba's Fidel] Castro. He was wrong. In March, when Cuban exile leader José Miró Cardona asked [National Security Adviser McGeorge] Bundy for help with an invasion, he refused. "Decisive action [cannot] be accomplished without the open involvement of U.S. armed forces," Bundy said. "This would mean open war against Cuba which in the U.S. judgment [is] not advisable in the present international situation." The following month Kennedy told Cardona the same thing. But even if the United States had no immediate invasion plan, Khrushchev felt that Castro's support of subversion would eventually persuade Kennedy to act against him. In addition, concern that Castro was moving closer to communist China gave Khrushchev another reason to strengthen Soviet-Cuban relations.

To do this, he decided to turn Cuba into a missile base from which he could more directly threaten the United States. In May and June, Khrushchev and Soviet military and political chiefs agreed to deploy on the island twenty-four medium-range R-12 missiles, which could travel 1,050 miles, and sixteen intermediate R-14 missiles, with a range of 2,100 miles. The forty missiles would double the number in the Soviet arsenal that could reach the continental United States. The plan also called for approximately forty-four thousand support troops and thirteen hundred civilian construction workers, as well as a Soviet naval base housing surface ships and "nuclear-missile equipped submarines."

Khrushchev saw multiple benefits from the deployment of Soviet missiles abroad. It would deter a U.S. attack on Cuba, keep the island in Moscow's orbit, and give him greater leverage in bargaining with Washington over Berlin. Yet such a substantial change in the balance of power seemed likely to provoke a crisis and possibly a war with the United States. Khrushchev convinced himself, however, that the "intelligent" Kennedy "would not set off a thermonuclear war if there were our warheads there, just as they put their warheads on missiles in Turkey." These seventeen intermediate-range Jupiter missiles under U.S. command, which became operational in 1962, had indeed frightened Moscow, but Khrushchev did not anticipate using his missiles. "Every idiot can start a war," Khrushchev told Kremlin associates, "but it is impossible to win this war. . . . Therefore the missiles have one purpose—to scare them, to restrain them . . . to give them back some of their own medicine." The deployment would equalize "what the West likes to call 'the balance of power.' The Americans had surrounded our country with military bases and threatened us with nuclear weapons, and now they would learn just what it feels like to have enemy missiles pointing at [them]." . . .

Khrushchev's aim was to hide the buildup in Cuba until after the American elections, when he planned to attend the U.N. General Assembly and see Kennedy. He would then reveal the existence of the Cuban missile base and extract concessions from the president over Berlin and Cuba. As historians Aleksandr Fursenko and Timothy Naftali concluded, borrowing from JFK, it was "one hell of a gamble." . . .

In August 1962, U.S. intelligence reported increased Soviet military equipment going to Cuba, where it was transported to the interior of the island under Soviet guards. U.S. national security officials concluded that the Soviets were installing SA-2 missiles, a modern anti-aircraft weapon with a thirty-mile range. The report noted that the SA-2s could be fit with nuclear warheads, "but there is no evidence that the Soviet government had ever provided nuclear warheads to any other state, on any terms. It seems unlikely that such a move is currently planned—but," the analysts warned, "there is also little reason to suppose that the Soviets would refuse to introduce such weapons if the move could be controlled in the Soviet interest."

Soviet private and public statements also gave Kennedy assurances that the military buildup represented a change in degree but not in kind. In April 1961, after the Bay of Pigs invasion, Khrushchev had told Kennedy, "We have no bases in Cuba, and do not intend to establish any." On July 30, 1962, in order to reduce the likelihood of exposure, Khrushchev asked Kennedy, "for the sake of better relations," to stop reconnaissance flights over Soviet ships in the Caribbean. Eager to avoid any international crisis during the election campaign, Kennedy ostensibly agreed. . . .

However much Kennedy wished to believe the Soviet professions of restraint, he could not take their assurances at face value; their deviousness in secretly preparing renewed nuclear tests had made him suspicious of anything they said. Besides, [CIA director John] McCone and Bobby [the president's brother and attorney general] were asserting that the "defensive" buildup might presage offensive missile deployments, and even if not, they saw the expanding Soviet presence in Cuba as reason to topple Castro's regime as quickly as possible. Complaints from Republicans about timid responses to the Cuban danger joined with the McCone-Bobby warnings to heighten Kennedy's concerns. . . .

On September 4, Kennedy and his advisers spent several hours preparing a statement about Soviet missiles in Cuba. To be as clear as possible, Kennedy expanded an admonition about "offensive weapons" to include a warning against "ground-to-ground missiles." He also eliminated any mention of the Monroe Doctrine and kept references to Cuba to a minimum. He wanted the statement to focus on Soviet aggression and not on U.S. power in the Western Hemisphere or on the administration's eagerness to topple Castro's regime. . . .

On October 1, [however, Secretary of Defense Robert S.] McNamara and the Joint Chiefs received disturbing information about offensive weapons in Cuba. On September 21, the Defense Intelligence Agency had learned of "a first-hand sighting on September 12 of a truck convoy of 20 objects 65 to 70 feet long which resembled large missiles." The convoy had "turned into an airport on the southwest edge of Havana." Because early reports of a similar nature had proved false, the DIA described the information as only "potentially significant." However, photographs received in the last week of September and reports of surface-to-air missile (SAM) sites produced "a hypothesis that MRBM [medium-range ballistic missile] sites were under preparation in Pinar del Rio province." . . .

October 9, Kennedy approved a U-2 [spy plane] mission to take place as soon as weather permitted. Clear visibility up to seventy-four thousand feet, the U-2's altitude, did not occur until October 14. In the meantime, on October 10, [Senator Kenneth] Keating [R-NY] publicly announced that he had evidence of six IRBM (intermediate-range ballistic missile) sites in Cuba. The IRBMs, which could reach targets twenty-one hundred miles away, had twice the range of MRBMs. . . .

To Kennedy's distress, the October 14 U-2 flight over the island, which lasted six minutes and produced 928 photographs, revealed conclusive evidence of offensive weapons: three medium-range ballistic missile sites under construction; one additional MRBM site discovered at San Cristobal; and two IRBM sites at Guanajay. The photos also revealed twenty-one crated IL-28 medium-range bombers capable of delivering nuclear bombs. The CIA's report on the discoveries reached Bundy on the evening of October 15, but he decided to wait until morning to present this "very big news" to the president, when enlargements of the photographs would be available. . . .

At 8:45 on the morning of the sixteenth, Bundy brought the bad news to Kennedy in his bedroom. The president ordered Bundy to set up a White House meeting in the

Cabinet Room before noon and ticked off the names of the national security officials he wanted there. He then called Bobby, who had been first on his list. "We have some big trouble. I want you over here," the president told him. Determined not to create a public crisis and demands for press comments before he had had a chance to consider his options, Kennedy kept his early-morning appointments. . . .

At 11:45 A.M., thirteen men joined the president in the Cabinet Room for an hour-and-ten-minute discussion. The group came to be called Ex Comm, the Executive Committee of the National Security Council. Kennedy sat in the center of an oblong table, with [Secretary of State Dean] Rusk, [Undersecretary of State George] Ball, and Deputy Undersecretary of State U. Alexis Johnson to his immediate right and McNamara, [Deputy Defense Secretary Roswell] Gilpatric, Joint Chiefs chairman Maxwell Taylor, and acting CIA director Marshall Carter (McCone was at a family funeral) to his immediate left. Bundy, [Treasury Secretary Douglas] Dillon, Bobby, and [Vice-president Lyndon] Johnson sat across from the president. Two experts on aerial photography, Arthur Lundahl and Sidney Graybeal, briefed the group on the U-2 photos, which were propped on easels. . . .

The principal focus on the meeting was on how to eliminate the missiles from Cuba. Rusk thought that they could do it by a "sudden, unannounced strike of some sort," or by a political track in which they built up the crisis "to the point where the other side has to consider very seriously about giving in." Perhaps they could talk sense to Castro through an intermediary, Rusk suggested. "It ought to be said to Castro that this kind of a base is intolerable. . . . The time has now come when he must, in the interests of the Cuban people . . . break cleanly with the Soviet Union and prevent this missile base from becoming operational." The alternative to the quick strike, Rusk said, was "to alert our allies and Mr. Khrushchev that there is an utterly serious crisis in the making here. . . . We'll be facing a situation that could well lead to a general war. . . . We have an obligation to do what has to be done, but to do it in a way that gives everybody a chance to pull away from it before it gets too hard."

For the moment, Kennedy was not thinking about any political or diplomatic solution; his focus was on military options and how to mute the crisis until they had some clear idea of what to do. He saw four possible military actions: an air strike against the missile installations; a more general air attack against a wide array of targets; a blockade; and an invasion. He wanted preparations for the second, third, and fourth possibilities, decisions on which could could later. But "we're certainly going to do number one," he said. "We're going to take out these missiles." Just when, he did not say, but he wanted knowledge of the missiles limited to as few officials as possible. He believed that the news would leak anyway in two or three days. But even when it became known, he wanted policy decisions to remain secret. "Otherwise," he said, "we bitch it up."

He scheduled another Ex Comm meeting for 6:30 that evening. . . .

The evening meeting included the morning's participants as well as [speech writer Theodore] Sorensen and Edwin Martin, a State Department expert on Latin America. Kennedy . . . [expressed] his puzzlement over Khrushchev's actions. Khrushchev had, all things considered, been cautious over Berlin, so how did the Russian experts explain his willingness to risk a war by putting nuclear missiles in Cuba, especially if, as some believed, it did not reduce America's military advantage over the USSR? "Well, it's a goddamn mystery to me," Kennedy admitted. "I don't know enough about the Soviet Union, but if anybody can tell me any other time since the Berlin blockade where the Russians have given so clear a provocation, I don't know when it's been, because they've been awfully cautious, really."

Ball, Bundy, and Alex Johnson saw the Soviets as trying to expand their strategic capabilities. But McNamara was not so sure. The Joint Chiefs thought the Soviet missile deployments "substantially" changed the strategic balance, but McNamara believed it made no difference. Taylor acknowledged that the missiles in Cuba meant "just a few more missiles targeted on the United States," but he considered them "a very, a rather important, adjunct and reinforcement" to Moscow's "strike capability." . . .

The question that remained, then, was how to remove the missiles without a full-scale war. Despite his earlier certainty, Kennedy had begun to have doubts about a surprise air strike and may already have ruled this out as a sensible option. When he asked at the morning meeting, "How effective can the take-out be?" Taylor had answered, "It'll never be 100 percent, Mr. President, we know. We hope to take out the vast majority in the first strike, but this is not just one thing—one strike, one day— but continuous air attack for whenever necessary, whenever we discover a target." Kennedy picked up on the uncertain results of such an operation: "Well, let's say we just take out the missile bases," he said. "Then they have some more there. Obviously they can get them in by submarine and so on. I don't know whether you just keep high strikes on." . . .

The only new idea put forth at the evening meeting came from McNamara. He suggested a middle ground between the military and political courses they had been discussing. He proposed a "declaration of open surveillance: a statement that we would immediately impose a blockade against offensive weapons entering Cuba in the future, and an indication that, with our open surveillance reconnaissance, which we would plan to maintain indefinitely for the future, we would be prepared to immediately attack the Soviet Union in the event that Cuba made any offensive move against this country."

After a long day of discussions, Kennedy was no closer to a firm decision on how to proceed. On Wednesday, the seventeenth, while he continued to hide the crisis from public view by meeting with West Germany's foreign minister, eating lunch with Libya's crown prince, and flying to Connecticut to campaign for Democratic candidates, his advisers held nonstop meetings. But first he saw McCone, who had returned to Washington, at 9:30 in the morning. The CIA director gained the impression that Kennedy was "inclined to act promptly if at all, without warning, targeting on MRBMs and possible airfields." McCone may have been hearing what he wanted to hear, or, more likely, Kennedy created this impression by inviting McCone to make the case for prompt air strikes.

As part of his balancing act, Kennedy invited [U.S. ambassador to the U.N.] Adlai Stevenson into the discussion. After learning about the crisis from the president, who showed him the missile photos on the afternoon of the sixteenth, Stevenson predictably urged Kennedy not to rush into military action. When Kennedy said, "I suppose the alternatives are to go in by air and wipe them out, or to take other steps to render the weapons inoperable," Stevenson replied, "Let's not go into an air strike until we have explored the possibilities of a peaceful solution." . . .

When Ex Comm met again on Thursday morning, October 18, additional reconnaissance photos revealed construction of IRBM launching pads. They had now discovered five different missile sites. McCone reported that the Soviets could have between sixteen and thirty-two missiles ready to fire "within a week or slightly more." Concerned about convincing the world of the accuracy of their information, Kennedy wanted to know if an untrained observer would see what the experts saw in the photos. Lundahl doubted it. "I think the uninitiated would like to see the missile, in the tube," he said.

Sensing the president's hesitancy about quick action without clear evidence to convince the world of its necessity, Rusk asked whether the group thought it "necessary to take action." He believed it essential. The Soviets were turning Cuba into "a powerful military problem" for the United States, he said, and a failure to respond would "undermine our alliances all over the world." Inaction would also encourage Moscow to feel free to intervene wherever they liked and would create an unmanageable problem in sustaining domestic support for the country's foreign policy commitments. Rusk then read a letter from [former U.S. ambassador to the Soviet Union Charles] Bohlen urging diplomatic action as a prelude to military steps. An attack on Cuba without a prior effort at diplomatic pressure to remove the missiles, Bohlen said, would alienate all America's allies, give Moscow credibility for a response against Berlin, and "greatly increase the probability of general war."

Bohlen's argument echoed Kennedy's thinking. People saw the United States as "slightly demented" about Cuba, the president said. "No matter how good our films are . . . a lot of people would regard this [military action] as a mad act by the United States." They would see it as "a loss of nerve because they will argue that taken at its worst, the presence of those missiles really doesn't change the [military] balance."

But the evidence of additional missile sites had convinced the Joint Chiefs to urge a full-scale invasion of Cuba. Kennedy stubbornly resisted. "Nobody knows what kind of success we're going to have with this invasion," he said. "Invasions are tough, hazardous. We've got a lot of equipment, a lot of—thousands of—Americans get killed in Cuba, and I think you're in much more of a mess than you are if you take out these . . . bases." And if Bobby's opinion remained a reflection of his brother's thinking, Kennedy also opposed unannounced air strikes. Ball made what Bobby called "a hell of a good point." "If we act without warning," Ball said, "without giving Khrushchev some way out . . . that's like Pearl Harbor. It's the kind of conduct that one might expect of the Soviet Union. It is not conduct that one expects of the United States." The way we act, Bobby asserted, speaks to "the whole question of . . . what kind of a country we are." Ball saw surprise air strikes as comparable to "carrying the mark of Cain on your brow for the rest of your life." Bobby echoed the point: "We've fought for 15 years with Russia to prevent a first strike against us. Now . . . we do that to a small country. I think it is a hell of a burden to carry."

Kennedy had not ruled out military action, but his remarks at the meetings on October 18 revealed a preference for a blockade and negotiations. He wanted to know what would be the best way to open talks with Khrushchev—through a cable, a personal envoy? He also asked, if we established a blockade of Cuba, what would we do about the missiles already there, and would we need to declare war on Havana?

[U.S. ambassador to the Soviet Union] Llewellyn Thompson, who had joined the Thursday morning discussion, addressed Kennedy's first concern by suggesting Kennedy press Khrushchev to dismantle the existing missile sites and warn him that if they were armed, our constant surveillance would alert us, and we would eliminate them. As for a declaration of war, Kennedy thought it would be unwise: "It seems to me that with a declaration of war our objective would be an invasion."

To keep up the facade of normality, Kennedy followed his regular schedule for the rest of the day, including a two-hour meeting with Soviet foreign minister Andrei Gromyko. Nothing was said about the offensive missiles by Gromyko or Kennedy. But they gave each other indirect messages. Gromyko ploddingly read a prepared statement. He emphasized that they were giving Cuba "armaments which were only defensive—and he wished to stress the word defensive—in character." After the meeting, Kennedy told [former Secretary of Defense] Bob Lovett about Gromyko, "who, in this very room not over ten minutes ago, told more barefaced lies than I have ever heard in so short a time. All during his denial that the Russians had any missiles or weapons, or anything else, in Cuba, I had the . . . pictures in the center drawer of my desk, and it was an enormous temptation to show them to him." Instead, Kennedy told Gromyko that the Soviet arms shipments had created "the most dangerous situation since the end of the war." . . .

Kennedy reconvened his advisers at a secret late-night meeting on the second floor of the executive mansion. He wanted to hear the results of the day's deliberations. Bundy now argued the case for doing nothing. He believed that any kind of action would bring a reprisal against Berlin, which would divide the NATO alliance. But Kennedy thought it was impossible to sit still. As he had said earlier in the day, "Somehow we've got to take some action. . . . Now, the question really is . . . what action we take which lessens the chances of a nuclear exchange which obviously is the final failure." They agreed that a blockade against Soviet shipments of additional offensive weapons would be the best starting point. Instead of air strikes or an invasion, which was tantamount to a state of war, they would try to resolve the crisis with "a limited blockade for a limited purpose."

On Friday, October 19, Kennedy kept his campaign schedule, which took him to Cleveland and Springfield, Illinois, and Chicago. . . .

In the morning, however, he held a secret forty-five-minute meeting with the Joint Chiefs. The discussion was as much an exercise in political hand-holding as in advancing a solution to the crisis. Kennedy knew that the Chiefs favored a massive air strike and were divided on whether to follow it with an invasion. He saw their counsel as predictable and not especially helpful. His memories of the navy brass in World War II, the apparent readiness of the Chiefs to risk nuclear war in Europe and their unhelpful advice before the Bay of Pigs . . . deepened his distrust of their promised results.

Nevertheless, Kennedy candidly discussed his concerns with the Chiefs. An attack on Cuba would provoke the Soviets into blocking or taking Berlin, he said. And our allies would complain that "we let Berlin go because we didn't have the guts to endure a situation in Cuba." Moreover, we might eliminate the danger in Cuba, but the Berlin crisis would likely touch off a nuclear war.

Taylor respectfully acknowledged the president's dilemma but asserted the need for military action. Without it, we would lose our credibility, he said, and "our strength anyplace in the world is the credibility of our response. . . . And if we don't respond here in Cuba, we think the credibility is sacrificed."

[Air Force general] Curtis LeMay was even more emphatic. He did not share the president's view "that if we knock off Cuba, they're going to knock off Berlin." Kennedy asked, "What do you think their reply would be?" LeMay did not think there would be one. He saw military intervention as the only solution. "This blockade and political action," he predicted, "I see leading into war. I don't see any other solution. It will lead right into war. This is almost as bad as the appeasement at Munich." . . .

At a late-morning gathering of the Ex Comm, [former Secretary of State Dean] Acheson, Bundy, Dillon, and McCone lined up with the Chiefs in favor of an air strike. McNamara, undoubtedly alerted to the president's preference, favored a blockade over air action. Bobby, grinning, said that he had spoken with the president that morning and thought "it would be very, very difficult indeed for the President if the decision were to be for an air strike, with all the memory of Pearl Harbor. . . . A sneak attack was not in our traditions. . . .

For two hours and forty minutes, beginning at 2:30 P.M., on Saturday, October 20, Kennedy and the National Security Council reviewed their options. None impressed him as just right, but under the president's prodding the group agreed to a blockade or, rather, a "quarantine," which could more readily be described as less than an act of war and seemed less likely to draw comparisons to the Soviets' 1948 Berlin blockade. The announcement of the quarantine was to coincide with a demand for removal of the offensive missiles from Cuba and preparations for an air strike should Moscow not comply. Kennedy was willing to discuss the removal of U.S. missiles from Turkey or Italy in exchange, but only if the Soviets raised the issue. Should the United States make this concession, he intended to assure the Turks and Italians that Polaris submarines would become their defense shield. . . .

Kennedy spent Monday working to create a national and international consensus for the blockade. . . . [H]e told Taylor, "I know you and your colleagues are unhappy with this decision, but I trust that you will support me." Kennedy telephoned former presidents Hoover, Truman, and Eisenhower and consulted advisers about messages to foreign heads of state and his planned evening address. . . .

A meeting with congressional leaders for an hour before he spoke to the nation heightened his doubts about being able to generate the strong support he felt essential in the crisis. Their opposition to a blockade was as intense as that voiced by the Chiefs and seemed more likely to become public; unlike the military, congressional barons were not under presidential command. Senator Richard Russell saw a blockade as a weak response to the Soviet action. "It seems to me that we are at a crossroads," he said. "We're either a first-class power or we're not." Since Russell believed that a war with Russia was "coming someday," he thought that the time to fight was now. William Fulbright also favored an invasion. . . .

Kennedy saw his speech to the country and the world explaining the crisis and his choice of a blockade as crucial not only in bringing Americans together but also in pressuring Khrushchev to accede to his demands. He also sent Khrushchev a letter, which [Soviet ambassador Anatoly] Dobrynin received at the State Department an hour before Kennedy spoke. He had an ongoing concern, Kennedy wrote, that "your Government would not correctly understand the will and determination of the United States in any given situation." He feared a Soviet miscalculation, "since I have not assumed that you or any other sane man would, in this nuclear age, plunge the world into war which it is crystal clear no country could win and which could only result in catastrophic consequences to the whole world, including the aggressor." . . .

Kennedy's seventeen-minute speech Monday night reached one hundred million Americans, who had been alerted to the crisis by the media; it was the largest audience ever up to that point for a presidential address. The president's words matched his grim demeanor. Looking drawn and tired, he spoke more deliberately than usual, making clear the gravity of what the United States and USSR, and, indeed, the whole world faced. Moscow had created a "nuclear strike capability" in Cuba. The missiles could hit Washington, D.C., or any other city in the southeastern United States. IRBMs, when installed, could strike most of the major cities in the Western Hemisphere. Kennedy bluntly condemned the Soviets for lying: The deployment represented a total breach of faith with repeated Soviet promises to supply Cuba with only defensive weapons. The United States, Kennedy announced, could not tolerate this threat to its security and would henceforth quarantine Cuba to block all offensive weapons from reaching the island. A Soviet failure to stop its buildup would justify additional U.S. action. Any use of the missiles already in Cuba would bring retaliatory attacks against the Soviet Union. Kennedy demanded prompt dismantling and withdrawal of all offensive weapons in Cuba under U.N. supervision. . . .

A reply from Khrushchev, which reached the president by noon [Tuesday], gave little hope of a peaceful settlement. Khrushchev complained that Kennedy's speech and letter to him represented a "serious threat to peace." A U.S. quarantine would be a "gross violation of . . . international norms." Khrushchev reaffirmed that the weapons going to Cuba were defensive and urged Kennedy to "renounce actions pursued by you, which could lead to catastrophic consequences." . . .

In his eagerness to find a way out of the crisis, Bobby had asked journalists Frank Holeman and Charles Barlett to tell [Soviet military attaché Georgi] Bolshakov that the White House might be receptive to dismantling Jupiter missiles in Turkey if the Soviets removed the missiles in Cuba. But the American move could come only after the Soviets had acted—"in a time of quiet and not when there is the threat of war." When Bobby reported to Kennedy, the president suggested that his brother directly approach Dobrynin, which he did that evening. Telling the ambassador that he was there on his own, without instructions from the president, Bobby angrily accused him and Khrushchev of "hypocritical, misleading and false" actions. Bobby asked "if the ships were going to go through to Cuba." Dobrynin believed they would. As he left, Bobby declared, "I don't know how all this will end, but we intend to stop your ships."

At the morning Ex Comm meeting on the twenty-fourth, the group feared that they were on the brink of an unavoidable disaster. The Soviets were making "rapid progress" in the completion of their missile sites and bringing their military forces "into a complete state of readiness." In fact, by the morning of the twenty-fourth, all of the Soviet MRBMs and their warheads were in Cuba and close to operational. In addition, Soviet ships were continuing on course, and two of them, which seemed to be carrying "offensive weapons," would approach the quarantine line by about noon, or in two hours. The presence of Soviet submarines screening the ships made it "a very dangerous situation." U.S. forces had increased their state of readiness from Defense Condition 3 to DEFCON2, only one level below readiness for a general war. . . .

Only a State Department intelligence report gave a glimmer of hope. Khrushchev's "public line," the analysts advised—which continued to be that Moscow had no offensive weapons in Cuba—"seems designed to leave him with some option to back off, if he chooses." A written report handed to McCone during the meeting suggested that Khrushchev might be doing just that. "Mr. President," McCone interrupted McNamara, who was explaining how the navy would deal with the Soviet subs, "I have a note just handed to me. . . . It says we've just received information through ONI [Office of Naval Intelligence] that all six Soviet ships currently identified in Cuban waters—and I don't know what that means—have either stopped or reversed course." McCone left the room to ask for clarification on what "Cuban waters" meant: Were these ships approaching or leaving Cuba? The good news that it was indeed ships heading toward Cuba momentarily broke the mood of dire concern. "We're eyeball to eyeball," Rusk whispered to Bundy, "and I think the other fellow just blinked." But no one saw this as an end to the crisis. . . .

In the afternoon, McNamara went to the navy's command center in the Pentagon, a secure room under constant marine guard. McNamara learned that it had taken hours for some of the information on Soviet ship movements to reach the White House. He began chiding the duty officers for the delay, when Admiral George Anderson, the navy's representative on the Joint Chiefs, entered. Mindful of the president's concern about unauthorized navy action, McNamara began interrogating Anderson about procedures for dealing with the Soviet ships. Anderson saw the president's instructions as an unwarranted interference in the navy's freedom to do its job. Anderson told McNamara that his local commanders would decide on the details of how to deal with Soviet ships crossing the quarantine line, and said, "We've been doing this ever since the days of John Paul Jones." He waved the navy regulations manual at McNamara, saying, "It's all in there." McNamara heatedly replied, "I don't give a damn what John Paul Jones would have done. I want to know what you are going to do, now." The objective was to deter Khrushchev and avert a nuclear war, McNamara explained. Anderson answered that they would shoot across the bow, and if the ship did not stop, they would disable its rudder. Anderson defiantly added, "Now, Mr. Secretary, if you and your deputy will go back to your offices, the navy will run the blockade." McNamara ordered him not to fire at anything without his permission and left. . . .

Khrushchev put a fresh damper on hopes that Moscow would not challenge the quarantine, with a letter arriving on the night of the twenty-fourth. His language was harsh and uncompromising. He objected to the U.S. "ultimatum" and threat of "force," described U.S. actions toward Cuba as "the folly of degenerate imperialism," and refused to submit to the blockade. We intend "to protect our rights," he wrote, and ominously declared, "We have everything necessary to do so." . . .

An unyielding reply from Kennedy to Khrushchev's letter, which reached Moscow on the morning of the twenty-fifth, plus indications that the Americans might invade Cuba, convinced Khrushchev it was time to negotiate an end to the crisis. More than anything else, it was Khrushchev's concern with Soviet military inferiority that compelled him to back down. "He could not go to war in the Caribbean with any hope of prevailing." Fursenko and Naftali write. . . .

Kennedy spent the twenty-fifth temporizing. Since a dozen Soviet ships had turned away from the quarantine line, the White House had some time to consider which remained Cuba-bound ships to stop and inspect. Kennedy told the morning Ex Comm meeting that he did not want "a sense of euphoria to get around. That [October 24] message of Khrushchev is much tougher than that." At the same time, however, a proposal from U.N. secretary general U Thant for a cooling-off period, during which Moscow and Washington would avoid tests of the quarantine, persuaded Kennedy to temporarily suspend a decision to board a Soviet ship. . . .

Yet Kennedy was doubtful that U Thant's initiative would come to much. On the afternoon of the twenty-fifth, he watched a televised confrontation at the U.N. between Stevenson and Soviet ambassador Valerian Zorin. When Stevenson pressed Zorin to say whether the Soviets had put offensive missiles in Cuba, he replied, "I am not in an American courtroom, and therefore I do not wish to answer a question that is put to me in the fashion in which a prosecutor puts questions." Stevenson would not let him evade the question. "You are in the courtroom of world opinion right now, and you can answer yes or no," Stevenson shot back. "You will have your answer in due course," Zorin answered. "I am prepared to wait for my answer until hell freezes over," Stevenson said. He then embarrassed the Russians by putting U-2 photos of the missiles before the Security Council. "I never knew Adlai had it in him," Kennedy said of his performance. . . .

At the Ex Comm meeting at 10:00 A.M. on the twenty-sixth, it was clear that the quarantine was no longer the central issue. There were no ships close to the quarantine line; nor did they expect any "quarantine activity with respect to Soviet ships . . . in the next few days." The concern now was the continuing missile buildup in Cuba. . . . He told [British prime minister Harold] Macmillan that evening, "If at the end of 48 hours we are getting no place, and the missile sites continue to be constructed, then we are going to be faced with some hard decisions."

But Kennedy did not have to wait two days. Within two hours after talking to Macmillan, he received a long, rambling letter from Khrushchev, which Llewellyn Thompson, who was with the president when he read it, believed Khrushchev had written in a state of near panic without consultation. It was an unmistakable plea for a settlement. He justified Soviet help to Cuba as preserving its right of self-determination against U.S. aggression, and he continued to dispute Kennedy's characterization of the missiles as offensive weapons, but declared, "Let us not quarrel now. It is apparent that I will not be able to convince you of this." He had no interest in mutual destruction. It was time for "good sense." To that end, he proposed an exchange: If the United States promised not to invade or support an invasion of Cuba and would recall its fleet, the Soviet Union would no longer see a need for armaments on the island—"the presence of our military specialists in Cuba would disappear." He urged Kennedy to avoid the catastrophe of a nuclear war, but warned, should there be one, "We are ready for this." . . .

But fresh evidence of Soviet progress on the missile sites, coupled with reports that six Soviet and three satellite ships remained on course toward the quarantine line, put a damper on Khrushchev's negotiating proposal. "We cannot permit ourselves to be impaled on a long negotiating hook while the work goes on on these bases," Kennedy told the Ex Comm at the October 27 morning meeting. They feared that Khrushchev's letter might be a ploy for engaging them in drawn-out talks that would allow Soviet completion of the missile sites.

A new initiative from Moscow, which reached Kennedy during the morning Ex Comm discussions, deepened their suspicions. The Kremlin had released a more polished version of Khrushchev's October 26 letter to the press. It now included a proposal that the United States remove its Jupiter missiles from Turkey in return for the dismantling of what "you regard as offensive weapons" in Cuba. The revised letter also maintained the demand for a pledge against invading Cuba and reliance on the U.N. as an intermediary. . . .

For almost four hours beginning at 4:00 P.M. on Saturday the twenty-seventh, the Ex Comm agonized over Khrushchev's Cuba-for-Turkey missile swap. With the Cuban missile sites nearing completion and reports that a SAM had shot down a U-2 flying over Cuba and killed its pilot, the Joint Chiefs were pressing for a massive air strike no later than Monday morning, the twenty-ninth, to be followed by an invasion in seven days. Kennedy and his advisers saw Khrushchev's proposal as possibly the last chance to reach a settlement and avoid military action that could lead to a nuclear exchange. . . .

Nevertheless, Kennedy's advisers convinced him to omit any mention of Turkey in his written reply to Khrushchev—in other words, to answer the first letter and largely ignore the second. He told Khrushchev that he first had to stop work on offensive missile bases in Cuba, make all offensive weapons systems there "inoperable," and halt the further introduction of such weapons. All of it was to be done under U.N. supervision. In return, the United States would end the quarantine and give assurances against an invasion of Cuba. Such a settlement "would enable us to work toward a more general arrangement regarding 'other armaments,' as proposed in your second letter which you made public. . . .

At the same time Kennedy cabled his letter to Moscow, he had Bobby hand deliver it to Dobrynin. By using his brother as the messenger, Kennedy was indicating that this was no committee or bureaucratic response but a statement of his personal eagerness to end the crisis on the terms described in the letter. Bobby's mission was also meant to signal the urgency of a positive response from Khrushchev to relieve Pentagon pressure on the president for military action. As is clear from a memo Bobby subsequently made of his conversation with Dobrynin, he left no question that a failure to agree to the proposed exchange would have disastrous consequences. Bobby told him that the attack on the U-2 and death of the pilot compelled the administration "to make certain decisions within the next 12 or possibly 24 hours. There was very little time left. If the Cubans were shooting at our planes, then we were going to shoot back." . . .

When Dobrynin asked about Khrushchev's proposal on Turkey, Bobby was ready with an answer. At a meeting with the president and several of his advisers just before he met with the ambassador, Bobby was instructed by Kennedy and Rusk to say that "while there could be no deal over the Turkish missiles, the President was determined to get them out and would do so once the Cuban crisis was resolved." The group agreed that knowledge of this commitment would be a closely guarded secret, since "this unilateral private assurance might appear to betray an ally." Bobby was also told to make plain to Dobrynin that if Moscow revealed this pledge, it would become null and void. On October 27, Kennedy secretly instructed Rusk to telephone Andrew Cordier, a Columbia University dean, who had served under U Thant at the U.N., and ask him to be prepared to give the secretary general a statement proposing the simultaneous removal of the missiles in Turkey and Cuba. Although this contingency plan was never activated and Rusk did not reveal its existence until 1987, it leaves no doubt that the president would have publicly given up the Jupiters for an end to the crisis. . . .

At a meeting of the entire Soviet presidium in a Moscow suburb, Khrushchev declared the need for a "retreat" in order to save Soviet power and the world from a nuclear catastrophe. As a prelude to a discussion on how to respond to Kennedy's offer, the presidium authorized Soviet forces to repel a U.S. attack on Cuba if there were no settlement. During the presidium discussion, the arrival of Dobrynin's report on his meeting with Bobby created a sense of urgency about ending the crisis. Khrushchev immediately dictated a letter accepting Kennedy's terms and instructed that it be broadcast on the radio to ensure its prompt receipt in Washington before some incident triggered military action. At the same time, Khrushchev sent the president a secret communication expressing satisfaction at Kennedy's promise to remove the Jupiters from Turkey in four or five months and promised to hold this agreement in confidence.

The Soviet broadcast, which was heard in Washington at 9:00 A.M. Sunday morning, lifted a pall of apprehension from Kennedy and his Ex Comm advisers. Only the Joint Chiefs refused to take Khrushchev's "surrender" at face value. Led by LeMay, they sent the president a letter recommending execution of the planned air strikes on Monday followed by the invasion unless there were "irrefutable evidence" of immediate Soviet action to remove the missile sites. . . .

Kennedy told his advisers that the quarantine would continue until they could be sure that the terms of the agreement were met. He would remain uncomfortable with the continued presence of Soviet IL-28 bombers in Cuba, which had been omitted from the required elimination of offensive weapons. He also anticipated no end to communist subversion in the hemisphere and expected the two sides would be "toe to toe on Berlin" by the end of November. But for the moment, the danger of a Soviet-American war had receded. . . .

In refusing to declare the crisis at an end, Kennedy wished to avoid an embarrassing possible reversal, which would be a political disaster and an irresistible prod to military action. He planned to officially end the quarantine after the Soviets dismantled the launching sites and shipped the missiles back to Russia. He also wanted the IL-28 bombers removed. . . .

Kennedy received justifiable plaudits for resolving the crisis. Yet he had no illusion that his response was the principal reason for success. Rather, America's local military superiority, Moscow's limited national security stake in keeping missiles in Cuba, and the Soviets' difficulty justifying to world opinion a possible nuclear conflict over Cuba were of greater importance in persuading Khrushchev to back down. Still, Kennedy's resistance to pressure from military chiefs for air attacks and an invasion, and his understanding that patient diplomacy and measured pressure could persuade the Soviets to remove the missiles were essential contributions to the peaceful outcome of the crisis. . . .

Forty years after the crisis, historians almost uniformly agree that this was the most dangerous moment in the forty-five-year Cold War. Moreover, despite his part in provoking the crisis, they generally have high praise for Kennedy's performance. His restraint in resisting a military solution that would almost certainly have triggered a nuclear exchange makes him a model of wise statesmanship in a dire situation. One need only compare his performance with that of Europe's heads of government before World War I—a disaster that cost millions of lives and wasted unprecedented sums of wealth—to understand how important effective leadership can be in times of international strife. October 1962 was not only Kennedy's finest hour in the White House; it was also an imperishable example of how one man prevented a catastrophe that may yet afflict the world.

Spinning Out of Control: Kennedy's War Against Cuba and the Missile Crisis

THOMAS G. PATERSON

"My God," muttered Richard Helms of the Central Intelligence Agency, "these Kennedys keep the pressure on about [Fidel] Castro." Another CIA officer heard it straight from John F. and Robert F. Kennedy: "Get off your ass about Cuba." Defense Secretary Robert McNamara remembered that "we were hysterical about Castro at the time of the Bay of Pigs and thereafter." When White House assistant Arthur Schlesinger, Jr., returned from an early 1962 overseas trip, he told the president that people abroad thought that the administration was "obsessed with Cuba." President Kennedy himself acknowledged during the missile crisis that "most allies regard [Cuba] as a fixation of the United States."

This essay seeks, first, to explain the U.S. "fixation" with Cuba in the early 1960s, identifying the sources and negative consequences of the Kennedy administration's multitrack war against Cuba. Second, to demonstrate the considerable American responsibility for the onset of the dangerous missile crisis of fall 1962. Third, to explore Kennedy's handling of the crisis, questioning the thesis of deft, cautious management. And, last, to illustrate the persistence of the "fixation" by studying the aftermath of the missile crisis, when the revitalization of the U.S. war against Castro's government set Cuban-American relations on a collision course for decades.

A knowledgeable and engaged President Kennedy spent as much or more time on Cuba as on any other foreign-policy problem. Cuba stood at the center of his administration's greatest failure, the Bay of Pigs, and its alleged greatest success, the missile crisis. Why did President Kennedy and his chief advisers indulge such an obsession with Cuba and direct so many U.S. resources to an unrelenting campaign to monitor, harass, isolate, and ultimately destroy Havana's radical regime? One answer springs from a candid remark by the president's brother, Robert F. Kennedy, who later wondered "if we did not pay a very great price for being more energetic than wise about a lot of things, especially Cuba." The Kennedys' famed eagerness for

Revised for this sixth edition, this essay is based on Thomas G. Paterson, "Fixation with Cuba: The Bay of Pigs, Missile Crisis, and Covert War Against Castro," in Thomas G. Paterson, ed., *Kennedy's Quest for Victory: American Foreign Policy, 1961–1963* (New York: Oxford University Press, 1989), 123–155, 343–352; Thomas G. Paterson, "The Defense-of-Cuba Theme and the Missile Crisis," *Diplomatic History,* XIV (Spring 1990), 249–256; and Thomas G. Paterson, *Contesting Castro: The United States and the Triumph of the Cuban Revolution* (New York: Oxford Univeristy Press, 1994); and documents declassified and studies published since the publication of these works.

action became exaggerated in the case of Cuba. They always wanted to get moving on Cuba, and Castro dared them to try. The popular, intelligent, but erratic Cuban leader, who in January 1959 overthrew the U.S. ally Fulgencio Batista, hurled harsh words at Washington and defiantly challenged the Kennedy model of evolutionary, capitalist development so evident in the Alliance for Progress. As charismatic figures charting new frontiers, Kennedy and Castro often personalized the Cuban-American contest. To Kennedy's great annoyance, Castro could not be wheedled or beaten.

Kennedy's ardent war against *fidelismo* may also have stemmed from his feeling that Castro had double-crossed him. As a senator, Kennedy had initially joined many Americans in welcoming the Cuban Revolution as an advancement over the "oppressive" Batista dictatorship. Kennedy had urged a "patient attitude" toward the new government, which he did not see as Communist. Denying repeatedly that he was a Communist, Castro had in fact proclaimed his allegiance to democracy and private property. But in the process of legitimizing his revolution and resisting U.S. pressure, Castro turned more and more radical. Americans grew impatient with the regime's highly-charged anti-Yankeeism, postponement of elections, jailing of critics, and nationalization of property. . . .

Richard N. Goodwin, the young White House and State Department official, provided another explanation for the Kennedy "fixation" with Cuba. He remarked that "the entire history of the Cold War, its positions and assumptions, converged upon the 'problem of Cuba.'" The Cold War dominated international politics, and as Cuban-American relations steadily deteriorated, Cuban-Soviet relations gradually improved. Not only did Americans come to believe that a once-loyal ally had jilted them for the tawdry embrace of the Soviets; they also grew alarmed that Castro sneered at the Monroe Doctrine by inviting the Soviet military to the island. When Castro, in late 1961, declared himself a Marxist-Leninist, Americans who had long denounced him as a Communist then felt vindicated. . . .

American politics also influenced the administration's Cuba policy. In the 1960 presidential campaign, Kennedy had seized the Cuban issue to counter Richard Nixon's charge that the inexperienced Democratic candidate would abandon Zinmen (Quemoy) and Mazu (Matsu) to Communism and prove no match for the hard-nosed Khrushchev. "In 1952 the Republicans ran on a program of rolling back the Iron Curtain in Eastern Europe," Kennedy jabbed. "Today the Iron Curtain is 90 miles off the coast of the United States." He asked in private, "How would *we* have saved Cuba if we had [had] the power," but he nonetheless valued the political payback from his attack. "What the hell," he informed his aides, "they never told us how they would have saved China." Apparently unaware that President Dwight D. Eisenhower had initiated a clandestine CIA program to train Cuban exiles for an invasion of the island, candidate Kennedy bluntly called for just such a project. After exploiting the Cuban issue, Kennedy, upon becoming president, could not easily have retreated.

Overarching all explanations for Kennedy's obsession with Cuba is a major phenomenon of the second half of the twentieth century: the steady erosion of the authority of imperial powers, which had built systems of dependent, client, and colonial governments. The strong currents of decolonization, anti-imperialism, revolutionary nationalism, and social revolution, sometimes in combination, undermined the instruments the imperial nations had used to maintain control and order. The Cuban Revolution exemplified this process of breaking up and breaking away. American leaders reacted so hostilely to this revolution not simply because Castro and his 26th of July Movement taunted them or because domestic politics and the Cold War swayed them, but also because Cuba, as symbol and reality, challenged U.S. hegemony in Latin America. The specter of "another Cuba" haunted President Kennedy, not just because it would hurt him politically, but because "the game would be up through a good deal of Latin America," as Under Secretary of State George Ball put it. The Monroe Doctrine and the U.S. claim to political, economic, and military leadership in the hemisphere seemed at stake. As Castro once remarked, "the United States *had* to fight his revolution."

The Eisenhower Administration bequeathed to its successor an unproductive tit-for-tat process of confrontation with Cuba and a legacy of failure. In November 1959, President Eisenhower decided to encourage anti-Castro groups within Cuba to "replace" the revolutionary regime and thus end an anti-Americanism that was "having serious adverse effects on the United States position in Latin America and corresponding advantages for international Communism." In March 1960 Eisenhower ordered the CIA to train Cuban exiles for an invasion of their homeland— this shortly after Cuba signed a trade treaty with the Soviet Union. The CIA, as well, hatched assassination plots against Castro and staged hit-and-run attacks along the Cuban coast. As Cuba undertook land reform that struck at American interests and nationalized American-owned industries, the United States suspended Cuba's sugar quota and forbade American exports to the island, drastically cutting a once-flourishing commerce. On January 3, 1961, fearing an invasion and certain that the U.S. embassy was a "nest of spies" aligned with counterrevolutionaries who were burning cane fields and sabotaging buildings, Castro demanded that the embassy staff be greatly reduced. Washington promptly broke diplomatic relations with Havana. . . .

The plan to invade Cuba at the Bay of Pigs began to unravel from the start. As the brigade's old, slow freighters plowed their way to the island, B-26 airplanes took to the skies from Nicaragua. On April 15, D-Day-minus-2, the brigade pilots destroyed several parked planes of Castro's meager air force. That same day, as part of a pre-invasion ploy, a lone, artificially damaged B-26 flew directly to Miami, where its pilot claimed that he had defected from the Cuban military and had just bombed his country's airfields. But the cover story soon cracked. Snooping journalists noticed that the nose cone of the B-26 was metal; Cuban planes had plastic noses. They observed too that the aircraft's guns had not been fired. The American hand was being exposed. The president, still insistent upon hiding U.S. complicity, decided to cancel a second D-Day strike against the remnants of the Cuban air force.

Shortly after midnight on April 17, more than 1,400 commandoes motored in small boats to the beaches at Bahía de Cochinos. The invaders immediately tangled with Castro's militia. Some commandoes never made it, because their boats broke apart on razor-sharp coral reefs. In the air, Castro's marauding airplanes shot down two brigade B-26s and sank ships carrying essential communications equipment and ammunition. Fighting ferociously, the brigade nonetheless failed to establish a beachhead. Would Washington try to salvage the mission? Kennedy turned down desperate CIA appeals to dispatch planes from the nearby U.S.S. *Essex,* but he did permit some jets to provide air cover for a new B-26 attack from Nicaragua. Manned this time by American CIA pilots, the B-26s arrived an hour after the jets had come and gone. Cuban aircraft downed the B-26s, killing four Americans. With Castro's boasting that the *mercenarios* had been foiled, the final toll proved grim: 114 of the exile brigade dead and 1,189 captured. One hundred-and-fifty Cuban defenders died. . . .

The most controversial operational question remains the cancelled second D-day air strike. Post-crisis critics have complained that the president lost his nerve and made a decision that condemned the expedition to disaster. Cuban air supremacy did prove important to Cuba's triumph. But was it decisive? A preemptive strike on D-Day against the Cuban air force would not have delivered victory to the invaders. After the first air attack, Castro had dispersed his planes; the brigade's B-26s would have encountered considerable difficulty in locating and destroying them. And, even if a D-Day assault had disabled all of Castro's planes, then what? The brigade's 1,400 warriors would have had to face Castro's army of 25,000 and the nation's 200,000 militia. The commandoes most likely would not have survived the overwhelming power of the Cuban military. . . .

Critical to understanding the frightening missile crisis of fall 1962 is the relationship between post–Bay of Pigs U.S. activities and the Soviet/Cuban decisions to place on the island nuclear-tipped missiles that could strike the United States, endangering the lives of 92 million people. In late April, after hearing from Cuban leaders that they expected a direct U.S. invasion and sought Soviet help to resist an attack, and after protesting the deployment of U.S. intermediate-range Jupiter missiles in Turkey, Nikita Khrushchev began to think about a missile deployment in Cuba; in late May, after dismissing the skepticism of some key advisers who judged his plan provocative to the United States and therefore highly explosive, he made the offer of missiles to Fidel Castro, who quickly accepted them. . . . The plan called for the Soviets' installation on the island of forty-eight medium-range ballistic missiles (SS-4s with a range of 1,020 miles), thirty-two intermediate-range ballistic missiles (SS-5s with a range of 2,200 miles), 144 surface-to-air missiles (SAMs), theater-nuclear weapons (Lunas), forty-eight IL-28 light bombers (with a range of 600 miles), and 42,000 Soviet combat troops.

After the Bay of Pigs, the Kennedy administration launched a multitrack program of covert, economic, diplomatic, and propagandistic elements calculated to overthrow the Castro government. This multidimensional project prompted the Cuban/Soviet decisions of mid-1962. Secretary of Defense Robert McNamara said later: "If I had been in Moscow or Havana at that time [1961–1962], I would have believed the Americans were preparing for an invasion." Indeed, Havana had to fear a successful Bay of Pigs operation conducted by U.S. forces.

Encouraged by the White House, the CIA created a huge station in Miami called JMWAVE to recruit and organize Cuban exiles. In Washington, Robert Kennedy became a ramrod for action. At a November 4, 1961, White House meeting, the Attorney General insisted: "stir things up on the island with espionage, sabotage, general disorder. . . ." The president himself asked Colonel Edward Lansdale to direct Operation Mongoose—"to use our available assets . . . to help Cuba overthrow the Communist regime." Operation Mongoose and JMWAVE, although failing to unseat Castro, punished Cubans. CIA-handled saboteurs burned cane fields and blew up factories and oil storage tanks. In a December 1961 raid, for example, a seven-man team blasted a railroad bridge, derailed an approaching train, and torched a sugar warehouse. One group, Agrupacíon Montecristi, attacked a Cuban patrol boat off the northern coast of the island in May 1962. Directorio Revolucionario Estudiantil, another exile organization, used two boats to attack Cuba in August, hoping to hit a hotel where Castro was dining.

The CIA, meanwhile, devised new plots to kill Castro with poisonous cigars, pills, and needles. To no avail. Did the Kennedys know about these death schemes? In May 1961, Federal Bureau of Investigation Director J. Edgar Hoover informed Robert Kennedy that the CIA had hired mafia boss Sam Giancana to do some "dirty business" in Cuba. Kennedy noted on the margin of the Hoover memorandum that this information should be "followed up vigorously." A year later, the CIA briefed the attorney general about its use of mafia gangsters to assassinate Castro. If his brother Robert knew about these CIA assassination plots, the president surely did, for Robert was John's closest confidant. They kept little if anything from one another. President Kennedy apparently never directly ordered the assassination of Castro—at least no trail of documents leads to the White House. But, of course, nobody uttered the word "assassination" in the presence of the president or committed the word to paper, thereby honoring the principle of plausible deniability. Advisers instead simply mentioned the need to remove Castro. "And if killing him was one of the things that was to be done in this connection," assassination was attempted because "we felt we were acting within the guidelines," said the CIA's Richard Helms.

Intensified economic coercion joined these covert activities. The Kennedy administration, in February 1962, banned most imports of Cuban products. Washington also pressed its North Atlantic Treaty Organization allies to support the "economic isolation" of Cuba. The embargo hurt. Cuba had to pay higher freight costs, enlarge its foreign debt, and suffer innumerable factory shut-downs due to the lack of spare parts once bought in the United States. Cuba's economic woes also stemmed from the flight of technicians and managers, a decline in tourism, high workers' absenteeism rates, the drying up of foreign capital investment, hastily conceived policies to diversify the economy, and suffocating government controls. . . .

[A] contemporary document, this one from the chairman of the Joint Chiefs of Staff, General Maxwell Taylor, noted in spring 1962 that the Mongoose plan to overthrow the Cuban government would be undertaken largely by "indigenous resources," but "recognizes that final success will require decisive U.S. military intervention." Because the plan also required close cooperation with Cuban exiles, it is very likely that Castro's spies picked up from the Cuban community in Miami leaks that the U.S. military contemplated military action against Cuba. As CIA agents liked to joke, there were three ways to transmit information rapidly: telegraph, telephone, and tell-a-Cuban. Cuban officials have claimed, in fact, that their intelligence agency had infiltrated anti-Castro exile groups and had learned about some of the activities associated with Lansdale's scheme. Although they surely did not know the details of President Kennedy's National Security Action Memorandum No. 181 (NSAM-181), dated August 23, a directive to engineer an internal revolt that would be followed by U.S. military intervention, the Cubans no doubt began to observe accelerated U.S. actions to achieve that goal. . . .

By the late spring and early summer of 1962, then, when Havana and Moscow discussed defensive measures that included missiles with nuclear warheads, Cuba felt besieged from several quarters. The Soviet Union had become its trading partner, and the Soviets, after the Bay of Pigs, had begun military shipments of small arms, howitzers, machine guns, armored personnel carriers, patrol boats, tanks, and MiG jet fighters. Yet all of this weaponry had not deterred the United States. And, given the failure of Kennedy's multitrack program to unseat Castro, "were we right or wrong to fear direct invasion" next, asked Fidel Castro. As he said in mid-1962, shortly after striking the missile-deployment agreement with the Soviets: "We must prepare ourselves for that direct invasion."

Had there been no exile expedition at the Bay of Pigs, no destructive covert activities, no assassination plots, no military maneuvers and plans, and no economic and diplomatic steps to harass, isolate, and destroy the Castro government in Havana, there would not have been a Cuban missile crisis. The origins of the October 1962 crisis derived largely from the concerted U.S. campaign to quash the Cuban Revolution. To stress only the global dimension (Soviet-American competition in the nuclear arms race) is to slight the local origins of the conflict. To slight these sources by suggesting from very incomplete declassified Soviet records that the "thought of deterring a U.S. invasion figured only incidentally" in Moscow's calculations, as argued by Ernest R. May and Philip D. Zelikow, editors of the tape recordings that Kennedy made during the crisis, is to overlook the substantial evidence of Soviet (and Cuban) preoccupation with the defense of Cuba and is to miss the central point that Premier Nikita Khrushchev would never have had the opportunity to install dangerous missiles in the Caribbean if the United States had not been attempting to overthrow the Cuban government. This interpretation does not dismiss the view that the emplacement of nuclear missiles in Cuba also served the Soviet strategic goal of catching up in the nuclear arms race. Rather, the interpretation in this essay emphasizes that both Cuba and the Soviet Union calculated that their interests would be served by putting nuclear-capable rockets on the island. . . .

Why did the Cubans and Soviets decide on nuclear-tipped ballistic missiles instead of a military pact, conventional (non-nuclear) forces, or just the battlefield Lunas—in short, weapons that Washington could not label "offensive" because they could not reach the United States? The Cubans sought effective deterrence, or what the historian Mark White has called "the *ultimate* deterrent." One thinks here of similar American thinking, near the end of the Second World War, that the Japanese were so fanatical that only the threat of annihilation from atomic bombs would persuade them to surrender. The Cubans, in fact, looking for an immediate deterrent effect, had wanted to make the 1962 missile agreement public, but the Soviets, guessing that the deployment could be camouflaged until the missiles became operational, preferred secrecy.

On October 14, an American U-2 plane photographed missile sites in Cuba, thus providing the first "hard" evidence, as distinct from the "soft" reports of exiles, that the island was becoming a nuclear base. "He can't do that to me!" snapped Kennedy when he saw the pictures on the 16th. He had warned the Soviets that the United States would not suffer "offensive" weapons in Cuba, although the warnings had come after the Cuban-Soviet agreement of early summer. Shortly before noon on October 16, the president convened his top advisers (a group eventually called the Executive Committee, or ExComm). His first questions focused on the firing readiness of the missiles and the probability that they carried nuclear warheads. The advisers gave tentative answers. All agreed that the missiles could become operational in a brief time. Discussion of military options (invasion? air strike?) dominated this first meeting. Kennedy's immediate preference became clear: "We're certainly going . . . to take out these . . . missiles." Kennedy showed little interest in negotiations. Perhaps his initial tilt toward military action derived from his knowledge of the significant U.S. military plans, maneuvers, and movement of forces and equipment undertaken after he signed NSAM-181, thus making it possible for the United States to respond with military effectiveness.

At a second meeting on the 16th, Secretary of State Dean Rusk argued against the surprise air strike that General Taylor had bluntly advocated. Rusk recommended instead "a direct message to Castro." At the close of Rusk's remarks, Kennedy immediately asked: "Can we get a little idea about what the military thing *is*?" Bundy then asked: "How gravely does this change the strategic balance?" McNamara, for one, thought "not at all," but Taylor disputed him. Kennedy himself seemed uncertain, but he did complain that the missile emplacement in Cuba "makes them look like they're co-equal with us." And, added Treasury Secretary C. Douglas Dillon, who obviously knew the president's competitive personality, the presence of the missiles made it appear that "we're scared of the Cubans."

Then the rambling discussion turned to Khrushchev's motivation. The Soviet leader had been cautious on Berlin, Kennedy said. "It's just as if we suddenly began to put a major number of MRBMs in Turkey," the President went on. "Now that'd be goddam dangerous. . . ." Bundy jumped in: "Well, we *did*, Mr. President." Not liking the sound of a double standard, Kennedy lamely answered, "Yeah, but that was five years ago." Actually, the American Jupiter missiles in Turkey were IRBMs (intermediate-range ballistic missiles) which, under a 1959 agreement with Ankara, had gone into launch position in mid-1961—during the Kennedy administration—and were turned over to Turkish forces on October 22, 1962, the very day Kennedy informed Moscow that it must withdraw its missiles from Cuba.

For the next several days, ExComm met frequently in tight secrecy and discussed four policy options: "talk them out," "squeeze them out," "shoot them out," or "buy them out." In exhausting sessions marked by frank disagreement and changing minds, the president's advisers weighed the advantages and disadvantages of invasion, bombing, quarantine, and diplomacy. The president gradually moved with a majority of ExComm toward a quarantine or blockade of Cuba: incoming ships would be stopped and inspected for military cargo. When queried if an air strike would knock out all of the known missiles General Taylor said that "the best we can offer you is to destroy 90%. . . ." In other words, some missiles in Cuba would remain in place for firing against the United States. Robert Kennedy also worried that the Soviets might react unpredictably with military force, "which could be so serious as to lead to general nuclear war." In any case, the attorney general insisted, there would be no "Pearl Harbor type of attack" on his brother's record.

By October 22 the president had made two decisions. First, to quarantine Cuba to prevent further military shipments and to impress the Soviets with U.S. resolve to force the missiles out. If the Soviets balked, other, more drastic, measures would be undertaken. Second, Kennedy decided to inform the Soviets of U.S. policy through a television address rather than through diplomatic channels. Several advisers dubiously argued that a surprise public speech was necessary to rally world opinion behind U.S. policy and to prevent Khrushchev from issuing an ultimatum, but some ExComm participants recommended that negotiations be tried first. Former ambassador to the Soviet Union Charles Bohlen advised that Moscow would have to retaliate against the United States if its technicians died from American bombs. A stern letter to Khrushchev should be "tested" as a method to gain withdrawal of the missiles. "I don't see the urgency of military action," Bohlen told the president. And ambassador to the United Nations Adlai Stevenson appealed to an unreceptive Kennedy: "the existence of nuclear missile bases anywhere is negotiable before we start anything." Stevenson favored a trade: withdrawing the U.S. Jupiter missiles from Turkey and evacuating the Guantánamo naval base, turning it over to Cuba, in exchange for withdrawal of the Soviet missiles from Cuba. The president, according to the minutes of an October 20 ExComm meeting, "sharply rejected" Stevenson's proposal, especially on the issue of Guantánamo. . . .

In his evening television speech of October 22, Kennedy demanded that the Soviets dismantle the missiles in Cuba, and he announced the Caribbean quarantine as an "initial" step. Later that evening, in a telephone conversation, he told British prime minister Harold Macmillan that U.S. credibility was on the line; if he had not acted, America's resolve to defend Berlin might be questioned and Soviet success in deploying the missiles "would have unhinged us in all of Latin America." The missile crisis soon became an international war of nerves. More than sixty American ships began patrols to enforce the blockade. The Strategic Air Command went on nuclear alert, moving upward to Defense Condition (DEFCON) 2 for the first time ever (the next level is deployment for combat). B-52 bombers, loaded with nuclear weapons, stood ready, while men and equipment moved to the southeastern United States to prepare for an invasion. The Soviets did not mobilize or redeploy their huge military, nor did they take measures to make their strategic forces less vulnerable. The Soviets also refrained from testing the quarantine: Their ships turned around and went home. But what next? On the 26th, Kennedy and some ExComm members, thinking that the Soviets were stalling, soured on the quarantine. Sentiment for military action strengthened.

On the afternoon of the 26th, an intelligence officer attached to the Soviet embassy, Aleksandr Feklisov (alias Fomin), met with ABC television correspondent John Scali and suggested a solution to the crisis: The Soviet Union would withdraw the missiles if the United States would promise not to invade Cuba. Scali scurried to Secretary of State Dean Rusk, who sent him back to Feklisov with the reply that American leaders were interested in discussing the proposal. As it turns out, and unbeknownst to American leaders, Feklisov was acting on his own and a report of his conversations with Scali did not reach the Soviet foreign secretary in Moscow until the late afternoon of October 27. Feklisov's independent intervention, in other words, did not influence the writing of the two critical letters that Khrushchev sent to Washington on the 26th and 27th, but ExComm thought the Feklisov initiative and Khrushchev's letters were linked, thus clearly signaling an earnest Soviet desire to settle.

Khrushchev's first letter, a rambling emotional private message that ruminated on the horrors of war, offered to withdraw the missiles if the United States pledged not to invade Cuba. The Soviet premier defended the initial installation of the missiles with the argument that the United States had been threatening the island. In the morning of October 27, another Khrushchev letter reached the president. Khrushchev now upped the stakes: He would trade the missiles in Cuba for the American missiles in Turkey. Kennedy felt boxed, because "we are now in the position of risking war in Cuba and in Berlin over missiles in Turkey which are of little military value." At first, Kennedy hesitated to accept a swap—because he did not want to appear to be giving up anything in the face of Soviet provocation; because he knew that the proud Turks would recoil from the appearance of being "traded off in order to appease an enemy"; and because acceptance of a missile trade would lend credence to charges that the United States all along had been applying a doubling standard. Kennedy told ExComm that Khrushchev's offer caused "embarrassment," for most people would think it "a very fair trade." Indeed, Moscow had played "a very good card."

In the afternoon of the 27th, more bad news rocked the White House. An American U-2 plane overflew the eastern part of the Soviet Union, probably because its equipment malfunctioned. "There is always some son of a bitch who doesn't get the word," the president remarked. Soviet fighters scrambled to intercept the U-2, and American fighter jets from Alaska, carrying Falcon missiles with nuclear warheads, took flight to protect the errant aircraft. Although the spy plane flew home without having sparked a dog fight, the incident carried the potential of sending the crisis to a more dangerous level.

Also on the 27th, a U-2 was shot down over Cuba and its pilot killed by a surface-to-air missile (SAM). The shoot-down constituted a serious escalation. A distressed McNamara, not knowing that the order to shoot was made independently by the Soviet air defense commander in Cuba without orders from Moscow, now thought "invasion had become almost inevitable." He urged that U.S. aircraft "go in and take out that SAM site." But Kennedy hesitated to retaliate, surely scared about taking a step in toward a nuclear nightmare. The president decided to ignore Khrushchev's second letter and answer the first. The evening of the 27th, he also dispatched his brother Robert to deliver an ultimatum to Soviet Ambassador Anatoly Dobrynin: Start pulling out the missiles within forty-eight hours or "we would remove them." After Dobrynin asked about the Jupiters in Turkey, Robert Kennedy presented an important American concession: They would be dismantled if the problem in Cuba were resolved. As the president had said in an ExComm meeting, "we can't very well invade Cuba with all its toil . . . when we could have gotten them out by making a deal on the same missiles in Turkey." But, should the Soviets leak word of a "deal," Robert Kennedy told the Soviet ambassador, the United States would disavow the offer. Dobrynin, who judged President Kennedy a "hot-tempered gambler," cabled an account of the meeting to Moscow, pointing out that the "very upset" president's brother insisted that "time is of the essence" and that if another U.S. plane were shot at, the United States would return fire and set off "a chain reaction" toward "a real war."

On October 28, faced with an ultimatum and a concession, and fearful that the Cubans might precipitate a greater Soviet-American conflagration, Khrushchev retreated and accepted the American offer: the Soviet Union would dismantle its missiles under United Nations supervision and the United States would pledge not to invade Cuba. The crisis had ended—just when the nuclear giants seemed about to stumble over the brink. . . .

Many analysts give John F. Kennedy high marks for his handling of the Cuban missile crisis, applauding a stunning success, noble statesmanship, and model of crisis management. Secretary Rusk lauded Kennedy for having "ice water in his veins." The journalist Hugh Sidey has gushed over "the serene leader who guides the nation away from nuclear conflict." Arthur Schlesinger, Jr., has effusively written that Kennedy's crisis leadership constituted a "combination of toughness and restraint, of will, nerve, and wisdom, so brilliantly controlled, so matchlessly calibrated." May and Zelikow celebrate Kennedy's "finest hours," sketching a "lucid" and "calm" president, who, in the end, steps back from the brink.

Kennedy's stewardship of policymaking during the crisis actually stands less as a supreme display of careful crisis management and more as a case of near misses, close calls, narrow squeaks, physical exhaustion, accidents, and guesses that together scared officials on both sides into a settlement, because, in the words of McGeorge Bundy, the crisis was "so near to spinning out of control." When McNamara recalled those weeks, he questioned the entire notion of crisis management because of "misinformation, miscalculation, misjudgment, and human fallibility." "We were in luck," Ambassador John Kenneth Galbraith ruminated, "but success in a lottery is no argument for lotteries." . . .

Danger lurked too in the way the commander of the Strategic Air Command issued DEFCON 2 alert instructions. He did so in the clear, instead of in code, because he wanted to impress the Soviets. Alerts serve to prepare American forces for war, but they may also provoke an adversary to think that the United States might launch a first strike. Under such circumstances, the adversary might be tempted to strike first. The Navy's antisubmarine warfare activities also carried the potential of escalating the crisis. Soviet submarines prowled near the quarantine line, and, following standing orders, Navy ships forced several of them to surface. In one case, a Navy commander exercised the high-risk option of dropping a depth charge on a Soviet submarine. As in so many of these examples, decisionmakers in Washington actually lost some control of the crisis to personnel at the operational level.

ExComm members represented considerable intellectual talent and experience, but a mythology of grandeur, illusion of control, and embellishment of performance have obscured the history of the committee. ExComm debated alternatives under "intense strain," often in a "state of anxiety and emotional exhaustion," recalled Under Secretary Ball. McGeorge Bundy told Ball on October 24 that he (Bundy) was getting "groggy." Two advisers may have suffered such stress that they became less able to perform their responsibilities. An assistant to Adlai Stevenson recalled that he had had to become an ExComm "back-up" for the ambassador because, "while he could speak clearly, his memory wasn't very clear. . . ." Asked if failing health produced this condition, Vice Admiral Charles Wellborn answered that the "emotional state and nervous tension that was involved in it [missile crisis] had this effect." Stevenson was feeling "pretty frightened." So apparently was Dean Rusk. The president scratched on a notepad during an October 22 meeting: "Rusk rather quiet & somewhat fatigued." Robert Kennedy remembered that the secretary of state "had a virtually complete breakdown mentally and physically." Once, when Rusk's eyes swelled with tears, Dean Acheson barked at him: "Pull yourself together, . . . you're the only secretary of state we have." We cannot determine how stress affected the advice ExComm gave Kennedy, but at least we know that its members struggled against time, sleep, exhaustion, and themselves, and they did not always think clearheadedly at a time when the stakes were very high.

What about the president himself, gravely ill from Addison's disease and often in severe pain because of his ailing back? Dr. Max Jacobson, known as "Dr. Feelgood" by the Hollywood crowd that paid for his services, and a frequent visitor to the White House, administered amphetamines and steroids to President Kennedy during the first days of the missile crisis. Medical doctors have reported that the effect of these unorthodox injections might have been supreme confidence and belligerence. One might speculate that JFK's inclination toward a bold military response at the start of the crisis was influenced by the doses of potent drugs he was taking. . . .

As for the Soviets, they too worried about their decisionmaking process and the crisis spinning out of control. Khrushchev, of course, had miscalculated from the outset. He somehow thought that the Americans would not discover the missiles until after all of them had become operational. He had no fallback plan once they were photographed. Because he had never informed his own embassy in Washington that missiles were being placed in Cuba, he had cut himself off from critical advice—counsel that would have alerted him to the certain vigorous U.S. response to the emplacement. . . .

Add to these worries the Soviet premier's troubles with Fidel Castro, who demanded a bold Soviet response to U.S. actions and who might provoke an incident with the United States that could escalate the crisis. Castro pressed the Soviets to use nuclear weapons to save Cuba should the United States attack. Soviet leaders urged Castro not to "initiate provocations" and to practice "self-restraint." Such "adventurists," remarked a Soviet decisionmaker about the Cubans. Khrushchev sternly told his advisers: "You see how far things can go. We've got to get those missiles out of there before a real fire starts."

President Kennedy helped precipitate the missile crisis by harassing Cuba through his multitrack program. Then he reacted to the crisis by suspending diplomacy in favor of public confrontation. In the end, with the management of the crisis disintegrating, he frightened himself. In order to postpone doomsday, or at least to prevent a high-casualty invasion of Cuba, he moderated the American response and compromised. Khrushchev withdrew his mistake, while gaining what ExComm member Ambassador Llewellyn Thompson thought was the "important thing" all along for the Soviet leader: being able to say, "I saved Cuba. I stopped an invasion." . . .

After the missile imbroglio, the pre-crisis "fixation" reasserted itself. For example, the State Department's Policy Planning Council on November 7 urged a "maximal U.S. strategy" to eliminate the Castro regime. The messy ending to the crisis—no formal accord was reached, no formal document signed—also left the Kennedy administration room to hedge on the no-invasion promise. Using the argument that the United States had agreed not to invade the island only if the missiles were withdrawn under United Nations inspection and that Castro had blocked such inspection, Kennedy refused to give an unqualified no-invasion pledge. . . .

Kennedy's retreat to an ambiguous no-invasion promise reflected his administration's unrelenting determination to oust Castro. In early January 1963, the CIA director noted that "Cuba and the Communist China nuclear threat" were the two most prominent issues on Kennedy's foreign-policy agenda. Later that month, the president himself told the National Security Council that Cuba must become a U.S. hostage. "We must always be in a position to threaten Cuba as a possible riposte to Russian pressure against us in Berlin. We must always be ready to move immediately against Cuba" should the Soviets move against Berlin. "We can use Cuba to limit Soviet actions," he concluded. The administration set about once again to threaten Cuba, to "tighten the noose" around Cuba, although Kennedy grew impatient with exile attacks, because they did not deliver "any real blow at Castro."

In June 1963, the National Security Council approved a new sabotage program. The CIA quickly cranked up destructive plots and revitalized its assassination option by making contact with a traitorous Cuban official, Rolando Cubela. Code-named AM/LASH, he plotted with CIA operatives to kill Fidel Castro. . . .

After President Kennedy's death, the new Johnson administration decided to put the "marginal" and "tenuous" Cuban-American contacts "on ice." President Johnson also instructed his advisers to avoid "high risk actions" toward Cuba. Throughout the 1960s, as the United States became hostage to the war in Vietnam, Cuba receded as a top priority. Fidel Castro may have been correct when he re-marked a decade after the missile crisis that Cuba "was saved by Vietnam. Who can say whether the immense American drive that went into Vietnam . . . would not have been turned against Cuba?" Except for a thaw in the mid to late-1970s, U.S.-Cuba relations remained frozen in hostility. Kennedy's "fixation" with Cuba fixed itself on U.S. Cuba policy for decades.

FURTHER READING

Graham Allison, *Essence of Decision* (1971)
——— and Philip Zelikow, *Essence of Decision* (1999; 2nd ed.)
Jules Benjamin, *The United States and the Origins of the Cuban Revolution* (1990)
Barton J. Bernstein, "The Cuban Missile Crisis: Trading the Jupiters in Turkey?" *Political Science Quarterly,* 95 (1980), 97–125
Michael Beschloss, *The Crisis Years* (1991)
James A. Bill, *George Ball* (1977)
Cole Blasier, *The Hovering Giant* (1976)
James G. Blight, *The Shattered Crystal Ball* (1990)
——— et al., *Cuba on the Brink* (2003)
——— and Philip Brenner, *Sad and Luminous Days* (2002)
Dino Brugioni, *Eyeball to Eyeball* (1991)
McGeorge Bundy, *Danger and Survival* (1988)
Laurence Chang and Peter Kornbluh, eds., *The Cuban Missile Crisis, 1962* (1992)
Jorge I. Domínguez, *Cuba: Order and Revolution* (1978)
———, *To Make a World Safe for Revolution* (1989)
Lawrence Freedman, *Kennedy's Wars* (2002)
Aleksandr Fursenko and Timothy Naftali, *"One Hell of a Gamble": Khrushchev, Castro, and Kennedy, 1958–1964* (1997)
Raymond L. Garthoff, "Berlin 1961: The Record Corrected," *Foreign Policy,* 84 (1991), 142–156
———, *Reflections on the Cuban Missile Crisis* (1989)
Alexander George, *Avoiding War: Problems of Crisis Management* (1991)
Alice L. George, *Awaiting Armageddon* (2003)
James N. Giglio, *The Presidency of John F. Kennedy* (1991)
——— and Stephen G. Rabe, *Debating the Kennedy Presidency* (2003)
Piero Gleijeses, *Conflicting Missions: Havana, Washington, and Africa, 1959–1976* (2001)
———, "Ships in the Night: The C.I.A., The White House, and the Bay of Pigs," *Journal of Latin American Studies,* 27 (1995), 1–42

Maurice Halperin, *The Rise and Decline of Fidel Castro* (1972)
———, *The Taming of Fidel Castro* (1981)
Mary N. Hampton, *The Wilsonian Impulse* (1996) (on U.S.-Germany)
Hope Harrison, "Ulbricht and the Concrete 'Rose': New Archival Evidence on the Dynamics
    of Soviet-East German Relations and the Berlin Crisis, 1958–1961," Working Paper #5
    (May 1993), *Cold War International History Project Bulletin,* Woodrow Wilson Inter-
    national Center for Scholars
Seymour Hersh, *The Dark Side of Camelot* (1997)
James G. Hershberg, "Before 'The Missiles of October': Did Kennedy Plan a Military
    Strike Against Cuba?" *Diplomatic History,* 14 (1990), 163–198
Trumbull Higgins, *The Perfect Failure* (1987) (on the Bay of Pigs invasion)
Irving L. Janis, *Groupthink* (1982)
Donna Rich Kaplowitz, *Anatomy of a Failed Embargo: U.S. Sanctions Against Cuba* (1998)
Montague Kern, Patricia W. Levering, and Ralph B. Levering, *The Kennedy Crises: The
    Press, the Presidency, and Foreign Policy* (1983)
Richard Ned Lebow, *Between Peace and War* (1981)
——— and Janice Gross Stein, *We All Lost the Cold War* (1993)
Ernest R. May and Philip D. Zelikow, *The Kennedy Tapes* (1997)
Frank A. Mayer, *Adenauer and Kennedy: A Study in German-American Relations,
    1961–1963* (1996)
Morris Morley, *Imperial State and Revolution: The United States and Cuba, 1952–1987*
    (1987)
Philip Nash, *The Other Missiles of October* (1997) (on Jupiters)
James A. Nathan, *Anatomy of the Cuban Missile Crisis* (2001)
Kendrick Oliver, *Kennedy, Macmillan, and the Nuclear Test Ban Treaty* (1998)
Herbert S. Parmet, *JFK* (1983)
Thomas G. Paterson, *Contesting Castro* (1994)
———, ed., *Kennedy's Quest for Victory* (1989)
——— and William T. Brophy, "October Missiles and November Elections: The Cuban
    Missile Crisis and American Politics, 1962," *Journal of American History,* 73 (1986),
    87–119
Louis A. Pérez, Jr., *Cuba and the United States* (1990)
Richard M. Pious, "The Cuban Missile Crisis and the Limits of Crisis Management,"
    Political Science Quarterly, 116 (2001), 81–105
Steven G. Rabe, *The Most Dangerous Area in the World* (1999)
Scott D. Sagan, *The Limits of Safety* (1993)
Arthur M. Schlesinger, Jr., *Robert Kennedy and His Times* (1978)
———, *A Thousand Days* (1965)
Thomas J. Schoenbaum, *Waging Peace and War* (1988) (on Rusk)
Len Scott and Steve Smith, "Lessons of October: Historians, Political Scientists, Policy-
    makers, and the Cuban Missile Crisis," *International Affairs,* 70 (1994), 659–684
Glenn T. Seaborg and Benjamin J. Loeb, *Kennedy, Khrushchev, and the Test Ban* (1981)
Sheldon Stern, *Averting the Final Failure* (2003)
Tad Szulc, *Fidel* (1986)
Marc Trachtenberg, *History and Strategy* (1991)
Lucien S. Vandenbroucke, "Anatomy of a Failure: The Decision to Land at the Bay of Pigs,"
    Political Science Quarterly, 99 (1984), 471–491
———, *Perilous Options* (1993)
Robert Weisbrot, *Maximum Danger* (2002)
Richard E. Welch, Jr., *Response to Revolution* (1985)
Mark J. White, *The Kennedys and Cuba* (1999)
———, *Missiles in Cuba* (1997)
Peter Wyden, *Bay of Pigs* (1979)

C H A P T E R
11

The Vietnam War

After World War II, the United States's engagement in the Indochinese country of Vietnam deepened over a thirty-year period. In 1945 the Truman administration tolerated the reimposition of French colonialism, and in 1950 Washington began giving massive aid to the French to quell the patriot Ho Chi Minh's nationalist, communist-led insurgency. After the French defeat in 1954, the United States supported the division of Vietnam at the seventeenth parallel, and the Eisenhower administration helped to organize, and to prop up, a noncommunist regime in the South. In 1961 President John F. Kennedy sent U.S. military personnel to fight in Vietnamese jungles; then in 1964, under Kennedy's successor, Lyndon B. Johnson, American bombers launched an air war against North Vietnam. The Johnson administration significantly increased the level of ground forces in South Vietnam in 1965. Following the North Vietnamese–Vietcong Tet offensive in 1968, peace talks began, and in 1973 Washington and Hanoi reached a peace settlement that permitted the United States to continue to support the South Vietnamese regime. But in 1975 communist forces drove Americans pell-mell from Vietnam and seized Saigon, the southern capital, which they renamed Ho Chi Minh City.

With each passing year, the war's costs had mounted. By the end, more than 58,000 American servicemen and women had died in Vietnam, and the United States had spent more than $175 billion in Southeast Asia. Millions of Asians perished, hundreds of thousands of others became refugees, and the countries of Indochina—Vietnam, Cambodia, and Laos—lay in ruins. The war also polarized Americans at home. Peace demonstrations swept the United States during the 1960s and early 1970s. U.S. leaders ultimately responded by withdrawing American forces, but the passionate Vietnam debate nonetheless unhinged a twenty-five-year-old Cold War consensus on foreign policy.

Considering the war's length and historical significance, it is not surprising that scholars debate all aspects of the conflict. Perhaps the most fundamental question is: Why did the United States intervene in the Vietnam War and become so deeply involved? Some scholars stress that a blinding Cold War anticommunism led U.S. officials to downplay Ho Chi Minh's anticolonial nationalism and exaggerate Hanoi's ties to Moscow and Beijing. Cold War calculations similarly made Washington conclude that America's prestige and credibility across the world required the survival of a noncommunist South Vietnam. Other analysts argue that a flawed decision-making process, a bureaucracy that prized consensus, a powerful "imperial" presidency, and a go-along-to-get-along Congress drew the United States into a

Southeast Asia and the Vietnam War

■ Major U.S. bases during the Vietnam War

0   100   200   300
miles

**The Tet Offensive
January-February
1968**

☆ Major battles

quagmire. Historians of a radical bent challenge the notion that the war stemmed from mistaken judgment or bureaucratic morass; they assert that the Americanization of the Vietnam War arose from an aggressive and deliberate drive for global hegemony—a post–World War II ambition to make the world safe for markets, capital investment, and military bases. Another school of thought posits that cultural arrogance, whether expressed in terms of race, machismo, or national mission, served as the principal motivating force for American intervention.

Of course, Americans have long debated the military conduct of the war. The most nagging question remains: Was the Vietnam War winnable? Some experts maintain that the United States was on the right track with its deployment of air power, "search and destroy" campaigns, and war of attrition, but that domestic political pressures, the antiwar movement, and the media forced U.S. leaders to retreat. Others argue that U.S. forces could have been victorious, but only with a change in strategy. A more rapid escalation, unrestricted bombing, an invasion of North Vietnam, the sealing of the Vietnamese-Laotian border, and a more vigorous counterinsurgency effort have all been cited as possible alternative strategies. Still, some analysts conclude that the American effort in Vietnam was doomed from the start. A corrupt and unpopular South Vietnamese government and military, a highly motivated and skilled guerrilla opponent, a debilitating climate and harsh terrain, and an inflexible U.S. command structure made the war unwinnable for the United States. Not only was the war unwinnable, but the widespread use of air power and intensive village warfare led to atrocities and a staggering level of civilian casualties.

Why did we fight? Why did we lose? What lessons can we learn? These questions have haunted an entire generation of Americans and continue to challenge historians in the twenty-first century.

🌐 D O C U M E N T S

Resistance to foreigners is an enduring theme in Vietnamese history. During World War II, the Vietnamese battled the Japanese. On September 2, 1945, Ho Chi Minh and other nationalists wrote a Declaration of Independence for the Democratic Republic of Vietnam. Reprinted here as Document 1, it resembled the 1776 American declaration. The French attempt to reimplement colonial rule during the early postwar period, however, led to the first Indochinese War between Ho Chi Minh's nationalist-communist insurgency and the French military. Fearing that a communist victory in Indochina would lead to a communist-dominated Asia—the so-called domino theory—the United States provided the French with assistance. The beleaguered French ultimately decided to withdrawn from Vietnam, and at the Geneva Conference of May 8–July 21, 1954, the warring parties and their allies, including the United States, prepared peace terms for Indochina. The Geneva Accords that were set down in the final declaration are reprinted here as Document 2. Thereafter, Ho's communists governed North Vietnam, and the United States, which refused to accept the Geneva Accords, backed a regime in the south.

Despite U.S. aid, the government of South Vietnam was plagued by rampant corruption, inefficiency, and inadequate popular support. By 1960 a communist-led insurgency, the National Liberation Front (NLF), had gained widespread support in the south and gained North Vietnamese assistance. In Document 3, dated from 1961, North Vietnamese general Vo Nguyen Giap explains the strategy of "people's war," whereby a smaller, weaker force could achieve military victory over a stronger, imperialist power. The Tonkin Gulf Resolution, Document 4, which the U.S. Senate passed on August 10, 1964, with only two dissenting votes, authorized the president to use the force he deemed necessary in Vietnam. American warmongers interpreted this important document as equivalent to a declaration of war. Just prior to President Lyndon Johnson's landslide victory at the polls in November 1964, a National Security Council Working Group weighed U.S. options for addressing the deteriorating political conditions in South Vietnam. Document 5, a memorandum to Undersecretary of State George Ball from his assistant Thomas Ehrlich, laments the Working Group's focus on military action and its neglect of proposals for a negotiated withdrawal: "these things seem quickly to develop a bureaucratic life of their own," he concludes. The Working Group ultimately sent its findings to an NSC Executive Committee consisting of Secretaries Dean Rusk and Robert McNamara, National Security Adviser McGeorge Bundy, and CIA chief John McCone; the committee made its final recommendations to President Johnson on December 2, 1964. The "Position Paper on Southeast Asia," reprinted here as Document 6, provided a blueprint for the first phase of U.S. military activity along North Vietnamese supply lines in Laos and north of the seventeenth parallel. It also laid plans for a more extensive second phase of "graduated military pressures" against the Democratic Republic of Vietnam, including U.S. air strikes in reprisal for Vietcong provocations. Johnson approved the policy paper the following day. Following a Vietcong attack against the U.S. helicopter base in Pleiku, South Vietnam, on February 7, 1965, the United States initiated Operation Rolling Thunder, a sustained bombing campaign against North Vietnam. An increase in U.S. combat troops followed. The American escalation was paralleled by increases in both Soviet and Chinese assistance to Hanoi. Document 7, drawn from Chinese archives, is a translation of Chairman Mao Zedong's presentation to a visiting delegation of North Vietnamese officials, dated October 20, 1965. Mao praises his Vietnamese comrades for fighting an "excellent war" against the United States, discourages negotiations, and confirms that Chinese assistance will continue.

J. William Fulbright, chair of the Senate Foreign Relations Committee, became a vocal critic of the Vietnam War. In Document 8, a speech of May 5, 1966, he protests an American "arrogance of power." In Document 9, an excerpt from Robert S. McNamara's controversial 1995 memoir, *In Retrospect,* the former secretary concludes that he and the Johnson administration erred badly in July 1965 when they escalated U.S. military intervention in Vietnam.

1. The Vietnamese Declaration of Independence, 1945

All men are created equal. They are endowed by their Creator with certain inalienable rights, among these are Life, Liberty and the pursuit of Happiness.

This immortal statement was made in the Declaration of Independence of the United States of America in 1776. In a broader sense, this means: All the peoples on the earth are equal from birth, all the peoples have a right to live, to be happy and free.

The Declaration of the French Revolution made in 1791 on the Rights of Man and the Citizen also states: "All men are born free and with equal rights, and must always remain free and have equal rights."

Those are undeniable truths.

Nevertheless, for more than eighty years, the French imperialists, abusing the standard of Liberty, Equality and Fraternity, have violated our Fatherland and oppressed our fellow-citizens. They have acted contrary to the ideals of humanity and justice.

This document can be found in Information Service, Viet-Nam Delegation in France, *The Democratic Republic of Viet-Nam* (Paris: Imprimerie Centrale Commerciale, 1948), pp. 3–5.

In the field of politics, they have deprived our people of every democratic liberty.

They have enforced inhuman laws; they have set up three distinct political regimes in the North, the Centre and the South of Viet Nam in order to wreck our national unity and prevent our people from being united.

They have built more prisons than schools. They have mercilessly slain our patriots; they have drowned our uprisings in rivers of blood.

They have fettered public opinion; they have practised obscurantism against our people.

To weaken our race they have forced us to use opium and alcohol.

In the field of economics, they have fleeced us to the backbone, impoverished our people and devastated our land.

They have robbed us of our ricefields, our mines, our forests and our raw materials. They have monopolized the issuing of banknotes and the export trade.

They have invented numerous unjustifiable taxes and reduced our people, especially our peasantry, to a state of extreme poverty.

They have hampered the prospering of our national bourgeoisie; they have mercilessly exploited our workers. . . .

For these reasons, we, members of the Provisional Government, representing the whole Vietnamese people, declare that from now on we break off all relations of a colonial character with France; we repeal all the international obligation[s] that France has so far subscribed to on behalf of Viet Nam and we abolish all the special rights the French have unlawfully acquired in our Fatherland.

The whole Vietnamese people, animated by a common purpose, are determined to fight to the bitter end against any attempt by the French colonialists to reconquer their country.

We are convinced that the Allied nations which at Teheran and San Francisco have acknowledged the principles of self-determination and equality of nations, will not refuse to acknowledge the independence of Viet Nam.

A people who have courageously opposed French domination for more than eighty years, a people who have fought side by side with the Allies against the fascists during these last years, such a people must be free and independent.

For these reasons, we, members of the Provisional Government of the Democratic Republic of Vietnam, solemnly declare to the world that Viet Nam has the right to be a free and independent country—and in fact it is so already. The entire Vietnamese people are determined to mobilize all their physical and mental strength, to sacrifice their lives and property in order to safeguard their independence and liberty.

2. Final Declaration of the Geneva Conference on Indochina, 1954

1. The Conference takes note of the agreements ending hostilities in Cambodia, Laos and Viet Nam and organising international control and the supervision of the execution of the provisions of these agreements. . . .

This document can be found in *Department of State Bulletin*, XXXI (August 2, 1954), p. 164.

4. The Conference takes note of the clauses in the agreement on the cessation of hostilities in Viet Nam prohibiting the introduction into Viet Nam of foreign troops and military personnel as well as of all kinds of arms and munitions. . . .

5. The Conference takes note of the clauses in the agreement on the cessation of hostilities in Viet Nam to the effect that no military base under the control of a foreign State may be established in the regrouping zones of the two parties [above and below the seventeenth parallel], the latter having the obligation to see that the zones allotted to them shall not constitute part of any military alliance and shall not be utilised for the resumption of hostilities or in the service of an aggressive policy. . . .

6. The Conference recognises that the essential purpose of the agreement relating to Viet Nam is to settle military questions with a view to ending hostilities and that the military demarcation line [at the seventeenth parallel] is provisional and should not in any way be interpreted as constituting a political or territorial boundary. The Conference expresses its conviction that the execution of the provisions set out in the present declaration and in the agreement on the cessation of hostilities creates the necessary basis for the achievement in the near future of a political settlement in Viet Nam.

7. The Conference declares that, so far as Viet Nam is concerned, the settlement of political problems, effected on the basis of respect for the principles of independence, unity and territorial integrity, shall permit the Vietnamese people to enjoy the fundamental freedoms, guaranteed by democratic institutions established as a result of free general elections by secret ballot. In order to ensure that sufficient progress in the restoration of peace has been made, and that all of the necessary conditions obtain for free expression of the national will, general elections shall be held in July 1956, under the supervision of an international commission composed of representatives of the Member States of the International Supervisory Commission, referred to in the agreement on the cessation of hostilities. Consultations will be held on this subject between the competent representative authorities of the two zones from July 20, 1955, onwards. . . .

12. In their relations with Cambodia, Laos and Viet Nam, each member of the Geneva Conference undertakes to respect the sovereignty, the independence, the unity and the territorial integrity of the above-mentioned States, and to refrain from any interference in their internal affairs.

3. North Vietnamese General Vo Nguyen Giap Outlines His People's War Strategy, 1961

The Vietnamese people's war of liberation [against France] was a just war, aiming to win back the independence and unity of the country, to bring land to our peasants and guarantee them the right to it, and to defend the achievements of the August [1945] Revolution. That is why it was first and foremost a people's war. To educate, mobilise, organise and arm the whole people in order that they might take part in the Resistance was a crucial question.

This document can be found in Vo Nguyen Giap, *People's War, People's Army* (Hanoi: Foreign Languages Publishing House, 1961), pp. 27–30.

The enemy of the Vietnamese nation was aggressive imperialism, which had to be overthrown. . . .

A backward colonial country which had only just risen up to proclaim its independence and install people's power, Viet Nam only recently possessed armed forces, equipped with still very mediocre arms and having no combat experience. Her enemy, on the other hand, was an imperialist power which has retained a fairly considerable economic and military potentiality despite the recent German occupation [during World War II] and benefited, furthermore, from the active support of the United States. The balance of forces decidedly showed up our weaknesses against the enemy's power. The Vietnamese people's war of liberation had, therefore, to be a hard and long-lasting war in order to succeed in creating conditions for victory. All the conceptions born of impatience and aimed at obtaining speedy victory could only be gross errors. It was necessary to firmly grasp the strategy of a long-term resistance, and to exalt the will to be self-supporting in order to maintain and gradually augment our forces, while nibbling at and progressively destroying those of the enemy; it was necessary to accumulate thousands of small victories to turn them into a great success, thus gradually altering the balance of forces in transforming our weakness into power and carrying off final victory. . . .

From the point of view of directing operations, our *strategy and tactics had to be those of a people's war and of a long-term resistance.*

Our strategy was, as we have stressed, to wage a long-lasting battle. A war of this nature in general entails several phases; in principle, starting from a stage of contention, it goes through a period of equilibrium before arriving at a general counter-offensive. In effect, the way in which it is carried on can be more subtle and more complex, depending on the particular conditions obtaining on both sides during the course of operations. Only a long-term war could enable us to utilise to the maximum our political trump cards, to overcome our material handicap and to transform our weakness into strength. To maintain and increase our forces, was the principle to which we adhered, contenting ourselves with attacking when success was certain, refusing to give battle likely to incur losses to us or to engage in hazardous actions. We had to apply the slogan: to build up our strength during the actual course of fighting.

The forms of fighting had to be completely adapted that is, to raise the fighting spirit to the maximum and rely on heroism of our troops to overcome the enemy's material superiority. In the main, especially at the outset of the war, we had recourse to guerilla fighting. In the Vietnamese theatre of operations, this method carried off great victories: it could be used in the mountains as well as in the delta, it could be waged with good or mediocre material and even without arms, and was to enable us eventually to equip ourselves at the cost of the enemy. Wherever the Expeditionary Corps came, the entire population took part in the fighting; every commune had its fortified village, every district had its regional troops fighting under the command of the local branches of the Party and the people's administration, in liaison with the regular forces in order to wear down and annihilate the enemy forces.

Thereafter, with the development of our forces, guerilla warfare changed into a mobile warfare—a form of mobile warfare still strongly marked by guerilla warfare—which would afterwards become the essential form of operations on the main front, the northern front. In this process of development of guerilla warfare and of accentuation of the mobile warfare, our people's army constantly grew and passed from the stage of combats involving a section or company, to fairly large-scale campaigns bringing into action several divisions. Gradually, its equipment improved, mainly by the seizure of arms from the enemy—the materiel of the French and American imperialists.

From the military point of view, *the Vietnamese people's war of liberation proved that an insufficiently equipped people's army, but an army fighting for a just cause, can, with appropriate strategy and tactics, combine the conditions needed to conquer a modern army of aggressive imperialism.*

4. The Tonkin Gulf Resolution Authorizes the President to Use Force, 1964

To promote the maintenance of international peace and security in southeast Asia.

Whereas naval units of the Communist regime in Vietnam, in violation of the principles of the Charter of the United Nations and of international law, have deliberately and repeatedly attacked United States naval vessels lawfully present in international waters, and have thereby created a serious threat to international peace; and

Whereas these attacks are part of a deliberate and systematic campaign of aggression that the Communist regime in North Vietnam has been waging against its neighbors and the nations joined with them in the collective defense of their freedom; and

Whereas the United States is assisting the peoples of southeast Asia to protect their freedom and has no territorial, military or political ambitions in that area, but desires only that these peoples should be left in peace to work out their own destinies in their own way: Now, therefore, be it *Resolved by the Senate and House of Representatives of the United States of America in Congress assembled,* That the Congress approves and supports the determination of the President, as Commander in Chief, to take all necessary measures to repel any armed attack against the forces of the United States and to prevent further aggression.

Sec. 2. The United States regards as vital to its national interest and to world peace the maintenance of international peace and security in southeast Asia. Consonant with the Constitution of the United States and the Charter of the United Nations and in accordance with its obligations under the Southeast Asia Collective Defense Treaty, the United States is, therefore, prepared, as the President determines, to take all necessary steps, including the use of armed force, to assist any member or protocol state of the Southeast Asia Collective Defense Treaty requesting assistance in defense of its freedom.

Sec. 3. This resolution shall expire when the President shall determine that the peace and security of the area is reasonably assured by international conditions created by action of the United Nations or otherwise, except that it may be terminated earlier by concurrent resolution of the Congress.

This document can be found in *Department of State Bulletin,* LI (August 24, 1964), 268.

5. A Bureaucratic Insider Laments the Momentum Against Negotiation, November 1964

Mr. Bundy has circulated the attached papers concerning "courses of action in Southeast Asia" to Secretary [of State Dean] Rusk, Secretary [of Defense Robert] McNamara, [CIA Director] Mr. [John] McCone, and General [Earl] Wheeler. A meeting with Secretary Rusk, Secretary McNamara, you, and McGeorge and William Bundy to review these papers is scheduled for next Tuesday. After further meetings next Thursday and Friday, a meeting with the President is scheduled for December 1.

I think that the approach taken in these papers will cause you serious concern. Three "broad options" are considered. *First,* to "continue present policies of maximum assistance with SVN [South Vietnam] and limited external actions in Laos and by the GVN [Government of Vietnam] coherently against North Viet-Nam;" and, possibly, specific individual reprisal actions. "Basic to this option is the continued rejection of negotiation in the hope that the situation will improve." *Second,* "present policies plus a systematic program of military pressures against the north, meshing at some point with negotiation, but with pressure actions to be continued until we achieve our central present objectives." *Third,* "present policies plus additional forceful measures and military moves, followed by negotiations in which we would seek to maintain a believable threat of still further military pressures but would not actually carry out such pressures to any marked degree during the negotiations."

These papers conclude with a proposed recommendation to the President that we follow "a program of immediate actions within the next few weeks" and that, "if the Communist side does not respond favorably" to these actions, we adopt the third alternative early next year. The "basic ingredients" of the "immediate actions during the next few weeks" would be: (1) "talking tough;" (2) "vigorous actions within our current policy" including: (a) a strong 34–A MAROPS [covert U.S.–South Vietnamese sabotage against North Vietnam] schedule; (b) continued strong air activity in the Panhandle area of Laos, including at least a few United States armed reconnaissance strikes; (c) continued strong air activity in central Laos; (d) perhaps a DeSoto patrol [a covert electronic spying program against North Vietnam] early in December; and (e) "consider explicit use of US air in South Viet-Nam if a lucrative target appears;" (3) reprisals in the event of future serious incidents; (4) "consultations with the GVN to improve its performance;" and (5) "miscellaneous actions clearly foreshadowing stronger actions."

Nowhere in these papers is there a consideration of your proposal for negotiations within the near future and without increased military action (although with the threat of such action). In fact, the first option (to continue present policies) specifically excludes negotiations. Furthermore, although the outline of the papers calls for a separate section concerning "alternative forms of negotiation" no draft of this

This document can be found in Memorandum from the Under Secretary of State's Special Assistant (Ehrlich) to the Under Secretary of State (Ball), 18 November 1964, *Foreign Relations of the United States, 1964–1968, I: Vietnam 1964* (Washington, D.C.: Government Printing Office, 1992), pp. 912–913.

section was prepared. Rather, "various working papers on negotiations . . . have been woven into" the other sections.

I think there are a number of significant gaps in reasoning and questions unanswered throughout these papers. As we have discussed, the third option is full of dangers—I do not believe that they have received sufficient consideration in these papers. Most serious, however, is the lack of any real analysis of a negotiating track. In my judgment, at the very least, a paper on this track should be prepared as a fourth option.

I am particularly concerned because policy proposals like these seem quickly to develop a bureaucratic life of their own unless immediate action is taken.

6. President Lyndon B. Johnson's Advisers Chart the Path to Military Escalation, December 1964

A. US objectives in South Vietnam (SVN) are unchanged. They are to:

1. Get Hanoi and North Vietnam (DRV) support and direction removed from South Vietnam, and, to the extent possible, obtain DRV cooperation in ending Viet Cong (VC) operations in SVN.

2. Re-establish an independent and secure South Vietnam with appropriate international safeguards, including the freedom to accept US and other external assistance as required.

3. Maintain the security of other non-Communist nations in Southeast Asia including specifically the maintenance and observance of the Geneva Accords of 1962 in Laos.

B. We will continue to press the South Vietnamese Government (GVN) in every possible way to make the government itself more effective and to push forward with the pacification program. We will also press upon leaders and members of all groups in that country the overriding need for national unity.

C. We will join at once with the South Vietnamese and Lao Governments in a determined action program aimed at DRV activities in both countries and designed to help GVN morale and to increase the costs and strain on Hanoi, foreshadowing still greater pressures to come. Under this program the *first phase* actions within the next thirty days will be intensified forms of action already under way, plus possibly U.S. air protection of Lao aircraft making strikes in the Corridor, US armed air reconnaissance and air strikes against infiltration routes in Laos, and GVN and possibly US air strikes against the DRV as reprisal against any major or spectacular Viet Cong action in the south, whether against US personal and installations or not. We would be prepared to stop the flow of dependents to Vietnam at the same time as US strikes in Laos were conducted.

This document can be found in paper prepared by the Executive Committee, "Position Paper on Southeast Asia," 2 December 1964, *Foreign Relations of the United States, 1964–1968, I: Vietnam 1964* (Washington, D.C.: Government Printing Office, 1992), pp. 969–970, 973.

D. Beyond the thirty-day period, first phase actions may be continued without change. Alternatively, additional military measures may be taken, including deployment of a large number of US aircraft to the area, low-level reconnaissance of infiltration targets in the DRV near the borders, and the possible initiation of strikes a short distance across the border against the infiltration routes from the DRV. . . .

E. Thereafter, if the GVN improves its effectiveness to an acceptable degree and Hanoi does not yield on acceptable terms, the US is prepared—at a time to be determined—to enter into a *second phase* program, in support of the GVN and RLG, of graduated military pressures directed systematically against the DRV. Such a program would consist principally of progressively more serious air strikes, of a weight and tempo adjusted to the situation as it develops (possibly running from two to six months) and of appropriate US deployments to handle any contingency. Targets in the DRV would start with infiltration targets south of the 19th parallel and work up to targets north of that point. This could eventually lead to such measures as air strikes on all major military-related targets, aerial mining of DRV ports, and a US naval blockade of the DRV. The whole sequence of military actions would be designed to give the impression of a steady, deliberate approach, and to give the US the option at any time (subject to enemy reaction) to proceed or not, to escalate or not, and to quicken the pace or not. Concurrently, the US would be alert to any sign of yielding by Hanoi, and would be prepared to explore negotiated solutions that attain US objectives in an acceptable manner. . . .

I. *Reprisal Actions*

For any VC provocation similar to the following, a reprisal will be undertaken, preferably within 24 hours, against one or more selected targets in the DRV. GVN forces will be used to the maximum extent, supplemented as necessary by US forces. The exact reprisal will be decided at the time, in accordance with a quick-reaction procedure which will be worked out.

The following may be appropriate occasions for reprisals, but we should be alert for any appropriate occasion:

1. Attacks on airfields.
2. Attack on Saigon.
3. Attacks on provincial or district capitals.
4. Major attacks on US citizens.
5. Attacks on major POL facilities.
6. Attacks on bridges and railroad lines after the presently damaged facilities have been restored and warning given.
7. Other "spectaculars" such as earlier attack on a US transport carrier at a pier in Saigon.

In these or similar cases, the reprisal action would be linked as directly as possible to DRV infiltration, so that we have a common thread of justification. VC attacks on transportation facilities, in addition to being related to DRV infiltration, would provide the occasion for attacks on DRV communications on a parallel basis.

A flexible list of reprisal targets has been prepared running from infiltration targets in the southern part of the DRV up to airfields, ports, and naval bases also located south of the 19th parallel.

7. Chinese Leader Mao Zedong Urges the North Vietnamese to Fight On, 1965

You are fighting an excellent war. Both the South and the North are fighting well. The people of the whole world, including those who have already awakened and those who have not awakened, are supporting you. The current world is not a peaceful one. It is not you Vietnamese who are invading the United States, neither are the Chinese who are waging an aggressive war against the United States.

Not long ago the Japanese *Asahi Shimbum* and *Yomiuri Shimbun* published several reports filed by Japanese correspondents from South Vietnam. U.S. newspapers described these reports as unfair, thus provoking a debate. I am not referring to the Japanese Communist newspaper, *Akahata*. I am talking about Japanese bourgeois newspapers. This shows that the direction of the media is not favorable to the United States. Recently the demonstration by the American people against the American government's Vietnam policy has developed. At the moment it is primarily American intellectuals who are making trouble.

But all this are external conditions. In fact what will solve the problem is the war you are fighting. Of course you can conduct negotiations. In the past you held negotiations in Geneva. But the American did not honor their promise after the negotiations. We have had negotiations with both Chiang Kai-shek and the United States. . . . But we stick to one point: the United States must withdraw from Taiwan, and after that all other problems can be easily resolved. The United States does not accept this point. China and the United States have been negotiating for ten years and we are still repeating the same old words. We will not give up that point. . . .

You withdrew your armed forces from the South in accordance with the Geneva Accords. As a result, the enemy began to kill people in the South, and you revived armed struggle. At first you adopted political struggle as a priority supplemented by armed struggle. We supported you. In the second stage when you were carrying out political and armed struggles simultaneously, we again supported you. In the third stage when you are pursuing armed struggle as a priority supplemented by political struggle, we still support you. In my view, the enemy is gradually escalating the war: so are you. In the next two and three years you may encounter difficulties. But it is hard to say, and it may not be so. We need to take this possibility into consideration. So long as you have made all kinds of preparations, even if the most difficult situation emerges, you will not find it too far from your initial considerations. Isn't this a good argument? Therefore there are two essential points: the first is to strive for the most favorable situation, and the second to prepare for the worst. . . .

I have not noticed what issues you have negotiated with the United States. I only pay attention to how you fight the Americans and how you drive the Americans out. You can have negotiations at certain time[s], but you should not lower your tones. You should raise your tones a little higher. Be prepared that the enemy may deceive you.

From "Mao's Conversation with the Party and Government Delegation of the Democratic Republic of Vietnam," 20 October, 1965, translated by Qiang Zhai, in *Cold War International History Project Bulletin* (Winter 1995–1996), pp. 245–246. Copyright © 1996. Reprinted with permission.

We will support you until your final victory. The confidence in victory comes from the fighting you have done and from the struggle you have made. For instance, one experience we have is that the Americans can be fought. We obtained this experience only after fighting the Americans. The Americans can be fought and can be defeated. We should demolish the myth that the Americans cannot be fought and cannot be defeated. Both of our two parties have many experiences. Both of us have fought the Japanese. You have also fought the French. At the moment you are fighting the Americans. . . .

The Chinese people and the people of the whole world support you. The more friends you have, the better you are.

8. Senator J. William Fulbright Decries the "Arrogance of Power," 1966

The attitude above all others which I feel sure is no longer valid is the arrogance of power, the tendency of great nations to equate power with virtue and major responsibilities with a universal mission. The dilemmas involved are preeminently American dilemmas, not because America has weaknesses that others do not have but because America is powerful as no nation has ever been before and the discrepancy between its power and the power of others appears to be increasing. . . .

We are now engaged in a war to "defend freedom" in South Vietnam. Unlike the Republic of Korea, South Vietnam has an army which [is] without notable success and a weak, dictatorial government which does not command the loyalty of the South Vietnamese people. The official war aims of the United States Government, as I understand them, are to defeat what is regarded as North Vietnamese aggression, to demonstrate the futility of what the communists call "wars of national liberation," and to create conditions under which the South Vietnamese people will be able freely to determine their own future. I have not the slightest doubt of the sincerity of the President and the Vice President and the Secretaries of State and Defense in propounding these aims. What I do doubt—and doubt very much—is the ability of the United States to achieve these aims by the means being used. I do not question the power of our weapons and the efficiency of our logistics; I cannot say these things delight me as they seem to delight some of our officials, but they are certainly impressive. What I do question is the ability of the United States, or France or any other Western nation, to go into a small, alien, undeveloped Asian nation and create stability where there is chaos, the will to fight where there is defeatism, democracy where there is no tradition of it and honest government where corruption is almost a way of life. Our handicap is well expressed in the pungent Chinese proverb: "In shallow waters dragons become the sport of shrimps."

Early last month demonstrators in Saigon burned American jeeps, tried to assault American soldiers, and marched through the streets shouting "Down with the

---

This document can be found in the *Congressional Record*, CXII (May 17, 1966), 10805–10810.

American imperialists," while one of the Buddhist leaders made a speech equating the United States with the communists as a threat to South Vietnamese independence. Most Americans are understandably shocked and angered to encounter such hostility from people who by now would be under the rule of the Viet Cong but for the sacrifice of American lives and money. Why, we may ask, are they so shockingly ungrateful? Surely they must know that their very right to parade and protest and demonstrate depends on the Americans who are defending them.

The answer, I think, is that "fatal impact" of the rich and strong on the poor and weak. Dependent on it though the Vietnamese are, our very strength is a reproach to their weakness, our wealth a mockery of their poverty, our success a reminder of their failures. What they resent is the disruptive effect of our strong culture upon their fragile one, an effect which we can no more avoid than a man can help being bigger than a child. What they fear, I think rightly, is that traditional Vietnamese society cannot survive the American economic and cultural impact. . . .

The cause of our difficulties in southeast Asia is not a deficiency of power but an excess of the wrong kind of power which results in a feeling of impotence when it fails to achieve its desired ends. We are still acting like boy scouts dragging reluctant old ladies across the streets they do not want to cross. We are trying to remake Vietnamese society, a task which certainly cannot be accomplished by force and which probably cannot be accomplished by any means available to outsiders. The objective may be desirable, but it is not feasible. . . .

If America has a service to perform in the world—and I believe it has—it is in large part the service of its own example. In our excessive involvement in the affairs of other countries, we are not only living off our assets and denying our own people the proper enjoyment of their resources; we are also denying the world the example of a free society enjoying its freedom to the fullest. This is regrettable indeed for a nation that aspires to teach democracy to other nations, because, as [Edmund] Burke said, "Example is the school of mankind, and they will learn at no other.". . .

There are many respects in which America, if it can bring itself to act with the magnanimity and the empathy appropriate to its size and power, can be an intelligent example to the world. We have the opportunity to set an example of generous understanding in our relations with China, of practical cooperation for peace in our relations with Russia, of reliable and respectful partnership in our relations with Western Europe, of material helpfulness without moral presumption in our relations with the developing nations, of abstention from the temptations of hegemony in our relations with Latin America, and of the all-around advantages of minding one's own business in our relations with everybody. Most of all, we have the opportunity to serve as an example of democracy to the world by the way in which we run our own society; America, in the words of John Quincy Adams, should be "the well-wisher to the freedom and independence of all" but "the champion and vindicator only of her own.". . .

If we can bring ourselves so to act, we will have overcome the dangers of the arrogance of power. It will involve, no doubt, the loss of certain glories, but that seems a price worth paying for the probable rewards, which are the happiness of America and the peace of the world.

9. Former Secretary of Defense Robert S. McNamara Concludes That He Erred, 1995

We of the Kennedy and Johnson administrations who participated in the decisions on Vietnam acted according to what we thought were the principles and traditions of this nation. We made our decisions in light of those values.

Yet we were wrong, terribly wrong. . . .

Looking back, I clearly erred by not forcing—then or later, in either Saigon or Washington—a knock-down, drag-out debate over the loose assumptions, unasked questions, and thin analyses underlying our military strategy in Vietnam. I had spent twenty years as a manager identifying problems and forcing organizations—often against their will—to think deeply and realistically about alternative courses of action and their consequences. I doubt I will ever fully understand why I did not do so here.

On July 21 [1965], I returned to Washington and presented the report I had prepared along the way to the president. It began with a frank but disturbing assessment:

> The situation in South Vietnam is worse than a year ago (when it was worse than a year before that). After a few months of stalemate, the tempo of the war has quickened. A hard VC push is now on to dismember the nation and to maul the army. . . . Without further outside help, the ARVN* is faced with successive tactical reverses, loss of key communication and population centers particularly in the highlands, piecemeal destruction of ARVN units . . . and loss of civilian confidence.

I continued:

> There are no signs that we have throttled the inflow of supplies for the VC or can throttle the flow while their material needs are as low as they are. . . . Nor have our air attacks in North Vietnam produced tangible evidence of the willingness on the part of Hanoi to come to the conference table in a reasonable mood. The DRV/VC [Democratic Republic of North Vietnam/Vietcong] seem to believe that South Vietnam is on the run and near collapse; they show no signs of settling for less than a complete take-over.

I then reviewed the three alternatives we had examined so many times before: (1) withdraw under the best conditions obtainable—almost certainly meaning something close to unconditional surrender; (2) continue at the present level—almost certainly forcing us into Option 1 later; or (3) expand our forces to meet Westy's request** while launching a vigorous effort to open negotiations—almost certainly staving off near-term defeat but also increasing the difficulty and cost of withdrawal later.

I was driven to Option 3, which I considered "prerequisite to the achievement of any acceptable settlement." I ended by expressing my judgment that "the course of action recommended in this memorandum—if the military and political moves are properly integrated and executed with continuing vigor and visible determination—stands a good chance of achieving an acceptable outcome within a reasonable time." Subsequent events proved my judgment wrong.

From *In Retrospect* by Robert S. McNamara. Copyright © 1995 by Robert S. McNamara. Used by permission of Times Books, a division of Random House, Inc.

*The Army of the Republic of South Vietnam
**General William Westmoreland requested 175,000 troops by year's end and another 100,000 in 1966.

 *E S S A Y S*

In the first essay, Robert Buzzanco of the University of Houston places the Vietnam War in a global context—the post–World War II competition between international capitalism and communism—and argues that the United States's pursuit of an integrated world capitalist market dictated U.S. opposition to Vietnam's nationalism and communism and ultimately direct military intervention. According to Buzzanco, U.S. policymakers, from Truman through Johnson, deemed Vietnam essential to U.S. efforts to promote post–World War II recovery in Europe and Japan. Although never a puppet to external communist powers, Vietnam became a Cold War battleground when the Soviet Union and the People's Republic of China began to aid Ho Chi Minh's anticolonial movement. Ironically, the war became so expensive that it generated a severe global monetary crisis and undermined American hegemony. It also unmasked deep divisions within the socialist camp.

In the second essay, Fredrik Logevall of the University of California at Santa Barbara disputes that Vietnam policy was driven primarily by either United States economic needs or Cold War containment. He instead deconstructs the decisionmaking process of late 1964 and concludes that President Johnson and his highest-ranking advisers equated U.S. national interests with their own personal reputations and therefore chose military escalation to forestall an embarrassing retreat. Johnson's ego and machismo led him to demand victory in Vietnam even though intelligence reports minimized the chances for military success and even though numerous foreign leaders, journalists, and Democrats urged disengagement. The administration's midlevel working group on Southeast Asia and its most senior advisers fell in line with the president's wishes, partly out of conviction, but also to maintain their status within the bureaucracy. Thus presidential power and bureaucratic politics set the stage for a military debacle in Vietnam.

In the final piece, Robert K. Brigham of Vassar College uses new Chinese and Vietnamese sources to reassess the U.S. military defeat in Vietnam. Brigham identifies three strategies commonly cited as alternatives to gradual escalation and attrition: a U.S. invasion of North Vietnam; American incursion into neighboring Laos; and the concentration of U.S. forces in defensive enclaves in South Vietnam. He concludes that none would have brought victory because each failed to take into account the indigenous nature of the South Vietnamese insurgency and the multiple deficiencies of the Saigon government. An attack on the north carried the added disadvantage of virtually guaranteeing a costly U.S. war with Hanoi's neighbor and ally, the People's Republic of China. Given the nature of a people's war, Brigham concludes that no American strategy could have reversed the war's outcome.

International Capitalism and Communism Collide with Vietnamese Nationalism

ROBERT BUZZANCO

Vietnam became an important *international* issue only after World War II. During those years in the late 1940s, U.S. officials were trying to reestablish a stable world system but at the same time restructure it according to U.S. needs. The United States believed it imperative to rebuild former enemies like Germany and Japan along

From Robert Buzzanco, "The United States and Vietnam: Capitalism, Communism, and Containment," in Peter Hahn and Mary Ann Heiss, eds., *Empire and Revolution: The United States and the Third World Since 1945* (Columbus: Ohio State University Press, 2001), pp. 95–105, 107–115. Copyright © 2001 by Ohio State University Press. Reprinted with permission.

capitalist and democratic lines. In this effort to create a new world (liberal) order, smaller countries, like Vietnam, became objects of interest. Future economic prosperity, if not hegemony, would depend on creating an integrated world market. Where colonial areas earlier in the twentieth century might have been attractive principally as sources of raw materials or cheap labor, in the postwar economic environment they would serve as important areas for investment and regional development. Vietnam's development along anticommunist lines, for instance, would be essential for the re-creation of capitalism in Japan and to keep the French appeased in Europe. Thus, this [essay] will, more than most studies, pay attention to the economic factors involved in the Vietnam War: the need to use all of Southeast Asia, not just Vietnam, as a means of rebuilding Japan, and ultimately the drain on U.S. resources that the war would become. It will also stress the global nature of the war. In the past few years, documents from archives in ex-communist nations and from China have begun to increase our understanding of the Cold War and, in the case of places like Vietnam, the hot wars that attended it. . . .

[P]erhaps the United States's greatest blunder was its inability to recognize both the nationalist *and* socialist nature of the Vietnamese resistance, later organized as the Viet Minh. Never doctrinaire, Ho merged a class analysis and a program for land redistribution (the key issue in Vietnamese society) with popular front politics and an appeal to *all* anti-French elements to join the cause. Ho himself had no inherent animus against the United States either; in fact, encouraged by Woodrow Wilson's call for self-determination during the Great War, the expatriate in Paris had tried to get an audience with the U.S. president during the postwar conference at Versailles. In 1945, when Ho declared Vietnamese independence after the defeat of the Japanese, he had positive relations with U.S. military and intelligence officials, quoted at length from the U.S. Declaration of Independence during his own address marking Vietnamese sovereignty on 2 September 1945, and even sent telegrams to President Harry S. Truman seeking U.S. amity and recognition. . . .

Though U.S. leaders had mounted anticolonial rhetoric in World War II, the White House and State Department had supported the return of France to power in Indochina in 1945–46. Fearing the emergence of communist parties and trade union movements in Western Europe, and especially in France where the Communist Party and labor were strong, the United States would placate the French by acquiescing in their renewed control over Vietnam. For U.S. foreign policy makers, this was a no-brainer, since a French role in containing the European Left was exponentially more important than Vietnamese autonomy. Ironically, however, U.S. military officials, who agreed on the primacy of French interests, argued *against* supporting their return to Indochina, claiming that it would divert resources and attention away from their principal mission, containment at home. The civilians won out, however, and the United States began to back the French, sending about $25 million in 1950, which rose to nearly $1 billion by 1954.

The Vietnamese, however, continued to resist the French, politically and militarily from 1946 to 1954, so the U.S. aid did not rescue France's position in Indochina. By 1954, then, the Viet Minh were on the verge of victory; hence the expedient agreement at Geneva to divide the country, *temporarily,* until nationwide elections could be held in 1956. That plebiscite never happened, though. Aware of Ho's popularity and support on both sides of the seventeenth parallel, U.S. officials and their

Vietnamese allies canceled the vote, ensuring the continued partition of Vietnam, with a disgruntled nationalist-communist state—the Democratic Republic of Vietnam (DRV)—in the north and an artificial "country"—the Republic of Vietnam (RVN)—cobbled together by the United States in the south. Complicating U.S. efforts at containment in Vietnam, the southern regime was led by an autocratic mandarin, Ngo Dinh Diem, whose repression and corruption would be a great recruiting tool for the enemy Viet Minh. By the mid-1950s, then, the United States was on a collision course with the forces of liberation and revolution in Vietnam. . . .

The most pressing [global] problem facing the United States after World War II was the so-called dollar gap. The United States was the only power to emerge from the hostilities stronger than it entered and was producing more goods than domestic markets could absorb (as in the 1890s). But European nations lacked adequate dollars to purchase the U.S. surplus. The United States needed to somehow get dollars into foreign hands so that other nations could in turn buy U.S. goods, but Congress, especially after appropriating $17 billion in Marshall Plan money in 1948, was reluctant to expend another huge sum of money on foreign aid. Still, without some type of support, U.S. officials feared, the Europeans would probably erect trade barriers against U.S. goods as they did during the 1930s, thereby exacerbating the Great Depression.

Complicating, and connecting, such matters, the United States had also been subsidizing Japanese recovery since 1945 but by 1950 was hoping to wean Japan off U.S. funding and to connect it, as before the war, with other Far Eastern economies such as those in Southeast Asia, including Vietnam. On this issue—the need for Southeast Asian markets—European and Japanese interests merged. Not only could the Japanese profit from trade with other Asians, especially since plans to link the Japanese and Chinese economies fell by the wayside with Mao's victory, but British recovery was linked to Southeast Asia as well. In the aftermath of the Second World War, British debt was growing rapidly, to a large extent because the flow of dollars from its colony in Malaya had been cut off, first because of the Japanese occupation during the war and then because of reconstruction difficulties afterward. To remedy Malaya's economic ills, the British began to pour money—£86 million between 1945 and 1949—into the country and to pressure the United States to offer economic aid and to increase imports of Malayan tin and rubber. U.S. purchases would then provide the dollars that the British could use to purchase goods from the United States. As Seymour Harris, an economist on the government dole at the time, explained, "A gradual transfer of aid from Western Europe to the underdeveloped areas [such as Southeast Asia] will contribute towards a solution of the dollar problems of both Europe and the underdeveloped areas." "A vigorous foreign aid program," Harris concluded, was necessary "for a prosperous America." Southeast Asia, then, could serve a dual purpose: providing markets and materials to Japan and helping fix the dollar gap for Europeans.

Vietnam was crucial to this process for two reasons. First, it too could provide raw materials and become a source of dollars for the French and could become a market for and offer materials to Japan. Second, the issue of communism in Asia touched directly on Vietnam. Within Southeast Asia after World War II, there were two communist insurgencies directed against European colonial powers—in Malaya against the British and in Vietnam against the French. While British leaders were not enthusiastic about France's return to Indochina, they even more feared that Ho's revolution would succeed and that Laos, Cambodia, Burma, and Thailand would then, like falling dominoes, fall to the Reds as well, thereby putting intense and direct pressure on Malaya. Once more, Ho's movement for national liberation became a target of U.S. opposition not because of events in Vietnam so much as because of the United States's need to develop a world system in which capitalist markets would be protected and nationalist-communist movements would be contained.

While the Vietnam War was being fought in the 1960s and 1970s, U.S. leaders contended that it was imperative to fight there to defeat communism. But there were then, and there remain today, important questions about Ho's own version of communism, his commitment to expand Vietnamese control elsewhere, and his relationship with other communist states. . . .

In the late 1950s, both the Soviet Union and the PRC were urging Ho to be cautious with regard to any forced attempt to unify Vietnam—advice that dovetailed nicely with Ho's own conservative tendencies on that matter. After a Vietnamese request to analyze their plans for the south, Chinese communist leaders responded that the "most fundamental, the most crucial, and the most urgent" task was to rebuild and develop socialism above the seventeenth parallel. In the south, PRC officials advised Ho, the anti-Diem activists should conduct "long-term" preparations and "wait for opportunities." Although dispensing advice freely, the communist powers, as General Tran Van Don, an aide to Diem in the south, conceded, were giving only limited material support to Ho, still dramatically less than the United States was supplying to the RVN. In the south, however, remnants of the Viet Minh, suffering under the Diemist repression, were pleading with the communist leadership in Hanoi to sponsor and fund an armed insurgency in the south. Ho, as [the historian] William Duiker's work over the years has shown, wanted to move more slowly than the southern insurgents, and the RVN itself did not fear northern aggression below the partition line or a significant increase in DRV aid to the anti-Diem movement. Apparently, the new documents show, the Chinese and Ho were on the same page.

By 1960, however, both Ho and the Chinese began to see the efficacy of armed struggle against Diem, with Hanoi acquiescing at the end of the year to the establishment of the southern-based National Liberation Front (NLF). It is not clear whether one side convinced the other or the PRC and DRV came to the same conclusion about armed insurgency on their own (which is probably more likely), but in a May 1960 meeting, [PRC Foreign Minister] Zhou Enlai, [Mao's eventual successor] Deng Xiaoping, and the Vietnamese now saw the need for combining intensified political organization with armed struggle. By 1961, with a new U.S. president ready to significant expand the U.S. role in Vietnam, communists in Vietnam, and China, were prepared to meet John Kennedy's challenge. During a 1961 visit by the DRV's premier, Pham Van Dong, to China, Mao Zedong expressed general support for armed struggle in southern Vietnam. The war in Vietnam was about to expand.

As U.S. support and aid to the RVN increased and its military involvement grew correspondingly, Ho continued to make contacts with the PRC and Soviet Union and looked to them for more assistance as well. The Chinese especially had been helping the Viet Minh and NLF in the 1950s and early 1960s, providing the DRV and NLF with 270,000 guns, over 10,000 artillery pieces and millions of artillery shells, thousands of wire transmitters, over 1,000 trucks, aircraft, warships, and uniforms; in fact, one of the U.S. justifications for its own increased role in Vietnam was such PRC involvement. . . . Remembering Korea, Mao feared a U.S. military role in Vietnam, so close to the PRC's own borders, and was ideologically committed to supporting the Vietnamese liberation movement. . . .

In October 1964, Pham Van Dong, Ho's closest adviser, met with Mao in Beijing and explained that his strategy was to restrict the war in the south "to the sphere of special war" (i.e., insurgency war), avoid provoking a larger U.S. intervention, and prevent the war from expanding above the seventeenth parallel. Mao was unimpressed by the U.S. potential to thwart the insurgency in the south and predicted that, if it engaged the DRV, the United States would "fight for one hundred years, and its legs will be trapped." Mao accordingly approved of the Vietnamese plans and suggested to Pham Van Dong that "you must not engage your main force in a head-to-head confrontation with [U.S. forces], and must well maintain our main force. My opinion is that so long as the green mountain is there, how can you ever lack firewood?" . . . General [Vo Nguyen] Giap already understood this approach and was adept throughout the war at drawing U.S. forces into battles in which the PAVN [Peoples Army of Vietnam] held the initiative and was able to inflict heavy casualties. Ironically, one U.S. war leader, Defense Secretary McNamara, saw the war in similar ways to Mao and Pham Van Dong. In November 1965, after the so-called victory of U.S. forces at Ia Drang, he recognized that the PAVN was avoiding main-force engagements and was attacking only at opportune moments. Even with a larger concentration of U.S. forces in Vietnam, as military commanders were requesting, Giap's strategic successes made it more likely "that we will be faced with a 'no-decision' at an even higher level."

McNamara's fear, an expanded war in Southeast Asia, was, conversely, China's threat and advantage. Promising to "go to Vietnam if Vietnam is in need, as we did in Korea," Zhou [Enlai] warned that "the war will have no limits if the US expands it into Chinese territory. The US can fight an air war. Yet, China can also fight a ground war." Lyndon Johnson understood that as well, and prudently . . . did avoid provoking the PRC to the point of intervention. Indeed, during discussions with his military chiefs regarding reinforcements in 1967, the president asked, "At what point does the enemy ask for [Chinese] volunteers?" General Earle Wheeler, the chair of the Joint Chiefs of Staff, could not reassure Johnson, agreeing that China could easily send troops into Vietnam in support of the DRV-NLF effort. . . .

While the PRC maintained a high level of interest in the war in Vietnam from the outset of the war of liberation in the 1950s, the other communist power, the Soviet Union (USSR), was initially more distant from the conflict. While offering recognition and some support to the DRV, the Soviets did not match the level of Chinese interest. In the aftermath of the 1962 Cuban missile crisis, U.S.-Soviet relations had improved noticeably, and the Soviets had minimized their role in Vietnam, which—along with Soviet suspicions that Ho was too close to Mao—caused a chill in the Kremlin's contacts with the DRV through 1964. That year, however, the ouster of Nikita Khrushchev and Leonid Brezhnev's assumption of power prompted the USSR to reevaluate its Vietnam policies and become more deeply involved in support of the DRV. In part, the Soviets did not want to lose influence in Southeast Asia or relinquish their role as primary communist power to the PRC. Toward that end, the Soviets began to publicly denounce the "American aggression" in Vietnam and to increase their military and economic assistance to the DRV and NLF. Between 1963 and 1967, the Soviets sent over one billion rubles worth of military supplies to the Vietnamese, shipped German-, and then Soviet-, made arms to their "Vietnamese friends," and sent surface-to-air missiles, jets, rockets, field artillery, and air defense technology to Ho. Economic aid flowed as freely, with the Soviets providing 50 percent of all aid to the DRV by 1968, with a total package to that point of over 1.8 billion rubles. The Vietnamese, while appreciative of Russian help, tried to exploit the friendship of both the Chinese and the Soviets. Vietnamese leaders Le Duan, Pham Van Dong, and Vo Nguyen Giap, among others, formed a working group in 1964–65 to determine ways to gain support from both communist powers while avoiding Chinese imperialism and an overreliance on the USSR. . . .

Ho, the master strategist who had played off France, China, Japan, and the United States for several decades already, had once again done so, acquiring significant aid from both the Soviet Union and China but never relinquishing Vietnamese sovereignty in the process. Meanwhile, the war against the United States raged on, with the stakes for all sides increasing on a steady basis.

By the late 1960s, U.S. leaders had been monitoring the economic effects of military intervention in Vietnam for some time already. The war was exacerbating a deep deficit in the U.S. balance of payments (BOP)—the amount of U.S. money moving abroad, in the form of tourist dollars, investment capital, or military spending, for instance—thereby weakening the dollar and prompting foreign governments to cash in their U.S. currency for gold, which in turn undermined the international monetary structure. The eminent business historian Louis Galambos has argued that Vietnam "was the most debilitating episode in the nation's entire history, more expensive in its own special way than World Wars I and II combined." An examination of the economic legacy of Vietnam in the 1960s offers ample evidence to support such claims.

After World War II, the United States had established global hegemony based on the confluence of its military power, economic growth, and political liberalism, and for a generation afterward it maintained a dominant position in the world political economy. By the mid-1960s, however, the United States's role was changing, principally as participation in the Vietnam War grew and caused greater BOP deficits and shortages in U.S. gold reserves. By 1968, the postwar system was entering a crisis phase as the Tet Offensive and the so-called gold crisis converged to transform the international system and create new political relationships at home. The events of 1967–68, it is not an exaggeration to suggest, marked the evolution of the United States's postwar role from that of unrivaled and prosperous imperial power to "first among equals" in a system of "shared hegemony." At home, the spiraling economic growth brought on by two decades of military Keynesianism could not be sustained in wartime, and U.S. capital began to flow overseas, to the detriment of domestic workers. By itself, Vietnam was calling into question the United States's military power and world leadership. At the same time, the Bretton Woods system experienced the greatest crisis since its founding. Created near the end of World War II, the Bretton Woods system established the dollar as the world's currency, fully convertible to gold at $35 per ounce and exchangeable with other currencies at stable rates based on the gold standard. Throughout the Vietnam War, however, the world monetary system was in disequilibrium or disarray, both as a result of the chronic and escalating BOP problem and, more critically, because of continuing runs on U.S. gold. . . .

Throughout 1966 and 1967 . . . the BOP deficits grew, [and] gold continued to leave the United States. . . . Inflation was rising as well, causing a major increase in the cost of the war, increasing import demand, and decreasing exports. The U.S. share of world trade, which had approached 50 percent after World War II, was down to 25 percent in 1964 and fell to just 10 percent by 1968. Treasury officials also estimated that the BOP deficit would continue to soar due "entirely to our intensified effort in Southeast Asia" while "a further $200 million increase in [military] expenditures may occur next year [FY 67] and worsen the projected deficit by that amount." . . .

Indeed, U.S. leaders could no longer avoid meeting the "overall problem" of Vietnam and economic calamity, and in early 1968 they had to confront the most serious U.S. crisis, military or economic, of the postwar era. In Vietnam, the enemy launched the Tet Offensive, a countrywide series of attacks that undermined [General William] Westmoreland's claim of "light at the end of the tunnel." Enemy forces, breaking a Tet holiday cease-fire, struck virtually every center of political or military significance in the RVN. Though suffering heavy losses—which U.S. officials would cite to claim victory during the offensive—the NLF and PAVN had in fact gained a major politico-strategic victory, exposing both the shaky nature of ARVN forces, who deserted in large numbers, and the bankruptcy of U.S. strategy, for U.S. forces could not even protect their own installations, even the embassy, in southern Vietnam. The shock of Tet, especially after respected newsman Walter Cronkite appeared on national television in late February 1968 urging an end to the war, forced U.S. leaders to finally reevaluate their approach to Vietnam. . . .

But, just as importantly, the world economic crisis peaked in early 1968 as well, and money and war were on a collision course. The military's request for massive reinforcement—206,000 more troops and the activation of 280,000 reserves—McNamara warned, would require additional appropriations of $25 billion in fiscal year 1969–70 alone, without the likelihood, let alone the promise, of turning the corner in Vietnam. At the same time, the Europeans, fearing the economic effects of another escalation in Vietnam, began cashing in their dollars for gold. During the last week of February, the gold pool sold $119 million in hard currency; on 3 and 4 March, losses totaled $141 million; and by early March the new chair of the Council of Economic Advisers, Arthur Okun, describing "a bad case of the shakes" in world financial markets, reported that the BOP deficit for the first week of March had risen to $321 million while gold losses soared to $395 million, including $179 million on 8 March alone. Should such withdrawals continue to mount, as [the historian] Thomas McCormick has explained, the depletion of gold reserves could have caused a devaluation of the dollar, which could have ignited a series of currency devaluations not unlike the 1930s. Then, with the absence of stable exchange rates, businesses would suffer globally.

With the crisis intensifying, the administration scrambled for a response. An Advisory Committee established by [Treasury Secretary] Henry Fowler, headed by Douglas Dillon and including various leaders of the Washington and Wall Street establishments, insisted that Johnson press hard for a 10 percent surcharge on corporate and individual income taxes, a move Johnson had been hoping to avoid since late 1965; retain the $35 price of gold despite European calls for an increase; and, if the problems deepened, consider closing the gold pool. "My own feeling," [National Security Adviser Walt] Rostow admitted, "is that the moment of truth is close upon us." He was right. On 14 March the gold pool lost $372 million—bringing the March losses to date to $1.26 billion—and U.S. officials anticipated that the next day's withdrawals could top $1 billion. The administration, as Rostow lamented, "can't go on as is, hoping that something will turn up." The Europeans were also pressuring the United States to act, so Johnson, on the 15th, closed the London gold market for the day, a Friday—typically the heaviest trading day of the week—and called an emergency meeting of central bankers. That weekend, governors of the central banks of the United States, the United Kingdom, Germany, Italy, Belgium, the Netherlands, and Switzerland—but not France [which had sharply criticized U.S. policy]—met in Washington to deliberate world monetary conditions. The governors, not for the first time, called on the United States and the United Kingdom to improve their BOP positions, urged the president to retain the official price of gold, and called for a "two-tiered" system for gold in which private markets could float their rates. Perhaps the major reform emerging from the crisis was the establishment of Special Drawing Rights (SDR). Created by the International Monetary Fund, these international reserve units—"paper" gold—provided the world monetary system with internationally managed liquid assets to avoid future massive hard currency withdrawals.

While the governors had stemmed the crisis with such action, LBJ was feeling more political heat than ever. . . . Rostow and Economic Adviser Ernest Goldstein told the president to anticipate additional costs for Vietnam in the $6 to $8 billion range for fiscal year 1969. And, in a biting analysis, Presidential Aide Harry McPherson berated Johnson for asking the U.S. people to keep supporting a war that was already excessively costly and had no end in sight. Lyndon Johnson, however, did not have to be told how bad the situation had turned. . . .

The alliance and military survived much better than Johnson. In a 31 March speech to the nation, he announced limited reinforcements for Vietnam, curtailed bombing above the twentieth parallel, discussed the world monetary crisis, and stressed the need for a tax surcharge. At the end of his address he stunned the nation by withdrawing from the 1968 campaign. Although the war in Vietnam would continue for five more years, Johnson was admitting failure in early 1968. . . .

The communist nations were not without their own crises in 1968, however, for the PRC, Soviet Union, and Vietnam all fell into conflict with each other just as the DRV-NLF war was attaining its greatest success. The Soviet Union was [now] trying to persuade Ho to negotiate with the United States and had denounced Hanoi for rejecting Lyndon Johnson's late 1967 "San Antonio Formula," which had promised a bombing pause if the Vietnamese would talk. The Soviet embassy even advised Moscow to inform the DRV that the USSR could not afford political brinksmanship with the United States by deepening its involvement in Vietnam and that an end to hostilities in 1968 would be in both Vietnamese and Soviet interests. But the PRC, wanting to maintain a high level of antagonism between the Soviet Union and the United States, feared that negotiations could end the war, which would raise the prospects of Chinese-Vietnamese tension again and would remove the U.S. counterbalance in Asia against the Soviets. . . .

For their part, the Vietnamese did not appreciate PRC pressure and began to distance themselves from the Chinese, especially during the Czech crisis of mid-1968. The USSR, believing it had to take a leadership role in global affairs regarding socialist countries, sent troops into Czechoslovakia to stem a liberalization movement there. The Chinese had repeatedly accused the Soviet Union of deviating from the Marxist, revolutionary line and of collusion with the West, so, as Ilya Gaiduk explained, "the Kremlin had to defend its policy not only by strong words, but also by deeds." The DRV, amid an intense anti-Soviet campaign out of Beijing, supported the Czech invasion, angering the Chinese but bringing praise from Moscow. Hanoi's support of the Soviets, open and explicit, was a signal to the USSR that the DRV was moving closer to it and remaining independent of the PRC. Thus the Soviet Union urged—and the Vietnamese agreed—that negotiations, then under way in Paris, should be taken seriously to try to end the war. . . .

What had begun in the aftermath of World War II as a war of national liberation waged by the Viet Minh against the French Union had become a global affair, with the world's major powers involved.

Because of the escalation of the conflict in Vietnam—by the United States, by Vietnam, by the Soviet Union, and by China too—the world was transformed. U.S. military and economic power, the events of the mid- to late 1960s showed, was limited. Washington no longer had fiat over the world as it seemed to have had in the 1940s and 1950s. Apparently unable or unwilling to distinguish between nationalism and communism, the United States, for reasons of credibility and capitalist expansion, tried to crush a liberation-cum-revolution in Vietnam with dire consequences. Not only was the United States's world position undermined, but, much worse, tens of thousands of U.S. citizens died fighting in Indochina, while, worse still, a small nation in Indochina was destroyed beyond feasible reconstruction. The Vietnamese, for their part, finally reached their goal. After 1968 it was clear that the United States did not possess the means or the will to "win" in Vietnam, and though troops remained until 1973 and the United States supported the RVN until 1975, Tet had effectively become the U.S. obituary in Vietnam. As for the communist world, the Vietnam War exposed divisions between the PRC and the USSR that were evident prior to the 1960s but not as obvious. By 1968, talk of "monolithic communism" was simply absurd; the major powers were more concerned with the political war they were fighting among themselves than with the shooting war between Vietnam and the United States.

Lyndon Johnson and His Bureaucracy Choose War

FREDRIK LOGEVALL

There can be no doubt that millions who cast their ballots for Johnson [in the 1964 presidential election] did so precisely because he was not Barry Goldwater. The Republican candidate scared them with his ideologically tinged speeches and his seeming proclivity for a direct confrontation with communist forces in Vietnam. In contrast, Johnson ran as the candidate of peace, as the man who would continue to support South Vietnam but also keep the United States out of a major war in Southeast Asia. Notwithstanding the attempt by White House speechwriters to leave slightly ajar the door to a larger American involvement in the conflict, the dominant impression left by LBJ in the final weeks of the campaign was that of a president telling

From Fredrik Logevall, *Choosing War: The Lost Chance for Peace and the Escalation of War in Vietnam* (Berkeley: University of California Press, 1999), pp. 253–260, 266–271, 383, 387–395. Reprinted by permission of the University of California Press.

voters that if they wanted to avoid a larger war in Vietnam, he was their man. "If any American president had ever promised anything to the American people," Thomas Powers has written, "then Lyndon Johnson had promised to keep the United States out of the war in Vietnam." . . .

And disengagement was a policy option that won many new adherents in the United States in the wake of the election, less because of American than because of South Vietnamese political developments. November and December 1964 witnessed the almost total unraveling of the South Vietnamese socio-political fabric. Internal factional struggles among Saigon officials reached new levels of intensity, and intelligence agencies reported widespread support for some form of neutralist settlement leading to a coalition government. War-weariness became still more pervasive among the peasantry and many urban dwellers, and there occurred a pronounced increase in anti-American rhetoric, some of it uttered by top GVN [Government of Vietnam] officials. To longtime proponents of early negotiations these developments only confirmed what they had always said: that any American attempt to secure a GVN military victory over the Vietcong would inevitably fail, and that it was foolish to pretend otherwise.

Significantly, these critics now found vastly increased support for their views. In December 1964, dozens of newspapers across the United States, some of which had hitherto been unquestioning supporters of the American commitment (and would be again after the Americanization of the war in 1965), began to express deep doubts about the enterprise. Many of them endorsed a negotiated disengagement from the war. Others would not go that far but still explicitly ruled out any deeper American involvement. A troubling question began to echo in editorials across the land: Just what was America doing supporting a government and a people so demonstrably unwilling to contribute to their own defense? On Capitol Hill, meanwhile, support increased for a full-fledged reexamination of the country's commitment to South Vietnam. . . .

On some level, Lyndon Johnson understood that he had options regarding Vietnam and that the immediate postelection period would present an opportunity to examine those options closely. The day before the election, he ordered the creation of an NSC "Working Group" to study "immediately and intensively" the American alternatives in Southeast Asia. The group, to be chaired by Assistant Secretary of State William P. Bundy, would be composed of eight middle-level officials from the State Department, the Pentagon, and the CIA—in addition to Bundy, they were Marshall Green, Robert H. Johnson, and Michael Forrestal, all from the State Department, John McNaughton and Vice Admiral Lloyd Mustin from the Pentagon, and Harold Ford and George Carver from the CIA. These men would report their conclusions to a group of NSC "principals" (Secretary of Defense Robert McNamara, Secretary of State Dean Rusk, National Security Adviser McGeorge Bundy, CIA Director John McCone, Undersecretary of State George Ball, and Joint Chiefs of Staff Chairman General Earle Wheeler), who would in turn make recommendations to the president. It resembled a bureaucratic layer cake, which suited the president fine—it allowed him to create something close to unanimity among his advisers.

Herein lay the crux of the matter. Lyndon Johnson not only wanted consensus on which way to proceed in Vietnam; he also wanted victory in the war, or at least something other than defeat. In the wake of his campaign triumph, he was no less adamant than before that he would not be the president who lost Vietnam. As William Bundy put it in a memorandum on 5 November, LBJ emerged from the election "clearly thinking in terms of maximum use of a Gulf of Tonkin rationale" to show American determination. Presidential advisers, whether in the top or middle level, understood this Johnsonian idée fixe perfectly well, and it must have hung like a heavy blanket over the planning that November. In addition, almost all of these advisers had developed a deep stake in the success of the war effort. For several years in many cases, they had trumpeted the need to stand firm and proclaimed the certainty of ultimate victory; to suggest a new course now would mean going against all their previous recommendations and analyses. Vested interest, in other words, produced bias.

These pressures explain what in hindsight is the most defining characteristic of the postelection deliberations: their highly circumscribed nature. Whatever freedom of action other observers may have thought Johnson possessed after the crushing victory over Goldwater, it quickly became clear that there remained little latitude for reopening the basic questions about American involvement in Vietnam—about whether the struggle needed to be won or whether it could be won. NSAM [National Security Action Memo] 288, issued in March 1964, which committed the United States to defending and preserving an independent, noncommunist South Vietnam, remained the bedrock upon which all proposals were to be built. . . .

Before the NSC Working Group held its first meeting, in fact even before the election, this future direction of American policy could be seen. On 1 November, a State Department cable approved by Secretary of Defense Robert McNamara and by the White House asked Ambassador Maxwell Taylor in Saigon to recommend actions that would give the "right signal level to the North and keep up morale in the South." The cable requested Taylor's opinion about the use of air strikes against Vietcong units in South Vietnam and about the deployment of American ground forces, suggesting that such forces could give "the desirable appearance of securing decks for action." The following day, on the eve of the election, a second cable, authored by the Working Group's chairman, William Bundy, and approved by the White House, informed Taylor that the administration intended to seek the "earliest possible preparation for a later decision" to begin expanded action, and to authorize "interim actions" that would demonstrate America's unbending determination in the war. The cable added that the administration would try to have the various alternatives for wider action ready as soon as possible. . . .

The Working Group thus began its work with the general assessment that an increase American participation in the war would be useful and necessary. The three basic options were outlined immediately and, with some modifications, were the ones presented to the principals in the final week of November. Option A would be to continue present policies, including, in John McNaughton's words, "maximum assistance within South Vietnam and limited external actions in Laos and by the GVN covertly against North Vietnam." Any American reprisal actions would be for the purpose of punishing large Vietcong actions in the South enough to deter future activity but not so much as to bring about strong international negotiating pressures. Basic to this option would be the "continued rejection of negotiating in the hope the situation will improve." Option B would be early, heavy military pressure against the North, called "fast/full squeeze" by McNaughton. The actions would continue at a rapid pace and without interruption until the United States achieved its present objectives (that is, an end to the insurgency). At some point, Option B activity would be meshed with negotiation, Bundy and McNaughton wrote, "but we would approach any discussions or negotiations with absolutely inflexible insistence on our present objectives."

Option C took the middle road between A and B. It called for a continuation of existing policies but with added military pressure. There would be communication with Hanoi, Beijing, or both, and graduated military moves against infiltration routes in Laos and North Vietnam and then against additional targets in the North. "The scenario should give the impression of a steady deliberate approach," McNaughton suggested. "It would be designed to give the U.S. the option at any point to proceed or not, to escalate or not, and to quicken the pace or not." Under Option C, the question of negotiations would be "played by ear," though the administration should probably indicate a willingness to talk under the right conditions. McNaughton and Bundy, the two dominant members of the Working Group, both preferred this option. Smart bureaucrats that they were, they plainly sought to control the outcome of the deliberations by utilizing what has been called the "Goldilocks principle," in which one choice is portrayed as too soft, one too hard, and one just right. The two men could reasonably expect the principals to join them in favoring the "just right" choice, Option C.

Though these three options framed the debate throughout the Working Group's deliberations, there are intriguing hints that early in the process at least fleeting consideration was given to a "fall-back" position, to what we might call an "Option D," under which the United States would seek to disengage from the war. The unspoken rationale behind this line of thinking was that defeat in Vietnam was certain, or almost certain, regardless of what the administration did. An early position paper, drafted by William Bundy . . . acknowledged that most of the world had written off South Vietnam and Laos in 1954; that South Vietnam was uniquely poor ground on which to make a stand, for reasons of geography, demography, and history; and that the present situation looked dismal. American policy had always been based on the notion that the South Vietnamese would care about defending themselves, the paper said, yet in the view of much of the world this will was precisely the lacking element in South Vietnam. . . .

It is not clear if any members of the Working Group actually thought this fall-back positions merited serious consideration, but the group's intelligence panel held views that, if nothing else, seemed to confirm its pessimistic conclusions. The panel members noted that "the basic elements of Communist strength in South Vietnam remain indigenous" and that "even if severely damaged," North Vietnam could continue to support the insurgency at a reduced level. Equally important, Hanoi would endure great pain in any "test of wills with the United States over the course of events in South Vietnam." . . .

Nevertheless, Bundy and McNaughton remained committed to pressing ahead, regardless of the odds. In this conviction they were joined by the Joint Chiefs of Staff's representative to the group, Vice Admiral Lloyd Mustin, who called for an end to the "dallying and delaying" in favor of expanded military action. Mustin's forceful advocacy no doubt helped remove any chance that serious consideration be given the "fall-back" position, but it meant less to the deliberations than the position articulated in the cables of his former boss, Saigon ambassador Maxwell Taylor. Still a voice of major influence in American policy making on Vietnam, Taylor by the last two months of 1964 had become fully convinced that an air campaign against the

North represented the magical missing ingredient in the war effort. . . . On 9 November, for example, the ambassador called such action the only way to revive a "despondent country grown tired of the strains of the counterinsurgency struggle." He theorized that bombing could inflict significant damage on "the sources of VC strength" in North Vietnam and along the infiltration routes in Laos and that this damage would boost southern morale. . . .

In reality, unstoppable momentum had developed in favor of bombing the North, and early negotiations leading to withdrawal had been ruled out. The fact that senior officials continued to refer to [Undersecretary of State George] Ball's activity as a "devil's advocate" exercise suggests how little intellectual weight they attached to it. . . . Likewise, Ball's mid-November suggestion that the administration develop a diplomatic strategy in the event of an imminent collapse by the Saigon regime got nowhere—the centerpiece of this strategy, an early great-power conference on the war convened by the British, at which the United States would play the best it could with lousy cards, was anathema to officials who still refused to contemplate seriously a retreat from core aims laid down in NSAM 288.

Nor was Ball alone in hoping to restrain the move to a larger war. Several mid-level officials shared his basis position, among them James C. Thomson Jr. of the NSC; Thomas L. Hughes, who headed the Bureau of Intelligence and Research at the State Department; Allen Whiting, deputy director of the East Asian desk at the State Department; Carl Salans of the Legal Adviser's Office at the State Department; and the Working Group's Robert Johnson. No less than Ball, these men were distressed by the continuing administration pursuit of a military solution and by the complete unwillingness to negotiate on any terms except those that amounted to Hanoi's unconditional surrender. The United States was in no position to bargain from strength, they believed, and yet the administration had adopted a totally unyielding position on the question of negotiations. . . .

Paul Kattenburg, whose suggestion of withdrawal back in the late summer of 1963 had been so swiftly quashed, later outlined the numerous disadvantages that such individuals worked from in terms of what he called the "bureaucratic-political warfare within the U.S. government." To begin with, Kattenburg argued, with the exception of Ball they were all middle- or lower-ranking officials, which meant that they lacked pulling power against the president's senior advisers. (Even Ball, Kattenburg might have noted, stood outside the inner circle occupied by only Rusk, McNamara, McGeorge Bundy, and perhaps Taylor.) In addition, these men did not make up a coherent group within the bureaucracy but rather worked individually and apart, and they did not actively try to alter this situation by seeking allies in other agencies like the Defense Department or the CIA. Finally, in Kattenburg's view, they were all "just sufficiently career oriented not to dare pit their personal futures" on the single aim of stopping the momentum toward bombing.

Kattenburg suggested that George Ball was the only one of the group not constrained by career considerations, but in fact the undersecretary was as anxious as anyone to preserve his position in the administration. Maintaining the posture to which he had adhered all year, Ball in November and December always took care not to rock the boat too much and to voice his strongest doubts outside Johnson's presence. This may explain why Ball, who attended the 19 November meeting at the White House, said nothing when McGeorge Bundy spoke of the growing consensus around Option C, and why he raised no objection to Bundy's use of the phrase "devil's advocate exercise" to describe what he was doing. . . .

By Thanksgiving, when Ambassador Taylor returned to Washington to take part in the shaping of the final report to be presented to Johnson on 1 December, a solid consensus had developed among the principals in favor of expanded action and against early negotiations. . . . The ambassador's visit was thus extraordinarily important . . . —he more than anyone could have challenged the consensus for escalation. He did not. He was, to be sure, a troubled man as he boarded the plane for Washington, and he carried with him a gloomy report he had written detailing the desperate military situation, the weakness of the GVN ("It is impossible to foresee a stable and effective government under any name in anything like the near future"), and the pronounced and mounting war-weariness and hopelessness that pervaded South Vietnam. At the same time, the report maintained that the United States should persist in its efforts in Vietnam and indeed should expand them, by working to "establish" a stronger Saigon government and by bombing the North. . . .

Johnson's top advisers were in agreement that, if necessary, the new measures should be undertaken regardless of the strength of the regime, but they conceded that a more viable political foundation in South Vietnam had to be in place before too long. They accordingly recommended a two-phase policy, consistent with the general approach outlined in Option C. The first phase involved "armed reconnaissance strikes" against infiltration routes in Laos as well as retaliatory strikes against the North in the event of a Vietcong "spectacular" such as the one at Bienhoa [site of a Vietcong rocket attack against a U.S. air base on November 1, 1964], and the second phase would see "graduated military pressure" against North Vietnam. Phase one would begin as soon as possible. Phase two would come later, after thirty days, provided the Saigon government had bettered its effectiveness "to an acceptable degree." However, unwilling to contemplate the implications if the regime should fail to meet this standard, the advisory team then proceeded to waive this requirement: "If the GVN can only be kept going by stronger action," the final recommendations read, then "the U.S. is prepared . . . to enter into a second phase program." Escalation, in other words, should be undertaken regardless of the political picture in Saigon, either to reward the GVN or to keep it from disintegrating.

Enter Lyndon Johnson. On 19 November, the president had indicated his general agreement with the Working Group's early thinking; now, almost two weeks later, he had the final recommendations in front of him. His decision was never in serious doubt, though he plainly did not relish making it. At a long White House meeting on 1 December, he worried about the absence of governmental stability in Saigon ("Basic to anything is stability," he said) and complained that he did not want to send "Johnson City boys" out to die for a bunch of politicians who could not get their act together. "Why not say, 'This is it?'" and withdraw, he wondered aloud. These comments could be taken as proof that LBJ in this period remained deeply uncertain about which way to proceed in the war, but his subsequent comments in the same meeting suggest that he still shared the same mixture of gloom and determination that he and his top aides had possessed throughout 1964. It would be "easy to get in or out," he lectured the men in the room, "but hard to be patient." The United States had to stick it out. The plans you've got now," he said, referring to the Working Group's recommendations, "[are] all right." Johnson insisted that Taylor "do [his] damnedest in South Vietnam" before the administration moved into the second phase, but he signaled his intention to go ahead regardless. If the Saigon situation failed to improve, he declared, looking at JCS chairman Wheeler, "then I'll be talking to you, General." . . .

It would be hard to overestimate the importance of this presidential decision. Johnson opted to fundamentally alter the American involvement in Vietnam. Like his ambassador in Saigon, he was unhappy about the prospect of moving against the North without a stronger South Vietnamese government, but like him, he was prepared to do so if necessary. The decision contained deep contradictions. Washington policymakers had for a long time conceded among themselves that the keys to victory in the war lay in the South, but now they were seeking a solution through striking the North, despite general skepticism in the intelligence community that such a policy would yield results. They had consistently preached the need for stable, effective government in Saigon prior to any action north of the seventeenth parallel, but now they were opting to try to bring about that stability by bombing the North. They had always declared that Americans should not be sent to fight in the war, and yet such a deployment looked more and more likely—the position paper that emerged out of the 1 December meeting included the cryptic but suggestive line that the escalatory program would include "appropriate U.S. deployments to handle any contingency."

And as always, there was the stark contradiction between the administration's publicly stated willingness to pursue a peaceful solution to the war and its profound private fear of such an outcome. American officials had always proclaimed their commitment to the notion of South Vietnamese self-determination, but the deliberations in November revealed just how empty that claim had become—"The U.S. would oppose any independent South Vietnamese moves to negotiate," said the report that Johnson approved. The establishment of a National Assembly in South Vietnam should be delayed as long as possible, because it might be dominated by pro-peace elements. It is clear that neither LBJ nor his top aides were prepared to accept the idea that to win the people, you had to let them express themselves, which meant risking a government that might negotiate an end to the war. Plainly put, the self-determination Washington claimed to be defending was what it feared most. . . .

Seen in this light, the Americanization of the war becomes difficult to understand. The isolation of the United States on the war among its international allies at the end of 1964; the thin nature of domestic American popular support for the Vietnam commitment; the downright opposition to a larger war among many elite American voices; the spreading war-weariness and anti-Americanism in urban and rural areas of South Vietnam; and the political chaos in Saigon—add all these elements together, along with the fact that senior officials in Washington knew of them and worried about them, and you have a policy decision that is far less easily explained than many would suggest (and this author used to believe). This does not mean it is impossible to explain. . . .

For the key consideration behind the decision for war we must look to [a] . . . rationale articulated by policymakers: *credibility* and the need to preserve it by avoiding defeat in Vietnam. This was the explanation typically advanced by officials when they addressed knowledgeable audiences in off-the-record meetings—one finds scant references to "moral obligations" or "defending world freedom" in the records of their interaction with congressional committees, with foreign government leaders, with journalists in private sessions. In these settings, the emphasis was almost always on abstract (and closely related) notions of prestige, reputation, and credibility and how these were on the line in Vietnam. Even here, however, the picture that emerges is incomplete, inasmuch as the "credibility" referred to was always a purely national concept, having to do with the position of the United States on the world stage. That is, it was *American* credibility that was at stake in Southeast Asia, *American* prestige that needed to be upheld there. Though it can be right and proper to define the credibility imperative in exclusively national terms; it will not suffice as an explanation for policy making in Vietnam. For Vietnam a broader definition is essential, one that also includes domestic political credibility and even personal credibility. For it was not merely the United States that had a stake in the outcome in Vietnam; so did the Democratic Party (or at least so Kennedy and Johnson believed), and so did the individuals who had helped shape the earlier commitment and who were now charged with deciding the next move.

We may go further and argue that, within this three-part conception of the credibility imperative, the national part was the least important. Geostrategic considerations were not the driving force in American Vietnam policy in . . . 1964, either before the election or after; partisan political considerations were; individual careerist considerations were. True, some officials did see Vietnam as a vital theater in the larger Cold War struggle against world communism, did see American credibility as very much on the line—Dean Rusk was one, Walt Rostow another. Most, however, ever, were more dubious. William Bundy and John McNaughton, two of the key players in the policy deliberations in late 1964, not only shared much of George Ball's pessimism about the long-term prospects in the war but on several occasions endorsed his relatively benign view of the likely consequences of defeat in South Vietnam. . . . So why did they favor Americanization? Less out of concern for America's credibility, I believe, than out of fears for their own personal credibility. For more than three years, McNamara and Bundy had counseled the need to stand firm in the war (a relatively easy thing to do in, say, 1962, when the commitment was small and the Cold War situation considerably more tense), and to go against that now would be to expose themselves to potential humiliation and to threaten their careers. . . .

Johnson was always first among equals, as the internal record makes clear. If his top Vietnam aides intimidated him with their accomplishments and academic pedigrees, he also intimidated them with his forceful presence and his frequent resort to bullying tactics, and he established firm control of his administration from the start. Furthermore, no president is a prisoner to his advisers—Eisenhower and Kennedy had rejected policy recommendations on Vietnam, and Johnson might have done the same had he so desired. (He showed a capacity to do so on non-Vietnam issues.) He did not. What, then, drove Johnson's approach to the Vietnam issue? Chiefly its potential to do harm to his domestic political objectives and to his personal historical reputation. Both concerns were there from the start—he determined already in late 1963 that Vietnam would be kept on the back burner in 1964, so as to avoid giving Republicans an issue with which to beat up on Democrats in an election year, and he vowed only hours after the Dallas assassination that he would not be the president who lost Vietnam.

Understanding this duality in Johnson's thinking about the war, in which partisan calculations competed for supremacy with concerns for his personal reputation, is essential to understanding the outcome of the policy process in Washington in the fifteen months that followed his taking office as president. The former explains his determination to keep Vietnam from being lost in an election year, a year in which he also sought to pass major pieces of the Democratic Party's legislative agenda. But it cannot by itself explain his willingness to proceed with a major military intervention—whose importance and viability he himself doubted—after the glorious election results, which brought not only a smashing victory over Barry Goldwater but also huge Democratic majorities in both houses of Congress. . . .

For this reason it would be wrong to overemphasize the importance of the Great Society in the decision to escalate the conflict—that is, to give too much weight to the idea that LBJ took the nation to war because of fears that if he did not, Republicans and conservative Democrats would oppose and possibly scuttle his beloved domestic agenda. Concerns along these lines certainly existed within Johnson, and they directly influenced the *way* in which he expanded the war—in particular, they dictated that the escalation be as quiet as possible so as to avoid the need for choosing between the war and the programs, between guns and butter. But strategizing of this sort cannot be considered the primary *cause* of the decision for escalation. . . .

Lyndon Johnson was a hawk on Vietnam, and he was so for reasons that went beyond immediate domestic political or geostrategic advantage. For it was not merely his country's and his party's reputation that Johnson took to be on the line, but also his own. His tendency to personalize all issues relating to the war, so evident in the later years, in 1966 and 1967 and 1968, was there from the start, from the time he vowed to not be the first American president to lose a war. From the beginning, he viewed attacks on the policy as attacks on himself, saw American credibility and his own credibility as essentially synonymous. In so doing he diminished his capacity to render objective judgment, to retain the necessary level of detachment. . . .

Had Johnson been concerned only with, or even primarily with, preserving *American* credibility and/or *Democratic* credibility, he surely would have ordered extensive contingency planning for some kind of fig leaf for withdrawal in the months leading up to escalation, when the outlook looked grimmer than ever. He would have actively sought, rather than actively avoided, the advice of allied leaders like [British prime minister] Harold Wilson and [Canadian prime minister] Lester Pearson and given much deeper reflection to the urgings of anti-Americanization voices on Capitol Hill and in the press community. His dislike of the war was hardly less intense than theirs, after all, his evaluation of the Saigon government's potential not significantly more rosy. But the end result of the scenario these critics espoused—American withdrawal without victory—was one Johnson could not contemplate, largely because of the damage such an outcome could do to his own personal reputation.

The concern here went deeper than merely saving his political skin. In private LBJ would sometimes say that he could not withdraw from Vietnam because it would lead to his impeachment, but he was too smart a politician to really believe such a thing. What he really feared was the personal humiliation that he believed would come with failure in Vietnam. He saw the war as a test of his own manliness. Many have commented on the powerful element of *machismo* in Johnson's world view, rooted in his upbringing and fueled by his hunting fear that he would be judged insufficiently manly for the job, that he would lack courage when the chips were down. In his world there were weak and strong men; the weak men were the skeptics, who sat around contemplating, talking, criticizing; the strong men were the doers, the activists, the ones who were always tough and always refused to back down. Thus [Senator Mike] Mansfield could be dismissed as spineless, as "milque-toast"; thus [Senator J. William] Fulbright could be castigated as a "crybaby." Though Johnson on occasion showed himself quite capable of asking probing questions in policy meetings, he had little patience with those who tried to supply probing answers. His macho ethos extended to relations among states. "If you let a bully come into your front yard one day," he liked to say, in reference to the lesson of Munich, "the next day he will be up on your porch and the day after that he will rape your wife in your own bed." In such a situation, retreat was impossible, retreat was cowardly. Johnson's approach did not make him reckless on Vietnam—he was, in fact, exceedingly cautious—but it made him quite unable to contemplate extrication as anything but the equivalent of, as he might put it, "tucking tail and running."

This personal insecurity in Johnson, so much a feature of the recollections of those who knew him and worked with him, might have been less important in Vietnam policy if not for the way it reinforced his equally well documented intolerance of dissent. Even in the early months of his presidency he was incredulous to learn that some Americans might be opposed to his policy of fully supporting South Vietnam; it was un-American, he believed, to make an issue during the Cold War of national security matters. Throughout his career Johnson had made his way in politics by intimidation, by dominating those around him, and he did not change this modus operandi once he got the White House. "I'm the only president you have," he told those who opposed his policies. His demand for consensus and loyalty extended to his inner circle of advisers, a reality that, when combined with his powerful personality, must have had a chilling effect on anyone inclined to try to build support for a contrary view. . . .

In this way, while responsibility for the outcome of the policy process rested with all of those who participated in it, it rested chiefly with the president. Johnson, no one else, ensured that the critical decisions on Vietnam were made by a small and insular group of individuals who by the latter part of 1964 had been involved in policy making for several years in most cases, who had overseen the steady expansion in the U.S. commitment to the war, and who had a large personal stake in seeing that commitment succeed. . . . Johnson was poorly served by his advisory system, but it was a system he in large measure created.

An Unwinnable War

ROBERT K. BRIGHAM

Three alternative military strategies have been put forward since the end of the Vietnam War as missed opportunities for a U.S. military victory. They are: (1) invasion of North Vietnam; (2) incursion into Laos; and (3) concentration of U.S. forces on defense of "enclaves."

When each is reexamined carefully, in light of recently released information from new Chinese and Vietnamese sources, we find that none of them would likely have produced a better outcome for the United States.

An invasion of North Vietnam was enthusiastically advanced by some in the U.S. Army. They believed that the United States should have attacked the North directly, north of the demilitarized zone (DMZ) at the 17th parallel. Military leaders who supported this strategy, however, overlooked the threat of China and, on occasion, even appeared eager for a direct confrontation. Secretary of Defense Robert S. McNamara was convinced, in contrast, that an invasion of the North carried an unacceptable risk of bringing the Chinese into the war. He reasoned that Beijing would act in its own self-interest and would never surrender its buffer area to the West. Gen. Bruce Palmer Jr., Gen. William Westmoreland's deputy in Vietnam, agrees. He argues in his book *The Twenty-Five Year War* that "one cannot quarrel with the decision not to invade North Vietnam because it was too close to China." In addition, as Palmer recognized, a war with China would have had little to do with American objectives in Vietnam and could even have led to millions of unnecessary deaths.

New documentary evidence from Hanoi and Beijing supports the worst U.S. predictions. We now know that North Vietnam asked for and received security commitments from Beijing from 1960 onward. In 1962 a Vietnamese delegation headed by Ho Chi Minh and Gen. Nguyen Chi Thanh visited China, requesting aid for the southern struggles. The Chinese communists pledged an additional 230 battalions to the Vietnamese if needed. The following year, Beijing's military chief of staff, Luo Ruiqing, visited Hanoi. He told Ho that if the Americans were to attack the North, China would come to its defense. In June 1964 the North Vietnamese Army's chief of staff, Van Tien Dung, received Beijing's pledge of "unconditional military support." During the Tonkin Gulf crisis of August 1964, Chinese communists placed their naval units stationed in the area on combat readiness and ordered them to "pay close attention to the movement of American forces" and be prepared to "cope with any possible sudden attack." The Chinese air command went on alert, and the Seventh Army's air force was moved to the Vietnamese border, where it remained for several years. Four other air divisions were also moved closer to the border, and Beijing built two new airstrips in anticipation of an American invasion. American intelligence reports also detected the Chinese movement of nearly forty MiG fighters to the North Vietnamese airfield at Phuc Yen.

In 1965, when the sustained bombing of the North began under Operation "ROLLING THUNDER," the Chinese agreed to step up their commitment to Vietnam as a rear area and deterrent. Beijing pledged repeatedly that it would avoid a direct military conflict with the United States as long as possible, but it would not back away from a confrontation. On March 25, 1965, an editorial in the Party's official newspaper announced that China had offered Hanoi "any necessary material support, including the supply of weapons and all kinds of military materials." It stated further that, if necessary, China was prepared to "send its personnel to fight together with the Vietnamese people to annihilate the American aggressors." Shortly after these statements, China sent the first wave of its combat engineers to Vietnam to aid in the construction of antiaircraft batteries, railroads, airports, bridges, and roads. By 1968, the number of Chinese serving within North Vietnam's borders reached 200,000. . . .

Some analysts have suggested that China may have backed away from its military commitments to Vietnam during the Cultural Revolution. New material from communist archives suggests, however, that China never would have allowed an American invasion of North Vietnam to go unanswered. In fact, as Beijing looked inward during the mid-1960s, its line concerning the United States in Vietnam actually hardened. Until the end of 1964, China's official policy concerning U.S. planes fly-ing into its airspace was to avoid a direct confrontation. By mid-1965, however, this policy had been reversed. Accordingly, there were nearly two hundred confrontations between China and the United States, resulting in the destruction of twelve American fighters. Even after relations between Vietnam and China had soured, the evidence indicates that Beijing's own self-interest would have led it to defend its "buffer zone" in Indochina. . . .

China was motivated to aid Vietnam by its own foreign policy needs. Beijing hoped to use its support of the war in Vietnam to stimulate mass mobilization within China for the Cultural Revolution. Chinese leaders claimed that Beijing was the cen-ter for continuous revolutions and that the United States threatened that central role. China repeatedly claimed that it would support Vietnam by any means necessary, "even at the expense of heavy national sacrifice." Accordingly, when a Vietnamese delegation visited Beijing in April 1965, China pledged to aid Hanoi economically and militarily. Aid came in the form of armored vehicles, small arms and ammuni-tion, uniforms, shoes, rice, and even recreation equipment for North Vietnamese soldiers. Chinese communist sources claim that more than $200 million in material aid was sent to Hanoi annually beginning in 1965.

At the time, other considerations were also thought to preclude taking the war to the North. During the early years of the war, the Sullivan Group, a presidential advisory group, had concluded that attacking the North would do little to reduce its support for the war in the South. For example, the group predicted:

> It is not likely that North Vietnam would (if it could) call off the war in the South even though U.S. actions would in time have serious economic and political impact. Overt ac-tion against North Vietnam would be unlikely to produce reduction in Viet Cong activity sufficiently to make victory on the ground possible in South Vietnam unless accompanied by new U.S. bolstering actions in South Vietnam and considerable improvement in the government there.

Indeed, the war had always been fundamentally about the political future of Vietnam south of the 17th parallel, and a direct attack by U.S. ground forces against North Vietnam would have had little or no positive effect on meeting this objective. The United States came to understand too late that the insurgency in the South was primarily indigenous. During the early days of the insurgency, we now know, it was the southern cadres who pressed Hanoi to allow them to move toward the armed struggle. Attacking the North to stop the insurgency was strategically meaningless, given the U.S. objective of preserving the *South* Vietnamese government in Saigon. By 1968 it was understood in Washington that the NLF would have continued to carry the fight to the South Vietnamese Army, and it would have remained in control in the countryside no matter what happened in North Vietnam.

Many southern cadres felt betrayed because of the 1954 partition of Vietnam, which left them vulnerable to the brutal efforts of the anticommunist Ngo Dinh Diem to exterminate them. Thereafter, the southerners tended to stress the need for a deci-sive battlefield victory prior to engaging in peace talks. Communist documents show overwhelmingly that southerners were more offensive-minded than many of their colleagues in Hanoi—in fact that they were prepared to carry on the struggle against the United States and its Saigon ally no matter what decisions were made by Hanoi.

Writing after the war in a special issue of a military history journal, Le Duc Tho, a longtime member of the Party's political bureau, noted that southerners often engaged in offensive struggles "in spite of orders to the contrary by northern cadres." This is especially true after Gen. Nguyen Chi Thanh became director of the Central Office South Vietnam—the mobile command post in the South—in 1965. Nguyen Chi Thanh was a southerner who had long advocated a more military pursuit of the war effort. During the early 1960s, he argued that victory over the South Vietnamese and their American backers would come only on the battlefield. "If we feared the United States," Nguyen Chi Thanh declared, "we would have called on the people of southern Vietnam to wait and coexist peacefully with the U.S.-Diem clique. We are not afraid of the United States. . . ."

An attack against the North, therefore, was a losing strategy on several counts. It virtually guaranteed a war with China. If China intervened, one could only surmise what the Soviets would do, in an attempt to retain their leadership of the world communist movement. Neither did such a strategy take account of the irrelevance of an invasion of the North regarding saving the South Vietnamese government from collapse. And finally, neither did such a strategy acknowledge the probable consequences—north and south—for U.S. forces. The probable casualties would have dwarfed the actual U.S. casualties from the war, leading in all likelihood to severely hostile reactions in the U.S. Congress and American body politic.

Former U.S. Army Col. Harry Summers has long been one of the most outspoken advocates of the invasion of Laos. Summers argues that a combined military action into Laos could have blocked the Laotian panhandle from being used as a base by North Vietnamese forces. After blocking the flow of men and supplies South, Summers contends, the South Vietnamese forces could have isolated the battlefield from communist incursions originating in Laos and destroyed the NLF.

The U.S. Army actually considered this proposal during the war but ultimately rejected it as unacceptable. When Army Chief of Staff Harold K. Johnson explored the option, he concluded that it would require support services beyond U.S. capabilities. For example, he found that such an operation demanded the astounding total of 18,000 engineer troops to make the operation feasible. Alas, the United States did not have available 18,000 engineer troops for assignment to Vietnam and Laos. Furthermore, U.S. intelligence reports reliably reported that, until mid-1969, the majority of communist forces in the South were actually southerners, who had not need of a sanctuary in Laos in which they might prepare to "invade" South Vietnam. They were already there.

The Trong Son, or Ho Chi Minh Trail, ran through the Laotian panhandle. Advocates of the Laotian invasion strategy believe that by invading Laos the United States could have effectively cut off the trail, stopped supplies heading from North Vietnam to South Vietnam, and thus won the war. But it is clear now, years later, that the southern insurgency could have survived without the Ho Chi Minh Trail. All the conditions that created the insurgency would still have been present.The NLF was never dependent on the North for its sustenance, in any case.

Finally, the force that Summers proposed would probably have met with the same fate as those U.S. forces who operated along the DMZ, nearest to North Vietnam's territory. These troops experienced unusually high casualty rates—mainly from mortars and heavy artillery. The same sort of phenomenon had already occurred in Laos, where U.S. combat losses were higher in a relative sense than those within the territory of Vietnam. Thus, the "barrier across Laos" strategy ignores the reality of jungle war and the extraordinary disadvantages the U.S. would have had in such a war with the NLF and North Vietnamese. . . .

Leading military strategists in Hanoi agree that cutting off the Ho Chi Minh Trail via an invasion of Laos would have accomplished nothing for the United States. Gen. Doan Chuong, director of Hanoi's Institute for Strategic Studies, recently addressed the issue as follows:

> If the supply route had been truly cut off during the war, this would have been a very serious development. That is why the strategic Truong Son Road [Ho Chi Minh Trail] was constructed and involved such elaborate precautions, as you know. We not only had trials on land, we also had a "sea trail." In addition to the East Truong Son Road, there was a West Truong Son Road, with numerous criss-cross pathways, like a labyrinth. So it would have been hard to cut it off completely. As you know the U.S. applied various measures to block it: bombing, defoliating, sending in commandos, setting up a fence called "McNamara's Line," concentrating air strikes on the panhandle area, and so on. Still, the route remained open. . . . We could not, and in fact did not, allow the Trail to be cut off. . . .

William C. Westmoreland, the U.S. field commander from 1964–1968, opposed the Laotian invasion strategy. In his memoirs, General Westmoreland recalls with amazement that many of his critics—within the military and without—"considered it practicable to seal land frontiers against North Vietnamese infiltration. . . . Yet small though South Vietnam is," he pointed out, "its land frontier extended for more than 900 miles." To have defended that entire frontier, according to General Westmoreland, would have required "many millions of troops."

A cardinal error of advocates of the Laos incursion, it would appear, is their use of the U.S. experience in Korea as a model for what they believe should have been done in Vietnam. But the Korean Peninsula presented problems for the infiltration of men and supplies far different from what was faced in Vietnam. Surrounded by water on three sides, the actual Korean *frontier* was quite limited. Not only is the Vietnamese frontier, in this sense, almost 1,000 miles long, or roughly the distance from Boston to Chicago; in addition, the Truong Son Mountains of Indochina, along which supplies moved north to south, are home to the largest triple-canopy jungle in the world outside of the Amazon Basin. Detection and interdiction of the movement of supplies is nearly impossible in such conditions, which can create almost total darkness at noon on a sunny day.

A third alternative U.S. strategy in Vietnam—gathering U.S. forces into enclaves located in or near strategic assets—is in some ways more sophisticated than the invasion strategies directed at North Vietnam and Laos. Those advocating this strategy showed that they understood the nature of the war on the ground in South Vietnam: a fundamentally indigenous insurgency that could be successfully combated, if at all, by the application of counterinsurgency techniques in the South.

At the heart of this notion is the idea that U.S. troops would occupy a supporting role by controlling the densely populated coastal areas. The South Vietnamese forces would thereby be free to move inland from coastal bases, where they would confront the NLF. Proponents of the enclave strategy argued that U.S. troops could join the fight as long as the coastal bases remained protected and secure.

This strategy was based on some realistic assumptions about the war: (1) Basically, the war in the countryside had to be won by the South Vietnamese; and (2) the communists would never be strong enough to drive the U.S. Army into the sea. At worst, its adherents claimed (as some still claim), the enclave strategy would have bought time for South Vietnam to become stabilized, at minimum cost in American lives and material. An added feature, it is claimed, is that the insurgency itself would actually weaken once U.S. troops secured the heavily populated coast.

The enclave strategy, however, like the other alternatives, has not been without its strident critics. They assert that herding U.S. forces into enclaves would have disallowed the Americans from taking maximum advantage of their most potent weapon—superior firepower. Considerable doubt has also been expressed as to the ability of the South Vietnamese Army to carry the battle inland to the NLF. Time and again, the South Vietnamese proved they were no match for the NLF's committed guerrillas.

General Westmoreland was absolutely opposed to the enclave strategy. He believed bringing American combat troops into the major coastal cities of the South, including Saigon, would constitute a huge mistake. He saw the potential for them to get embroiled in the daily street demonstrations and other political conflicts that plagued the South. When Gen. Earle Wheeler, the chairman of the Joint Chiefs of Staff, recommended the enclave strategy to Westmoreland as one that would free the South Vietnamese for offensive operations in the countryside, the field commander pointed out that approximately 40 percent of the South Vietnamese forces were always available for, or committed to, combat operations in any case. . . .

In fact, a variant of the enclave strategy had been tried before, by the French, and it had failed miserably. Col. Quach Hai Luong, deputy director of Hanoi's Institute for Strategic Studies, recently argued that the Americans would have met a similar fate if they had withdrawn to enclaves: "That would conjure up a situation that was similar to what happened during the French war. The French had also concentrated their forces in the big cities. If you do that, then you would be able to control various outlets [i.e., ports] and economic and political headquarters. If you want to occupy a country for a long time, as the French did, then that's what you would do." As Quach Hai Luong went on to point out, however, the Americans had no wish to occupy Vietnam in the traditional sense, as the French did. To him, this meant that the strategy of enclaves would make even less sense for the Americans than it did for the French. At least the French goal—long-term occupation of Vietnam—was consistent with the strategy, even though it failed. But for the Americans, he could see no benefits to it whatsoever.

Many who have compared the American and French military experiences in Vietnam agree. Bernard Fall, a French journalist and scholar with vast experience in Indochina, wrote in 1961 that the enclave strategy invited disaster because it concentrated conventional forces in an area where it could not dispense its weapons, for fear of alienating the local population. Revolutionaries, according to Fall, could isolate enemy forces for attack and simply use the village or rural area as a sanctuary. This was certainly the French experience along the central Vietnamese coast on Highway 1—*La Rue Sans Joie,* or "The Street Without Joy."

After the war, Harry Summers recalled an encounter with a North Vietnamese general in which Summers said that the Americans won every battle in Vietnam. The general replied, "That may be so, but it is also irrelevant." *Why* it was irrelevant is something that has been insufficiently grasped by advocates of one or more of the alternative strategies just reexamined. In short, the U.S. forces arrived in Vietnam prepared to turn back an invasion of South Vietnam by North Vietnam. If that had been the nature of the problem, the United States might have been successful. But what they encountered, and what some analysts still find it impossible to accept, is a war in the South that was fundamentally a war among southerners. Each side had a more powerful patron—the NLF was allied to Hanoi and the South Vietnamese government to the United States. And in this kind of war, the United States, along with its uninspired and hapless South Vietnamese allies, did not "know the territory."

Any strategy, including those just reexamined, would have required for its success a viable South Vietnamese government with credibility in the eyes of the South Vietnamese people. No government in Saigon after November 1963, when Diem was assassinated, was credible in this sense. From 1965, therefore, when U.S. combat troops first arrived, the situation in Saigon was politically untenable. In the end, no American strategy could have reversed the outcome in Vietnam, because the NLF and its North Vietnamese allies had committed to total war. Each was prepared to sustain casualties, far beyond American estimates, without giving up the fight. Any war would have been a war of attrition on the ground. And it is obvious, looking back, which side was willing, as John Kennedy said during his inaugural address, to "pay any price, bear any burden."

FURTHER READING

David L. Anderson, ed., *The Human Tradition in the Vietnam Era* (2000)

———, *Shadow on the White House* (1993)

———, *Trapped by Success: The Eisenhower Administration and Vietnam, 1953–1961*
   (1991)

Christian Appy, *Working-Class War* (1993)

Loren Baritz, *Backfire* (1985)

Richard J. Barnet, *Intervention and Revolution* (1972)

David M. Barrett, *Uncertain Warriors* (1993)

Eric M. Bergerud, *The Dynamics of Defeat* (1991)

———, *Red Thunder, Tropic Lightning* (1993)

Larry Berman, *Lyndon Johnson's War* (1989)

William C. Berman, *William Fulbright and the Vietnam War* (1988)

Irving Bernstein, *Guns or Butter: The Presidency of Lyndon Johnson* (1996)

Michael R. Beschloss, *Taking Charge* (1997) (on the LBJ White House)

Melanie Billings-Yun, *Decision Against War: Eisenhower and Dien Bien Phu, 1954* (1988)

Anne Blair, *Lodge in Vietnam* (1995)

Mark Philip Bradley, *Imagining Vietnam* (2000)

Peter Braestrup, *Big Story* (1977)

———, ed., *Vietnam as History* (1984)

Robert Brigham, *The NLF's Foreign Relations and the Vietnam War* (1999)

Peter Busch, *All the Way with JFK?* (2003)

Robert Buzzanco, *Masters of War* (1996)

Larry Cable, *Unholy Grail* (1991)

Timothy Castle, *At War in the Shadow of Vietnam* (1993) (on Laos)

Noam Chomsky, *Rethinking Camelot* (1993) (on JFK and Vietnam)

James W. Clinton, *The Loyal Opposition* (1995)

Warren I. Cohen, *Dean Rusk* (1980)

Warren I. Cohen and Nancy Bernkopf Tucker, eds., *Lyndon Johnson Confronts the World*
   (1995)

Chester Cooper, *The Lost Crusade* (1970)

Robert Dallek, *Flawed Giant* (1998) (on LBJ)

Charles DeBenedetti with Charles Chatfield, *An American Ordeal: The Antiwar Movement of the Vietnam Era* (1990)

William J. Duiker, *Ho Chi Minh* (2000)

——, *Sacred War* (1995)

Bernard Fall, *The Two Vietnams* (1967)

Frances FitzGerald, *Fire in the Lake* (1972)

Marc Frey et al., *The Transformation of Southeast Asia* (2003) (on decolonization)

Ilya V. Gaiduk, *The Soviet Union and the Vietnam War* (1996)

Lloyd C. Gardner, *Approaching Vietnam* (1988)

——, *Pay Any Price* (1995) (on LBJ)

Leslie H. Gelb and Richard K. Betts, *The Irony of Vietnam* (1979)

William C. Gibbons, *The U.S. Government and the Vietnam War* (1986–1987)

James William Gibson, *The Perfect War* (1986)

Marc Jason Gilbert, ed., *Why the North Won the Vietnam War* (2002)

Daniel P. O'C. Greene, "John Foster Dulles and the End of Franco-American Entente in Indochina," *Diplomatic History,* 16 (1992), 551–572

Fred I. Greenstein and Richard H. Immerman, "What Did Eisenhower Tell Kennedy About Indochina? The Politics of Misperception," *Journal of American History,* 79 (1992), 568–587

David Halberstam, *The Best and the Brightest* (1972)

Daniel C. Hallin, *The "Uncensored War"* (1986)

Ellen J. Hammer, *A Death in November: America in Vietnam, 1963* (1988)

David Harris, *Our War* (1996)

James P. Harrison, ed., *The Endless War* (1989)

Patrick L. Hatcher, *The Suicide of an Elite* (1990)

Kenneth Heineman, *Campus Wars* (1993)

John Hellman, *American Myth and the Legacy of Vietnam* (1986)

Herbert Hendin and Ann P. Haas, *Wounds of War: The Psychological Aftermath of Combat in Vietnam* (1985)

George C. Herring, *America's Longest War* (1996)

——, *LBJ and Vietnam* (1994)

Gary R. Hess, *Vietnam and the United States* (1990)

Michael H. Hunt, *Lyndon Johnson's War* (1996)

Richard H. Immerman, "The United States and the Geneva Conference of 1954: A New Look," *Diplomatic History,* 14 (1990), 43–66

—— and George Herring, "Eisenhower, Dulles, and Dienbienphu: The Day We Didn't Go to War," *Journal of American History,* 71 (1984), 343–363

"International Dimensions of the Vietnam War," *Diplomatic History,* 27 (2003), 35–149

Maurice Isserman, *Witness to War* (1995)

Susan Jeffords, *The Remasculinization of America: Gender and the Vietnam War* (1989)

Howard Jones, *Death of a Generation* (2002) (on the JFK and Diem assassinations)

Matthew Jones, *Conflict and Confrontation in Southeast Asia* (2001)

George McT. Kahin, *Intervention* (1986)

David Kaiser, *American Tragedy* (2000)

Lawrence S. Kaplan, Denise Artaud, and Mark R. Rubin, eds., *Dienbienphu and the Crisis in Franco-American Relations, 1954–1955* (1990)

Stanley Karnow, *Vietnam* (1983)

Douglas Kinnard, *The Certain Trumpet: Maxwell Taylor and the American Experience in Vietnam* (1991)

Katherine Kinney, *Friendly Fire* (2000)

Gabriel Kolko, *Anatomy of a War* (1985)

Andrew F. Krepinevich, Jr., *The Army and Vietnam* (1986)

Diane B. Kunz, ed., *The Diplomacy of the Crucial Decade* (1994)

Alan J. Levine, *The U.S. and the Struggle for Southeast Asia* (1995)

David W. Levy, *The Debate over Vietnam* (1991)

Guenter Lewy, *America in Vietnam* (1978)

Michael Lind, *Vietnam: The Necessary War* (2000)

Robert Mann, *A Grand Delusion* (2001)

David Maraniss, *They Marched into Sunlight* (2003)

Robert J. McMahon, "Contested Memory: The Vietnam War and American Society, 1975–2001," *Diplomatic History,* 26 (2002), 159–184

———, "U.S.-Vietnamese Relations: A Historiographical Survey," in Warren I. Cohen, ed., *Pacific Passages* (1996)

H. R. McMaster, *Dereliction of Duty* (1997)

Edwin F. Moise, *Tonkin Gulf and the Escalation of the Vietnam War* (1996)

James W. Mooney and Thomas R. West, *Vietnam* (1994)

Richard R. Moser, *The New Winter Soldiers* (1996)

Charles E. Neu, *After Vietnam* (2000)

Don Oberdofer, *Tet* (2001)

Gregory A. Olson, *Mansfield and Vietnam* (1995)

James S. Olson and Randy Roberts, *Where the Domino Fell* (1996)

Robert E. Osgood, *Limited War Revisited* (1979)

Bruce Palmer, Jr., *The 25-Year War* (1984)

Douglas Pike, *History of Vietnamese Communism* (1978)

———, *PAVN: People's Army of Vietnam* (1986)

———, *Vietnam and the Soviet Union* (1987)

Norman Podhoretz, *Why We Were in Vietnam* (1982)

John Prados, *The Blood Road: The Ho Chi Minh Trail and the Vietnam War* (1998)

———, *Operation Vulture* (2002) (on Eisenhower)

William Prochnau, *Once Upon a Distant Star* (1995)

Jeffrey Record, *The Wrong War* (1998)

Andrew J. Rotter, *The Path to Vietnam* (1987)

William J. Rust, *Kennedy in Vietnam* (1985)

Howard B. Schaffer, *Ellsworth Bunker* (2003)

Thomas J. Schoenbaum, *Waging Peace and War* (1988) (on Rusk)

Robert D. Schulzinger, *A Time for War* (1997)

Orrin Schwab, *Defending the Free World* (1998)

Robert Shaplen, *Time Out of Hand* (1970)

———, *A Turning Wheel* (1979)

William Shawcross, *Sideshow: Kissinger, Nixon, and the Destruction of Cambodia* (1979)

Neil Sheehan, *A Bright Shining Lie* (1988)

Anthony Short, *The Origins of the Vietnam War* (1989)

Melvin Small, *Antiwarriors: The Vietnam War and the Battle for America's Hearts and Minds* (2002)

——— and William D. Hoover, eds., *Give Peace a Chance* (1992)

Ronald H. Spector, *After Tet* (1992)

———, *The United States Army in Vietnam* (1983)

Shelby L. Stanton, *The Rise and Fall of an American Army* (1985)

Harry G. Summers, *On Strategy* (1981)

Sandra Taylor, *Vietnamese Women at War* (1999)

James C. Thomson, *Rolling Thunder* (1980)

Robert R. Tomes, *Apocalypse Then: American Intellectuals and the Vietnam War* (1998)

William S. Turley, *The Second Indochina War* (1986)

Kathleen J. Turner, *Lyndon Johnson's Dual War* (1985) (on the press)

Brian VanDeMark, *Into the Quagmire* (1991)

Francis X. Winters, *The Year of the Hare* (1997)

Randall Woods, *Fulbright* (1995)

———, ed., *Vietnam and the American Political Tradition* (2003)

Marilyn B. Young, *The Vietnam Wars* (1991)

Nancy Zaroulis and Gerald Sullivan, *Who Spoke Up?* (1984)

Qiang Zhai, *China and the Vietnam Wars* (2000)

Richard M. Nixon,
Henry A. Kissinger,
the Grand Strategy, and Détente

By the late 1960s the United States no longer dominated global affairs as it had during the two decades immediately following World War II. Defeat in Vietnam, the Soviet Union's achievement of parity in nuclear weapons, and the rise of a multipolar world order—characterized by America's relative decline and a diffusion of global economic and political power—spurred the Nixon administration to reconfigure the nation's foreign policy. President Richard M. Nixon and Henry A. Kissinger designed a grand strategy for achieving stability in the international environment. As self-described realists, they sought to make U.S. diplomacy less ideological and more adaptive to balance-of-power diplomacy. As an influential assistant for national security affairs (1969–1973) and secretary of state (1973–1977), Kissinger worked closely with Nixon to pursue détente with both the People's Republic of China and the Soviet Union. Their management of the Strategic Arms Limitation Talks (SALT) produced major agreements. Secret negotiations helped to extricate the United States from Vietnam. And Kissinger's "shuttle diplomacy" temporarily cooled the Arab-Israeli crisis in the Middle East. Admirers and critics alike applauded the Nixon administration's apparent diplomatic achievements in the 1970s.

But the Nixon-Kissinger team compiled a mixed record, as scholars have shown. Interventions and crises in Indochina, Chile, Cyprus, Bangladesh, Angola, and elsewhere sidetracked détente and undermined global stability. The White House's soft selling of human rights and emphasis on power politics raised doubts about the administration's morality and judgment. The Nixon Doctrine, which tried to reduce U.S. obligations abroad by relying on allies to promote stability, often hinged on U.S. ties to unsavory clients such as the Shah of Iran, Mohammad Reza Pahlavi, and the Philippine dictator Ferdinand Marcos. The international economy, meanwhile, continued to deteriorate, and, despite SALT, the nuclear arms race accelerated. Nixon and Kissinger claimed too much for détente, and the public felt disappointed every time the Cold War heated up. Congress, resentful of being

*shut off from policymaking, increasingly contested Nixon's "imperial presidency."
Nixon eventually resigned and the administration fell because of the array of
corruptions revealed in the Watergate crisis.*

*The Nixon-Kissinger diplomacy, still a part of living memory for many scholars,
has generated spirited debate. In some ways, it provides an opportunity to weigh
the strengths and weaknesses of foreign-policy realism and balance-of-power diplomacy. While some writers have applauded détente as a significant departure from
the traditional Cold War diplomacy—perhaps even a necessary precursor to the end
of the Cold War two decades later—others have concluded that it represented little
more than a change in tactics, or a new style of anticommunist containment. The
administration's defenders perceive SALT and arms control as an important step
toward nuclear arms reduction, the opening to the People's Republic of China as a
diplomatic triumph, and the promotion of trade and cultural exchanges with Moscow
and Beijing as a harbinger of change in the communist world. Critics focus on the
continued arms buildup that SALT allowed, the administration's blind spot on
international human rights, the agonizing delay in ending the Vietnam War, and
the ongoing Soviet-American competition in the Third World. To sum up in the form
of a question, how fully did Nixon and Kissinger understand global change and
the limits to American power in the 1960s and 1970s, and how far were they willing
to go in adjusting Cold War policy and U.S. commitments abroad?*

*The Nixon foreign policy has also raised questions centered on power and pro-
cedure. Wary of the public's understanding of complex international issues, some
analysts defend the Nixon-Kissinger penchant for secrecy and covert action and
their frequent circumvention of Congress. The savvy exercise of executive power prevented hard-line conservatives from derailing arms control and détente, contained
popular division over the Vietnam War, and produced impressive achievements such
as SALT and rapprochement with China. Others see a direct line connecting Nixon's
heavy-handed conduct of foreign policy to the abuses of presidential power evident
in the Watergate scandal. From a pragmatic perspective, some argue that a more
open relationship with Congress and the public might have helped build long-term
public support for détente and other foreign-policy initiatives. In short, could the
United States have adjusted more successfully to international change by adhering
more consistently to democratic values and constitutional procedures?*

*As this chapter's selections suggest, Nixon and Kissinger share an ambiguous
legacy that invites searching debate.*

 D O C U M E N T S

Richard M. Nixon, elected president in November 1968, assumed office with a reputation as a hard-line Cold Warrior. But Document 1, from his memoirs, shows that he recognized new diplomatic opportunities to contain the Soviet Union and to end the war in
Vietnam. One method of gaining these objectives was the exploitation of the Sino-Soviet
split, sometimes called the "China card." Document 2, a Nixon statement on Asian self-
help given during an interview on July 25, 1969, became known as the Nixon Doctrine.
Nixon also acknowledged changes in the international economy during his presidency.
Document 3 is an excerpt from a speech he gave in Kansas City, Missouri, on July 6,
1971, in which he discussed the five economic superpowers and America's role in the
new global economy. In 1972 the Soviet Union and the United States signed the Strategic Arms Limitation Talks agreement, or SALT-I. In a September 19, 1974, appearance
before the Senate Foreign Relations Committee, Henry A. Kissinger defined détente and
its accomplishments. His statement is reprinted here as Document 4.

Chile became a trouble spot from the Nixon-Kissinger perspective in 1970 when a Marxist, Salvador Allende, was elected president of that South American nation. The United States had attempted to block his election through covert operations but had failed. The Nixon administration then plotted to destabilize Allende's government. Document 5 is a 1975 report from the U.S. Senate Select Committee on Intelligence Activities—the Church Committee, named for its chair, Idaho Democrat Frank Church—on covert activities in Chile, 1963–1973. Document 6 is a January 13, 1977, editorial by Anthony Lewis of the *New York Times,* a writer who sharply indicted Kissinger's diplomatic record.

1. President Richard M. Nixon Recalls His Initial Goals (1968), 1978

For twenty-five years, I had watched the changing face of communism. I had seen prewar communism, luring workers and intellectuals with its siren call of equality and justice, reveal itself as an aggressive imperialistic ideology during the postwar period of the Marshall Plan. Despite the most nobly ringing rhetoric, the pattern was tragically the same: as soon as the Communists came to power, they destroyed all opposition. I had watched the Soviets' phenomenal recovery from the devastation of war and their costly but successful struggle to achieve for communism the selling point of potential prosperity. At home I had seen the face of underground subversive communism when it surfaced in the [Alger] Hiss case, reminding people not only that it existed, but that its purpose was deadly serious. . . .

Never once in my career have I doubted the Communists mean it when they say that their goal is to bring the world under Communist control. Nor have I ever forgotten [Alger Hiss's accuser] Whittaker Chamber's chilling comment that when he left communism, he had the feeling he was leaving the winning side. But unlike some anticommunists who think we should refuse to recognize or deal with the Communists lest in doing so we imply or extend an ideological respectability to their philosophy and their system, I have always believed that we can and must communicate and, when possible, negotiate with Communist nations. They are too powerful to ignore. We must always remember that they will never act out of altruism, but only out of self-interest. Once this is understood, it is more sensible—and also safer—to communicate with the Communists than it is to live in icy cold-war isolation or confrontation. In fact, in January 1969 I felt that the relationship between the United States and the Soviet Union would probably be the single most important factor in determining whether the world would live at peace during and after my administration.

I felt that we had allowed ourselves to get in a disadvantageous position vis-à-vis the Soviets. They had a major presence in the Arab states of the Middle East, while we had none; they had Castro in Cuba; since the mid-1960s they had supplanted the Chinese as the principal military suppliers of North Vietnam; and except for Tito's Yugoslavia they still totally controlled Eastern Europe and threatened the stability and security of Western Europe.

There were, however, a few things in our favor. The most important and interesting was the Soviet split with China. There was also some evidence of growing, albeit limited, independence in some of the satellite nations. There were indications that the Soviet leaders were becoming interested in reaching an agreement on strategic arms limitation. They also appeared to be ready to hold serious talks on the anomalous situation in Berlin, which, almost a quarter century after the war had ended, was still a divided city and a constant source of tension, not just between the Soviets and the United States, but also between the Soviets and Western Europe. We sensed that they were looking for a face-saving formula that would lessen the risk of confrontation in the Mideast. And we had some solid evidence that they were anxious for an expansion of trade.

It was often said that the key to a Vietnam settlement lay in Moscow and Peking rather than in Hanoi. Without continuous and massive aid from either or both of the Communist giants, the leaders of North Vietnam would not have been able to carry on the war for more than a few months. Thanks to the Sino-Soviet split, however, the North Vietnamese had been extremely successful in playing off the Soviets and the Chinese against each other by turning support for their war effort into a touchstone of Communist orthodoxy and a requisite for keeping North Vietnam from settling into the opposing camp in the struggle for domination within the Communist world. This situation became a strain, particularly for the Soviets. Aside from wanting to keep Hanoi from going over to Peking, Moscow had little stake in the outcome of the North Vietnamese cause, especially as it increasingly worked against Moscow's own major interests vis-à-vis the United States. While I understood that the Soviets were not entirely free agents where their support for North Vietnam was concerned, I nonetheless planned to bring maximum pressure to bear on them in this area. . . .

During the transition period [Henry] Kissinger and I developed a new policy for dealing with the Soviets. Since U.S.-Soviet interests as the world's two competing nuclear superpowers were so widespread and overlapping, it was unrealistic to separate or compartmentalize areas of concern. Therefore we decided to link progress in such areas of Soviet concern as strategic arms limitation and increased trade with progress in areas that were important to us—Vietnam, the Mideast and Berlin. This concept became known as linkage.

Lest there be any doubt of my seriousness in pursuing this policy, I purposely announced it at my first press conference when asked a question about starting SALT [Strategic Arms Limitation Treaty] talks. I said, "What I want to do is to see to it that we have strategic arms talks in a way and at a time that will promote, if possible, progress on outstanding political problems at the same time—for example, on the problem of the Mideast and on other outstanding problems in which the United States and the Soviet Union acting together can serve the cause of peace."

Linkage was something uncomfortably new and different for the Soviets, and I was not surprised when they bridled at the restraints it imposed on our relationship. It would take almost two years of patient and hard-nosed determination on our part before they would accept that linkage with what we wanted from them was the price they would have to pay for getting any of the things they wanted from us. . . .

The most pressing foreign problem I would have to deal with as soon as I became President was the war in Vietnam. During the transition Kissinger began a review of all possible policies toward Vietnam, distilling them into specific options that ran the gamut from massive military escalation to immediate unilateral withdrawal. . . .

I began my presidency with three fundamental premises regarding Vietnam. First, I would have to prepare public opinion for the fact that total military victory was no longer possible. Second, I would have to act on what my conscience, my experience, and my analysis told me was true about the need to keep our commitment. To abandon South Vietnam to the Communists now would cost us inestimably in our search for a stable, structured, and lasting peace. Third, I would have to end the war as quickly as was honorably possible. . . .

The Vietnam war was complicated by factors that had never occurred before in America's conduct of a war. Many of the most prominent liberals of both parties in Congress, having supported our involvement in Vietnam under Kennedy and Johnson, were now trying to back off from their commitment. Senators and congressmen, Cabinet members and columnists who had formerly supported the war were now swelling the ranks of the antiwar forces. In 1969 I still had a congressional majority on war-related votes and questions, but it was a bare one at best, and I could not be sure how long it would hold. Another unusual aspect of this war was that the American news media had come to dominate domestic opinion about its purpose and conduct and also about the nature of the enemy. The North Vietnamese were a particularly ruthless and cruel enemy, but the American media concentrated primarily on the failings and frailties of the South Vietnamese or of our own forces. In each night's TV news and in each morning's paper the war was reported battle by battle, but little or no sense of the underlying purpose of the fighting was conveyed. Eventually this contributed to the impression that we were fighting in military and moral quicksand, rather than toward an important and worthwhile objective. . . .

As I prepared to enter the presidency, I regarded the antiwar protesters and demonstrators with alternating feelings of appreciation for their concerns, anger at their excesses, and, primarily, frustration at their apparent unwillingness to credit me even with a genuine desire for peace. But whatever my estimation of the demonstrators' motives—and whatever their estimate of mine—I considered that the practical effect of their activity was to give encouragement to the enemy and thus prolong the war. They wanted to end the war in Vietnam. So did I. But they wanted to end it immediately, and in order to do so they were prepared to abandon South Vietnam. That was something I would not permit.

2. The Nixon Doctrine Calls on Asian Nations to Take Responsibility for Their Own Security, 1969

I believe that the time has come when the United States, in our relations with all of our Asian friends, [must] be quite emphatic on two points: One, that we will keep our treaty commitments, our treaty commitments, for example, with Thailand under SEATO [Southeast Asia Treaty Organization]; but, two, that as far as the problems of internal security are concerned, as far as the problems of military defense, except for the threat of a major power involving nuclear weapons, that the United States is going to encourage and has a right to expect that this problem

---

This document can be found in *Public Papers of the Presidents: Richard Nixon, 1969* (Washington, D.C.: U.S. Government Printing Office, 1971), p. 549.

will be increasingly handled by, and the responsibility for it taken by, the Asian nations themselves.

I believe, incidentally, from my preliminary conversations with several Asian leaders over the past few months that they are going to be willing to undertake this responsibility. It will not be easy, but if the United States just continues down the road of responding to requests for assistance, of assuming the primary responsibility for defending these countries when they have internal problems or external problems, they are never going to take care of themselves.

3. Nixon Explains the Five Power Centers of the New Global Economy, 1971

Many of you, a few of you, are old enough to remember what America was 24 years ago.

We were number one in the world militarily, with no one who even challenged us because we had a monopoly on atomic weapons. We also at that point, of course, were number one economically by all odds. In fact, the United States of America was producing more than 50 percent of all the world's goods.

That was just 25 years ago. Now, 25 years having passed, let's look at the situation today and what it may be 5 years from now or 10 years from now. I will not try to limit myself to 5 or 10 years except to say that in the next decade we are going to see changes that may be even greater than what have occurred in the last 25 years, and very great ones have occurred in that respect.

First, instead of just America being number one in the world from an economic standpoint, the preeminent world power, and instead of there being just two super powers, when we think in economic terms and economic potentialities, there are five great power centers in the world today. Let's look at them very briefly.

There is, of course, the United States of America. There is, second, Western Europe—Western Europe with Britain in the Common Market. That means 300 million of the most advanced people in the world, with all the productivity and all the capacity that those people will have and, of course, with the clout that they have when they will act together, as they certainly will. That is a new factor in the world scene that will come, and come very soon, as we all know.

Then in the Pacific, looking also at free world countries, we have a resurgent Japan. I met with steel leaders this morning—leaders of industry and leaders of unions. I pointed out what had happened to Japan in terms of their business: Just 20 years ago Japan produced 5 million tons of steel a year; this year they produced 100 million tons of steel; 2 years from now Japan will produce more steel than the United States of America.

That is what has happened. It has happened in the case of Japan, in the case of Germany, our two major enemies in World War II, partly as a result of our help in getting them on their feet. But it has happened since that time as a result of their own energy and their own ability. . . .

This document can be found in *Public Papers of the Presidents: Richard Nixon, 1971* (Washington, D.C.: U.S. Government Printing Office, 1972), pp. 804–807.

Now we turn to the other two super powers, economic super powers I will say for the moment. The Soviet Union, of course, first comes to mind. Looking at the Soviet Union, we are entering a period which only time will tell may be successful in terms of creating a very new relationship or a very different relationship than we have had previously.

I referred to the need for an era of negotiation rather than confrontation when I made my inaugural speech. . . . I am not suggesting that these negotiations are going to lead to instant peace and instant relationships with the Soviet Union such as we presently have with our friends in Western Europe and with our friends in Asia who may be allied with us, or who may have systems of government that are more closely aligned to ours. What we have to recognize is that even as we limit arms, if we do reach an agreement in that field, and even if we find ways to avoid confrontation in other areas, and perhaps work out negotiated settlements for mutual force reductions in Europe, the problem of Berlin, all the others that come to mind, we must recognize that the Soviet Union will continue to be a very potent, powerful, and aggressive competitor of the United States of America. And, ironically—and this is also true of Mainland China, as I will point out in a moment—as we have more and more success on the negotiation front, as for example the Soviet Union, like the United States, may be able if we have a limitation in nuclear arms, if we are able to turn our eyes more toward our economic development and our economic problems, it simply means that the competition changes and becomes much more challenging in the economic area than it has been previously. . . .

Mainland China is, of course, a very different situation. First in terms of its economic capacity at the present time, a pretty good indication of where it is is that Japan, with 100 million people, produces more than Mainland China, with 800 million people. But that should not mislead us, and it gives us, and should give none of the potential competitors in world markets of Mainland China, any sense of satisfaction that it will always be that way. Because when we see the Chinese as people—and I have seen them all over the world, and some of you have, too, whether in Hong Kong, or whether in Taiwan, or whether they are in Singapore or Bangkok, any of the great cities, Manila, where Chinese are there—they are creative, they are productive, they are one of the most capable people in the world. And 800 million Chinese are going to be, inevitably, an enormous economic power, with all that that means in terms of what they could be in other areas if they move in that direction.

That is the reason why I felt that it was essential that this Administration take the first steps toward ending the isolation of Mainland China from the world community. We had to take those steps because the Soviet Union could not, because of differences that they have that at the present time seem to be irreconcilable. We were the only other power that could take those steps. . . .

Now, I do not suggest, in mentioning these five, that Latin America is not important, that Africa is not important, that South Asia is not important. All nations are important, and all peoples in underdeveloped or less developed countries will play their role. But these are the five that will determine the economic future and, because economic power will be the key to other kinds of power, the future of the world in other ways in the last third of this century.

Now let's see what this means to the United States. It means that the United States, as compared with that position we found ourselves in immediately after

World War II, has a challenge such as we did not even dream of. Then we were talking about the dollar gap; then we were talking about the necessity of—putting it in terms of a poker game—that the United States had all the chips and we had to spread a few of the chips around so that others could play.

We did it. One hundred billion dollars worth to Western Europe, for example, to rebuild them, and billions of others to other countries, and it was the correct policy as it turned out. But now when we see the world in which we are about to move, the United States no longer is in the position of complete preeminence or predominance. That is not a bad thing. As a matter of fact, it can be a constructive thing. The United States, let us understand, is still the strongest nation in the world; it is still the richest nation in the world. But now we face a situation where four other potential economic powers have the capacity, have the kind of people—if not the kind of government, but at least the kind of people—who can challenge us on every front.

4. Secretary of State Henry A. Kissinger Defines Détente, 1974

There can be no peaceful international order without a constructive relationship between the United States and the Soviet Union. There will be no international stability unless both the Soviet Union and the United States conduct themselves with restraint and unless they use their enormous power for the benefit of mankind.

Thus, we must be clear at the outset on what the term "détente" entails. It is the search for a more constructive relationship with the Soviet Union. It is a continuing process, not a final condition. And it has been pursued by successive American leaders though the means have varied as have world conditions.

Some fundamental principles guide this policy:

The United States does not base its policy solely on Moscow's good intentions. We seek, regardless of Soviet intentions, to serve peace through a systematic resistance to pressure and conciliatory responses to moderate behavior.

We must oppose aggressive actions, but we must not seek confrontations lightly.

We must maintain a strong national defense while recognizing that in the nuclear age the relationship between military strength and politically usable power is the most complex in all history.

Where the age-old antagonism between freedom and tyranny is concerned, we are not neutral. But other imperatives impose limits on our ability to produce internal changes in foreign countries. Consciousness of our limits is a recognition of the necessity of peace—not moral callousness. The preservation of human life and human society are moral values, too.

We must be mature enough to recognize that to be stable a relationship must provide advantages to both sides and that the most constructive international relationships are those in which both parties perceive an element of gain. . . .

To set forth principles of behavior in formal documents is hardly to guarantee their observance. But they are reference points against which to judge actions and set goals.

This document can be found in U.S. Senate, Committee on Foreign Relations, *Détente* (Washington, D.C.: U.S. Government Printing Office, 1975), pp. 247–248, 251–254, 256.

The first of the series of documents is the Statement of Principles signed in Moscow in 1972. It affirms: (1) the necessity of avoiding confrontation; (2) the imperative of mutual restraint; (3) the rejection of attempts to exploit tensions to gain unilateral advantages; (4) the renunciation of claims of special influence in the world; and (5) the willingness, on this new basis, to coexist peacefully and build a firm long-term relationship.

An Agreement on the Prevention of Nuclear War based on these Principles was signed in 1973. But it emphasizes that this objective presupposes the renunciation of any war or threat of war not only by the two nuclear superpowers against each other, but also against allies or third countries. In other words, the principle of restraint is not confined to relations between the United States and the U.S.S.R. It is explicitly extended to include all countries.

These statements of principles are not an American concession; indeed, we have been affirming them unilaterally for two decades. Nor are they a legal contract; rather, they are an aspiration and a yardstick by which we assess Soviet behavior. We have never intended to rely on Soviet compliance with every principle; we do seek to elaborate standards of conduct which the Soviet Union would violate only to its cost. And if over the long term the more durable relationship takes hold, the basic principles will give it definition, structure, and hope.

One of the features of the current phase of United States–Soviet relations is the unprecedented consultation between leaders either face to face or through diplomatic channels. . . .

It was difficult in the past to speak of a United States–Soviet bilateral relationship in any normal sense of the phrase. Trade was negligible. Contacts between various institutions and between the peoples of the two countries were at best sporadic. Today, by joining our efforts even in such seemingly apolitical fields as medical research or environmental protection, we and the Soviets can benefit not only our two peoples, but all mankind.

Since 1972 we have concluded agreements on a common effort against cancer, on research to protect the environment, on studying the use of the ocean's resources, on the use of atomic energy for peaceful purposes, on studying methods for conserving energy, on examining construction techniques for regions subject to earthquakes, and on devising new transportation methods. . . .

We have approached the question of economic relations with deliberation and circumspection and as an act of policy not primarily of commercial opportunity. As political relations have improved on a broad basis, economic issues have been dealt with on a comparably broad front. A series of interlocking economic agreements with the U.S.S.R. has been negotiated, side by side with the political progress already noted. The 25-year-old lend-lease debt was settled; the reciprocal extension of the most-favored-nation treatment was negotiated, together with safeguards against the possible disruption of our markets and a series of practical arrangements to facilitate the conduct of business; our Government credit facilities were made available for trade with the U.S.S.R.; and a maritime agreement regulating the carriage of goods has been signed. . . .

Over time, trade and investment may leaven the autarkic tendencies of the Soviet system, invite gradual association of the Soviet economy with the world economy, and foster a degree of interdependence that adds an element of stability to the political relationship.

We cannot expect to relax international tensions or achieve a more stable international system should the two strongest nuclear powers conduct an unrestrained strategic arms race. Thus, perhaps the single most important component of our policy toward the Soviet Union is the effort to limit strategic weapons competition.

The competition in which we now find ourselves is historically unique:

Each side has the capacity to destroy civilization as we know it.

Failure to maintain equivalence could jeopardize not only our freedom but our very survival. . . .

The prospect of a decisive military advantage, even if theoretically possible, is politically intolerable; neither side will passively permit a massive shift in the nuclear balance. Therefore, the probable outcome of each succeeding round of competition is the restoration of a strategic equilibrium, but at increasingly higher and more complex levels of forces.

The arms race is driven by political as well as military factors. While a decisive advantage is hard to calculate, the appearance of inferiority—whatever its actual significance—can have serious political consequences. Thus, each side has a high incentive to achieve not only the reality but the appearance of equality. In a very real sense each side shapes the military establishment of the other.

If we are driven to it, the United States will sustain an arms race. But the political or military benefit which would flow from such a situation would remain elusive. Indeed, after such an evolution it might well be that both sides would be worse off than before the race began.

The Soviet Union must realize that the overall relationship with the United States will be less stable if strategic balance is sought through unrestrained competitive programs. Sustaining the buildup requires exhortations by both sides that in time may prove incompatible with restrained international conduct. The very fact of a strategic arms race has a high potential for feeding attitudes of hostility and suspicion on both sides, transforming the fears of those who demand more weapons into self-fulfilling prophecies. . . .

Détente is admittedly far from a modern equivalent to the kind of stable peace that characterized most of the 19th century. But it is a long step away from the bitter and aggressive spirit that has characterized so much of the post-war period. When linked to such broad and unprecedented projects as SALT, détente takes on added meaning and opens prospects of a more stable peace. SALT agreements should be seen as steps in a process leading to progressively greater stability. It is in that light that SALT and related projects will be judged by history.

5. U.S. Covert Action in Chile (1963–1973), 1975

The pattern of United States covert action in Chile is striking but not unique. It arose in the context not only of American foreign policy, but also of covert U.S. involvement in other countries within and outside Latin America. The scale of CIA involvement in Chile was unusual but by no means unprecedented. . . .

This document can be found in U.S. Senate, Select Committee to Study Governmental Operations with Respect to Intelligence Activities, Staff Report, *Covert Action in Chile (1963–1973)* (Washington, D.C.: U.S. Government Printing Office, 1975).

The most extensive covert action activity in Chile was propaganda. It was relatively cheap. In Chile, it continued at a low level during "normal" times, then was cranked up to meet particular threats or to counter particular dangers.

The most common form of a propaganda project is simply the development of "assets" in media organizations who can place articles or be asked to write them. The Agency provided to its field Stations several kinds of guidance about what sorts of propaganda were desired. For example, one CIA project in Chile supported from one to five media assets during the seven years it operated (1965–1971). Most of those assets worked for a major Santiago daily which was the key to CIA propaganda efforts. . . .

The covert propaganda efforts in Chile also included "black" propaganda—material falsely purporting to be the product of a particular individual or group. In the 1970 election, for instance, the CIA used "black" propaganda to sow discord between the Communists and the Socialists and between the national labor confederation and the Chilean Communist Party.

In some cases, the form of propaganda was still more direct. The Station financed Chilean groups who erected wall posters, passed out political leaflets (at times prepared by the Station) and engaged in other street activities. . . .

Of thirty-odd covert action projects undertaken [in] Chile by the CIA between 1961 and 1974, approximately a half dozen had propaganda as their principal activity. Propaganda was an important subsidiary element of many others, particularly election projects. (See Table 1.) Press placements were attractive because each placement might produce a multiplier effect, being picked up and replayed by media outlets other than the one in which it originally came out.

In addition to buying propaganda piecemeal, the Station often purchased it wholesale by subsidizing Chilean media organizations friendly to the United States. Doing so was propaganda writ large. Instead of placing individual items, the CIA supported—or even founded—friendly media outlets which might not have existed in the absence of Agency support. . . .

By far, the largest—and probably the most significant—instance of support for a media organization was the money provided to *El Mercurio,* the major Santiago daily, under pressure during the Allende regime. . . . A CIA project renewal memorandum concluded that *El Mercurio* and other media outlets supported by the Agency had played an important role in setting the stage for the September 11, 1973, military coup which overthrew Allende.

Table 1   Techniques of Covert Action: Expenditures in Chile, 1963–73*

TECHNIQUES	AMOUNT
Propaganda for elections and other support for political parties	$8,000,000
Producing and disseminating propaganda and supporting mass media	4,300,000
Influencing Chilean institutions (labor, students, peasants, women) and supporting private sector organizations	900,000
Promoting military coup d'etat	<200,000

*Figures rounded to nearest $100,000.

Through its covert activities in Chile, the U.S. government sought to influence the actions of a wide variety of institutions and groups in Chilean society. The specific intent of those activities ran the gamut from attempting to influence directly the making of government policy to trying to counter communist or leftist influence among organized groups in the society. That most of these projects included a propaganda component is obvious. . . .

Projects were directed, for example, toward:

• Wresting control of Chilean university student organizations from the communists;

• Supporting a women's group active in Chilean political and intellectual life;

• Combating the communist-dominated *Central Unica de Trabajadores Chilenos* (CUTCh) and supporting democratic labor groups; and

• Exploiting a civic action front group to combat communist influence within cultural and intellectual circles.

Covert American activity was a factor in almost every major election in Chile in the decade between 1963 and 1973. In several instances the United States intervention was massive.

The 1964 presidential election was the most prominent example of a large-scale election project. The Central Intelligence Agency spent more than $2.6 million in support of the election of the Christian Democratic candidate, in part to prevent the accession to the presidency of Marxist Salvador Allende. More than half of the Christian Democratic candidate's campaign was financed by the United States, although he was not informed of this assistance. . . .

In Washington, an inter-agency election committee was established, composed of State Department, White House and CIA officials. That committee was paralleled by a group in the embassy in Santiago. No special task force was established within the CIA, but the Station in Santiago was reinforced. The Station assisted the Christian Democrats in running an American-style campaign, which included polling, voter registration and get-out-the-vote drives, in addition to covert propaganda.

The United States was also involved in the 1970 presidential campaign. That effort, however, was smaller and did not include support for any specific candidate. It was directed more at preventing Allende's election than at insuring another candidate's victory. . . .

Most covert American support to Chilean political parties was furnished as part of specific efforts to influence election outcomes. However, in several instances the CIA provided subsidies to parties for more general purposes, when elections were not imminent. Most such support was furnished during the Allende years, 1970–1973, when the U.S. government judged that without its support parties of the center and right might not survive either as opposition elements or as contestants in elections several years away.

In a sequence of decisions in 1971 through 1973, the 40 Committee [a sub-cabinet body of the executive branch which reviewed covert plans] authorized nearly $4 million for opposition political parties in Chile. Most of this money went to the Christian Democratic Party (PDC), but a substantial portion was earmarked for the National Party (PN), a conservative grouping more stridently opposed to the Allende government than was the PDC. An effort was also made to split the ruling Popular Unity coalition by inducing elements to break away. . . .

As part of its program of support for opposition elements during the Allende government, the CIA provided money to several trade organizations of the Chilean private sector. In September 1972, for instance, the 40 Committee authorized $24,000 in emergency support for an anti-Allende businessmen's organization. At that time, supporting other private sector organizations was considered but rejected because of the fear that those organizations might be involved in anti-government strikes. . . .

United States covert efforts to affect the course of Chilean politics reached a peak in 1970: the CIA was directed to undertake an effort to promote a military coup in Chile to prevent the accession to power of Salvador Allende [a project known as Track II]. . . . A brief summary here will demonstrate the extreme in American covert intervention in Chilean politics.

On September 15, 1970—after Allende finished first in the election but before the Chilean Congress had chosen between him and the runner-up, [Jorge] Alessandri—President Nixon met with Richard Helms, the Director of Central Intelligence, Assistant to the President for National Security Affairs Henry Kissinger and Attorney General John Mitchell. Helms was directed to prevent Allende from taking power. This effort was to be conducted without the knowledge of the Department of State and Defense or the Ambassador. Track II was never discussed at a 40 Committee meeting.

It quickly became apparent to both White House and CIA officials that a military coup was the only way to prevent Allende's accession to power. To achieve that end, the CIA established contact with several groups of military plotters and eventually passed three weapons and tear gas to one group. The weapons were subsequently returned, apparently unused. The CIA knew that the plans of all groups of plotters began with the abduction of the constitutionalist Chief of Staff of the Chilean Army, General René Schneider. The Committee has received conflicting testimony about the extent of CIA/White House communication and of White House officials' awareness of specific coup plans, but there is no doubt that the U.S. government sought a military coup in Chile.

On October 22, one group of plotters attempted to kidnap Schneider. Schneider resisted, was shot, and subsequently died. The CIA had been in touch with that group of plotters but a week earlier had withdrawn its support for the group's specific plans.

The coup plotting collapsed and Allende was inaugurated President. After his election, the CIA and U.S. military attachés maintained contacts with the Chilean military for the purpose of collecting intelligence. Whether those contacts strayed into encouraging the Chilean military to move against Allende; or whether the Chilean military—having been goaded toward a coup during Track II—took encouragement to act against the President from those contacts even though U.S. officials did not intend to provide it: these are major questions which are inherent in U.S. covert activities in the period of the Allende government. . . .

In addition to providing information and cover to the CIA, multinational corporations also participated in covert attempts to influence Chilean politics. . . .

A number of multinational corporations were apprehensive about the possibility that Allende would be elected President of Chile. Allende's public announcements indicated his intention, if elected, to nationalize basic industries and to bring under Chilean ownership service industries such as the national telephone company, which was at that time a subsidiary of ITT [International Telephone and Telegraph].

In 1964 Allende had been defeated, and it was widely known both in Chile and among American multinational corporations with significant interests in Chile that his opponents had been supported by the United States government. John McCone, a former CIA Director and a member of ITT's Board of Directors in 1970, knew of the significant American government involvement in 1964 and of the offer of assistance made at that time by American companies. Agency documents indicate that McCone informed Harold Geneen, ITT's Board Chairman, of these facts.

In 1970 leaders of American multinational corporations with substantial interests in Chile, together with other American citizens concerned about what might happen to Chile in the event of an Allende victory, contacted U.S. government officials in order to make their views known.

In July 1970, a CIA representative in Santiago met with representatives of ITT and, in a discussion of the upcoming election, indicated that Alessandri could use financial assistance. The Station suggested the name of an individual who could be used as a secure channel for getting these funds to the Alessandri campaign.

Shortly thereafter John McCone telephoned CIA Director Richard Helms. As a result of this call, a meeting was arranged between the Chairman of the Board of ITT and Chief of the Western Hemisphere Division of the CIA. Geneen offered to make available to the CIA a substantial amount of money to be used in support of the Alessandri campaign. In subsequent meetings ITT offered to make $1 million available to the CIA. The CIA rejected the offer. The memorandum indicated further that CIA's advice was sought with respect to an individual who might serve as a conduit of ITT funds to the Alessandri campaign.

The CIA confirmed that the individual in question was a reliable channel which could be used for getting funds to Alessandri. A second channel of funds from ITT to a political party opposing Allende, the National Party, was developed following CIA advice as to a secure funding mechanism utilizing two CIA assets in Chile. These assets were also receiving Agency funds in connection with the "spoiling" operation.

During the period prior to the September election, ITT representatives met frequently with CIA representatives both in Chile and in the United States and CIA advised ITT as to ways in which it might safely channel funds both to the Alessandri campaign and to the National Party. CIA was kept informed of the extent and the mechanism of the funding. Eventually at least $350,000 was passed by ITT to this campaign. A roughly equal amount was passed by other U.S. companies; the CIA learned of this funding but did not assist in it.

6. The Journalist Anthony Lewis Blasts Kissinger's Record, 1977

Henry Kissinger is leaving office in a blaze of adulation. The National Press Club produces a belly dancer for him and gives standing applause to his views on world peace. The Harlem Globetrotters make him an honorary member. Senators pay tribute to his wisdom.

Historians of the next generation will find it all very puzzling. Because they will not have seen Mr. Kissinger perform, they will have to rely on the record. And the record of his eight years in Washington is likely to seem thin in diplomatic achievement and shameful in human terms.

The one outstanding accomplishment is Mr. Kissinger's Middle East diplomacy. He restored United States relations with the Arab world, and he set in motion the beginnings of an Arab-Israeli dialogue. Of course, the work is incomplete. But to start something after so many years of total failure was a great breakthrough and it was essentially the work of one man: Henry Kissinger.

The other undoubtedly positive entry on the record is the opening to China, but that was in good part Richard Nixon's doing. Also, the beginnings of a relationship with the People's Republic were not followed up as they might have been, and the failure may prove damaging.

With the Soviet Union, Mr. Kissinger took the familiar idea of easing tensions and glamorized it as détente. The glamor was dangerous. It fostered the illusion that détente could prevent conflict all over the world, and many Americans turned sour on the whole idea when it did not. At times Mr. Kissinger himself seemed to believe the illusion—and became apoplectic when it failed as in Angola. Détente's real achievements are scant; not much more than a halting step toward nuclear arms control.

Ignorance and ineptitude marked his policy in much of the rest of the world. In Cyprus, his blundering led to human tragedy and left America's reputation damaged in both Greece and Turkey. His insensitivity to Japanese feelings had traumatic effects on a most important ally.

In dealing with Portugal and its African territories Mr. Kissinger decided in succession that (1) the Portuguese were in Africa to stay, (2) the U.S. should help Portugal's dictatorship, (3) after the dictatorship's fall the Communists were bound to prevail in Portugal and (4) the U.S. could decide the outcome in Angola by covert aid. That parade of folly was matched in his African policy generally: years of malign neglect, then last-minute intervention for majority rule in Rhodesia.

He often talked about freedom, but his acts show a pre-eminent interest in order. Millions lost their freedom during the Kissinger years, many to dictatorships that had crucial support from his policies, as in Chile and the Philippines. He expressed little open concern for the victims of Soviet tyranny, and he did little to enforce the human rights clauses of the Helsinki Agreement.

The American constitutional system of checks and balances he treated as an irritating obstacle to power. In his valedictory to the Press Club his only reference to Watergate was an expression of regret at "the disintegration of Executive authority that resulted."

Secrecy and deceit were levers of his power; he had no patience for the democratic virtues of openness and consultation. By keeping all the facts to himself and a few intimates, he centralized control. He practiced deceit with a kind of gusto, from petty personal matters to "peace is at hand."

His conduct in the wiretapping of his own staff gave ugly insight into his character. He provided names for investigation—and then, when the story came out, wriggled and deceived in order to minimize his role. He never expressed regret, even to those who had been closest to him, for the fact that their family conversations had been overheard for months. But when someone ransacked his garbage, he said his wife had suffered "grave anguish."

History will remember him most of all for his policy in Indochina. In the teeth of evidence well known by 1969, this supposed realist pressed obsessively for indefinite maintenance of the status quo. To that end, in his time, 20,492 more Americans died in Vietnam and hundreds of thousands of Vietnamese. The war was expanded into Cambodia, destroying that peaceable land. And all for nothing.

With such a record, how is it that people vie to place laurels on the head of the departing Secretary of State? The answer became clear the other night during an extraordinarily thoughtful Public Broadcasting television program on Mr. Kissinger's career: He has discovered that in our age publicity is power, and he has played the press as Dr. Miracle played his violin. He is intelligent and hard-working and ruthless, but those qualities are common enough. His secret is showmanship.

Henry Kissinger is our P. T. Barnum—a Barnum who plays in a vastly larger tent and whose jokes have about them the air of the grave. That we honor a person who has done such things in our name is a comment on us.

 E S S A Y S

In the first essay, Joan Hoff, a Nixon biographer who teaches at Montana State University, presents a positive appraisal of Nixon's Grand Design. Although Hoff faults the administration for conducting foreign policy under a veil of secrecy, particularly when combating suspected communism in the Third World, she places much of the blame for the administration's shortcomings on the president's adviser, Henry A. Kissinger. She praises Nixon, on the other hand, for his bold and imaginative policy of détente toward the People's Republic of China and the Soviet Union, his pursuit of arms control, and his ability to adjust U.S. policy to the realities of a more competitive world economy. Nixon, according to Hoff, deserves credit for initiating a foreign policy that transcended constraints imposed by Cold War ideology, deftly balanced détente with U.S. security goals in Western Europe, and effectively managed a Democratic Congress. Détente broke down, according to Hoff, largely because Moscow did not seek at the time to end the Cold War, and détente's opponents exploited popular distaste for Soviet human-rights violations.

In the second essay, Raymond L. Garthoff, a former foreign service officer and ambassador who is currently a senior fellow at the Brookings Institution in Washington, D.C., advances a more negative interpretation, finding détente a failure. He criticizes the Nixon-Kissinger team for not defining the meaning of détente more clearly and for not developing with Moscow a viable code of conduct and collaborative measures for managing the superpower rivalry. Each side expected too much from détente and misperceived the other's continued military buildup and interventions as threatening and destabilizing. The United States, Garthoff argues, maintained a particularly idealized concept of détente that condemned aggressive Soviet behavior but failed to acknowledge that the vigorous foreign policy of the United States itself at times violated the spirit of détente.

The last selection is drawn from Walter Isaacson's lengthy biography of Henry A. Kissinger. In the excerpt, Isaacson, an editor at *Time* magazine, examines Kissinger's foreign policy "realism." In contrast to Hoff, Isaacson respects Kissinger's intellectual brilliance and political savvy. Isaacson, however, emphasizes that Kissinger's concern for U.S. credibility led to imprudent interventions in the Third World. Most important, according to Isaacson, Kissinger's European style of diplomacy clashed with America's democratic traditions and moral values and thus weakened public backing for détente.

Nixon's Innovative Grand Design
and the Wisdom of Détente

JOAN HOFF

Any revisionist approach to Nixon's management of foreign policy must begin by attempting to place in perspective the complex interaction developed between Nixon and Kissinger, whose "advanced megalomania remains legendary." In retrospect, I believe that one of the most unfortunate decisions the president-elect made during the interregnum was to appoint Kissinger, about whom he knew only that, as a Nelson Rockefeller supporter, Kissinger had been openly disdainful of Nixon and his bid for the Republican nomination in 1968. If Nixon thought Kissinger's views on U.S. policy were important, he could have employed him as consultant to the NSC, as the Kennedy administration had briefly done. This opinion, however, [was] not shared by Nixon or most of his former advisers, one of whom defended Kissinger's appointment by saying that "the care and feeding of Henry" was worth all the paranoia, backbiting, leaking, rumor-mongering, and pseudo-intellectual posturing that he brought to the White House. . . .

On the surface Nixon and Kissinger—an American Quaker and a German-American Jew—appear to have been the odd couple of U.S. foreign policy. Given his long personal and professional association with the Rockefeller family and his blunt criticisms of Nixon, Kissinger apparently did not think he would last even six months in the new Nixon administration. Yet when these two men came together in 1968, they actually shared many viewpoints and had developed similar operational styles. Both relished covert activity and liked making unilateral decisions; both distrusted bureaucracies; both resented any attempt by Congress to interfere with initiatives; and both agreed that the United States could impose order and stability on the world only if the White House controlled policy by appearing conciliatory but acting tough. While neither had headed any complex organization, both thought "personalized executive control" and formal application of procedures would lead to success. Even more coincidental, perhaps, each had a history of failure and rejection, which made them susceptible to devising ways of protecting themselves and their positions of power. Often the concern for protection appeared as obsession with eavesdropping, whether wiretaps or reconnaissance flights. They even eavesdropped on themselves: Nixon by installing an automatic taping system in the Oval Office, Kissinger by having some of his meetings and all of his phone conversations taped or transcribed from notes. In a word, instead of compensating for each other's weaknesses and enhancing strengths, Nixon and Kissinger shared their worst characteristics. . . .

Kissinger did not share Nixon's optimistic approach to diplomacy and proclivity for taking risky, far-reaching foreign policy actions. As vice president under Eisenhower, Nixon had said: "I am not necessarily a respecter of the *status quo* in foreign affairs. I am a *chance taker* in foreign affairs. I would take chances for peace." Along these same lines, Nixon told Kissinger in August 1969: "just because [I] supported [something] as a private individual does not mean [I] will as president." In contrast, practically every analyst of Kissinger's ideas points out their essentially conservative (and profoundly pessimistic), nineteenth-century European roots. When he joined the Nixon administration, Kissinger seems not to have changed his ideas (and dense writing style) much from the time he wrote his Ph.D. dissertation, in which he recommended the Metternichian [in reference to the nineteenth century Austrian count Klemens von Metternich] system of alliances among conservative regimes to check the forces of revolution in the modern, Western world. Kissinger's early writings presaged what his memoirs confirmed: the mind of "a middle-level manager who has learned to conceal vacuity with pretentious verbiage." His pre-1968 political science writings convey very conventional cold warrior ideas about Vietnam, anti-Communist views that opposed ideologically driven grand designs in foreign policy and at best paid only occasional lip service to the necessity for some risk taking. And as an "inveterate conceptualizer," he was seldom on top of specific contemporary issues in his search for global solutions. . . .

It remained for the president to lead the way toward genuinely innovative, grand designs for redirecting of U.S. diplomacy. . . . Henry Kissinger was a geopolitical follower rather than a leader, although his talent for dramatic, back-channel diplomacy may have made the execution of some of Nixon's policies exemplary rather than simply ordinary. The scholar Richard Falk, among a variety of contemporary commentators, noted specifically that "Nixon deserves the main credit, and bore the main responsibility, for shifts in political direction implicit in the moves toward accommodation with China and détente with the Soviet Union. In both instances there had been receptivity on the Sino-Soviet side . . . [but] it was Nixon who decided to respond affirmatively." In addition, Washington aficionados as politically and socially diverse as [Nixon cabinet member] Elliot Richardson and Ralph de Toledano (biographer of the rich and famous) agreed that Nixon's diplomacy was, indeed, "his own." . . .

In Kansas City on July 6, 1971, Nixon announced his five-power, or "northern tier" strategy, which he hoped would replace the bipolar, confrontational aspects of the cold war. Instead of continuing to deal only bilaterally with the Soviet Union, Nixon wanted to bring the five great economic regions of the world—the United States, the USSR, mainland China, Japan, and Western Europe—into constructive negotiation and mutually profitable economic competition. Admitting that the United States could not long maintain its post–World War II position of "complete pre-eminence or predominance," Nixon outlined a "pentagonal strategy" for promoting peace and economic progress by linking the interests of the major regional powers. Kissinger never officially endorsed this plan, preferring the more exclusive Rockefeller "trilateral" approach that included only the U.S., Japan, and the Common Market nations of Western Europe (including the United Kingdom). . . .

This meant, of course, that from the beginning of the Nixon administration, entire areas of the Third World—southern Asia, the Middle East, Africa, Latin America—occupied a secondary place in the president's (and his national security adviser's) political approach to foreign policy. In particular, Nixon and Kissinger largely ignored economic foreign policy considerations in dealing with the Third World, preferring instead to link events in such countries to power relations among the major nations. "Linkage," therefore, accounts for many of the seemingly erratic aspects of U.S. foreign policy in Third World areas that fell outside the parameters of pentagonal strategy. Nixon was more interested in maintaining American spheres of influence in the Third World than in the economic needs of these developing nations. Thus, the United States promoted the overthrow of [Salvador] Allende in Chile; restrained Egyptian and Syrian aggression in the Middle East, while ignoring the potential instability of the shah's [(Mohammed Reza Pahlavi)] regime in Iran and indirectly encouraging the rise in OPEC oil prices; continued to oppose [Fidel] Castro in Cuba; and supported Pakistan against India [in their 1971 war]. The "grand design" may have been grand by superpower standards, but it remained ineffectual with respect to the Third World. . . .

Long before Nixon and Kissinger formally adopted the word *détente* to describe their diplomatic strategies and goals, the president's use of the term in early foreign policy statements and in private notes for speeches clearly indicates that he thought the relationship between NATO and détente with the USSR problematic. This uncertainty was considerably exacerbated when the bilateral, back-channel methods used to achieve rapprochement with China and détente with the Soviet Union bypassed the North Atlantic Treaty countries. In particular, both the ABM [Anti Ballistic Missile] and SALT I [Strategic Arms Limitation Treaty] agreements were negotiated with a minimum of consultation with NATO nations. The same was true of the New Economic Policy announced by Nixon in August 1971. Among other things, the NEP unilaterally "floated" the U.S. dollar on international financial markets, setting the stage for its subsequent devaluation and ending the post–World War II Bretton Woods international monetary system. . . .

Nixon almost immediately resorted to sporadic back-channel dealings with, or neglect of, NATO nations. For example, he told Kissinger on February 4, 1969, that he wanted "to go forward with a heads of government meeting" during the NATO twentieth-anniversary gathering in April, but that this plan should be "very closely held until we complete our European trip. I will discuss this matter of other NATO heads of government and then make the announcement on my return from the trip." Not until he and Kissinger proclaimed 1973 to be the Year of Europe did the president concentrate on concrete ways to improve relations with NATO. By that time they thought they had secured relations with both China and the Soviet Union and successfully ended the war in Vietnam.

The United States was on the verge of developing a defensive antiballistic missile system just as LBJ and Soviet Premier Alexei Kosygin had agreed in the summer of 1967 to discussions about reducing their countries' respective nuclear arsenals. It was obvious to both Nixon and Kissinger that the ABM might prove counterproductive if it resulted in an increased number of missiles (as did indeed occur later with the multiple independently targeted reentry vehicles, or MIRVs), but the president, in particular, was convinced that he had to have the ABM as a "bargaining chip" because intelligence reports indicated a buildup in Soviet offensive nuclear weapons. Unable to reveal these reports, the administration had to rationalize the ABM system to critics on Capitol Hill on other grounds. Consequently, Nixon publicly said that opposition from Congress to the ABM system threatened the possibility of détente and continued U.S. conventional arms support for the North Atlantic Treaty nations. Liberal, Democratic senators who opposed ABM tended to be the aame senators who wanted to reduce U.S. troop contributions to NATO through what was known at the time as the Mansfield amendment. So he ordered the Departments of Defense and State to close ranks behind the ABM, instead of encouraging more dissent among senators with "informed sources leaks."

The administration also did not place as much emphasis as its opponents within Congress and the arms-control community on the danger of the ABM system jeopardizing the ongoing negotiations between Gerard C. Smith, head of the U.S. Arms Control and Disarmament Agency (ACDA), and his Soviet counterpart, Vladimir Semenov, who were meeting in Vienna. As head of the U.S. SALT delegation as well, Smith wanted the development and deployment of MIRVs and ABM systems to be limited. This placed him immediately in opposition with Nixingerism [the Nixon-Kissinger policy] on two counts because the administration was in the process of striking a private bargain with the Joint Chiefs of Staff in which they would receive MIRVs in exchange for their agreement to limit ABM sites. (Smith was to add a third point of opposition in 1972, when he disagreed with specific provisions of SALT I.) But in 1970 the administration tried its best to downplay disagreement with Smith because he could sway so many congressional votes. . . .

During the spring and summer of 1969, Nixon dealt publicly and privately with NATO nations and his gradually emerging détente policy while battling senators over the ABM. The president's handwritten comments and memoranda testify to his personal involvement in the domestic political fight over the ABM issue. From telling his staff to "raise hell with CBS" for its anti-ABM television coverage when polls showed 64 percent of the American public in favor, to criticizing members of his own cabinet, like Secretary of Defense [Melvyn] Laird, for not "doing enough," he alternately cajoled his supporters and berated his opponents. After informing Congress on March 14 of his decision to go forward with a "substantial modification in the ABM system submitted by the previous administration," Nixon privately called [Democratic] Senator Edmund Muskie's proposal to use the $6.6 billion proposed for the ABM on hunger and poverty at home and abroad "unbelievable nonsense from a national leader!" When he read that [another Democrat,] Senator John Glenn, the former astronaut, had called the ABM a "false hope" because "no one knows if it works," the president sarcastically asked: "did he know the first space shot would absolutely work?" These private outbursts notwithstanding, Nixon, always the hardball politician, told [presidential aide H. R.] Haldeman, "this is war," and issued heavy-handed orders to his staff to "concentrate on those [senators] who are on the fence and *only* on those where we have a chance to win." Nonetheless, on August 6 he only narrowly won the battle on this antiballistic missile system in three separate amendment votes, with Vice President [Spiro T.] Agnew breaking a tie on the crucial amendment providing "spending for Safeguard deployment." The struggle left bitterness on both sides that did not bode well for future White House–Capitol Hill cooperation on other foreign or domestic issues, and the press treated it "as an anticlimactic victory for the administration."

While carefully monitoring and refusing to compromise his basic ABM proposal, Nixon authorized back-channel meetings between Kissinger and Anatoly Dobrynin, garnered support for the ABM from NATO nations, and decided to go ahead with MIRV testing despite the opposition of nonmilitary experts—all before leaving for his June 8 meeting with South Vietnamese President Nguyen Van Thieu on Midway Island in the Pacific. Then a month later, on July 25, at the beginning of a trip around the world, the president informally presented to reporters what became known as the Nixon Doctrine, noting that the United States would no longer commit U.S. troops to East Asia, although it continued to support regional security and national self-sufficiency in the area. Hence, the Nixon Doctrine was more necessary from an American perspective as a foundation block upon which to build the détente agreements with the Soviet Union (and China) than was the ABM legislation, despite the greater domestic attention that the latter received in the United States during the spring and summer of 1969. . . .

As a defense system, the ABM was more important to Soviet foreign policy than it was to the American grand design. The relative unimportance of the ABM issue for Nixingerism became more evident after Kissinger and Dobrynin agreed to divide the issues of the defensive weapons (the ABM) and offensive weapons (ultimately SALT I) in May 1971. By that time, the president and his national security adviser had decided that it would be easier to come to an agreement over future deployment of their respective ABM systems, which primarily existed only on paper, than it would be to conclude a treaty limiting the deployment of existing nuclear weapons. After campaigning against congressmen who opposed the ABM in the 1970 midterm elections, Nixon continued his "war" against Capitol Hill in the spring of 1971 by deciding it was time to "break the back of the establishment and Democratic leadership . . . [and] then build a strong defense in [our] second term" When the president wrote this to Kissinger, he faced stiff opposition in Congress over three military issues: U.S. NATO troop commitments, suspicion about a Soviet ABM system, and, of course, the ongoing Strategic Arms Limitation Talks. Even under this domestic political duress, the president did not forget the dual nature of détente; from his perspective, despite its public call for arms limitations and economic exchanges with the USSR, it privately meant continued military buildup—except in Vietnam. . . .

From 1949 until 1979 the United States refused to recognize the Communist government of the People's Republic of China. Not until the early 1970s, during Nixon's first administration, did the U.S. government begin to reverse this standard cold war policy of nonrecognition with a number of unilateral gestures of reconciliation, which ultimately brought about rapprochement (the establishment of friendly relations) under Nixon and recognition under Jimmy Carter in 1979. Setting in motion a process that ended in recognition of China remains one of Nixon's longest-lasting diplomatic accomplishments. Normalization of U.S. relations with China was part of Nixon's grand design to bring this giant Communist nation into the ranks of the superpowers. . . .

Opening relations with China . . . appears to have been on Nixon's mind from the beginning of his presidency. By the mid-1960s China specialists had openly begun to complain about continuing to isolate the People's Republic and, even though anti-Chinese sentiments loomed large in the public mind because of China's support for the North Vietnamese, China had been gaining international credibility for over twenty years and was recognized by over fifty countries when Nixon assumed office. As leader of the nonaligned nations, China challenged the superpowers' right to dictate to Third World nations. Its ties with the Soviet Union had been severely strained, if not actually broken, by 1969. And the cultural revolution inside China had subsided.

Thus, conditions were propitious for rethinking Chinese-American relations—a fact not lost on Nixon. It was time to bring China into the international fold of civilized nations, along with the Soviet Union through rapprochement. There was even the slight possibility that, despite Soviet and U.S. military advantages over China, that country might launch an irrational attack against one of them. In rationalizing his new approach to the Chinese, Nixon argued to his top foreign policy adviser in April 1969 that "the tragic fact of history [is] that most of the great wars were not started by responsible men and that we have to base our assumptions on what potentially irresponsible or irrational men may do, rather than simply on what we, as responsible leaders, might do." Rapprochement might help make "irrational" Communist Chinese leaders more rational, or so the president ethnocentrically implied. . . .

By the time Nixon became president he had decided to establish a new policy toward the People's Republic of China in several stages. First, American anti-Chinese rhetoric had to be toned down in order to bring about a more rational discourse than had prevailed in fifteen years of discussion largely conducted through the mediation of Poland. Second, trade and visa restrictions needed to be reduced. Third, the number of U.S. troops at bases surrounding China and in Vietnam would be reduced. Finally, Nixon wanted the Communist leaders to know that he would personally consider revising the rigid cold war position of the United States on Taiwan and its heretofore unstinting support of Chiang. These attitude changes and low-level diplomatic actions initially took place without fanfare. Nixon underscored this approach in a memorandum to Kissinger on February 1, 1969, wanting "to give every encouragement to the attitude that this Administration is 'exploring the possibilities of rapprochement with the Chinese.' This should be done privately and under no circumstances get into public prints from this direction." Around the same time, Nixon privately told Senate majority leader Mike Mansfield that he wanted to involve China in "global responsibility." Then, on February 18, 1969, he instructed Secretary of State William Rogers to make a public announcement that the United States now favored a program of cultural and scientific exchanges with the People's Republic. . . .

Peking's slow response was fortunate in that it allowed Kissinger to come up to speed on Nixon's rapprochement policy. In August 1969, Kissinger finally invited Allen S. Whiting, a former State Department specialist on China, to brief him personally about Sino-Soviet border clashes that had occurred in March. Up to this point Kissinger had only generally endorsed Nixon's idea of rapprochement, but did not contribute specifically to it. Whiting convinced Kissinger that the administration had reacted to these military skirmishes much too casually, and that it was inaccurate to think that China would attack Russia. In fact, China so feared a Soviet attack that this was a historic opportunity to change traditional U.S. cold war policy, which had been more "favorably" disposed toward the USSR than toward China. "Belatedly, Kissinger became a convert—a latter-day Marco Polo discovering the new China," according to Marvin and Bernard Kalb, "and he plunged into his subject with all of the eagerness and occasional naiveté of the newcomer to Asia." . . .

The stage was set for a breakthrough in Sino-American relations. An encouraging message from China through Romania at the beginning of 1971 prompted the United States in March and April to terminate all restrictions on American travel to the Chinese mainland and the twenty-year-old embargo on trade. Following the highly publicized Ping-Pong games between Chinese and American teams in April, the Pakistan ambassador to the United States also delivered a message from Chinese Premier Chou En-lai [Zhou Enlai] to Nixon (replying to one from the president on January 5), asking him to send a representative to China for direct discussions. The message noted that "the Chinese government reaffirms its willingness to receive publicly in Peking a special envoy of the President of the United States . . . for direct meetings and discussions."

It has never been made absolutely clear by either Nixon or Kissinger why the contacts after this note had to be conducted in secret. The obvious reasons are that the mission might have failed and that it might have provoked both the Russians and the Japanese—neither of whom knew about the previously secret contacts with the Chinese. Thus secrecy bred secrecy. Additionally, Nixon paid lip service in his memoirs to the realization that there would be conservative opposition to open, direct contacts; Kissinger gives no reason for keeping his mission secret. He does, however, manage to exaggerate both his initial role in the policy and its potential danger: "I felt immense relief [at being chosen as envoy] after so long a preoccupation with its design I would be able to bring the enterprise to fruition. . . . Assisted only by his security adviser, without the alibi provided by normal processes of bureaucratic clearance, [Nixon] authorized a mission that, had it failed, would surely have produced a political catastrophe for him and an international catastrophe for his country." More likely, covert foreign policy operations had simply become so common that Kissinger was the obvious choice as secret envoy, even though others mentioned for the mission were more qualified. Secrecy certainly made Nixon's July 15, 1971, announcement of Kissinger's undercover trip and of his own decision to visit China early in 1972 more dramatic. . . .

Although various government officials denied that Nixon courted China in order to bring pressure to bear on the Soviet Union, the president's triumphant visit to the People's Republic of China in February 1972 (with its attendant joint "Shanghai Communiqué") was clearly part of the Nixinger "triangularization" policy. Moreover, in July 1971 when Nixon announced the visit, there is some indication that possible Sino-American rapprochement made the Soviets more amenable to moving ahead with détente in the fall of 1971. It is often forgotten, however, that the original purpose behind improved relations with both China and the USSR was to bring leverage to bear on both nations to improve the situation for the United States in Vietnam. Like so many other attempts at linkage, this one did not prove successful.

There is no direct evidence that because of Soviet concern over the results of Nixon's trip to China, rapprochement became indirectly linked to the success of negotiations leading to the ten formal summit agreements signed in Moscow between the United States and the USSR in May 1972. . . . They provided for prevention of military incidents at sea and in the air; scholarly cooperation and exchange in the fields of science and technology; cooperation in health research; cooperation in environmental matters; cooperation in the exploration of outer space; facilitation of commercial and economic relations; and, most important, the Anti-Ballistic Missile Treaty, the Interim Agreement on the Limitations on Strategic Arms (SALT I), and the Basic Principles of U.S.-Soviet Relations.

In the area of arms control, Nixinger détente policy contained the potential not only to substitute for containment—the standard way the United States had fought the cold war against the Soviet Union since the late 1940s—but also to transcend the procrustean ideological constraints at the very heart of the post–World War II conflict between these two nations. This potential was never fully realized, in large measure because Nixon and Kissinger chose to give priority to SALT talks over MIRV talks. To a smaller extent it was never realized because, until the collapse of communism in central and eastern Europe and the Soviet Union almost thirty years later, their immediate successors proved unable (or unwilling) to build upon the delicate distinction between containment and détente that they left behind. Also, there was no changed leadership or structural base in the USSR (or the former Soviet bloc countries) to reinforce the concept of détente inside or outside its borders during the last half of the 1970s, as there began to appear at the end of the 1980s. It must be remembered that the Nixon-Brezhnev détente remained essentially tactical because the cold war had not yet significantly begun to recede. Hence, there was no basic change in conflicting cold war strategies under Nixingerism—only a temporary blurring of hostilities that Reagan revived to a fever pitch in the 1980s.

SALT I, conducted in Helsinki in 1969 and Vienna in 1970, led to two arms-control documents at the 1972 Moscow summit—both in keeping with the tactical aspects of Nixon's détente. These included a treaty limiting the deployment of antiballistic missile systems (ABMs) to two for each country, and an agreement freezing the number of offensive intercontinental ballistic missiles (ICBMs) at the level of those then under production or deployed. Unlike SALT I, the ABM Treaty was of "unlimited duration . . . and not open to material unilateral revision," despite attempts by the Reagan administration to do just this beginning in 1985. Until the Strategic Defense Initiative (SDI) efforts in the last half of the 1980s, however, the ABM Treaty essentially succeeded in relegating deployment of conventional ballistic missile defense systems to minor strategic significance.

SALT I, on the other hand, was an agreement of limited, five-year duration that attempted to establish a rough balance or parity between the offensive nuclear arsenals of the two superpowers, despite the "missile gaps" that continued to exist between them in specific weapons. For example, when Nixon signed SALT I, the United States had a total of 1,710 missiles: 1,054 land-based ICBMs and 656 on submarines (sub-launched ballistic missiles, or SLBMs). The USSR had a total of 2,358 missiles: 1,618 landbased ICBMs and 740 SLBMs. SALT I not only recognized the strategic parity of the USSR but gave it a numerical edge in missiles and a slight throw-weight [a measurement of rocket thrust] advantage. The United States retained a numerical advantage in warheads and a superiority in strategic bombers— 460 in 1972 to 120 for the Soviets. SALT I by no means stopped the nuclear arms race, but it recognized that unregulated weapons competition between the two superpowers could no longer be rationally condoned. By freezing further missile buildup, SALT I meant that by the time SALT II was signed in 1979, total American-Soviet missile strength remained essentially unchanged: 2,283 to 2,504, respectively. From 1972 until the mid-1980s, therefore, SALT talks were regarded as a barometer of relations between the two countries, contrary to the claims of critics, even though the "MIRVing" engaged in by both sides has tended to obscure their generally parallel buildup since 1972. . . .

Nixon and Kissinger returned from the May 1972 Moscow summit meeting triumphant, but more vulnerable than ever on three fronts: military, economic, and moral and ideological. All three boded ill for the SALT II talks that would begin six months later. Critics immediately asserted that the United States had been "hoodwinked" by the Soviet Union into a disadvantageous military deal with respect to SLBMs. With Helsinki CSCE [Conference on Security and Cooperation in Europe, a comprehensive political conference pursued by European advocates of détente] agreements still three years away and no mutual and balanced force reductions [(MBFR), on conventional forces in Europe] in sight, as negotiations over SALT II dragged on into the 1970s, an additional military criticism became that the Soviets were violating the terms of both the ABM and SALT I agreements. . . . Moral criticism of Nixingerism based on ideological hostility to the USSR became more credible in the wake of Watergate, but had always been strong in the minds of particular Republican and Democratic conservatives in Congress and across the country. It was this criticism that Nixon and Kissinger found the hardest to answer, because their approach to détente had not, in fact, been based on moral or ideological considerations, but on very pragmatic ones. . . .

Beginning in 1972 certain members of Congress insisted that in return for most-favored-nation treatment (MFN), the Soviet Union should liberalize emigration policies affecting Jews. As late as March 1974, Kissinger referred to "domestic obstacles, some of a highly irresponsible nature," after Brezhnev brought up [Democratic] Senator "Scoop" Jackson's opposition to granting MFN status to the USSR. When Brezhnev said that Jackson was linking "something [the question of Jewish migration] that bears no relation to this entire matter [MFN]," Kissinger agreed, saying: "We don't consider this a proper subject of inquiry by the United States Government." The general secretary's fears, which he had expressed the previous year to [Treasury Secretary] George Shultz, proved more realistic than the secretary of state's optimism on this question.

Once again, as on NATO troop reductions and arms control, Senator Jackson orchestrated a Senate amendment to counter the Soviet-American trade agreement. After two and a half years of haggling over various versions of the Jackson-Vanik amendment, which was extended in 1974 to include a ceiling on loans to the Soviet Union from the Export-Import Bank, [President Gerald R.] Ford signed the Trade Reform Bill with the amendment on January 3, 1975, and the Soviet government officially refused to comply with it on January 10. Later that month the president withdrew his support for the MFN treatment of the USSR because of Soviet intervention into the Angolan civil war. Thus ended the move toward liberalizing trade with the Communist world (at least as represented by the Soviet Union) in the name of détente that had begun so optimistically under the Nixon administration with the passage of the Export Administration Act of 1969, liberalizing export controls.

In the interim, the October 1973 war in the Middle East not only misleadingly contributed to the popular impression in the United States that détente was not working with the Soviet Union; it also exacerbated all the underlyng differences between the European and American conceptions of détente—placing even more strain on the Atlantic Alliance. . . .

In July 1975, with American-Soviet trade relations temporarily on hold and NATO allies restive over having been bypassed at the Moscow summit and uncertain over how the United States would respond to talk of increasing Soviet military strength, the long-awaited Conference on Security and Cooperation in Europe began. The declaration of ten principles signed by thirty-five nations at Helsinki on August 1 was important to the United States and the Soviet Union for different reasons. Consequently, they differed over how best to implement the Final Act of the CSCE because they each emphasized different sections of it. This had not been the case in 1974 when Kissinger and [Soviet foreign minister Andrei] Gromyko frankly agreed to thwart the "impossible proposals" for "military détente" being put forward by the Western allies of the United States at CSCE and MBFR meetings. The Soviet Union, for example, opposed supplying . . . information about troop maneuvers. "I have told you we will not support this proposal," Kissinger assured Gromyko with Brezhnev listening, adding, "we can weaken these proposals substantially." Kissinger even assured the Soviet foreign minister and secretary general in this 1974 meeting that the United States would "use its influence not to embarrass the Soviet Union or raise provocative issues" with respect to Basket III, which called for humanitarian and cultural cooperation, including the freer movement of people, which the Soviets opposed.

By the time President Ford traveled to Helsinki to sign the CSCE agreements before the election of 1976, Basket III had been not only included in them but "linked" to further East-West economic cooperation at the insistence of Western Europe. Significantly, Ford's political opponents within the Republican party, such as Ronald Reagan and members of his own staff, implied in press statements that the Helsinki Accords represented "another Kissinger deal that was forced down the President's throat." They simply didn't understand how much these agreements differed from the promises Kissinger had made to Gromyko in 1974. Gone were the halcyon days of détente under the Nixon administration. . . .

The U.S. government, especially under President Carter, stressed the human rights provision of the CSCE and used it as a standard by which to measure the treatment of citizens in foreign countries, including the USSR and its satellite nations. This principle became a bone of contention between the United States and the Soviet Union in ways not anticipated by the Nixon administration. Moscow, on the other hand, logically preferred to focus on those segments of the Final Act that granted implied recognition of Soviet hegemony in eastern Europe. A major legacy of Nixinger foreign policy from 1975 until the disintegration of the Soviet Union has been manifested by agreement to disagree over the importance of the Helsinki Accords. Little wonder that Nixon's successors (including Ford) quickly retreated from a defense of Nixon's brand of détente to the point of dropping the use of the word. Yet, in light of the fall of communism, it deserved more credit than it received before Nixon's death. Détente was more than "deals with Moscow in return for no demonstrable Soviet restraint," as some commentators in the early 1990s asserted.

Why Détente Failed

RAYMOND L. GARTHOFF

Foremost among the causes of the ultimate failure of détente in the 1970s was a fatal difference in the conception of its basic role by the two sides. The American leaders saw it (in [Henry] Kissinger's words) as a way of "managing the emergence of Soviet power" into world politics in an age of nuclear parity. The Soviet leaders envisaged it as a way of managing the transition of the United States from its former superiority to a more modest role in world politics in an age of nuclear parity. Thus each saw itself as the manager of a transition of the other. Moreover, while the advent of parity ineluctably meant some decrease in the ability of the United States to manage world affairs, this fact was not sufficiently appreciated in Washington. And while it meant a relatively more important role for the Soviet Union, it did not mean acquisition of the kind of power the United States wielded. Finally, both had diverging images of the world order, and although that fact was well enough understood, its implications were not. Thus, underlying the attempts by each of the two powers to manage the adjustment of the other to a changing correlation of forces in the world there were even more basic parallel attempts by both to modify the fundamental world order— in different directions.

The Soviet leaders, conditioned by their Marxist-Leninist ideology, believed that a certain historical movement would ultimately lead to the replacement of cap- italism (imperialism) in the world by socialism (communism). But they realized this transition would have to occur in a world made incalculably more dangerous by massive arsenals of nuclear weapons. Peaceful coexistence and détente were seen as offering a path to neutralize this danger by ruling out war between states, permitting historical change to occur, as the Soviets believed it must, through fun- damental indigenous social-economic-political processes within states. While Marxist-Leninists did not shun the use of any other instrument of power if it was expedient, they did not see military power as the fundamental moving force of his- tory. On the contrary, they saw it as a possible ultimate recourse of the doomed capitalist class ruling the imperialist citadels of the West. There was, therefore, no ideological barrier to or reservation about pursuing a policy of détente aimed at preventing nuclear war. Quite the contrary—détente represented a policy aimed at providing stability to a world order that allowed progressive historical change.

The American leadership and the American people, not holding a deterministic ideology, while self-confident, were much less sure of the trend of history. Insofar as they held an ideology for a global order, it was one of pluralism. That ideology did not assume the whole world would choose an American-style democratic and free enterprise system. The world order has been seen as one that should provide stability and at least protect the democratic option for peoples. Occasionally during the Cold War there were crusades to extirpate communism in the world. . . . But the dominant American aim was to contain and deter Soviet or Soviet-controlled communist ex- pansion at the expense of a pluralistic and, in that sense, "free" world order. What varied and periodically was at issue was the relative weight to be placed, on the one hand, on containment achieved by building positions of counterposing power, and on the other, on cooperation, pursued by seeking common ground for mutual efforts to reduce tension and accommodate the differing interests of the two sides. There were varied judgments in both countries about whether objective circumstances permit the latter approach or require the former, and therefore about whether détente was feasible or confrontation was necessary.

When [Richard] Nixon and Kissinger developed a strategy of détente to replace a strategy of confrontation, the underlying expectation was that as the Soviet Union became more and more extensively engaged in an organic network of relations with the existing world order, it would gradually become reconciled to that order. Ideo- logical expectations of global revolutionary change would become attenuated and merely philosophical rather than actively political. Avoidance of the risks of nuclear war was essential; hence there was acceptance of peaceful coexistence and of efforts at strategic arms limitations and other negotiations to reduce the risks.

The common American and Soviet recognition of the need to avert war was . . . of fundamental significance. But there remained radically different visions of the course world history would follow and, therefore, of the pattern of world politics. This divergence in their worldviews naturally affected the policies of the two powers. The difference was well-known in a general way; its implications for the two superpowers' respective actions, and therefore for their mutual relations and for détente, were not, however, sufficiently understood. And this gap led to unrealistic expectations that were not met and that undermined confidence in détente. . . .

The United States did not analyze critically the underlying postulates of either American or Soviet conceptions—nor, indeed, could that be done before they were more clearly articulated. For example, consider the proposition held by the Soviet leaders until 1986 that "the class struggle" and "national liberation struggle" were not and could not be affected by détente. With the exception of a minuscule minority that accepted the Soviet line uncritically, almost all Americans saw that proposition as communist mumbo jumbo being used as a transparently self-serving argument to excuse pursuit of Soviet interests. In fact, Soviet leaders considered that proposition to be a self-evident truth: détente was a policy, while the class struggle was an objective phenomenon in the historical process that could not be abolished by policy decision, even if the Soviet leaders wanted to do so. While there *was* a self-serving dimension to the Soviet proposition, it was not cynical artifice. To the contrary, it was sincerely believed. On a logical plane, to whatever extent the Soviet premise was true, it was crystal clear that any inevitable historical process could not be stopped by any state's policy or agreement between the two states.

It was not necessary to assume a prior meeting of the minds of the leaders of the two powers on ideological conceptions as a prerequisite to agreements based on calculated mutual advantage. While ideological conditioning and belief did influence policy, they did not determine it. Questions about the historical process can and should be left to history. The critical question was not whether there was a global class struggle or national liberation struggle, as defined by Marxism-Leninism, but what the Soviet leadership was going to do about it. While the Soviet leadership accepted a moral commitment to aid the world revolutionary process, it was also ideologically obliged to do so only in ways that did not weaken or risk the attainments of socialism in the USSR. Moreover, the ideology also held that world revolutionary processes were indigenous. Revolution could not be exported. Neither could counterrevolution. But both could be aided by external forces. . . .

In approaching the question of what was a proper and consistent code of conduct with respect to Soviet—and American—behavior in the third world, each side needed to understand the perspective of the other. Each, naturally, retained its own view of the historical process, as well as its own national interests. Differences of concrete interests remained to be reconciled, but failure to understand each other's viewpoint seriously compounded the problem.

A second cause of the collapse of détente was the failure to turn to greater use of collaborative measures to meet the requirements of security. National military power was bound to remain a foundation of national security in the foreseeable future. But it did not need to be the first, or usual, or sole, recourse. The American-Soviet détente involved efforts to prevent and to manage crises, and to regulate the military balance through arms control and arms limitation. In the final analysis, however, those efforts—while useful and potentially significant—were almost entirely dependent on the political relationship, and in large measure withered with it.

The effort to achieve strategic arms limitations marked the first, and the most daring, attempt to follow a collaborative approach in meeting military security requirements. It involved an unprecedented joint consideration of ways to control the most vital (or fatal) element of national power—the arsenals of strategic nuclear weaponry. Early successes held great promise—but also showed the limits of readiness of both superpowers to take this path. SALT [Strategic Arms Limitation Talks] generated problems of its own and provided a focal point for objection by those who did not wish to see either regulated military parity or political détente. The final lesson of the failure to ratify SALT II was that arms control could not stand alone nor sustain a political détente that did not support itself. Indeed, even the early successes of SALT I, which contributed to an upsurge of détente and were worthwhile on their own merits, became a bone of contention as détente came under fire.

The widely held American view that SALT tried to do too much was a misjudgment: the *real* flaw was the failure of SALT to do enough. There were remarkable initial successes in the agreement on parity as an objective and on stability of the strategic arms relationship as a necessary condition, and the control imposed on strategic defensive competition in ABM [Anti-Ballistic Missile] systems. But there was insufficient political will (and perhaps political authority) to bite the bullet and ban or sharply limit MIRVs [Multiple Independently-targetable Reentry Vehicles]— the key to controlling the strategic offensive arms race. Both sides share the blame for this failure, but especially the United States because it led a new round of the arms competition when it could safely have held back (in view of the ABM Treaty) long enough to make a real effort to ban MIRVs. The failure to control MIRVs was ultimately the key to the essential failure in the 1970s to stabilize the military dimension of parity, and it contributed indirectly to the overall fall of détente.

Too little attention has been paid to the efforts in the 1970s to devise a regime of crisis management and crisis avoidance. Paradoxically, the relatively more successful steps in this direction are rarely remembered because they do not seize attention as do political frictions. The agreements of 1971 on averting war by accident or miscalculation and on upgrading the hot line, the agreement of 1972 on avoiding incidents at sea between the U.S. and Soviet navies, and the agreement of 1973 on prevention of nuclear war played a positive role. (In addition, so did multilateral confidence-building measures in the European security framework.) The one instance sometimes charged to have been a failure of collaboration was in fact, if anything, a success: the defusing of the pseudocrisis between the two superpowers in October 1973 at the climax of the fourth Arab-Israeli war.

A third cause of the failure of American-Soviet détente in the 1970s was the inability of the superpowers to transform the recognition of strategic parity into a common political standard to govern their competitive actions in the world. The divergent conceptions of détente and of the world order underlay this failure, but these were compounded by other factors. One was the unreadiness of the United States, in conceding nominal strategic parity, also to concede political parity. Another was a reciprocated hubris in which each superpower applied a one-sided double standard in perceiving, and judging, the behavior of the other. The basic principles of mutual relations and a code of conduct were never thrashed out with the necessary frank discussion of differing views, a failure that gave rise to a facade of agreement that not only affected public, but to some extent even leadership, expectations. Expectations based on wishful thinking about the effects of the historical process, or based on overconfidence about a country's managerial abilities to discipline the behavior of the other side, were doomed to failure. Paradoxically, these inflated expectations coexisted—on both sides—with underlying excessive and projected fears and imputations of aggressive hostility, which resurfaced when the expectations were not met. That this process influenced wider political constituencies (a much wider body politic in the United States) only compounded a situation that affected the leadership as well. . . .

In the United States, many in the 1970s saw a cumulative series of Soviet interventions, involving military means, often with proxies—Angola, Ethiopia, Kampuchea, Afghanistan—that they believed formed a pattern of Soviet expansion and aggrandizement inconsistent with the Basic Principles [a May 1972 Soviet-American agreement to practice restraint in their relations] and détente. Moreover, many believed that these expansionist moves were encouraged by détente, or were at least induced by a weakness of U.S. will and military power. Hence the need to rebuild that power and reassert that will; hence the heightened suspicion of détente.

In fact, the history of diplomatic, political, and interventionist activity during the last decade [1970s] is much more extensive and complex—and much less one-sided. Certainly from the Soviet perspective, not only was the Soviet role more limited and more justified than the United States would concede, but the American role was more active and less benign. . . .

In the Middle East, the United States arranged the defection of Sadat's Egypt—and of the Sudan, Somalia, and to some degree Iraq. It effectively squeezed the Soviet Union out of a role in the Middle East peace process, despite repeated assurances that it would not do so. . . . In Africa, U.S. allies and proxies repeatedly and blatantly intervened with military force—Portugal before 1974; France in numerous cases; France, Belgium, Morocco, and Egypt in Zaire; Zaire, South Africa and others in Angola in 1975–76, albeit unsuccessfully; and so forth. Using covert operations, the United States assisted in the overthrow of an elected Marxist, [Salvador] Allende, in Chile and, with European assistance, of the Marxist-supported [Arelino] Gonçalves in Portugal. . . .

There were . . . also conscious policies of assertive competition by both powers throughout the period of nominal détente. Recall, for example, the U.S. policy initiatives in the immediate aftermath of the first summit meeting in Moscow in 1972, the summit that launched détente. President Nixon flew directly from the Soviet Union to Iran. One purpose of his visit was to establish the shah [of Iran] as, in effect, American proconsul in the region, in keeping with the Nixon Doctrine. The shah was promised virtually any American arms he wanted. A contributory reason for the shah's deputation that was not apparent was to follow through on some conversations with the Chinese and to signal to them U.S. intention to build regional positions of strength around the Soviet Union, détente notwithstanding. In addition, while in Tehran the president accepted the shah's proposal covertly to arm the Iraqi Kurds. (Iraq had just signed a Treaty of Friendship with the Soviet Union.) Thus the Kurds became proxies of the United States and Iran (and of Israel, which joined in providing support in order to tie the Iraqi army down). And there was a later chapter to this American initiative: the shah persuaded and induced President Mohammad Daoud of Afghanistan in 1975–78 to move away from his previous close alignment with the Soviet Union, to improve relations with Pakistan, and to crack down on Afghan leftists. . . . That led the [pro-Soviet] Khalq military faction to mount a coup and depose him, turning the government over to the People's Democratic Party and setting in train the developments within Afghanistan that culminated in the Soviet intervention.

From Iran President Nixon flew to Poland, where he was greeted by stirring public acclaim, demonstratively showing not only that the United States would support more or less nonaligned communist regimes (Nixon had visited Romania in 1969 and Yugoslavia in 1970, as well as China in 1972), but also that no part of the Soviet alliance was out of bounds to American interest under détente.

As a direct result of the U.S. handling of the Middle East question at the détente summit meeting, [Anwar el-]Sadat [president of Egypt]—who was already secretly in touch with the United States—six weeks later expelled the 20,000 Soviet military advisers (and Soviet reconnaissance aircraft) from Egypt.

Only a few months later, in September 1972, China and Japan—with American encouragement—renewed diplomatic relations. And in December new armed clashes occurred on the Sino-Soviet border.

Further, upon President Nixon's return to Washington from the summit he urged not only ratification of the SALT I agreements, but also an increase in strategic arms. Secretary of Defense [Melvin R.] Laird even conditioned his support for SALT on congressional approval of new military programs, which he justified as necessary so as to be able to negotiate "from a position of strength," wittingly or not invoking a key symbol of the Cold War.

It is not the purpose of this brief recapitulation of some examples of vigorous American competitive activity to argue either that the *Soviet* perception of American responsibility for the decline and fall of détente is justified, or that the United States was wrong to compete with the Soviet Union (individual actions were wise or unwise on their merits, and good or bad in their consequences—as is true of various Soviet actions). But Americans need to recognize that not only the Soviet Union but also the United States was "waging détente" in the 1970s—and that it was not justified in concluding that the Soviet Union was violating some agreed, clear, and impartial standard to which the United States in practice adhered. This same point about the application of a double standard equally needed to be recognized in the Soviet Union, and equally was not. . . .

Both the United States and the Soviet Union acted in ways contrary to the spirit and letter of a code of conduct for détente as set forth in the Basic Principles to which both had committed themselves in 1972. Each saw its own actions as compatible with pursuit of a *realistic* policy of détente. Each, however, sought to hold the other side to its own *idealized* view of détente. As a result, each was disappointed in and critical of the actions of the other. The Soviet leaders, however, adjusted their expectations more realistically, seeing no better alternative than to continue an imperfect détente. This was the Soviet judgment even though the United States was seen as taking advantage of détente in the continuing competition, and even though détente proved less of a restraint on the United States than the Soviets had hoped and expected. . . .

Many developments during the period under review bear witness to the importance of evaluating correctly the intentions, and not merely the capabilities or ambitions, of the other power. . . . If one side is in fact motivated by an expansionist impulse, then a forceful advance stand in opposition or retaliatory response *is* called for and can sometimes be effective. If, however, the action—no matter how reprehensible and forcible—is motivated by fear of a threat or loss, a vigorous show of strength and threats of counteraction may in fact *contribute* to the perceived threat and hence to the very moves that the other side wants to deter. By contrast, measures to allay the unfounded fears might have been a more effective course. It thus becomes highly important to assess, and assess correctly, the intentions and motivations of the other side.

The importance of assessment is that it not only applies to a specific situation, but also affects the lessons drawn from that experience. The easy conclusion often reached about Soviet moves adverse to American interests (especially by critics but sometimes also by incumbent administrations) was to question whether the United States possessed sufficient strength and had demonstrated clearly enough its readiness to use it. Sometimes that may have been the relevant question. But the record strongly suggests that more often it was not American strength and resolve that Soviet leaders have doubted, but American restraint and recognition of Soviet interests. . . .

Both powers also were reluctant to acknowledge, even to recognize, failures of their own political systems. Instead, they were only too ready to project responsibility onto the other side. Thus, for example, Soviet claims of American responsibility for internal opposition in Afghanistan and Poland served (among other purposes) as an alibi for failures of Soviet-style socialism. American charges of Cuban and Soviet responsibility for revolution in Central America were similarly more convenient than acknowledging failures of reactionary regimes to provide for needed peaceful change. In addition to reflecting genuine fears based on perceived vulnerabilities, it was simply easier to project hostile intervention than to admit failures to facilitate or permit peaceful change within respective areas of predominant influence.

Thus, apart from differing conceptions of détente, there were very important differences in perceptions not only of the motivations of the other side, but of the very reality of world politics. Détente should have been recognized as one complex *basis* for a competitive relationship, not as an alternative to competition. That was the reality, and the fact should have been recognized.

During much of the 1970s American perceptions of what was occurring in the world failed to reflect reality. One example was the failure of the United States to see that it was waging a vigorous competition along with the Soviet Union. And the U.S. leadership to varying degrees was more aware of the realities than the public. . . . But even the practitioners of hardheaded détente often failed to recognize the whole reality. Political critics also either did not see, or did not wish to acknowledge, reality. The desire to sustain public support for policy by using a myth of détente (and of conformity with idealistic goals) also inhibited public awareness that the United States was competing as much as the Soviet Union. The result was a shift of public opinion as détente *seemed* not to be safeguarding and serving American interests. Ronald Reagan's challenge to President [Gerald] Ford in 1976 marked the first significant political manifestation of this shift. Although the challenge did not succeed, it did lead Ford to shelve SALT and to jettison the very word détente. By 1980 this shift contributed (along with domestic economic and other concerns, and President [Jimmy] Carter's ineptness and plain bad luck) to Reagan's victory and open American renunciation of détente.

Naiveté was charged to the advocates of détente. But while some may have had unrealistic aims and expectations, the American leaders and practitioners of détente ... were not as naive as were the critics and challengers who preferred to remain blind both to the strength and vigor of U.S. global competition and to the limits on Soviet power and policy. The critics of détente saw both American and Soviet power and its exercise from opposite ends of a telescope—a greatly exaggerated image of relentless Soviet buildup and use of power in a single-minded offensive expansionist policy, and a grossly distorted image of U.S. passivity and impotence in the world.

This U.S. perspective contributed to American-European differences and frictions. The European powers (and most other countries in the world as well) had a much more balanced perception. Although they still exaggerated the Soviet threat, at least they recognized more accurately the active American role in competition—often they were concerned over what they saw as excessive competition. For the Europeans had (and have) a very different view of the cooperative element in détente, valuing more highly than most Americans the potential for economic, political, social, and arms control gains and the realities of cooperation under détente. . . . Even as such key European countries as Britain and West Germany turned to conservative governments in the early 1980s, support for East-West détente (and criticism of American confrontational policies, for example, in the Caribbean basin) continued, to the perplexity, dismay and sometimes anger of leaders in Washington. . . .

A fourth cause of the decline in confidence in détente in the 1970s was the view widely held on both sides that the other side was acquiring military capabilities in excess of what it needed for deterrence and defense, and therefore was not adhering to détente. This is a complex question. For example, the limits under SALT reduced some previously important areas of concern and uncertainties in projecting the military balance—notably with respect to ABMs. But another effect was that the rather complex *real* strategic balance was artificially simplified in the general understanding (and not just of the general public) to certain highlighted indexes, thereby increasing sensitivity to a symbolic arithmetical "balance." And national means of intelligence, which were given high credibility when it came to identifying a threat, were regarded with a more jaundiced eye when called upon to monitor and verify compliance with an arms limitation agreement.

In any event, during the latter half of the 1970s concern mounted in the United States over why the Soviet Union was engaged in what has been termed a relentless continuing arms buildup. At the same time U.S. military programs were justified as meeting that buildup. In turn the Soviet Union saw the American buildup as designed to restore the United States to a position of superiority.

Throughout the preceding two decades of Cold War and cold peace, the United States had maintained a clear strategic nuclear superiority. As the Soviet Union continued to build its strategic forces, despite earlier agreed strategic arms limitations, new fears and suspicions arose in the United States. Unfortunately, the actual consolidation of parity in the latter 1970s was not in synchronization with the political acceptance and public impression of parity in the early 1970s. What the Soviets saw as finally closing the gap through programs of weapons deployment, which they saw as fully consonant both with the terms of the SALT agreement and with achievement of parity, many in the United States saw as a Soviet pursuit of advantages that violated at least the spirit, if not the letter, of SALT and that threatened to go beyond parity to superiority. The real inconsistency was between the continuing Soviet deployments and the American public's *expectation* derived from SALT. The interim freeze of 1972 had set a level with respect to the deployment of forces, including some construction under way that had not yet been completed by the Soviet Union. In addition, it had limited only the level of strategic missile launchers, not of warheads, and the Soviets, who were behind in terms of arming their strategic missile force with MIRVs, sought to catch up in the years following. If the Soviet strategic deployments had occurred more nearly at the time of American deployment, and both countries had agreed to accept parity and stop at the same time (and not merely at the same level), the public perception would have been quite different.

While a desire to influence public opinion played a part in inflating presentations of the military threat posed by the other side, there were real buildups on both sides. In part, then, perceptions on both sides of a hostile arms buildup were genuine. But both sides were unduly alarmist in exaggerating the military capabilities—and imputed intentions—of the other. . . .

In addition to major gaps in mutual understanding of such key elements of détente as behavior in international politics and in managing the arms race, a fifth cause of the decline of détente was a failure to understand its crucial relationship to the internal politics of the two countries. In part this failure was reflected in errors, in particular by the Soviet Union, in comprehending the domestic political processes and dynamics of the other country. There was also some failure by political leaders, especially in the United States, to gauge the degree of their own authority. The Soviet leaders also put too much trust in the ability of an American president to carry out policy. This situation was true in the whole matter of normalization of trade and repeatedly with SALT II from 1975 to 1980. While Nixon, Kissinger, and Ford were careful to relate linkages to foreign policy issues, Congress attempted to make its own linkages with Soviet internal affairs. It failed in the effort, creating in the process new issues in U.S.-Soviet relations and reducing support for détente in the United States. The Soviet leaders also had difficulty understanding the sudden changes and discontinuities between (and occasionally within) administrations. On the other hand, American leaders, especially Presidents Carter and Reagan, . . . had little understanding of the Soviet political leadership or of Soviet political processes. President Carter was especially insensitive to the necessary limits on détente as a medium for influencing the internal political affairs of the Soviet Union.

Leaders on both sides, especially the Soviet leaders, frequently and seriously underestimated the impact of their own actions on the perceptions and policy of the other side, and the extent to which the actions of one side have been responses to real or perceived challenges. And again, Soviet secrecy, and self-serving justifications on both sides, compounded this problem.

Finally, the failure in the United States to sustain a political consensus in support of détente also ranked as a major cause of its collapse. This conclusion is particularly clear when the role of domestic political factors in the United States in torpedoing the attempt at détente is considered. Most blatant, but far from unique, was the attempt to tie trade, and thus the whole economic dimension of détente, to what amounted to interference in the internal affairs of the Soviet Union. The approach was all the more tragic but no less lethal because of the high moral motivations of many of the supporters of the effort. In this respect, the Soviet leaders were more successful in the less difficult, though not easy, task of maintaining a consensus in their quite different political process.

One reason for the disintegration of the consensus in favor of détente in the United States was the failure of the leadership to explain its limits as well as its promises to the public. To the extent that the leaders themselves failed to gauge the differences in conceptions about détente and were prisoners of their own view of the world order, they could not make this limitation clear to others. But Nixon and Kissinger did understand very well at least that there was a continuing active competition—not only in the Soviet conception, but in their own policy—a competition that was, however, masked by too much talk about a new structure of peace. When the expectations of the public, aroused by the hyperbole about the benefits of peace and détente, were not met, disillusion set in—and so did a natural temptation to blame the other side. This reaction against détente, based on disillusionment (in the pure meaning of the term), was thus in part engendered by both Nixon's and Kissinger's overestimation of their ability to manipulate and manage both international and national affairs. It should also be noted that the public (including the broader congressional and active political constituencies) has been little aware of or prepared to understand the subtleties of international politics, or even the basic idea of a political relationship of mixed cooperation and competition with the Soviet Union. In addition, the political process in the United States not only does not provide a tradition of continuity or cushion against sudden changes in foreign policy, but invites domestic political exploitation of apparent and actual adversities in the course of international relations.

The decade of détente in American-Soviet relations was in fact one of mixed confrontation and détente, of competition and cooperation, with a remarkable if ill-starred attempt to build—too rapidly—a structure for peaceful coexistence between powerful adversaries.

Kissinger's Realism Without Morality

WALTER ISAACSON

"Americans," he [Henry A. Kissinger] once wrote, "are comfortable with an idealistic tradition that espouses great causes, such as making the world safe for democracy, or human rights." But it was not in the country's nature, he often lamented, to sit still for the unedifying work of tending to imperfect alliances or the never-ending meddling necessary to maintain a balance of power. The U.S. has historically been, in [the political scientist] Stanley Hoffmann's words "traditionally hostile to balance of power diplomacy with its closets of partitions, compensations, secret treaties and gunboats."

To Kissinger, this excessive aversion to secret treaties and gunboats, and to all the other trappings of realpolitik and balance-of-power diplomacy, stemmed from the simple, often simplistic, naiveté and decency of most Americans. With a jarring use of the first-person plural that belies the fact that the descriptions scarcely apply to him, Kissinger once wrote that "our native inclination for straightforwardness, our instinct for open, noisy politics, our distrust of European manners and continental elites, all brought about an increasing impatience with the stylized methods of European diplomacy and with its tendency toward ambiguous compromise."

This idealistic streak in the American character, this desire to seek moral perfection rather than messy accommodations, was what caused the nation to lurch over the years between isolationism and interventionism, to embark on crusades (World War I, Vietnam), and then to recoil into self-righteous withdrawal. "Emotional slogans, unleavened by a concept of the national interest, had caused us to oscillate between excesses of isolation and overextension," Kissinger wrote. The way to moderate these pendulum swings, he said, was "by making judgments according to some more permanent conception of national interest."

One key component of Kissinger's brand of realism was his special emphasis on the role of military might. "Throughout history," he once wrote, "the influence of nations has been roughly correlative to their military power." This view led him to favor great displays and pretenses of power: bombings, incursions, aircraft carriers steaming toward trouble spots, nuclear alerts.

Even from a realist perspective, this emphasis on military power was subject to criticism. Other sophisticated realists, such as George Kennan and Hans Morgenthau, emphasized that economic vitality and political stability are equally important elements of national power. Kissinger's best diplomacy came in China, the Middle East, and later Africa, where the direct threat of American force played little role; his greatest failures came in Vietnam, Cambodia, and Pakistan, where displays of force abounded. There was also a political constraint: the brutal and cold application of force was incompatible with America's self-conception and what its citizenry in the 1970s was willing to countenance.

Another component of Kissinger's realism was the stress he put on the role that "credibility" played in determining a nation's influence and power. An emphasis on credibility is why realism in foreign policy is not always the same thing as pragmatism. In dealing with Vietnam, for example, a pragmatist would have come more quickly to the conclusion that the war was simply not worth the effort, that the costs were greater than any potential benefits. Realists such as Kissinger, however, emphasized that America could not abandon its commitments or else it would undermine its influence elsewhere in the world.

From his *Foreign Affairs* piece [on Vietnam negotiations] in 1968, to his analysis of Vietnam options in 1969, to his arguments in early 1975 as Saigon was falling, Kissinger put enormous weight on the credibility argument. The problem with an emphasis on credibility is that it can—and in the case of Vietnam did—result in an inability to discriminate between vital interests and ones that are merely peripheral.

A third aspect of Kissinger's realism was his lack of concern about supporting democratic forces and human rights movements in authoritarian countries. He was more comfortable dealing with strong rulers—Brezhnev, Zhou Enlai, the shah of

Iran, [Syrian leader Hafez] Assad, and [Egyptian president Anwar el-]Sadat—than with the messy democracies in Europe and Israel.

In office and after, he opposed the crusades of moral activists who wanted the U.S. to push for domestic reforms in the Soviet Union, China, Pakistan, and the shah's Iran. "Why is it our business how they govern themselves?" an annoyed Kissinger asked at a meeting in 1971 when State Department bureaucrats were recommending pressure on Pakistan. This attitude was later reflected when Kissinger refused to join in the criticism of China after the 1989 crackdown in Tiananmen Square.

Though complex, even ingenious, in its design, Kissinger's realism began with a simple premise: any event should be judged foremost by whether it represented a gain for the Soviets or for the West in the overall global balance. That was the basis of his credibility argument in Vietnam: the war would show the rest of the world whether Washington had the will to stand up to Soviet expansion elsewhere. He embarked on the Middle East peace process partly as a way to undermine Soviet influence there. In the India-Pakistan war, the U.S. became involved on the losing side partly because Kissinger insisted on viewing the regional war as a proxy struggle between a Soviet and an American client.

This tendency to see global disputes through an East-West prism provided his foreign policy with a coherent framework, but it could also be distorting, as he later admitted. "We must outgrow the notion that every setback is a Soviet gain or every problem is caused by Soviet action," he said in May 1975, after setbacks in Vietnam, Cambodia, Portugal, and the Middle East put him on the defensive about his policy of détente with the Soviets. Yet the "we" in his speech fit snugly, for he had spent six years pushing that notion. . . .

At an emotional press conference in Salzburg in 1974, when he brooded about resigning because of stories about the wiretaps [of aides], Kissinger became unusually maudlin. He had been identified, he said, as someone who cared more about stabilizing the balance of power than about moral issues. "I would rather like to think," he added, "that when the record is written, one may remember that perhaps some lives were saved and perhaps some mothers can rest more at ease. But I leave that to history."

This historical judgment is unlikely ever to be a simple one. The structure of peace that Kissinger designed places him with Henry Stimson, George Marshall, and Dean Acheson atop the pantheon of modern American statesmen. In addition, he was the foremost American negotiator of this century and, along with George Kennan, the most influential foreign policy intellectual.

But Kissinger never had an instinctive feel for American values and mores, such as the emphasis that a Stimson would place on honor over intrigue or on idealism over national interests. Nor did he have an appreciation of the strengths to be derived from the healthy raucousness of American politics or from open decision-making in a democratic society. "Henry is a balance-of-power thinker," said Lawrence Eagleburger, one of his closest colleagues. "He deeply believes in stability. These kind[s] of objectives are antithetical to the American experience. Americans tend to want to pursue a set of moral principles. Henry does not have an intrinsic feel for the American political system, and he does not start with the same basic values and assumptions."

Kissinger came to power at a perilous moment for the foreign policy of his adoptive nation. America's isolationist reflexes were twitching as a result of its ill-conceived involvement in Vietnam. Congress and the public were in no mood to pay for new weapons or to engage the Soviets in marginal confrontations in the third world.

By ushering in an era of détente, Kissinger helped to assure that the competition with the Soviets would be more manageable and the showdowns less dangerous. And by devising a web of linkages, he provided the U.S. with some diplomatic leverage to compensate for its loss of military resolve. Looking back twenty years later, he could claim with some justification that "we perhaps deserve some credit for holding together the sinews of America at a time of fundamental collapse."

Some of the initiatives that he pursued along the way were enlightened and imaginative, others impulsively brutal and blunt. Some were clever, others too clever by half. As the only European-style realist ever to guide U.S. foreign policy, a power practitioner unencumbered by the sentimental idealism that suffuses American history, he seemed painfully amoral at times. But he was able to take a clear-eyed approach to the creation of a new global balance, one that helped to preserve American influence in the post-Vietnam era and eventually contributed to the end of the cold war.

Although he was too likely to see a Moscow-inspired threat in every regional crisis, Kissinger was correct in resisting the dovish and isolationist forces of the period that sought to abandon the competition with the Soviets. And he was equally correct in resisting the hawkish and neoconservative pressure to abandon cooperation with the Soviets. As Kennan had pointed out in the late 1940s—and Kissinger had reiterated in the early 1970s—the rulers in the Kremlin could prop up their system only by expanding their empire or by invoking foreign threats. If denied these opportunities, the Soviet system would eventually disintegrate, as it did.

In addition, Kissinger and Nixon turned the world's bipolar tug-of-war into a three-dimensional chess game that provided the U.S. with more opportunities for creative diplomacy. The new relationship with China, which previous presidents had barely contemplated, gave both of the world's communist giants an incentive to maintain better relations with the U.S. than they had with one another.

It added up to a fundamental change in America's postwar foreign policy: for the first time since the Potsdam Conference of 1945, cooperation as well as competition with both Moscow and Beijing could be part of a great-power strategy of balance. That alone was a triumph of hard-edged realism worthy of a Metternich [the nineteenth-century Austrian prince Klemens von Metternich].

This new framework incorporated a recognition of America's limits with a belief that the nation still had a major role to play in resisting the spread of Soviet influence. Less ardently anti-Soviet than his conservative critics desired, and more interventionist than most liberals could abide, Kissinger was able to create an American role that kept the pendulum from careening too rapidly in one direction or the other after Vietnam.

The main lines of this policy were followed for the next two decades: a blend of containment and cooperation with Moscow that allowed the internal contradictions of the Soviet system to play out; a step-by-step process in the Middle East that kept the U.S. the dominant player in the region; and a realistic attitude toward China that created a global balance that was more stable and gave Washington more leverage. When the cold war ended, this dose of realism would help the U.S. operate in a new global environment based on multiple power centers and balances.

But Kissinger's power-oriented realism and focus on national interests faltered because it was too dismissive of the role of morality. The secret bombing and then invasion of Cambodia, the Christmas bombing of Hanoi, the destabilization of Chile—these and other brutal actions betrayed a callous attitude toward what Americans like to believe is the historic foundation of their foreign policy: a respect for human rights, international law, democracy, and other idealistic values. The setbacks Kissinger encountered as a statesman, and the antagonism he engendered as a person, stemmed from the perceived amorality of his geopolitical calculations.

Kissinger's approach led to a backlash against détente; the national mood swung toward both the moralism of Jimmy Carter and the ideological fervor of Ronald Reagan. As a result, not unlike Metternich, Kissinger's legacy turned out to be one of brilliance more than solidity, of masterful structures built of bricks that were made without straw.

To Kissinger, an emphasis on realism and national interests—even though it might seem callous in its execution—was not a rejection of moral values. Rather, he saw it as the best way to pursue the stable world order that he believed was the ultimate moral imperative, especially in a nuclear age.

He tried to explain this relationship between realism and morality at a Paris gathering of Nobel Prize laureates in 1988. After being attacked in a closed-door session for his power-oriented and amoral approach—Argentine Adolfo Perez Esquivel, a former Peace Prize winner, accused him of "genocide and collective massacre"—Kissinger began to talk about his childhood. The room hushed.

More than a dozen of his relatives had been killed in the holocaust, he said, so he knew something of the nature of genocide. It was easy for human rights crusaders and peace activists to insist on perfection in this world. But the policymaker who has to deal with reality learns to seek the best that can be achieved rather than the best that can be imagined. It would be wonderful to banish the role of military power from world affairs, but the world is not perfect, as he had learned as a child. Those with true responsibility for peace, unlike those on the sidelines, cannot afford pure idealism. They must have the courage to deal with ambiguities and accommodations, to realize that great goals can be achieved only in imperfect steps. No side has a monopoly on morality.

But Kissinger's realpolitik was ill-suited to an open and democratic society, where it is difficult to invoke distant ends to justify unpalatable means. A belief that America's actions are moral and noble is necessary to rally a naturally isolationist people. Whether marching off to war or rousing itself to counter the spread of communism, America draws its motivation from a desire to defend its values—rather than from a cold calculation of its geopolitical interests. Even when an American involvement is partly based on economic self-interest, such as the Persian Gulf War of 1991, the more high-minded goals are the ones that tend to be publicly emphasized.

Kissinger considered this idealistic aspect of the American spirit a weakness in terms of sustaining policies in a messy world. To some extent he was right—but it was also a source of strength. The greatest triumph of political influence in the modern age was that of democratic capitalism over communism in the early 1990s.

This occurred partly because Kissinger and others helped to create a new global balance during the 1970s, one that preserved American influence in the post-Vietnam era. But the main reason that the United States triumphed in the cold war was not because it won a competition for military power and influence. It was because the values offered by its system—among them a foreign policy that could draw its strength from the ideals of its people—eventually proved more attractive.

FURTHER READING

Robert J. Alexander, *The Tragedy of Chile* (1978)

Dana H. Allin, *Cold War Illusions* (1995)

Stephen E. Ambrose, *Nixon* (1987–1991)

Peter Asselin, *A Bitter Peace* (2002) (on Vietnam)

Richard J. Barnet, *The Giants* (1977)

———, *The Lean Years* (1980)

Robert L. Beisner, "History and Henry Kissinger," *Diplomatic History,* 14 (1990), 511–527

Larry Berman, *Vietnam: No Peace, No Honor* (2001)

George W. Breslauer, "Why Détente Failed: An Interpretation," in Alexander L. George, ed., *Managing Soviet-American Relations* (1983)

Seyom Brown, *The Faces of Power* (1983)

William Bundy, *A Tangled Web* (1998)

Anne H. Cahn, *Killing Détente: The Right Attacks the C.I.A.* (1998)

Dan Caldwell, ed., *Henry Kissinger* (1983)

David Calleo, *The Imperious Economy* (1982)

Gregory D. Cleva, *Henry Kissinger and the American Approach to Foreign Policy* (1989)

Thomas M. Franck and Edward Weisband, *Foreign Policy by Congress* (1979)

Leon Friedman and William F. Levantrosser, eds., *Cold War Patriot and Statesman: Richard M. Nixon* (1993)

Michael B. Froman, *The Development of the Idea of Détente* (1992)

John L. Gaddis, *Russia, the Soviet Union, and the United States* (1990)

———, *Strategies of Containment* (1982)

Lloyd C. Gardner, ed., *The Great Nixon Turnaround* (1973)

Raymond L. Garthoff, *The Great Transition* (1994)

Charles Gati and Toby Trister Gati, *The Debate over Détente* (1977)

Michael Genovese, *The Nixon Presidency* (1990)

Matti Golan, *The Secret Conversations of Henry Kissinger* (1976)

Stephen Graubard, *Kissinger: Portrait of a Mind* (1973)

David Greenberg, *Nixon's Shadow* (2003)

John Robert Greene, *The Limits of Power* (1992)

Jussi M. Hanhimäki, *The Flawed Architect* (2004) (on Kissinger)

Seymour M. Hersh, *The Price of Power: Kissinger in the White House* (1983)

Christopher Hitchens, *The Trial of Henry Kissinger* (2001)

Stanley Hoffmann, *Primacy or World Order* (1978)

William G. Hyland, *Mortal Rivals* (1987)

Robert C. Johansen, *The National Interest and the Human Interest* (1980)

Loch K. Johnson, *A Season of Inquiry: The Senate Intelligence Investigation* (1985)

Bernard Kalb and Marvin Kalb, *Kissinger* (1974)

Jeffrey Kimball, *Nixon's Vietnam War* (1999)

———, *The Vietnam War Files* (2003)

David Landau, *Kissinger: Uses of Power* (1972)

Thomas B. Larson, *Soviet-American Rivalry* (1978)

Robert S. Litwak, *Détente and the Nixon Doctrine* (1984)

Michael Mandelbaum, *The Nuclear Question* (1979)

James Mann, *About Face* (1999) (on China)

Iwan Morgan, *Nixon* (2002)

Roger Morris, *Richard Milhous Nixon* (1989)

———, *Uncertain Greatness: Henry Kissinger and American Foreign Policy* (1977)

Keith L. Nelson, *The Making of Détente* (1995)

John Newhouse, *Cold Dawn: The Story of SALT* (1973)

———, *War and Peace in the Nuclear Age* (1988)

Herbert S. Parmet, *Richard Nixon and His America* (1990)

James Petras and Morris Morley, *The United States and Chile* (1975)

Richard Pipes, *U.S.-Soviet Relations in the Era of Détente* (1981)

Richard Reeves, *President Nixon* (2001)

Mary E. Sarotte, *Dealing with the Devil* (2001) (on East Germany)

Walter F. Sater, *Chile and the United States* (1990)

Robert D. Schulzinger, *Henry Kissinger* (1989)

Franz Schurmann, *The Foreign Politics of Richard Nixon* (1987)

David Shambaugh, *Beautiful Imperialist* (1991) (on Sino-U.S. relations)

Edward R. F. Sheehan, *The Arabs, Israelis, and Kissinger* (1976)

Paul E. Sigmund, *The United States and Democracy in Chile* (1993)

Melvin Small, *The Presidency of Richard Nixon* (1999)

Lewis Sorley, *Arms Transfers Under Nixon* (1983)

Harvey Starr, *Henry Kissinger* (1984)

Richard Stevenson, *The Rise and Fall of Détente* (1985)

John G. Stoessinger, *Henry Kissinger: The Anguish of Power* (1976)

Gerald S. Strober and Deborah Hart Strober, *Nixon: An Oral History of His Presidency* (1996)

Anthony Summers, *The Arrogance of Power* (2000)

Jeremi Suri, *Power and Protest* (2003)

Tad Szulc, *The Illusion of Peace* (1978)

Terry Terriff, *The Nixon Administration and the Making of U.S. Nuclear Policy* (1995)

Patrick Tyler, *A Great Wall* (on China)

Adam B. Ulam, *Dangerous Relations: The Soviet Union in World Politics, 1970–1982* (1983)

Garry Wills, *Nixon Agonistes* (1970)

C H A P T E R
13

The Cold War Ends and the
Post–Cold War Era Begins

After Vietnam, the Watergate crisis, and the waning of détente, President Jimmy
Carter attempted to reenergize Soviet-American arms control, but at the close of
his administration (1977–1981), the Cold War had become as contentious as ever:
Strategic Arms Limitations Talks (SALT) had stalled; the Soviet Union had invaded
Afghanistan; and plans had been set in motion to install American Pershing II and
cruise missiles in NATO countries in Western Europe to counter Moscow's SS-20
missiles. Iran's Islamic revolution, dramatic spikes in oil and gasoline prices, and
the taking of fifty-two U.S. embassy personnel hostage in Tehran added to Carter's
list of setbacks. Some scholars wrote of America's decline in the world system.

Contemptuous of the message of decline and brandishing a 1950s-style anticommunism, Republican candidate Ronald Reagan charged during the 1980 presidential election that Carter had let American power slip. Following his decisive
electoral victory, Reagan spurned arms control talks, introduced the largest peacetime
military budget in history, stepped up aid to anticommunist movements around the
world, and announced the Strategic Defense Initiative (SDI, a space-based anti-missile
defense system). Democrats criticized the soaring budget deficits, denounced Washington's neglect of mounting domestic social ills, and ridiculed SDI, or "Star Wars"
as they tagged it, as science fiction. Pressured by critics at home and abroad, Reagan
proposed a new approach: arms reduction instead of arms control.

Then, a new, younger, reform-minded generation of Soviet officials came
to power in Moscow in 1985, led by General Secretary of the Communist Party
Mikhail Gorbachev. Under the "new thinking" in the Kremlin Gorbachev worked to
restructure the moribund Soviet economy (perestroika), liberalize politics (glasnost),
reduce military forces, and loosen controls over the Eastern European satellite states.
Soon Gorbachev and Reagan were arranging summit meetings, discussing substantial cuts in nuclear weapons.

Long-simmering protest in the Communist-ruled dictatorships of Eastern Europe
and East Germany exploded in this new atmosphere of reform. Having reduced
Soviet forces in the region, Gorbachev did not suppress dissent in the Warsaw Pact
nations. Thus Communist regimes collapsed one after another, in domino fashion,
in 1989—Poland, Hungary, East Germany, Czechoslovakia, and Romania. In

November, one of the infamous pillars of the Cold War, the Berlin Wall, came down. And by the end of the year, Gorbachev had pulled Soviet troops out of Afghanistan. In his State of the Union address in 1990, the new American president, George Bush, proclaimed communism to be a remnant of the past. The Soviet Communist party disbanded, and the Union of Soviet Socialist Republics dissolved in 1991.

In the decade that followed, U.S. power was unmatched. When the Iraqi dictator Saddam Hussein sent invading forces to annex his oil-rich neighbor Kuwait in August 1990, Bush assembled an international military coalition that in early 1991 ousted Hussein's troops. Bush boasted that the "gloomsayers" who predicted decline for America had been proven wrong and that the United States stood poised to lead a "new world order" based on self-determination and collective security. But over the next decade, a proliferation of challenges arose to test U.S. power and resiliency. Ethnic and religious wars in the former Yugoslavia, tribal bloodletting in African Rwanda, famine in Somalia, and drug trafficking in Latin America defied easy solutions. Acid rain, global warming, and deforestation endangered the world's environment. The spread of weapons of mass destruction cast an ominous shadow across the Middle East, on the Indian subcontinent, and on the Korean peninsula.

Throughout the tenure of three presidential administrations—the Republican George Bush senior (1989–1993), the Democrat Bill Clinton (1993–2001), and the younger Republican George W. Bush (2001–)—U.S. officials struggled to define America's role in the post–Cold War era. At times the United States deployed its power unilaterally to bring American values and order to the rest of the world, as in 1989–1990 when President Bush dispatched U.S. troops to Panama and arrested Panamanian president Manuel Noriega on narcotics charges. At other times, the United States worked with other states and multilateral institutions to promote global security. To keep the peace between the emergent states of Bosnia and Croatia and the Serbian-led government in Yugoslavia, President Clinton deployed a U.S.-led NATO peacekeeping force in 1995. Then, in response to Serbian attacks against ethnic Albanians in the Yugoslav province of Kosovo, the Clinton administration and NATO in March 1999 conducted air strikes against Yugoslavia to force a negotiation of Kosovo's political status.

American economic dominance also came into question. The end of the Cold War sparked a renewed American dedication to the expansion of capitalism. President Clinton placed special emphasis on trade treaties such as the North American Free Trade Agreement, or NAFTA (approved by Congress in 1993), and the establishment of the World Trade Organization, or WTO (1994). When critics on the home front charged that trade liberalization undermined U.S. industries and jobs, the administration denounced the "new isolationism" and drew analogies to the 1930s, when high tariffs had spawned depression, dictatorships, and war. The younger George W. Bush succeeded Clinton in 2001, touting the free enterprise system. Citing their stifling impact on economic growth, the new administration abandoned the multilateral Kyoto Protocol (1997), which aimed to reduce atmospheric emissions linked to global warming, and won congressional approval for large domestic tax cuts to stimulate investment. The economic boom of the 1990s nonetheless slowed, joblessness increased, and U.S. budget deficits soared.

Although few predicted the startling turnarounds that produced the post–Cold War era, historians and political scientists—along with news commentators and former officials—have offered numerous competing explanations for the end of the Cold War. One school of thought claims that President Reagan's tough anti-communism, especially his military expansion and strategy of negotiating through strength, broke the bank and the spirit of the Soviet system. Others look inside the

*Soviet system itself for an explanation, stressing communism's failure to spur pro-
ductivity as the key factor in ending the Cold War. According to this perspective, it
was Mikhail Gorbachev who took the initiative in Soviet-American relations as he
tried to accompany internal reforms with reduced arms expenditures in order to
revive a decaying command economy. Still others have emphasized the importance
of external, or international, developments: the relative decline of both the Soviet
Union and the United States in the international system.*

*Nor is there agreement on the state of the world following the Cold War's demise.
Many commentators have proclaimed a new unipolar era in which a triumphant
United States wields overwhelming military, economic, and cultural strength. Thus
the United States has an unprecedented opportunity to impose unilaterally its preference for Open Door economics and to dictate political solutions to troubled states and
regions. Others see a more murky global reality in which America's power remains
limited. According to this view, the dispersal of international economic power and
global cultural differences have constrained Washington and forced it to seek allies
and multilateral arrangements to safeguard its overseas interests.*

*Why and how did the Cold War end? What were the key characteristics of the
post–Cold War Era? The debate over these questions will undoubtedly shape American foreign relations in the twenty-first century.*

 D O C U M E N T S

In Document 1, comprising press conference comments from January 19, 1981, the
newly inaugurated president Ronald Reagan denounces the Soviet Union, setting
the Cold War confrontational style of his administration. In a March 23, 1983, speech,
Reagan explains U.S. military expansion. Portions of his case, including his call for
a new defensive system to blunt nuclear weapons (later called the Strategic Defense
Initiative, or SDI), are reprinted here as Document 2.

Reagan and Gorbachev met at Geneva in 1985, and again at Reykjavík, Iceland, in
October 1986. At Reykjavík, they came close to a major agreement on terminating the
nuclear arms race, but Gorbachev would not accept SDI, which he saw as threatening,
and Reagan would not abandon the system, which he saw as defensive. Their opposing
positions are presented in Documents 3 and 4, both televised addresses—Reagan's on
October 13 and Gorbachev's on October 22. Document 5, from interviews conducted
during 1987–1989 with Georgi Arbatov, one of the reformers who emerged with
Gorbachev, provides a glimpse of the "new thinking" in the Soviet Union. A member
of the Communist party's Central Committee and his nation's preeminent Americanist
scholar, Arbatov headed the USA Institute, a think tank in Moscow.

President George Bush officially ushered in the post–Cold War era in September
1990, roughly one year following the collapse of the Berlin Wall. In Document 6, the
president's State of the Union address, Bush applauded the rebirth of freedom in formerly Soviet-dominated Eastern Europe, rallied Americans to support the ideal of
liberty worldwide, and credited Harry Truman's policy of anticommunist containment
for patiently outlasting Soviet communism. The administration of President William J.
Clinton committed itself to advancing American influences and values abroad. Document 7 consists of remarks given by Clinton at a breakfast meeting on October 6, 1995,
a day after signing a cease-fire agreement for war-torn and ethnically divided Bosnia.
In his comments, the president trumpeted America's role as a peacemaker and world
leader, and warned against the danger of isolationism. Document 8 is a letter from
President George W. Bush to Senate Republican leaders, dated March 13, 2001, in

which the president explains his opposition to the international Kyoto Protocol on carbon dioxide emissions. It demonstrates the growing importance of environmental issues in world affairs, the new administration's emphasis on free enterprise, and American opposition to intrusive government regulation. It also serves as an example of President Bush's skepticism about multilateral initiatives, especially when they impinge on U.S. interests.

1. President Ronald Reagan Denounces the Soviet Union, 1981

So far détente's been a one-way street that the Soviet Union has used to pursue its own aims. I don't have to think of an answer as to what I think their intentions are; they have repeated it. I know of no leader of the Soviet Union since the revolution, and including the present leadership, that has not more than once repeated in the various Communist congresses they hold their determination that their goal must be the promotion of world revolution and a one-world Socialist or Communist state, whichever word you want to use.

Now, as long as they do that and as long as they, at the same time, have openly and publicly declared that the only morality they recognize is what will further their cause, meaning they reserve unto themselves the right to commit any crime, to lie, to cheat, in order to attain that, and that is moral, not immoral, and we operate on a different set of standards, I think when you do business with them, even at a détente, you keep that in mind.

2. Reagan Touts U.S. Military Power and Introduces the Strategic Defense Initiative (SDI), 1983

Since the dawn of the atomic age, we've sought to reduce the risk of war by maintaining a strong deterrent and by seeking genuine arms control. "Deterrence" means simply this: making sure any adversary who thinks about attacking the United States, or our allies, or our vital interests, concludes that the risks to him outweigh any potential gains. Once he understands that, he won't attack. We maintain the peace through our strength; weakness only invites aggression. . . .

For 20 years the Soviet Union has been accumulating enormous military might. They didn't stop when their forces exceeded all requirements of a legitimate defensive capability. And they haven't stopped now. During the past decade and a half, the Soviets have built up a massive arsenal of new strategic nuclear weapons—weapons that can strike directly at the United States. . . .

Another example of what's happened: In 1978 the Soviets had 600 intermediate-range nuclear missiles based on land and were beginning to add the SS-20—a new, highly accurate, mobile missile with 3 warheads. We had none. Since then the Soviets have strengthened their lead. By the end of 1979, when Soviet leader Brezhnev

Document 1 can be found in *Public Papers of the Presidents, Ronald Reagan, 1981* (Washington, D.C.: U.S. Government Printing Office, 1982), p. 57.

Document 2 can be found in *Public Papers of the Presidents, Ronald Reagan, 1983* (Washington, D.C.: U.S. Government Printing Office, 1984), Book I, pp. 437–443.

declared "a balance now exists," the Soviets had over 800 warheads. We still had none. A year ago this month, Mr. Brezhnev pledged a moratorium, or freeze, on SS-20 deployment. But by last August, their 800 warheads had become more than 1,200. We still had none. Some freeze. At this time Soviet Defense Minister [Dmitri] Ustinov announced "approximate parity of forces continues to exist." But the Soviets are still adding an average of 3 new warheads a week, and now have 1,300. These warheads can reach their targets in a matter of a few minutes. We still have none. So far, it seems that the Soviet definition of parity is a box score of 1,300 to nothing, in their favor.

So, together with our NATO allies, we decided in 1979 to deploy new weapons, beginning this year, as a deterrent to their SS-20's and as an incentive to the Soviet Union to meet us in serious arms control negotiations. We will begin that deployment late this year. At the same time, however, we're willing to cancel our program if the Soviets will dismantle theirs. This is what we've called a zero-zero plan. The Soviets are now at the negotiating table—and I think it's fair to say that without our planned deployments, they wouldn't be there. . . .

Some people may still ask: Would the Soviets ever use their formidable military power? Well, again, can we afford to believe they won't? There is Afghanistan. And in Poland, the Soviets denied the will of the people and in so doing demonstrated to the world how their military power could also be used to intimidate.

The final fact is that the Soviet Union is acquiring what can only be considered an offensive military force. They have continued to build far more intercontinental ballistic missiles than they could possibly need simply to deter an attack. Their conventional forces are trained and equipped not so much to defend against an attack as they are to permit sudden, surprise offensives of their own. . . .

I know that all of you want peace, and so do I. I know too that many of you seriously believe that a nuclear freeze would further the cause of peace. But a freeze now would make us less, not more, secure and would raise, not reduce, the risks of war. It would be largely unverifiable and would seriously undercut our negotiations on arms reduction. It would reward the Soviets for their massive military buildup while preventing us from modernizing our aging and increasingly vulnerable forces. With their present margin of superiority, why should they agree to arms reductions knowing that we were prohibited from catching up? . . .

The calls for cutting back the defense budget come in nice, simple arithmetic. They're the same kind of talk that led the democracies to neglect their defenses in the 1930's and invited the tragedy of World War II. We must not let that grim chapter of history repeat itself through apathy or neglect. . . .

This approach to stability [deterrence] through offensive threat [retaliation] has worked. We and our allies have succeeded in preventing nuclear war for more than three decades. In recent months, however, my advisers, including in particular the Joint Chiefs of Staff, have underscored the necessity to break out of a future that relies solely on offensive retaliation for our security. . . .

If the Soviet Union will join with us in our effort to achieve major arms reduction, we will have succeeded in stabilizing the nuclear balance. Nevertheless, it will still be necessary to rely on the specter of retaliation, on mutual threat. And that's a sad commentary on the human condition. Wouldn't it be better to save lives than to avenge them? Are we not capable of demonstrating our peaceful intentions by applying all our abilities and our ingenuity to achieving a truly lasting stability? I think we are. Indeed, we must.

After careful consultation with my advisers, including the Joint Chiefs of Staff, I believe there is a way. Let me share with you a vision of the future which offers hope. It is that we embark on a program to counter the awesome Soviet missile threat with measures that are defensive. Let us turn to the very strengths in technology that spawned our great industrial base and that have given us the quality of life we enjoy today.

What if free people could live secure in the knowledge that their security did not rest upon the threat of instant U.S. retaliation to deter a Soviet attack, that we could intercept and destroy strategic ballistic missiles before they reached our own soil or that of our allies?

I know this is a formidable, technical task, one that may not be accomplished before the end of this century. Yet, current technology has attained a level of sophistication where it's reasonable for us to begin this effort. It will take years, probably decades of effort on many fronts. There will be failures and setbacks, just as there will be successes and breakthroughs. And as we proceed, we must remain constant in preserving the nuclear deterrent and maintaining a solid capability for flexible response. But isn't it worth every investment necessary to free the world from the threat of nuclear war? We know it is. . . .

I clearly recognize that defensive systems have limitations and raise certain problems and ambiguities. If paired with offensive systems, they can be viewed as fostering an aggressive policy, and no one wants that. But with these considerations firmly in mind, I call upon the scientific community in our country, those who gave us nuclear weapons, to turn their great talents now to the cause of mankind and world peace, to give us the means of rendering these nuclear weapons impotent and obsolete.

Tonight, consistent with our obligations of the ABM [Anti-Ballistic Missile] treaty and recognizing the need for closer consultation with our allies, I'm taking an important first step. I am directing a comprehensive and intensive effort to define a long-term research and development program to begin to achieve our ultimate goal of eliminating the threat posed by strategic nuclear missiles. This could pave the way for arms control measures to eliminate the weapons themselves. We seek neither military superiority nor political advantage. Our only purpose—one all people share—is to search for ways to reduce the danger of nuclear war.

3. Reagan Defends SDI After the Reykjavík Summit Meeting, 1986

We proposed the most sweeping and generous arms control proposal in history. We offered the complete elimination of all ballistic missiles—Soviet and American— from the face of the Earth by 1996. While we parted company with this American offer still on the table, we are closer than ever before to agreements that could lead to a safer world without nuclear weapons. . . .

Some years ago, the United States and the Soviet Union agreed to limit any defense against nuclear missile attacks to the emplacement in one location in each

---

This document can be found in *Public Papers of the Presidents, Ronald Reagan, 1986* (Washington, D.C.: U.S. Government Printing Office, 1989), Book II, pp. 1367–1370.

country of a small number of missiles capable of intercepting and shooting down incoming nuclear missiles, thus leaving our real defense—a policy called mutual assured destruction, meaning if one side launched a nuclear attack, the other side could retaliate. And this mutual threat of destruction was believed to be a deterrent against either side striking first. So here we sit, with thousands of nuclear warheads targeted on each other and capable of wiping out both our countries. The Soviets deployed the few antiballistic missiles around Moscow as the treaty permitted. Our country didn't bother deploying because the threat of nationwide annihilation made such a limited defense seem useless.

For some years now we've been aware that the Soviets may be developing a nationwide defense. They have installed a large, modern radar at Krasnoyarsk, which we believe is a critical part of a radar system designed to provide radar guidance for antiballistic missiles protecting the entire nation. Now, this is a violation of the ABM treaty. Believing that a policy of mutual destruction and slaughter of their citizens and ours was uncivilized, I asked our military, a few years ago, to study and see if there was a practical way to destroy nuclear missiles after their launch but before they can reach their targets, rather than just destroy people. Well, this is the goal for what we call SDI, and our scientists researching such a system are convinced it is practical and that several years down the road we can have such a system ready to deploy. Now incidentally, we are not violating the ABM treaty, which permits such research. If and when we deploy, the treaty also allows withdrawal from the treaty upon 6 months' notice. SDI, let me make it clear, is a nonnuclear defense. . . .

I offered a proposal that we continue our present [SDI] research. And if and when we reached the stage of testing, we would sign, now, a treaty that would permit Soviet observation of such tests. And if the program was practical, we would both eliminate our offensive missiles, and then we would share the benefits of advanced defenses. I explained that even though we would have done away with our offensive ballistic missiles, having the defense would protect against cheating or the possibility of a madman, sometime, deciding to create nuclear missiles. After all, the world now knows how to make them. I likened it to our keeping our gas masks, even though the nations of the world had outlawed poison gas after World War I. We seemed to be making progress on reducing weaponry, although the General Secretary [Gorbachev] was registering opposition to SDI and proposing a pledge to observe ABM for a number of years. . . .

The Soviets had asked for a 10-year delay in the deployment of SDI programs. In an effort to see how we could satisfy their concerns—while protecting our principles and security—we proposed a 10-year period in which we began with the reduction of all strategic nuclear arms, bombers, air-launched cruise missiles, intercontinental ballistic missiles, submarine-launched ballistic missiles and the weapons they carry. They would be reduced 50 percent in the first 5 years. During the next 5 years, we would continue by eliminating all remaining offensive ballistic missiles, of all ranges. And during that time, we would proceed with research, development, and testing of SDI—all done in conformity with ABM provisions. At the 10-year point, with all ballistic missiles eliminated, we could proceed to deploy advanced defenses, at the same time permitting the Soviets to do likewise.

And here the debate began. The General Secretary wanted wording that, in effect, would have kept us from developing the SDI for the entire 10 years. In effect, he was killing SDI. And unless I agreed, all that work toward eliminating nuclear weapons would go down the drain—canceled. I told him I had pledged to the American people that I would not trade away SDI, there was no way I could tell our people their government would not protect them against nuclear destruction. . . .

I realize some Americans may be asking tonight: Why not accept Mr. Gorbachev's demand? Why not give up SDI for this agreement? Well, the answer, my friends, is simple. SDI is America's insurance policy that the Soviet Union would keep the commitments made at Reykjavík. SDI is America's security guarantee if the Soviets should—as they have done too often in the past—fail to comply with their solemn commitments. SDI is what brought the Soviets back to arms control talks at Geneva and Iceland. SDI is the key to a world without nuclear weapons. The Soviets understand this. They have devoted far more resources, for a lot longer time than we, to their own SDI. The world's only operational missile defense today surrounds Moscow, the capital of the Soviet Union.

What Mr. Gorbachev was demanding at Reykjavík was that the United States agree to a new version of a 14-year-old ABM treaty that the Soviet Union has already violated. I told him we don't make those kinds of deals in the United States. And the American people should reflect on these critical questions: How does a defense of the United States threaten the Soviet Union or anyone else? Why are the Soviets so adamant that America remain forever vulnerable to Soviet rocket attack? As of today, all free nations are utterly defenseless against Soviet missiles—fired either by accident or design. Why does the Soviet Union insist that we remain so—forever?

4. Soviet General Secretary Mikhail Gorbachev Criticizes SDI After the Reykjavík Summit Meeting, 1986

Reykjavík generated not hopes alone. Reykjavík also highlighted the hardships on the road to a nuclear-free world. . . .

Quarters linked with militarism and arms race profits are clearly scared. They are doing their utmost to cope with the new situation and, coordinating their actions, are trying in every way to mislead the people, to control the sentiment of broad sections of the world public, to suppress their quest for peace, to hinder governments from taking a clear-cut position at this decisive moment in history. . . .

Far-reaching and interconnected, they [the Soviet proposals presented at the Reykjavík meeting] constitute an integrated package and are based on the program we announced on 15 January for the elimination of nuclear weapons by the year 2000.

The first proposal is to cut by half all strategic arms, without exception.

The second proposal is to fully eliminate Soviet and US medium-range missiles in Europe and immediately set about talks on missiles of this type in Asia, as well as on missiles with a range of less than a thousand kilometres. We suggested freezing the number of such missiles immediately.

This document can be found in M. S. Gorbachev, *Speeches and Writings* (Oxford: Pergamon Press, 1986), II, 64–70.

The third proposal is to consolidate the ABM Treaty and to start full-scale talks on a total ban on nuclear tests. . . .

The US Administration is now trying in every possible way to convince people that a possible major success with concrete agreements was not achieved owing to Soviet unyieldingness over the program of the so-called Strategic Defence Initiative (SDI).

It is even being asserted that we allegedly lured the President into a trap by putting forward "breathtaking" proposals on cutting down strategic offensive arms and medium-range missiles, and that later on we ostensibly demanded in an ultimatum form that SDI be renounced.

But the essence of our stand and of our proposals is as follows: we are for reduction and then complete elimination of nuclear weapons and are firmly against a new stage in the arms race and against its transfer to outer space.

Hence we are against SDI and are for consolidation of the ABM Treaty.

It is clear to every sober-minded person that if we embark upon the road of deep cuts and then complete elimination of nuclear weapons, it is essential to rule out any opportunity for either the Soviet or US side to gain unilateral military superiority.

We perceive the main danger of SDI precisely in a transfer of the arms race to a new sphere, and in endeavours to go out into space with offensive arms and thereby achieve military superiority.

SDI has become an obstacle to ending the arms race, to getting rid of nuclear weapons, and is the main obstacle to a nuclear-free world. . . .

In upholding the position that thwarted the reaching of agreement in Reykjavík, the President asks rhetorical questions: Why do the Russians so stubbornly demand that America forever remain vulnerable to a Soviet missile strike? Why does the Soviet Union insist that we remain defenceless forever?

I am surprised at such questions, I must say. They have the air of indicating that the American President has an opportunity to make his country invulnerable, to give it secure protection against a nuclear strike.

As long as nuclear weapons exist and the arms race continues, he does not have such an opportunity. The same, naturally, applies to ourselves.

If the President counts on SDI in this respect, he does so in vain. The system would be effective only if all missiles were eliminated. But then, one might ask, why the anti-missile defence altogether? Why build it? I need not mention the money wasted, the cost of the system—according to some estimates, it will run into several trillion dollars.

So far, we have been trying to persuade America to give up that dangerous undertaking. We are urging the American Administration to look for invulnerability and for protection in another way—the way of total elimination of nuclear weapons and the establishment of a comprehensive system of international security that would preclude all war—nuclear and conventional. . . .

It is hard to reconcile oneself to the loss of a unique chance—that of saving mankind from the nuclear threat. Bearing precisely this in mind, I told the press conference in Reykjavík that we did not regard the dialogue as closed and hoped that President Reagan, on returning home, would consult Congress and the American people and adopt decisions logically necessitated by what had been achieved in Reykjavík.

Quite a different thing has happened. Besides distorting the entire picture of the Reykjavík negotiations—I will speak about that later—they have in recent days taken actions that look simply wild in the normal human view after such an important meeting between the two countries' top leaders.

I mean the expulsion of another fifty-five Soviet embassy and consular staff from the United States. We will take measures in response, of course—very tough measures on an equal footing. We are not going to put up with such outrageous practices. But for now let me say the following.

What kind of government is this? What can one expect from it in other affairs in the international arena? To what limits does the unpredictability of its actions go?

It turns out that it has no constructive proposals on key disarmament issues and that it does not even have a desire to maintain the atmosphere essential for a normal continuation of the dialogue. It appears that Washington is not prepared for any of these. . . .

An unattractive portrait of the Administration of that great country, of an Administration quick to take disruptive actions, is coming into view. Either the President is unable to cope with an entourage which literally breathes hatred for the Soviet Union and for everything that may lead international affairs into a calm channel or he himself wants that. At all events, there is no keeping the "hawks" in the White House in check. And this is very dangerous. . . .

Let me say once again: when SDI is preferred to nuclear disarmament, only one conclusion is possible: it is that through that military program efforts are being made to disprove the axiom of international relations of our epoch expressed in the simple and clear-cut words under which the US President and I put our signatures last year [at the Geneva summit conference]. Here are those words: nuclear war must not be fought and it cannot be won.

Let me say in conclusion: the Soviet Union has put the maximum of goodwill into its proposals. We are not removing these proposals, they still stand! Everything that has been said by the way of their substantiation and development remains in force.

5. Soviet Reformer Georgi Arbatov Explains the "New Thinking" in the Soviet Union, 1989

Personally I share the radical view that *perestroika* means building a new model of Soviet socialism. We have to go all the way in democratization, *glasnost,* and economic reforms, not halfway. This bothers some people, but the reasons aren't hard to understand. The Soviet Union is a young country—just over seventy years old. During those years we have lived through so many extraordinary circumstances—the Revolution, the Civil War, Stalinism, the world war, the Cold War—that our structures, psychology, and behavior acquired extraordinary characteristics. It was like growing up under martial law. Even Stalinism was shaped by extraordinary circumstances—the threats of German fascism and Japanese militarism in the

---

1930s, the burden of the Cold War. So it's not surprising that we haven't yet built the socialist model we intended and believe in.

Now we have to rid ourselves of all those things that arose in those extraordinary times—things in which we used to believe, things we thought were intrinsic to socialism. This isn't easy, partly because many people will believe in all those things but also because the old economic model worked rather well in its time and for certain purposes. If the old economic model had completely failed, if the country had not developed from being a very backward country, it would be easier to change today. It would be easier to give up the obsolete thinking and policies that led the country into a dead end and that had such a negative impact on international relations. I can't think of any other country or government that now is so self-critical and demanding in looking at its own past and learning from the sufferings of the past.

That's why I argue against some of our officials who are guarded or worried about *glasnost*. The anti-*glasnost* tradition was imposed on the country during Stalinism, and it has had very negative effects in our domestic policies—but also in foreign policy. In fact, improvements brought by the Twentieth Party Congress back in the 1950s barely touched foreign policy. I don't mean that everything in our foreign policy stagnated in the years that followed. There were achievements— the beginnings of détente, arms control steps, and other things. But the tradition of secrecy, silence, and the absence of *glasnost* fossilized much of our defense and foreign policy thinking and decision making. When I argue for greater openness, some of our people say that exposing our problems will hurt us abroad. I tell them that the world knew about our problems before *glasnost;* we can't hide them. Moreover, *glasnost* has helped us abroad because more people there understand we are serious about our reforms. If there is an attempt to curtail *glasnost*, it will be harmful and counterproductive. . . .

The main priority of our foreign policy is to create the best international circumstances for the reforms going on inside our country. For us, economic and social progress is the most important thing. Of course, there still are some people here who cling to old ideas about the priority of promoting revolutions abroad—people who still think we can work miracles when foreign Marxists ask us for help. But it doesn't work. The best way to influence other countries is by reforming our own system. *Perestroika* involves a new way of thinking about foreign policy which begins with seeing realities as they are, not as we want them to be. We must face the truth, no matter how bitter it is. Our basic conception of the world has changed. We no longer view it in terms of "we" and "they" but as one humanity that has to live or die together. The nuclear world is too fragile for the use of military force, any kind of serious misbehavior, any geopolitical adventures, or an unlimited arms race. That is a basic principle of our new thinking. . . .

[W]e now believe that what unites different countries, their common interests, is more important than the conflicts and differences between them. We also realized that we relied too much on military power for security. Both the Soviet Union and the United States have far more military power than they can use for any reasonable purpose. Militarism on the part of all countries is the real danger. We all must rely for security more on political means—on negotiations, for example. Our mutual task is to reverse the militarization of life. We have no need for all these weapons and huge armies. We also now understand that we cannot obtain national security at the expense of the other side—at your [U.S.] expense—and the same is true for you. This is our concept of mutual security. Our security depends on you feeling secure, and yours depends on us feeling secure. Now we also understand better that the lagging economic development of the Third World is a global problem, and despite our limited resources we have to make our contribution to solving this problem.

More generally, the Soviet Union no longer can live in economic autarchy, isolated from the world economy. Interdependence can only increase. All of these new perceptions make us favor more multilateral efforts, particularly through the United Nations. My own view is that the two superpowers have to be more democratic in their thinking about the world. The Soviet Union and the United States represent only about 10 percent of the world population. We can't and shouldn't try to do everything. And the rest of the world should not be held hostage to U.S.-Soviet relations. . . .

We think [military] sufficiency is enough. Of course, we want some kind of equality, but not in numerical terms. We don't have to have as many airplanes as you have. We don't need them. All we need is enough so that you know it would be folly to start a war.

But we have gone beyond this. We want to create a nonnuclear world or a world with very few nuclear weapons. And we understand that we cannot have these major reductions in nuclear weapons without major reductions in conventional weapons. You can see how serious we are about this from Gorbachev's unilateral reductions in our conventional forces. So far as we are concerned, the door is wide open for even larger reductions through negotiations.

Unfortunately, there is a good deal of hypocrisy on your side. Your authorities complain that we have superiority in conventional weapons. Perhaps we do in some categories and we are prepared to build down in these areas. But you've been complaining about this for forty years, despite the fact that the West's GNP is two and a half times bigger than ours. If you really thought we had such superiority, why didn't you catch up? Your automobile and tractor industries are much stronger than ours. Why didn't they build tanks? No, I think you've used this scare about alleged Soviet superiority to hold your NATO alliance together and to justify building an absolutely irrational number of nuclear weapons. . . .

I know that some Americans dislike them [Soviet domestic reforms] and I understand why. Since 1945 many American institutions have needed a foreign enemy—an evil empire. Indeed, the general framework of American foreign policy has been constructed on the premise of this enemy. The Cold War was built on a kind of black-and-white, religious fundamentalism. There was the American paradise and the Soviet hell. When hell disappears, when the enemy image erodes, the whole structure becomes shaky. Some Americans fear this. But they will just have to find ways to live without the image of the Soviet enemy. America also needs *perestroika* and new thinking of her own. . . .

But, you know, there is so much ideology about us in America. It's a great irony. You've always accused us of being too ideological, but there's no country in the world more ideological than the Untied States, despite your professed pragmatism. Mr. Reagan's presidency brought this ideological impulse to the fore. We too tended to over-ideologize our foreign policy, but our new thinking is based on realism. For example, that all these weapons are dangerous and useless. Your ideology—or illusions—seem to persist, which is one reason why you can't let go of the enemy image so easily. . . .

The Cold War is a living corpse. It died sometime in the 1960s and has been kept alive by political injections of myths and fantasies about the Soviet threat— like a body kept alive on an artificial heart-and-lung machine. It is time to lay it to rest. Neither of us can any longer afford to squander money on fake problems, false stereotypes, and pointless suspicions. Both of us have plenty of real problems at home.

6. President George Bush Proclaims Cold War Victory, 1990

Tonight I come not to speak about the state of the Government, not to detail every new initiative we plan for the coming year nor to describe every line in the budget. I'm here to speak to you and to the American people about the state of the Union, about our world—the changes we've seen, the challenges we face—and what that means for America.

There are singular moments in history, dates that divide all that goes before from all that comes after. And many of us in this Chamber have lived much of our lives in a world whose fundamental features were defined in 1945; and the events of that year decreed the shape of nations, the pace of progress, freedom or oppression for millions of people around the world.

Nineteen forty-five provided the common frame of reference, the compass points of the postwar era we've relied upon to understand ourselves. And that was our world, until now. The events of the year just ended, the Revolution of '89, have been a chain reaction, changes so striking that it marks the beginning of a new era in the world's affairs.

Think back—think back just 12 short months ago to the world we knew as 1989 began.

One year—one year ago, the people of Panama lived in fear, under the thumb of a dictator. Today democracy is restored; Panama is free. Operation Just Cause has achieved its objective. The number of military personnel in Panama is now very close to what it was before the operation began. And tonight I an announcing that well before the end of February, the additional numbers of American troops, the brave men and women of our Armed Forces who made this mission a success, will be back home.

A year ago in Poland, Lech Walesa declared that he was ready to open a dialog with the Communist rulers of that country; and today, with the future of a free Poland in their own hands, members of Solidarity lead the Polish Government.

A year ago, freedom's playwright, Václav Havel, languished as a prisoner in Prague. And today it's Václav Havel, President of Czechoslovakia.

And 1 year ago, Erich Honecker of East Germany claimed history as his guide, and he predicted the Berlin Wall would last another hundred years. And today, less than 1 year later, it's the Wall that's history.

From "Address Before a Joint Session of the Congress on the State of the Union," 31 January 1990, *Public Papers of the Presidents, George Bush 1990* (Washington, D.C.: Government Printing Office, 1991), Book I, pp. 129–134.

Remarkable events—events that fulfill the long-held hopes of the American people; events that validate the longstanding goals of American policy, a policy based on a single, shining principle: the cause of freedom.

America, not just the nation but an idea, alive in the minds of people everywhere. As this new world takes shape, America stands at the center of a widening circle of freedom—today, tomorrow, and into the next century. Our nation is the enduring dream of every immigrant who ever set foot on these shores, and the millions still struggling to be free. This nation, this idea called America, was and always will be a new world—our new world.

At a workers' rally, in a place called Branik on the outskirts of Prague, the idea called America is alive. A worker, dressed in grimy overalls, rises to speak at the factory gates. He begins his speech to his fellow citizens with these words, words of a distant revolution: "We hold these truths to be self-evident, that all men are created equal, that they are endowed by their Creator with certain unalienable Rights, and that among these are Life, Liberty and the pursuit of Happiness."

It's no secret that here at home freedom's door opened long ago. The cornerstones of this free society have already been set in place: democracy, competition, opportunity, private investment, stewardship, and of course leadership. And our challenge today is to take this democratic system of ours, a system second to none, and make it better. . . .

I began tonight speaking about the changes we've seen this past year. There is a new world of challenges and opportunities before us, and there's a need for leadership that only America can provide. Nearly 40 years ago, in his last address to the Congress, President Harry Truman predicted such a time would come. He said: "As our world grows stronger, more united, more attractive to men on both sides of the Iron Curtain, then inevitably there will come a time of change within the Communist world." Today, that change is taking place.

For more than 40 years, America and its allies held communism in check and ensured that democracy would continue to exist. And today, with communism crumbling, our aim must be to ensure democracy's advance, to take the lead in forging peace and freedom's best hope: a great and growing commonwealth of free nations. And to the Congress and to all Americans, I say it is time to acclaim a new consensus at home and abroad, a common vision of the peaceful world we want to see.

Here is our own hemisphere, it is time for all the peoples of the Americas, North and South, to live in freedom. In the Far East and Africa, it's time for the full flowering of free governments and free markets that have served as the engine of progress. It's time to offer our hand to the emerging democracies of Eastern Europe so that continent—for too long a continent divided—can see a future whole and free. It's time to build on our new relationship with the Soviet Union, to endorse and encourage a peaceful process of internal change toward democracy and economic opportunity.

We are in a period of great transition, great hope, and yet great uncertainty. We recognize that the Soviet military threat in Europe is diminishing, but we see little change in Soviet strategic modernization. Therefore, we must sustain our own strategic offense modernization and the Strategic Defense Initiative.

But the time is right to move forward on a conventional arms control agreement to move us to more appropriate levels of military forces in Europe, a coherent defense program that ensures the U.S. will continue to be a catalyst for peaceful change in Europe. And I've consulted with leaders of NATO. In fact, I spoke by phone with President Gorbachev just today.

I agree with our European allies that an American military presence in Europe is essential and that it should not be tied solely to the Soviet military presence in Eastern Europe. But our troop levels can still be lower. And so, tonight I am announcing a major new step for a further reduction in U.S. and Soviet manpower in Central and Eastern Europe to 195,000 on each side. This level reflects the advice of our senior military advisers. It's designed to protect American and European interests and sustain NATO's defense strategy. A swift conclusion to our arms control talks—conventional, chemical, and strategic—must now be our goal. And that time has come.

Still, we must recognize an unfortunate fact: In many regions of the world tonight, the reality is conflict, not peace. Enduring animosities and opposing interests remain. And thus, the cause of peace must be served by an America strong enough and sure enough to defend our interests and our ideals. It's this American idea that for the past four decades helped inspire this Revolution of '89.

7. President William J. Clinton Applauds America's Globalism and Warns Against a New Isolationism, 1995

You know, in 1991 I sought the presidency because I believed it was essential to restore the American dream for all Americans and to reassert America's leadership in the post-cold-war world. As we move from the industrial to the information age, from the cold war world to the global village, we have an extraordinary opportunity to advance our values at home and around the world. But we face some stiff challenges in doing so as well. . . .

We see the benefits of American leadership in the progress now being made in Bosnia. In recent weeks, our military muscle through NATO, our determined diplomacy throughout the region, have brought the parties closer to a settlement than at any time since this terrible war began 4 years ago. Yesterday, we helped to produce an agreement on a Bosnia-wide cease-fire. Now, the parties will come to the United States to pursue their peace talks mediated by our negotiating team and our European and Russian counterparts.

We have a long way to go, and there's no guarantee of success. But we will use every ounce of our influence to help the parties make a peace that preserves Bosnia as a single democratic state and protects the rights of all citizens, regardless of their ethnic group. . . .

We also saw the benefits of America's leadership last week at the White House where leaders from all over the Middle East gathered to support the agreement between Israel and the Palestinian Authority. For nearly a half-century now, Democratic and Republican administrations have worked to facilitate the cause of peace in the Middle East. The credit here belongs to the peacemakers. But we should all

This document can be found in "Remarks at Freedom House," 6 October 1995, *Public Papers of the Presidents of the United States, William J. Clinton, 1995* (Washington, D.C.: U.S. Government Printing Office, 1996), Book II, pp. 1544–1551.

be proud that at critical moments along the way, our efforts helped to make the difference between failure and success.

It was almost exactly a year ago that the United States led the international effort to remove Haiti's military regime and give the people of Haiti a real chance at democracy. We've succeeded because we've backed diplomacy with sanctions and ultimately with force. We've succeeded because we understood that standing up for democracy in our own hemisphere was right for the Haitian people and right for America.

American efforts in Bosnia, the Middle East, and Haiti and elsewhere have required investments of time and energy and resources. They've required persistent diplomacy and the measured use of the world's strongest military. They have required both determination and flexibility in our efforts to work as leaders and to work with other nations. And sometimes they've called on us to make decisions that were, of necessity, unpopular in the short run, knowing that the payoff would not come in days or weeks but in months or years. Sometimes they have been difficult for many Americans to understand because they have to be made, as many decisions did right after World War II, without the benefit of some overarching framework, the kind of framework the bipolar cold war world provided for so many years.

To use the popular analogy of the present day, there seems to be no mainframe explanation for the PC world in which we're living. We have to drop the abstractions and dogma and pursue, based on trial and error and persistent experimentation, a policy that advances our values of freedom and democracy, peace, and security. . . .

Throughout what we now call the American century, Republicans and Democrats disagreed on specific policies, often heatedly from time to time, but we have always agreed on the need for American leadership in the cause of democracy, freedom, security, and prosperity. Now that consensus is truly in danger, and interestingly enough, it is in danger in both parties. Voices from the left and the right are calling on us to step back from, instead of stepping up to, the challenges of the present day. They threaten to reverse the bipartisan support for our leadership that has been essential to our strength for 50 years. Some really believe that after the cold war the United States can play a secondary role in the world, just as some thought we could after World War II, and some made sure we did after World War I.

But if you look at the results from Bosnia to Haiti, from the Middle East to Northern Ireland, it proves once again that American leadership is indispensable and that without it our values, our interests, and peace itself would be at risk.

It has now become a truism to blame the current isolationism on the end of the cold war because there is no longer a mainframe threat in this PC world. . . .

The isolationists are simply wrong. The environment we face may be new and different, but to meet it with the challenges and opportunities it presents and to advance our enduring values, we have to be more engaged in the world, not less engaged in the world. That's why we have done everything we could in our administration to lead the fight to reduce the nuclear threat, to spread democracy in human rights, to support peace, to open markets, to enlarge and defend the community of nations around the world, to share our aspirations and our values. . . .

The American people are good people. They have common sense. They care when people are being murdered around the world. They understand that a war somewhere else could one day involve our sons and daughters. They know that we cannot simply pretend that the rest of the world is not there. But many of them have their own difficulties. We must work and work and work on the basic values and interests and arguments until we beat back the forces of isolation, with both intense passion and reason.

8. President George W. Bush Jettisons the Multilateral Kyoto Protocol on the Environment, 2001

Thank you for your letter of March 6, 2001, asking for the Administration's view on global climate change, in particular the Kyoto Protocol and efforts to regulate carbon dioxide under the Clean Air Act. My Administration takes the issue of global climate change very seriously.

As you know, I oppose the Kyoto Protocol because it exempts 80 percent of the world, including major population centers such as China and India, from compliance, and would cause serious harm to the U.S. economy. The Senate's vote, 95–0, shows that there is a clear consensus that the Kyoto Protocol is an unfair and ineffective means of addressing global climate change concerns.

As you also know, I support a comprehensive and balanced national energy policy that takes into account the importance of improving air quality. Consistent with this balanced approach, I intend to work with the Congress on a multipollutant strategy to require power plants to reduce emissions of sulfur dioxide, nitrogen oxides, and mercury. And such strategy would include phasing in reductions over a reasonable period of time, providing regulatory certainty, and offering market-based incentives to help industry meet the targets. I do not believe, however, that the government should impose on power plants mandatory emissions reductions for carbon dioxide, which is not a "pollutant" under the Clean Air Act.

A recently released Department of Energy Report, "Analysis of Strategies for Reducing Multiple Emissions from Power Plants," concluded that including caps on carbon dioxide emissions as part of a multiple emissions strategy would lead to an even more dramatic shift from coal to natural gas for electric power generation and significantly higher electricity prices compared to scenarios in which only sulfur dioxide and nitrogen oxides were reduced.

This is important new information that warrants a reevaluation, especially at a time of rising energy prices and a serious energy shortage. Coal generates more than half of America's electricity supply. At a time when California has already experienced energy shortages, and other Western states are worried about price and availability of energy this summer, we must be very careful not to take actions that could harm consumers. This is especially true given the incomplete state of scientific knowledge of the causes of, and solutions to, global climate change and the lack of commercially available technologies for removing and storing carbon dioxide.

Consistent with these concerns, we will continue to fully examine global climate change issues—including the science, technologies, market-based systems, and innovative options for addressing concentrations of greenhouse gases in the atmosphere. I am very optimistic that, with the proper focus and working with our friends and

This document can be found at George W. Bush to Senators Hagel, Helms, Craig, and Roberts, 13 March 2001, *Public Papers of the Presidents of the United States, George W. Bush, 2001* (Washington, D.C.: U.S. Government Printing Office, 2002), Book I, p. 235.

allies, we will be able to develop technologies, market incentives, and other creative ways to address global climate change.

I look forward to working with you and others to address global climate change issues in the context of a national energy policy that protects our environment, consumers, and economy.

 E S S A Y S

In the first essay, Thomas G. Paterson, professor emeritus at the University of Connecticut, probes the external and internal factors that intersected to change both American and Soviet policies, end the Cold War, and usher in the post–Cold War era. He studies the costs of the long conflict between the United States and the Soviet Union and the changes in the international system that undermined the power of both countries. Moscow and Washington reversed course and ended the Cold War to stem their decline and recover their sagging international positions. Although the dawning of the post–Cold War era witnessed a renewed U.S. drive for influence, Paterson concludes that, given their substantial domestic problems by the early 1990s, it can hardly be said that either the United States or the Soviet Union won the Cold War.

In the second essay, a statement representative of the Reagan victory school, the historian John Lewis Gaddis disagrees with Paterson's perspective on the ending of the Cold War. Gaddis credits Reagan's political leadership skills, especially his ability to balance ideological vision with operational pragmatism, for reducing Cold War tensions. Reagan capitalized on Soviet decline and shrewdly used America's military buildup and his SDI initiative to bring the Soviets to the bargaining table. In the new Soviet leader Mikhail Gorbachev, Reagan gained a Russian partner who shared his goal of reducing, not just controlling, nuclear weapons. Gaddis concludes that Reagan's critics—on both the right and the left—vastly underestimated the president's determination to negotiate from strength and to build a domestic political base in favor of détente.

The final essay, by Joseph S. Nye Jr., former assistant secretary of defense in the Clinton administration and a professor of international relations at Harvard University, analyzes America's quest for global hegemony in the post–Cold War era. Nye acknowledges America's overwhelming international power, but he also stresses that modern communications and the information revolution have shrunk the globe and challenged American hegemony. According to Nye, new international realities require that the United States seek the cooperation of other states, nongovernmental organizations, and multilateral institutions in managing world affairs.

Superpower Decline and Hegemonic Survival

THOMAS G. PATERSON

Simply put, the Cold War ended because of the relative decline of the United States and the Soviet Union in the international system from the 1950s through the 1980s. The Cold War waned because the contest had undermined the power of its two major protagonists. In acts of hegemonic survival in a world of mounting challenges on several fronts, they gradually moved toward a cautious cooperation whose urgent

From *On Every Front: The Making and Unmaking of the Cold War,* Revised Edition by Thomas G. Paterson. Copyright © 1992, 1979 by W. W. Norton & Company, Inc. Reprinted by permission of W. W. Norton & Company, Inc.

goals were nothing less than the restoration of their economic well-being and the preservation of their diminishing global positions.

At least three sources or trends explain this gradual decline and the consequent attractions of détente. The first was the burgeoning economic costs of the Cold War. Challenges to the leadership of the two major powers from within their spheres of influence constitute the second source. The third was the emergence of the Third World, which brought new players into the international game, further diffused power, and eroded bipolarism. The three elements combined to weaken the standing of the two adversaries and ultimately to persuade Soviet and American leaders to halt their nations' descent by ending the Cold War. The Soviet Union fell much harder than the United States, but the implications of decline became unmistakable for both: The Cold War they made in the 1940s had to be unmade if the two nations were to remain prominent international superintendents.

The first source was the economic burden that the long confrontation inflicted on the United States and the Soviet Union. . . . In the postwar years the United States used its abundant economic resources to spur the recovery of its allies and to build an international military network. The costs of maintaining and expanding its global interests climbed dramatically: $12.4 billion for the Marshall Plan, $69.5 billion for the Korean War, $22.3 billion for the Alliance for Progress, $172.2 billion for the Vietnam War. In the years from 1946 through 1987 the United States dispensed more than $382 billion in economic and military foreign aid. International organizations in which the United States was prominent, such as the World Bank, offered another $273 billion in assistance.

The United States also spent billions of dollars for CIA operations. . . . Expenses also mounted for the maintenance of occupying forces in Germany, Japan, and elsewhere. U.S. Information Agency propaganda activities proved expensive, too, as witnessed by the Voice of America's $640 million expenditure in the 1970s.

Security links stretched across the globe. After the Rio Pact (1947) and NATO (1949) came the ANZUS Pact with Australia and New Zealand (1951), the defense treaty with Japan (1952), the South East Asia Treaty Organization (SEATO, 1954), and the Baghdad Pact for the Middle East (1955). . . . In 1959, moreover, one million Americans were stationed overseas; in 1970 the number was nearly nine hundred thousand; and by 1985 the United States still had more than half a million armed forces personnel abroad.

Alliance building, military expansion, clandestine operations, and interventionism spawned galloping defense budgets amounting to trillions of dollars over four decades. U.S. military spending stood at $13.5 billion in 1949, averaged $40 billion a year in the 1950s, rose to $54 billion in 1960 and $90 billion in 1970 (largely because of the Vietnam War), and soared to $155 billion in 1980. By 1988 the military budget alone had reached more than $300 billion. In the mid-1980s the Defense Department was spending an average of $28 million an hour, twenty-four hours a day, seven days a week. Nuclear-arms development and ever more sophisticated technology [also] drove up the cost of waging the Cold War. . . .

America's massive military spending chipped away at the nation's infrastructure, contributing to the relative decline of the United States and stimulating the movement toward Soviet-American détente. Defense spending demanded capital, which the federal government had to borrow, forcing up interest rates, which in turn slowed economic development. Persistent deficit spending by the federal government drove up the federal debt, which stood at $257 billion in 1950, $286 billion in 1960, $371 billion in 1970, and $908 billion in 1980. By 1986 the debt had reached a staggering $2.1 trillion. . . .

Military spending constantly drew funds away from other categories so essential to the overall well-being of the nation—what economists call "opportunity costs." Domestic troubles mounted: lower productivity, falling savings rate, sagging agricultural sector, inadequately skilled labor force with an increasing number of functional illiterates, drug abuse, decaying cities, growing high school dropout rates, a health care system that failed to cover large numbers of people, and weak conservation programs that left the U.S. economy vulnerable to sharp swings in prices of imported raw materials. . . .

The United States also became a debtor nation with a serious balance of payments problem and a widening trade deficit. . . . International economic crises—high oil prices in the 1970s and massive Third World debt in the 1980s—added to America's woes. Debt-ridden nations curbed their purchases of American products and suspended debt payments. By 1985 the U.S. trade deficit had reached a remarkable $148.5 billion. . . . By 1989 the U.S. foreign debt hit $650 billion. . . .

Although the American economy during the Cold War grew in absolute numbers, the U.S. share of the world's material resources declined relative to other nations. . . . Between 1960 and 1973 the U.S. economic growth rate compared with that of all other countries was 4 percent versus 5.6 percent, and from 1973 to 1980 2 percent versus 3.6 percent. In the decade of the 1970s ninety-eight nations had higher rates of economic growth than the United States. In 1979 and 1980 the U.S. growth rate dropped to minus 0.2 percent; by comparison, Japan's stood at 4.2 percent and West Germany's at 1.8, and the world rate was 2 percent. The U.S. share of gross world product also declined: from approximately 40 percent in 1950 to about 22 percent in 1980. Japan doubled its share in the same period to 9 percent. From the 1950s to the 1980s the American share of world exports slumped while West Germany's and Japan's shares jumped. The American rate for productivity growth (output per worker) also descended; for 1950–1970 the rate was 2.68 percent, then for 1970–1980 it dropped to 1.17 percent, and for 1980–1986 it stood at 1.53 percent. For the same periods Japan's and West Germany's rates ranked higher than the U.S. rate. The American share of world industrial production also fell, and the United States lost its lead in televisions, automobiles, semiconductors, and machine tools. . . .

Measurable economic decline compelled American policy makers, however reluctantly at times, to take steps toward ending the Cold War. By relieving domestic troubles, détente seemed to offer continuation of America's world-class status. Détente might make expensive interventions and ever-growing arsenals less necessary. It also promised greater trade with both the Soviet Union and the People's Republic of China. . . .

The Cold War also cost the Soviet Union a great deal—indeed, much more than it cost the United States—and this burden persuaded Moscow to seek détente. . . . The Soviet Union also became a big military spender, in part to catch up in the strategic arms race. . . .

Foreign ventures, too, strained Soviet resources. In the 1950s Moscow began to lend funds to Third World nations—to India for a steel plant, to Egypt for the

Aswan Dam. The Warsaw Pact; aid to the People's Republic of China (until halted by Moscow in the early 1960s); support for Egypt (until the Soviets were evicted in 1972), Syria, and other Middle Eastern states; and subsidies to Fidel Castro's Cuba (which averaged close to five billion dollars during the 1980s) also drew heavily on Soviet funds. North Vietnam received more than eight billion dollars in Soviet aid from 1965 to 1975. The Soviet Union subsidized its Eastern European client states, probably spending at least seventeen billion dollars a year by the early 1980s. The invasions of Hungary in 1956 and Czechoslovakia in 1968 and the ten-year war in Afghanistan from 1979 to 1989 cost dearly. . . .

To pay for its large Red Army encamped in Eastern Europe and along the tense border with China, the considerable expansion of its navy, and its interventions, foreign aid, and nuclear weaponry, the Kremlin shortchanged the nation's domestic development. . . . The nation's overall industrial and agricultural rates of growth slackened. In the 1950s the rate of Soviet economic growth stood at 5.9; from 1960 to 1973 the rate declined to 4.9 percent; from 1973 to 1980 the rate dropped even more to 2.6 percent; and for 1981 to 1985 the rate plummeted further to 1.9. . . .

Low productivity and shoddy craftsmanship stemmed from poor labor morale, alcoholism, high absenteeism, and a stultifying Communist party bureaucracy. "They pretend to pay us and we pretend to work" went the joke. Air and water pollution, crumbling plants, inefficient and hence dismal agricultural output, and declining life expectancy rates also plagued the Soviet Union through the Cold War decades. Shabbily manufactured tractors and trucks required inordinate maintenance; factory breakdowns and lack of spare parts slowed production. . . .

"There are real sources of trouble" in the Soviet Union, admitted Georgi Arbatov, director of Moscow's Institute for United States and Canadian Studies. "The Cold War just prevents us from dealing with them," he explained. "Neither of us can any longer afford to squander money on fake problems, false stereotypes, and pointless suspicions. Both of us have plenty of real problems at home." In 1987, for example, the Chernobyl nuclear plant accident spewed radioactive fallout across Europe and raised anew doubts about Soviet workmanship, management skills, and governmental competence. . . .To save the Soviet economy, the expensive arms race had to be stopped, for military spending was eating up at least a quarter of the nation's budget. . . .

In addition to the economic burden of the Cold War, another significant source accounted for the great powers' decline and their movement toward détente: challenges to their hegemony from independent-minded client states and allies. Some allies, such as West Germany and France, advanced détente on their own. Others made so much trouble that the hegemonic powers welcomed détente as a means to discipline them—Moscow's eagerness to build Soviet-American cooperation as a counterweight to China, for example. The two great powers also embraced détente as a means to reassert mastery, as in the 1970s, when Moscow hoped that the United States would accept the Soviet Union's preeminent influence in Eastern Europe and Washington hoped that détente would create a great-power "equilibrium" that would help reduce radical revolution in the American sphere. Sometimes détente afforded a great power an apparent opportunity to exploit division within a sphere in order to contain or weaken its adversary. The USSR, for example, attempted to encourage France to spoil U.S. plans for Western Europe, and the United States played its "China card" against the Soviet Union. . . .

The United States, too, faced challenges from within its far-flung sphere of influence, although with less disarray than that experienced by the Soviets [in dealing with Eastern European nationalism and the Sino-Soviet schism]. Europe became for Americans a source not only of friends but also of rivals, who themselves marched in the direction of ending the Cold War. . . .

Such expressions of independence by allies became common during the Vietnam era, when NATO partners failed to support the long U.S. war in Southeast Asia. The British, complained the always pungent President Lyndon B. Johnson, could at least have sent a platoon of bagpipers. . . . Some jittery Europeans also believed that American policy makers preferred to use European territory as a nuclear battleground. Under the weight of such strains the American sphere of influence in Europe progressively frayed.

The nationalism and independent decision making of West Germany also shook the American sphere and advanced détente. Many West Germans scorned Americans when the United States did not knock down the Berlin Wall after it went up in 1961, and Chancellor Konrad Adenauer became suspicious that Moscow and Washington would cut deals at Germany's expense. Soon France and Germany seemed to be competing to see which could first establish détente with the Soviet Union. When Willy Brandt became chancellor in 1969, the Federal Republic of Germany displayed unusual independence by making overtures to Moscow. Brandt's Eastern policy *(Ostpolitik)* led in 1970 to a Soviet-German nonaggression treaty, which especially reduced friction over Berlin. Two years later, in an early gesture toward reunification, the two Germanys opened diplomatic channels. Kissinger bristled at this "new form of classic German nationalism," but he nonetheless endorsed Brandt's efforts because most allies did. "We could best hold the Alliance together," he recalled, "by accepting the principle of détente. . . ."

Greatly expanded Western European trade with and investment in the Soviet sphere of influence beginning in the late 1940s also drew back the "iron curtain" in a seemingly irreversible process of economic détente. After the divisive Suez crisis, for example, America's European allies sought more energy independence from the Middle East—and from the United States. The Soviet Union, to Washington's dismay, became an alternative oil and natural gas source. . . .

The diminution of America's power could be measured even in the most conspicuous arena of its hegemony—Latin America. . . . Clear signs of hemispheric independence became evident when Venezuela helped found the Organization of Petroleum Exporting Countries (OPEC) [in 1960] and nationalized American-owned oil companies. American-owned multinational corporations faced higher taxes, terrorism, expropriation, and regulations on the hiring of nationals. . . . During the Vietnam War, when the United States appeared "unreliable as a security partner," Brazil began to import weapons from European suppliers; later it developed its own profitable weapons-exporting business. U.S. hegemony in the Western Hemisphere had rested in part on U.S. dominance in arms production and weapons sales. Washington witnessed another setback in the 1970 election of the Marxist President Salvador Allende in Chile and in Peru's defiant 1970s purchases of Soviet MiGs. The 1979 victory of the radical Sandinistas over the longtime U.S. ally Anastasio Somoza in Nicaragua and Argentina's selling of grain to the Soviet Union in 1980 during a U.S.-imposed embargo against the Soviets provided further evidence of diminished U.S.

power in the hemisphere. Although the CIA helped depose Allende in 1973, this American success and the U.S. military interventions in the Dominican Republic (1965), Grenada (1983), and Panama (1989) attested not to U.S. strength but to the loosening of its imperial net. Western Hemispheric nations, overall, boldly questioned the "hegemonic presumption" of the United States.

The most serious defiance to the United States came from Cuba's Fidel Castro.... Castro survived the [missile] crisis, consolidated his power, and promised revolution all over Latin America. Cuba remained a Soviet ally, although Havana frequently followed an independent foreign policy. Cuban-American hostility persisted despite some steps toward improved relations in the 1970s.

As he cultivated détente in the early 1970s, President Nixon identified five power centers in the world: the United States, the Soviet Union, China, Japan, and the Common Market. Under détente, he declared, each center should maintain order among smaller states in its region of responsibility. Because the "five great economic superpowers will determine the economic future," Nixon explained, "and, because economic power will be the key to other kinds of power, [they will determine] the future of the world. . . ." For the United States, détente seemed to offer opportunities to determine the future—to discipline its Latin American sphere under a global system of great-power management and to deter Soviet inroads or assistance to rebel groups like the insurgent Sandinistas in Nicaragua by threatening to withdraw the economic benefits the Soviets sought from détente. Détente beckoned as a means to reestablish U.S. control of its most traditional sphere. In 1984 the President's Commission on Central America warned that if the United States ever revealed symptoms of decline in its own neighborhood, it would experience the "erosion of our power to influence events worldwide that would flow from the perception that we were unable to influence vital events close to home."

If the erosion of American and Soviet power stemmed from the fracturing of their spheres, so, too, was it due to the rise of the Third World. After the Second World War a cavalcade of colonies broke from their imperial rulers. From 1943 to 1989 no fewer than ninety-six countries gained independence and entered the international system as new states. . . . Undersecretary of State George W. Ball recalled [that diplomats] necessarily had to focus "on problems involving the bits and pieces of disintegrating empires." . . .

When many Third World nations formed a nonaligned movement to challenge the two Cold Warriors and to press for an end to their dangerous competition, the international system fragmented, bipolarism eroded, and the relative power of the United States and the Soviet Union diminished accordingly. After the 1955 Bandung Conference, many Third World nations in Asia, Africa, and the Middle East declared their neutralism in the Cold War. Third World expressions of alienation from the two superpowers came in many other forms, including Pan-Arabism and Muslim fundamentalism, [and] the Group of 77 in the United Nations. . . .

By sheer force of numbers Third World states became a formidable bloc in world forums. The United States gradually became isolated in the United Nations. In the Security Council, for example, the United States, losing the majority vote its sphere members had long provided, had to cast its first veto in 1970, and by the 1980s it was averaging four vetoes a year. The United States became the largest caster of nay votes in the General Assembly, where it frequently had to contend with setbacks like the 108–9 vote to condemn its invasion of Grenada. In the 1950s

General Assembly members voted 70 percent of the time with the United States; in the 1970s the coincidence rate fell to 30 percent, and by the early 1980s to 20 percent. . . .

All of this tugging and pulling jolted the international system. . . . International affairs became more fluid, more unpredictable, less secure, and less manageable. . . . Détente was born in part as a response to this disorderly, pluralistic world. With the United States suffering Third World setbacks in Vietnam, Iran, Nicaragua, and elsewhere, and the Soviet Union stumbling in Egypt and Afghanistan, among other places, Washington and Moscow looked less and less like superpowers. The declining powers in this transforming international system sought to hold their positions by moving from confrontation to cooperation. Détente seemed to promise a restoration of great-power control, a reassertion of great-power tutelage. If détente was embraced as a means to reduce the costs of the Cold War and to meet challenges from sphere members, it also became attractive as a means to deal with the volatile Third World. As President Jimmy Carter once said, Americans had to put their "inordinate fear of Communism" behind them in order to address long-term Third World crises. For the United States, détente with the Soviet Union also offered a "fulcrum or base from which to exert American diplomatic leverage" in the Third World. In 1990, during the Gulf War, when Soviet-American cooperation marshaled a worldwide condemnation of Iraq after it had invaded neighboring Kuwait, Secretary of State James Baker expressed what leaders before him had been saying about the virtues of détente: "When the United States and the Soviet Union lead, others are likely to follow.". . .

The United States and the Soviet Union, bedeviled by Cold War–induced economic problems, independent-minded allies, and contentious Third World nations, gradually moved in fits of truculence and accommodation toward détente and the ultimate end of the Cold War. By the late 1960s, remembered Henry Kissinger, America had to operate "in much more complex conditions than we had ever before faced." That time "marked the end of the period of American predominance based on overwhelming nuclear and economic supremacy." Indeed, he continued, "the Soviet nuclear stockpile was inevitably approaching parity. The economic strength of Europe and Japan was bound to lead them to seek larger political influence. The new, developing nations pressed their claims to greater power and participation." If the world further "tilted against us," he feared, America's strong, if no longer preeminent, position in the international balance of power would falter. In this unsettled environment, détente became even more attractive. Détente did not mean that Soviet-American rivalry would cease, but rather that judicious great-power cooperation, located somewhere between hostile obstructionism and friendly coexistence, would reduce world tensions. Moscow and Washington cautiously endorsed détente as a process to stem the erosion of their power. . . .

U.S. entry into the Persian Gulf War of 1990 and 1991, following Iraq's brutal invasion and annexation of oil-rich Kuwait, exposed a core feature of the immediate post–Cold War international order: the U.S. drive to recoup lost influence, to reestablish credibility, to reaffirm a counterrevolutionary posture, to reassert the great-power status that the prolonged Cold War had eroded. . . . President George Bush claimed that the new war in the Middle East was the first post–Cold War "test of our mettle." The president claimed that "recent events have surely proven that there is no substitute for American leadership" in the world. And "let no one doubt our staying power." The *Wall Street Journal* welcomed the outbreak of war because a U.S. victory "lets America, and above all its elite, recover a sense of self-confidence and self-worth." During Operation Desert Storm proud Americans ballyhooed the destructive power of their high-tech air war, the credibility of their military forces, the skill with which an international coalition was created, and the swiftness of victory. "This is the end of the decline," cheered an official of the conservative American Enterprise Institute. . . .

Although it became fashionable to say that America had won "the sucker and won it big," and it became evident that democratization and capitalism were ascending, the Cold War actually had no winners. Both the United States and the Soviet Union had spent themselves into weakened conditions. Both had paid tremendous prices for making and waging the Cold War. That is why President Gorbachev launched his restructuring programs and why President Bush, echoing Carter and Reagan, made the case for American "renewal" and "renewed credibility." Each major power, in groping for an end to the Cold War, was seeking structures of stability at home and abroad to stem the decline—and collapse—that other complex societies had suffered in the past.

President Ronald Reagan's Successful Strategy of Negotiating from Strength

JOHN LEWIS GADDIS

To say that the Reagan administration's policy toward the Soviet Union is going to pose special challenges to historians is to understate the matter: rarely has there been a greater gap between the expectations held for an administration at the beginning of its term and the results it actually produced. The last thing one would have anticipated at the time Ronald Reagan took office in 1981 was that he would use his eight years in the White House to bring about the most significant improvement in Soviet-American relations since the end of World War II. I am not at all sure that President Reagan himself foresaw this result. And yet, that is precisely what happened, with—admittedly—a good deal of help from Mikhail Gorbachev. . . .

President Reagan in March, 1983, made his most memorable pronouncement on the Soviet Union: condemning the tendency of his critics to hold both sides responsible for the nuclear arms race, he denounced the U.S.S.R. as an "evil empire" and as "the focus of evil in the modern world." Two weeks later, the President surprised even his closet associates by calling for a long-term research and development program to create defense against attacks by strategic missiles, with a view, ultimately, to "rendering these nuclear weapons impotent and obsolete." The Strategic Defense Initiative was the most fundamental challenge to existing orthodoxies on arms control since negotiations on that subject had begun with the Russians almost three decades earlier. Once again it called into question the President's seriousness in seeking an end to—or even a significant moderation of—the strategic arms race.

From John Lewis Gaddis, *The United States and the End of the Cold War: Implications, Reconsiderations, Provocations* (Oxford University Press, 1992), pp. 119, 122–132. Copyright © 1992 by John Lewis Gaddis. Used by permission of Oxford University Press, Inc.

Anyone who listened to the "evil empire" speech or who considered the implications of "Star Wars" might well have concluded that Reagan saw the Soviet-American relationship as an elemental confrontation between virtue and wickedness that would allow neither negotiation nor conciliation in any form; his tone seemed more appropriate to a medieval crusade than to a revival of containment. Certainly there were those within his administration who held such views, and their influence, for a time, was considerable. But to see the President's policies solely in terms of his rhetoric, it is now clear, would have been quite wrong.

For President Reagan appears to have understood—or to have quickly learned—the dangers of basing foreign policy solely on ideology: he combined militancy with a surprising degree of operational pragmatism and a shrewd sense of timing. To the astonishment of his own hard-line supporters, what appeared to be an enthusiastic return to the Cold War in fact turned out to be a more solidly based approach to detente than anything the Nixon, Ford, or Carter administrations had been able to accomplish.

There had always been a certain ambivalence in the Reagan administration's image of the Soviet Union. On the other hand, dire warnings about Moscow's growing military strength suggested an almost Spenglerian gloom about the future: time, it appeared, was on the Russians' side. But mixed with this pessimism was a strong sense of self-confidence, growing out of the ascendancy of conservatism within the United States and an increasing enthusiasm for capitalism overseas, that assumed the unworkability of Marxism as a form of political, social, and economic organization: "The West won't contain communism, it will transcend communism," the President predicted in May, 1981. "It won't bother to . . . denounce it, it will dismiss it as some bizarre chapter in human history whose last pages are even now being written." By this logic, the Soviet Union had already reached the apex of its strength as a world power, and time in fact was on the side of the West.

Events proved the optimism to have been more justified than the pessimism, for over the next four years the Soviet Union would undergo one of the most rapid erosions both of internal self-confidence and external influence in modern history; that this happened just as Moscow's long and costly military buildup should have begun to pay political dividends made the situation all the more frustrating for the Russians. It may have been luck for President Reagan to have come into office at a peak in the fortunes of the Soviet Union and at a trough in those of the United States: things would almost certainly have improved regardless of who entered the White House in 1981. But it took more than luck to recognize what was happening, and to capitalize on it to the extent that the Reagan administration did.

Indications of Soviet decline took several forms. The occupation of Afghanistan had produced only a bloody Vietnam-like stalemate, with Soviet troops unable to suppress the rebellion, or to protect themselves and their clients, or to withdraw. In Poland a long history of economic mismanagement had produced, in the form of the Solidarity trade union, a rare phenomenon within the Soviet bloc: a true workers' movement. Soviet ineffectiveness became apparent in the Middle East in 1982 when the Russians were unable to provide any significant help to the Palestinian Liberation Organization during the Israeli invasion of Lebanon; even more embarrassing, Israeli pilots using American-built fighters shot down over eighty Soviet-supplied Syrian jets without a single loss of their own. Meanwhile, the Soviet domestic economy which [former Soviet premier Nikita] Khrushchev had once predicted would overtake that of the United States, had in fact stagnated during the early 1980s, Japan by some indices actually overtook the U.S.S.R. as the world's second largest producer of goods and services, and even China, a nation with four times the population of the Soviet Union, now became an agricultural exporter at a time when Moscow still required food imports from the West to feed its own people.

What all of this meant was that the Soviet Union's appeal as a model for Third World political and economic development—once formidable—had virtually disappeared, indeed as Moscow's military presence in those regions grew during the late 1970s, the Russians increasingly came to be seen, not as liberators, but as latter-day imperialists themselves. The Reagan administration moved swiftly to take advantage of this situation by funneling military assistance—sometimes openly sometimes covertly—to rebel groups (or "freedom fighters," as the President insisted on calling them) seeking to overthrow Soviet-backed regimes in Afghanistan, Angola, Ethiopia, Cambodia, and Nicaragua; in October, 1983, to huge domestic acclaim but with dubious legality Reagan even ordered the direct use of American military forces to overthrow an unpopular Marxist government on the tiny Caribbean island of Grenada. The Reagan Doctrine, as this strategy became known, sought to exploit vulnerabilities the Russians had created for themselves in the Third World: this latter-day effort to "roll back" Soviet influence would, in time, produce impressive results at minimum cost and risk to the United States.

Compounding the Soviet Union's external difficulties was a long vacuum in internal leadership occasioned by [President Leonid] Brezhnev's slow enfeeblement and eventual death in November, 1982; by the installation as his successor of an already-ill Yuri Andropov, who himself died in February 1984; and by the installation of his equally geriatric successor, Konstantin Chernenko. At a time when a group of strong Western leaders had emerged—including not just President Reagan but also Prime Minister Margaret Thatcher in Great Britain, President François Mitterrand in France, and Chancellor Helmut Kohl in West Germany—this apparent inability to entrust leadership to anyone other than party stalwarts on their deathbeds was a severe commentary on what the sclerotic Soviet system had become. "We could go no further without hitting the end," one Russian later recalled of Chernenko's brief reign. "Here was the General Secretary of the party who is also the Chairman of the Presidium of the Supreme Soviet, the embodiment of our country, the personification of the party and he could barely stand up."

There was no disagreement within the Reagan administration about the desirability under these circumstances, of pressing the Russians hard. Unlike several of their predecessors, the President and his advisers did not see containment as requiring the application of sticks and carrots in equal proportion; wielders of sticks definitely predominated among them. But there were important differences over what the purpose of wielding the sticks was to be.

Some advisers, like [Secretary of Defense Casper] Weinberger, [Assistant Secretary of Defense for International Security Policy Richard] Perle, and [chief Soviet specialist on the National Security Council Richard] Pipes, saw the situation as a historic opportunity to exhaust the Soviet system. Noting that the Soviet economy was already stretched to the limit, they advocated taking advantage of American technological superiority to engage the Russians in an arms race of indefinite duration and indeterminate cost. Others, including [the arms negotiator Paul] Nitze, the

Joint Chiefs of Staff, career Foreign Service officer Jack Matlock, who succeeded Pipes as chief Soviet expert at the NSC, and—most important—[Secretary of State Alexander M.] Haig's replacement after June, 1982, the unflamboyant but steady George Shultz, endorsed the principle of "negotiation from strength": the purpose of accumulating military hardware was not to debilitate the other side, but to convince it to negotiate.

The key question, of course, was what President Reagan's position would be. Despite his rhetoric, he had been careful not to rule out talks with the Russians once the proper conditions had been met: even while complaining, in his first press conference, about the Soviet propensity to lie, cheat, and steal, he had also noted that "when we can, . . . we should start negotiations on the basis of trying to effect an actual reduction in the numbers of nuclear weapons. That would be real arms reduction." But most observers—and probably many of his own advisers—assumed that when the President endorsed negotiations leading toward the "reduction," as opposed to the "limitation," of strategic arms, or the "zero option" in the INF [intermediate-range nuclear forces] talks, or the Strategic Defense Initiative, he was really seeking to avoid negotiations by setting minimal demands above the maximum concessions the Russians could afford to make. He was looking for a way they believed, to gain credit for cooperativeness with both domestic and allied constituencies without actually having to give up anything.

That would turn out to be a gross misjudgment of President Reagan, who may have had cynical advisers but was not cynical himself. It would become apparent with the passage of time that when the Chief Executive talked about "reducing" strategic missiles he meant precisely that; the appeal of the "zero option" was that it really would get rid of intermediate-range nuclear forces; the Strategic Defense Initiative might in fact, just as the President had said, make nuclear weapons "impotent and obsolete." A simple and straightforward man, Reagan took the principle of "negotiation from strength" literally: once one had built strength, one negotiated.

The first indications that the President might be interested in something other than an indefinite arms race began to appear in the spring and summer of 1983. Widespread criticism of his "evil empire" speech apparently shook him: although his view of the Soviet system itself did not change, Reagan was careful, after that point, to use more restrained language in characterizing it. Clear evidence of the President's new moderation came with the Korean airliner incident [downed when it strayed into Soviet airspace] of September, 1983. Despite his outrage, Reagan did not respond—as one might have expected him to—by reviving his "evil empire" rhetoric; instead he insisted that arms control negotiations would continue, and in a remarkably conciliatory television address early in 1984 he announced that the United States was "in its strongest position in years to establish a constructive and realistic working relationship with the Soviet Union." The President concluded this address by speculating on how a typical Soviet couple—Ivan and Anya—might find that they had much in common with a typical American couple—Jim and Sally: "They might even have decided that they were all going to get together for dinner some evening soon."

It was possible to construct self-serving motives for this startling shift in tone. With a presidential campaign under way the White House was sensitive to Democratic charges that Reagan was the only postwar president not to have met with a

Soviet leader while in office. Certainly it was to the advantage of the United States in its relations with Western Europe to look as reasonable as possible in the face of Soviet intransigence. But events would show that the President's interest in an improved relationship was based on more than just electoral politics or the needs of the alliance: it was only the unfortunate tendency of Soviet leaders to die upon taking office that was depriving the American Chief Executive—himself a spry septuagenarian—of a partner with whom to negotiate.

By the end of September, 1984—and to the dismay of Democratic partisans who saw Republicans snatching the "peace" issue from them—a contrite Soviet Foreign Minister Andrei Gromyko had made the pilgrimage to Washington to re-establish contacts with the Reagan administration. Shortly after Reagan's landslide re-election over Walter Mondale in November, the United States and the Soviet Union announced that a new set of arms control negotiations would begin early the following year, linking together discussions on START [Strategic Arms Reduction Talks], INF, and weapons in space. And in December, a hitherto obscure member of the Soviet Politburo, Mikhail Gorbachev, announced while visiting Great Britain that the U.S.S.R. was prepared to seek "radical solutions" looking toward a ban on nuclear missiles altogether. Three months later, Konstantin Chernenko, the last in a series of feeble and unimaginative Soviet leaders, expired, and Gorbachev—a man who was in no way feeble and unimaginative—became the General Secretary of the Communist Party of the Soviet Union. Nothing would ever be quite the same again. . . .

Whatever the circumstances that led to it, the accession of Gorbachev reversed almost overnight the pattern of the preceding four years: after March, 1985, it was the Soviet Union that seized the initiative in relations with the West. It did so in a way that was both reassuring and unnerving at the same time: by becoming so determinedly cooperative as to convince some supporters of containment in the United States and Western Europe—uneasy in the absence of the intransigence to which they had become accustomed—that the Russians were now seeking to defeat that strategy by depriving it, with sinister cleverness, of an object to be contained.

President Reagan, in contrast, welcomed the fresh breezes emanating from Moscow and moved quickly to establish a personal relationship with the new Soviet leader. Within four days of Gorbachev's taking power, the President was characterizing the Russians as "in a different frame of mind than they've been in the past. . . . [T]hey, I believe, are really going to try and, with us, negotiate a reduction in armaments." And within four months, the White House was announcing that Reagan would meet Gorbachev at Geneva in November for the first Soviet-American summit since 1979.

The Geneva summit, like so many before it, was long on symbolism and short on substance. The two leaders appeared to get along well with one another: they behaved, as one Reagan adviser later put it, "like a couple of fellows who had run into each other at the club and discovered that they had a lot in common." The President agreed to discuss deep cuts in strategic weapons and improved verification, but he made it clear that he was not prepared to forgo development of the Strategic Defense Initiative in order to get them. His reason—which Gorbachev may not have taken seriously until this point—had to do with his determination to retain SDI as a means ultimately of rendering nuclear weapons obsolete. The President's stubbornness on this point precluded progress, at least for the moment, on what was coming to be called the "grand compromise": Paul Nitze's idea of accepting limits on SDI in return for sweeping reductions in strategic missiles. But it did leave the way open for an alert Gorbachev, detecting the President's personal enthusiasm for nuclear abolition, to surprise the world in January, 1986, with his own plan for accomplishing that objective: a Soviet-American agreement to rid the world of nuclear weapons altogether by the year 2000.

It was easy to question Gorbachev's motives in making so radical a proposal in so public a manner with no advance warning. Certainly any discussion of even reducing—much less abolishing—nuclear arsenals would raise difficult questions for American allies, where an abhorrence of nuclear weapons continued to coexist uneasily alongside the conviction that only their presence could deter superior Soviet conventional forces. Nor was the Gorbachev proposal clear on how Russians and Americans could ever impose abolition, even if they themselves agreed to it, on other nuclear and non-nuclear powers. Still, the line between rhetoric and conviction is a thin one: the first Reagan-Gorbachev summit may not only have created a personal bond between the two leaders; it may also have sharpened a vague but growing sense in the minds of both men that, despite all the difficulties in constructing an alternative, an indefinite continuation of life under nuclear threat was not a tolerable condition for either of their countries, and that their own energies might very well be directed toward overcoming that situation.

That both Reagan and Gorbachev were thinking along these lines became clear at their second meeting, the most extraordinary Soviet-American summit of the postwar era, held on very short notice at Reykjavik, Iceland, in October, 1986. The months that preceded Reykjavik had seen little tangible progress toward arms control; there had also developed, in August, an unpleasant skirmish between intelligence agencies on both sides as the KGB, in apparent retaliation for the FBI's highly publicized arrest of a Soviet United Nations official in New York on espionage charges, set up, seized, and held *USNEWS* correspondent Nicholas Daniloff on trumped-up accusations for just under a month. It was a sobering reminder that the Soviet-American relationship existed at several different levels, and that cordiality in one did not rule out the possibility of confrontation in others. The Daniloff affair also brought opportunity though, for in the course of negotiations to settle it Gorbachev proposed a quick "preliminary" summit, to be held within two weeks, to try to break the stalemate in negotiations over intermediate-range nuclear forces in Europe, the aspect of arms control where progress at a more formal summit seemed likely. Reagan immediately agreed.

But when the President and his advisers arrived at Reykjavik, they found that Gorbachev had much more grandiose proposals in mind. These included not only an endorsement of 50 percent cuts in Soviet and American strategic weapons across the broad, but also agreement not to demand the inclusion of British and French nuclear weapons in these calculations—a concession that removed a major stumbling block to START—and acceptance in principle of Reagan's 1981 "zero option" for intermediate-range nuclear forces, all in return for an American commitment not to undermine SALT I's ban on strategic defenses for the next ten years. Impressed by the scope of these concessions, the American side quickly put together a compromise that would have cut ballistic missiles to zero within a decade in return for the right, after that time, to deploy strategic defenses against the bomber and cruise missile forces that would be left. Gorbachev immediately countered by proposing the abolition of *all* nuclear weapons within ten years, thus moving his orig-inal deadline from the year 2000 to 1996. President Reagan is said to have replied: "*All* nuclear weapons? Well, Mikhail, that's exactly what I've been talking about all along. . . . That's always been my goal."

A series of events set in motion by a Soviet diplomat's arrest on a New York sub-way platform and by the reciprocal framing of an American journalist in Moscow had wound up with the two most powerful men in the world agreeing—for the mo-ment, and to the astonishment of their aides—on the abolition of all nuclear weapons within ten years. But the moment did not last. Gorbachev went on to insist, as a con-dition for nuclear abolition, upon a ban on the laboratory testing of SDI, which Rea-gan immediately interpreted as an effort to kill strategic defense altogether. Because the ABM treaty does allow for some laboratory testing, the differences between the two positions were not all that great. But in the hothouse atmosphere of this cold-climate summit no one explored such details, and the meeting broke up in disarray, acrimony, and mutual disappointment. . . .

Negotiations on arms control continued in the year that followed Reykjavik, however, with both sides edging toward the long-awaited "grand compromise" that would defer SDI in return for progress toward a START agreement. Reagan and Gorbachev did sign an intermediate-range nuclear forces treaty in Washington in December, 1987, which for the first time provided that Russians and Americans would actually dismantle and destroy—literally before each other's eyes—an entire category of nuclear missiles. There followed a triumphal Reagan visit to Moscow in May, 1988, featuring the unusual sight of a Soviet general secretary and an Ameri-can president strolling amiably through Red Square, greeting tourists and bouncing babies in front of Lenin's tomb, while their respective military aides—each carrying the codes needed to launch nuclear missiles at each other's territory—stood dis-creetly in the background. Gorbachev made an equally triumphal visit to New York in December, 1988, to address the United Nations General Assembly: there he an-nounced a *unilateral* Soviet cut of some 500,000 ground troops, a major step toward moving arms control into the realm of conventional forces. . . .

[A]s the Reagan administration prepared to leave office the following month, in an elegaic mood very different from the grim militancy with which it had as-sumed its responsibilities eight years earlier, the actual prospect of a nuclear holo-caust seemed more remote than at any point since the Soviet-American nuclear rivalry had begun. Accidents, to be sure, could always happen. Irrationality though blessedly rare since 1945, could never be ruled out. There was reason for optimism, though, in the fact that as George Bush entered the White House early in 1989, the point at issue no longer seemed to be "how to fight the Cold War" at all, but rather "is the Cold War over?"

The record of the Reagan years suggests the need to avoid the common error of trying to predict outcomes from attributes. There is no question that the President and his advisers came into office with an ideological view of the world that appeared to allow for no compromise with the Russians; but ideology has a way of evolving to accommodate reality especially in the hands of skillful political leadership. Indeed a good working definition of leadership might be just this—the ability to accommo-date ideology to practical reality—and by that standard, Reagan's achievements in relations with the Soviet Union will certainly compare favorably with, and perhaps even surpass, those of Richard Nixon and Henry Kissinger.

Did President Reagan intend for things to come out this way? That question is, of course, more difficult to determine, given our lack of access to the archives. But a careful reading of the public record would, I think, show that the President was expressing hopes for an improvement in Soviet-American relations from the moment he entered the White House, and that he began shifting American policy in that direction as early as the first months of 1983, almost two years before Mikhail Gorbachev came to power. Gorbachev's extraordinary receptiveness to such initiatives—as distinct from the literally moribund responses of his predecessors—greatly accelerated the improvement in relations, but it would be a mistake to credit him solely with the responsibility for what happened: Ronald Reagan deserves a great deal of the credit as well.

Critics have raised the question, though, of whether President Reagan was responsible for, or even aware of, the direction administration policy was taking. This argument is, I think, both incorrect and unfair. Reagan's opponents have been quick enough to hold him personally responsible for the failures of his administration; they should be equally prepared to acknowledge his successes. And there are points, even with the limited sources now available, where we can see that the President himself had a decisive impact upon the course of events. They include, among others: the Strategic Defense Initiative, which may have had its problems as a missile shield but which certainly worked in unsettling the Russians; endorsement of the "zero option" in the INF talks and real reductions in START, the rapidity with which the President entered into, and thereby legitimized, serious negotiations with Gorbachev once he came into office; and, most remarkably of all, his eagerness to contemplate alternatives to the nuclear arms race in a way no previous president had been willing to do.

Now, it may be objected that these were simple, unsophisticated, and, as people are given to saying these days, imperfectly "nuanced" ideas. I would not argue with that proposition. But it is important to remember that while complexity, sophistication, and nuance may be prerequisites for intellectual leadership, they are not necessarily so for political leadership, and can at times actually get in the way. President Reagan generally meant precisely what he said: when he came out in favor of negotiations from strength, or for strategic arms reductions as opposed to limitations, or even for making nuclear weapons ultimately irrelevant and obsolete, he did not do so in the "killer amendment" spirit favored by geopolitical sophisticates on the right; the President may have been conservative but he was never devious. The lesson here ought to be to beware of excessive convolution and subtlety in strategy, for sometimes simplemindedness wins out, especially if it occurs in high places.

Finally President Reagan also understood something that many geopolitical sophisticates on the left have not understood: that although toughness may or may not be a prerequisite for successful negotiations with the Russians—there are arguments for both propositions—it is absolutely essential if the American people are to lend their support, over time, to what has been negotiated. Others may have seen in the doctrine of "negotiation from strength" a way of avoiding negotiations altogether, but it now seems clear that the President saw in that approach the means of constructing a domestic political base without which agreements with the Russians would almost certainly have foundered, as indeed many of them did in the 1970s.

For unless one can sustain domestic support—and one does not do that by appearing weak—then it is hardly likely that whatever one has arranged with any adversary will actually come to anything.

There is one last irony to all of this: it is that it fell to Ronald Reagan to preside over the belated but decisive success of the strategy of containment George F. Kennan had first proposed more than four decades earlier. For what were Gorbachev's reforms if not the long-delayed "mellowing" of Soviet society that Kennan had said would take place with the passage of time? The Stalinist system that had required outside adversaries to justify its own existence now seemed at last to have passed from the scene; Gorbachev appeared to have concluded that the Soviet Union could continue to be a great power in world affairs only through the introduction of something approximating a market economy, democratic political institutions, official accountability, and respect for the rule of law at home. And that, in turn, suggested an even more remarkable conclusion: that the very survival of the ideology Lenin had imposed on Russia in 1917 now required infiltration—perhaps even subversion—by precisely the ideology the great revolutionary had sworn to overthrow.

I have some reason to suspect that Professor Kennan is not entirely comfortable with the suggestion that Ronald Reagan successfully completed the execution of the strategy he originated. But as Kennan the historian would be the first to acknowledge, history is full of ironies, and this one, surely, will not rank among the least of them.

The Limits of American Post–Cold War Power

JOSEPH S. NYE JR.

The tragedy on September 11, 2001, was a wake-up call for Americans. We became complacent during the 1990s. After the collapse of the Soviet Union, no country could match or balance us. We had unsurpassed global military, economic, and cultural power. The Gulf War at the beginning of the decade was an easy victory; and at the end of the decade, we bombed Serbia without suffering a single casualty. The economy grew and the stock market boomed. We resembled Britain in its mid-Victorian glory, but with even greater global reach.

But Americans were largely indifferent and uncertain about how to shape a foreign policy to guide this power. Polls showed the American public focused on domestic affairs and paying little attention to the rest of the world. Between 1989 and 2000, the television networks closed foreign bureaus and cut their foreign news content by two-thirds. TV executives found that "young adults cared more about the Zone diet than the subtleties of Middle East diplomacy." The president of MSNBC blamed "a national fog of materialism and disinterest and avoidance." And many of those Americans who did pay attention to foreign policy became arrogant about our power, arguing that we did not need to heed other nations. We seemed both invincible and invulnerable.

All that changed on September 11. The decision of the change, if not the timing could have been foreseen. Earlier in the year, the final report of a commission on national security chaired by former senators Gary Hart and Warren Rudman warned that America's military superiority would not protect us from hostile attacks on our homeland: "Americans will likely die on American soil, possibly in large numbers." The report was largely ignored. In 1997, [CIA director] James Woolsey and I had written that the highest priority in U.S. national security policy should be given to catastrophic terrorism, but we feared that "the very nature of U.S. society makes it difficult to prepare for this problem. Because of our 'Pearl Harbor mentality,' we are unlikely to mount an adequate defense until we suffer an attack."

The terrorist attack was a terrible symptom of deeper changes that are occurring in the world. . . . [A] technological revolution in information and communications has been diffusing power away from governments and empowering individuals and groups to play roles in world politics—including wreaking massive destruction—that were once reserved for the governments of states. Privatization has been increasing, and terrorism is the privatization of war. Moreover, the processes of globalization have been shrinking distances, and events in faraway places—such as Afghanistan—are having a greater impact on American lives. The world has been changing from the Cold War era to the global information age, but until very recently, American attitudes and policies were not keeping pace.

Where do we go from here? Americans are still wrestling with how best to combine our power and our values while reducing our vulnerabilities. As the largest power in the world, we excite both longing and hatred among some, particularly in the Muslin world. As one Pakistani physician and religious leader put it, "You are blind to anyone beyond your borders. . . . America is the world's biggest bully. Is it any wonder that so many cheer when the bully finally gets a bloodied nose?" At the same time, the tragedy also produced an enormous upwelling of sympathy for the United States in most parts of the world.

Some Americans are tempted to believe that we could reduce these hatreds and our vulnerability if we would withdraw our troops, curtail our alliances, and follow a more isolationist foreign policy. But isolationism would not remove our vulnerability. Not only are the terrorists who struck on September 11 dedicated to reducing American power, but in the words of Jordan's King Abdallah, "they want to break down the fabric of the U.S. They want to break down what America stands for." Even if we had a weaker foreign policy, such groups would resent the power of the American economy, which would still reach well beyond our shores. American corporations and citizens represent global capitalism, which is anathema to some.

Moreover, American popular culture has a global reach regardless of what we do. There is no escaping the influence of Hollywood, CNN, and the Internet. American films and television express freedom, individualism, and change (as well as sex and violence). Generally, the global reach of American culture helps to enhance our soft power—our cultural and ideological appeal. But not for everyone. Individualism and liberties are attractive to many people but repulsive to some, particularly fundamentalists. American feminism, open sexuality, and individual choices are profoundly subversive of patriarchal societies. One of the terrorist pilots is reported to have said that he did not like the United States because it is "too lax. I can go anywhere I want and they can't stop me." Some tyrants and fundamentalists will always hate us because of our values of openness and opportunity, and we will have no choice but to deal with them through more effective counterterrorism policies. But those hard nuggets of hate are unlikely to catalyze broader hatred unless we abandon our values and pursue arrogant and overbearing policies that let the extremists appeal to the majority in the middle.

What policies should guide our power, and can we preserve it? The United States has been compared to the Roman Empire, but even Rome eventually collapsed. A decade ago, the conventional wisdom lamented an America in decline. Best-seller lists featured books that described our fall. The cover of a popular magazine depicted the Statue of Liberty with a tear running down her cheek. Japan was eating our lunch and would soon replace us as number one. That view was wrong at the time, and I said so. When I wrote *Bound to Lead* in 1989, I predicted the continuing rise of American power. But power has its perils.

In his election campaign, President George W. Bush said, "If we are an arrogant nation, they'll view us that way, but if we're a humble nation, they'll respect us." He was right, but unfortunately, many foreigners saw the United States in 2001 as arrogantly concerned with narrow American interests at the expense of the rest of the world. They saw us focusing on the hard power of our military might rather than our soft power as we turned our backs on many international treaties, norms, and negotiating forums. In their eyes, the United States used consultations for talking, not listening. Yet effective leadership requires dialogue with followers. American leadership will be more enduring if we can convince our partners that we are sensitive to their concerns. September 2001 was a start toward such sensitivity, but only a start.

The problem is more than a partisan one. President Bush has declared that he is not a unilateralist, and President Clinton originally touted "assertive multilateralism" but subsequently backed away from United Nations peacekeeping efforts. Nor was he able to follow through on many of his multilateral initiatives. One reason was that Americans were internally preoccupied and relatively indifferent to our extraordinary role in the world. Both Republicans and Democrats in Congress responded largely to domestic special interests and often treated foreign policy as a mere extension of domestic politics. Congress tried to legislate for the rest of the world and imposed sanctions when others did not follow American law—for example, on trade with Iran or Cuba. Not only did Congress refuse to ratify more than a dozen treaties and conventions over the last decade, but it reduced foreign aid, withheld our dues to the United Nations and other international agencies, slashed spending at the State Department, and abolished the U.S. Information Agency. We must do better than that.

I am not alone in warning against the dangers of a foreign policy that combines unilateralism, arrogance, and parochialism. A number of American adherents of realist international relations theory have also expressed concern about America's staying power. Throughout history, coalitions of countries have arisen to balance dominant powers, and the search for new state challengers is well under way. Some see China as the new enemy; others envisage a Russia-China-India coalition as the threat. Still others see a uniting Europe becoming a nation-state that will challenge us for primacy. . . [W]hile the realists have a point, they are largely barking up the wrong tree.

In fact, the real challenges to our power are coming on cat's feet in the night, and ironically, our desire to go it alone may ultimately weaken us. The contemporary information revolution and its attendant brand of globalization are transforming and shrinking our world. At the beginning of this new century, these two forces have increased American power, including our ability to influence others through our attractive or "soft" power. But with time, technology spreads to other countries and peoples, and our relative preeminence will diminish. For example, today our twentieth of the global population represents more than half of the Internet. Many believe that in a decade or two, Chinese will be the dominant language of the Internet. It will not dethrone English as a lingua franca, but at some point the Asian market will loom larger than the American market. Or to take other examples, in international trade and antitrust matters the European Union already balances American economic power, and Europe's economic and soft power is likely to increase in years to come.

Even more important, the information revolution is creating virtual communities and networks that cut across national borders. Transnational corporations and nongovernmental actors (terrorists included) will play larger roles. Many of these organizations will have soft power of their own as they attract our citizens into coalitions that ignore national boundaries. As one of America's top diplomats observed, NGOs are "a huge and important force. . . . In many issues of American policy, from human rights to the environment, NGOs are in fact the driving force." By traditional measures of hard power, compared to other nations, the United States will remain number one, but being number one ain't gonna be what it used to.

Globalization—the growth of networks of worldwide interdependence—is putting new items on our national and international agenda whether we like it or not. Many of these issues we cannot resolve by ourselves. International financial stability is vital to the prosperity of Americans, but we need the cooperation of others to ensure it. Global climate change, too, will affect Americans' quality of life, but we cannot manage the problem alone. And in a world where borders are becoming more porous than ever to everything from drugs to infectious diseases to terrorism, we are forced to work with other countries behind their borders and inside ours. To rephrase the title of my earlier book, we are not only bound to lead, but bound to cooperate.

How should we guide our foreign policy in a global information age? Some in the current foreign policy debates look at our preponderance in power and see a modern empire. For example, self-styled neo-Reaganites advocate a foreign policy of "benign American hegemony." Since American values are good and we have the military power, we should not feel restrained by others. In their eyes, "Americans should understand that their support for American pre-eminence is as much a boost for international justice as any people is capable of giving. It is also a boon for American interests and for what might be called the American spirit."

But many conservatives realists as well as liberals believe that such views smack of hubris and arrogance that alienate our friends. Americans have always viewed our nation as exceptional, but even our Declamation of Independence expressed "a decent respect for the opinions of mankind." If we are truly acting in the interests of others as well as our own, we would presumably accord to others a substantial voice and, by doing so, end up embracing some form of multilateralism. As our allies point out, even well-intentioned Americans are not immune to Lord Acton's famous warning that power can corrupt. . . .

Americans are divided over how to be involved with the rest of the world. At the end of the Cold War, many observers were haunted by the specter of the return of American isolationism. The debate today, however, is not only between isolationists and internationalists but also within the internationalists camp, which is split between unilateralists and multilateralists. Some urge a new unilateralism in which we refuse to play the role of docile international citizen, instead unashamedly pursuing our own ends. They speak of a unipolar world because of our unequaled military power. But . . . military power alone cannot produce the outcomes we want on many of the issues that matter to Americans.

As a former assistant secretary of defense, I would be the last to deny the continuing importance of military power. Our military role is essential to global stability. And the military is part of our response to terrorism. But we must not let the metaphor of war blind us to the fact that suppressing terrorism will take years of patient, unspectacular work, including close civilian cooperation with other countries. On many of the key issues today, such as international financial stability, drug smuggling, or global climate change, military power simply cannot produce success, and its use can sometimes be counterproductive. As President Bush's father said after the September tragedy, "Just as Pearl Harbor awakened this country from the notion that we could somehow avoid the call of duty and defend freedom in Europe and Asia in World War II, so, too, should this most recent surprise attack erase the concept in some quarters that America can somehow go it alone in the fight against terrorism or in anything else for that matter."

The initial American response followed this advice. Congress suddenly approved a big dues payment and confirmed our ambassador to the United Nations. The president sought UN support and stressed coalition building. The Treasury and White House, which earlier had undercut international cooperation on money-laundering tax havens, rapidly became proponents of cooperation. But unilateralism is far from banished. At first, the Pentagon was even unwilling to have NATO invoked the alliance's mutual-defense clause. The allies were desperately trying to give us political cover and the Pentagon was resisting it. Eventually Secretary of Defense Donald Rumsfeld understood it was a plus, not a minus, and was able to accept it. Other officials, however, worried that coalitions would shackle the United States and that invoking the international authority of the UN or NATO would set a bad precedent. Internal debates about how to implement the Bush doctrine of eliminating the scourge of terrorism raised concerns in other countries that the United States would be the unilateral judge of whether a country is supporting terrorism and the appropriate methods of response. In the Congress, at the same time that our ally Britain was ratifying the treaty creating an international criminal court, Senator Jesse Helms was pressing legislation that would authorize "any necessary action to free U.S. soldiers improperly handed over to the court, a provision dubbed by some delegates as 'the Hague invasion clause.'" How long the new multilateralism will last and how deep it goes remains an open question.

Any retreat to a traditional policy focus on unipolarity, hegemony, sovereignty, and unilateralism will fail to produce the right outcomes, and its accompanying arrogance will erode the soft power that is often part of the solution. We must not let the illusion of empire blind us to the increasing importance of our soft power.

How should we act in this time of unparalleled power and peril? Can we learn how to use our hard and soft power in productive combination to not only defeat terrorism but deal with the other issues of a global information age? Can we wisely use our lead during these years early in the century to build a framework for the long term? Can we promote and ensure our basic values of freedom and democracy? Are our domestic attitudes and institutions up to the challenge, or will we fritter away our advantage through inattention or arrogance? Why are we having such a hard time defining our national interest in this global information age? . . .

Our historical test will be to develop a consensus on principles and norms that will allow us to work with others to create political stability, economic growth, and democratic values. American power is not eternal. If we squander our soft power through a combination of arrogance and indifference, we will increase our vulnerability, sell our values short, and hasten the erosion of our preeminence.

 # FURTHER READING

David Armstrong and Erik Goldstein, eds., *The End of the Cold War* (1990)
Anders Åslund, *Gorbachev's Struggle for Economic Reform* (1989)
Andrew J. Bacevich, *American Empire* (2002)
Robert H. Baker, *Hollow Victory* (2001)
Richard J. Barnet and John Cavanaugh, *Global Dreams: Imperial Corporations and the New World Order* (1994)
Donald C. Baucom, *The Origins of SDI, 1944–1983* (1992)
Larry Berman, ed., *Looking Back at the Reagan Presidency* (1990)
Paul Berman, *A Tale of Two Utopias* (1996)
William G. Berman, *America's Right Turn* (1994)
———, *From the Center to the Edge* (2001) (on the Clinton presidency)
Michael A. Bernstein et al., *Understanding America's Economic Decline* (1994)
Michael R. Beschloss and Strobe Talbott, *At the Highest Levels* (1993)
Seweryn Bialer and Michael Mandlebaum, eds., *Gorbachev's Russia and American Foreign Policy* (1988)
Jane Boulden, *Peace Enforcement: The United Nations Experience in Congo, Somalia, and Bosnia* (2002)
Paul Boyer, ed., *Reagan as President* (1990)
Seyom Brown, *The Illusion of Control* (2003)
Lester H. Brune, *The United States and Post Cold War Interventions* (1998)
David Callahan, *Between Two Worlds* (1994) (on post–Cold War affairs)
David P. Calleo, *Beyond American Hegemony* (1987)
Fraser Cameron, *U.S. Foreign Policy After the Cold War* (2002)
Colin Campbell and Bert A. Rockman, *The Bush Presidency* (1991)
Lou Cannon, *President Reagan* (1991)
James Chace, *The Consequences of Peace* (1992)
Stephen Cohen, *Failed Crusade,* (2000)
Michael Cox, *U.S. Foreign Policy After the Cold War* (1999)
Ivo H. Daalder and James M. Lindsay, *America Unbound* (2003) (on George W. Bush)
Dusko Doder and Louise Branson, *Gorbachev* (1990)
Theodore Draper, *A Very Thin Line* (1991) (on Iran-Contra)
Michael Duffy and Dan Goodgame, *Marching in Place* (1992)
Matthew Evangelista, *Unarmed Forces: The Transnational Movement to End the Cold War* (1999)
John Feffer, ed., *Power Trip* (2003)
Beth A. Fisher, *The Reagan Reversal* (1997)
Frances Fitzgerald, *Way Out There* (2000) (on *Star Wars*)
Frederick H. Fleitz, Jr., *Peacekeeping Fiascos of the 1990s* (2002)
Jeffrey E. Garten, *A Cold Peace* (1992)

Raymond L. Garthoff, *The Great Transition* (1995)

Robert Gates, *From the Shadows* (1996)

Charles Gati, *The Bloc That Failed* (1990)

Misha Glenny, *The Fall of Yugoslavia* (1992)

John Robert Greene, *The Presidency of George Bush* (2000)

David Halberstam, *War in a Time of Peace* (2001)

Jim Hanson, *The Decline of the American Empire* (1993)

Erwin C. Hargrove, *Jimmy Carter as President* (1988)

Jonathan Haslam, *The Soviet Union and the Politics of Nuclear Weapons in Europe* (1990)

Stanley Hoffman, *World Disorders* (1999)

Michael J. Hogan, ed., *The End of the Cold War* (1992)

Samuel P. Huntington, *The Clash of Civilizations and the Remaking of World Order* (1996)

William G. Hyland, *Clinton's World* (1999)

John G. Ikenberry, ed., *America Unrivaled* (2002)

William M. D. Jackson, "Soviet Assessments of Ronald Reagan," *Political Science Quarterly,*
    113 (1998–1999), pp. 617–644

Robert Jervis and Seweryn Bialer, eds., *Soviet-American Relations After the Cold War* (1991)

Haynes Johnson, *The Best of Times: America in the Clinton Years* (2002)

———, *Sleepwalking Through History* (1991) (on Reagan)

Robert H. Johnson, *Improbable Dangers* (1995)

Charles O. Jones, *The Trusteeship Presidency* (1988) (on Carter)

Robert Kagan, *Of Paradise and Power* (2003) (on the U.S. and Europe)

Robert G. Kaiser, *How Gorbachev Happened* (1991)

William W. Kaufmann, *Glasnost, Perestroika, and U.S. Defense Spending* (1990)

George F. Kennan, "On American Principles," *Foreign Affairs,* 75 (1995), 116–126

Paul Kennedy, *Preparing for the Next Century* (1993)

———, *The Rise and Fall of the Great Powers* (1987)

Henry A. Kissinger, *Does America Need a Foreign Policy?* (2000)

Stephen Kotkin, *Armageddon Averted* (2001)

Charles A. Kupchan, *The End of the American Era* (2002)

David E. Kyvig, *Reagan and the World* (1990)

Richard Ned Lebow, *We All Lost the Cold War* (1994)

Robert J. Leiber, *Eagle Adrift* (1997)

Edwin T. Linenthal, *Symbolic Defense* (1989) (on SDI)

Thomas Lippman, *Madeleine Albright and the New American Diplomacy* (2000)

Allen Lynch, *The Cold War Is Over—Again* (1992)

Sean M. Lynn-Jones, ed., *The Cold War and After* (1991)

Matthew McAllester, *Beyond the Mountains of the Damned: The War Inside Kosovo* (2002)

Michael McCgwire, *Perestroika and Soviet National Security* (1991)

Robert J. McMahon, "Making Sense of American Foreign Policy During the Reagan
    Years," *Diplomatic History,* 19 (1995), 367–384

John J. Mearshimer, *The Tragedy of Great Power Politics* (2001)

Morris Morley, *Crisis and Confrontation* (1988)

Henry R. Nau, *The Myth of America's Decline* (1990)

John Newhouse, *War and Peace in the Nuclear Age* (1989)

Joseph S. Nye Jr., *Bound to Lead* (1990)

Don Oberdorfer, *From the Cold War to a New Era* (1998)

William E. Odom and Robert Dujarric, *America's Inadvertent Empire* (2004)

Kenneth A. Oye et al., ed., *Eagle in a New World* (1992)

S. Victor Papacosma et al., *NATO After Fifty Years* (2001)

Herbert S. Parmet, *George Bush* (1998)

Joseph E. Persico, *Casey* (1990)

Kevin Phillips, *American Dynasty* (2004) (on the Bush family)

Ronald E. Powaski, *Return to Armageddon* (2003)

John Prados, *President's Secret Wars* (1996)

Miron Rezan, *Europe's Nightmare: The Struggle for Kosovo* (2001)

Michael Rogin, *Ronald Reagan* (1987)

Richard Rosencrance, *America's Economic Resurgence* (1990)

Michael Schaller, *Reckoning with Reagan* (1992)

Arthur M. Schlesinger Jr., "Back to the Womb?: Isolationism's Renewed Threat," *Foreign Affairs,* 74 (1995), 2–8

Peter Schweitzer, *Reagan's War* (2002)

Gaddis Smith, *Morality, Reason, and Power* (1986) (on Carter)

Leonard S. Spector, *Nuclear Ambitions*(1990)

James Gustave Speth, *Red Sky at Morning* (2004) (on the global environment)

Ronald Steel, *Temptations of a Superpower* (1996)

Robert Strong, *Working in the World* (2002) (on Carter)

Ralph Summy and Michael E. Salla, *Why the Cold War Ended* (1995)

Strobe Talbot, *The Russian and Reagan* (1984)

Gregory E. Treverton, *America, Germany, and the Future of Germany* (1992)

Robert W. Tucker and David C. Hendrickson, *The Imperial Temptation* (1992)

Peter Wallison, *Ronald Reagan* (2002)

Garry Wills, "Habits of Hegemony," *Foreign Affairs,* 78 (1999), 50–59

Philip Zelikow and Condoleeza Rice, *Germany Unified and Europe Transformed* (1995)

Vladislav M. Zubok, "New Evidence on the 'Soviet Factor' in the Peaceful Revolutions of 1989," *Cold War International History Project Bulletin,* 12/13 (2001), 5–14

CHAPTER
14

September 11, 2001,
and Anti-Americanism
in the Muslim World

*On September 20, 2001, nine days after the horrific attacks on the World Trade
Center in New York City and the Pentagon in Washington, D.C., President George W.
Bush addressed a joint session of Congress. Over the previous week the press reported
that the deadliest terrorist attack in U.S. history, with nearly 3,000 casualties, had
been executed by an Islamic group known as al Qaeda, a shadowy, global network
led by a wealthy Saudi Arabian named Osama bin Laden. "Why do they hate us?"
the president implored. He reviewed the possibilities: resentment of American
freedom, hatred for U.S.-backed governments in the Middle East, intolerance for
Christians and Jews. In the following weeks, the questions multiplied. Was Islamic
culture inherently violent? Or had al Qaeda hijacked the religion? Did American
support for oil-rich monarchs and Israel generate the hatred? Did the attack stem
from a global conflict between modern and traditional societies, rich versus poor?*

*The United States is only the most recent external power to exercise influence
in the Middle East. From the sixteenth century until World War I, the Ottoman
Turks ruled most of the region. Following the Turks' defeat in World War I, the
victorious British and French forged a new political order in the Middle East by
creating new states, redrawing boundaries, and striking alliances with local rulers.
American missionaries established a presence in the Arab world during the nineteenth and early twentieth centuries, but it was World War II that eroded European
colonialism and ushered U.S. power into the region. During the war, President
Franklin Roosevelt anointed King Ibn Saud's Saudi Arabia as America's favored
Middle East oil supplier. Then, in 1946, after blunting Soviet influence in oil-rich
Iran, Washington initiated a partnership with another oil kingdom, that of Shah
Mohammed Reza Pahlavi. While oil fueled America's military, facilitated European
and Japanese postwar recovery, and drove global capitalism, petroleum politics
also generated antagonism. Prime Minister Mohammed Mossadeq's nationaliza-
tion of Iranian oil led to a CIA-backed coup in 1953 that removed him from power.
But a quarter of a century later, the reinstated Shah's pro-Western, modernizing*

autocracy had widened the gap between rich and poor in Iran and embittered con-servative Islamic clerics.

U.S. support for Israel also stirred discord. After World War II, the United Nations backed a partition of the British mandate in Palestine and the creation of two political entities—one Jewish and one Palestinian. Arabs protested, but Israelis in May 1948 declared the creation of a Jewish state, and won diplomatic recognition from both Washington and Moscow. Hundreds of thousands of Palestinian refugees spilled across borders, and Egypt, Jordan, and Syria sent armies into Palestine to engage Israeli forces in the first Arab-Israeli War (1948–1949). Although the Truman administra-tion rebuffed Israel's requests for military aid, the United States gradually established a commitment to the new state, based on sympathy for the victims of Nazi genocide, political lobbying by Jewish Americans, and strategic Cold War considerations.

During the 1950s U.S. military interests increasingly impinged on the region. The U.S.-sponsored Baghdad Pact—an anti-Soviet alliance that included Britain, Iran, Iraq, Pakistan, and Turkey—aggravated relations with Egypt's nationalist Gamal Abdel Nasser. President Eisenhower and Secretary of State John Foster Dulles tried to appease Nasser by promising aid to build the High Aswan Dam on the Nile River, but abruptly withdrew the offer when Nasser accepted Eastern bloc arms. Nasser nationalized the British- and French-run Suez Canal in 1956, and withstood a British-French-Israel invasion. Ike and Dulles applied diplomatic and economic pressure on U.S. allies to abandon their military operations, but viewed Nasser's rising stature with alarm. In 1957 the Congress approved the Eisenhower Doctrine, authorizing the dispatch of U.S. troops to any Middle Eastern nation that requested help in resisting international Communism. The following year U.S. Marines landed on Lebanon's shores to bolster a pro-Western regime.

Arab frustrations mounted following Nasser's devastating setback in the Six Day War of June 1967 when Israel won a stunning victory and seized Jordan's West Bank, including the Holy City of Jerusalem, Syria's Golan Heights, and Egypt's Sinai Peninsula and Gaza Strip. Washington's growing willingness to supply Israel with advanced weaponry, and Tel Aviv's cool response to U.N.-sponsored peace talks, fed a growing anti-Americanism in the region. Palestinians living under Israeli rule in the West Bank and Gaza looked to Yasir Arafat and the militant, anti-Israeli Palestinian Liberation Organization (PLO) for leadership. But neither a third major Arab-Israeli clash, the Yom Kippur War of October 1973, nor a globally destabilizing oil embargo orchestrated by the Organization of Petroleum Exporting Countries (OPEC), dislodged the Israelis. The Camp David Accords between Egypt's Anwar Sadat and Israel's prime minister Menachem Begin in 1978, brokered by President Jimmy Carter (1977–1981), provided for Israel's withdrawal from the Sinai, and Egypt's recogni-tion of the Jewish state, but left unresolved the status of other occupied territories.

In early 1979, Iran's Islamic revolution in Iran unseated Shah Pahlavi and unleashed a torrent of anti-American fury. The decade-long Soviet invasion of Afghanistan (1979–1989) produced bitter new social tensions that facilitated the eventual Islamic Taliban takeover in Kabul. Israel's invasion of Lebanon in 1982 and a cycle of terrorism conducted by the PLO, Hamas, and Hezbollah—including the bombing of U.S. Marine barracks in Lebanon—further unhinged the region. Meanwhile, Iraqi leader Saddam Hussein, armed with chemical weapons, em-barked on a war with neighboring Iran (1980–1985). Iraq's invasion of oil-rich Kuwait in the summer of 1990 momentarily aligned Israel, Egypt, Saudi Arabia, and Syria in a U.S.-led coalition that turned back Saddam Hussein's war machine, but neither the administration of George Bush (1989–1993) nor Bill Clinton (1993–2001) succeeded in sealing an Arab-Israeli peace. Clinton brought Prime

Minister Yitzhak Rabin and Yasir Arafat to the White House in September 1993 to sign an accord that committed Israel to withdraw from Gaza and the West Bank city of Jericho. Additional portions of the West Bank would gradually transfer to the Palestinian Authority. But efforts to achieve a lasting peace floundered.

Nor did the U.S. triumph over Iraq in 1991 bring peace to the Gulf. Saddam Hussein survived the war, and the Saudi kingdom, a base for U.S. military operations, became a recruiting ground for al Qaeda. When the attacks of September 11, 2001 came, the younger George Bush administration (2001–) vowed an unrelenting war against terrorism. From October through December 2001, the U.S. military demolished the Taliban regime in Afghanistan, which had provided haven to al Qaeda, but Osama bin Laden eluded capture. In January 2002, Bush denounced what he termed an "axis of evil," citing Iran, Iraq, and North Korea for their nuclear weapons programs and their links to terrorism. The White House gained Congressional approval for the use of force to make Iraq comply with post–Gulf War terms for disarmament, and in November 2002 the U.N. Security Council found Baghdad in breach of U.N. resolutions prohibiting development of weapons of mass destruction. Hussein denied the charges and readmitted U.N. weapons inspectors, whom he had ousted in 1998, but Washington still demanded Saddam's removal. When Security Council members threatened to veto a resolution for war, Bush assembled a coalition of willing allies and launched a second Persian Gulf War on March 20, 2003. U.S. troops quickly toppled the Iraqi regime, but Hussein loyalists organized a deadly guerrilla resistance. A costly U.S. occupation began.

The chronology of events supports conflicting explanations for Middle Eastern anti-Americanism. Some scholars argue that deep cultural differences separate the West and the Muslim world. The "clash of civilizations" thesis posits that Islamic leaders have dodged the need for democratic reform and deflected criticism by denouncing all vestiges of Westernization. Others trace Muslim rage primarily to U.S. policies in the Middle East: the pursuit of oil, single-minded anti-Communism, support for corrupt Arab autocracies, and Washington's staunch backing for Israel. Some analysts fault European and U.S. officials for feeding into cultural stereotypes by interpreting the Muslim world through the prism of "orientalism," a set of perceptions that highlight the Middle East's exoticism and "otherness." Finally, some see in Arab terrorism an anguished response to the dislocation inflicted by economic, political, and cultural globalization—the revenge of the territorially dispossessed and economically disadvantaged.

Why do they hate us? Everyone, it seems, has a different answer. America's ability and willingness to formulate a historically-based understanding of Muslim anger may determine the outcome of the war on terror and the long-term security of the United States.

DOCUMENTS

The United States first intruded upon European hegemony in the Middle East in 1933 when King Abdul Aziz Ibn Saud, head of the recently formed state of Saudi Arabia, granted a concession to the Standard Oil Company of California. Recognizing the importance of the kingdom's oil reserves, President Roosevelt made Saudi Arabia eligible for Lend-Lease aid in 1943 and in February 1945 met with Ibn Saud aboard the USS *Quincy* in the Suez Canal. At that meeting the fundamentals of the relationship were established: the United States pledged to provide for Saudi security needs in exchange for access to Saudi oil. The monarch also raised concerns about the growing presence of Jewish settlers in Palestine. Document 1 is a reprint of a letter from Roosevelt to Ibn Saud, dated April 5, 1945, in which FDR reassured the king that no decision would be taken on Palestine's future without consultation with both Jews and Arabs. World War II and Nazi genocide, however, increased pressure for a Jewish homeland in the British mandate of Palestine. Unable to reconcile Jewish and Arab demands, the British announced their intention to withdraw from the holy land. The United States then backed a UN resolution passed on November 29, 1947, to partition Palestine into separate Jewish and Arab states. But mounting violence between Jews and Arabs in the territory made many State Department and Pentagon officials fear that partition would drive angry Arabs into the Soviet camp, jeopardize Western oil supplies, and perhaps require UN military intervention. Document 2 is a draft National Security Council memorandum, penned in February 1948, that weighs the pros and cons of partition and its alternatives. The NSC ultimately recommended that partition be delayed, but President Harry Truman overruled his foreign-policy advisers. Many observers at the time suspected that Truman was seeking Jewish votes in the upcoming election. The president maintained that he acted out of concern for the oppressed Jewish people. On May 14, 1948, the state of Israel was proclaimed, and the White House extended diplomatic recognition within hours.

During the mid-1950s and early 1960s Egyptian president Gamal Abdel Nasser emerged as the voice of Third World nationalism in the Arab world. In 1955, when the Cold War neutralist accepted arms from the Soviet camp, President Dwight D. Eisenhower and Secretary of State John Foster Dulles canceled loans to help build the Aswan Dam. Nasser, in turn, nationalized the Suez Canal. Document 3 is drawn from a July 28, 1956, speech in which Nasser blasts European imperialism and justifies Egypt's takeover of the canal. Israel's decisive victory over Egypt and its allies and its occupation of Arab lands in the Six Day War of June 1967 badly tarnished Nasser's image. Viewing Nasser and the Soviet Union as largely responsible for the outbreak of the war, the administration of Lyndon Johnson backed Israel. The United States tried to counteract anti-American sentiment among Arabs by supporting UN Resolution 242, adopted on November 22, 1967, which called upon Israel to relinquish the occupied territories in exchange for official recognition and peace. Meanwhile, the Palestinian Liberation Organization (PLO) took up the cause of Arabs displaced by Israel's policies and issued its National Covenant, Document 4, in July 1968. Although the covenant does not mention Israel by name, it denounces a "Zionist invasion" as a tool of Western imperialism and calls for military and political action to regain Palestine for its Arab inhabitants.

During the 1970s Islamic extremism shook the Middle East landscape. In 1979 America's ally, the Shah of Iran, was swept aside by the Ayatollah Khomeini's Islamic fundamentalism. In November, America's troubles with Iran reached a boiling point when Iranian students stormed the U.S. embassy in Tehran and took U.S. citizens hostage. The excruciating hostages crisis lasted fourteen months until January 1981. Meanwhile, in December 1979, Moscow sent seventy-five thousand Soviet troops into neighboring Afghanistan to bolster a client Marxist government. President Jimmy Carter initiated covert support for the anticommunist Afghan *mujahadeen,* a program that was expanded by the Reagan administration. Document 5 is an excerpt from Carter's State of the Union address delivered on January 23, 1980. In that speech, the president lamented the Iranian hostage crisis, denounced Soviet military actions, and enunciated the "Carter Doctrine": the United States would use military force to counter aggression by any outside forces in the Persian Gulf. In Document 6, an address to Congress on September 11, 1990, the elder President George Bush emphasized both principle and U.S. interest in Persian Gulf oil to rally the nation to overturn Iraq's conquest of Kuwait and build a "new world order" based on the rule of law.

Saddam Hussein's defeat in the first Persian Gulf War was followed by momentary progress in the Arab-Israeli peace process. In September 1993 President Bill Clinton welcomed Israeli prime minister Yitzhak Rabin and PLO chairman Yasir Arafat to Washington. The two rivals signed a peace treaty committing Tel Aviv to withdraw from Gaza and parts of the West Bank and the Palestinian Authority to denounce terrorism. Document 7 is Rabin's eloquent plea for peace made at the White House signing ceremony on September 13, 1993. Rabin was later assassinated by an Israel extremist, the peace process sputtered, and his Labor party was voted out of office and replaced by a conservative Likud government.

The 1990s produced a new wave of violence. In the aftermath of the Soviet withdrawal from Afghanistan, Saudi millionaire Osama bin Laden assembled his al Qaeda organization in the Taliban-ruled Southwest Asian state. The group formed links with other Islamist groups and developed a global network. The first al Qaeda attack on New York's World Trade Center came in 1993, when a bomb detonated in the underground car park killed seven and injured more than one thousand others. Five years later, bin Laden's forces engineered the simultaneous bombing of U.S. embassies in Dar es Salaam, Tanzania, and Nairobi, killing 258 people. In 2000 a suicide attack on the USS *Cole* in the Yemeni port of Aden killed 17 U.S. servicemen. Then came the attacks on the World Trade Center and Pentagon on September 11, 2001. On September 20, the younger President George Bush (2001–) addressed the Congress and the nation. The president identified al Qaeda as the group responsible for the tragedy, demanded that the Taliban deliver the organization's leaders to U.S. authorities, and declared a "war on terror." In his address, Bush also posed the essential question: Why do they hate us? The speech is reprinted here as Document 8. On October 7, 2001, after the United States launched its attack on Afghanistan's leaders, the Arab television news network al Jazeera broadcast a defiant speech from Osama bin Laden (Document 9). Al Qaeda's leader praised god and the prophet Mohammed, and he claimed that justice had been meted out to those responsible for suffering and death in the Muslim world. Following the successful overthrow of the Taliban regime in Afghanistan, the Bush administration turned its sights on Iraq, charging that Saddam Hussein threatened the world at large with his weapons of mass destruction and his support for terrorism. Facing strong opposition to his demand for "regime change" in Baghdad, the president made his case for U.S. military action—without specific UN sanction—in a televised speech on March 17, 2003. Excerpts from the speech are reprinted here as Document 10.

1. President Franklin D. Roosevelt Befriends King Ibn Saud, 1945

I have received the communication which Your Majesty sent me under date of March 10, 1945, in which you refer to the question of Palestine and to the continuing interest of the Arabs in current developments affecting that country.

I am gratified that Your Majesty took this occasion to bring your views on this question to my attention and I have given the most careful attention to the statements which you make in your letter. I am also mindful of the memorable conversation which we had not so long ago and in the course of which I had an opportunity to obtain so vivid an impression of Your Majesty's sentiments on this question.

Your Majesty will recall that on previous occasions I communicated to you the attitude of the American Government toward Palestine and made clear our desire

This document can be found in *Department of State Bulletin,* 21 October 1945, p. 623.

that no decision be taken with respect to the basic situation in that country without full consultation with both Arabs and Jews. Your Majesty will also doubtless recall that during our recent conversation I assured you that I would take no action, in my capacity as Chief of the Executive Branch of this Government, which might prove hostile to the Arab people.

It gives me pleasure to renew to Your Majesty the assurances which you have previously received regarding the attitude of my Government and my own, as Chief Executive, with regard to the question of Palestine and to inform you that the policy of this Government in this respect is unchanged.

I desire also at this time to send you my best wishes for Your Majesty's continued good health and for the welfare of your people.

2. The National Security Council Weighs U.S. Options in the Middle East, 1948

The United States Government, on the basis of high motives and in consideration of conditions existing at the time, voted in favor of the General Assembly Resolution of 29 November 1947, recommending the Plan for Partition of Palestine. In so doing our government assumed a moral obligation, along with the other members of the UN who voted for the resolution, to lend its support honestly and courageously to the implementation of that resolution. Our government cannot without cause fail to fulfill this moral obligation. The most impelling cause for any change in our position on the Palestine problem would be a demonstration of the incompatibility of our present position with the security of our own nation.

The greatest threat to the security of the United States and to international peace is the USSR and its aggressive program of Communist expansion.

In meeting this threat, the United States cannot take steps which disregard the following considerations:

   a. Unrestricted access to the oil resources of the Middle east is essential to the complete economy of the United States and to the economic recovery of Europe under the ERP [European Recovery Program].
   b. In the event of war, the oil and certain strategic areas of the Middle East will figure prominently in the successful prosecution of such a war by the United States.
   c. A friendly or at least a neutral attitude by the Arab peoples toward the US and its interests is requisite to the procurement of adequate quantities of oil for the purposes as stated and to the utilization of strategic areas without prohibitive cost in the event of war.

The United States cannot afford to allow the USSR to gain a lodgment in the Eastern Mediterranean. The Joint Chiefs of Staff have emphasized their view that,

---

This document can be found at Draft: "The Position of the United States with Respect to Palestine," 17 February 1948, Papers of Clark M. Clifford, Harry S. Truman Library, Independence, Missouri. It can also be found in Dennis Merrill, ed., *Documentary History of the Truman Presidency,* (Bethesda, Md.: University Publications of America, 1998) XXVI, 49–64.

of all the possible eventualities in the Palestine situation, the most unfavorable in the security interests of the United States would be the intrusion of Soviet forces and, second only to that the introduction of US troops in opposition to possible Arab resistance. . . .

The affirmative vote of the United States upon the UN Plan for Partition of Palestine, and the pressure applied to other governments by various US groups and individuals, have antagonized the Arab peoples to an unprecedented degree. Competent observers of Arab psychology predict that increasing animosity will attend each further manifestation of US leadership in or support of implementation of the Plan for Partition. Consideration must be given to the fact that the Arab people sincerely believe in the righteousness of their opposition to Palestine partition, which imposes upon them the major initial cost of attempting a solution to the international problem of Zionism. . . .

Fundamental to the Plan for Partition of Palestine is economic union between the proposed Jewish and Arab States. The Arabs have announced their implacable opposition to the establishment of the contemplated Arab State in Palestine, and there is no indication that the Jews and Arabs of Palestine have made any conciliatory moves to effect a compromise solution. Severe fighting has broken out between the Jews and Arabs of Palestine. These and other developments, since the General Assembly adoption of the Palestine resolution, raise grave doubts that the proposed solution to the Palestine problem is the one most conducive to the security of the US, the increased prestige of the UN, and to the peace of the world. . . .

The security of the United States, the peace of the world, and the preservation of the UN, dictate that all possible courses of action by this government be reexamined to determine the one with most promise of success to each of these objectives.

Alternative US courses of action with respect to the Palestine question are:

a. Fully support the partition plan with all the means at our disposal, including the use of armed forces under the United Nations.

Under this course of action, the United States would have to take steps to grant substantial economic assistance to the Jewish authorities and to afford them support through the supply of arms, ammunition and implements of war. In order to enable the Jewish state to survive in the face of wide-scale resistance from the Arabs in Palestine, from the neighboring Arab States, and possibly from other Moslem countries, the United States would be prepared ultimately to utilize its naval units and military forces for this purpose. . . .

(1) Advantages.

    (a) Maintains UN and US policy constant in the eyes of the world.

    (b) Contributes to the settlement of the displaced Jews of Europe.

(2) Disadvantages.

    (a) Alienates the Moslem world with the resultant threat of:

        1. Suspension or cancellation of US air base rights and commercial concessions including oil, and drastic curtailment of US trade in the area.

        2. Loss of access to British air, military and naval facilities in the area, affecting our strategic position in the Middle East and Mediterranean.

3. Closing of our educational, religious and philanthropic institutions in the area.
4. Possible deaths, injuries and damages arising from acts of violence against individual US citizens and interests throughout the Middle East.
5. A serious impediment to the success of the European Recovery Program, which is dependent on increased production of Middle East oil.

(b) Provides a vehicle for Soviet expansion into an area vital to our security interests.
(c) Deploys US troops in a situation where there is high probability of loss of American lives and which might result in war. . . .

b. Continuation of support for the Partition Plan in the United Nations by all measures short of the use of outside armed force to impose the Plan upon the people of Palestine.

In this course of action United States representatives in the UN Security Council, the Trusteeship Council and the Economic and Social Council would continue to support the implementation of the General Assembly recommendations on Palestine. Such support should take into account, however, that the Charter does not authorize the imposition of a recommended settlement upon the people directly concerned by armed action of the United Nations or its Members. . . .

(1) Advantages.
(a) Maintains the announced policy of the United States with respect to Palestine so long as such policy appears to have any reasonable opportunity for implementation.
(b) Retains the responsibility for consideration of the Palestine question within the framework of the United Nations, distributes the responsibility throughout the UN membership, and prevents it from becoming still further a matter of United States responsibility.
(c) Assures a certain amount of political support from elements in the major political parties within the United States.
(d) Contributes to the settlement of the displaced Jews of Europe.

(2) Disadvantages.
(a) Leads to continued deterioration of Arab relations with the United States. . . .
(b) Permits further exploitation of the interests of world Zionism by the USSR.
(c) Entails further loss of life while waiting for a conclusive demonstration that outside force will be required to preserve law and order within Palestine.
(d) Encourages the Arabs within Palestine to increase their resistance by all available means.
(e) In the event of implementation of partition, provides a vehicle for Soviet expansion into an area vital to our interests.
(f) Threatens the success of the European Recovery Program, which is dependent on increased production of Middle East oil.

c. Adopt a passive or neutral role, taking no further steps to aid or implement partition.

This course of action would involve maintenance and enforcement of the present United States embargo on arms to Palestine and the neighboring countries. The United States would give no unilateral assistance to either the proposed Jewish or Arab States financially, militarily or otherwise, and insofar as possible, the United States would require an attitude of neutrality to be observed by all persons or organizations under US jurisdiction. The United States would oppose sending armed forces into Palestine by the United Nations or any member thereof for the purpose of implementing partition, and would oppose the recruitment of volunteers for this purpose.

Such a course of action would rest on the assumption that implementation of the General Assembly resolution was a collective responsibility of the United Nations and that no leadership in the matter devolved upon the United States. . . .

(1) Advantages.
   (a) Maintains United Nations and United States policy constant in the eyes of the world.
   (b) Avoids employment of US troops in Palestine.
(2) Disadvantages.
   (a) Surrenders US initiative in the solution of the Palestine problem.
   (b) Permits communist encouragement of chaos.
   (c) Possibly results in Russian intervention on a unilateral basis.
   (d) Exposes the United States to possible curtailment of air base rights and commercial concessions including oil, and to a lesser degree to drastic curtailment of US trade in the area.

d. Alter our previous policy of support for partition and seek another solution to the problem.

This course of action would call for a special session of the General Assembly to reconsider the situation. Abandoning US support of partition as impracticable and unworkable in view of the demonstrated inability of the people of Palestine to assume the responsibilities of self-government, and in view of the report of the [UN] Palestine Commission that outside military forces would be required, the United States would, under this course of action, attempt to seek a constructive solution of the problem. . . .

Specifically the United States would endeavor to bring about conciliation of the problem. The United States would propose that while working for such conciliation or arbitration, a special session of the General Assembly be called to consider a new solution in the form of

(1) An international trusteeship or
(2) A federal state,

with provision for Jewish immigration in either case, and preferably excluding the use of either US or USSR troops.

A trusteeship could take one of several forms; a three-power trusteeship of the US, UK and France, and joint US-UK trusteeship either with or without some of the smaller states, or a general UN trusteeship with the Trusteeship Council as administering authority. Alternatively, a federal state with cantonization, a plan which the British originally favored as having the greatest chance of success, could be discussed.

(1) Advantages.

  (a) Assists in preventing Communist expansion into the Middle East and the Mediterranean.

  (b) Improves our strategic position in the Middle East, thereby enhancing our overall national security.

  (c) Opens the way for restorations of US friendship and influence in the Arab world.

  (d) Opens the way for a solution to the Palestine problem more acceptable to the people of Palestine.

  (e) Lessens probability of use of US military forces in combat in Palestine.

  (f) Protects our philanthropic and educational interests, investments and oil interests.

(2) Disadvantages.

  (a) Produces violent Zionist opposition.

  (b) Gives Russia and its Communist satellites a sounding board for further vitriolic vituperations.

  (c) Requires the General Assembly to find another solution for the Palestine question without any present assurance of success.

3. Egypt's Gamal Abdel Nasser Justifies Nationalizing the Suez Canal, 1956

The uproar which we anticipated has been taking place in London and Paris. This tremendous uproar is not supported by reason or logic. It is backed only by imperialist methods, by the habits of blood-sucking and of usurping rights, and by interference in the affairs of other countries. An unjustified uproar arose in London, and yesterday Britain submitted a protest to Egypt. I wonder what was the basis of this protest by Britain to Egypt? The Suez Canal Company is an Egyptian company, subject to Egyptian sovereignty. When we nationalized the Suez Canal Company, we only nationalized an Egyptian limited company, and by doing so we exercised a right which stems from the very core of Egyptian sovereignty. What right has Britain to interfere in our internal affairs? What right has Britain to interfere in our affairs and our questions? When we nationalized the Suez Canal Company, we only performed an act stemming from the very heart of our sovereignty. The Suez Canal Company is a limited company, awarded a concession by the Egyptian Government in 1865 to carry out its tasks. Today we withdraw the concession in order to do the job ourselves.

Although we have withdrawn this concession, we shall compensate shareholders of the company, despite the fact that they usurped our rights. Britain usurped 44 per cent of the shares free of charge. Today we shall pay her for her 44 per cent of the shares. We do not treat her as she treated us. We are not usurping the 44 per cent as

---

This document can be found in the *Summary of World Broadcasts,* Part IV, Daily Series, 6, 30 July 1956, British Broadcasting Corporation, London, UK. It can also be found in T. G. Fraser, *The Middle East, 1914–1979* (New York: St. Martin's Press, 1980), pp. 88–89.

she did. We do not tell Britain that we shall usurp her right as she usurped ours, but we tell her that we shall compensate her and forget the past.

The Suez Canal would have been restored to us in 12 years. What would have happened in 12 years' time? Would an uproar have been raised? What has happened now has disclosed hidden intentions and has unmasked Britain. If the canal was to fall to us in 12 years, why should it not be restored to us now? Why should it cause an uproar? We understand by this that they had no intention of fulfilling this pledge 12 years from now. What difference is it if the canal is restored to us now or in 12 years' time? Why should Britain say this will affect shipping in the canal? Would it have affected shipping 12 years hence?

Shipping in the Suez Canal has been normal for the past 48 hours from the time of nationalization until now. Shipping continued and is normal. We nationalized the company. We have not interfered with shipping, and we are facilitating shipping matters. However, I emphatically warn the imperialist countries that their tricks, provocations and interference will be the reason for any hindrance to shipping. I place full responsibility on Britain and France for any curtailment of shipping in the Suez Canal when I state that Egypt will maintain freedom of shipping in the Suez Canal, and that since Egypt nationalized the Suez Canal Company shipping has been normal. Even before that we maintained freedom of shipping in the canal. Who has protected the canal? The canal has been under Egyptian protection because it is part of Egypt and we are the ones who should ensure freedom of shipping. We protect it today, we protected it a month ago, and we protected it for years because it is our territory and a part of our territory. Today we shall continue to protect the canal. But, because of the tricks they are playing, I hold Britain and France responsible for any consequences which may affect shipping.

Compatriots, we shall maintain our independence and sovereignty. The Suez Canal Company has become our property, and the Egyptian flag flies over it. We shall hold it with our blood and strength, and we shall meet aggression with aggression and evil with evil. We shall proceed towards achieving dignity and prestige for Egypt and building a sound national economy and true freedom. Peace be with you.

4. The Palestinian National Covenant Calls for the Liberation of Palestine, 1968

Palestine is the homeland of the Palestinian Arab people and an integral part of the great Arab homeland, and the people of Palestine is a part of the Arab nation.

Palestine with its boundaries that existed at the time of the British mandate is an integral regional unit.

The Palestinian Arab people possesses the legal right to its homeland, and when the liberation of its homeland is completed it will exercise self-determination solely according to its own will and choice.

The Palestinian personality is an innate, persistent characteristic that does not disappear, and it is transferred from fathers to sons. The Zionist occupation, and the dispersal of the Palestinian Arab people as a result of the disasters which came

---

This document can be found in Walter Laqueur and Barry Rubin, eds., *The Israel-Arab Reader: A Documentary History of the Middle East Conflict* (New York: Penguin Books, 1995), pp. 218–222.

over it, do not deprive it of its Palestinian personality and affiliation and do not nullify them.

The Palestinians are the Arab citizens who were living permanently in Palestine until 1947, whether they were expelled from there or remained. Whoever is born to a Palestinian Arab father after this date, within Palestine or outside it, is a Palestinian.

Jews who were living permanently in Palestine until the beginning of the Zionist invasion will be considered Palestinians.

The Palestinian affiliation and the material, spiritual and historical tie with Palestine are permanent realities. The upbringing of the Palestinian individual in an Arab and revolutionary fashion, the undertaking of all means of forging consciousness and training the Palestinian, in order to acquaint him profoundly with his homeland, spiritually and materially, and preparing him for the conflict and the armed struggle, as well as for the sacrifice of his property and his life to restore his homeland, until the liberation of all this is a national duty.

The phase in which the people of Palestine is living is that of national struggle for the liberation of Palestine. Therefore, the contradictions among the Palestinian national forces are of secondary order which must be suspended in the interest of the fundamental contradiction between Zionism and colonialism on the one side and the Palestinian Arab people on the other. On this basis, the Palestinian masses, whether in the homeland or in places of exile, organizations and individuals, comprise one national front which acts to restore Palestine and liberate it through armed struggle.

Armed struggle is the only way to liberate Palestine and is therefore a strategy and not tactics. The Palestinian Arab people affirms its absolute resolution and abiding determination to pursue the armed struggle and to march forward towards the armed popular revolution, to liberate its homeland and return to it [to maintain] its right to a natural life in it, and to exercise its right of self-determination in it and sovereignty over it. . . .

The Palestinian Arab people believes in Arab unity. In order to fulfill its role in realizing this, it must preserve, in this phase of its national struggle, its Palestinian personality and the constituents thereof, increase consciousness of its existence and resist any plan that tends to disintegrate or weaken it. . . .

The destiny of the Arab nation, indeed the very Arab existence, depends upon the destiny of the Palestine issue. The endeavour and effort of the Arab nation to liberate Palestine follows from this connection. The people of Palestine assumes its vanguard role in realizing this sacred national aim.

The liberation of Palestine, from an Arab viewpoint, is a national duty to repulse the Zionist, Imperialist invasion from the great Arab homeland and to purge the Zionist presence from Palestine. Its full responsibility falls upon the Arab nation, peoples and governments, with the Palestinian Arab people at their head. For this purpose, the Arab nation must mobilize all its military, human, material and spiritual capacities to participate actively with the people of Palestine in the liberation of Palestine. They must especially in the present stage of armed Palestinian revolution, grant and offer the people of Palestine all possible help and every material and human support, and afford it every sure means and opportunity enabling it to continue to assume its vanguard role in pursuing its armed revolution until the liberation of its homeland.

The liberation of Palestine, from a spiritual viewpoint, will prepare an atmosphere of tranquillity and peace for the Holy Land in the shade of which all the Holy

Places will be safeguarded, and freedom of worship and visitation to all will be guaranteed, without distinction or discrimination of race, colour, language or religion. For this reason, the people of Palestine looks to the support of all the spiritual forces in the world.

The liberation of Palestine, from a human viewpoint, will restore to the Palestinian man his dignity, glory and freedom. For this, the Palestinian Arab people looks to the support of those in the world who believe in the dignity and freedom of man.

The liberation of Palestine, from an international viewpoint is a defensive act necessitated by the requirements of self-defence. For this reason the Arab people of Palestine, desiring to befriend all peoples, looks to the support of the states which love freedom, justice and peace in restoring the legal situation to Palestine, establishing security and peace in its territory, and enabling its people to exercise national sovereignty and national freedom. . . .

To realize the aims of this covenant and its principles the Palestine Liberation Organization will undertake its full role in liberating Palestine.

The Palestine Liberation Organization, which represents the forces of the Palestinian revolution, is responsible for the movement of the Palestinian Arab people in its struggle to restore its homeland, liberate it, return to it and exercise the right of self-determination in it. This responsibility extends to all military, political and financial matters, and all else that the Palestine issue requires in the Arab and international spheres.

The Palestine Liberation Organization will cooperate with all Arab States, each according to its capacities, and will maintain neutrality in their mutual relations in the light of and on the basis of, the requirements of the battle of liberation and will not interfere in the internal affairs of any Arab State.

5. The Carter Doctrine Announces U.S. Intention to Repel Aggression in the Persian Gulf, 1980

This last few months has not been an easy time for any of us. As we meet tonight, it has never been more clear that the state of our Union depends on the state of the world. And tonight, as throughout our own generation, freedom and peace in the world depend on the state of our Union. . . .

At this time in Iran, 50 Americans are still held captive, innocent victims of terrorism and anarchy. Also at this moment, massive Soviet troops are attempting to subjugate the fiercely independent and deeply religious people of Afghanistan. These two acts—one of international terrorism and one of military aggression— present a serious challenge to the United States of America and indeed to all the nations of the world. Together, we will meet these threats to peace. . . .

Three basic developments have helped to shape our challenges: the steady growth and increased projection of Soviet military power beyond its own borders; the overwhelming dependence of the Western democracies on oil supplies from the Middle East; and the press of social and religious and economic and political change in the many nations of the developing world, exemplified by the revolution in Iran. . . .

This document can be found in "President Jimmy Carter's State of the Union Address Before Congress, 23 January 1980," *Public Papers of the Presidents, 1980–1981* (Washington, D.C.: Government Printing Office, 1981), pp. 194–199.

In response to the abhorrent act in Iran, our nation has never been aroused and unified so greatly in peacetime. Our position is clear. The United States will not yield to blackmail.

We continue to pursue these specific goals: first, to protect the present and long-range interests of the United States; secondly, to preserve the lives of the American hostages and to secure, as quickly as possible, their safe release, if possible, to avoid bloodshed which might further endanger the lives of our fellow citizens; to enlist the help of other nations in condemning this act of violence, which is shocking and violates the moral and the legal standards of a civilized world; and also to convince and to persuade the Iranian leaders that the real danger to their nation lies in the north, in the Soviet Union and from the Soviet troops now in Afghanistan, and that the unwarranted Iranian quarrel with the United States hampers their response to this far greater danger to them.

If the American hostages are harmed, a severe price will be paid. We will never rest until every one of the American hostages are released.

But now we face a broader and more fundamental challenge in this region because of the recent military action of the Soviet Union. . . .

The Soviet Union has taken a radical and an aggressive new step. It's using its great military power against a relatively defenseless nation. The implications of the Soviet invasion of Afghanistan could pose the most serious threat to the peace since the Second World War. . . .

While this invasion continues, we and the other nations of the world cannot conduct business as usual with the Soviet Union. That's why the United States has imposed stiff economic penalties on the Soviet Union. . . .

The region which is now threatened by Soviet troops in Afghanistan is of great strategic importance: It contains more than two-thirds of the world's exportable oil. The Soviet effort to dominate Afghanistan has brought Soviet military forces to within 300 miles of the Indian Ocean and close to the Straits of Hormuz, a waterway [connecting the Persian Gulf to the Indian Ocean] through which most of the world's oil must flow. The Soviet Union is now attempting to consolidate a strategic position, therefore, that poses a grave threat to the free movement of Middle East oil.

This situation demands careful thought, steady nerves, and resolute action, not only for this year but for many years to come. It demands collective efforts to meet this new threat to security in the Persian Gulf and in Southwest Asia. It demands the participation of all those who rely on oil from the Middle East and who are concerned with global peace and stability. And it demands consultation and close cooperation with countries in the area which might be threatened.

Meeting this challenge will take national will, diplomatic and political wisdom, economic sacrifice, and, of course, military capability. We must call on the best that is in us to preserve the security of this crucial region.

Let our position be absolutely clear: An attempt by any outside force to gain control of the Persian Gulf region will be regarded as an assault on the vital interests of the United States of America, and such an assault will be repelled by any means necessary, including military force.

We are working with our allies to prevent conflict in the Middle East. The peace treaty between Egypt and Israel [framed at Camp David and finalized in March 1979] is a notable achievement which represents a strategic asset for America and which also enhances prospects for regional and world peace. We are now engaged in further negotiations to provide full autonomy for the people of the West Bank and Gaza, to resolve the Palestinian issue in all its aspects, and to preserve the peace and security of Israel. Let no one doubt our commitment to the security of Israel. In a few days we will observe an historic event when Israel makes another major withdrawal from the Sinai and when Ambassadors will be exchanged between Israel and Egypt. . . .

We've increased and strengthened our naval presence in the Indian Ocean, and we are now making arrangements for key naval and air facilities to be used by our forces in the region of northeast Africa and the Persian Gulf. . . .

In the weeks ahead, we will further strengthen political and military ties with other nations in the region. We believe that there are no irreconcilable differences between us and any Islamic nation. We respect the faith of Islam, and we are ready to cooperate with all Moslem countries. . . .

The crises in Iran and Afghanistan have dramatized a very important lesson: Our excessive dependence on foreign oil is a clear and present danger to our Nation's security. The need has never been more urgent. At long last, we must have a clear, comprehensive energy policy for the United States. . . .

The single biggest factor in the inflation rate last year, the increase in the inflation rate last year, was from one cause: the skyrocketing prices of OPEC [Organization of Petroleum Exporting Countries] oil. We must take whatever actions are necessary to reduce our dependence on foreign oil.

6. President George Bush Declares a New World Order During the Persian Gulf Crisis, 1990

We stand today at a unique and extraordinary moment. The crisis in the Persian Gulf, as grave as it is, also offers a rare opportunity to move toward an historic period of cooperation. Out of these troubled times, . . . a new world order can emerge: a new era—freer from the threat of terror, stronger in the pursuit of justice, and more secure in the quest for peace. An era in which the nations of the world, East and West, North and South, can prosper and live in harmony. A hundred generations have searched for this elusive path to peace, while a thousand wars raged across the span of human endeavor. Today that new world is struggling to be born, a world quite different from the one we've known. A world where the rule of law supplants the rule of the jungle. A world in which nations recognize the shared responsibility for freedom and justice. A world where the strong respect the rights of the weak. This is the vision that I shared with [Soviet] President Gorbachev in Helsinki. He and other leaders from Europe, the Gulf, and around the world understand that how we manage this crisis today could shape the future for generations to come.

The test we face is great, and so are the stakes. This is the first assault on the new world that we seek, the first test of our mettle. Had we not responded to this first provocation with clarity of purpose, if we do not continue to demonstrate our

---

This document can be found in "Address to Congress on Persian Gulf Crisis," 11 September 1990, *Public Papers of the Presidents of the United States, George Bush, 1990* (Washington, D.C.: U.S. Government Printing Office, 1991), Book II, pp. 1218–1222.

determination, it would be a signal to actual and potential despots around the world. America and the world must defend common vital interests—and we will. America and the world must support the rule of law—and we will. America and the world must stand up to aggression—and we will. And one thing more: In the pursuit of these goals America will not be intimidated.

Vital issues of principle are at stake. Saddam Hussein is literally trying to wipe a country [Kuwait] off the face of the Earth. We do not exaggerate. Nor do we exaggerate when we say Saddam Hussein will fail. Vital economic interests are at risk as well. Iraq itself controls some 10 percent of the world's proven oil reserves. Iraq plus Kuwait controls twice that. An Iraq permitted to swallow Kuwait would have the economic and military power, as well as the arrogance, to intimidate and coerce its neighbors—neighbors who control the lion's share of the world's remaining oil reserves. We cannot permit a resource so vital to be dominated by one so ruthless. And we won't.

Recent events have surely proven that there is no substitute for American leadership. In the face of tyranny, let no one doubt American credibility and reliability.

7. Israeli Prime Minister Yitzhak Rabin Pleads for Peace, 1993

We, the soldiers who have returned from battles stained with blood; we who have seen our relatives and friends killed before our eyes; we who have attended their funerals and cannot look in the eyes of their parents; we who have come from a land where parents bury their children; we who have fought against you, the Palestinians—we say to you today, in a loud and a clear voice: enough of blood and tears. Enough.

8. President George W. Bush Asks, "Why Do They Hate Us?" 2001

On September the 11th, enemies of freedom committed an act of war against our country. Americans have known wars, but for the past 136 years they have been wars on foreign soil, except for one Sunday in 1941. Americans have known the casualties of war, but not at the center of a great city on a peaceful morning.

Americans have known surprise attacks, but never before on thousands of civilians. All of this was brought upon us in a single day, and night fell on a different world, a world where freedom itself is under attack.

Americans have many questions tonight. Americans are asking, "Who attacked our country?"

Document 7 can be found at Israeli Prime Minister Speech at the White House, 13 September 1993, *http://www.bartleby.com/66/28/45828.html.*

Document 8 can be found at President Bush Address to Congress, 20 September 2001, *Journal of the House of Representatives,* 107th Congress, 1st Session, Vol. 1 (Washington, D.C.: Government Printing Office), pp. 1081–1083.

The evidence we have gathered all points to a collection of loosely affiliated terrorist organizations known as al Qaeda. They are some of the murderers indicated for bombing American embassies in Tanzania and Kenya and responsible for bombing the USS Cole.

Al Qaeda is to terror what the Mafia is to crime. But its goal is not making money, its goal is remaking the world and imposing its radical beliefs on people everywhere.

The terrorists practice a fringe form of Islamic extremism that has been rejected by Muslim scholars and the vast majority of Muslim clerics; a fringe movement that prevents the peaceful teachings of Islam.

The terrorists' directive commands them to kill Christians and Jews, to kill all Americans and make no distinction among military and civilians, including women and children. This group and its leader, a person named Osama bin Laden, are linked to many other organizations in different countries, including the Egyptian Islamic Jihad, the Islamic Movement of Uzbekistan.

There are thousands of these terrorists in more then 60 countries.

They are recruited from their own nations and neighborhoods and brought to camps in places like Afghanistan where they are trained in the tactics of terror. They are sent back to their homes or sent to hide in countries around the world to plot evil and destruction. The leadership of al Qaeda has great influence in Afghanistan and supports the Taliban regime in controlling most of that country. In Afghanistan we see al Qaeda's vision for the world. Afghanistan's people have been brutalized, many are starving and many have fled.

Women are not allowed to attend school. You can be jailed for owning a television. Religion can be practiced only as their leaders dictate. A man can be jailed in Afghanistan if his beard is not long enough. The United States respects the people of Afghanistan—after all, we are currently its largest source of humanitarian aid—but we condemn the Taliban regime.

It is not only repressing its own people, it is threatening people everywhere by sponsoring and sheltering and supplying terrorists.

By aiding and abetting murder, the Taliban regime is committing murder. And tonight the United States of America makes the following demands on the Taliban:
•   Deliver to United States authorities all of the leaders of Al Qaeda who hide in your land.
•   Release all foreign nationals, including American citizens you have unjustly imprisoned.
•   Protect foreign journalists, diplomats and aid workers in your country.
•   Close immediately and permanently every terrorist training camp in Afghanistan. And hand over every terrorist and every person and their support structure to appropriate authorities.
•   Give the United States full access to terrorist training camps, so we can make sure they are no longer operating.

These demands are not open to negotiation or discussion.

The Taliban must act and act immediately.

They will hand over the terrorists or they will share in their fate. I also want to speak tonight directly to Muslims throughout the world. We respect your faith. It's practiced freely by many millions of Americans and by millions more in countries that America counts as friends. Its teachings are good and peaceful, and those who commit evil in the name of Allah blaspheme the name of Allah.

The terrorists are traitors to their own faith, trying, in effect, to hijack Islam itself.

The enemy of America is not our many Muslim friends. It is not our many Arab friends. Our enemy is a radical network of terrorists and every government that supports them.

Our war on terror begins with al Qaeda, but it does not end there.

It will not end until every terrorist group of global reach has been found, stopped and defeated.

Americans are asking "Why do they hate us?"

They hate what they see right here in this chamber: a democratically elected government. Their leaders are self-appointed. They hate our freedoms: our freedom of religion, our freedom of speech, our freedom to vote and assemble and disagree with each other.

They want to overthrow existing governments in many Muslim countries such as Egypt, Saudi Arabia and Jordan. They want to drive Israel out of the Middle East. They want to drive Christians and Jews out of vast regions of Asia and Africa.

These terrorists kill not merely to end lives, but to disrupt and end a way of life. With every atrocity, they hope that America grows fearful, retreating from the world and forsaking our friends. They stand against us because we stand in their way.

We're not deceived by their pretenses to piety.

We have seen their kind before. They're the heirs of all the murderous ideologies of the 20th century. By sacrificing human life to serve their radical visions, by abandoning every value except the will to power, they follow the path of fascism, Nazism and totalitarianism. And they will follow that path all the way to where it ends in history's unmarked grave of discarded lies. Americans are asking, "How will we fight and win this war?"

We will direct every resource at our command—every means of diplomacy, every tool of intelligence, every instrument of law enforcement, every financial influence, and every necessary weapon of war—to the destruction and to the defeat of the global terror network.

Now, this war will not be like the war against Iraq a decade ago, with a decisive liberation of territory and a swift conclusion. It will not look like the air war above Kosovo two years ago, where no ground troops were used and not a single American was lost in combat.

Our response involves far more than instant retaliation and isolated strikes. Americans should not expect one battle, but a lengthy campaign unlike any other we have ever seen. It may include dramatic strikes visible on TV and covert operations secret even in success.

We will starve terrorists of funding, turn them one against another, drive them from place to place until there is no refuge or no rest.

And we will pursue nations that provide aid or safe haven to terrorism. Every nation in every region now has a decision to make: Either you are with us or you are with the terrorists.

From this day forward, any nation that continues to harbor or support terrorism will be regarded by the United States as a hostile regime. Our nation has been put on notice, we're not immune from attack. We will take defensive measures against terrorism to protect Americans. Today, dozens of federal departments and agencies, as well as state and local governments, have responsibilities affecting homeland security.

These efforts must be coordinated at the highest level. So tonight, I announce the creation of a Cabinet-level position reporting directly to me, the Office of Homeland Security. . . .

This is not, however, just America's fight. And what is at stake is not just America's freedom. This is the world's fight. This is civilization's fight. This is the fight of all who believe in progress and pluralism, tolerance and freedom.

We ask every nation to join us. . . .

Our nation, this generation, will lift the dark threat of violence from our people and our future. We will rally the world to this cause by our efforts, by our courage. We will not tire, we will not falter and we will not fail.

It is my hope that in the months and years ahead life will return almost to normal. We'll go back to our lives and routines and that is good.

Even grief recedes with time and grace.

But our resolve must not pass. Each of us will remember what happened that day and to whom it happened. We will remember the moment the news came, where we were and what we were doing. . . .

I will not forget the wound to our country and those who inflicted it. I will not yield, I will not rest, I will not relent in waging this struggle for freedom and security for the American people. The course of this conflict is not known, yet its outcome is certain. Freedom and fear, justice and cruelty, have always been at war, and we know that God is not neutral between them.

9. Osama bin Laden Proclaims, "God Has Given Them Back What They Deserve," 2001

Thanks to God, he who God guides will never lose. And I believe that there's only one God. And I declare I believe there's no prophet but Mohammed.

This is America, God has sent one of the attacks by God and has attacked one of its best buildings. And this is America filled with fear from the north to south and east to west, thank God.

And what America is facing today is something very little of what we have tasted for decades. Our nation, since nearly 80 years is tasting this humility. Sons are killed, and nobody answers the call.

And when God has guided a bunch of Muslims to be at the forefront and destroyed America, a big destruction, I wish God would lift their position.

And when those people have defended and retaliated to what their brothers and sisters have suffered in Palestine and Lebanon, the whole world has been shouting.

And there are civilians, innocent children being killed every day in Iraq without any guilt, and we never hear anybody. We never hear any fatwah from the clergymen of the government.

And every day we see the Israeli tanks going to Jenin, Ramallah, Beit Jalla and other lands of Islam. And, no, we never hear anybody objecting to that.

So when the swords came after eight years to America, then the whole world has been crying for those criminals who attacked. This is the least which could be said about them. They are people. They supported the murder against the victim, so God has given them back what they deserve.

I say the matter is very clear, so every Muslim after this, and after the officials in America, starting with the head of the infidels, Bush. And they came out with their men and equipment and they even encouraged even countries claiming to be Muslims against us.

So, we run with our religion. They came out to fight Islam with the name of fighting terrorism.

People—event of the world—in Japan, hundreds of thousands of people got killed. This is not a war crime. Or in Iraq, what our—who are being killed in Iraq. This is not a crime. And those, when they were attacked in my Nairobi, and Dar es Salaam, Afghanistan, and Sudan were attacked.

I say these events have split the whole world into two camps: the camp of belief and the disbelief. So every Muslim shall take—shall support his religion.

And now with the winds of change has blown up now, has come to the Arabian Peninsula.

And to America, I say to it and to its people this: I swear by God the Great, America will never dream nor those who in America will never taste security and safety unless we feel security and safety in our land and in Palestine.

10. President Bush Makes the Case for War on Iraq, 2003

My fellow citizens, events in Iraq have now reached the final days of decision. For more than a decade, the United States, and other nations have pursued patient and honorable efforts to disarm the Iraqi regime without war. That regime pledged to reveal and destroy all its weapons of mass destruction as a condition for ending the Persian Gulf War in 1991.

Since, then, the world has engaged in 12 years of diplomacy. We have passed more than a dozen resolutions in the United Nations Security Council. We have sent hundreds of weapons inspectors to oversee the disarmament of Iraq. Our good faith has not been returned.

The Iraqi regime has used diplomacy as a ploy to gain time and advantage. It has uniformly defied Security Council resolutions demanding full disarmament. Over the years, U.N. weapon inspectors have been threatened by Iraqi officials, electronically bugged, and systematically deceived. Peaceful efforts to disarm the Iraqi regime have failed again and again—because we are not dealing with peaceful men.

Intelligence gathered by this and other governments leaves no doubt that the Iraq regime continues to possess and conceal some of the most lethal weapons ever

This document can be found at "President Says Saddam Hussein Must Leave Iraq Within 48 Hours," 17 March 2003, *www.whitehouse.gov/news/releases/2003/03*

devised. This regime has already used weapons of mass destruction against Iraq's neighbors and against Iraq's people.

The regime has a history of reckless aggression in the Middle East. It has a deep hatred of America and our friends. And it has aided, trained and harbored terrorists, including operatives of al Qaeda.

The danger is clear: using chemical, biological or, one day, nuclear weapons, obtained with the help of Iraq, the terrorists could fulfill their stated ambitions and kill thousands or hundreds of thousands of innocent people in our country, or any other.

The United States and other nations did nothing to deserve or invite this threat. But we will do everything to defeat it. Instead of drifting along toward tragedy, we will set a course toward safety. Before the day of horror can come, before it is too late to act, this danger will be removed.

The United States of America has the sovereign authority to use force in assuring its own national security. That duty falls to me, as Commander-in-Chief, by the oath I have sworn, by the oath I will keep.

Recognizing the threat to our country, the United States Congress voted overwhelmingly last year to support the use of force against Iraq. America tried to work with the United Nations to address this threat because we wanted to resolve the issue peacefully. We believe in the mission of the United Nations. One reason the U.N. was founded after the second world war was to confront aggressive dictators, actively and early, before they can attack the innocent and destroy the peace.

In the case of Iraq, the Security Council did act, in the early 1990s. Under Resolutions 678 and 687—both still in effect—the United States and our allies are authorized to use force in ridding Iraq of weapons of mass destruction. This is not a question of authority, it is a question of will.

Last September, I went to the U.N. General Assembly and urged the nations of the world to unite and bring an end to this danger. On November 8th, the Security Council unanimously passed Resolution 1441, finding Iraq in material breach of its obligations, and vowing serious consequences if Iraq did not fully and immediately disarm.

Today, no nation can possibly claim that Iraq has disarmed. And it will not disarm so long as Saddam Hussein holds power. For the last four-and-a-half months, the United States and our allies have worked within the Security Council to enforce that Council's long-standing demands. Yet, some permanent members of the Security Council have publicly announced they will veto any resolution that compels the disarmament of Iraq. These governments share our assessment of the danger, but not our resolve to meet it. Many nations, however, do have the resolve and fortitude to act against this threat to peace, and a broad coalition is now gathering to enforce the just demands of the world. The United Nations Security Council has not lived up to its responsibilities, so we will rise to ours.

In recent days, some governments in the Middle East have been doing their part. They have delivered public and private messages urging the dictator to leave Iraq, so that disarmament can proceed peacefully. He has thus far refused. All the decades of deceit and cruelty have now reached an end. Saddam Hussein and his sons must leave Iraq within 48 hours. Their refusal to do so will result in military conflict, commenced at a time of our choosing. . . .

It is too late for Saddam Hussein to remain in power. It is not too late for the Iraqi military to act with honor and protect your country [Iraq] by permitting the peaceful entry of coalition forces to eliminate weapons of mass destruction. Our forces will give Iraqi military units clear instructions on actions they can take to avoid being attacked and destroyed. I urge every member of the Iraqi military and intelligence services, if war comes, do not fight for a dying regime that is not worth your own life.

And all Iraqi military and civilian personnel should listen carefully to this warning. In any conflict, your fate will depend on your action. Do not destroy oil wells, a source of wealth that belongs to the Iraqi people. Do not obey any command to use weapons of mass destruction against anyone, including the Iraqi people. War crimes will be prosecuted. War criminals will be punished. And it will be no defense to say, "I was just following orders." . . .

We are now acting because the risks of inaction would be far greater. In one year, or five years, the power of Iraq to inflict harm on all free nations would be multiplied many times over. With these capabilities, Saddam Hussein and his terrorist allies could choose the moment of deadly conflict when they are strongest. We choose to meet that threat now, where it arises, before it can appear suddenly in our skies and cities.

The cause of peace requires all free nations to recognize new and undeniable realities. In the 20th century, some chose to appease murderous dictators, whose threats were allowed to grow into genocide and global war. In this century, when evil men plot chemical, biological and nuclear terror, a policy of appeasement could bring destruction of a kind never before seen on this earth.

Terrorists and terror states do not reveal these threats with fair notice, in formal declarations—and responding to such enemies only after they have struck first is not self-defense, it is suicide. The security of the world requires disarming Saddam Hussein now.

 E S S A Y S

The first essay, by Bernard Lewis, a professor emeritus at Princeton University, is representative of the "clash of civilizations" thesis that attributes much of Muslim anti-Americanism to the vast cultural differences that separate the West and the Middle East. According to Lewis, the religiously based Muslim civilization is tradition bound and resistant to modernity, secularism, and democracy. Unable to form stable, popularly based nation-states in the postcolonial era, most of the region's rulers have blamed outsiders for their shortcomings, especially Britain, France, Israel, and the United States. Although some Muslims admire America for its promise of human rights and free institutions, a historical consciousness based on anti-Westernism and antimodernity has become central to Muslim identity, and in recent years has fueled the rise of Islamic extremism and terrorism.

Ussama Makdisi of Rice University strongly disagrees with the clash of civilizations thesis. In the second essay, Makdisi argues that hatred of the United States and the West is not embedded in Muslim culture, but finds expression among a growing segment of Arabs who oppose America's foreign policies. The United States was widely admired by Arabs in the nineteenth and early twentieth centuries as a consequence of its educational philanthropy and Woodrow Wilson's support for self-determination after World War I. But as its power grew with the passing decades, the United States increasingly allied itself with corrupt oil kingdoms, opposed popular nationalist movements, and abandoned all pretense of neutrality in the Arab-Israeli conflict by its strong backing of Tel Aviv. Makdisi concludes that September 11 was ultimately a perverted, or hijacked, expression of widespread Arab anger at the United States.

The last selection, by Robert Wright, a journalist and visiting scholar at the University of Pennsylvania's Psychology Department, appeared in the *New York Times* on September 11, 2003, the second anniversary of the al Qaeda attacks on New York and Washington. Wright explains Arab hatred for the United States as a response to the economic and cultural incongruities of globalization and modernity. According to Wright, terrorism is not primarily an outgrowth of Muslim culture. Instead, it constitutes a weapon for those who have not been fully integrated into a technologically and economically advanced world. Wary of the Bush administration's propensity for unilateral military action, as illustrated by the U.S. invasion of Iraq in March 2003, Wright calls for new forms of multilateral global governance to police nuclear materials, prevent future terrorist tragedies, and defend American liberty. Wright concludes that cultural tolerance and an understanding of the root cause of hatred are essential to any antiterror strategy.

The Revolt of Islam

BERNARD LEWIS

I. Making History

President Bush and other Western politicians have taken great pains to make it clear that the war in which we are engaged is a war against terrorism—not a war against Arabs, or, more generally, against Muslims, who are urged to join us in this struggle against our common enemy. Osama bin Laden's message is the opposite. For bin Laden and those who follow him, this is a religious war, a war for Islam and against infidels, and therefore, inevitably, against the United States, the greatest power in the world of the infidels.

In his pronouncements, bin Laden makes frequent references to history. One of the most dramatic was his mention, in the October 7th videotape, of the "humiliation and disgrace" that Islam has suffered for "more than eighty years." Most American—and, no doubt, European—observers of the Middle Eastern scene began an anxious search for something that had happened "more than eighty years" ago, and came up with various answers. We can be fairly sure that bin Laden's Muslim listeners—the people he was addressing—picked up the allusion immediately and appreciated its significance. In 1918, the Ottoman sultanate, the last of the great Muslim empires, was finally defeated—its capital, Constantinople, occupied, its sovereign held captive, and much of its territory partitioned between the victorious British and French Empires. The Turks eventually succeeded in liberating their homeland, but they did so not in the name of Islam but through a secular nationalist movement. One of their first acts, in November, 1922, was to abolish the sultanate. The Ottoman sovereign was not only a sultan, the ruler of a specific state; he was also widely recognized as the caliph, the head of all Sunni Islam, and the last in a line of such rulers that dated back to the death of the Prophet Muhammad, in 632 A.D. After a brief experiment with a separate caliph, the Turks, in March, 1924, abolished the caliphate, too. During its

---

"The Revolt of Islam" first appeared in *The New Yorker,* November 19, 2001 and then a more extended version was published in Professor Lewis's book entitled *The Crisis of Islam: Holy War and Unholy Terror,* New York 2003. Reprinted with permission of the author.

nearly thirteen centuries, the caliphate had gone through many vicissitudes, but it remained a potent symbol of Muslim unity, even identity, and its abolition, under the double assault of foreign imperialists and domestic modernists, was felt throughout the Muslim world.

Historical allusions such as bin Laden's, which may seem abstruse to many Americans, are common among Muslims, and can be properly understood only within the context of Middle eastern perceptions of identity and against the background of Middle Eastern history. Even the concepts of history and identity require redefinition for the Westerner trying to understand the contemporary Middle East. In current American usage, the phrase "that's history" is commonly used to dismiss something as unimportant, of no relevance to current concerns, and, despite an immense investment in the teaching and writing of history, the general level of historical knowledge in our society is abysmally low. The Muslim peoples, like everyone else in the world, are shaped by their history, but, unlike some others, they are keenly aware of it. In the nineteen-eighties, during the Iran-Iraq war, for instance, both sides waged massive propaganda campaigns that frequently evoked events and personalities dating back as far as the seventh century. These were not detailed narratives but rapid, incomplete allusions, and yet both sides employed them in the secure knowledge that they would be understood by their target audiences—even by the large proportion of that audience that was illiterate. Middle Easterners' perception of history is nourished from the pulpit, by schools, and by the media, and, although it may be—indeed, often is—slanted and inaccurate, it is nevertheless vivid and powerfully resonant.

But history of what? In the Western world, the basic unit of human organization is the nation, which is then subdivided in various ways, one of which is by religion. Muslims, however, tend to see not a nation subdivided into religious groups but a religion subdivided into nations. This is no doubt partly because most of the nation-states that make up the modern Middle East are relatively new creations, left over from the era of Anglo-French imperial domination that followed the defeat of the Ottoman Empire, and they preserve the state-building and frontier demarcations of their former imperial masters. Even their names reflect this artificiality: Iraq was a medieval province, with borders very different from those of the modern republic; Syria, Palestine, and Libya are names from classical antiquity that hadn't been used in the region for a thousand years or more before they were revived and imposed by European imperialists in the twentieth century; Algeria and Tunisia do not even exist as words in Arabic—the same name serves for the city and the country. Most remarkable of all, there is no word in the Arabic language for Arabia, and modern Saudi Arabia is spoken of instead as "the Saudi Arab kingdom" or "the peninsula of the Arabs," depending on the context. This is not because Arabic is a poor language—quite the reverse is true—but because the Arabs simply did not think in terms of combined ethnic and territorial identity. Indeed, the caliph Omar, the second in succession after the Prophet Muhammad, is quoted as saying to the Arabs, "Learn your genealogies, and do not be like the local peasants who, when they are asked who they are, reply: 'I am from such-and-such a place.'"

In the early centuries of the Muslim era, the Islamic community was one state under one ruler. Even after that community split up into many states, the ideal of a single Islamic polity persisted. The states were almost all dynastic, with shifting frontiers, and it is surely significant that, in the immensely rich historiography of the

Islamic world in Arabic, Persian, and Turkish, there are histories of dynasties, of cities, and, primarily, of the Islamic state and community, but no histories of Arabia, Persia, or Turkey. Both Arabs and Turks produced a vast literature describing their struggles against Christian Europe, from the first Arab incursions in the eighth century to the final Turkish retreat in the twentieth. But until the modern period, when European concepts and categories became dominant, Islamic commentators almost always referred to their opponents not in territorial or ethnic terms but simply as infidels (*kafir*). They never referred to their own side as Arab or Turkish; they identified themselves as Muslims. This perspective helps to explain, among other things, Pakistan's concern for the Taliban in Afghanistan. The name Pakistan, a twentieth-century invention, designates a country defined entirely by its Islamic religion. In every other respect, the country and people of Pakistan are—as they have been for millennia—part of India. An Afghanistan defined by its Islamic identity would be a natural ally, even a satellite, of Pakistan. An Afghanistan defined by ethnic nationality, on the other hand, could be a dangerous neighbor, advancing irredentist claims on the Pashto-speaking areas of northwestern Pakistan and perhaps even allying itself with India.

II. The House of War

In the course of human history, many civilizations have risen and fallen—China, India, Greece, Rome, and, before them, the ancient civilizations of the Middle East. During the centuries that in European history are called medieval, the most advanced civilization in the world was undoubtedly that of Islam. Islam may have been equalled—or even, in some ways, surpassed—by India and China, but both of those civilizations remained essentially limited to one region and to one ethnic group, and their impact on the rest of the world was correspondingly restricted. The civilization of Islam, on the other hand, was ecumenical in its outlook, and explicitly so in its aspirations. One of the basic tasks bequeathed to Muslims by the Prophet was jihad. This word, which literally means "striving," was usually cited in the Koranic phrase "striving in the path of God" and was interpreted to mean armed struggle for the defense or advancement of Muslim power. In principle, the world was divided into two houses: the House of Islam, in which a Muslim government ruled and Muslim law prevailed, and the House of War, the rest of the world, still inhabited and, more important, ruled by infidels. Between the two, there was to be a perpetual state of war until the entire world either embraced Islam or submitted to the rule of the Muslim state.

From an early date, Muslims knew that there were certain differences among the peoples of the House of War. Most of them were simply polytheists and idolaters, who represented no serious threat to Islam and were likely prospects for conversion. The major exception was the Christians, whom Muslims recognized as having a religion of the same kind as their own, and therefore as their primary rival in the struggle for world domination—or, as they would have put it, world enlightenment. It is surely significant that the Koranic and other inscriptions on the Dome of the Rock, one of the earliest Muslim religious structures outside Arabia, built in Jerusalem between 691 and 692 A.D., include a number of directly anti-Christian polemics: "Praise be to God, who begets no son, and has no partner," and "He is God, one, eternal. He does not beget, nor is he begotten, and he has no peer." For the early

Muslims, the leader of Christendom, the Christian equivalent of the Muslim caliph, was the Byzantine emperor in Constantinople. Later, his place was taken by the Holy Roman Emperor in Vienna, and his in turn by the new rulers of the West. Each of these, in his time, was the principal adversary of the jihad.

In practice, of course, the application of jihad wasn't always rigorous or violent. The canonically obligatory state of war could be interrupted by what were legally defined as "truces," but these differed little from the so-called peace treaties the warring European powers signed with one another. Such truces were made by the Prophet with his pagan enemies, and they became the basis of what one might call Islamic international law. In the lands under Muslim rule, Islamic law required that Jews and Christians be allowed to practice their religions and run their own affairs, subject to certain disabilities, the most important being a poll tax that they were required to pay. In modern parlance, Jews and Christians in the classical Islamic state were what we would call second-class citizens, but second-class citizenship, established by law and the Koran and recognized by public opinion, was far better than the total lack of citizenship that was the fate of non-Christians and even of some deviant Christians in the West. The jihad also did not prevent Muslim governments from occasionally seeking Christian allies against Muslim rivals—even during the Crusades, when Christians set up four principalities in the Syro-Palestinian area. The great twelfth-century Muslim leader Saladin, for instance, entered into an agreement with the Crusader king of Jerusalem, to keep the peace for their mutual convenience.

Under the medieval caliphate, and again under the Persian and Turkish dynasties, the empire of Islam was the richest, most powerful, most creative, most enlightened region in the world, and for most of the Middle Ages Christendom was on the defensive. In the fifteenth century, the Christian counterattack expanded. The Tatars were expelled from Russia, and the Moors from Spain. But in southeastern Europe, where the Ottoman sultan confronted first the Byzantine and then the Holy Roman Emperor, Muslim power prevailed, and these setbacks were seen as minor and peripheral. As late as the seventeenth century, Turkish pashas still ruled in Budapest and Belgrade, Turkish armies were besieging Vienna, and Barbary corsairs were raiding lands as distant as the British Isles and, on one occasion, in 1627, even Iceland.

Then came the great change. The second Turkish siege of Vienna, in 1683, ended in total failure followed by headlong retreat—an entirely new experience for the Ottoman armies. A contemporary Turkish historian, Silihdar Mehmet Aga, described the disaster with commendable frankness: "This was a calamitous defeat, so great that there has been none like it since the first appearance of the Ottoman state." This defeat, suffered by what was then the major military power of the Muslim world, gave rise to a new debate, which in a sense has been going on ever since. The argument began among the Ottoman military and political élite as a discussion of two questions: Why had the once victorious Ottoman armies been vanquished by the despised Christian enemy? And how could they restore the previous situation?

There was good reason for concern. Defeat followed defeat, and Christian European forces, having liberated their own lands, pursued their former invaders whence they had come, the Russians moving into North and Central Asia, the Portuguese into Africa and around Africa to South and Southeast Asia. Even small European powers such as Holland and Portugal were able to build vast empires in the East and to establish a dominant role in trade.

For most historians, Middle Eastern and Western alike, the conventional beginning of modern history in the Middle East dates from 1798, when the French Revolution, in the person of Napoleon Bonaparte, landed in Egypt. Within a remarkably short time, General Bonaparte and his small expeditionary force were able to conquer, occupy, and rule the country. There had been, before this, attacks, retreats, and losses of territory on the remote frontiers, where the Turks and the Persians faced Austria and Russia. But for a small Western force to invade one of the heartlands of Islam was a profound shock. The departure of the French was, in a sense, an even greater shock. They were forced to leave Egypt not by the Egyptians, nor by their suzerains the Turks, but by a small squadron of the British Royal Navy, commanded by a young admiral named Horatio Nelson. This was the second bitter lesson the Muslims had to learn: not only could a Western power arrive, invade, and rule a will but only another Western power could get it out.

By the early twentieth century—although a precarious independence was retained by Turkey and Iran and by some remoter countries like Afghanistan, which at that time did not seem worth the trouble of invading—almost the entire Muslim world had been incorporated into the four European empires of Britain, France, Russia, and the Netherlands. Middle Eastern governments and factions were forced to learn how to play these mighty rivals off against one another. For a time, they played the game with some success. Since the Western allies—Britain and France and then the United States—effectively dominated the region, Middle Eastern resisters naturally looked to those allies' enemies for support. In the Second World War, they turned to Germany; in the Cold War, to the Soviet Union.

And then came the collapse of the Soviet Union, which left the United States as the sole world superpower. The era of Middle Eastern history that had been inaugurated by Napoleon and Nelson was ended by [Soviet President Mikhail] Gorbachev and the elder George Bush. At first, it seemed that the era of imperial rivalry had ended with the withdrawal of both competitors: the Soviet Union couldn't play the imperial role, and the United States wouldn't. But most Middle Easterners didn't see it that way. For them, this was simply a new phase in an old imperial game, with America as the latest in a succession of Western imperial overlords, except that this overlord had no rival—no Hitler or Stalin—whom they could use either to damage or influence the West. In the absence of such a patron, Middle Easterners found themselves obligated to mobilize their own force of resistance. Al Qaeda—its leaders, its sponsors, its financiers—is one such force.

III. "The Great Satan"

America's new role—and the Middle East's perception of it—was vividly illustrated by an incident in Pakistan in 1979. On November 20th, a band of a thousand Muslim religious radicals seized the Great Mosque in Mecca and held it for a time against the Saudi security forces. Their declared aim was to "purify Islam" and liberate the holy land of Arabia from the royal "clique of infidels" and the corrupt religious leaders who supported them. Their leader, in speeches played from loudspeakers, denounced Westerners as the destroyers of fundamental Islamic values and the Saudi government as their accomplices. He called for a return to the old Islamic traditions of "justice and equality." After some hard fighting, the rebels were suppressed. Their leader was executed on January 9, 1980, along with sixty-two of his followers, among them Egyptians, Kuwaitis, Yemenis, and citizens of other Arab countries.

Meanwhile, a demonstration in support of the rebels took place in the Pakistani capital, Islamabad. A rumor had circulated—endorsed by Ayatollah Khomeini, who was then in the process of establishing himself as the revolutionary leader in Iran— that American troops had been involved in the clashes in Mecca. The American Embassy was attacked by a crowd of Muslim demonstrators, and two Americans and two Pakistani employees were killed. Why had Khomeini stood by a report that was not only false but wildly improbable?

These events took place within the context of the Iranian revolution of 1979. On November 4th, the United States Embassy in Teheran [was] seized, and fifty-two Americans were taken hostage; those hostages were then held for four hundred and forty-four days, until their release on January 20, 1981. The motives for this, baffling to many at the time, have become clearer since, thanks to subsequent statements and revelations from the hostage-takers and others. It is now apparent that the hostage crisis occurred not because relations between Iran and the United States were deteriorating but because they were improving. In the fall of 1979, the relatively moderate Iranian Prime Minister, Mehdi Bazargan, had arranged to meet with the American national-security adviser, Zbigniew Brzezinski, under the aegis of the Algerian government. The two men met on November 1st, and were reported to have been photographed shaking hands. There seemed to be a real possibility—in the eyes of the radicals, a real danger—that there might be some accommodation between the two countries. Protesters seized the Embassy and took the American diplomats hostage in order to destroy any hope of further dialogue.

For Khomeini, the United States was "the Great Satan," the principal adversary against whom he had to wage his holy war for Islam. America was by then perceived—rightly—as the leader of what we like to call "the free world." Then, as in the past, this world of unbelievers was seen as the only serious force rivalling and preventing the divinely ordained spread and triumph of Islam. But American observers, reluctant to recognize the historical quality of the hostility, sought other reasons for the anti-American sentiment that had been intensifying in the Islamic world for some time. One explanation which was widely accepted, particularly in American foreign-policy circles, was that America's image had been tarnished by its wartime and continuing alliance with the former colonial powers of Europe.

In their country's defense, some American commentators pointed out that, unlike the Western European imperialists, America had itself been a victim of colonialism; the United States was the first country to win freedom from British rule. But the hope that the Middle Eastern subjects of the former British and French Empires would accept the American Revolution as a model for their own anti-imperialist struggle rested on a basic fallacy that Arab writers were quick to point out. The American Revolution was fought not by Native American nationalists but by British settlers, and, far from being a victory against colonialism it represented colonialism's ultimate triumph—the English in North America succeeded in colonizing the land so thoroughly that they no longer needed the support of the mother country.

It is hardly surprising that former colonial subjects in the Middle East would see America as being tainted by the same kind of imperialism as Western Europe. But Middle Eastern resentment of imperial powers has not always been consistent.

The Soviet Union, which extended the imperial conquests of the tsars of Russia, ruled with no light hand over tens of millions of Muslim subjects in Central Asian states and in the Caucasus; had it not been for American opposition and the Cold War, the Arab world might well have shared the fate of Poland and Hungary, or, more probably, that of Uzbekistan. And yet the Soviet Union suffered no similar backlash of anger and hatred from the Arab community. Even the Russian invasion of Afghanistan in 1979—a clear case of imperialist aggression, conquest, and domination—triggered only a muted response in the Islamic world. The P.L.O. observer at the United Nations defended the invasion, and the Organization of the Islamic Conference did little to protest it. South Yemen and Syria boycotted a meeting held to discuss the issue, Libya delivered an attack on the United States, and the P.L.O. representative abstained from voting and submitted his reservations in writing. Ironically, it was the United States, in the end, that was left to orchestrate an Islamic response to Soviet imperialism in Afghanistan.

As the Western European empires faded, Middle Eastern anti-Americanism was attributed more and more to another cause: American support for Israel, first in its conflict with the Palestinian Arabs, then in its conflict with the neighboring Arab states and the larger Islamic world. There is certainly support for this hypothesis in Arab statements on the subject. But there are incongruities, too. In the nineteen-thirties, Nazi Germany's policies were the main cause of Jewish migration to Palestine, then a British mandate, and the consequent reinforcement of the Jewish community there. The Nazis not only permitted this migration; they facilitated it until the outbreak of the war, while the British, in the somewhat forlorn hope of winning Arab good will, imposed and enforced restrictions. Nevertheless, the Palestinian leadership of the time, and many other Arab leaders, supported the Germans, who sent the Jews to Palestine, rather than the British, who tried to keep them out.

The same kind of discrepancy can be seen in the events leading to and following the establishment of the State of Israel, in 1948. The Soviet Union played a significant role in procuring the majority by which the General Assembly of the United Nations voted to establish a Jewish state in Palestine, and then gave Israel immediate de-jure recognition. The United States, however, gave only de-facto recognition. More important, the American government maintained a partial arms embargo on Israel, while Czechoslovakia, at Moscow's direction, immediately sent a supply of weaponry, which enabled the new state to survive the attempts to strangle it at birth. As late as the war of 1967, Israel still relied for its arms on European, mainly French, suppliers, not on the United States.

The Soviet Union had been one of Israel's biggest supporters. Yet, when Egypt announced an arms deal with Russia, in September of 1955, there was an overwhelmingly enthusiastic response in the Arab press. The Chambers of Deputies in Syria, Lebanon, and Jordan met immediately and voted resolutions of congratulation to President [Gamal Abdel] Nasser; even Nuri Said, the pro-Western ruler of Iraq, felt obliged to congratulate his Egyptian colleague—this despite the fact that the Arabs had no special love of Russia, nor did Muslims in the Arab world or elsewhere wish to invite either Communist ideology or Soviet power to their lands. What delighted them was that they saw the arms deal—no doubt correctly—as a slap in the face for the West. The slap, and the agitated Western response, reinforced the mood of hatred and spite toward the West and encouraged its exponents. It also encouraged the

United States to look more favorably on Israel, now seen as a reliable and potentially useful ally in a largely hostile region. Today, it is often forgotten that the strategic relationship between the United States and Israel was a consequence, not a cause, of Soviet penetration.

The Israeli-Palestinian conflict is only one of many struggles between the Islamic and non-Islamic worlds—on a list that includes Nigeria, Sudan, Bosnia, Kosovo, Macedonia, Chechnya, Sinkiang, Kashmir, and Mindanao—but it has attracted far more attention than any of the others. There are several reasons for this. First, since Israel is a democracy and an open society, it is much easier to report—and mis-report—what is going on. Second, Jews are involved, and this can usually secure the attention of those who, for one reason or another, are for or against them. Third, and most important, resentment of Israel is the only grievance that can be freely and safely expressed in those Muslim countries where the media are either wholly owned or strictly overseen by the government. Indeed, Israel serves as a useful stand-in for complaints about the economic privation and political repression under which most Muslim people live, and as a way of deflecting the resulting anger.

IV. Double Standards

This raises another issue. Increasingly in recent decades, Middle Easterners have articulated a new grievance against American policy: not American complicity with imperialism or with Zionism but something nearer home and more immediate—American complicity with the corrupt tyrants who rule over them. For obvious reasons, this particular complaint does not often appear in public discourse. Middle Eastern governments, such as those of Iraq, Syria, and the Palestine Authority, have developed great skill in controlling their own media and manipulating those of Western countries. Nor, for equally obvious reasons, is it raised in diplomatic negotiation. But it is discussed, with increasing anguish and urgency, in private conversations with listeners who can be trusted, and recently even in public. (Interestingly, the Iranian revolution of 1979 was one time when this resentment was expressed openly. The Shah was accused of supporting America, but America was also attacked for imposing an impious and tyrannical leader as its puppet.)

Almost the entire Muslim world is affected by poverty and tyranny. Both of these problems are attributed, especially by those with an interest in diverting attention from themselves, to America—the first to American economic dominance and exploitation, now thinly disguised as "globalization"; the second to America's support for the many so-called Muslim tyrants who serve its purposes. Globalization has become a major theme in the Arab media, and it is almost always raised in connection with American economic penetration. The increasingly wretched economic situation in most of the Muslim world, relative not only to the West but also to the tiger economies of East Asia, fuels these frustrations. American paramountcy, as Middle Easterners see it, indicates where to direct the blame and the resulting hostility.

There is some justice in one charge that is frequently leveled against the United States: Middle Easterners increasingly complain that the United States judges them by different and lower standards than it does Europeans and Americans, both in what is expected of them and in what they may expect—in terms of their financial well-being and their political freedom. They assert that Western spokesmen repeatedly overlook or even defend actions and support rulers that they would not tolerate in their own countries. As many Middle Easterners see it, the Western and American governments' basic position is: "We don't care what you do to your own people at home, so long as you are coöperative in meeting our needs and protecting our interests."

The most dramatic example of this form of racial and cultural arrogance was what Iraqis and others see as the betrayal of 1991, when the United States called on the Iraqi people to revolt against Saddam Hussein. The rebels of northern and southern Iraq did so, and the United States forces watched while Saddam, using the helicopters that the ceasefire agreement had allowed him to retain, bloodily suppressed them, group by group. The reasoning behind this action—or, rather, inaction—is not difficult to see. Certainly, the victorious Gulf War coalition wanted a change of government in Iraq, but they had hoped for a coup d'état, not a revolution. They saw a genuine popular uprising as dangerous—it could lead to uncertainty or even anarchy in the region. A coup would be more predictable and could achieve the desired result—the replacement of Saddam Hussein by another, more amenable tyrant, who could take his place among America's so-called allies in the coalition. The United States' abandonment of Afghanistan after the departure of the Soviets was understood in much the same way as its abandonment of the Iraqi rebels.

Another example of this double standard occurred in the Syrian city of Hama and in refugee camps in Sabra and Shatila. The troubles in Hama began with an uprising headed by the radical group in Muslim Brothers in 1982. The government responded swiftly. Troops were sent, supported by armor, artillery, and aircraft, and within a very short time they had reduced a large part of the city to rubble. The number killed was estimated, by Amnesty International, at somewhere between ten thousand and twenty-five thousand. The action, which was ordered and supervised by the Syrian President, Hafiz al-Assad, attracted little attention at the time and did not prevent the United States from subsequently courting Assad, who received a long succession of visits from American Secretaries of State James Baker, Warren Christopher, and Madeleine Albright, and even from President [Bill] Clinton. It is hardly likely that Americans would have been so eager to propitiate a ruler who had perpetrated such crimes on Western soil, with Western victims.

The massacre of seven hundred to eight hundred Palestinian refugees in Sabra and Shatila that same year was carried out by Lebanese militiamen, led by a Lebanese commander who subsequently became a minister in the Syrian-sponsored Lebanese government, and it was seen as a reprisal for the assassination of the Lebanese President Bashir Gemayyel. Ariel Sharon, who at the time commanded the Israeli forces in Lebanon, was reprimanded by an Israeli commission of inquiry for not having foreseen and prevented the massacre, and was forced to resign from his position as Minister of Defense. It is understandable that the Palestinians and other Arabs should lay sole blame for the massacre on Sharon. What is puzzling is that Europeans and Americans should do the same. Some even wanted to try Sharon for crimes against humanity before a tribunal in Europe. No such suggestion was made regarding either Saddam Hussein or Hafiz al-Assad, who slaughtered ten of thousands of their compatriots. It is easy to understand the bitterness of those who see the implication here. It was as if the militia who had carried out the deed were animals, not accountable by the same human standards as the Israelis.

Thanks to modern communications, the people of the Middle East are increasingly aware of the deep and widening gulf between the opportunities of the free world outside their borders and the appalling privation and repression within them. The resulting anger is naturally directed first against their rulers, and then against those whom they see as keeping those rulers in power for selfish reasons. It is surely significant that most of the terrorists who have been identified in the September 11th attacks on New York and Washington come from Saudi Arabia and Egypt—that is, from countries whose rulers are deemed friendly to the United States.

V. A Failure of Modernity

If America's double standards—and its selfish support for corrupt regimes in the Arab world—have long caused anger among Muslims, why has that anger only recently found its expression in acts of terrorism? In the nineteenth and twentieth centuries, Muslims responded in two ways to the widening imbalance of power and wealth between their societies and those of the West. The reformers or modernizers tried to identify the sources of Western wealth and power and adapt them to their own use, in order to meet the West on equal terms. Muslim governments—first in Turkey, then in Egypt and Iran—made great efforts to modernize, that is, to Westernize, the weaponry and equipment of their armed forces; they even dressed them in Western-style uniforms and marched them to the tune of brass bands. When defeats on the battlefield were matched by others in the marketplace, the reformers tried to discover the secrets of Western economic success and to emulate them by establishing industries of their own. Young Muslim students who were sent to the West to study the arts of war also came back with dangerous and explosive notions about elected assemblies and constitutional governments.

All attempts at reform ended badly. If anything, the modernization of the armed forces accelerated the process of defeat and withdrawal, culminating in the humiliating failure of five Arab states and armies to prevent a half million Jews from building a new state in the debris of the British Mandate in Palestine in 1948. With rare exceptions, the economic reforms, capitalist and socialist alike, fared no better. The Middle Eastern combination of low productivity and high birth rate makes for an unstable mix, and by all indications the Arab countries, in such matters as job creation, education, technology, and productivity, lag ever farther behind the West. Even worse, the Arab nations also lag behind the more recent recruits to Western-style modernity, such as Korea, Taiwan, and Singapore. Out of a hundred and fifty-five countries ranked for economic freedom in 2001, the highest-ranking Muslim states are Bahrain (No. 9), the United Arab Emirates (No. 14), and Kuwait (No. 42). According to the World Bank, in 2000 the average annual income in the Muslim countries from Morocco to Bangladesh was only half the world average, and in the nineties the combined gross national products of Jordan, Syria, and Lebanon—that is, three of Israel's Arab neighbors—were considerably smaller than that of Israel alone. The per-capita figures are worse. According to United Nations statistics, Israel's per-capita G.D.P. was three and a half times that of Lebanon and Syria, twelve times that of Jordan, and thirteen and a half times that of Egypt. The contrast with the West, and now also with the Far East, is even more disconcerting.

Modernization in politics has fared no better—perhaps even worse—than in warfare and economics. Many Islamic countries have experimented with democratic institutions of one kind or another. In some, as in Turkey, Iran, and Tunisia, they were introduced by innovative native reformers; in others, they were installed and then bequeathed by departing imperialists. The record, with the possible exception of Turkey, is one of almost unrelieved failure. Western-style parties and parliaments almost invariably ended in corrupt tyrannies, maintained by repression and indoctrination. The only European model that worked, in the sense of accomplishing its purpose, was the one-party dictatorship. The Baath Party, different branches of which have rules Iraq and Syria for decades, incorporated the worst features of its Nazi and Soviet models. Since the death of Nasser, in 1970, no Arab leader has been able to gain extensive support outside his own country. Indeed, no Arab leader has been willing to submit his claim to power to a free vote. The leaders who have come closest to winning pan-Arab approval are Qaddafi in the seventies and, more recently, Saddam Hussein. That these two, of all Arab rulers, should enjoy such wide popularity is in itself both appalling and revealing.

In view of this, it is hardly surprising that many Muslims speak of the failure of modernization. The rejection of modernity in favor of a return to the sacred past has a varied and ramified history in the region and has given rise to a number of movements. The most important of these, Wahhabism, has lasted more than two and a half centuries and exerts a significant influence on Muslim movements in the Middle East today. Its founder, Muhammad ibn Abd al-Wahhab (1703–87), was a theologian from the Najd area of Arabia. In 1744, he launched a campaign of purification and renewal. His purpose was to return the Muslim world to the pure and authentic Islam of the Prophet, removing and, where necessary, destroying all later accretions. The Wahhabi cause was embraced by the Saudi rulers of Najd, who promoted it, for a while successfully, by force. In a series of campaigns, they carried their rule and their faith to much of central and eastern Arabia, before being rebuffed, at the end of the eighteenth century, by the Ottoman sultan, whom the Saudi ruler had denounced as a backslider from the true faith and a usurper in the Muslim state. The second alliance of Wahhabi doctrine and Saudi force began in the last years of the Ottoman Empire and continued after the collapse. The Saudi conquest of the Hejaz, including the holy cities of Mecca and Medina, increased the prestige of the House of Saud and gave new scope to the Wahhabi doctrine, which spread, in a variety of forms, throughout the Islamic world.

From the nineteen-thirties on, the discovery of oil in the eastern provinces or Arabia and its exploitation, chiefly by American companies, brought vast new wealth and bitter new social tensions. In the old society, inequalities of wealth had been limited, and their effects were restrained, on the one hand, by the traditional social bonds and obligations that linked rich and poor and, on the other hand, by the privacy of Muslim home life. Modernization has all too often widened the gap, destroyed those social bonds, and, through the universality of the modern media, made the resulting inequalities painfully visible. All this has created new and receptive audiences for Wahhabi teachings and those of other like-minded groups, among them the Muslim Brothers in Egypt and Syria and the Taliban in Afghanistan.

It has now become normal to designate these movements as "fundamentalist." The term is unfortunate for a number of reasons. It was originally an American Protestant term, used to designate Protestant churches that differed in some respects from the mainstream churches. These differences bear no resemblance to those that divide Muslim fundamentalists from the Islamic mainstream, and the use of the term can therefore be misleading. Broadly speaking, Muslim fundamentalists are those who feel that the troubles of the Muslim world at the present time are the result not of insufficient modernization but of excessive modernization. From their point of view, the primary struggle is not against the Western enemy as such but against the Westernizing enemies at home, who have imported and imposed infidel ways on Muslim peoples. The task of the Muslims is to depose and remove these infidel rulers, sometimes by defeating or expelling their foreign patrons and protectors, and to abrogate and destroy the laws, institutions, and social customs that they have introduced, so as to return to a purely Islamic way of life, in accordance with the principles of Islam and the rules of the Holy Law.

VI. The Rise of Terrorism

Osama bin Laden and his Al Qaeda followers may not represent Islam, and their statements and their actions directly contradict basic Islamic principles and teachings, but they do arise from within Muslim civilization, just as Hitler and the Nazis arose from within Christian civilization, so they must be seen in their own cultural, religious, and historical context.

If one looks at the historical record, the Muslim approach to war does not differ greatly from that of Christians, or that of Jews in the very ancient and very modern periods when the option was open to them. While Muslims, perhaps more frequently than Christians, made war against the followers of other faiths to bring them within the scope of Islam, Christians—with the notable exception of the Crusades, which were themselves an imitation of Muslim practice—were more prone to fight internal religious wars against those whom they saw as schismatics or heretics. Islam, no doubt owing to the political and military involvement of its founder, takes what one might call a more pragmatic view than the Gospels of the realities of societal relationships. Because war for the faith has been a religious obligation within Islam from the beginning, it is elaborately regulated. Islamic religious law, or the Sharia, deals in some detail with such matters as the opening, conclusion, and resumption of hostilities, the avoidance of injury to noncombatants, the treatment of prisoners, the division of booty, and even the types of weapons that may be used. Some of these rules have been explained away by modern radical commentators who support the fundamentalists; others are simply disregarded.

What about terrorism? Followers of many faiths have at one time or another invoked religion in the practice of murder, both retail and wholesale. Two words deriving from such movements in Eastern religions have even entered the English language: "thug," from India, and "assassin," from the Middle East, both commemorating fanatical religious sects whose form of worship was to murder those whom they regarded as enemies of the faith. The question of the lawfulness of assassination in Islam first arose in 656 A.D., with the murder of the third caliph, Uthman, by pious Muslim rebels who believed they were carrying out the will of God. The first of a succession of civil wars was fought over the question of whether the rebels were fulfilling or defying God's commandment. Islamic law and tradition are very clear on the duty of obedience to the Islamic ruler. But they also quote two sayings attributed to the Prophet: "There is no obedience in sin" and "Do not obey a creature against his creator." If a ruler orders something that is contrary to the law of God, then the duty of obedience is replaced by a duty of disobedience. The notion of tyrannicide—the justified removal of a tyrant—was not an Islamic innovation; it was familiar in antiquity, among Jews, Greeks, and Romans alike, and those who performed it were often acclaimed as heroes.

Members of the eleventh-to-thirteenth-century Muslim sect known as the Assassins, which was based in Iran and Syria, seem to have been the first to transform the act that was named after them into a system and an ideology. Their efforts, contrary to popular belief, were primarily directed not against the crusaders but against their own leaders, whom they saw as impious usurpers. In this sense, the Assassins are the true predecessors of many of the so-called Islamic terrorists of today, some of whom explicitly make this point. The name Assassins, with its connotation of "hashish-taker," was given to them by their Muslim enemies. They called themselves *fidayeen*—those who are ready to sacrifice their lives for their cause. The term has been revived and adopted by their modern imitators. In two respects, however—in their choice of weapons and of victims—the Assassins were markedly different from their modern successors. The victim was always an individual—a highly placed political, military, or religious leader who was seen as the source of evil. He, and he alone, was killed. This action was not terrorism in the current sense of that term but, rather, what we would call "targeted assassination." The method was always the same: the dagger. The Assassins disdained the use of poison, crossbows, and other weapons that could be used from a distance, and the Assassin did not expect—or, it would seem, even desire—to survive his act, which he believed would insure him eternal bliss. But in no circumstance did he commit suicide. He died at the hands of his captors.

The twentieth century brought a renewal of such actions in the Middle East, though of different types and for different purposes, and terrorism has gone through several phases. During the last years of the British Empire, imperial Britain faced terrorist movements in its Middle Eastern dependencies that represented three different cultures: Greeks in Cyprus, Jews in Palestine, and Arabs in Aden. All three acted from nationalist, rather than religious, motives. Though very different in their backgrounds and political circumstances, the three were substantially alike in their tactics. Their purpose was to persuade the imperial power that staying in the region was not worth the cost in blood. Their method was to attack the military and, to a lesser extent, administrative personnel and installations. All three operated only within their own territory and generally avoided collateral damage. All three succeeded in their endeavors.

Thanks to the rapid development of the media, and especially of television, the more recent forms of terrorism are targeted not at specific and limited enemy objectives but at world opinion. Their primary purpose is not to defeat or even to weaken the enemy militarily but to gain publicity—a psychological victory. The most successful group by far in this exercise has been the Palestine Liberation Organization. The P.L.O. was founded in 1964 but became important in 1967, after the defeat of the combined Arab armies in the Six-Day War. Regular warfare had failed; it was time to try other methods. The targets in this form of armed struggle were not military or other government establishments, which are usually too well guarded, but public places and gatherings of any kind, which are overwhelmingly civilian, and in which the victims do not necessarily have a connection to the declared enemy. Examples of this include, in 1970, the hijacking of three aircraft—one Swiss, one British, and one American—which were all taken to Amman; the 1972 murder of Israeli athletes at the Munich Olympics; the seizure in 1973 of the Saudi Embassy in Khartoum, and the murder there of two Americans and a Belgian diplomat; and the takeover of the Italian cruise ship Achille Lauro, in 1985. Other attacks were directed against schools, shopping malls, discothèques, pizzerias, and even passengers waiting in line at European airports. These and other attacks by the P.L.O. were immediately and remarkably successful in attaining their objectives—the capture of newspaper headlines and television screens. They also drew a great deal of support in some-times unexpected places, and raised their perpetrators to starring roles in the drama of international relations. Small wonder that others were encouraged to follow their example—in Ireland, in Spain, and elsewhere.

The Arab terrorists of the seventies and eighties made it clear that they were waging a war for an Arab or Palestinian cause, not for Islam. Indeed, a significant proportion of the P.L.O. leaders and activists were Christian. Unlike socialism, which was discredited by its failure, nationalism was discredited by its success. In every Arab land but Palestine, the nationalists achieved their purposes—the defeat and departure of imperialist rulers, and the establishment of national sovereignty under national leaders. For a while, freedom and independence were used as more or less synonymous and interchangeable terms. The early experience of independence, however, revealed that this was a sad error. Independence and freedom are very different, and all too often the attainment of one meant the end of the other.

Both in defeat and in victory, the Arab nationalists of the twentieth century pio-neered the methods that were later adopted by religious terrorists, in particular the lack of concern at the slaughter of innocent bystanders. This unconcern reached new proportions in the terror campaign launched by Osama bin Laden in the early nineties. The first major example was the bombing of two American embassies in East Africa in 1998. In order to kill twelve American diplomats, the terrorists were willing to slaughter more than two hundred Africans, many of them Muslims, who happened to be in the vicinity. The same disregard for human life, on a vastly greater scale, underlay the action in New York on September 11th.

There is no doubt that the foundation of Al Qaeda and the consecutive declara-tions of war by Osama bin Laden marked the beginning of a new and ominous phase in the history of both Islam and terrorism. The triggers for bin Laden's actions, as he himself has explained very clearly, were America's presence in Arabia during the Gulf War—a desecration of the Muslim Holy land—and America's use of Saudi Arabia as a base for an attack on Iraq. If Arabia is the most symbolic location in the world of Islam, Baghdad, seat of the caliphate for half a millennium and the scene of some of the most glorious chapters in Islamic history, is the second.

There was another, perhaps more important, factor driving bin Laden. In the past, Muslims fighting against the West could always turn to the enemies of the West for comfort, encouragement, and material and military help. With the collapse of the Soviet Union for the first time in centuries there was no such useful enemy. There were some nations that had the will, but they lacked the means to play the role of the Third Reich or the Soviet Union. Bin Laden and his cohorts soon realized that, in the new configuration of world power, if they wished to fight America they had to do it themselves. Some eleven years ago, they created Al Qaeda, which included many veterans of the war in Afghanistan. Their task might have seemed daunting to anyone else, but they did not see it that way. In their view, they had already driven the

Russians out of Afghanistan, in a defeat so overwhelming that it led directly to the collapse of the Soviet Union itself. Having overcome the superpower that they had always regarded as more formidable, they felt ready to take on the other; in this they were encouraged by the opinion, often expressed by Osama bin Laden, among others, that America was a paper tiger.

Muslim terrorists had been driven by such beliefs before. One of the most surprising revelations in the memoirs of those who held the American Embassy in Teheran from 1979 to 1981 was that their original intention had been to hold the building and the hostages for only a few days. They changed their minds when statements from Washington made it clear that there was no danger of serious action against them. They finally released the hostages, they explained, only because they feared that the new President, Ronald Reagan, might approach the problem "like a cowboy."

Bin Laden and his followers clearly have no such concern, and their hatred is neither constrained by fear nor diluted by respect. As precedents, they repeatedly cite the American retreats from Vietnam, from Lebanon, and—the most important of all, in their eyes—from Somalia. Bin Laden's remarks in an interview with John Miller, of ABC News, on May 28, 1998, are especially revealing:

> We have seen in the last decade the decline of the American government and the weakness of the American soldier, who is ready to wage cold wars and unprepared to fight long wars. This was proven in Beirut when the Marines fled after two explosions. It also proves they can run in less than twenty-four hours, and this was also repeated in Somalia. . . . The youth were surprised at the low morale of the American soldiers. . . . After a few blows, they ran in defeat. . . . They forgot about being the world leader and the leader of the new world order. [They] left, dragging their corpses and their shameful defeat, and stopped using such titles.

Similar inferences are drawn when American spokesmen refuse to implicate— and sometimes even hasten to exculpate—parties that most Middle Easterners believe to be deeply involved in the attacks on America. A good example is the repeated official denial of any Iraqi involvement in the events of September 11th. It may indeed be true that there is no evidence of Iraqi involvement, and that the Administration is unwilling to make false accusations. But it is difficult for Middle Easterners to resist the idea that this refusal to implicate Saddam Hussein is due less to a concern for legality than to a fear of confronting him. He would indeed be a formidable adversary. If he faces the prospect of imminent destruction, as would be inevitable in a real confrontation, there is no knowing what he might do with his already considerable arsenal of unconventional weapons. Certainly, he would not be restrained by any scruples, or by the consideration that the greatest victims of any such attack would be his own people and their immediate neighbors.

For Osama bin Laden, 2001 marks the resumption of the war for the religious dominance of the world that began in the seventh century. For him and his followers, this is a moment of opportunity. Today, America exemplifies the civilization and embodies the leadership of the House of War, and, like Rome and Byzantium, it has become degenerate and demoralized, ready to be overthrown. Khomeini's designation of the United States as "the Great Satan" was telling. In the Koran, Satan is described as "the insidious tempter who whispers in the hearts of men." This is the essential point about Satan: he is neither a conqueror nor an exploiter—he is, first and last, a tempter. And for the members of Al Qaeda it is the seduction of America that represents the greatest threat to the kind of Islam they wish to impose on their fellow-Muslims.

But there are others for whom America offers a different kind of temptation—the promise of human rights, of free institutions, and of a responsible and elected government. There are a growing number of individuals and even some movements that have undertaken the complex task of introducing such institutions in their own countries. It is not easy. Similar attempts, as noted, led to many of today's corrupt regimes. Of the fifty-seven member states of the Organization of the Islamic Conference, only one, the Turkish Republic, has operated democratic institutions over a long period of time and, despite difficult and ongoing problems, has made progress in establishing a liberal economy and a free society and political order.

In two countries, Iraq and Iran, where the regimes are strongly anti-American, there are democratic oppositions capable of taking over and forming governments. We could do much to help them, and have done little. In most other countries in the region, there are people who share our values, sympathize with us, and would like to share our way of life. They understand freedom, and want to enjoy it at home. It is more difficult for us to help those people, but at least we should not hinder them. If they succeed, we shall have friends and allies in the true, not just the diplomatic, sense of these words.

Meanwhile, there is a more urgent problem. If bin Laden can persuade the world of Islam to accept his views and his leadership, then a long and bitter struggle lies ahead, and not only for America. Sooner or later, Al Qaeda and related groups will clash with the other neighbors of Islam—Russia, China, India—who may prove less squeamish than the Americans in using their power against Muslims and their sanctities. If bin Laden is correct in his calculations and succeeds in his war, then a dark future awaits the world, especially the part of it that embraces Islam.

A Clash with U.S. Foreign Policy

USSAMA MAKDISI

[T]his essay turns to history to answer the oft-asked question "Why do they hate us?" It offers a brief, synthetic, interpretive account of Arab and American interactions over the past two centuries. I recognize from the outset the limits of generalizing about 280 million Arabs, living in a host of Arab countries, each with its own tradition and history. Nonetheless, I seek to place the rise of anti-American sentiment in the Arab world within a historical and political context often neglected, misunderstood, or ignored by proponents of a "clash of civilizations" thesis.

Anti-Americanism is a recent phenomenon fueled by American foreign policy, not an epochal confrontation of civilizations. While there are certainly those in both the United States and the Arab world who believe in a clash of civilizations

From Ussama Makdisi, "Anti-Americanism in the Arab World: An Interpretation of a Brief History," *Journal of American History,* 89 (September 2002), 538–557. Copyright © 2002 by the Organization of American Historians. Reprinted with permission.

and who invest politically in such beliefs, history belies them. Indeed, at the time of World War I the image of the United States in the Arab provinces of the Ottoman Empire was generally positive; those Arabs who knew of the country saw it as a great power that was not imperialist as Britain, France, and Russia were. Those Americans who lived in the region—missionaries and their descendants and collaborators— were pioneers in the realm of higher education. Liberal America was not simply a slogan; it was a reality encountered and experienced by Arabs, Turks, Armenians, and Persians in the hallways of the Syrian Protestant College (later renamed the American University of Beirut), Robert College in Istanbul, the American College in Persia, and the American University in Cairo. But over the course of the twentieth century, American policies in the region profoundly complicated the meaning of America for Arabs.

Among the vast majority of Arabs today, the expression of anti-American feelings stems less from a blind hatred of the United States or American values than from a profound ambivalence about America: at once an object of admiration for its affluence, its films, its technology (and for some its secularism, its law, its order) and a source of deep disappointment given the ongoing role of the United States in shaping a repressive Middle Eastern status quo. Anti-Americanism is not an ideologically consistent discourse—its intensity, indeed, its coherence and evidence, vary across the Arab world. Yet to the extent that specifically anti-American sentiments are present, never more obviously so to Americans than in the aftermath of the attacks of September 11, 2001, it is imperative to understand their nature and origins.

American involvement with the Arab world began inauspiciously in 1784 when an American ship, the *Betsey,* was seized in the Mediterranean Sea by Moroccan privateers. A year later Algerians captured more American vessels and imprisoned their crews. Thus were inaugurated the negotiations, skirmishes, and legends known collectively as the Barbary wars, which culminated in the capture of the U.S. frigate *Philadelphia* in 1803, Stephen Decatur's famous but quite ineffectual raid on Tripoli in 1804, and the ransom and release of the American captives in 1805. The episodes sparked debates between Thomas Jefferson and John Adams about whether it was necessary to go to war, rather than pay ransom to the Barbary states, in order to uphold the values of the newly independent republic. As Robert J. Allison has noted in his work on the image of Islam in the early-nineteenth-century United States, the Barbary wars, and especially the myriad captivity narratives that emerged from them, crystallized existing negative Western images of the Muslim and Ottoman world. The discourse of the despotic "Turk" functioned as one foil to early republican identity just as the more entrenched discourse of "Mohammedanism" as imposture signified the antithesis of true religion, that is to say, Christianity, at a time when complex political and sectarian battle lines were being etched into a rapidly changing American landscape.

Such perspectives were amplified in the nineteenth century by the advent of U.S. travelers' discourses of the Orient and, specifically, of Palestine. Hilton Obenzinger has described a "Holy Land mania" that gripped American travelers, artists, and writers who toured and laid claim to Palestine. The Arab inhabitants of Palestine (and the surrounding areas) were acknowledged to be paradoxically there—animating accounts of the Holy Land as Levantine dragomans, dirty natives, impious Mohammedans, or "nominal" Christians—yet not there in any meaningful historical or spiritual sense. During his post–Civil War tour of the Ottoman Empire, for example, Mark Twain irreverently satirized American travelers' religious obsession with Palestine and their enchantment with the East more generally.

In the United States itself books by Twain and by missionaries, landscapes by such artists as Frederic Church, as well as novels such as Robert Smythe Hichens's 1904 *The Garden of Allah* (which went into forty-four editions over the next forty years), contributed to the rise of a specifically American genre of orientalism. It exoticized the East as premodern, conceived of it as dreamy yet often experienced it as squalid, separated the sacred landscape of the Holy Land from its native Arab inhabitants, and commodified the Orient through promotions, advertisements, trinkets, novels, photographic exhibits, postcards, and ultimately films.

There was, however, an American encounter with the Arabs that was far more direct and had a far greater impact on early Arab attitudes toward the United States. This was the missionary encounter led mostly by New England men and women. They shared many of the prejudices that characterized nineteenth-century American travelers; indeed, the roots of their missionary effort lay in part in their disavowal of a growing liberalism in New England religious thought. They were impelled by a sense of patrimony in the Holy Land and feelings of superiority to the natives as they sought to reclaim the lands of the Bible from Muslim and Eastern Christian control. Yet, motivated by "disinterested benevolence," they were also the first Americans to engage with the local populations in a serious and sustained manner— they wanted to change the Ottoman world, not just to describe or experience it. Their spiritual preoccupation with the Holy Land was premised, not on overlooking the natives, but on recognizing their presence on the land and on proclaiming the urgent need to save the "perishing souls" of the East. The first American missionaries to the Arab world were associated with the American Board of Commissioners for Foreign Missions. They departed Boston in 1819 and arrived in the Levant in 1820. Failing to establish themselves in Jerusalem, they settled on Beirut as the center of a missionary enterprise to Syria in 1823. . . .

Had the missionaries devoted themselves only to direct proselytizing, their impact on the region would have been scarcely noticeable and their later achievements impossible. But the missionaries also functioned as a bridge between cultures. Not only did they seek to introduce the Ottoman Arab world to Protestant notions of piety and individual salvation, they also brought with them American manners and customs, clothes, education, and medicine. Simultaneously, they sought to introduce Americans to a world unknown to them—to actually inhabitants, societies, histories, and geographies normally excluded by the alternatively sacred and exotic discourse of American orientalism. . . .

The missionaries . . . served as ethnographers of Arabs to Americans. . . . The missionaries themselves changed in the crucible of encounter, especially after it became clear that the proselytizing dimension of their enterprise had failed. Thus an evangelical effort that rejected a current liberalism growing in early-nineteenth-century New England was transformed—by the labors of missionaries and natives alike— into a major project of essentially secular liberal higher education embodied in institutions such as the 1866 Syrian Protestant College in Beirut and in 1863 Robert College in Istanbul. Nowhere was the fruit of this transformation by actual experience in the Orient more evident than in the words of the famous American missionary-turned-college president Daniel Bliss. When he laid the cornerstone of College Hall at the Syrian Protestant College in 1871, Bliss spoke words as revolutionary in America as they were in the Ottoman Empire:

> This College is for all conditions and classes of men without regard to colour, nationality, race or religion. A man white, black or yellow; Christian, Jew, Mohammedan or heathen, may enter and enjoy all the advantages of this institution for three, four, or eight years; and go out believing in one God, or in many Gods, or in no God. But it will be impossible for any one to continue with us long without knowing what we believe to be the truth and our reasons for that belief.

This conversion from direct proselytization that was openly intolerant of other faiths to more liberal persuasion was fraught with tension. The secularization of the missionary enterprise coincided with and reflected a dramatic increase in Western ascendancy in the non-Western world in the late nineteenth century. That ascendancy led to a codification of national and racial prejudices—from designations of professors, to differential pay scales, to the insistence that only the English language could be a medium of modern instruction—that discriminated against Arabs even as it offered them educational opportunities that they readily grasped. Students of the Syrian Protestant College—known locally as the "American college" long before it changed its name to the American University of Beirut in 1920—played a crucial role in building a thriving late Ottoman Arab print culture, and its medical graduates greatly contributed to the development of modern health care in Lebanon and the Arab world. Innovative modern education and the absence of American government imperialism in the late Ottoman Empire contributed to the benevolent image of the United States in such places as Beirut, Istanbul, and Tehran. For example, the famous nineteenth-century Egyptian advocate of women's liberation, Qasim Amin, extolled American virtues and praised the freedom of women in America. . . .

The influence of an idea of a benevolent America reached its apex among Arabs during and immediately after World War I. Not only were Americans identified with educational efforts in the region, they were also central to relief efforts amid a terrible wartime famine in Beirut and the surrounding region of Mount Lebanon. Moreover, President Woodrow Wilson's proclamations on self-determination reinforced a notion among nationalist elites in the Arab world that the United States was different from the European powers, which had agreed to partition the postwar Middle East much as they had partitioned Africa in the late nineteenth century, with the notable difference that Africa was partitioned openly while the Arab world was carved up secretly. Most egregious from an Arab perspective was the Balfour Declaration of 1917, which promised British support for the establishment of a Jewish "national home" in Palestine despite the fact that the overwhelming majority of the native inhabitants—90 percent—were Arabs who opposed what they saw as European colonialism bent on dispossessing them of their land. . . . In 1919 Howard Bliss, son of Daniel Bliss and then president of the Syrian Protestant College, urged Wilson to form a mission to find out what the Arab peoples wanted, an idea that squarely contradicted the spirit of the Balfour Declaration and the colonial wisdom on which it was based.

The American section of the resultant Inter-Allied Commission on Mandates in Turkey was popularly known as the King-Crane commission, headed as it was by two Americans: Charles Crane, a Chicago industrialist and contributor to Wilson's presidential campaign, and Henry King, president of Oberlin College. The British and the French opposed it from the outset, reluctant to participate in what they regarded as American meddling in their imperial spheres of influence. Zionist leaders regarded it with "deepest disquietude," for travel to Palestine and interviews with natives threatened to expose a fundamental (and still often unacknowledged) problem of the Zionist project in Palestine: Namely, by what right could one create a Jewish state in a land where the vast majority of the indigenous population was not Jewish? The King-Crane commission represented the tension between two strands of nineteenth-century American experience of the Arab world. On the one hand, the commissioners by their own admission began with a "predisposition" to the Zionist perspective: they were well informed about the passionate claims to Palestine made by Jews. At the outset of their mission, therefore, they reflected a dominant nineteenth-century American view of Palestine that overlooked the Arab reality on the ground or dismissed it as marginal to the allegedly true Judeo-Christian heritage of the land or to its modern civilized future. . . .

[However] After conducting interviews with local mayors and municipal councils and professional and trade organizations and making an extensive tour of Palestine and Syria, the King-Crane commission issued a final report that outraged British and French imperial sentiments as well as Zionist aspirations. It recommended an independent unified Arab state in Syria, Palestine, and Lebanon that, if necessary, should be placed under American mandatory control. In recommending an American mandate, the commissioners drew on a discourse of American exceptionalism and a history of American missionary contributions to higher education in the region that, they claimed, had led Arabs to know and trust the United States. The Arab people, noted the final report, "declared that their choice was due to knowledge of America's record: the unselfish aims with which she had come into the war; the faith in her felt by multitudes of Syrians who had been in America; the spirit revealed in American educational institutions in Syria, especially the College in Beirut, . . . their belief that America had no territorial or colonial ambitions;" and finally "her genuinely democratic spirit; and her ample resources." . . .

The King-Crane report fell on deaf ears in Washington, London, and Paris. Wilson, who had already committed himself to the Balfour Declaration and to British imperial interests, did not publish the report officially. The British and the French proceeded with their predetermined partition of the Arab world. In 1920 Palestine became a British mandate formally committed to the terms of the Balfour Declarations, and the French dismantled the fledgling Arab state in Syria, exiling its leader, who became instead king of the newly constituted British-dominated state of Iraq. . . .

The discovery of oil in Saudi Arabia in 1938 pushed the United States into a more direct role in the Middle East. It was in oil, not in mandatory Palestine or Syria, that the United States had a strategic stake. And unlike the largely passive U.S. Middle Eastern policy of the immediate post–World War I decades, post–World War II policy was far more extensive and direct. The result was a symbiotic relationship between American oil companies, the U.S. government, and the emerging Saudi state. The brilliant novel *Cities of Salt* (1984) by Abdelrahman Munif depicts the extraordinary political transformations entailed by the almost overnight conversion of an Arab tribal society into an oil kingdom, the corruption it induced, and the alienation created as rulers became increasingly independent of their subjects and dependent on oil companies and foreign protection. The novel explores the historical tensions between the American racialist paternalism toward Arabs, epitomized in the white American compounds from which natives were barred, and the collaboration between Americans and Arabs to explore for, market, and profit from oil.

The Saudi state became an oil frontier not only for American companies, as the political scientist Robert Vitalis has argued, but also for thousands of Arabs from the Levant and tens of thousands of migrant workers from South Asia. It was from this oil frontier that the Saudi regime emerged in its present form, on the one hand deeply dependent on expatriates and on the government of the United States, and on the other hand constantly emphasizing its Islamic (and hence non-American) heritage and mandate in an effort to maintain its legitimacy with its own people. The autocratic Saudi state has sought to co-opt and outflank domestic opposition both by appearing to uphold a "pure" version of Islam and by using oil profits to build a modern infrastructure of highways, hospitals, airports, schools, and electricity grids for its citizens. The American-Saudi relationship inaugurated a U.S. involvement with the Arab world far more secular in form, strategic in conception, and nationalist in interest than the nineteenth-century spiritual and educational missionary enterprise. Henceforth, while the United States remained a land of opportunity for many Arabs and American oil companies were instrumental in realizing the undreamed-of profits for many Gulf Arab states (as well as for themselves), the U.S. government saw itself far less as a force for liberal or democratic change than as a guarantor of the status quo.

The Cold War exacerbated the suspicion felt by U.S. policy makers toward any potentially destabilizing force in the Middle East, particularly populist secular Iranian and Arab nationalisms. In Iran, for example, after the parliament nationalized the British-dominated Anglo-Iranian Oil Company in 1951, the Central Intelligence Agency (CIA) organized the overthrow in 1953 of the nationalist prime minister Mohammed Mossadeq. Thereafter, the United States supported the absolutist dictatorship of Mohammed Reza Shah Pahlavi, rationalizing or ignoring the tremendous popular disaffection with Pahlavi rule. As late as New Year's Eve 1978, Jimmy Carter lavishly praised "the great leadership of the Shah," which, he insisted, had turned Iran into "an island of stability in one of the more troubled areas of the world." The United States helped the shah establish (with Israeli advisers) the infamous SAVAK internal security agency that rounded up and tortured political prisoners. The historian Nikki R. Keddie concluded her study of the Iranian revolution of 1979 by noting that it was American policies in Iran that led to a marked increase in anti-American feeling.

A similar process unfolded in the Arab world. American hostility to Mossadeq paralleled American animosity toward the secular Pan-Arab nationalism of Gamal Abdel Nasser in Egypt. Despite some initial sympathy, American policy makers were ultimately unwilling to interpret his nationalist Pan-Arab rhetoric within the context of the recent history of British and French colonial exploitation of the Arab world. Nasser saw Israel as the greatest threat to the Arabs, whereas the Americans focused on the dangers of alleged Soviet intrusion into the Middle East. Thus they perceived Nasser within a Cold War logic that dismissed his attempt at nonalignment. Although much of the Arab world, indeed, the Third World, saw in Nasser a genuinely charismatic leader and an authentic voice for Arab aspirations, for the Palestinian people, and for Egypt, Americans portrayed him as dangerously ambitious. They regarded his 1955 decision to seek arms from the eastern block (after being rebuffed by the West) and his 1956 nationalization of the Suez Canal (after the United States suddenly pulled out of financing the Aswan Dam project) as destabilizing to pro-Western regimes in the region, including Saudi Arabia and Iraq (whose monarchy was indeed overthrown). When the Iraqi monarchy fell in July 1958, 14,000 American troops were immediately dispatched to a Lebanon embroiled in civil conflict. They were sent to shore up the pro-Western regime of Camille Chamoun and also to signal U.S. determination to stave off perceived radical Arab nationalism and Soviet expansionism. This politicization of the United States on the side of conservative autocratic regimes fostered a first round of anti-American sentiment in the Arab world that was similar to the anti-Americanism then evident in Latin America and Asia, where the United States more often than not sided with dictatorships in the name of fighting Communism and radical nationalism.

This anti-Americanism was not characterized by hatred of America or things American as much as by a relatively new identification of American power as a force for repression rather than liberation in the Arab world. . . .

The secular anti-imperialist rhetoric of student movements, leftist intellectuals, and "progressive" governments such as Nasser's now regarded the U.S. government as a representative of the historic force of colonialism and imperialism (and capitalism) and as a power holding the Arab world back from its rightful place at the eagerly anticipated postcolonial "rendezvous of victory." Enormous differences within the secularist camp notwithstanding (Nasser's regime, for example, persecuted Communists), this secular criticism of perceived American imperialism was based ultimately, not on a theory about a clash of civilizations, but on a discourse about a historic clash between the reactionary forces of imperialism and the progressive forces of revolution. It interpreted politics as a struggle between two stages of a single teleological reading of history in which the United States supported allegedly retrograde regimes, be it in the shah's Iran or in Chamoun's Lebanon and Nuri Said's Iraq in 1958 against supposedly more progressive ones. Anti-imperialist mobilization involved anti-American rhetoric, but its characterizations were broad, its criticism tempered by the fact that the United States as a nation remained a promised land for many, a source of admiration for still more, and on occasion—as during the Suez crisis in 1956 when President Dwight D. Eisenhower reversed a British, French, and Israeli invasion of Egypt following Nasser's nationalization of the Suez Canal—a symbol of hope for a new kind of relationship between the Third World and the great powers.

For the most part secular anti-imperialist rhetoric prevailed from Cairo to Baghdad, especially in the 1960s as the secular Arab nationalism represented by Nasser remained ascendant. But there also existed an undercurrent of Islamist dissidence from the autocratic governments of the Arab world and Iran. Unlike secularists, Islamists (who were also split into many ideological factions) framed their politics as a response to the violation of an alleged tradition and envisioned a revival of an ostensibly pure Islamic state and society. Unlike many of the great nineteenth-century Islamist reformers such as Jamal al-Din al-Afghani and Muhammad 'Abdu, who had tried to reconcile Islam and the West, many Islamists now regarded the West as a representative of an antagonistic secular and un-Islamic history, culture, and civilization. They witnessed the Arab inability to prevent the loss of Palestine and the dispersion of the Palestinian people—the first of which was justified, and the second largely ignored, by the West. They also seethed at the corruption of post-colonial Arab regimes. [Egypt's Sayyid] Qutb, who had once awkwardly admired certain facets of the United States, turned away from it in the 1950s because of its materialism and its support for Israel. He was further radicalized following his arrest in 1954 after a failed assassination attempt on Nasser by a member of the Muslim Brotherhood to which Qutb belonged. Qutb suffered, as did many other Egyptians, at the hands of Nasser's secret police. . . . It was not freedom or temptation per se that Qutb opposed; it was what he saw as the degradation, corruption, injustice, authoritarianism, and materialism imposed on Muslims by their enemies. Qutb was hanged by Nasser's regime in 1966.

A year later Nasser's regime and secular Arab nationalism were shaken by Israel's success in the June 1967 war. The Israeli defeat of Nasser and secular Arab nationalism, which by then had amassed a dismal human rights and economic record, and the Iranian revolution of 1979 sapped secularist rhetoric and galvanized the Islamist alternative. What Qutb, an adherent of the dominant Sunni branch of Islam, advocated in Egypt, Ayatollah Ruhollah Khomeini succeeded in accomplishing in predominantly Shiite Iran. Not surprisingly, when the shah of Iran finally fell in 1979, an intense power struggle between Islamists and secularists and among Islamists themselves began not only in Iran but also in the Arab world. Many self-styled spokesmen for Islam denounced American and Western culture, and some have also criticized and on occasion persecuted those women, minorities, and Muslim men who did not conform to "proper" Islamic codes of conduct. In the Arab world, however, Islamist movements have remained oppositional forces to authoritarian governments. In Iran the Islamists led by Khomeini triumphed and ushered in the "Islamic Revolution" and with it the most sustained challenge to U.S. regional hegemony. Khomeini did not hide his antipathy to the West and the United States in particular for propping up the shah's repressive regime. "With the support of America," Khomeini wrote in 1978, "and with all the infernal means at his disposal, the Shah has fallen on our oppressed people, turning Iran into one vast graveyard."

But unlike Nasser, and unlike Islamists such as Ali Shariati who promoted an Islamic liberation theology, Khomeini mobilized and channeled revolutionary aspirations into a Manichaean theocracy that viewed Islam and America as totally antithetical civilizations. The taking of American hostages in 1980 dramatically illustrated the gulf that separated the revolutionary Iranian sense of an "imperialist" America and the U.S. image of itself as a benevolent nation. Khomeini's fiery denunciation of America in 1980 drew on a history of American overseas politics of which most Americans were ignorant but that Iranians and Arabs encountered on a daily basis. "The most important and painful problem confronting the subjugated nations of the world, both Muslim and non-Muslim," Khomeini said, "is the problem of America." . . .

The Islamist anti-American sentiment that came to the fore during the Iranian revolution was ironically and unintentionally exacerbated by covert U.S. and Saudi mobilization, training, and financing of Muslim fighters to repel the Soviet invasion of Afghanistan. Their victory over one "imperialist" superpower turned their attention to another. Indeed, the United States loomed in the 1980s and 1990s ever more clearly as the unequivocal regional hegemon, the largest arms seller to the

Middle East (particularly the gulf Arab states), an increasingly staunch supporter of Israel, and the guarantor of the authoritarian status quo in the gulf states (the wealthiest Arabs) and, since [the peace accords at] Camp David, in Egypt (the most populous Arab nation). And the United States military firmly planted itself in Saudi Arabia following the Gulf War . . . to oversee a stringent sanctions regime against Iraq. It is in this context of Iranian revolutionary upheaval, the defeat of the Soviets in Afghanistan, and the rise of U.S. dominance in the Persian Gulf that some Saudi Islamists, for example, have incorporated a militant anti-Americanism into their opposition to an increasingly obvious dependency of Saudi Arabia and to the "unjust" regional order that the United States has overseen. Their specific political anti-Americanism is inextricably bound up with their religious defensiveness and their more general repudiation of secular culture. Their anti-Americanism is not, however, simply a reaction against the basing of U.S. "infidels" near Mecca and Medina; nor is it simply fury at long-lost Muslim ascendancy. Such Islamists see the United States as a leader of a new crusade, a term that in the Arab world is replete not only with religious connotations of spiritual violation but equally with political ideas of occupation and oppression, in short, of worldly *injustice*. . . .

On no issue is Arab anger at the United States more widely and acutely felt than that of Palestine. And on *no* issue, arguably, has there been more misunderstanding and less candor in mainstream commentaries purporting to explain Arab anger to American audiences following September 11. For it is over Palestine that otherwise antithetical Arab secularist and Islamist interpretations of history converge in their common perception of an immense gulf separating official American avowals of support for freedom from actual American policies. No account of anti-Americanism in the Arab world that does not squarely address the Arab understanding of Israel can even begin to convey the nature, the depth, and the sheer intensity of Arab anger at the United States.

Viewed from an exclusively Western perspective, the creation of the state of Israel represented Jewish national redemption, both because of a history of European anti-Semitism (especially the Holocaust) and because of the centrality of the Jewish presence (and the marginality of Islam) in Christian, particularly evangelical, thought about Palestine. But from an Arab perspective, Israel never has been and never could have been so understood. Zionism in Palestine, a land whose overwhelming majority was Arab at the turn of the twentieth century and for over a thousand years before that, caused the destruction of Palestinian society and the dispossession of its Arab inhabitants. . . .

Compounding the original uprooting of the Palestinians in 1948 from their homes and lands—what Palestinians refer to as the *nakba* (catastrophe)—has been Israel's 1967 military occupation of the West Bank, Gaza, East Jerusalem, and the Golan Heights, an occupation that remains in full force today. Successive Israeli governments, Labor and Likud alike, have steadily confiscated more and more Palestinian land, demolished Palestinian homes, and exiled Palestinians, thus dismantling an Arab reality in Palestine and transforming it into a Jewish one. In the immediate aftermath of the 1948 war, for example, the new state of Israel razed approximately four hundred Palestinian villages; today Jewish settlements continue to be built on expropriated Palestinian land in East Jerusalem and the West Bank. Because of this, Israel represents, for Arabs, a gross injustice. The contradictions and nuances within Israeli society are lost in the fact that Israel's creation and its persistence in its present form came and *continues* to come at the expense of the indigenous inhabitants of the land. From an Arab perspective, the creation of Israel marked the triumph of Western colonialism over native Arabs at a time when India and much of Africa and Asia were freeing themselves from European colonial rule. The specific question of Palestine has always been a broader Arab one as well, both because of the hundreds of thousands of Palestinian refugees in several Arab countries and because of a common history, language, culture, and politics that leads Arabs—Muslim and Christian—to identify with Palestinians.

American support for Israel has several foundations, ranging from the evangelical to the secular, from putative Judeo-Christian affinity to Cold War strategy, from passionate belief in the necessity of a Jewish state to opportunistic appeal to American Jewish voters, and from memory of the Holocaust to a perception of Israel as a small democratic nation surrounded by hostile Arab nations. For those reasons American financial support for Israel currently stands at nearly $3 billion a year, making it by far the single largest recipient of U.S. foreign aid. But as Kathleen Christison, a former CIA analyst, has recently put it, "the singular U.S. focus on Israel's perspective in the conflict renders the United States unable to perform the role it has always set for itself as ultimate mediator and peacemaker." In the United States (unlike most other parts of the world, including Europe) and among most Americans, the cumulative costs borne by Palestinians particularly and Arabs more generally for the violent creation of a Jewish state in the Arab world against the explicit wishes of the indigenous population are rarely acknowledged in public debate. To the extent that Arab hostility to Israel is known, it is often assumed to be based on age-old or irrational hatreds, anti-Semitism, or an intrinsic antidemocratic Arab sensibility. Just as support for Israel has become fundamental to an American imagination of the Middle East, particularly following the 1967 war, it is largely through Israel that most Arabs have come to judge the United States politically (although within often contradictory secular and Islamist narratives and hence with different implications). Satellite television stations such as Al-Jazeera daily beam pictures of Palestinian *suffering* under Israeli *occupation* directly into Arab households at a time when American television represents the Palestinian-Israeli conflict largely as Arab *violence* against Israel and Israeli *retaliation* against this violence.

It is not lost on Arabs that current American government officials describe the United States as an "honest broker." But those officials (and those in administrations before them) have explicitly condemned Palestinian terror against Israeli civilians while remaining largely silent when Palestinian civilians in far greater numbers are killed by Israeli terror. This American silence is seen in the Arab world as complicity in Israeli occupation—particularly when it is American planes, helicopters, and bombs that enforce the thirty-five-year-old occupation. The dominant view in the Arab world is that American foreign policy regarding the Arab-Israeli conflict is shaped by the pro-Israel lobby, notably the American Israel Public Affairs Committee (AIPAC). Even regimes considered "pro-American" such as those of Saudi Arabia, Jordan, and post–Camp David Egypt are embarrassed by their apparent inability to make any significant impact on this state of affairs. . . .

[C]ondemnations of an evident U.S. bias toward Israel rarely acknowledge the Arabs own role in solidifying that affinity, given the lack of democratic governance in the Arab world and the consequent inability of Arab leaders (and recently of Yasir Arafat) to articulate the moral and political nature of the Palestinian struggle for self-determination in terms that will resonate with the American public. Nor is it to deny that many Arab regimes and opposition parties have ruthlessly exploited the Palestinian question or that those regimes treat Palestinians and their own citizens callously. Nor is it to suggest that Arab convergence on the question of Palestine indicates unanimity on how to resolve the Arab-Israeli conflict. On that question, as on so many others, Arabs are deeply divided. Nor is it to deny that the Palestinians' own leadership under Yasir Arafat has successively alienated Arab people after people, beginning in Jordan, going on to Lebanon, and most recently in Kuwait, both tarnishing the image and immensely complicating the meaning of the Palestinian struggle within the Arab world. Nor is it, finally, to deny that criticism of Israel covers up a multitude of Arab sins, from the suppression of democratic opposition, the torture and banishment of dissidents, and the rampant corruption of state institutions to the cultivation of one-party and, indeed, one-family rule in Arab regimes (pro-American or not) from Saudi Arabia to Syria. Yet it *is* testament to the unresolved simplicity of the basic underlying issue that fuels this struggle—Arab natives evicted from their homes by Zionists, languishing stateless in refugee camps, and still suffering under Israeli occupation—that Arabs, from Morocco to Yemen and from all walks of life, still strongly sympathize with the Palestinians as a people for their half century of tribulations and exile from their land.

Whatever good Americans and the United States as a nation do in the region—from food aid to technological assistance to educational outreach to efforts at bilateral Arab-Israeli peacemaking—has been constantly overshadowed and tainted in Arab eyes by the continuation of the Arab-Israeli conflict, in which Arabs do not see the United States as evenhanded. Anti-American sentiment stemming from American support for Israel has been compounded in the past decade by the punitive American-dominated United Nations (UN) sanctions regime against Iraq put in place following the second Gulf War [in 1991]. The sanctions have contributed—according to UN statistics—to the deaths of several hundred thousand Iraqi civilians. In 1996 CBS correspondent Lesley Stahl noted a report that "half a million children" had died in Iraq as a result of sanctions and asked then secretary of state Madeleine Albright, "Is the price worth it?" Albright replied, "I think this is a very hard choice, but the price, we think the price is worth it." Americans see the image of Saddam Hussein and hear about frightening "weapons of mass destruction." Arabs see a flagrant double standard—Iraq punished and humiliated for invading Kuwait; Israel effusively supported despite its far longer occupation of Lebanon (which began in 1978 and ended in April 2000 because of a successful resistance campaign waged by Hezbollah), both occupations in clear defiance of UN resolutions. In the Arab world, therefore, the hope in America evident at the beginning of the twentieth century was transformed by the mid-twentieth century into disillusionment and by the end of the twentieth century into outright anger and hostility.

Most Arabs do not and will not act on this anger at U.S. policy in the region, like other people, most Arabs try to get on with their daily lives and, when they do turn to politics, can and do separate what they think of American culture, of Americans, and of American foreign policy. Yet September 11 is ultimately a mutilated and hijacked expression of immense Arab anger at the United States. Osama bin Laden is no more representative of Arabs than David Koresh or Timothy McVeigh were representative of Americans. But bin Laden *is* a manifestation of a deeply troubled Arab world beset by Arab government authoritarianism, a rise of Islamic fundamentalism, Israeli occupation and settlement of Arab lands, continuing Palestinian exile, and, finally, by American policies toward the region during and after the Cold War that have done little to encourage justice or democracy. . . .

The merest familiarity with modern history, then, would indicate that widespread Arab opposition to America is a sign of the times. It is based, not on *long-standing hatred* of "American" values, but on more *recent anger* at American policies in the region, especially toward Israel. Anti-Americanism is therefore not civilizationally rooted, even if it is at times expressed in civilizational terms.

A Clash Between Globalization and Tradition

ROBERT WRIGHT

Among the ideas that seemed to collapse along with the twin towers two years ago was a view of globalization as a kind of manifest destiny. Unlike the 19th-century version of manifest destiny, this vision didn't involve expanding America's borders. Rather, America's values—notably economic and political liberty—would spread beyond those borders, covering the planet. And this time around America's mission didn't have the widely assumed blessing of God. But it had the next best thing: the force of history. Globalization was seen by some as a nearly inevitable climax of the human story—destiny of a secular sort.

In some versions of this scenario, like neoconservative ones, tough American guidance might be needed—coercing China, say, toward democracy. In other versions, international economic competition would do the coercing. After all, microelectronics was making free markets a more essential ingredient in prosperity, and free markets work best with free minds. As some libertarians saw things, all you had to do was end trade barriers and then sit back and enjoy the show.

Some show. As commentators started noting around Sept. 12, 2001, the terrorists had turned the tools of globalization—cellphones, e-mail, international banking—against the system. What's more, their grievances had grown partly out of globalization, with its jarringly modern values. It started to seem as if globalization, far from being a benign culmination of history, had carried the seeds of its own destruction all along.

Two years later, that view is still defensible. Though the United States has been free from serious terrorism, anti-American terrorist networks are intact—and the war in Iraq has given them both a new rallying cry and conveniently located targets. Further, Islamist terrorism is assuming more global form; one can imagine a chain of attacks setting off a worldwide economic tailspin. With biotechnology and nuclear materials emphatically not under control, out-and-out collapse in some future decade is possible.

From Robert Wright, "Two Years Later, a Thousand Years Ago," *New York Times,* 11 September 2003.

Still, viewed against the backdrop of history, the case for a kind of manifest destiny is stronger than ever. In this version, America's mission is different from the ones libertarians and neoconservatives have in mind—passive role model or aggressive evangelizer, respectively. It is in some ways a grander mission, carrying a deep and subtle moral challenge. Indeed, the challenge is so deep, and so natural an outgrowth of history, that the idea of destiny in some nonsecular sense isn't beyond the pale. In any event, Sept 11, 2001, illustrates the challenge in painfully vivid form.

Globalization dates back to prehistory, when the technologically driven expansion of commerce began. Early advances in transportation—roads, wheels, boats—were used to do deals (when they weren't used to fight wars). So too with information technology. Writing seems to have evolved in Mesopotamia as a recorder of debts. Later, in the form of contracts, it would lubricate long-distance trade.

All this is grounded in human nature. People instinctively play nonzero-sum games—games, like economic exchange, in which both players can win. And technological advance lets them play more complex games over longer distances. Hence globalization.

What makes globalization precarious is that nonzero-sum relationships typically have a downside: both players can lose as well as win. Their fortunes are correlated, their fates partly shared, for better or worse. As a web of commerce expands and thickens, this interdependence deepens. The ancient world saw prosperity spread but also saw vast downturns—like collapse across the eastern Mediterranean around 1200 B.C.

One reason trouble can spread so broadly is that it often uses the economic system's conduits of transportation or communication. The collapse of 1200 B.C. seems to have been abetted by raiders who exploited shipping lanes. In the Middle Ages, the bubonic plague moved from city to city along avenues of commerce. Today a bioweapon could spread death globally the same way. And support for terrorism proliferates via the very satellites that convey stock prices, as appeals from Osama bin Laden, or images of civilian casualties in Iraq or Gaza, are beamed around the world.

One way to protect an expanding realm of interdependence is through expanded governance. The Roman Empire, in its heyday, kept vast trade routes secure. But governance needn't come in the form of a full-fledged state. In the late Middle Ages, merchants in German cities formed the Hanseatic League to repel pirates and brigands.

Today the globalization of commerce, and of threats to it, has created the rudiments of international governance, from the World Health Organization to arrangements for policing nuclear weapons. Global governance sounds radical, but it's just history marching on—commerce making the world safe for itself.

In light of 9/11, there is room for improvement. For starters, we need more routine and forceful means of policing the world's nuclear materials and, more challenging still, its biotechnology infrastructure. This will involve rethinking national sovereignty—for example, accepting visits from international inspectors in exchange for the reassuring knowledge that they visit other countries, too. But we have little choice. The aftermath of the Iraq war suggests that even a superpower can't afford to invade every country that may have illicit weapons.

History's expansion of commerce has entailed the growth not just of governance, but of morality. Doing business with people, even at a distance, usually involves acknowledging their humanity. This may not sound like a major moral breakthrough. But prehistoric life seems to have featured frequent hostility among groups, with violence justified by the moral devaluation, even dehumanization, of the victims. And recorded history is replete with such bigotry. The modern idea that people of all races and religions are morally equal is often taken for granted, but viewed against the human past, it is almost bizarre.

Can moral enlightenment really be rooted in crass self-interest as mediated by the nonzero-sum logic of expanding economic interdependence? Certainly that would explain why an ethos of ethnic and religious tolerance is most common in highly globalized nations like the United States. And it would help explain why, in contrast, open hatred of Christians or Jews is found in some Muslim countries that aren't deeply, organically integrated into the global economy. . . .

Some favor a different explanation, blaming belligerent passages in the Koran for radical Islam's intolerance. But during the Middle Ages, when Islamic civilization was at the forefront of globalization, and co-existence with Christians and Jews made economic sense, Islamic scholars devised the requisite doctrines of tolerance. Muslims can read Scripture selectively when conditions warrant, just as many cosmopolitan Christians and Jews are profitably unaware of the jihads advocated in Deuteronomy.

Globalization, then, might eventually dampen the appeal of radical Islam, especially if economic liberty indeed tends to bring political liberty. In a world of economically intertwined free-market democracies, not only will more Muslim elites rub elbows with non-Muslims in business class, but also more young Muslims will have non-lethal outlets for their energies, thanks to a new avenues for political activism and economic ambition.

Sounds great—and, in fact, it's a prospect that has been hopefully invoked by many, including some hawks in advocating war with Iraq. But before deciding how to get from here to there, we might ponder one of history's lessons: bursts of technological progress can bring great instability. A particularly unsettling parallel with the current moment lies in a previous revolution in information technology, the coming of the movable-type printing press to Europe in the 15th century.

When transmitting information gets cheaper, groups that lack power can gain it. Within weeks of Martin Luther's unveiling his 95 Theses in 1517, German printers in several cities took it upon themselves to sell copies. An amorphous and largely silent interest group—people disenchanted with the Roman Catholic Church—crystallized and found its voice. Protest was now feasible. (Hence the term Protestant.)

The ensuing erosion of central authority went beyond the church. The "wars of religion" that ravaged Europe during the 16th and 17th centuries were about politics, too, and by their end the Hapsburgs, not just the pope, had lost possessions. If Europe's powers had adjusted more gracefully to the decentralizing force of print, much bloodshed might have been averted.

Today, similarly, new information technologies allow previously amorphous or powerless groups to coalesce and orchestrate activities, from peaceful lobbying to terrorist slaughter. And the revolution is young. As the Internet goes broadband, Osama bin Laden's potent recruiting videos will get more accessible—viewable on demand from more and more parts of the world. Other terrorist televangelists may spring up, too. As in the age of print, far-flung discontent will grow more powerful—often through peaceful means, but sometimes not.

Paradoxically, the increasing volatility of intense discontent puts Americans in a more nonzero-sum relationship with the world's discontented peoples. If, for example, unhappy Muslims overseas grow more unhappy and resentful, that's good for Osama bin Laden and hence bad for America. If they grow more secure and satisfied, that's good for America. This is history's drift: technology correlating the fortunes of ever-more-distant people, enmeshing humanity in a web of shared fate. . . .

The architects of America's national security policy at once grasp this cross-cultural interdependence and don't. They see that prosperous and free Muslim nations are good for America. But they don't see that the very logic behind this goal counsels against pursuing it crudely, with primary reliance on force and intimidation. They don't appreciate how easily, amid modern technology, resentment and hatred metastasize. Witness their planning for postwar Iraq, with spectacular inattention to keeping Iraqis safe, content and well informed.

Nor do they seem aware, as they focus tightly on state sponsors of terrorism that technology lets terrorists operate with less and less state support. Anarchic states—like the ones that may now be emerging in Iraq and Afghanistan—could soon be as big a problem as hostile states.

Grasping the new challenge of terrorism doesn't render the problem simple or undermine President Bush's entire terrorism strategy. Obviously, we can't grow so concerned with grassroots opinion that we give in to specific terrorist demands. And sometimes we may have to use force in ways that, in the short run, inflame anti-Americanism. And so on.

Still, only if we see the growing power of grassroots sentiment will we give due attention to the subject that hawks so disdain: "root causes." With hatred becoming Public Enemy No. 1, a successful war on terrorism demands an understanding of how so much of the world has come to dislike America. When people who are born with the same human nature as you and I grow up to commit suicide bombings—or applaud them—there must be a reason. And it's at least conceivable that their fanaticism is needlessly encouraged by American policy or rhetoric.

Putting yourself in the shoes of people who do things you find abhorrent may be the hardest moral exercise there is. But it would be easier to excuse Americans who refuse to try if they didn't spend so much time indicting Islamic radicals for the same refusal. Somebody has to go first, and if no body does we're all in trouble.

Even if we dawdle, and make no progress on either the moral or governmental fronts—fail to move toward a global norm of tolerance and toward sound global governance—history will eventually concentrate our minds. A nuclear explosion, or epic bioterrorism, will lead even some hardened unilateralists to embrace arms control and other multilateral actions.

But it would be nice to avoid the million deaths. Besides, if we wait until an American city is erased, by then hatred of America will be broad and deep. One can imagine national and global policing regimes that could keep us fairly secure even then, but they would be severe, with expanded monitoring of everyday life and shrinking civil liberties.

In other words, the age-old tradeoff between security and liberty increasingly involves a third variable: antipathy. The less hatred there is in the world, the more security we can have without sacrificing personal freedom. Assuming we like our liberty, we have little choice but to take an earnest interest in the situation of distant and seemingly strange people, working to elevate their welfare, exploring their discontent as a step toward expanding their moral horizons—and in the process expanding ours. Global governance without global moral progress could be very unpleasant.

As the world's most powerful nation, and one of the world's most ethnically and religiously diverse nations, America is a natural leader of this moral revolution. America is also well positioned to lead in shaping a judicious form of global governance.

This role wasn't inevitable. But for a few quirks of history, some other nation might be on top at this moment of challenge. What was more or less inevitable, in my view, is the challenge itself. All along, technological evolution has been moving our species toward this nonzero-sum moment, when our welfare is crucially correlated with the welfare of the other, and our freedom depends on the sympathetic comprehension of the other.

That history has driven us toward moral enlightenment—and then left the final choice to us, with momentous stakes—is scary but inspiring. Some, indeed, may see this as evidence of the higher purpose that was widely assumed back in the 19th century. But a religious motivation isn't necessary. Simple self-interest will do. That's the beauty of the thing.

FURTHER READING

Fouad Ajami, *The Arab's Predicament* (1992)

———, *The Dream Palace of the Arab's Dream* (1999)

M. J. Akbar, *The Shades of Swords* (2002) (on Islam and Christianity)

Hamid Algar, *Wahhabism* (2002)

Robert J. Allison, *The Crescent Obscured: The United States and the Muslim World, 1776–1815* (1995)

Isaac Alteras, *Eisenhower and Israel* (1993)

Robert Baer, *Sleeping with the Devil* (2003) (on Saudi Arabia)

George Ball and Douglas Ball, *The Passionate Attachment* (1992) (on Israel)

Daniel Benjamin and Steven Simon, *The Age of Sacred Terror* (2003)

Michael Benson, *The United States and the Founding of Israel* (1997)

Abraham Ben-Zvi, *Decade of Transition: Eisenhower, Kennedy, and the Origins of the American-Israeli Alliance* (1998)

Paul Berman, *Terror and Liberalism* (2003)

Hans Blix, *Disarming Iraq* (2004)

H. W. Brands, *Into the Labyrinth* (1994)

Teresa Brennan, *Globalism and Its Terrors* (2002)

Zbigniew K. Brzezinski, *The Choice: Global Domination or Global Leadership* (2004)

Richard J. Chasdi, *Tapestry of Terror* (2002)

Noam Chomsky, *Power and Terror* (2003)

Kathleen Christison, *Perceptions of Palestine* (1999)

Nathan Citino, *From Arab Nationalism to OPEC* (2002) (on Saudi Arabia)

Richard A. Clarke, *Against All Enemies* (2004)

Michael Cohen, *Truman and Israel* (1990)

Steve Coll, *Ghost Wars* (2004) (on the C.I.A. and Afghanistan)
Anthony H. Cordesman, *The Iraq War* (2003)
———, *Terrorism, Asymmetric Warfare, and Weapons of Mass Destruction* (2001)
Richard Crockett, *America Embattled* (2003)
Ivo H. Daalder and James M. Lindsay, *America Unbound* (2003)
Alan Dershowitz, *The Case for Israel* (2003)
Herbert Druks, *The Uncertain Alliance* (2001) (on Israel)
Khaled Abou El Fadl, *The Place of Tolerance in Islam* (2002)
Charles Enderlin, S*hattered Dreams* (2003) (on the Oslo peace process)
David L. Esposito, *Unholy War: Terror in the Name of Islam* (2002)
"Fifty Years of U.S.-Israeli Relations: A Roundtable," *Diplomatic History,* 22 (1998),
    231–283
Glen Frankel, *Beyond the Promised Land* (1996)
Lawrence Freedman and Ephraim Karsh, *The Gulf Conflict, 1990–1991* (1993)
Steven Z. Freiberger, *Dawn over Suez* (1992)
Thomas L. Friedman, *Longitudes and Attitudes* (2003)
———, *The Olive Tree and the Lexus* (2000)
David Fromkin, *A Peace to End All Peace* (2001) (on the Ottoman Empire)
Fawaz A. Gerges, *America and Political Islam* (1999)
Dore Gold, *Hatred's Kingdom* (2003) (on Saudi Arabia)
Peter L. Hahn, *United States, Great Britain, and Egypt, 1945–1956* (1991)
Parker T. Hart, *Saudi Arabia and the United States* (1999)
Dilip Hiro, *War Without End* (2002) (on terrorism)
Christopher Hitchens, *A Long Short War* (2003) (on the Iraq War)
Matthew F. Holland, *America and Egypt* (1996)
Fereydoun Hoveyda, *The Broken Cresent* (2002) (on Islamic fundamentalism)
Robert F. Hunter, *The Palestinian Uprising* (1993)
Samuel P. Huntington, *The Clash of Civilizations and the Remaking of the World Order*
    (1996)
Bruce Jentleson, *With Friends like These: Reagan, Bush, and Saddam* (1994)
Chalmers Johnson, *Blowback* (2000)
Robert Kaplan, *The Arabists* (1996)
Burton I. Kaufman, *The Arab Middle East and the United States* (1995)
Gilles Kepel, *Jihad* (2002)
Jane E. Krasno and James D. Sutterlin, *The United Nations and Iraq* (2002)
Audrey Kurth, "Behind the Curve: Globalization and International Terrorism," *International
    Security,* 3 (Winter 2002–2003), pp. 30–58
Walter LaQueur, *The New Terrorism* (1999)
Bernard Lewis, *The Crisis of Islam* (2003)
———, *What Went Wrong?* (2001)
Douglas Little, *American Orientalism* (2002)
Robert S. Litwak, *Rogue States and US Foreign Policy* (2000)
David Makovsky, *Making Peace with the PLO* (1996)
William Maley, *The Afghanistan Wars* (2002)
Mahmood Mamdani, *Good Muslim, Bad Muslim* (2004)
James Mann, *Rise of the Vulcans* (2004) (on the Bush administration)
Michelle Mart, "Tough Guys and American Cold War Policy: Images of Israel, 1948–1960,"
    Diplomatic History, 20 (Summer 1996), pp. 357–380
Melani McAlister, *Epic Encounters* (2001) (on the U.S. media and the Middle East)
Joanne Meyerowitz, ed., *History and September 11th* (2003)
John P. Migetta, *American Alliance Policy in the Middle East* (2002)
Benny Morris, *Israel's Border Wars, 1949–1956* (1993)
Williamson Murray and Robert H. Schlesinger Jr., *The Iraq War* (2003)
Donald Neff, *Fallen Pillars: US Policy Toward Palestine and Israel Since 1945* (1995)
David S. New, *Holy War* (2002)
Michael B. Oren, *Six Days of War* (2002)

David Painter, *Oil and the American Century* (1986)

Ibn Pappe, *The Israel/Palestine Question* (1999)

Richard B. Parker, *The Politics of Miscalculation in the Middle East* (1993)

Daniel Pipes, *Militant Islam Reaches America* (2002)

Gerald L. Posner, *Why America Slept* (2004) (on 9/11)

John Prados, ed., *America Confronts Terrorism* (2002)

William B. Quandt. *Peace Process* (1993)

Ahmed Rashid, *Jihad* (2002) (on Central Asia)

———, *Taliban* (2001)

Bernard Reich, *Securing the Covenant* (1995) (on Israel)

"The Road to and from September 11th: A Roundtable," *Diplomatic History,* 26 (Fall 2002), 541–644

Jeffrey J. Roberts, *The Origins of Conflict in Afghanistan* (2002)

Barry Rubin, *Cauldron of Turmoil* (1992)

———, *The Fragmentation of Afghanistan* (2002)

Edward W. Said, *The Question of Palestine* (1979)

Yezid Sayigh, *Armed Struggle and the Search for State* (1998) (on the Palestinians)

David Schoenbaum, *The United States and the State of Israel* (1993)

Stephen Schwartz, *The Two Faces of Islam* (2003)

David K. Shipler, *Arab and Jew* (2002)

Avi Shlaim, *War and Peace in the Middle East* (1994)

Geoff Simons, *Libya and the West* (2003)

Strobe Talbot and Nayan Chanda, eds., *The Age of Terror* (2002)

Shibley Telhami, *The Stakes: America and the Middle East* (2003)

Mark Tessler, *A History of the Israeli-Palestinian Conflict* (1995)

Bernard E. Trainor, *The General's War* (1995) (on the 1990 Gulf War)

Robert Vitalis, "Black Gold, White Crude: An Essay on American Exceptionalism, Hierarchy, and Hegemony in the Gulf," *Diplomatic History,* 26 (Spring 2002), 185–213

Bob Woodward, *Bush at War* (2003)

———, *Plan of Attack* (2004)

Daniel Yergin, *The Prize* (1991) (on oil)